THE FOCUS.

No. 1.]   SATURDAY, DECEMBER 1, 1821.   [Vol. I.

On an ancient Monument of Sculpture in Stone, representing the Theban Sphinx; which was recently discovered at Colchester, in Essex. By E. W. A. HAY, Esq. A. B., F. A. S.   Journal of Science, &c. No. 23.

A Monument of the Theban Sphinx has been discovered at Colchester, and which is described as being in a state of excellent preservation. There is every reason to believe it is Roman workmanship; Colchester being, beyond all doubt, the Colonia Camulodunum of the Romans. Besides, around the site of its deposit were discovered antique remains, such as pottery, tiles, bricks, fragments of bronze, &c., that display the true Roman character. And what may constitute almost a certainty of that fact is, that a portion of a sepulchral inscription, to the memory of one or more legionary soldiers, was, a few days before, dug up, within twenty-five paces from the spot where the Sphinx was found.

Around the site of the Sphinx, were many fragments of a stone, unknown as the produce of the vicinity of Colchester, commonly called Swanage; from the place where such stone is dug, in the Isle of Purbeck. The Sphinx, itself, is of Portland stone, of a good quality. The figure is stated to be extremely beautiful: the adjustment of its hair resembling that of the youngest Empress Faustina: wherefrom we may infer the work to have been of date posterior to her time, or at least to her birth. We may, too, presume, from the material being Portland stone, that the Sphinx was not brought hither from Italy; but executed by some eminent Roman artist, then in Britain. The Sphinx is represented as in a sitting attitude, with a human head between her paws, and bones under her belly. Mr. Hay states the dimensions of the antique to be as follows:—

"Length of the base .... 25½ inches.
Medium breadth of the base 10
Height from base to top of Sphinx's head.... 25
The face of the Sphinx, measuring from under the chin to the crown of the head........ 5

"The stone was found at the depth of about two feet from the surface of the soil, in trenching the ground around the General Hospital lately erected at Colchester. It was discovered in an almost perfect state, there being only a few marks of injury, and those slight; excepting upon the left side of the work that lay uppermost. The fracture of the nose of the Sphinx, as well as a blow upon the man's forehead, were, with some other less material bruises, the almost unavoidable effects of the labour upon discovery."

The sepulchral fragment is a curiosity, as distinctly mentioning the *Third* Imperial Legion, (LEGionis III. AVgustæ) "a portion of the Roman forces," says Mr. H., "of which I cannot find any trace by any references I have been able to make."

Another Sphinx was also found last summer, within a few yards of the spot where the former lay. This is of bronze, and much smaller than the stone one. It is simply a compound of the Lion and Virgin, without any destructive symbol accompanying it: and Mr. H. says, "from the arrangement of the hair resembling that of Julia Mæsa, or of her daughter Julia Sœmias (mother of the Emperor Heliogabalus), as well as from its inferiority of style and execution, it is doubtless of a later time than the large Sphinx; not appearing to claim any earlier date than about the beginning of the third century of our era."

In order to account for the presence of these remains of Roman art, Mr. Hay reasons thus:—

"We know that it was a custom with the Romans, as with the Greeks and the Egyptians, to place images of the Sphinx in the *pronaos* of their temples.—It is precisely to such a purpose, that I suspect our beautiful sculpture in stone to have been dedicated, in the vestibule of the temple of Claudius.

"But it may be asked, Why, in such a situation, should a mutilated victim be exhibited under the fangs of the Theban Sphinx? I cannot certainly venture in an unhesitating tone to attempt an explanation of this peculiarity. Yet, if we adopt the views of Hoffmann, this exhibition of the utter destruction of the victim may be fairly accounted for, and may be shown to have been perfectly adapted to the supposed situation of this Sphinx, as a warning emblem for all who presumed to pass the holy precincts, to enter even the porch of the temple. Hoffmann considers the fable of the Sphinx destroying such as did not understand her mysteries, to intimate that those who observed not the precepts of the gods, were abandoned to her, as to the infernal minister of that divine wrath, which would not fail to consign the disobedient to torments and to death.

"In reply to any hesitation that may be felt in granting the claims advanced for the Roman origin of our antique stone, upon the ground of the victim being thus introduced; I beg leave to observe, that it is only requisite to turn to Montfaucon, to Hoffmann, to Raspe, or to Millin, among the mass of antiquarian authority to which we might refer, for the exhibition of a victim conjoined with the image of the Grecian Sphinx. Yet, in the careful attachment, which is sometimes perhaps too exclusively retained, for precedent; we may be called upon to give an example from antiquity, of the destruction of a victim of the Sphinx, being shown as already completed."

Mr. Hay then proceeds to show, on the authority of Tacitus, that there was a Roman temple at Camulodunum; and as that city may be granted to have occupied the site of our present Colchester, there is much plausibility in his conjecture as to the position of the Sphinx, and its subsequent fall, during the indiscriminate ruin brought down on Camulodunum, in some partial triumph of the Britons over their Roman lords.

Some additional Facts relating to the Division of the Eighth Pair of Nerves, communicated in a Letter to the Editor of the Journal of the Royal Institution, by A. P. W. PHILIP, M.D., F.R.S. Ed., &c.

Journal of Science, Literature and Arts. No. 23.

On this interesting topic, there has already been much controversy, and probably there will be much more, before the question be fully determined. Would it not be advisable, in such a case as this, where simple experiments must, at last, settle the dispute, that such experiments were instituted in the joint presence of the contending parties? What more easy than for gentlemen, residing within the same city, to meet, and carry on a course of investigation, on a matter of interest to them mutually? The cause of science is always benefited by personal communion; and we take it for granted, that gentlemen, engaged in scientific controversy, are reciprocally anxious to establish truth; rather than contend for the frivolous glory of victory.

A gentleman named Broughton, lately instituted some experiments with a view to ascertain the justice of Dr. Philip's previous determination, relative to the influence of the eighth pair of nerves on the digestive functions, and the identity of galvanic with nervous power. Mr. B. came to the conclusion, that the digestive process does not cease immediately on the division of the par vagum; and that dyspnœa varies, both in time and degree, after such division.

Dr. P., after acknowledging the candour of Mr. B., contends that, on the latter gentleman's own experiments, we may conclude the digestive processs to be nearly annihilated, if the divided ends of the nerve are separated, and thrown widely apart: but when, after the incision, the ends are suffered to remain in contact, the digestive functions are comparatively vigorous. Dr. Philip then goes on to state, that he made two experiments on recently fed rabbits, by dividing the par vagum, and leaving the incised portions in contact, or nearly so. In one, the ends contracted spontaneously, and separated about the sixth of an inch; in the other, the contraction was one-fourth of an inch—the former died in eight hours; the latter in six. Mr. Brodie, and Mr.

Cutler, Assistant Surgeon in the Guards, authorize Dr. Philip to state, that " they are satisfied that the nervous influence had, in the foregoing experiments, passed from the upper to the lower portion of the divided nerves."

As we may have occasion to recur to this question, so interesting in its nature as to make us deviate a little from our rule of avoiding controversial matter, we will detail rather more at length what Dr. Philip holds to be proved.

1st. That separation of the divided surfaces prevents digestion.

2d. That if the stomachic, or lower portion of the divided nerve, be brought into contact with the positive pole of a voltaic battery, and the negative end with the skin over the stomach, no efforts to vomit follow the division of the nerve, and digestion proceeds as in health.

3d. That when the divided ends of the nerve are placed in contact, or not exceeding the distance apart one-fourth of an inch, digestion proceeds to a considerable degree.

4th. That dyspnœa after the division, is prevented by such galvanic application, as above mentioned.

The Doctor urges the propriety of assenting to these points; namely, that nervous influence is only chemical agency, not vital power; and that voltaic electricity is not merely the best stimulus to muscular fibre, but also capable of raising the temperature of arterial blood, while it cannot effect such power on venous blood, or even arterial that has lost vital principle.

Dr. Philip emphatically calls the experiment, wherein the divided nerve is not separated, and the digestive functions appear but little impaired, the Experimentum Crucis, as to his discussion with Dr. Alison.

We think that the experiment related by Dr. P. as having been made by Mr. Field, may be explained either for or against the Doctor's principles; but be this as it may, we cannot conclude without expressing a hope that these points may all be settled shortly, by a full revision of the most lucid experiments; or by the institution of new ones; for we consider the result as involving practical consequences of the first importance to the healing art.

Some Experiments made with a view to the Detection and Prevention of Frauds in the Sale of skimmed Milk; together with an Account of a simple Lactometer for effecting that Purpose. By EDMUND DAVY, Esq. Professor of Chemistry and Secretary to the Royal Cork Institution.

Philosophical Magazine, No. 282.

Skimmed milk constitutes a large portion of the daily food of the poor classes in Ireland; and therefore Dr. Davy merits their gratitude for his researches in their behalf. Were competent men to turn their attention to subjects of this nature, more than they do, Philosophy would better claim the esteem of the world; for after all the labour of intellect, and consumption of lamp oil, that is but empty speculation which produces no practical good. Philosophy is like wealth, to be valued principally as it becomes fixed in the ameliorated condition of man. Dr. Davy says that the weekly consumption of milk, in Cork alone, is estimated in market price, at £1000.; and the public having been long exposed to the dishonest practices of milk venders, he kindly set about to devise the best means of detecting them, at the solicitation of the Magistracy, who, to their honour, stepped forward in protection of the poor. The principle of the hydrometer suggested itself to Dr. D. as applicable to identify the strength of milk: but previously to the construction of such an instrument, it was necessary to determine whether there was any marked difference in density of skimmed milk. He subjected the milk obtained from various dairies to experiment, and was gratified in finding so uniform a density, as to render the purity determinable by an hydrometrical scale. He says the greater number of those specimens were of the specific gravity 1·037 and 1·0375. Some where higher, but the highest was 1·040, and the lowest 1·036, the thermometer being at 50°. " These experiments, confirmed by others which I afterwards made, led me to conclude that a considerable degree of uniformity prevails in the density of genuine skimmed milk; and this uniformity, I presume, would be still greater, if due allowance were made for accidental circumstances connected with the experiments, which, though not easy to appreciate, must, to a certain extent, influence the specific gravity of milk; as, for example, slight variations of temperature and of the balance employed; to which must be added the unequal exposure to the atmosphere of the several specimens of milk examined. In reference to this last particular, it is proper to state that I found only one specimen of milk of so high a specific gravity as 1·040; and in this instance the cream had been suffered to remain on the milk for above three days, and its specific gravity was not taken until some hours after it had been skimmed. These circumstances incline me to refer its superior density to evaporation, owing to protracted exposure to the atmosphere."

Water was found to be the adulterating article, and those milks which were most adulterated, bore the specific gravity of 1·026, " the highest of the genuine milks from the markets was 1·039, the thermometer being at 50°."

The Doctor never found the commonly suspected articles, as chalk, flour, starch, &c.; and he gives good reasons why they are not likely to be used for adulteration.—" Skimmed milk and water (says the Doctor) combine without undergoing any sensible alteration of volume, or condensation. Skimmed milk is of much greater specific gravity than water, and its density is diminished in direct proportion to the quantity of water added to it. On those facts the Lactometer I have made depends; it is exclusively adapted to skimmed milk, in which respect, as well as in simplicity of construction, it differs from the ingenious instrument of Mr. Dicas."

Dr. Davy then proceeds to describe his Lactometer, which is, as said before, on the hydrometer principle. It has been found fully equal to its intention; 2000 pottles of skimmed milk were seized by the Magistracy, the first morning it was used. In order to meet inaccuracies with an indulgent spirit, 5°. below purity in standard, are allowed. The Lactometer is graduated to concur with 60°. of temperature, Fah. " an allowance of 2 or 3°. below 0, would be amply sufficient for our warmest summer weather."

Dr. D. concludes thus, " I have made several experiments in the hope of being able to apply a similar instrument to detect the frauds practised in the sale of new milk; but I fear this is impracticable, because both water and skimmed milk are employed to adulterate new milk; and as the one is lighter and the other heavier than new milk, there would be no difficulty in so proportioning both, as to make the adulterated correspond with genuine new milk in density."

With this effective example before our eyes, we cannot but earnestly wish that some philanthropic experimentalist would devote a portion of time to the detection of those frauds we are suffering from, by the milk venders, in this metropolis; and when they shall be so detected, we trust that our Magistracy will be active in the suppression of the custom.

Remarks tending to facilitate the Analysis of Spring and Mineral Waters. By JOHN DALTON.

Manchester Memoirs.

The analysis of waters has a practical value of no small moment: for surely whatever extraneous matter may be mingled with, or dissolved in, the menstruum we are perpetually taking into our systems, must have some eventual effect on our health, especially on the urinary emunctory. Probably one of the most direful diseases that close the life of man, (we mean the stone,) may sometimes be attributable to the quality of the water drank by the sufferer; at all events, it will be wisdom to avoid water that is loaded with earthy solutions, that by deposition in the bladder may cause, or aggravate, disease in a delicate organ. We admit, that in constitutions not prone to calculous concretions, our fears would be modified; but, still we hold, that the less foreign matter is contained in water, the better, for all the purposes of diet and health.

Mr. Dalton does not enter into a profound consideration of the various waters, their contents, and tests; he merely states the sensible properties, commonly observed on testing with the common agents. After observing that, to carbonate and sulphate of lime, we principally owe the *hardness* of waters, he justly calls it " a very singular and astonishing quality, when it is considered as produced by so extremely small a portion of the earthy salt." The first he speaks of, is—

Soap Test.—Pure soap dissolved in pure water, produces a milky liquid, remaining many days unaltered. When soap be agitated with spring water, it immediately forms into curdly masses, rising to the surface; understood to be the fat of the soap, combined with the earthy matter of the water. This separated matter is glutinous, and gives a smearing soil to surfaces.

Lime-Water.—When the water (as generally) contains super-carbonate of lime, the addition of lime-water neutralizes the super-abundant carbonic acid, thereby forming an insoluble compound; which, precipitating, gives a milky appearance. By adding a little excess of lime-water, the entire matter may be precipitated, and easily ascertained. Or, when the whole has subsided, the clear liquid should be poured away and tested, &c.

If what is called super-carbonate of lime be really an *alkaline*, rather than *acid* compound, the term *super*-carbonate is a palpable misnomer. We consider the fact of super-carbonate of lime indicating the alkaline character, by test colours, as singularly deserving a scrutinizing pursuit; and as likely to lead to some new views in the composition of calcareous neutrals,—perhaps to other saline classes also. We do not consider the precipitation of ferruginous and cuprous metallic oxides, by common spring water, " just the same as by free lime," to be so conclusive, as to the fact alluded to by Mr. Dalton; but we feel a confidence that this matter will not sleep in the hands of such an active philosopher.

Acetate and Nitrate of Lead.—The lead combines with the acid of the sulphates and carbonates, forming insoluble precipitates. " If the precipitate be treated with nitric acid, the carbonate of lead is instantly dissolved, and the sulphate of lead (if present) remains undissolved; and may be collected and dried: from which the quantity of sulphuric acid may be determined."

Nitrate and Muriate of Barytes.—Best tests to determine presence of free or combined sulphuric acid.

Oxalic Acid.—To determine presence of lime: A little

ammonia should be added when lime in a state of combination. Amount of lime ascertained by known quantity of oxalic acid used; or by carefully collecting precipitate.

Nitrates of Silver and Mercury.—Tests for muriatic acid, free or combined; but this acid, and its compounds, are seldom met with; except in sea water, or lime springs.

Sulphuretted Hydrogen Water and Hydro-Sulphurets.— To detect lead, mercury, and some other metals: Conversely, solutions of lead are sensible tests of sulphurous waters.

Tincture of Galls, and Prussiates of Iron and Lime.—To detect iron: With the former, a black precipitate; with the latter, blue. A small quantity of solution of oxymuriate of lime to be added to the water, if it contain green oxide of iron in solution; in order to convert it to the red oxide.

Mr. Dalton makes the following judicious remarks, and with them we shall close the paper.—" The improvements I would propose in the use of tests are, that the exact quantities of the ingredients in each test should be previously ascertained and marked on the label of the bottle; this might easily be done, in most of them, in the present state of chemical science. We should then drop in certain known quantities of each, from a dropping tube, graduated into grains, till the required effect was produced; then, from the quantity of the test required, the quantity of saline matter in the water might be determined without the trouble of collecting the precipitate; or, if this was done, the one method would be a check upon the other."

On Lime, as Manure.
Sir John Sinclair's Code of Agriculture.

Sir John Sinclair, to whom the farmer is perhaps more indebted than to any other living author or experimentalist, in his Code of Agriculture, thus explains the principle on which lime acts as manure:—

" Quick-lime in powder, or dissolved in water, is injurious to plants; hence grass, watered with lime-water, is destroyed. But lime, freshly burnt or slacked, forms a compost with vegetable matter, which is partly soluble in water and nutritive to plants. When applied to land in a powdery state, lime tends to bring any hard animal or vegetable substance into a more rapid state of decomposition. It also renders salts and other matters not easily decomposed, miscible in water, thus promoting vegetation. If used, in a hot or caustic state, to strong and retentive soils, it will not only subdue their tenacity, but will communicate a certain degree of warmth to the ground. Light soils, from the application of lime, become adhesive and more retentive of moisture.

"Sometimes limestone is almost perfectly pure, as is the case with marble. But several sorts of limestone have mixtures of clay and sand in various proportions, by which the efficacy of the manure is considerably diminished. It is necessary, therefore, to analyze limestone, to ascertain the proportion of pure lime, before using so expensive an article in great quantities; more especially if it must be conveyed from a distance. Bituminous limestone makes good manure. But the magnesian is the species which requires the greatest attention. Limestone sometimes contains from 20·3 to 23·5 of magnesia, in which case it would be injurious to weak soils, from the peculiar qualities of the lime, to apply more than from twenty-five to thirty bushels per statute acre; though in rich soils double that quantity may be used, and still more with peat, on which soil it would have a most powerful effect in producing fertility.

"Limestone is burnt in kilns of various construction, and with various sorts of fuel. It is applied with advantage to soils recently reclaimed, in a caustic state; but is generally *slacked,* by throwing water upon the lumps until they crack and swell, and fall down into a fine powder. This operation, when it is to be done, should not be delayed: for, if properly burnt, it is easily reduced to a fine powder, which may not be the case if the slacking be postponed. If water cannot be easily obtained, the lumps may either be divided into small heaps and covered with earth, by the moisture of which they are soon pulverized; or they may be made into large heaps, the lumps and earth in alternate strata, the lumps four inches and the earth six inches thick, and the whole covered with earth. Where it can be easily had, it is a great advantage to slack the calcined limestone for manure with sea-water. Summer is the proper season for applying lime: for the land ought not only to be dry, but the surface as free from moisture as possible, so as to promote the equal distribution of the manure. The most profitable period for applying lime, is, Mr. Rennie of Phantassie thinks, when the land is under summer fallow, in the months of June and July, that it may be completely mixed with the soil before the crop is sown. This is also the general practice in other districts. For a turnip crop, it should be laid on in the spring, or early in the summer, before the turnips are drilled. When applied to old ley, it is a good practice to spread it on the surface previously to the land being broken up, by which it is fixed firmly on the sward. One year has been found of use, but when done three years before, greater advantages have been produced. The quantity applied must vary according to the soil: from 240 to 300 bushels of unslacked lime may be applied on strong lands with advantage. Even 600 bushels have been laid on at once on strong clays with great success. On light soils, a much smaller quantity will answer, say from 150 to 200 bushels; but these small doses ought to be more frequently repeated. When applied to the surface of bogs or moors, the quantity used is very considerable; and provided the land is naturally dry, or has been thoroughly drained, the more that is laid on, the greater the improvement. The real quantity, however, of calcareous matter used, depends upon the quality of the lime."

We do not quote the above as containing any thing new; but as a plain statement of the opinion formed by a gentleman of acknowledged experience.

On Smut.

So much has been said, written, declared, and retracted, on this important subject, that we cannot resist giving Sir John's judgment respecting it: he says—

"The nature of smut is now well known. It is a small and delicate microscopic plant, which would soon be destroyed by the variations of the atmosphere, if wheat did not offer an asylum where it could propagate itself. While it is only attached *externally* to the grain, and before its seeds or germs have penetrated into the plant, its germination may be effectually prevented by any operation which will clear the grain of the smutty powder, or that destroys it by acrid, corrosive, or poisonous applications. If nothing effectual is done for that purpose, the smut penetrates into the plant of the wheat while it is still very young. There it produces globules, which increase with the ear, and become perfect seeds when the wheat approaches maturity. If, however, the seed is fortified by a solution of copper, it not only destroys the germination of any smutty powder attached to the grain, but it likewise prevents its being attacked through the root by any other parasitical plant that may be found in the soil, and thus may escape other accidents or disorders to which wheat is liable.

" The best mode of using the BLUE VITRIOL (sulphate of copper) is as follows: Into eight quarts of boiling water put one pound of blue vitriol; while it is quite hot, mix three bushels of wheat with five quarts of the liquid, and at the end of three hours add the other three quarts. The three bushels of wheat are to remain three hours longer, or six hours in all, in the liquid. The whole should be stirred three or four times during the six hours, and the light grains taken off. Then add a sufficient quantity of slacked lime to make the wheat perfectly dry. It may remain in a heap for six hours; it may then be spread open, and used the next day, but not sooner. Wheat thus prepared may remain unsown for any space of time without injury. This application does not prevent the rust or mildew, yet for the smut it is an *infallible antidote*. The grain should be perfectly dry when the solution of copper is applied."

Relative to the subject of soaking seed grain, as a preventive of smut or mildew, we beg leave to call the attention of the practical agriculturist to a well written paper in the Farmer's Journal of the 12th November. It is therein stated, that a prolonged IMMERSION of grain in urine, is destructive of its vitality; and we would be disposed to think, that a thorough soaking, or *parboiling*, of the seed, as recommended by Sir John Sinclair, may sometimes have an injurious effect, especially if the seed grain be not old, and indurated. We are somewhat fortified in this opinion by a fact given in the Annals of Philosophy, by Mr. Phillips; who says, " Some time since, I accidentally spilled some solution, and oxide, of copper, near the root of a young poplar tree: in a short time, the tree began to droop; the leaves on the lower branches dying first; and, eventually, those on the upper ones. On cutting a branch from the tree, I observed that the knife was covered with copper, the whole breadth of the branch; showing that the copper had been absorbed, and had, undoubtedly, proved fatal to the life of the tree."

On the Aëriform Compounds of Charcoal and Hydrogen.
Journal of Science and Literature, No. 23,
Also Monthly Mag. No. 360.

The extended use of coal and oil gas, for the production of light, renders these compounds truly interesting to the public. We are happy to find that so able an experimentalist, as Dr. Henry, pursues his chemical researches into their nature; and hope he will not rest satisfied while any thing remains to be done, that can further contribute to our knowledge respecting them; or aid us in the best possible modes of their application to practical purposes. There is, in the body of the Doctor's paper, a remark that we think worthy of particular selection, and well deserving the attention of practical chemists, namely, " As far as my experience goes, no temperature, short of ignition, is sufficient for the decomposition of oil into permanent combustible gases; but the lower the heat that is employed, provided it be adequate to the effect, the heavier and more combustible is the gas; and the better suited to artificial illumination."

" It is evident, from these facts, that the aëriform ingredient of oil gas and coal gas, which is reducible to a liquid form by chlorine, is not identical with the olefiant gas obtained by the action of sulphuric acid on alcohol, but considerably exceeds that gas in specific gravity and combustibility. Two views may be taken of its nature; for it may either be a gas, *sui generis*, hitherto unknown, and constituted of hydrogen and charcoal in different proportions from those composing any known compound of these elements; or it may be merely the vapour of a highly volatile oil, mingled in various proportions with olefiant gas, carburetted hydrogen, and the other combustible gases. Of these two opinions, Mr. Dalton is inclined to the first, considering it as supported by the fact, that oil gas, or coal gas, may be passed through water, without being deprived of the ingredient in question; and that this anomalous elastic fluid is absorbed by agitation with water, and again expelled by heat or other gases, unchanged as to its chemical properties; as we have both satisfied ourselves by repeated experiments. On the other hand, I have found that hydrogen gas, by remaining several days in narrow tubes in contact with fluid naphtha, acquires the property of being affected by chlorine, precisely as if it were mixed with a small proportion of olefiant gas; and I am informed by Dr. Hope, that oil gas, when forcibly compressed in Gordon's portable gas lamp, deposits a portion of a highly volatile essential oil. The smell also of the liquid which is condensed on the inner surface of a glass receiver, in which oil gas or coal gas has been mixed with chlorine, denotes the presence of chloric ether,—evidently, however, mingled with the odour of some other fluid, which seems to me to bear most resemblance to that of spirit of turpentine. This part of the subject is well worthy of further investigation; but having devoted to the inquiry all the leisure which I am now able to command, I must remain satisfied at present with such conclusions as are safely deducible from the foregoing investigation."

The following is a recapitulation of Dr. Henry's results:—

1. "That carburetted hydrogen gas must still be considered as a distinct species, requiring, for the perfect combustion of each volume, two volumes of oxygen, and affording one volume of carbonic acid; and that if olefiant gas be considered as constituted of one atom of charcoal united with one atom of hydrogen, carburetted hydrogen must consist of one atom of charcoal in combination with two atoms of hydrogen.

2. "That there is a marked distinction between the action

of chlorine on olefiant gas, (which in certain proportions, is entirely independent of the presence of light, and is attended with the speedy condensation of the two gases into chloric ether,) and its relation to hydrogen, carburetted hydrogen, and carbonic oxide gases; on all of which it is inefficient, provided light be perfectly excluded from the mixture.

3. "That since chlorine, under these circumstances, condenses olefiant gas, without acting on the other three gases, it may be employed in the correct separation of the former from one or more of the three latter.

4. "That the gases evolved by heat from coal and from oil, though extremely uncertain as to the proportions of their ingredients, consist essentially of carburetted hydrogen, with variable proportions of hydrogen and carbonic oxide; and that they owe, moreover, much of their illuminating power to an elastic fluid, which resembles olefiant gas in the property of being speedily condensed by chlorine.

5. "That the proportion of oil gas and coal gas, which chlorine thus converts into a liquid form, does not precisely agree with olefiant gas in its other properties; but requires, for the combustion of each volume, nearly two volumes of oxygen more than are sufficient for saturating one volume of olefiant gas, and affords one additional volume of carbonic acid. It is probably, therefore, either a mixture of olefiant gas with a heavier and more combustible gas or vapour, or a new gas, *sui generis*, consisting of hydrogen and charcoal in proportions that remain to be determined."

Philosophical Transactions.

Description of Bridges of Suspension. By ROBERT STEVENSON, Esq. F. R. S. E., Civil Engineer.

Edinburgh Philosophical Journal, No. 10.

In this paper, Mr. Stevenson gives us a succinct description of the various Chain and Wire Bridges, that have been erected in Scotland; where, as it appears, they are likely to come into extensive use. The facility of applying this mode of construction, in many places, where the more bulky material of stone could not be so well adopted, and the small expense of the chain supports, as compared with that of masonry, are objects of no trifling importance. We cannot follow Mr. S. through his individual remarks, on each of the Bridges of Suspension that he presents to our notice; but must content ourselves with stating that the catenarian curve is the line of support. In some instances, this line is run *above* the horizontal roadway, and sustains it by perpendicular suspensory rods, let fall from the curve; in others, the curve runs *below* the roadway, the perpendiculars supporting it upwards. Though both are bridges of suspension, and on similar principle, yet the former would seem, to the vulgar eye, as most decidedly such. A few of the Scotch bridges, Galashiels, King's Meadows, and Thirlstane, are suspended by diagonal braces, proceeding from perpendiculars at each end. These bridges are liable to vibratory motion, both laterally and perpendicularly; and that too in an alarming degree: insomuch, that the Dryburgh Bridge was broken by three or four persons imprudently playing it into strong undulations. And it was again broken by the vibration produced by the wind. The motion produced by the passenger is sensible to him in all the smaller bridges; and, indeed, in the larger, measured stepping is perhaps equally so, where there is a large passing company, as a regiment of foot.

We consider this undulatory motion a great objection applying to suspension bridges; for where the span be great, the mass of material, if not dividing the friction of motion along the suspensory line, must have enormous effect in wear at the points of bearing. This effect must be still more powerful in the horizontal vibrations excited by the impulse of violent winds, on the entire body of the bridge; because the friction will be limited to comparative points. We cannot better elucidate our ideas on this matter, than by quoting Mr. Stevenson's, as follows:—

" But the effect we have to provide against in bridges of suspension, is not merely what is technically termed *deadweight*. A more powerful agent exists in the sudden impulses, or jerking motion of the load, which we have partly noticed in the description of Dryburgh Bridge. The greatest trial, for example, which the timber bridge at Montrose, about 500 feet in extent, has been considered to withstand, is the passing of a regiment of foot, marching in *regular time*. A troop of cavalry, on the contrary, does not produce corresponding effects, owing to the irregular step of the horses. The same observations apply to a crowd of persons walking promiscuously, or a drove of cattle, which counteract the undulating and rocking motion, observed on some occasions at the bridge of Montrose, when infantry has been passing along it. Hence also the effects of gusts of wind, often and violently repeated, which destroy the equilibrium of the parts of a bridge of suspension; and the importance of having the whole roadway and side-rails framed in the strongest possible manner."

We consider Mr. Stevenson entitled to the thanks of the public, for laying before it some facts that were very little known in South Britain: and although we, perhaps, have not here so many inducements as our northern brethren for adopting the use of bridges of suspension, yet we cannot doubt the propriety of their application, in cases where stone may be scarce, expense an object, or the elegant lightness of taste desirable.

Analysis of Mr. Barlow's Essay on Magnetic Attraction.
Edinburgh Philosophical Journal, No. 10.

The philosophical world begins to attach a paramount importance to the laws of Electricity, Galvanism, and Magnetism; not merely as to their individual relations with each other, but, also, as to their influence in the operations of nature. Without incurring the risk of any imputation on our scientific credulity, we may boldly announce our conviction, that whether their identity shall be hereafter proved to be respectively distinct, or but simple modifications of action of one and the same fluid; chemical experiment will determine them to be the most powerful and diffusive agents of material transformations. Through electrical instrumentality we have already resolved doubts that seemed to set improvement at defiance; we have analyzed presumed elements into the very elements of their unsuspected composition; we have shown water as a compound, by analysis and synthesis; and even demonstrated earths themselves to be combinations of oxygen with metallic bases. These are splendid instances of human intellect, tracing, by cautious experiment, and deducing, by critical logic. We will trust that the day of philosophical delusion (if we may so express ourselves) is gone by—rigid experiment now tests every plausible suggestion; and while this be the tone of mind pervading general science, we shall not have much to fear from the occasional dreamer, however fancifully he may decorate his visions.

In papers of the electrical and magnetic class that we may have to analyze, we anticipate no little labour; for experimentalists are starting up on all sides: and as there must necessarily be a wide diversity of opinion, on a subject hitherto but little, or but imperfectly, explored, we must bespeak the indulgence of our readers, while we attempt the arduous task of selecting the most lucid demonstrations that shall be found in this field of inquiry.

As we profess to give our readers the spirit of the journals, only, we shall usually take our remarks from the matter of such journals, rather than from the original essays, or books, out of, or from, which those journals may have drawn their inferences.

It appears that Mr. Barlow is making a series of experiments, to prove some facts relating to magnetic attraction; but that his deductions are said to have been anticipated. We think this is not true; or, rather, we are not satisfied that it is; nor shall we be, until it can be shown when and where these anticipations stand in print. We shall here extract the description of Mr. Barlow's apparatus:—

It consists, " first, of a solid iron ball, of nearly thirteen inches diameter, weighing about 288 lbs. This is suspended by a system of pulleys, which enables the experimenter to raise or lower it at pleasure. Immediately under the ball is placed a strong, firm, round table, about 5 feet in diameter, having a hole in its centre, through which the ball may be made to pass when required. The plane of this table is divided into equal portions of $2°\frac{1}{2}$ each, and properly numbered, proceeding from the line forming the magnetic meridian; and the whole rendered perfectly secure and steady, by placing the apparatus on piles driven into the earth, through the floor of the model room of the Royal Military Academy at Woolwich." With this machine, it is obvious, the compass might be placed at any azimuth from the magnetic meridian; at any distance from the centre of the table, and the ball itself placed at any height above, or depth below, the plane of the table.

Mr. Barlow had, previously, ascertained a fact of much practical value to mariners; namely, that balls of unmagnetized iron have a plane of *no attraction* passing from North to South, and forming, in our latitude, an angle of $19°\frac{1}{2}$ with the horizon; as complement of the dip. To confirm this, he subjects a very sensible magnet to trial; and finds the mean inclination of the plane $19° 24'$, and the actual dip $70° 30'\frac{1}{4}$; the complement of which being $19° 29'\frac{1}{4}$, leaves an error of only $5'\frac{1}{2}$, easily accountable for. He now goes on to show, as the result of varied positions and magnitudes in the compass and ball, the simple law, that " the tangent of deviation is proportional to the rectangle of the sine of the double latitude, and the cosine of the longitude." Next, at varied distances of 12, 15, 18, and 20 inches on the *minimum square* he found, that " the tangents of the angle of deviation are reciprocally proportional to the cubes of the distance." Also, by using balls of different magnitudes, " the tangents of deviations proportional to the cubes of the diameters." These mathematical proportions obtaining in a *particular* latitude, fortifies our hope that we really are coming to some determinate knowledge of the absolute laws of magnetism; and that the above theorems may solve the magnetic diversities of *every* latitude.

But we are indebted to Mr. Barlow for another magnetic law, of no less importance than the above, in a practical view; that is, "the tangents of the angles of deviation to be proportional to the cubes of the diameters"; whence, inferring they were " proportional to the masses," he was led to an experiment with a 10-inch *shell,* and "found it gave precisely the same deviations, as a *solid ball* of the same dimensions." Following up the train of reasoning, elicited by these demonstrated facts, he next ascertained, by experiments on balls, plates, and shells, that the attracting power resides wholly in the *surface*, perhaps not exceeding $\frac{1}{20}$ of an inch deep; and independent of the *mass*. From hence we shall learn what figure to give to a body of iron, to render it capable of receiving the greatest possible quantity of magnetic power.

As all the masses of iron Mr. Barlow had hitherto experimented with, were of regular mathematical forms, he now proceeded to try the effect of "an iron 24-pounder, mounted on a traversing carriage and platform, which, together with its iron trucks, &c. weighed 58 cwt.: on which the laws were found to be the same as on the most regular body;" and hence it followed " that they might be made immediately applicable to the correction of the local attraction of vessels; the object for which the course of experiments was undertaken."

Captain Parry carries out with him, in the Fury, an instrument of Mr. Barlow's construction, with a view to test the principles laid down by the latter gentleman. We shall anxiously seek for the result of the trial, when Captain Parry returns, and lay it before our readers.

Experiments and Observations on the Effects produced on the Rates of Chronometers, by the proximity of Iron Bodies. By JOHN BARLOW, Esq. Royal Military Academy, Woolwich.   Edinburgh Philosophical Journal, No. 10.

Occupying an insular territory, and being the greatest commercial people in the world, the British nation must ever be deeply interested in the developement of the laws of magnetic attraction, as subservient to the art of navigation.—Therefore, in our pages, we shall always give this subject its merited share of attention. We have, again, to present the indefatigable Mr. Barlow to the reader, where he will be found to stamp his theorems with the sanction of effect in practical application.

Chronometers at Sea have always been found to vary from others on land; this has generally been attributed to the vessel's motion; but it being observed by Mr. Fisher, in his voyage with Captain Buchan, that the rates on board, did not accord with those on shore, although the vessel was immoveably imbedded in ice, a suspicion arose that the *iron* of the vessel caused the variation; and to elucidate the mystery, Mr. Barlow commenced a series of experiments. Around a suspended iron ball, weighing nearly 300 lbs., at different distances, and in different situations, with reference to the magnetic equator, "*or plane of no attraction,*" he placed six excellent chronometers, where they remained three or four days; he then removed them, east, west, north, and south, observing the direction of position; the twelve o'clock mark pointing first to the north, then to the east, west, &c. They varied considerably, but always resumed the same rate in the same position. The difference of rate, in some, equalled 5" per day. This variation was presumed to arise from some magnetic property in the balance, or spring, of the chronometer. Mr. Frodsham, of the firm of Gaskinson and Frodsham, whose chronometers were found so accurate in the late northern voyage, went down to Woolwich, with detached balances and springs; and, there, in conjunction with Mr. Barlow, subjected them to experiment, which satisfied both parties that they were influenced by magnetic power.

Mr. Barlow having before discovered (as related in the preceding paper) that the power exerted by iron on the needle, was confined to its *surface*, independent of the *mass*, presumed its action on chronometers must be governed by a similar law; and proved the matter thus,—a circular plate of iron, 12 inches diameter, at the distance of 15 inches, retarded, in one instance, 4", in another 3". A very ingenious means was suggested to Mr. Barlow's mind, as arising out of the experiments hinted at in the preceding paper, to measure the effect of the general mass of iron of the vessel on the compass; and that was by presenting to the compass a plate of iron, so situated, as to equal the influential effect of the combined mass of iron on board. His Majesty's ship Leven has adopted this plan, during a voyage of sixteen months, with the most satisfactory result. Mr. Barlow now proposes a similar principle to regulate the chronometer.— May the event be equally happy!

On the Air Pump.

It is worthy of remark, that a philosophical truth, or implement, shall be fully appreciated at a certain time, in so far as the state of science may admit; and then be laid aside on the shelf unnoticed, as though obsolete and insignificant. So it has been with the air pump. In the time of Boyle, this instrument carried away the palm of fashion in philosophy. Electricity then succeeded in all its brilliancy, and the air pump became but a secondary play-thing in the hands of men of science. In these days of investigation, every means is called in to aid the searcher after truth; and the air pump is likely to resume its due rank, both in the scale of demonstrative experiment, and as an instrument to serve the purposes of the artisan.

This instrument has been lately used in the sizeing and wetting of paper. The material is inclosed in an air-tight vessel, into which the size or water is admitted, the air being previously withdrawn by the pump; of course, the fluid permeates the substance of the paper on re-admission of the atmospheric air, which presses on the liquid with a force proportioned to the foregoing exhaustion.

In dyeing, also, similar means have been used, and with decided advantage, as we might reasonably expect: for the fibre is the more capable of receiving colouring matter in a degree measured by the abstraction of air from its pores, which become occupied by the dye stuff in a plenary proportion. These simple facts only require to be reported among manufacturers, in order to pave the way for adoption of similar instruments in a vast variety of the arts. Whether it be that artisans partake in the generally improved state of public intellect, and thereby are divested of many of those prejudices that formerly operated to exclude the assistance of science; or that the mode of demonstrating fundamental principles is better comprehended by the professors, we will not venture to determine; but we do certainly witness less reluctance on the part of the workman to take science by the hand as his teacher or protector, than was formerly the case; and we hope, that art and philosophy will always maintain a good understanding.

Education of Mechanics.

As analogous with the foregoing remarks, we cannot resist mentioning, that a school has been established in Edinburgh, for the purpose of imparting to mechanics the philosophical principles on which their respective trades are founded. Two hundred members have already enrolled themselves. From such Institutions as this, the happiest effects *must* ensue. The workman will feel himself dignified in character, by a philosophical perception of the nature of his processes. By a knowledge of principles, he will know how to improve or to modify his means; and last, though not least, his vacant hours will be devoted to attendance on his preceptor, or in an emulous discussion of the truths imparted to him: to the exclusion of pot-house enjoyment, or a listless lounging out of painful time.

A scientific school has for some time been instituted at Glasgow, under the superintendance of Dr. Ure, who gives lectures on the various branches of science that can be conducive to the improvement of the artisan. The Doctor speaks highly of the general deportment and assiduous attention of the pupils. But, to the honour of the Scotch character, we must observe, that they are far more likely, by their sedater habits, to derive benefit from such Institutions, than their southern fellow subjects. It is warmly urged by some, that there is great risk incurred by imparting knowledge to the poorer classes; for the scientific artist, if obliged to plod on in a humble circle, is but the more miserable by his consciousness of meriting a better fate; and that if we qualify all to be masters, we shall have but few inclined to be servants. Let us, however, have a more benevolent opinion of our fellow beings, and trust, that as Providence has been pleased to make no distinction in natural intellect among men, considered as classes,—so, to cultivate that intellect by a display of the laws, so far as they can be known, whereby he forms, transforms, or sustains, matter, must have a direct tendency to improve, rather than debase his creatures.

Geological Fact.

Silliman's Journal.

During the years 1786-7, and 8, they were occupied near Aix, in Provence, in France, in quarrying stone for the rebuilding, upon a vast scale, of the Palace of Justice. The stone was a deep grey lime-stone, and of that kind which are tender when they come out of the quarry, but harden by exposure to the air. The strata were separated from one another by a bed of sand, mixed with clay more or less calcareous. The first which were wrought presented no appearance of any foreign bodies, but after the workmen had removed the first ten beds, they were astonished, when taking away the eleventh, to find its inferior surface, at the depth of forty or fifty feet, covered with shells. The stone of this bed having been removed, as they were taking away the sand which separated the eleventh bed from the twelfth, they found stumps of columns and fragments of stones half wrought, and the stone was exactly similar to that of the quarry. They found moreover, coins, handles of hammers, and other tools, or fragments of tools, of wood. But that which principally commanded their attention was a board, about an inch thick, and seven or eight feet long; it was broken into many pieces, of which none were missing; it was possible to join them again one to another, and to restore its original form, which was that of the boards of the same kind used by the masons and quarrymen; it was worn in the same manner, rounded and waving on the edges. The stones, which were partly wrought, had not changed in their nature, but the fragments of the board and the instruments, and the pieces of instruments of wood, had been changed into agates, which were very fine, and agreeably coloured. Here then (observes Count Bournon) we have the traces of a work, executed by the hand of man, placed at the depth of fifty feet, and covered with eleven beds of compact limestone; every thing tended to prove that this work had been executed upon the spot where the traces existed. The presence of man had then preceded the formation of this stone, and that very considerably, since he was already at such a degree of civilization that the arts were known to him, and that he wrought the stone, and formed columns out of it.

Much information is wanted to enable us to form a plausible conjecture as to the cause of this deposition of implements, so exactly resembling those in modern use. We should have been told whether there be any records of the date of the quarry; the quality and order of the surrounding earthy strata; whether there be any perpendicular openings, or shafts, denoting former subterranean excavation; and, if so, with what matter these excavations and shafts have been filled up. Indeed, the whole statement demands largely on our credulity. We should be glad to have it authenticated by some indisputable authority; such as the report of a public body, after investigation on the spot.

Description of a new Balance. By W. HERAPATH, Esq.
Annals of Philosophy.

The fine workmanship of our artists, has, from time to time, supplied us with exquisitely delicate balances, but we do not recollect any instance wherein friction, at the point of suspension, was reduced to nothing; as, in this very ingenious little instrument, it is nearly, if not quite. We think, however, that the effect has its limit, and indeed Mr. H. seems sensible of it, by intimating the expediency of having a set of magnets, of various powers; whereby, the weight to be suspended, and the attractive force, shall be duly apportioned. We can conceive that a very strong magnet, operating on a light weight, may produce sensible resistance to motion at the point of suspension. We beg leave to suggest, that the beam be made of matter not capable of being influenced by magnetic power; for we presume that some effect on the balance may be made if it become magnetized, especially if a mass of iron be near one end of the line of beam. The perpendicular, or axis, must necessarily be of iron. The scales, made of jewellers' foil, are suspended on the points of needles, rivetted into moveable pieces; and, with the beam, weigh 62·75 grains. When loaded with 5 grains in each scale, $1,100^{th}$. grain moves the middle index through an arc of 10°. The axis has knife edges; but Mr. H. intends making one with points, and two brass rings surrounding it, as a guard against its accidental fall. The extremities of the magnet are convex, to reduce the points of contact. He has used the balance with 165 grains in each scale; and is confident 250 might have been borne. The friction on the axis diminishes as the weight increases, so as to render the balance most sensible at the maximum of weight.

On the Phosphorescence of Marine Animals. By Dr. MACCULLOCH. Edinburgh Philosophical Journal, No. 10.

Dr. MacCulloch found, in most of the harbours of Shetland and Orkney, a vast quantity of a species of phosphorescent animals, not previously described; a cubic inch of water containing about 100 of them. There were many varieties of species, and of varied magnitudes. The light of the whole disappeared when they died. The Doctor adds more than 190 species to our catalogue of phosphorescent animals; among which are about 20 small medusæ.

" In the ancient genus Cancer, a considerable number of Squillæ were also found possessed of phosphorescence. In the genera Scolopendra and Nereis, five or six were luminous, which were all the species observed by Dr. MacCulloch. The other known genera in which luminous species were observed, were Phalangia, Monoculus, Oniscus, Iulus, Vorticella, Cercaria, Vibrio; Volvox, to these Dr. MacCulloch adds, among the fishes, a new species of Leptocephalus. The remaining luminous animals consisted of new genera, or at least of animals which could not be referred to any as yet to be found in authors. Dr. MacCulloch seems to think, that the ling and other fish which inhabit the submarine vallies, at depths to which the light of day cannot penetrate, must perceive their food, and pursue their avocations, by the phosphorescence of their prey, or of the animals which abound in the sea, or by phosphorescence elicited from their own bodies."

In confirmation of Dr. MacCulloch's conjecture respecting the phosphorescent light of marine animals being intended for the purpose of prey, we would urge the fact of fishes being easily attracted by artificial light, during the darkness of midnight.

Some remarks on the phosphorescence of the lampyris, noctiluca, and splendidula, by M. Macaire; published in the Bibliotheque Universelle last May, may be properly introduced here, as the result of numerous experiments on the effulgent emission. He states, 1st, what indeed no one would doubt, That a certain degree of heat is necessary to the effect;—2d, That high temperature is destructive to the phosphorescence, perhaps by the death of it;—3d, All bodies capable of coagulating albumen, destroy the phosphorescence;—4th, The presence of oxygen is indispensable to the luminous effect;—5th, Phosphorescence excited by the galvanic pile; but no effect produced by electricity;—6th, Luminous matter is principally albumen.

We confess that the 5th result puzzles us; because the voltaic electricity *coagulates albumen:* and keeping this fact in view, we cannot reconcile the 3d result to belief. We should have been glad to have had the entire series of experiments before us, that we might have collated them with some of our own; but we shall seek for M. Macaire's paper in the Bibliotheque Universelle itself. The above results we have taken as we found them in the Edinburgh Philosophical Journal. A future opportunity will be noticed to enlarge on this subject.

As relating to animal phosphorescence, we may here remark on some facts given by Baron Percy, an Officer on the French Medical Staff, whose opportunities of observation in the French Army, during twenty-five years of sanguinary war, have perhaps not been surpassed by any other medical veteran of the age. In the performance of his professional duties, he has occasionally been deprived of light, and it was under such a circumstance that the Baron first observed a phosphorescence on a slight wound of the leg for more than fifteen days. The soldier had applied compresses wet with urine to the sore, and possibly this contributed to the effect. The fact, however, impressing Baron Percy's mind, led him to remark, some time afterwards, a vivid light, or true ignis fatuus, diffused over the wound of an officer, at the siege of Manheim. In this case, pure water only had been applied to the part. Many similar facts occurred to the Baron afterwards, and would, probably, to all other surgeons, were opportunities created of observing wounds in the dark. In these cases, the phosphoric light may have been evolved by some chemical changes taking place in the secreted matter. and so distinguishing the mode of evolution from that exhibited by some living animals; the latter, we should presume, either directly secrete phosphorus, or phosphuretted hydrogen; or they evolve the light by electro-galvanic power. Contending, as we ever shall, that there is no such thing in nature as an anomaly; so we think that some practical benefit may be derived from a course of careful experiment on the subject of animal phosphorescence; for we cannot scruple to declare that we consider the result of M. Macaire's inquiry, before remarked on, to be contradictory, and therefore not satisfactory.

Ceylon Leech.

Dr. Davy, in his account of the interior of Ceylon, notices a small animal of singular voracity for blood. It is about half an inch in length, semitransparent, active, capable of great extreme in elongation and contraction, with a sharp pointed extremity. It seems to possess the sense of smell, for when a person advances near to their abode, they rush forward as expecting prey. Dr. Davy says that " those who have had no experience of these animals, of their immense numbers in their favourite haunts, of their activity, keen appetite, and love of blood, can have no idea of the kind and extent of annoyance they are to travellers in the interior, of which they may be truly said to be the plague. In rainy weather, it is almost shocking to see the legs of men on a long march, thickly beset with them, gorged with blood, and the blood trickling down in streams. In attempting to keep them off, they crowd to the attack, and fasten on quicker than they can be removed. I do not exaggerate, when I say that I have occasionally seen at least fifty on a person at a time. Their bites are apt to fester, and become sores, and frequently degenerate into extensive ulcers, which, in too many instances, have occasioned the loss of limb, and even of life."

The effects of their bite are apparently poisonous. We wish the Doctor had noticed whether this virulence was influenced by season.

Eruption of Carbonized Wood.

Mr. Bringier was in the vicinity of New Madrid at the time of the earthquake that destroyed it. The shock was felt two hundred miles round. The extraordinary spectacle that presented, and the personal peril by which Mr. B. was surrounded, are well expressed by the editor of the Edinburgh Philosophical Journal. "The violence of the earthquake having disturbed the earthy strata impending over the subterraneous cavities existing probably in an extensive bed of wood, highly carbonized, occasioned the whole superior mass to settle. This mass, pressing upon the water which had filled the lower cavities, forced it out, and blew up the earth, with loud explosions. It rushed out in all directions, bringing with it an *enormous quantity of carbonized wood reduced mostly into dust, which was ejected to the height of from 10 to 15 feet*, and fell in a black shower, mixed with the sand which its rapid motion had forced along: at the same time, the roaring and whistling, produced by the impetuosity of the air escaping from its confinement, seemed to increase the horrible disorder of the trees, which every where encumbered each other, being blown up, cracking and splitting, and falling by thousands at a time. In the mean time, the surface was sinking, and a black liquid was rising up to the belly of Mr. Bringier's horse, which stood motionless, struck with panic and terror. These occurrences occupied nearly two minutes. The trees kept falling here and there, and the whole surface of the country remained covered with holes, which, to compare small things with great, resembled so many craters of volcanoes, surrounded with a ring of carbonized wood and sand, which rose to the height of about seven feet. The depth of several of these holes, when measured some time after, did not exceed twenty feet, but the quicksand had washed into them. Mr. Bringier noticed a tendency to carbonization in all the vegetable substances that had been soaking in the ponds, produced by these eruptions." — *American Journal of Science*, vol. iii. No. 1, p. 20.

Mr. Bringier does not give us an account of any trial that he put the combustibility of this carbonized wood to; we are, therefore, ignorant of its purity. It is a matter of curious speculation, as to what the properties of this buried mass of vegetable coal might have been, after a lapse of distant centuries,—probably much must have depended on the quality of the superincumbent strata.

Egyptian Pigment.

The Pigment subjected to experiment was taken from the hieroglyphics cut into the sarcophagus, discovered by Belzoni, in the tomb of Psammis. The stone is a large mass of translucent matter, denominated Arragonite. The pigment is now nearly black at the surface; but of a dirty olive green when powdered. In some parts it is light blue. Heated in a glass tube, a dark coloured oil came over, with dense brown and inflammable vapours. A black residuum remained: the loss about 10 per cent. Diluted muriatic and nitric acid (or both) digested on the residuum, gave a slight effervescence, taking up about 17 per cent., with a blueish green solution, found to contain copper and lime: perhaps the lime may have come from a portion of the arragonite. About three-fourths remained insoluble, and, when dry, exhibited a beautiful blue colour, not much inferior to the finest ultramine; but rather deeper, and indestructible by a red heat. By farther process, Mr. Children determined the pigment to be oxide of copper, a large portion of silica, and a small portion of lime and potassa.

In the name of the artists, we thank Mr. Children for this analysis; and, also, beg leave to call to the attention of our readers how exactly this composition agrees with that recommended by the illustrious Sir Humphry Davy, as the result of experiment in his analysis of the pigments of the ancients. We cannot conclude this paper without adverting to the desideratum of some substitute for the oils, commonly used in painting. It is plain that the deterioration of colour, in the above pigment, is imputable to the oil; which would necessarily assume the black tinge in the close and dark cavity of the tomb.

Brilliant Red Pigment.

As, in the subject of the last paper, we stand indebted to chemistry, so do we here. M. Grotthus, in Les Bulletins de la Societe d'Encouragement, states a very simple process, whereby a brilliant red may be prepared, surpassing the lustre of common carmine. Vermilion being used in fraudulent mixture with carmine, artists have commonly dissolved the latter in ammonia; which leaves the vermilion as residue. This solution has a purple tinge at first; but as the ammonia volatilizes, the red becomes brilliant. Still, from the experiment of M. Grotthus, we may infer that some portion of the ammonia remains in combination with the colouring matter. In order to abstract the ammonia totally, he added to the solution, by degrees, another solution of concentrated acetic acid. The precipitate produced, he states to be of such an exquisite lustre, that the eye could scarcely bear to dwell on it. But this precipitate was so fine as to require the addition of a little alcohol, to diminish its density: the colouring matter then again depositing itself, and being dried, became the admirable pigment alluded to.

On Matter and Form for the Compass Needle.
Philosophical Transactions.

Captain Kater undertook the experiments, from whence the subsequent deductions were made, in order to render the needle as sensible of, and permanent in, power, as possible: for the needles carried out by Captain Ross, in his northern voyage, had become nearly useless, by their approximation to the magnetic pole. We would particularly notice Captain Kater's inference as to the best form for the magnet, because it corroborates that we drew ourselves (at page 21 of this number) from Mr. Barlow's proof that the magnetic influence was confined to the surface:—

1. "That the best material for compass-needles is clock spring; but care must be taken in forming the needle to expose it as seldom as possible to heat, otherwise its capability of receiving magnetism will be much diminished.

2. "That the best form for a compass-needle is the pierced rhombus, in the proportion of about five inches in length to two inches in width, this form being susceptible of the greatest directive force.

3. "That the best mode of tempering a compass-needle is, first to harden it at a red heat, and then to soften it from the middle to about an inch from each extremity, by exosing it to a heat sufficient to cause the blue colour which arises again to disappear.

4. "That in the same plate of steel of the size of a few square inches only, portions are found varying considerably in their capability of receiving magnetism, though not apparently differing in any other respect.

5. "That polishing the needle has no effect on its magnetism.

6. "That the best mode of communicating magnetism to a needle, appears to be by placing it in the magnetic meridian, joining the opposite poles of a pair of bar magnets (the magnets being in the same line) and laying the magnets so joined flat upon the needle with their poles upon its centre; then having elevated the distant extremities of the magnets, so that they may form an angle of about two or three degrees with the needle, they are to be drawn from the centre of the needle to the extremities, carefully preserving the same inclination, and having joined the poles of the magnets at a distance from the needle, the operation is to be repeated ten or twelve times on each surface.

7. "That in needles from five to eight inches in length, their

weights being equal, the directive forces are nearly as the lengths.

8. "That the directive force does not depend upon extent of surface, but in needles of nearly the same length and form, is as the mass.

9. "That the deviation of a compass-needle occasioned by the attraction of soft iron, depends, as Mr. Barlow has advanced, on extent of surface, and is wholly independent of the mass, except a certain thickness of the iron, amounting to about two-tenths of an inch, which is requisite for the complete developement of its attractive energy."

Electro Magnetism.

Philosophical Transactions.

This paper, by Sir H. Davy, bears some affinity of character to Captain Kater's, on the subject of imparting magnetic power to the needle. Whatever may be even suggested, by such an authority as the President of the Royal Society, will be held in as high respect as can be compatible with cautious philosophy; so we shall always seize opportunities of recording his valuable opinions. Sir Humphry, in noticing M. Ampere's view of the identity of magnetism and electricity, says, " I shall beg permission to mention two circumstances which seem to me unfavourable to the idea of the identity of electricity and magnetism: 1st, the great distance to which magnetism is communicated by common electricity (I found a steel bar was made magnetic at fourteen inches distance from a wire transmitting an electric shock from about seventy feet of charged surface); and 2d, that the effect of magnetizing at a distance by electricity, takes place with the same readiness through air and water, glass, mica, or metals; *i. e.* through conductors and non-conductors."

We confess we are not satisfied that we exactly understand the President, as to whether he means that lines of communication were made between the electrical battery and the steel bar; or that planes of the respective conductors and non-conductors were interposed perpendicularly.

But to revert to the specific object of Sir H. Davy's paper, which was that of exciting great power in magnets: he tells us, that the simple mode of effecting such power may be in fixing bars of steel *across*, or circular pieces of steel for making horse-shoe magnets *around*, the electrical conductors of buildings, in elevated situations.

Supply of Water.

Monthly Magazine, No. 360.

The inhabitants of Tottenham having long been distressed for water, are now supplied by the very simple means of boring; but we apprehend that the small capacity of the perforation will render it particularly liable to be choaked up, by malignancy or negligence. The perforation is effected thus:— " by the mere use of iron rods, forced into the earth by a windlass. The workmen (only three) in a few days get to a genuine spring of pure water, fit for every purpose of life; after the water is found, they merely put tin pipes down the aperture, and it throws up a fine stream from four to five feet high. The parish, observing its utility, have, much to their credit, sunk one, which they have ornamented very prettily with a bronze pillar, &c. The first that was formed gives a supply of twenty-nine gallons a minute. But the most important circumstance is the smallness of the expense. Several artisans have agreed, and will agree to perform the work for from twenty to twenty-five pounds; from this statement it will immediately occur to you, how easily large neighbourhoods may be supplied with water."

" Independently of the difference of the expense, the water from these springs must be more wholesome than that supplied from sluggish streams, exposed to receive all the filth which carelessness or malice, may throw into them."

On Musty Flour, and Bread.

E. Davy, Esq., of the Cork Institution, has found that carbonate of magnesia, (*i. e.* common magnesia,) will correct the musty smell and taste of damaged flour. The proportions to be used are thirty grains of magnesia to one pound of the flour. The process of making and baking to be the same as usual; from which results bread more light and spongy, whiter, more agreeable in flavour, and capable of keeping better, than that in common use. Magnesia has been recommended by Mr. Mackenzie, as a substitute for alum in the forming of bread; partly on the ground that as it corrects mustiness, so it must add to the good quality of even good flour. Now, we are not quite convinced that any chemical addition to the flour, supposing it pure in quality, and perfect in condition, is requisite. Nor are we more so that alum is used in a pernicious abundance by common bakers. Subject bread to the simple test of infusing it in distilled water for an hour: strain the fluid clear, and add a few drops of muriate of barytes; which, with alum, will throw down a dense white precipitate according to the proportion of aluminous matter present. It will, however, be found that there is but a small quantity of alum in bread,—not exceeding a few grains in the quartern loaf, and incapable of producing any bad effect by constipating, or otherwise, even if a person live on bread alone. It is the *bad quality* of the *flour*, from which we have so much to fear, in the London bread; and when this have arisen from mustiness, the admixture of magnesia may correct the evil: but we must earnestly remonstrate against the use of magnesia, as a constant ingredient in bread; even supposing it to have the properties ascribed to it; because we know, on the authority of Mr. Brande, how dangerous the habitual use of magnesia may be, on the digestive organs,—we may add, too, on the urinary, where a white sediment deposits from the secretion; for magnesia will almost invariably augment it.

THE FOCUS

OF

PHILOSOPHY, SCIENCE, AND ART.

No. II.]   Saturday, December 8, 1821.   [Vol. I.

On Pitchstone. By J. MacCulloch, M. D., F. R. S., &c.
Journal of Science, No. 23.

The very reason given by Dr. MacCulloch for not effecting all that geologists might wish on the subject of pitchstone, impels us to select all that we can meet with under the stamp of a respectable authority. Such we consider the Doctor to be; and shall gladly avail ourselves of the advantages resulting from his spirit of observation. Pitchstone, it is remarked, bears strong analogy with Trap; both as to its mineral characters, and geological connections: besides, it is usually found where trap exists. Dr. MacCulloch considers that the stratification of pitchstone remains to be proved: for we have not any example of it in this island; and the presumed instances in the isle of Arran, he states to be only veins conformable to the rocks which govern their position. Nor does he allow the reported stratification on the European continent, to be other than mineralogical error; by confounding resinous-looking jaspers with true pitchstone. Throughout Scotland, pitchstone occurs in veins, (with only one exception,) intersecting the strata in angular lines. In but one instance do they ramify; namely, the veins of Egg, round a mass of chert. The scuir of Egg would constitute but a solitary exception, in Scotland, were the position of the mass of pitchstone really what it appears to be. Dr. M., however, states it to be a porphyritic substance, intermediate between pitchstone and basalt. It forms a narrow irregular wall, on the surface of a mass of trap. He judges that it is neither a bed, nor stratified rock; because the very trap that supports it, reposes upon, and penetrates, the latest secondary stratum of coal.

In further proof that pitchstone is never to be considered as in regular rocky stratification, Dr. M. urges, that it is found in granite, in red, and in recent, sandstone; as well as in the latest trap rocks: and it will be obvious that, in the first and last of these, it could not be stratified;—in short, it must be always considered as a mere vein. Pitchstone is also analogous with trap, in its sometimes bearing the porphyritic character; and this is the common structure of the Scotch pitchstone. There is also an analogy in another respect; and that is, the pitchstone very rarely assumes the amygdaloid formation. Trap is inferred to intrude on the rocky strata, because masses of them have been found imbedded in the trap itself. This is uncommon in pitchstone; but Dr. MacC. says there is a solitary example in the vein at the end of Brodick wood, in Arran. Still, this exception, in the case of pitchstone, strengthens the analogous rule; for trap, too, very rarely forms in a similar manner.

The igneous origin of pitchstone is as justly presumed as that of trap; and, perhaps, more surely; as relates to porphyritic trap and pitchstone: for, in the latter, the feldspar is apparently vitrified into enamel, on the surface of the larger crystals, as if they had been subjected to the momentary action of the blow-pipe; the smaller are vitrified to their centres.

The Doctor next traces the casual resemblance of pitchstone to pearl-stone; but he does not intimate any apparent existence of obsidian: he merely enforces the similarity of spheroidal concretion; and remarks on the casual union of the enamel spherule, with the matter of the pitchstone; thereby forming a peculiar kind of pearl-stone. In Arran, an example of a very rare species occurs, wherein, he says, that "the feldspar crystals consist of successive concentric prisms, a layer of pitchstone being interposed between each; so as to produce a compound crystal."

If further proof of the propriety in concluding that trap and pitchstone are analogous, were wanting, we might recur to the common transition into basalt. Dr. MacC. presents us with a well marked instance at Loch Scavig, in Sky, where the basaltic veins, ramifying through the hyperstene rock, terminate their fine extremities in perfect pitchstone.

In the Cuchullin Hills of Sky, a large vein of basalt bears outer laminæ of pitchstone, which graduates into the basaltic matter of the vein. At Lamlash, the most particular example presents; for a vein of basalt penetrates through one of greenstone; the outer walls of the basalt being of glossy black pitchstone, half an inch thick. This covering case of pitchstone is, in part, distinct; the lamina being decided: in other part, it graduates down with the basaltic matter of the body of the vein, by an intermediate substance, similar to that of the scuir of Egg. In one of the veins of Egg, the body of this very substance is incased with perfect and brittle pitchstone. It would seem, then, that in these instances of united basalt, intermediate substance, and pitchstone, they were all of similar character in composition; but had assumed these forms, and yielded these appearances, through the comparative degree of their fusion, respectively.

Dr. MacC. does not remark on this point himself, his paper being rather descriptive than doctrinal; but we think it no great stretch of conjecture to draw such an inference. The composition of pitchstone and trap is, however, maintained, by the Doctor, to be analogous; and by easy gradation we include basalt; as all are, most likely, of similar origin. Dr. MacC. notices one point wherein trap and pitchstone differ; and that is, trap can often be traced to a fundamental mass; while pitchstone has not yet been found connected with any principal body of rock. The veins of the latter vary much in extent of range; ramifying from yards to inches, and sometimes are drawn out into thread-like branches. The pitchstone veins vary, too, in composition, colour, texture, and aspect; for different qualities will occur in the same; but the outer layer is always more perfectly vitrified than the interior of the mass.   (To be continued.)

Experimental Researches on Water Cements, Mortar, and Lime. By. S. J. VICAT, Engineer of the Corps Royal des Ponts et Chaussees, of France.

Scarcely any practical subject of more general application than that of cements, could be selected as matter of investigation. We appeal to all men of observation, whether every new street in London does not testify the ignorance, negligence, or knavery of the compounders of mortar. We witness all sorts of filth as ingredients; the lime in all sorts of condition, but what it should be; and the working of the mass so hastily, and so slovenly done, as to render the eventual compound any thing but a cement. Indeed, when we consider the bad quality of the mortar; and the no less poverty of the bricks; we may wonder that the houses stand at all. Perhaps it is by the mere mass of matter, accumulated longitudinally, when formed into streets, that principally enables them to support each other.

M. Vicat treats his subject practically, and scientifically too; therefore we shall gladly seek information, and not at all apprehend disappointment. He sets out with considering the qualities of the lime, which are commonly distinguished by the terms fat and lean lime. When lime reduced to powder, and absorbing so much water as to triple its bulk, during its conversion into quick-lime, (slack-lime?) he terms fat. If the bulk be augmented to from one to one and a fifth, he calls it lean.

The denomination of *lean* lime has been applied, exclusively, to all those species which have the property of hardening, or setting under water. "To define, more exactly, these several species, I shall give the name of hydraulic limes to those which, when burnt, have the property of hardening, in a short time, under water. I shall call *common* limes, those which have not this quality. And *fat* limes, those which, when calcined, and plunged under water, absorb, in slacking, 260 to 360 per cent. of their weight of water. *Middling* limes, those that absorb 230 to 260 per cent. And *lean* limes, those that absorb 100 to 230." The hydraulic limes are white, grey, or clay coloured, and when mixed with water to the consistence of thin soup, and plunged under water, *part with*, in setting, a portion of that with which they had been mixed. When of the thickness of paste, they *absorb* water in setting. Therefore, a determinate portion of water, it seems, is necessary to the proper setting. M. V. says, that " common limes slacked under water, take up more than they can solidify; and cannot reject the superfluity,— therefore do not set." There are some intermediate limes, taking consistency, but never setting. The quality of lime varies, not only in the same district, but in the same quarry; some being perfectly hydraulic, and some slacking soft. The setting of lime is not owing to manganese, silex, or alumine, as supposed by Guiton, Descotils, and Senorches. The hydraulic lime is also preferable, for common building; but disliked by the mason, because it requires a smaller portion of sand, consequently the more of lime. Guiton has recommended two processes for artificial hydraulic lime. The one consists of " four parts of grey clay, six of black oxyd of manganese, ninety of lime-stone in powder: the mixture to be calcined." The other thus, " add to common quicklime a certain portion of white iron ore, consisting principally of magnesian carbonate of lime." The first method requires too much labour, and the last could not be much used. M. Vicat, pursuing a hint of Saussure's, was led to this process. He mingles air-slacked lime with brick-clay, and a little water, and forms the mass into balls; then dries, and afterwards calcines them. Fat lime, powdered by exposure to air, may combine with about 20 per cent. of clay. Inferior lime requiring proportionally less clay. It is requisite that fragments of pebbles, if any, should be washed away, before the mixture with lime. A very common share of ingenuity will enable the manufacturer to establish his processes on a large scale.

There are three modes of slacking lime. The first, is by throwing a portion of water on the lime;—this the masons usually do to excess, rendering it a mere milk of lime. The common fat limes, when cream-like, augment three and a tenth in volume: the natural water-setting limes, only one and a fifth. Experiment determined that the leanest hydraulic lime absorbed 118 per cent. of water. The fattest lime, took up 357 per cent. One specimen, of very lean lime, not hydraulic, absorbed 144.

It should be well understood, that if lime be slacked by interrupted portions of water, it will not fall well to powder. It should either receive its full and proper portion at once; or be suffered to cool, before each successive affusion. When lime have been exposed to the air a few days before it is slacked, it will remain immersed in water, some time, before the slacking commences: especially hydraulic limes; and they, in this case, will evolve but little heat.

The second method of slacking is, to plunge the lime in water, and immediately withdraw it. It may be kept a long time in the powder, if dry; and does not evolve heat, when afterwards mixed with water. Fat lime takes up about 18 per cent. of water, to form powder. Hydraulic limes absorb from 20 to 35. Fat lime should be broken small, before it be processed this way, or it will divide in hard immiscible fragments. Common limes, after immersion, augment in bulk, about 50 to 70 per cent. The hydraulic limes from 80 to 118.

The third method consists in simple exposure of lime to a dry atmosphere. Very little heat evolves in this process. And by it, the fat limes augment their weights two-fifths; and from 75 to 155 per cent. of their volume.

These are the three modes of slacking lime. The first is generally practised; the second is merely experimental; and the third is rejected,—but how judiciously, will be hereafter exposed. (To be continued.)

On some new Electro-Magnetical Motions, and on the Theory of Magnetism. By Mr. FARADAY, Chemical Assistant in the Royal Institution. Journal of Science, No. 23.

Mr. Faraday's official situation affords him superior opportunities of aiding the cause of philosophy; and he seems resolved that they shall not be lost on him: for he engages in the pursuit of science with a zeal and judgment, that must be beneficial to the community, as well as honourable to himself. Mr. F. considers his experiments as tending to reconcile some discordant opinions now existing: how far this may be the case, we will leave to experimentalists to determine; foreknowing how tenaciously particular modes of reasoning are retained, when parties are once committed by them with the public, we presume that nothing short of positive demonstration can prevail; nor indeed should it.

The instrument used by Mr. Faraday was, Dr. Hare's calorimoter. The first thing noticed by Mr. F. is, that on bringing the needle towards the galvanized perpendicular wire, he found the attractive and repulsive positions, instead of being four, " one attractive and one repulsive for each pole," to be eight,—" two attractive and two repulsive for each pole." On approaching with the above wire to one pole of the needle, the pole passes off according to the attractive or repulsive quality of its extremity: but, as the wire is passed up towards the centre of motion, the directive tendency diminishes; and when at the centre, becomes indifferent to the wire: at last the motion is reversed; and the needle passes the opposite way. From hence Mr. F. infers that the true pole is not at the extremity of the needle, but at a point, a little distant from the end. Supposing this to be the case, may not the relative distances between the centre of motion, the true pole, and the extremity, vary, or be modified by the proportionate masses, magnitudes, forms, and powers, of the needles? Or, are they invariable, as to their comparative distances respectively? We would beg leave to suggest this to Mr. F., as a matter worthy of his future inquiry; because it may, in some degree, indicate the best form for the compass needle. He says that this point in the axis of the needle, or the true pole, as he infers it, had a tendency to revolve round the wire; and, by consequence, the wire round the point. To determine these relative tendencies, by experiment, he caused a copper wire, bent in the form of a crank, and revolving with little friction (by having its extremities moving in mercury, both at the top and the bottom,) to approach a magnetic pole; the wire immediately revolved on its axis, and struck against " the magnet; and that being rapidly brought round to the other side, the wire again made a revolution;" showing that it would have continued revolving, had it not been mechanically impeded by the magnet. This obstruction to the free revolution of the wire, Mr. F. ingeniously devised a means of obviating; and then, " the wire immediately began to revolve round the pole of the magnet; and continued to do so, so long as the connection was continued." By extending the distance of the radial extremity, the velocity was diminished. By reversing the contacts at the copper and zinc poles of the apparatus, the revolving direction was reversed. And by varying the position of the magnetic pole, relatively as to the wire, within and without; or from the centre of motion, up the side of the wire; it was found that the revolving tendency still displayed itself.

Mr. Faraday next proceeded to satisfy himself that the revolving power, between the wire and the magnet, was mutual; and constructed a very ingenious, but simple, means to demonstrate that fact. We will borrow his own description of it. He says, " The next object was to make the magnet revolve round the wire. This was done by so loading one pole of the small magnet with platinum, that the magnet would float upright in a bason of mercury, with the other pole above its surface; then connecting the mercury with one plate, and bringing a wire from the other, perpendicularly, into it, in another part, near the floating magnet, the upper pole immediately began to float round the wire; whilst the lower pole, being removed away, caused no interference, or counteracting effect." Here, again, the revolving direction was governed by the voltaic contact: for, as in the case of the wire revolutions before stated, the magnetic ones were now found to be reversed, as the reversed contacts were made with the zinc and copper poles.

Mr. Faraday now proceeds to relate that he endeavoured to make a wire, and a magnet, revolve on their own respective axes, by preventing the circular rotation. But he could not effect his purpose in the smallest degree. He says, " The motions evidently belong to the current, or whatever else it be, that is passing through the wire, and not to the wire itself; except as the vehicle of the current. When that current is made a curve, by the form of the wire, it is easy to conceive how, in revolving, it should take the wire with it:

but when the wire is straight, the current may revolve without any motion being communicated to the wire through which it passes."

The results of the experiments, by M. Ampere, are considered by Mr. Faraday, on the authority of Dr. Wollaston's opinion, to be complicated; not simple: Dr. W. judging, from the north pole of a needle on one side of the wire, and the south pole on the other side, being both attracted, that there was what he called a vertiginous magnetism; or an electro-magnetic current passing round the axis of the conjunctive wire. In the case of the wire being in the form of a helix, it is presumed (on the vertiginous principle) that there is a concentration in the axis of the helix, while the contrary kind is diffused and weakened, on the opposite side of the wire. When the pole of the magnetic needle be placed on one side of the wire, connected with a battery, it revolves round it, " passing towards that side by which it is attracted, and from that side by which it is repelled: *i. e.* the pole is at once attracted and repelled, and therefore neither recedes nor approaches."

M. Ampere having demonstrated that two similar wires attract each other, Sir H. Davy has pursued the fact, and shown that filings adhering to them attract from one to the other, on the same side; so that they condense the power towards the exterior wires, and may be said to resemble the effect of a ribbon of wire; the lateral margins of which are affected similarly with those of a longitudinal plate.

(To be continued.)

M. Bockman *on the Intensity of Magnetism produced by Electricity.* Bibliotheque Universelle.

M. Bockman used a plate machine, 26 inches diameter, and, by shocks, imparted to a steel rod a repulsive force, on the magnetic needle, of 7°.

By the charge of a Leyden surface, 3·7 square inches, he obtained, at one discharge, a repulsion of the north pole of the needle, 9°; of the south pole, 12°. At 2, 6, and 24 discharges, the repulsions were less at the north than at the south pole: but the difference diminished in an inverse proportion to the number of discharges; until, at 36, the repulsion on the north pole was 20°·5: at the south, 21°·5.

With 48 square inches of coating, the north pole was repelled 17°·5; the south, 19°. At 2 and 6 discharges, the proportionate effect on the respective poles, was in a direct ratio. And at 14 and 24, their effect was similar; i. e. repulsion on the north, 27°,—on the south, 30°.

With a Leyden phial of 300 square inches of coating, and at two discharges, the repulsion on the north was 21°·5; on the south, 23°. At 4, 6, and 18 discharges, northern repulsion was alike, 29°. On the southern, at four discharges, was 33°; but at 6 and 18 was alike, 34°.

With a battery of five jars, with about 300 square inches each, say 1500 square inches in the total: At one discharge, the repulsion of the north pole was 25°·5; of the south, 26°·5. At two discharges, the repulsion became 29° on the north, and 30° on the south pole. Thence through 3, 4, 5, 6, and 7, the rates gradually became up to the last number, 35° of repulsion on the north, and 36°·5 on the south pole.

We learn from the above experiments,—

That the repulsive power is not equal on the two poles of the needle; it being uniformly greater at the south than at the north.

That the greater the number of discharges from the same electrical surface, the less is that repulsive disparity.

That when the electrical surface be 300 inches, the maximum of repulsive effect is obtained under fewer discharges, and the disparity on the different poles is greatest.

Under the discharges from 1500 inches, we not only find the gradation of effect more regular, as to the number of discharges; but, also, that the disparity of influence on the north and south poles is less in quantity.

Lastly, we find that the effect produced is by no means proportionate to the extent of electric surface charged.

But M. Bockman tried if the diameter of the steel needles influenced the effect; and using the proportions of 1, 2, and 3 lines in diameter, the larger ones received magnetism in the highest degree, the maximum lying between the 12th and

18th discharge; and the highest repulsive power was 52°·5 on the north pole, 46°·5 on the south. In this result, the extended surface of the magnet probably denotes the measure of power.

To determine the effect of the number of spires, he varied them in nearly double order from one up to 174, with 3, 9, and 15 discharges on the respective number of spires. At 1 and 2 of the latter, not any effect was produced by any number of discharges. At 4 spires, 3 discharges gave of repulsion on the north pole 9°, and on the south 10°. 9 discharges gave of repulsion on the north pole 13°, on the south 14°. 15 discharges gave 13°·5 northern, and 15° southern repulsion.

The effect gradually augments up to 128 spires, when 3 discharges gave 24° northern repulsion, and 26° southern; 9 discharges 28° north and 28° south; 15 discharges 28°·5 north, and 28°·5 south. At 174 spires, the scale begins to descend. We should observe again, that the southern repulsion exceeded the northern, until it came near the maximum of effect.

We now come to an experiment worth all the others, instructive as they may be; and that is, When a spiral of 58 turns had half of the spires turned to the right, and the other half to the left, the two extremities of the steel needle, placed in the tube, *became north poles; and the two south poles appeared in the middle of the needle.* The repulsion of the north poles was 19° and 17°·5.

We consider this result extremely valuable, because it exactly coincides with what, it will be seen, in this number, Mr. Faraday has found; and what would scarcely have been conjectured; namely, that a needle may have four poles, or rather, that one line of steel may be two distinct magnets. We consider this fact to be one of the most extraordinary that has lately been discovered; and meriting further pursuit. It should not be overlooked that these two gentlemen have influenced the needle alike, in production of a double magnet, by different means. M. Bockman employed common electricity; but Mr. Faraday used the voltaic.

Among other experiments with glass tubes and spirals, varied in many ways, wherein the steel needle was always rendered magnetic, these two deserve especial notice. A needle was placed in a tube of glass, and this within another tube, of white iron, an inch in diameter: the whole within another glass tube, surrounded with a spiral. The first electrical discharge rendered the iron tube magnetic, the north pole showing a repulsive force of 21°; the south pole lost its magnetism rapidly. In a few minutes the tube ceased to show magnetic signs. The steel needle within the inner glass tube was totally insensible. But when a tube of lead was substituted for the iron one, the needle acquired magnetic power, and gave a repulsive force of 14° and 16°. The first of these experiments shows that the iron tube intercepted the magnetic fluid from the needle; the second, that the lead proved an effectual conductor.

A needle of nickel, in a glass tube, with the usual spiral, was subjected to several strong electrical discharges, without any perceptible effect.

M. Bockman next tried the relative effects of spirals of different diameters; the needle being placed in a glass tube, and subjected to discharges from a Leyden electrical surface of 300 square inches. With a spiral of 34 inches diameter, the maximum of effect was at five discharges; the repulsion of the southern pole being, as usual, superior to that of the northern,—the former being, at five discharges, 16° north, and 19° at the south.

With a spiral of 84, and of one between that and the 34 above mentioned, a barely sensible effect was produced; so that the diameter of 34 was, or nearly so, the maximum.

When steel needles were placed *without* the spiral, but near to it, they became more or less magnetic by electrical discharges; but had poles opposite to those placed within the spiral.

We place a high value on M. Bockman's experiments, but our estimation would have been greatly enhanced, if he had, in every case, tried the comparative effect of voltaic electricity. Indeed we are rather surprised that gentlemen do not sufficiently advert to the expediency of observing what correspondence, or difference, in effect may result from the same needle, under the same circumstances, when operated on by the common electrical, and the voltaic, forces respectively.

On the Black Rete Mucosum being a Defence against the Scorching Effects of the Sun's Rays. By Sir E. HOME, Bart.   Philosophical Transactions.

Sir Everard instituted a set of simple experiments, easy to be repeated by any person desirous to verify them, or to be pursued, if further inquiry be intended. We should not, *a priori*, have come to such a conclusion, by aid of mere reason, as these experiments warrant. The scorching and heating effect, which we should have thought must have been produced in a like degree, are evidently in a reversed. The third experiment was thus:—

"*Exp.* 3.—I exposed the backs of my two hands to the sun's rays, with a thermometer upon each; the one hand was uncovered; the other had a covering of black cloth, under which the ball of the thermometer was placed. After ten minutes, the degree of heat of each thermometer was marked, and the appearance on the skin examined. This was repeated three different times. The

1st time the thermometer under the cloth was	91° the other	85°
2d time	94° . . .	91°
3d time	106° . . .	98°

"In every one of these trials the skin was scorched that was uncovered; the other had not suffered in the slightest degree; there was no appearance of perspiration on either hand."

"*Exp.* 4.—The back of a negro's hand was exposed to the sun with a thermometer upon it, which stood at 100°; at the end of ten minutes the skin had not suffered in the least."

This last experiment shows in a remarkable degree the superior power of the black cutis in resisting the scorching effects of the sun. Some allowance should be made for the comparative delicacy of a gentleman's hand, with the hardier condition of the negro's, both in a nervous and fibrous sense.

" *Exp.* 7.—September 9, eleven o'clock, the thermometer in the sun at 90°. The concentrated rays applied to a piece of black kerseymere cloth, made tight round my arm, for fifteen minutes, gave me no real pain, and left no impression whatever on the skin, although the nap of the cloth had been destroyed.

" This experiment was repeated with white kerseymere, the heat at 86°; in fifteen minutes a blister was formed.

" Repeated with Irish linen, the thermometer 86°. In fifteen minutes a blister was formed, and coagulable lymph thrown out, which had become vascular."

These experiments show, very distinctly, that white cloth, and white linen, excite greater sense of heat, and scorching effect, than black cloth does.

" From these experiments, (observes Sir E. Home,) it is evident that the power of the sun's rays to scorch the skin of animals is destroyed, when applied to a black surface, although the absolute heat; in consequence of the absorption of rays, is greater.

" I have stated the fact of the scorching power of the sun's rays being destroyed, when they are applied to black surfaces, but have not gone further. Sir Humphry Davy, to whom I showed these observations, immediately explained it. He said that the radiant heat in the sun's rays was absorbed by the black surface, and converted into sensible heat."

Much as we admire Sir H. Davy's discrimination, we must say that we hesitate to yield an implicit credit to that explanation which so immediately satisfied Sir E. Home.

Tanning with Larch Bark.
Monthly Magazine, No. 360.

In the Journal last quoted, there is a paper connected with a matter of great practical importance; we allude to the larch bark, as a substitute for oak bark in tanning. It is high time that some succedaneum were found, if such can be; for our oak forests are fast disappearing under the axe; and the high value of land will deter its proprietors from planting trees, that can afford profit to remote descendants only. Mr. Enort Smith (the communicant) says, that amazing quantities of tanning are obtainable from the larch bark. We would recommend to gentlemen to avoid emphatic superlatives; because they lead to suspicion of a rather over sanguine temperament, however facts may really justify them; but should the strong recommendations given of the larch bark prove eventually just, the public cannot be too thankful for the benefit conferred by its friends. Mr. S. states, " that the said species of bark possesses those genuine astringent qualities which are necessary for the purpose of converting the raw material into leather, and that of the most excellent quality likewise, I ascertained when I resided in Newcastle-upon-Tyne. My friend, Mr. Richard Embleton, made an experiment, as to its actual strength, upon some hides and skins of different qualities and weights. At the ensuing August Leather Fair, in that town, he produced an exhibition of his novel experiment before a considerable number of country master tanners there assembled ; and the result of the closest scrutiny on their part, was, that '*better leather than Mr. E. then produced, was never tanned.*'"

Some doubts, and indeed denials, of the stated powers of larch bark have been put forth. Mr. Smith says "whereas, some of those hides which Mr. Embleton produced at the period 1 allude to, were of that kind which are denominated backs, and several (a hide divided in two) weighed upwards of sixty pounds each pair. Now, as respects the wearing properties of leather so tanned, Mr. John Sillick, jun. nephew to Mrs. Sillick, the principal currier of the town, informed me that the craft (shoemakers) spoke in the most favourable terms of the kindness of this leather, in working,—a sure sign of its goodness ; and Mr. Embleton, to carry the demonstrative effect of leather tanned with the larch bark, to the greatest practicable evidence, had on one of his boots a sole of Valonia tannage, and one on the other of larch bark tannage, and he frequently afterwards declared that the latter imbibed less moisture, and made a better resistance in the wear, than the tanners' favourite, the Valonia tannage did; needs there

Dutch or German bark to be imported, after this successful trial on the part of Mr. E?"

We cannot omit adding; what may not be so generally known, as, for the reasons above stated, it ought to be; namely, that the wood of chesnut contains twice as much tannin as cleansed oak bark; and six-sevenths as much colouring matter as logwood.

On an Elastic Admixture of Hair with Tar.
New Monthly Magazine.

We are here presented with a fabric that certainly bids fair to rival the common modes of excluding aqueous penetration, provided it eventually prove to be as efficacious as the inventor announces. And if so, we presume that it may be adaptable to many purposes of common life, as well as the important one for which it is particularly recommended; that is, to form a water-proof case for shipping.

Mr. Wm. Wood, of Bow, Middlesex, is the inventor of this prepared texture. It consists of a light felt of hide or hair; or mixture of hide hair and wool; which, when *saturated* with tar, is elastic, and water-proof. Mr. Wood proposes to sheath shipping with it, by nailing it on the outside of the ship's side and bottom. He does not at all advert to the ship's coppering, and therefore we infer that he means to place this water-proof garment between the copper sheathing and the longitudinal planking; for, to suppose that it should be endangered by the mechanical violence to which a ship's bottom is perpetually exposed, would be to totally destroy all reasonable expectation of its practical benefit. Its elasticity is so great as to admit of considerable extension of the fibre, without laceration; and, therefore, Mr. W. conceives that when the seams of the ship be opened, by strain of the timbers, the felt will not only re-assume its original space, but be occasionally interposed between the receded edges of the planks; and, thereby, constitute a kind of elastic caulking. Not having seen any of the manufactured substance, we cannot, of course, say whether its elasticity be equal to the stretch it may be occasionally put to, when a vessel may be said to yield at every seam; but, still, we can conceive its value, in a modified degree, as an elastic water-proof case, for a machine perpetually subjected to the penetrable action of water, proportioned to its weight of pressure on the element,—that is, we would consider it to produce the effect of a flexible and moveable varnish, over the surface to which it may be adapted.

The inventor, moreover, attributes to the adhesive felt, the very important advantage of completely protecting the ship from every species of worm, in all climates. He says, this animal is never known to penetrate the material, in the slightest degree. A small portion of practical effect is certainly worth many pages of doctrine; but we confess our surprise at this fact; taking it for granted that it be such; for why should the mere circumstance of saturating a texture, not in itself deleterious, with tar, produce an effect that tar itself, although saturating, as it were, the very surface of the timber is not found equal to. Whether a ship be strained, or not, in her seams, she will equally take the worm; so that the preventive efficacy against the worm, residing in the adhesive felt, cannot consist in its plugging up the space of the opening timbers. Besides, it has been proved that the pyrolignous acid, in tar, is a common cause of rot. At all events, we would take the liberty to recommend to Mr. Wood to use the tar that has had its aqueous, and acetous, matter distilled off; or been mingled with lime; if the latter be not found to affect the properties which specifically constitute its usefulness.

There are some other purposes to which we can conceive an elastic water-proof coating, like this, more adaptable than that of casing ships; such as a covering for the roofs of buildings, where its lightness, and impermeability to water, would constitute it a valuable protection.

Laws of the Propagation of Heat.

Journal of Science. No. 23.

M. Emer was led by M. Bellevue's inquiry into the nature of aërolites, to investigate how intense heat is suddenly propagated in dense bodies. He considers the points of equal heat and of equal motion of heat in bodies that fracture by the action of fire, and are uniform in all their parts. He then deduces the law governing the form of the violently ruptured surfaces, and concludes:—

1st. That it is at protuberances, and particularly at corners and edges, that this sort of mutilation should commence.

2d. That the fragments should generally affect mammillary forms; or those of pyramids, complete or truncated; or prisms.

3d. That the bases of the pyramids, and one face of the prisms, are the surfaces of the fracture; and are always convex towards their middle, and over the larger part of their surface.

4th. That the other faces are often concave, as if for the most part they were the fractured surfaces of the previous fragments.

5th. That in general the fractured surface of a principal fragment is its largest face, and that it is only the smaller fragments which are occasioned by the breaking up of these that present anomalies.

6th. That each fragment separated, is impelled by the result of the forces of dilatation; which result is perpendicular to the surface of the fracture.

M. Emer has made many useful applications of his theory to the arts and sciences.—Journ. de Phys. xcii. p. 158.

Steam Valves.

Steam is become so universal in its application to the purposes of art, whether by operating as a prime mover, superseding animal labour; as a means of promoting our comfort in numerous domestic processes; or, as adaptable where other powers could not be competent or convenient; that we must consider it an object of the very first interest. We shall therefore always seize with avidity any improved mode of using it; or any means that can render it still further convertible to the welfare of man. The only drawback on the practical value of steam power, consists in the danger of its occasionally bursting through its prescribed bounds; and as we have not any other security against this destructive evil, than that of the Safety Valve, we with pleasure observe human ingenuity at work to make the preventive principle more simple and perfect. We now present our readers with two different sorts of valve; both simple, and, as we think, either of them effective.

The description of the first, we have in the Edinburgh Journal of Arts. It is suggested by a Mr. Adie, that a piece of plate copper be introduced into the manhole of the boiler, and adjusted so as to yield to the pressure of steam at an expansion of about one half of what the boiler might be estimated to bear. But as the steam, when very largely generated, might, on passing through the valve, be dispersed on all sides, to the injury of the workman, it is proposed to carry up a tube from the manhole, 12 or 14 feet above the boiler; at the bottom of which tube, we suppose the manhole and valve to be situate. This would direct the escaping steam upwards, and effectually secure the attendants. The only objection we can consider this valve liable to, is, that proprietors will not choose to waste so much power as one-half of the expansive force that the boiler is calculated to sustain. The valve is perhaps a security; but we fear that it will also be held as requiring too great a sacrifice of that power which is convertible into profit.

The other valve, to which we have alluded, is described in the London Journal of Science and Art. It consists of a cylinder communicating with the interior of the boiler. Within this cylinder is a solid piston, from the upper side of which rises a piston-rod, that passes through a plate closing the upper end of the cylinder. From the upper side of the piston, and spirally round the rod, runs a serpentine spring, which governs the degree of pressure that the solid piston makes downwards in resistance to the escape of the steam.

At a distance from the lower end of the cylinder, and proportioned to the intended effect of the spring, is a bulging out of the cylinder; from which part arises an eduction pipe, to carry the waste steam up the chimney. When the pressure of steam increases so as to equal the force of the spring, it forces the solid piston upwards, as high as the bulging part of the cylinder, whence, diffusing itself, it passes off by the eduction tube. There is also a little reservoir of oil at the bottom of the cylinder, that perpetually lubricates the piston.

This latter valve is more complicated than the former, and therefore more liable to be out of order; as well as less sensible, by the greater amount of its friction. We would earnestly exhort all manufacturers to never suffer the valves, of whatever construction they may be, to possess a resisting power approaching to the presumed strength of the boiler within at least one-third. We know that power is profit: but we also trust, that policy will insure mercy. What, indeed, can be more cruel than to expose our labourer to the momentary hazard of destruction, in order to gain the motive power of an additional horse or two?

Propagation of Sound in Elastic Fluids.

The following is the result of Mr. Van Rees's experiments on the propagation of sound in elastic fluids.—

Velocity at 10° of centig. therm.

Hydrogen	1238·3 metres
Ammonia	432·0
Vapour of water temp. 54° cent.	422·6
Carbonic oxide	341·1
Azote	339·0
Carburetted Hydrogen	377·4
Oxygen	317·7
Deutoxide of azote	317·4
Sulphuretted hydrogen	305·7
Hydrochloric acid	298·8
Carbonic acid	270·7
Protoxide of azote	270·6
Vapour of alcohol	262·7
Sulphurous acid	229·2

The velocity of sound in traversing these gases, seems to have been governed by their respective gravities, making due allowance for that inaccuracy which must always pervade our best imagined experiments; and where any deviation from this result appears, it may probably be in some measure attributable to the impurity of the gases. If, however, that be not the case, and the above tabular order of succession in velocity be correct, we shall probably have to revise our tables of specific gravities of the gases. Calculating from Dr. Ure's General Table of Gaseous Bodies, we shall find, taking hydrogen for the standard, that the velocities given by Van Rees, are inversely as the square root of the specific gravities of the volumes.

Thus, taking the specific gravity of 100 cubic inches of hydrogen gas at 2·118, and of ammonical at 18·000; we find the gravities about 1 of the former to 8·5 of the latter: now, the square root of 8·5 is nearly 2·9;—and on multiplying Van Rees's ratio of velocity in ammonia, 432, by 2·9, we shall have the sum of 1252·8; no very wide variance from 1233·3, the number he gives for the velocity in hydrogen. Again, taking sulphurous acid, at the bottom of the scale, the rule holds, as it does also in those intermediate numbers that we have calculated. Dr. Ure's number for the specific gravity of 100 cubic inches of sulphurous acid gas, is 67·77; the ratio of which with hydrogen, is about 32·47 of the former to 1 of the latter. The square root of 32·47 being about 5·6,—multiply 229·2, Van Rees's number for the velocity in sulphurous gas, by this root 5·6, and you have 1249·44.—This comes still nearer the sum of velocity for hydrogen.

We lay these remarks before our readers as not altogether unworthy of their attention; and as an inducement to some gentleman, who can command leisure, to pursue the matter. On comparing Van Rees's Numbers of Velocity with Dr. Ure's Table of Gaseous Bodies, we were struck with an idea that the proportions of velocities bore some certain relative ratio with the gravities, and found as we have stated. We repeat, that we consider any little discrepancies, as arising from the respective impurities of the gases; or rather, that the deviations from exact coincidence are so small, as to not invalidate the law of the velocity being inversely as the square root of the specific gravity of the volume.

Gelatinous Meteor.

On the 13th of August, 1819, between eight and nine o'clock in the evening, a fire-ball, of the size of a large blown bladder, and of a brilliant white light, was seen in the atmosphere, at Amherst, in Massachussets; it fell near a house, and was examined by Rufus Graves, Esq. formerly Lecturer of Chemistry at Dartmouth College. It was of a circular form, resembling a solid dish, bottom upwards, about eight inches in diameter, and about one in thickness, of a bright buff colour, with a fine nap upon it, similar to that in milled cloth. On removing this nap, a buff coloured pulpy substance, of the consistence of soft soap, appeared, having an offensive suffocating smell, producing nausea and giddiness. After a few minutes' exposure to the air, the buff colour was changed into a livid colour, resembling venous blood. It attracted moisture readily from the air. A quantity of it in a tumbler soon liquified, and formed a mucilaginous substance, of the consistence, colour, and feeling of starch, when prepared for domestic use. The tumbler was then set in a safe place, where it remained undisturbed for two or three days, and it was found to have all evaporated, except a small dark coloured residuum adhering to the bottom and sides of the glass, which, when rubbed between the fingers, produced about a thimble-full of fine ash-coloured powder, without taste or smell, with concentrated and diluted muriatic and nitric acids: no chemical action was observed, and the matter remained unchanged. With the concentrated sulphuric acid, a violent effervescence ensued, a gas evolved, and the whole substance nearly dissolved.

This fact calls to our recollection that in early life we have often seen small masses of gelatinous matter, from the magnitude of an egg to that of as much as would fill a large tea cup, lying in the fields. The country people, in Staffordshire, used to call it *star-shot*. A term which, as we grew older, we considered to arise from the superstition of ignorance. Although the hinds could not point to any direct proof of the star-shot being really what its name imported, yet, the analogy of the matter with that herein described, is so strong, as to justify a presumption that it also was a meteoric production.

On the Advantages which trained Peach-Trees derive from their Roots being allowed to penetrate the Border on the North-side of the Wall. By Mr. J. ROBERTSON, F. H. S.
Transactions of the London Horticultural Society.

Having observed the benefit which trained trees derive from their roots having a communication with the ground on both sides of the wall, I beg leave to report an instance of it to the Horticultural Society.

Colonel Gore, of Barrowmount, in the county of Kilkenny, when building his garden-walls, about sixteen years ago, formed, in the foundation of those with a southern aspect, arches about three feet wide, by two feet deep, against which he planted peach-trees; he did this with the hope that the trees would be benefited by their roots thus having access to the exterior soil, and the result showed that his hopes were well-founded; for, from that time until this last year, when Colonel Gore changed his residence, and the trees were neglected, they have continued remarkably healthy and vigorous, and have borne abundant crops of well-flavoured fruit; although, within the period above-mentioned, there has occurred a succession of bad seasons in Ireland, which, in other gardens, were attended not only with the failure of the fruit, but, in many instances, with the loss of the trees also: nor can this instance of success be attributed to any local advantage of soil or situation, as the latter is a dead level, and the former a strong loam.

The objection will probably present itself, that the roots of peach-trees, when near a northern aspect, must there imbibe an ungenial nourishment, more likely to produce a cankered and spongy growth of wood, than well-ripened fertile shoots. To this the best answer is, that experience has proved the contrary; and a little reflection will show, that such a result might have been expected.

The temperatures of the earth in shade and sunshine, are not to be judged of by those of the air under similar circumstances, as they bear no relative proportion to each other; the extremes of the latter being more variable, and widely distant, than those of the earth, which, deriving its degree of warmth from the general state of the surrounding atmosphere, possesses it more equally, and with less difference in either situation; so that while the head of the peach would perish against a North wall, its roots would enjoy nearly as great a degree of warmth, as if in the South borders; and even that difference insensibly lessens, as the distance recedes from the wall, and in a short space becomes imperceptible. The roots of peach-trees, when undisturbed, soon reach this point, for in the instance above-mentioned, they were found to have run ten or twelve feet from the wall at the North side. In the North border also, which we may suppose wholly appropriated to the use of the trees, their roots will rise to the surface, and occupy it entirely; but in the South border, the ground being constantly cropped and tilled, they are cut and damaged by the spade, and forced down into the under stratum, and thence alone derive their nourishment; the ground there, too, is soon exhausted of that natural fertility and freshness, so essential to the peach.

The borders without should, in the first instance, be properly prepared for the roots of the trees, and be afterwards left entirely in their possession, and no other tool than a fork should be used about them, to avoid doing them an injury; such is the practice at Montreuil, near Paris, where the gardeners cultivate the peach to a greater extent, perhaps, and with more success, than in any other part of Europe.

Should the expense of building arches be objectionable, piers, at intervals of twelve or eighteen inches, the spaces between them being covered with large stones or flags, may be substituted with equal advantage.

On Raising Apple Trees.

In raising these trees, the wild crab kernels are said to be the most suitable; but the seeds obtained from the apples, after the cider is pressed out of them, will produce young plants equally useful with the crab. Some of which will, no doubt, yield many new varieties of fruit; but it is not, in general, wise to trust to the accident, or to wait for the uncertainty, when a decisive mode of obtaining what kind of fruit you might choose, can be adopted by *grafting*.

The method, therefore, generally adopted, is, of course, by grafting. Very large and even old trees, if unproductive, may be grafted with different fruit to great advantage. New orchards are raised by planting wilding apple trees, of two or three, or more years' growth, and grafting them a year or two after they have been so transplanted. We venture, however, to recommend a still more advantageous method. Let the space, in which every tree is designed to stand in the orchard about to be planted, be well dug, about one foot deep, and in a circle of about eight or ten feet diameter. Then let a proper quantity of apple-seed be strewn over each circle, and let the earth be raked over the seed so as to cover it properly. This process may be effected any time between November and March. We think November is the best time. During the next year, a great variety of plants will grow up in each circle; as the summer proceeds, let the weak and small plants be pulled up, so as to make room for the strong and vigorous ones. The next year let them be further reduced, so that if there be in each circle half a dozen, or at most ten, vigorous plants, there will be more than enough. The third or fourth year they may be all grafted, and, in the course of a year or two, the strongest and best graft in each of the circles being suffered to remain, the rest must be either thrown away, or removed to other plantations; and we do not hesitate to affirm, that a valuable orchard may be reared more early, by many years, than by the plans now usually adopted. For, do what we will, transplantation, in general, retards the growth of trees two or three, and sometimes many years.

The best kind of graft for the young plants is, beyond a doubt, the saddle-graft; and, in old or grown up trees, it is by no means advisable to split the stock with a knife; for in every case of splitting the stock, the growth of the tree is materially impeded. If the trees to be grafted, are full-sized, the tops of them should be cut off in winter, as sometimes when grafted without having been previously so cut, they will, as it is termed, *bleed* so much, that the grafts will not succeed; but even this depends, frequently, upon circumstances over which the gardener has not always control. We have known grafts to succeed worse by the trees being so previously cut. At any rate, they should not be cut down to the trunk, but as many branches should be left as look kind, and about the thickness of one's arm, or less. If the trees are previously cut before grafting, it is scarcely necessary to add, that some inches of each stock must be cut off again at the time of grafting, in order to arrive at the living and healthy wood.

Preservation of Fruits.

Annals of Philosophy.

M. Berard informs us that "Fruits act upon atmospherical air in a different manner to leaves. The former at all times, both in light and darkness, part with carbon to the oxygen of the atmosphere, [to produce carbonic acid, and this loss of carbon is essential to ripening, since the process stops, if the fruit is immersed in an atmosphere deprived of oxygen, and the fruit itself shrivels and dies. This occurs equally to those fruits which, when gathered green, are able to ripen of themselves, though separated from their parent tree; but in these, the ripening process may be by this means delayed for a certain time, and be completed by restoring them to an oxygenized atmosphere. In this manner, peaches, plums, apples, pears, &c. may be preserved unspoiled from three to ten or twelve weeks, inclosed in an air-tight jar, with a quantity of lime and sulphate of iron worked up into a paste with water, which has the property of abstracting oxygen from the air which is in contact with it. The passing from ripeness to decay in fruits is also characterized by the production and evolution of much carbonic acid, and equally requires the presence of an oxygenized medium. The internal changes produced in fruits by the ripening process are particularly distinguished by the production of sugar, which does not exist in any considerable quantity in immature fruits; and it appears to be produced at the expense of part of the gum, and especially of the ligneous fibre."—(Philosophical Magazine.)

We should think that any means which excluded oxygen totally, would be preferable to the mode proposed for the preservation of fruits. Why introduce water at all, if oxygen be required to make the fruit pass from ripeness to decay? Would it not be better to imbed the fruit in fine charcoal?

Preservation of Cauliflowers.

New Monthly Magazine, No. 12.

We extract the two following papers from the Memoirs of the Caledonian Horticultural Society, because they relate to objects of great importance; and hope that the modes of preservation pointed out, will be found efficacious by those persons who may be led to adopt them.

"As cauliflower is a most desirable vegetable, so it deserves to be kept as long for use as possible. In 1808 I had a large quantity of this vegetable in full head in the beginning of November. Being at a loss for a shed, or such place as is commonly used for hanging it up, in order to preserve it, I dug a pit along the bottom of a wall, about eighteen inches in depth, and much about the same breadth. On a dry day, I pulled up the stocks of cauliflower, keeping the leaves as entire as possible, and lapping them round the flower. I began at one end of the above mentioned pit, laying in my cauliflower with the roots uppermost, and the tops inclining downwards, the roots of the one layer covering the tops of the other, and so on with the whole of my stock. The pits were then covered closely up with earth, and beaten smooth with the back of the spade, in order that the rain might run off. It is to be observed that the covering had a considerable slope from the wall. The experiment succeeded to my wish; and I was able occasionally to give a dish of fine cauliflower till the middle of January 1809."

Preservation of Potatoes.

"For some years I have bestowed considerable attention on the mode of preserving the potato. I have tried various ways of keeping it, but have found none so good as the following, which I have employed these two last years with the best success. That part of my potatoes which I mean to keep longest, that is, for spring and summer use, before the succeeding crop be ready, I put into small pits, holding about two bolls each, heaped up and covered, in the usual mode, with straw and earth. In April or May, according to the heat of the season, these potatoes are turned over into other pits; after carefully rubbing off, or picking out the shoots or buds, and laying aside every one that has any blemish or tendency to spoil. The evening before, a new pit is dug, or an old one cleaned out, in some dry spot; and, if possible, under the shade of some tree, wall, or stack of hay, &c. This is filled nearly full of water; which by next morning is all drunk in, and the earth well cooled all round in the pit. The potatoes, carefully picked of all their shoots, are put into the pit thus prepared; and every quantity of a firlot or half a boll, is watered as it is put in, till the potatoes are level with the surface of the ground; they are then covered with live turf, the green side next the potatoes, and a hearty watering given; when the whole is covered, to the depth of two feet, with earth, watered, and well beaten together with the spade. This process is repeated every time the potatoes are turned over, which is about once in three weeks, less or more, according to the weather. When it is very hot, and the pits or heaps not in the shade, it is proper sometimes to cover the pit or heap with a mat, supported on a few sticks, so as to allow a free current of air between the mat and the heap. In this way I have been enabled to preserve potatoes quite plump, and entire in taste, to the end of September, or till the succeeding crop be sufficiently ripe to be used without loss; and loss must always be sustained in the quantity, when potatoes are largely used before they are nearly ripe. Nay, in this way, potatoes may be recovered in plumpness and taste, when they have suffered by injudicious exposure to air or heat, or by necessary carriage. In July last, I had occasion to send some potatoes for the use of my family, at sea-bathing quarters, a distance of sixteen or seventeen miles. They were taken out of the pit, and put into a sack; but it was three or four days before they were sent off; and, when they came to be used, they were found to have lost much of their fine taste, and somewhat of their mealiness. I immediately made a small pit in the back ground belonging to the house I possessed; into which, when well watered, the potatoes were put, watered and covered, as already described. In five days, the pit was opened, and the potatoes had recovered both their dryness and taste."

New Chemical Apparatus.

New Monthly Magazine, No. 12.

"An apparatus has been invented at Glasgow, for the manufacture of any mineral water requiring to be charged with carbonic acid gas, which amounts, in fact, to the developement of a power hitherto unknown, but equal to that of steam. This machine is described as having neither gasometer nor air-pump, yet the strength of a boy is asserted to be capable of compressing into any vessel from thirty to forty atmospheres of gas in a few minutes; while, to effect the same with a forcing-pump, would occupy the strength of several men as many hours. A machine equal in force to an engine of forty-horse power, and requiring neither fire nor water, would not occupy a space more than four feet square. For many purposes it would be more applicable than steam; but, by reason of the present price of sulphuric acid, greatly more expensive."

It is rather tantalizing to just throw out a hint of such a valuable power as this is said to be, without giving us some hope of its being eventually carried into effect; and we only extract it in order to set ingenious heads to work.

Improvement in Woulfe's Apparatus.

The following improved form of Woulfe's apparatus is due to the Marquess Ridolfi. The bottles have three apertures as usual; and the middle one, intended for the purpose of cleansing the bottle, or the introduction of materials, is closed either by a cork or a stopper; tubes descend by the other two into the bottles, one a little way in, the other nearly to the bottom; these tubes are small; they are fastened into the neck of the bottle, and do not rise far above. Each of these is surrounded on the exterior of the bottle by a larger tube as high as themselves, and fastened by cement on the tops of the necks or tubulars, so as to form a little vessel to receive mercury round the outside of the smaller tube. The connexion is then easily made between one or more of these bottles by glass tubes bent twice at right angles, and of such size as easily to slip in between the two tubes before described. When the lower ends are immersed in the mercury, all is tight, and the apparatus may be set to work. This contrivance allows a little motion to the bottles without endangering them; they are instantly connected or unconnected at pleasure, and they act to a certain extent as tubes of safety. (Journal of Science.)

Every suggested improvement in the form of this apparatus must be thankfully received by the practical chemist. We therefore take pleasure in presenting him with the above.

Congreve Rockets.

These destructive missiles have lately been employed with considerable effect in the whale fisheries. Capt. Scoresby, who is well known in the scientific world for his observations on the polar basin, was, we believe, the first to adopt this ingenious mode of capturing the " monarch of the ocean." The Fame has brought home nine fish, the whole of which were taken by this means. In one case, instant death was produced by a single rocket; and in all cases the speed of the fish was much diminished, and its power of sinking limited to three or four fathoms. The peculiar value and importance of the rocket in the fisheries is, that by means of it all the destructive effects of a six or even a twelve pounder piece of artillery, may be given with an apparatus not heavier than a musket, and with scarcely any shock or re-action on the boat. It appears that some of the smallest rockets employed in the Fame penetrated completely through the body of the fish, so that the effect of the explosion was visible on the opposite side. On the score of humanity, the employment of these rockets is also very desirable, as their fierce and destructive fire acting on the vitals of the animal, almost instantly destroys life; and saves the linger g tortures of the harpoon, axe, and even saw, which are occasionally resorted to.

Whenever we are under the necessity of destroying animal life, it is a duty incumbent on us to do so with the least possible pain; therefore, the application of the rocket to the taking of the whale, instead of the old mode by the harpoon, is most praiseworthy, and has also the advantage of being the most effectual.

Atmospheric Phenomenon.

At Letterkenny, (Ireland) Aug. 31, about eleven, A. M. there was a weak breeze from the south-west, the barometer at 'changeable,' with an appearance of heavy rain, which began to fall about forty minutes after eleven, and continued until twelve, at which time there was a dead calm, and the rain ceased. The sun had not shone during the morning, but a few minutes after twelve the darkness increased in a most extraordinary manner. At one there was not sufficient light to transact business; the domestic fowls went to roost; and mechanics and labourers quitted their work. Neither barometer nor thermometer changed a line from what they had been at ten o'clock. There was a dead calm, and the chimney smoke rose in perpendicular columns, till lost in masses of dark clouds, with which the concave surface of the heavens was covered. The appearance of these clouds was something like those dark blue volumes of smoke which arise from an explosion of gunpowder, and they seemed piled on each other, tier above tier, from the horizon to the zenith, where they concentrated so as to form the apparent vertex of a Gothic arch. Through small interstices, where those gigantic masses appeared to lap over each other, appeared to issue a faint gleam of sulphurous light.

At one o'clock, the meadows of a light green, appeared dark green—objects of a dark green seemed quite a dark bottle-green, and the dark gravel of some roads appeared of a blackish blood colour. Men's faces and dresses were changed in the same manner, so that people looked at each other with astonishment and awe. The colours were all of the finest tint and shade, very rich and mellow. The clouds which, though they seemed to the naked eye perfectly still, when viewed through a telescope, appeared to oscillate after the manner of *aurora borealis*, without changing their relative positions. This darkness continued till two o'clock, and to such a degree as that scarcely any person could read or write within doors without approaching close to the windows. A little after two there was observed a gentle motion of the clouds from the south-west; they moved almost imperceptibly to the north and east, and about three the darkness was dispelled, and cocks began to crow, and the swallows to fly about, as though it had been early in the morning.

New African Traveller.

Monthly Mag. No. 361.

The Monthly Magazine announces to the world a new traveller, whose progress through Africa, from Egypt to the Cape of Good Hope, has been accomplished in triumph, over hardships that have destroyed three out of four of his fellow-travellers. The following is the account given by the Editor of the above-named publication:—

"Mr. Waldeck, a German, has recently arrived in England from India, and is preparing an account of his travels through Africa, from Egypt to the Cape of Good Hope. Of the authority of his journey there is no doubt. It appears that at the foot of the Mountains of the Moon, he found an inscribed pillar, erected by a Roman consul, about the period of the reign of Vespasian. He found a level on the top of those mountains nearly 400 miles broad, on which he discovered a temple of the highest antiquity, and in fine preservation, and still used for religious purposes by the inhabitants. South of the level, he passed a descent of fifty-two days' journey, and when advanced about nine days, he found the skeleton of a man, with a telescope slung on his shoulder, marked with the name of Harris, and also a chronometer made by Marchand. There were also two other skeletons, and it was supposed the owners perished for the want of water. The manuscript is preparing, and the work will speedily appear in London, accompanied by engravings. Mr. Waldeck was accompanied by four European companions, only one of whom survived the hardships of the journey, and now resides in Paris."

Fire Shield.

London Journal of Arts, No. 12.

"Mr. RALPH BUCKLEY, of New York, has invented and obtained a patent for a *fire-shield*, which is said to be the most effectual protection of property from fire ever invented. This invention is intended to arrest the evil on the spot whence it originates, by enabling firemen to approach so near the flames, as to protect surrounding property. The fire shield is made of a metallic substance; thin, light, and impervious to heat; it is of a length and breadth sufficient to cover the whole person; it may be used in several different positions."

Should this promise be made good, the patentee will deserve the cordial thanks of all men. We have long enslaved water and air, and now it seems we shall walk forth into fire, like Salamanders.

PATENTS.

To ROBERT FRITH, *of Salford, Lancashire, for improvements in the method of Dyeing and Printing various colours, so as to fix, or make the same permanent, or fast, on Cottons, Linens, Silks, Mohair, Worsted and Woollens, Straw, Chip, and Leghorn.*

The principal novelty in this, seems to consist in the composition of the mordants; which are rather expensive, on account of the silver that constitutes an ingredient.

Mr. Frith's specification leaves us in doubt as to quantities, in some of the processes; and this very vagueness may ruin his views of security in the patent. Inrolled April 1821.

To JAMES FOSTER, *of Stourbridge, for certain Improvements in the Manufacture of Wrought or Malleable Iron.*

This is liable to precisely the same objections as the above, respecting the loose manner in which the specification is worded.

To CHARLES NEWMAN, *of Brighton, in the County of Sussex, for a new and original Invention in the Construction of the Body of a Stage or other Coach, by placing a certain proportion of the Outside Passengers in the Centre of the Carriage, and a proportion of the Luggage under the same, producing thereby Safety to the Coach and Convenience to the Passengers.*

This is a Safety Coach; but whether safer than others, so denominated, time and its passengers must prove. Inrolled Aug. 1821.

To JAMES SIMPSON, *of the Strand, London, for an Improvement in the Manufacture of Snuffers.*

We think that Mr. S. accomplishes his purpose, though by complex means; that is, by cross levers between the handles, which on closing, force a stopper down the chamber, and drive the snuff into a recess. Inrolled Sept. 1821.

To ALEXANDER LAW, *of the Commercial Road, London, for an Improvement in the Form of Bolts and Nails for Ships, and other Fastenings.*

The object of this patent is of superior importance. It consists in "making the sides and angles to wind round the axis of the bolt, or nail, in a screw form; so that the said bolt, or nail, when in the act of being driven into a hole of proper size, shall revolve on its axis, as it is made to advance by the force applied to it."

We apprehend that this screw-bolt must require additional labour in being driven home. It appears to us, however, that the bolt will fully accomplish the intention. Inrolled Sept. 1821

To AARON MANBY, *of Horseley, near Tipton, Staffordshire, for certain Improvements in the making and manufacturing of Steam Engines.*

The Steam Engine is so noble a monument of human ingenuity as to throw into distance almost every other production of intellect. Indeed it seems almost to possess intellect itself, and every mechanist feels proud to add a spark of Promethean fire. Mr. Manby's proposed improvements are two-fold—first, by rendering the cylinder oscillatory on pivots, he can effect rotatory motion; and secondly, by heating the water in the boiler by means of oil pipes, he can save fuel and lessen the risk of explosion. Inrolled July 1821.

To WILLIAM CARTER, *of St. Agnes Circus, Old Street Road, London, for certain Improvements in Steam Engines.*

Our principal objection is, that the extreme edges of the leaves, working within the cylinder, must speedily wear. They, who are conversant with Steam Engines, will form some judgment of the patentee's object, and mode, from the following extract:—

" My improvement on that engine consists in the particular construction of the engine as hereinbefore described, and in which it differs from Mr. Hornblower's engine. (viz.) First, my method of introducing and distributing the steam, and conveying it away. Second, my method of applying clamps to prevent the retrograde motion. Third, in making the cylinder revolve, in order to give motion to the machinery: And fourthly, in applying two pair of leaves instead of two single leaves, whereby the force is made equal on the opposite sides of the centre or axis of motion." Inrolled May 1821.

To ROBERT BURTON COOPER, *of the Strand, London, for Improvements on, or Substitutes for Stoppers, Covers, or Lids, such as are used for, Bottles, Tobacco and Snuff Boxes, Ink-Holders, and various other Articles requiring Stoppers, Covers, or Lids.*

We believe that these covers will answer the intended purpose; but we cannot help expressing our fears as to the profit they may realize for the patentee. We do not hesitate to assert that an object of petty importance, as to market demand, can never repay the expense of a patent. Inrolled Sept. 1821.

To WILLIAM ANNESLEY, *of Belfast, in Ireland, for certain Improvements in the Construction of Ships, Boats, and other Vessels.*

The spirit of this patent claims on the merit of planking with three or more alternate layers: the grain of the timber of one layer being longitudinal as to the vessel; that of the other transverse—also in constructing the keel of three thicknesses or bodies—and lastly, from a given model to construct a set of temporary frames, or moulds, for the purpose of giving to the bulk of the vessel the same figure and relative proportion as the model. Inrolled June 1821.

To WILLIAM CHAPMAN, *of Newcastle upon Tyne, for his method of Transferring the Ladings of Lighters and Barges into Ships or Vessels, or from Ships or Vessels into Lighters and Barges.*

Mr. Chapman's machinery is, apparently, competent to effect its purpose: which is that of preventing the breakage of coal, in the act of lading the brig. Mr. C. informs us that the waste in breakage amounts to *one-third of the coal shipped!* This is, indeed, an enormous loss—but we would beg leave to ask why the small coal cannot be sent to market? Small coal, of the agglutinating quality, such as we have from the Durham Collieries, burns well, when wetted; and radiates more heat than the larger masses—surely it would pay profit on freight. Inrolled June 1821.

THE FOCUS

OF

PHILOSOPHY, SCIENCE, AND ART.

No. III.]   Saturday, December 15, 1821.   [Vol. I.

On Pitchstone. By J. MacCulloch, M. D., F. R. S., &c.

(Continued from page 39.)

The veins of pitchstone sometimes assume the lamellar form, as trap occasionally does; the lamellæ lying parallel, and changing quality at the lines of union; passing into chalcedony and chert. Sometimes again they have prismatic tendency, at right angles to the vein. If the scuir of Egg be deemed a vein, they have also a parallel columnar structure.

As a rock, Dr. MacC. says, the pitchstone varies much in its internal structure. In Arran, large prisms stand at right angles to the line of the vein. In Egg, the prisms are smaller, but may be detached: and they present themselves in all directions; the ends of some being lengthened by the overlaying pressure of others. Sometimes, too, the laminar formation is so decided as to scale the vein into two or more planes. Among the smaller varieties, a laminar concretionary form is noticed; the laminæ varying in size, line, or curve: some, thin as paper; others, thick, jointed across the lamellæ; and, sometimes, taking a minutely prismatic form. Again, the prisms will form small columns, jointed; and, rarely, by surfaces alternately concave and convex. Where the joints are near together, the parts separate into irregular spheroidal forms. A central atom of feldspar, or enamel, will be found in each joint of the columnar structure. Here is a resemblance of pearl-stone, and sometimes an actual transition into it.

Occasionally, pitchstone assumes a concretionary, spheroidal, structure, of aggregated, minute, and granular formation; becoming completely analogous with pearl-stone: the spherules, too, confirm the analogy, by containing central atoms of feldspar, or enamel.

We come now to the porphyritic character of pitchstone; which varies much, as to the magnitude, perfection, and number of the crystals; the larger being rounder, and converted into a white, or grey, enamel; the smaller, are spheroidal enamel. On exposure to the atmosphere, some of them become white, enamel like, and scale away. At length, becoming decomposed into a fine clay, forming, with water, a tenacious mass or paste. Sometimes, but rarely, black; and, occasionally, assuming a plum-like bloom. It is rather singular that, although it has so vitreous a character, it contains much uncombined water; and, on drying, becomes brittle. Its lustre varies from perfectly vitreous, to the dull aspect of basalt. The darker colours, as olive greens, prevail in Scotland; but it has been found greyish white, dull yellow brown, olive brown, olive green, dark reddish brown, dark bottle blue, and black.

The customary transitions of pitchstone are, into Chalcedony, Chert, Semi-opal; also into a substance resembling conchoidal shining jasper, found in clay strata, entangled in trap, or volcanic rock; and lastly, into Trap.

Generally speaking, we may say, that pitchstone is identified by its vitreous, or resinous, aspect; and, as the Doctor says, differing " from obsidian, by its inferior hardness, and with which it has no affinity or transition."

Dr. MacC. concludes with a synopsis; of which we present our readers with an abstract.

Synopsis of Pitchstone.

First Division. Simple.

A   Amorphous, massive. Fracture. Conchoidal. Flat conchoidal. Splintery conchoidal. Splintery granular. Mixed fracture. Mixed, the large conchoidal presenting smaller conchoidal. Conchoidal, scaly, porphyritic aspect.

B Concretionary. Flat lamellar. Curved lamellar. Prismatic, simple or jointed. Columnar, simple or jointed, partly columnar and partly prismatic. Spheroidal, large, with columnar. Small concretionary, pearl-stone character. Imperfectly spheroidal, passing into porphyritic.

Structures vary by intermixture in the same rock.

Second Division. Porphyritic.

A Pitchstone porphyry. With glassy crystals of feldspar; sometimes nearly transparent. With common crystals of feldspar. Rounded or shapeless particles of feldspar. With spherules of feldspar, surrounded by grey enamel, or the enamel alone. When spherules numerous, passing into pearl-stone. Imbedded crystals or grains of quartz, or of quartz and feldspar. Granular quartz, surrounded by chert; or with granular chert. Porphyritic, granular quartz, and chert, condensed with lamellæ; alternating with slightly porphyritic pitchstone.

Third Division. Concretionary-spheroidal. Pearl-stone.

A Irregularly granular pitchstone, compressing, as coccolite.

B Grains with centers of other quality. Pearl-stone porphyry, with granular feldspar, or enamel, or both. Quartz and chert, or singly. Quartz and feldspar. Central atom of clay.

Fourth Division. Amygdaloidal, with imbedded Nodules of another Mineral.

A Pitchstone with imbedded zeolites. In Baffin's Bay only. Colours, dull white, pale ochre, pink, pale green, greenish grey, ochre yellow, ochre red, yellow brown, fawn, red brown, greenish brown, olives, dark blue, and black, or intermixed.

Porphyritic varieties variously modified as to base.'

Pitchstone passes into chert, cherty chalcedony, basalt, and, as is supposed, into opal, and semi-opal. When into chert, sometimes microscopical grains of chalcedony present, and often remarkably spheroidal concretionary.

We cannot close this paper without expressing the pleasure we have received in perusing Dr. MacCulloch's perspicuous description of pitchstone. This paper is evidently the result of that kind of knowledge which observation and discrimination can alone confer.

On Water Cements, Mortar, and Lime.
(Continued from page 42.)

It has already been seen that lime of different denominations bears different qualities, as to its absorption of water, and increase of volume. Below is a table of the relative powers, according to the three modes of slacking.

	Weight of Water absorbed.	Volume of Cream of Lime.
100 parts, by weight, of common fat lime slacked by affusion	236	310
Immersion	131	104
Atmospheric exposure	148	100
100 parts of lean coloured hydraulic lime slacked by affusion	105	137
Immersion	71	127
Atmospheric exposure	68	100
100 parts of lean white hydraulic lime slacked by affusion	110	130
Immersion	80	117
Atmospheric moisture	70	108

These results show that the mode of process has a decided influence in qualifying the effect:—for, although equal quantities of the same lime may be worked to the same consistence, under all the varieties of slacking, yet the required portions of water are widely different. With fat lime, we find that the water absorbed, by affusion, is nearly double the quantity taken up by immersion. The disproportion is not quite so great in the air-slacked lime; but still very wide.

Fat lime affords by affusion a sum, in volume, nearly equal

to the combined sums of water and lime: thus 100 parts of the lime absorbed 236 water=336; which is not far from the given sum for volume of cream of lime, or 310. Slacked by immersion, the result is, in volume of cream of lime, 104; which approximates to only *one half* the sum of lime and water, or 115. Again, slacked by atmospheric moisture, we find the sum of volume of cream, or 176, nearly *exact* that of half the combined water and lime, or 174. Agreeing with those who attach much importance to strict observation of arithmetical proportion, in all chemical researches, we could have wished M. Vicat had turned his attention a little to this point. These ratios of proportion do not obtain in the lean coloured hydraulic lime; nor in the lean white hydraulic; for in those the volume is nearly as the quantity of water absorbed. M. Vicat contends that the difference in quantity of water absorbed, depends on the " degree of tenuity which the particles of lime contract by extinction: the swelling and superior quantity of water absorbed in the first process, show that it is this in which the division of its particles are carried to its highest degree;" consequently, a greater proportion in mortar is required, when the lime be slacked by immersion, or by atmospheric exposure, than by affusion.

On the Combination of Water with Lime.

When milk of lime be dried at a moderate heat, it becomes a white powder, attracting carbonic acid, and increasing in weight nearly one-fourth,—termed by M. Thenard hydrate of lime. The quantity of water employed influences the hardness of hydrate.

	Water.	Hardness.
100 parts common fat lime slacked with	137 give	0·126
	183	0·222
	315	0·068
100 parts of hydraulic slacked with....	70	0·014
	92	0·051
	246	0·010

The hardest hydrate M. V. thinks, is obtainable by about 183 water to 100 of fat lime; and 92 water to 100 hydraulic.

From all the modes of slacking, M. V. obtained crystals of carbonate of lime in quadrangular prisms of indeterminate lengths, having for their section " a rectangle of 0·04 metre for its base, to 0·025 metre in height." He tried their tenacity by the force required to break them; and their hardness by Peyronnet's borer.

	Tenac.	Hardness.
Hydrates of fat lime by affusion, gave	2490	0·1696
Atmospheric exposure	1709	0·0850
Immersion	450	0·0713
Hydrates of hydraulic lime by affusion	864	0·0488
Immersion	392	0·0446
Atmospheric exposure	245	0·0358
The standard of comparison for tenacity and hardness, was a good brick giving	5690	0·096

We may observe here, that tenacity and hardness of the respective hydrates seem to bear a proportion with the relative powers of lime to absorb water and expand. Or, agreeably to the well known axiom of chemistry, that union is the more perfect as the tenuity of matter increases.

Hydrates of lime absorb carbonic acid from the atmosphere very slowly; that is, at about the rates of six millimetres, in thickness, during a year, with the hydraulic qualities. With the common sorts, two or three years are necessary. These crusts of regenerated lime-stone are always harder, and darker coloured, than the unchanged lime that lies under. The ratios of hardness were found to be about thus:—

	Hardness.
Common fat limes slacked by affusion	0·400
Atmospheric exposure	0·170
Immersion	0·130
Hydraulic limes slacked by affusion	0·087
Immersion	0·081
Atmospheric exposure	0·044

We consider this subject too important, in a practical sense, to be slightly treated; therefore we shall reserve our further detail of M. Vicat's labours for another number.

(To be continued.)

Tickell's Cement.

The proper elements for the composition of cement are, as yet, but imperfectly known. Much conjecture has been wasted by heads, presumedly wise, but in vain. Of this we have proof in the preceding paper, by M. Vicat, who shows that Bergman, Guiton, Saussure, and Descotils, have all imagined particular kinds of matter requisite, that have been found wanting in earths which afforded good cementing properties. Mr. Tickell is, perhaps, in error as well as all these great luminaries; when he supposes that his powder owes its qualities to the oxide of iron. Of all things, perhaps some sort of calcareous earth may be deemed most indispensable. We observe Mr. T. represents his cement to contain calcareous matter. We wish he had given an account of the specific gravity of the mass; the fracture of the smaller formations, the hardness and the splendour of the surface, especially whether there were any appearance of vitrification. But we will quote that part of his specification which alone can have an interest in a work devoted to practical science:—

"The material which I apply to the purpose of making cement is a mineral substance, raised in great abundance from the collieries and iron stone mines in Staffordshire and elsewhere, which is at present thrown aside as useless, except being lately occasionally broken into pieces, and in that crude state made use of to repair the walls with. This material is a mixture of certain iron ores, and is found at various depths in getting the coals and iron ores, being found also above as well as below the strata of each. It is of a most peculiar nature and figure, being of a blueish-grey colour, and found in large ponderous masses, presenting a very compact hard stone, forming horizontal series of conical shaped bodies, having nearly round or oval bases, and the lines forming the boundaries of their sides not straight, but curved inwardly and concave; and the interior of the bodies themselves, as well as the interstices between them, consisting of similar but smaller conical bodies, closely united and wedged together. It consists principally of calcareous and argillaceous earths, with an admixture of oxid of iron, not, however, in sufficient quantity to make it worth smelting to extract the iron, but fully sufficient in combination with the other materials of which it is composed, and after the treatment to which I subject it, to form the valuable cement which is the object of this patent.

"I convert this material into this cement in the following manner: the stone is broken into small pieces, and calcined in proper kilns, stratum super stratum, with the small refuse coal, called in Staffordshire *slack*, interposed, until a considerable portion of its volatile parts are driven off, (which, however, must be so regulated as not to produce vitrification,) and the material has assumed a bright yellow colour; it is then broken into smaller pieces, either under tilt hammers or otherwise, until it is sufficiently small to be capable of being ground by mill-stones into a fine smooth powder, which is to be put into ovens or iron pots, placed over fires, and kept stirred continually during the action of the heat so applied, in order to promote the further expulsion of any carbonic acid or water which it might have absorbed in the grinding process, and which would have materially injured its efficacy. The powder is then to be closely packed, whilst hot, from the ovens or pots, in casks or cases, so constructed of sheet iron as to secure it from the injurious action of the external air, and thus preserve its activity and usefulness as a most tenacious and durable cement, to be used in aquatic and other buildings and stucco works, when mixed with a proportion of clean-washed sand, the proportional quantity of which must be regulated for the different purposes it may be intended to be applied to, at the discretion of the workman; if for flooring, one-third part of sand to two-third parts of cement is sufficient to be mixed to warrant its firm durability; if for stucco-work, one-half of each, or a larger quantity of sand is admissible, with a suitable quantity of water, to render the composition fit for its various purposes.

"In witness whereof, &c."

Mr. Faraday, on new Electro-Magnetical Motions, and on the Theory of Magnetism.

(Continued from page 46.)

Mr. Faraday's next position is, that the pole placed between two wires, having reversed currents, when equidistant from them, is propelled in a line perpendicular to that which would join them; whether receding or approaching. If it approach, passing between, and then receding; so that it seems to be first attracted by the wires, and then repelled. Change the pole, and the direction changes. Bend a silk wire at the middle, parallel on itself; with the north pole it attracts strongly on one side, in the line between the two currents; but repels to the right and left: On the other side, the line repels the north, and attracts to the right or left. Actions are reversed with the south pole. When both poles are brought to bear, as by placing the needle on water, the effects are analogous. The perpendicular wire brought near to the needle, made it approach, not by its *poles*, but by its *centre;* and positing itself at right angles across the wire. Placing the wire on the opposite side of the needle, the latter was repelled; evincing the different lateral polarities. With two dissimilar wires, and both poles of the magnet free, the latter fixes across between them; but if not equidistant from them, or their powers be unequal, it slowly advances to one; and acts as with the single one, last noticed. If one of the poles be brought near either wire, in the position wherein it appears to attract most strongly, it will, if free, resume its position midway across the wire.

Mr. Faraday speaks in high approbation of a little apparatus invented by M. de la Rive, a description of which, the reader shall have in this number. This instrument, when placed on acidulated water, is extremely sensible to the magnet; and facilitates experimental parallel between straight wires and helices. If the magnet be brought near, and level with its axis, it recedes, or turns round, until that side of the curve, next to the nearest pole, be attracted by it; resting, like an equator, around it; and, however its position may be disturbed by force, it will resume it, when at freedom to act. Should the magnet be placed without, and over, the curve, it will stand in a plane perpendicular to the magnet; but in a reversed direction.

Mr. F. says, " From the central situation of the magnet, in these experiments, it may be concluded, that a strong and powerful curve, or helix, would suspend a powerful needle in its centre. By making a needle almost float on water, and putting the helix over a glass tube, this result has, in part, been obtained." The full success of this experiment, if we exactly comprehend Mr. Faraday's meaning, would lead us to no longer ridicule the principle, though we must disbelieve the tale of the suspension of Mahomet's tomb. In all these cases of magnetic attraction and repulsion, two poles and one wire, or two wires and one pole, were indispensable. With single poles and wires, the results may be deceptive. The poles of helices offer the purest instances; because the states of the opposite sides of the wire are nearly independant of one another: we can therefore excite two of those, to the exclusion of the rest; similar producing repulsion, and dissimilar, attraction, as shown by M. Ampere. So two cases of repulsion, and one of attraction, are produced by combination.

The opposite sides of similar wires, also, attract: as when similarly electrified; the four powers, of the four sides, constituting a double attraction.

With two dissimilar poles and a wire, the latter essays to describe opposite circles, round opposite poles. If on the sides where the circles close, it is attracted. On the opposite, where the circles are open, it is repelled.

Two wires and one pole, the wires being dissimilar, produce similar results to those of two dissimilar poles and one wire. Two poles and two dissimilar wires, show several powers combining to produce effect.

Following up M. Ampere's theory, of a concentric current of electricity round the axis of the wire, and the consequent effect on the circulation by the helix, Mr. F. was led to think that it might be possible to form artificial electro-magnets, and analyze natural ones: and, he presumes that by pursuing the idea, he has traced the action of an electro-magnetic pole to the concentric direction, whether attractive or repulsive.

As the absolute illustration of the presumed concentric motion of the electric matter, round the axis of the wire, cannot be too strongly impressed, we are unwilling to risk error in our expression of Mr. Faraday's position; and, therefore, we shall, for security sake, present the matter in his own words:—

"If three inches of connecting wire be taken, and a magnetic pole be allowed to circulate round the middle of it, describing a circle of little less than one inch in diameter, it will be moved with equal force in all parts of the circle.

"Bend the wire into a circle, leaving that part round which the pole revolves perpendicularly, undisturbed; and make it a condition that the pole be restrained from moving round the circle by a radius. It will immediately be evident that the wire now acts very differently on the pole, in the different parts of the circle it describes. Every part of it will be active, at the same time, on the pole, to make it move through the centre of the wire ring: while, as it passes away from that position, the powers diverge from it, and it is either removed from their action, or submitted to opposing ones; until, on its arriving at the opposite part of the circle, it is urged by a very small portion indeed of those which moved it before. As it continues to go round, its motion is accelerated; the forces rapidly gather together on it, until it again reaches the centre of the wire ring; where they are at their highest; and, afterwards, diminish as before. Thus the pole is perpetually urged in a circle; but with powers changing.

"If the wire ring be conceived to be occupied by a plane, then the centre of that plane is the spot where the powers are most active on the poles; and move it with the most force. Now, this spot is actually the pole of this magnetic apparatus. It seems to have powers over the circulating pole, making it approach, or attracting it, on the one side; and making it recede, or repelling it, on the other; with powers varying, as the distance: but its powers are only apparent; for the force is in the ring; and this spot is merely the place where they are most accumulated: and, though it seems to have opposite powers, namely those of attracting and repelling, yet this is merely a consequence of its situation in the circle, the motion being uniform in its direction, and really, and truly, impressed on the pole by its motor, the wire."

That the wire must be the motor is palpable; but whether the forces operating on the needle at the centre of the circle, are to be considered as the focal condensation of powers emanating from the wire line, forming the circumference; or whether the central point should be considered as in a negative sense magnetically, is not quite clear to our comprehension.

In the next paragraph, Mr. Faraday takes a little for granted, that does not appear to be proved; at least we think not; but we differ from him with all due respect. Alluding to the fact of the magnetic powers seeming to accumulate at the external sides of parallel wires; or at the outer margins of a metallic ribbon; he infers, that if concentric rings were placed within each other, having the electric fluid sent through them in the same direction; or if, "*which is the same thing*," a flat spiral of silked wire pass from the centre to the circumference, with its extremities in voltaic contact; then, the circle of revolution would still pass through the centre of the rings, or spiral; but the power would be increased. Indeed, such a spiral, when made, Mr. F. tells us, does take up an enormous quantity of iron filings, approaching the form of cones; so strong is its action at the centre. And its action on the needle, by different sides, is eminently powerful.

Now we must remark that, we are ignorant as to whether Mr. F., by concentric circles, means ribbons, or wires; and if the former, whether their surfaces be in the plane of the magnetic equator, or perpendicular thereto. At all events, we cannot subscribe to the conclusion that insulated concentric circles, and helices, must, in effect, be *the same thing*, until it be shown by direct experiment. We will, too, humbly hope that we are not too sturdy in our scepticism, by not taking it for granted that the decided effect produced on the iron filings, at the centre of the helix, arises from *positive*, rather than *negative* power; but we submit our doubts with perfect respect to this active experimentalist.

(To be continued.)

Account of the Electro-Magnetic Apparatus of Lieut. Col. Offerhaus. By G. MOLL, A.L.M., &c. &c. &c.

Professor Moll informs Dr. Brewster that being desirous to repeat the experiments of Oersted on Electro-Magnetism, he, in conjunction with others, first subjected the needle to a voltaic combination, containing 120 four-inch zinc plates, each placed between two copper ones. The effect on a sensible needle did not exceed 14°. Next they used a long, deep, and narrow trough, made of copper; within which was fixed a plate of zinc, 3600 square decimetres,* and sustained by wooden tarsels, to prevent contact with the copper. The space was filled with water, containing $\frac{1}{60}$ of its weight of nitric acid, and as much of sulphuric. A wire arose from the zinc, and another from the copper: which were united by a third of copper, placed in the magnetic meridian. Under this last wire the needle was put. The battery did not testify any power of chemical decomposition. The poles were reversed; that is, the copper was found to be positively, and the zinc negatively, electrified. It imparted high power to needles, suspended in spirals, between the wires connected with the poles of the battery: and the deviation, when the magnet was placed under, or above, the conductive wire, was considerable.

Not satisfied with the power obtained, Lieut. Col. Offerhaus devised the following form of apparatus, whereby the extent of metallic surface was increased, and the effect, of course, augmented. In the centre of a cylindrical case of wood, 51 centimetres high,† and 38 in diameter, is placed a solid wooden cylinder, to which is nailed one extremity of a cop-

---

* The Decimetre is nearly equal to four inches.
† The Centimetre nearly two-fifths of an inch.

per plate, 4·67 metres long, and 0·40 metres high,* so that the superfices may be about 2 square metres. This ribbon of copper was wound spirally round the central wooden cylinder, and within whose coils was placed a ribbon of zinc, 3·37 metres long, and 0·4 metres high, which follows the spirals of copper; but prevented from coming into contact with them by small wooden rods, interposed perpendicularly within the spirals of the helix. A copper wire projected from that end of the zinc spiral which was nearest to the central wooden nucleus; and another from that end of the copper, which terminated the copper coil outwardly; or at the end most remote from the nucleus; therefore, these wires arose from the opposite extremities of the concentric ribbons. At the top of each of these perpendicular wires was a small vessel, containing a little mercury. The conductive wire, communicating with the two perpendiculars, had, at each extremity, a small pin, which, being immersed in the vessels of mercury, rendered the contact more perfect. This horizontal conductive wire being placed in the magnetic meridian, and the interstices of the spiral plates filled with diluted acid, the action commenced. As in the former instance, the copper pole was positive, and the zinc negative. A needle 0·168 metres long, being placed at the distance of 43 millimetres† under the conducive wire, declined easterly as much as 80°. Above the wire, and at a similar distance, it declined 80° westerly.

Professor Moll remarks, that when the galvanic energy of the instrument be powerful, iron filings, brought closely under the conductive copper wire, will instantly become erected on their extremities, as if near a magnet; and when brought quite close, will adhere to the wire; but immediately fall off, when one end of the conductive wire be raised from its contact with the mercurial vessel. The diameter of the conductive should be about 5 millimetres.

With this instrument, a wire of platinum, $\frac{1}{4}$ of a millimetre in diameter, communicating with the copper and zinc poles, was fused. And it was observed that the intensity of mag-

---

* The Metre is about equal to thirty-nine inches and a third.
† The Millimetre is about one-fortieth of an inch.

netic power in the needle was increased, when placed under the conductive wire, in the ratio of 34 oscillations to 12, in the minute.

The first point worthy of notice is, that of the galvanic poles being reversed; the copper being positive, and the zinc negative: and that too, in both of the latter apparatuses constructed by Professor Moll and his friends. As this is not noticed to have been the case with the first battery, constructed as directed in Brande's Chemistry, we presume that the poles therein, displayed their usual characters. Secondly, the experimenters did not observe any inequality of power to effect deviation between the positions of the magnet above and below the conductive wire; the deviation being in each position 80°, though in reversed directions, as above or below. Thirdly, the conductive wire seems to have assumed the specific qualities of the magnet, during the period of its exposure to the voltaic current, and not longer.

In experiments with such an instrument, we would beg leave to suggest the expediency of trying on all occasions whether any, and what, difference of effect may be produced by conductive wires of different metallic qualities. We wish too, that the Professor had changed the relative attachments of the wires at the extremities of the metallic ribbons, *i. e.* by placing the wire in contact with the zinc ribbon at the end, next to the circumference of the helix,—and that with the copper, at the nucleus or central end; and thereby have determined if such reversed positions could influence the character of the voltaic poles. Not that we hold it probable such demonstration would have arisen; but that we think an experimental course should be varied in every possible form, when an apparent discordance in results is displayed.

Electro-Magnetism.

In further detail of this exhaustless subject, and as bearing close affinity with the foregoing paper, we place this in immediate succession. We have seen that Colonel Offerhaus' apparatus caused a deviation of 80° easterly or westerly, according as the magnet was placed, *above* or *below* the conductive wire; and the following facts will show that the magnetic circulation is governed by the character of the pole. Indeed, experiments on all hands evince such decided modifications of effect, by mere circumstance of relative locality. The Chevalier Yelin discovered that, when electrical matter was transmitted by sparks, or Leyden discharge, through a spiral, enveloping a steel needle, placed in a glass tube, the needle became magnetic. If the spiral were turned from the left to the right, and the electrical stream passed from the positive conductor, the end of the needle coming into contact with it, assumes a southern pole; the other extremity of the needle is of course the northern; and vice versa.

If a third needle, reckoning from its middle, be surrounded, spirally, with waxed taffeta, the poles appear at the points where the taffeta begins and ends.

This latter fact is analogous with that determined by Mr. Faraday, as related by us in our last number, in so far as it shows that the poles may not be in the extreme points of the needles. It were desirable that a steel wire should have two spirals encircling it, one at each half portion of its length; and leaving perhaps a fourth of its length in the middle, free. Then, on transmitting the electrical or galvanic current through the spiral, we should ascertain whether the double pole of each half could be imparted, to corroborate one of Mr. Faraday's other positions, viz. that each needle has two poles, as deduced by Mr. F., from the action of the conductive wire on it.

That the electro magnetic current has a tendency to spiral direction, and perhaps flows with an augmented intensity in that curve, may be inferred from another result presented by the Chevalier, namely, that if a straight rod be substituted for the spiral, the needle will be but slightly magnetic, even after repeated electrical discharges. Another curious fact is also stated, *i. e.* repeated electrical discharges along the spiral, reversed the poles of a magnetic needle.

With all due deference to our scientific readers, we beg leave to earnestly recommend that in an experimental course of inquiry, into the laws of electro-magnetism, they would never lose sight of the necessity of collating trials with galvanic, electrical, and magnetical powers to investigate the same fact, in every case where they can be severally applied. For instance, we think that Mr. Faraday, and the Chevalier, might have elicited some corroborative, or qualifying information, on the matter of their research. The discoveries made under one isolated principle, certainly have their value; but we humbly conceive that, in tracing a fact governed by voltaic electricity, (for instance,) we ought to test it by any other principle that bears analogous character: for, by observing the agreement and difference of each active principle, in its operation under similar circumstances, we shall the more clearly discern, in what their specific peculiarities, or their identities, may consist.

To illustrate, we will say that one experimentalist, applying common electricity to verify the poles of a magnetic needle, may produce exactly the same result as another, applying the voltaic fluid; and an analogy, almost amounting to identity of the two fluids, may be inferred. But in experiments so delicate as those of electro-magnetism, we hold the slightest difference of condition, even the line of contact, or the form, extent, and power of the needle, as influential on the conclusion; and therefore the same objects should be subjected to the operation of the three powers, whenever it be practicable.

On the Magnetic Influence of the Islands of St. Mayo, and the Great Salvage. By Lieut. W. MUDGE, R. N.
Edinburgh Phil. Journal, No. 10.

We have here a striking proof of local action on the magnetic needle; but whether produced by the purely magnetic character of the matter, composing the islandic mass; or by its merely containing an unusual portion of ferruginous ore, we have not any experiments before us to determine from. Lieut. M. says, indeed, that portions of the rock exhibit strong marks of polarity; but it is one thing to possess the real magnetic character, and another to have the simple power of influencing the magnetic needle. It is well known that masses of iron may have this power, without being, in themselves, specifically magnetic. Certainly there is nothing at variance with sound philosophy, in supposing an entire island to be possibly composed of loadstone; but it is more *probable* that terrestrial influence on the magnetic needle is to be ascribed to unpolarized ore, or masses of metallic iron. Mr. M. remarks that a large fragment of this rock, about 20 pounds weight, which he brought away with him, has lost much of its power, though its " effect on the compass is still strong, and its polarity well defined." It would have given us pleasure to have been informed by this gentleman how he determined the polarity, as belonging to the mass. We do not, however, hesitate to concur with Lieut. Mudge, that these islands, as masses, may really partake in the magnetic character; but what we principally desire to impress on navigators, and others, is, that an influence on the needle does not *necessarily* imply the existence of magnetic polarity, in the influential masses.

In the year 1819, Lieut. Mudge, with Lieut. Vidal, while employed in the survey of St. Mayo, found the dip of the needle of the theodolite so great, that it could not traverse, without the face of the instrument being brought down to a considerable angle from the horizon: and even then, from the uncertainty and varying effect produced by difference in station, rendered the theodolite totally useless. A similar circumstance occurring to Lieut. M. when off the island of Great Salvage, near Teneriffe, he entered into a more scrutinizing inquiry; and, at two different stations, less than a mile apart, the variation of the needle amounted to 72°.

We are told by him that the island is of volcanic origin; consisting of dark black rock, all presenting strong marks of fixed polarity. From this rock he took the specimen before mentioned. The dust of the roads, and that of the floors of the cottages, may be collected, like iron filings, on presenting a bar magnet. Lieut. M. further states an occurrence of a very remarkable character, provided the timepiece of which he speaks were esteemed to be generally correct. That is, Mr. Durnford, who was of Lieut. M.'s party, laid down his watch at one of their surveying positions, and on their return found it had gained two hours. This is ascribed to magnetic influence, and indeed with apparent propriety: for by recurring to Mr. Barlow's experiments on the influence of iron on the magnet, as given in our first number, we saw that a large mass of that metal, unpolarized, did not influence excellent chronometers more than four or five seconds in some days, although placed close to the ball.

Lieut. Mudge's paper contains a copy of a letter to him from Mr. Barlow, on this subject, wherein is narrated an analogous fact, which, we think, must be acceptable to our readers, especially they who are occupied in maritime pursuits.

Mr. Duncan, now Master Attendant in the Chatham Dock Yard, in the year 1791, commanded a ship belonging to the Hudson's Bay Company; and while in pursuit of a north west passage, in lat. 61° 52' N., long. 92° 23' W., being then 20 leagues from land, and with soundings of from 60 to 65 fathoms on a blue mud, found his azimuth compass influenced in a singular manner; the card revolving as if it had totally lost all magnetic power. This was an excellent instrument, and he ordered up seven other compasses to ascertain whether accident had disordered it; but they were all affected in a similar manner. He then stood farther off from land, and the compasses resumed their due positions. He had a dipping needle, furnished by the Royal Society, which varied, in a short time, from 78° to 86°; the mean dip, by one series of observations, was 81° 40', by another 83° 45'.

As every apparent anomaly is but a fact governed by the immutable laws of matter, and is anomalous to our judgment, only in so far as our ignorance of those laws extends; so we fully confide that the energies now applied by men of science to those branches of philosophy, which have an evident connection with magnetism, will be productive of results of high practical importance.

Electro-Magnetic Apparatus.
Journal of Science.

The two instruments, of which the subjoined descriptions are given, were suggested to the mind of M. de la Rive by the floating needle of M. Naef, which was a ribbon of silver and another of zinc in contact, bent, and floated by cork on acidulated water; whereby the magnetic pole was attracted and repelled.

M. de la Rive's instruments are cheap, simple, and easily applicable to the experimental purposes of electro-magnetism.

The first consists of a small voltaic combination attached to a cork; the plate of zinc is nearly half an inch wide, and extends about an inch and a half below the cork, its upper end passing through the cork to the upper surface; the slip of copper is the same width as the zinc, but passes round the zinc, being opposed to both its surfaces as in Dr. Wollaston's construction, its upper end also appears through the cork. A piece of copper wire, covered with silk thread, is coiled five or six times, and tied together, so as to form a ring about an inch in diameter, and the ends of the wire are connected, one with the zinc, and the other with the copper slip above the cork. When this small apparatus is placed in water slightly acidulated by sulphuric acid, the voltaic apparatus is active enough to make the ring highly magnetic; and by presenting a magnet to it in different directions, it may be attracted and repelled, and presents all the phenomena of a mobile conducting wire.

The other apparatus is also a little voltaic combination hung from a cork, but the plates are connected together, not by a ring of wire, but by a helix. The helix is made of similar wire to the ring, it is about one-third of an inch in diameter, and the two ends of the wire are returned through the helix till near the middle, when they are made to pass to the outside between the spirals; then being connected with the upper ends of the plates, the helix lies on the cork, with its two ends equally distant from the centre, the course of the electricity being along the wire, from one end of the helix to the other, and then back to the plates. When placed on acidulated water, the helix becomes magnetic, and its extremities become opposite magnetic poles, being attracted and repelled by the poles of a magnet, just as another magnet would be in the same situation.—*Bib. Univer.* xvi. p. 201.

In our next number we shall give a description of another apparatus, constructed for Mr. Faraday, of the Royal Institution, by Mr. Newman, of Lisle Street.

Previous to dismissing the subject of electro-magnetism, we have to state that Mr. Faraday recommends, in making experiments in voltaic and electro-magnetism, where repeated contacts be requisite, and if the wires be copper, to apply a little nitrate of mercury to their extremities; whereby an amalgam will be formed, which will prevent oxidation, and thereby render the contact more perfect.

We would beg leave also to hint to experimentalists, that by using short portions of the finest wire procurable, instead of iron filings, some demonstration of the magnetic current might be indicated by the direction such a pile of metallic bristles would assume. Filings are too heavy, and too short.

On the Decomposition of Metallic Salts by the Magnet. By Mr. J. MURRAY. Philosophical Magazine. No. 283.

Mr. Murray favours the scientific world by presenting further experiments on the very interesting subject of chemical agency by the magnet. He says, " I continue to receive renewed evidence of the truth of my conclusions." Does he mean, from concurrent experiments made by his friends; or by an extension of his own? And adds, " I confess that they appear to *me* quite satisfactory." It is impossible to abridge this valuable paper, without injury to the author; we shall therefore take the liberty to use his own words:—

" A solution of permuriate of mercury was by the magnet soon reduced into running or metallic mercury, and the supernatant fluid was not affected by the albumen of the egg.

" Hence, fine steel filings magnetized and administered in syrup will be an admirable antidote to corrosive sublimate.

" Nitromuriate of platinum was decomposed with a brisk effervescence, distinctly audible, and with a visible spray between the eye and light.

" Fine Dutch steel wire was selected, and proved to be non-magnetic.—It was thrown into nitrate of silver, where it remained for 14 hours without being affected; part of this was made the uniting wire between the N. and S. poles of two bar magnets; when, it became speedily plumed with crystals of silver.

"A portion of the same wire was snapped in twain, and the magnet passed over one of the fragments, and both projected into solution of nitrate of silver—that which was magnetized reduced the silver, while the other remained inert.

"The magnetic bar was coated with copal varnish, and placed into solution of muriate of mercury, but reduction took place as if no such film had interposed.

"Two magnetic bars were left for two days in phosphorous acid. The acid was decomposed—the north pole of one of the bars was scarcely affected, but the south pole of the other was corroded $\frac{1}{8}$ inch deep, and developed the fasciculated structure described by Mr. Daniel.

"The two magnetic poles (N. and S.) of two bar magnets immersed in nitrate of silver, were united about $\frac{1}{2}$ inch from their extremities by a thread of steel; a precipitation of crystals of reduced silver took place about the uniting wire (very few below), and the uniting wire itself became so invested.

"I have succeeded in decomposing every metallic salt in this way, to which I have applied the magnet; and I have yet to be informed that steel, simply as a carburet of iron, will attract all acids whatever from every metal whatsoever.

"A portion of platinum wire that suffered no change in nitrate of silver, in solution, was made the uniting wire between the poles of a powerful horse-shoe magnet (that supported 12lbs. weight). When this was immersed into nitrate of silver it soon became discoloured and acted upon.

"When a magnetic bar is plunged into solution of nitrate of silver, it accomplishes its complete reduction, however considerable the quantity; the surface of the magnet in contact with the solution is not abraded, but the surface above the solution is much corroded, from the escape of the acid vapour, the consequence of decomposition.

"When in the nitrate of silver, the N. pole became instantly studded with brilliant pallets of silver, and formed more rapidly and more copiously round it than round the south pole. These crystalline pallets exhibited evident polarity, and were affected by the approach of a fine steel plate.

"When the magnet is plunged into a solution of muriate of mercury, and the decomposition takes place which yields globules of fluid metallic mercury, it will be seen that the action is most intense at the angles and base of the bar, and the reduction there more copious and prompt. This phenomenon is manifested when a magnetic bar is rolled in iron filings; for it will then be perceived that the quantity of adhering particles is much greater in these places than in any other parts of the surface.

"It is an interesting spectacle to witness the reduction of minute metallic balls around the poles, particularly the north and its base, with a square floor reflecting the form or impress of the inclined bar—the reduction commences at the edges, and is striking and beautiful."

We think there will not be one dissentient opinion from the conclusion Mr. Murray has himself come to; and as we daily learn some new fact indicative of the important connection subsisting between electricity, galvanism, and magnetism; or approximating to a proof of their identity; we feel more anxious for a zealous pursuit, by rigid experiment, of their respective powers; whether as relative to the laws of motion, or of chemical action.

Account of some Experiments in Pickling Seed Wheat with Blue Vitriol, or Sulphate of Copper. By Mr. BARCLAY.
Farmer's Magazine, No. 88.

In our first number, wherein we gave the opinion of Sir John Sinclair, respecting the efficacy of immersing the seed grain in a solution of copper; we not only expressed our apprehensions on the subject of the solution being too warm; but, also, intimated the possible danger of soaking the seed too long; as well as pointing at Mr. Phillip's case of the destruction of vegetable life by cupreous matter. We candidly confess that these subjects are not so familiar to us as to render us dogmatic on them; but, we should trust that other metallic salts might be found to have as full a preventive effect, without having a deleterious action on the grain. Would not some of the ferruginous salts answer the purpose? Iron pervades almost every soil, in a slight degree, and, therefore, may not be injurious to grain within moderate limits. A strengthened dose of it might possibly be efficacious. In the case before us, Mr. Barclay shall speak for himself. He is to be supposed as addressing his correspondent, the Secretary to the Morayshire Farmer Club:—

"Having read last autumn, in the Farmer's Journal, some strong recommendations of blue vitriol as a pickle for wheat, I resolved, having tried several other pickles, to make trial of this also. For this purpose I bought 11 lib. of it, which cost me as many shillings; and with this quantity pickled seven bolls, which I sowed in seven acres, on the 6th of November. I washed the wheat before putting it into the pickle, in which part of it was steeped three hours, part two, and part only one. I did not remark any difference in the brairding: it came up I thought slowly, and rather thin; but I supposed this might be partly owing to the circumstance that the field was after two years' grass, and (though it had been dunged and break-furrowed in September) could not be brought to a sufficiently free mould.

"It happened that the seed which I used contained a considerable quantity of papple, (*Agrostemma githago*), which no farmer should sow; but I had no other wheat ready at that time; and the season being far advanced, I chose, rather than delay, to sow it, and weed out the papple in the spring. It was long, however, ere I saw a single plant of papple in the field; and in the beginning of April, when I weeded some other fields, I found that this did not require weeding for the papple: I did not see six plants of it in the whole seven acres. It seemed evident that it must have been destroyed by the pickle; and it was probable that a good deal of my wheat, which continued too thin, had also been destroyed by it. I resolved to make an experiment in my garden; and dissolved a piece of blue vitriol, something less than two beans, in nearly a gill of hot water, and, after it was cool, put into it 24 grains of wheat, and 24 seeds of papple, previously washed, and let them stand about nine hours in the solution. I then sowed them in a plot in my garden; and in another plot, 24 grains of wheat, and 24 of papple, washed and steeped the same time in pure water. This was on the 2d of June. From the unpickled seed I had soon 24 plants of wheat, and 22 of papple, healthy and vigorous. In the other plot, the pickled wheat came up slowly, and produced but sickly plants; they are only 21 in number; and three of them did not appear till nineteen days after the seed was put in the ground. Had it been sown in the field, late in the year, I am convinced a much greater proportion of it would never have brairded. The papple seemed to be destroyed by the pickle, it was so long ere any of it appeared,—only *one* sickly plant of it ever brairded, and that at the distance of six weeks from the time it was sown.

"To try the effect of a weaker solution of the vitriol, I dissolved a small piece, of the size of two peas, in about two gills of hot water, which, judging by the colour, I supposed to be about the strength of what I used for the seven bolls, and, after the solution was cool, put into it 24 grains of wheat and 24 of papple, with three seeds of the common field vetch (*Vicia sativa*), all previously washed, and left them 12 hours in it, when I sowed them in my garden; and in another plot, the same number of each sort, steeped the same time in pure water. This was on the 19th of June. On the 29th the whole 24 grains of unpickled wheat were brairded, while there were only 14 plants from the pickled seed; only 21 of these ever brairded, and some of them as late as the 5th of July. The papple used in the experiment was taken from the *dressings*, or small corn, (no other being at hand,) and does not seem to have been sound. There are only six plants of it from the unpickled seed; but there is none from the pickled. Neither has any of the pickled seeds of vetch grown, while there is a plant for each of those that were not pickled.

"Not having preserved the number of the Farmer's Journal alluded to, I cannot now recollect how far, in pickling the seven bolls, I deviated from the mode recommended there; my impression is, that I did not exceed the strength of pickle recommended, nor the time of steeping; and if my memory does not deceive me, the gentleman, whose letter in that journal was my guide, (though I am aware I did not follow his directions to the letter,) said he was convinced a stronger solution than he used would not injure the seed;— and I think he recommended steeping longer than I did. The experiments I have made in the field and garden, have satisfied me that blue vitriol is a pickle which requires to be used *with caution*. As a preventive of smut, I have found it, in the trial I have made, perfectly effectual.

"It was a thing I did not expect, to find any pickle more injurious to papple, that hardy weed, than to corn. Is it not likely that other pickles are, in some degree, destructive of the small seeds among wheat, though this has never, so far as I know, been urged as an argument in favour of pickling?"

On Dry Rot in Timber.

The following is taken from the same Journal; which, although written, in some degree, in the spirit of quackery, is worthy of notice, by the accuracy with which it describes this formidable evil. It would seem that Mr. Service, the writer, is occupied in curing the dry rot as a business, and therefore preserves the secret of his process. We consider his paper, addressed to the conductor of the Farmer's Magazine, as sheer advertisement; but still we derive a value from it, for the reason before stated. Mr. S. announces his secret process as infallible; and, as he does not intimate that he varies it at all according to the form under which the disease may appear in the timber, we are left to infer that the general character of dry rot is uniform, however varied the appearance may be. Mr. S. refers to the Bishop of Winchester—Wm. Manning, Esq. M. P.—Francis Fane, Esq. M. P., and others, in proof of the efficacy of his processes. By laying his description of the appearances of dry rot before our readers, we shall enable them to detect the evil in its earlier stages; and that is the sole object of our noticing what is held forth to the public from a motive of self interest, rather than of liberal communication. Mr. S. expresses himself thus:—"Of the various incidents and calamities to which houses and other buildings are subject, none is more justly to be dreaded, than that destructive decay in timber, usually called the DRY ROT, which, when once it has taken place, destroys, though not with the speed, yet with all the certainty, of a consuming fire. And what adds still more to the magnitude of the evil is, that in all places or situations liable thereto, however carefully and however frequently the affected timber be removed, and replaced by that which is perfectly sound, the deadly disease is ever ready to break out afresh, and extend its ravages over the whole building, unless its principle, as well as its effects, be completely exterminated from it. The heavy expense in maintaining continual repairs, without even the hope of a cure, which is severely felt by many owners of houses in different parts of the kingdom, is not the only evil attending the Dry Rot: it is injurious to the health of the persons inhabiting the affected house, and particularly so to children, whose tender frames are but ill adapted to resist the subtle and pernicious effluvia arising from the rot, which are found to be so destructive to every kind of wood, and even capable of penetrating the hardest stone.

" This distemper in timber manifests itself in a variety of forms. In some cases it appears like a mere spider's web, or mildew, spreading itself along the surface of the timber, and insidiously preparing it for certain dissolution. In other cases it assumes the form of a flat fungous cake, in texture somewhat like the honey-comb, in colour partly white and partly yellow, and in smell resembling the common field fungus. Sometimes it is found in the form of a vine, or sea weed, creeping along the joists, plates, flooring, skirting-boards, and wainscoting, and extracting therefrom all the medullary substance of the wood; in consequence of which, they crack as if parched with fire, and are soon afterwards reduced to powder. There is also frequently deposited, at small distances from the fungous cake, a kind of pollen, or reddish powder, like brick-dust, supposed to be the seeds of the fungus, which convey the devastation to the surrounding timber.—In general, where the rot has made any considerable progress, there is a combination of these and other appearances, either of which, singly, is sufficient to excite the most serious apprehensions on the part of those who are the owners of such infected buildings; but, when united, they bespeak an enemy too powerful to be tampered with any longer; being no less than *the plague in a house*, which, like a cancer or gangrene in the human body, must be instantly extirpated, or destruction will inevitably follow.

"The symptoms which usually indicate the existence of the dry rot, previous to its breaking through the flooring, skirting-boards, or dado, are the following; viz. dampness and discoloration of the parts affected; cracking and warping of the floors, wainscoting, and skirting-boards; and where the distemper has seized upon stone or marble pavements, which it will do, in like manner as upon timber, though not with equal rapidity and effect, large white or yellow blotches may be seen on their surface, not unlike leprous spots upon the skin. By these and similar appearances, the extent and progress of the rot may be easily traced: and whenever any such tokens begin to exhibit themselves, no time ought to be lost in removing the diseased timber, and applying a proper remedy to effect a permanent cure. For long experience has proved, that no repairs in the timber alone, no mere change of unhealthy materials for those which are perfectly sound, will be a sufficient security against the return of the rot while the seeds of the disorder are permitted to remain in any part of the building."

We cannot dismiss this subject without remarking on the particular condition in which timber, that suffers from this fungus, is placed: that is, it is excluded from air and light. It is said that, in some cases, the mere exposure to the sun and atmosphere will stop the fungous vegetation. How far this may be true, we know not from direct experience in this particular disease; but we think there are some analogies presenting daily to our eyes, from which a little wisdom may be gleaned. In all structures where the air and light be generally excluded, if moisture be present, we observe, on the surface of timber, a fungous or mouldy coating; that will spread rapidly; changing the colour to a grey or greenish grey, and which, when pressed upon, feels clammy to the fingers. On slicing into the superfices of the timber, we find it softened, and darkened a slight depth in its substance. If then, this effect be producible so injuriously, where the operating causes are but partial in degree, we may apprehend the worst, where their intensity exists. Some remedies, such as clearing the surface of the diseased film; and re-exposing the wood to the air and light, so as to dry it thoroughly; may afford partial or temporary relief; but we are not among those who would consider these means as fully effectual, and to be relied on: for we think that the absence of air and light are mere secondary causes, exciting the disease into maturity. We are inclined to believe that it frequently arises from the vegetable acid, the mucilaginous, or the saccharine matter contained in the timber; and which is so prone to assume the vegetable fungosity, that we cannot long preserve vinegar, or pyrolignous acid, in the state in which we usually procure them, without a fungous matter being generated. The same with all vegetable infusions and decoctions, containing mucilage, sugar, or extract.

The larger fungi, as mushrooms, &c. have been proved, by Braconnot, to contain a considerable quantity of a particular kind of acid; which he denominates fungic; and which, like many other of the vegetable acids, is probably only a modification of the acetic. As vegetable matter, the fungus constituting dry rot would doubtless yield acid also; were it subjected to experiment with the specific purpose of ascertaining the fact.

If then timber be exposed to *moisture*, not *soaked*, for the latter has a tendency to dissolve and wash away the nidus, we shall have a fungous surface generated in time; and that, too, the earlier, if we exclude air and light. The rot that assails privies, and all places where sulphuretted hydrogen and ammonical gas be occasionally generated, may be supposed to arise from various causes: that is, partly from the moisture, partly, perhaps, from the very quality of the gases to decompose the vegetable fibre of the wood; and partly from the animalcules generated in the decomposing fæcal matter.

We have been informed, on authority to which we attach respect, that the mineral acids are efficacious in dry rot; and we recollect, many years since, witnessing a case wherein diluted muriatic acid was really so: but we must candidly acknowledge that the disease had not made much progress. Our views of the causes of dry rot are rather sanctioned by this fact: for the mineral acids retard, or destroy the tendency of vegetable infusions and decoctions to form mouldy fungus. We throw out our ideas at a risk of their being eventually found erroneous, as we freely admit they may be; but we hope to stand excused for hazarding a simple conjecture on a subject of such importance.

Mr. Daniells' Platinum Pyrometer for High Temperatures.

Mr. Wedgewood's pyrometer was long held in the highest esteem of all the instruments proposed as a scale to measure the degrees of intense heat by; but it had its defects: for at a great intensity, it would become vitrified; and then cease to show that contraction in bulk which constituted it the scale of temperature. This defect was, of course, again governed by the comparative purity of the aluminous earth; which could not, under varying circumstances, be ever the same. Philosophers then naturally rested their further hopes on platinum, as a matter not fusible nor destructible, by any degrees of heat requisite for practical purposes. Guiton, and Dr. Ure, have given forms for platinum pyrometers, and now Mr. Daniells presents us with his. This instrument is simple in structure, which is one advantage in recommendation of it. It will enable us to measure to an intensity at least as high as the fusing point of cast iron; its sensibility indicating increments or decrements of about 7° of Fahr.

The pyrometer consists of a bar of platinum, 10¼ inches long, and 0·14 in. in diameter, placed in a tube of black-lead earthen-ware. The expansive difference between the bar and the tube, is indicated upon a circular scale, thus—a platinum wire, one-hundredth of an inch in diameter, is fixed to the end of the platinum bar; and is coiled three or four times round the axis of a small wheel, fixed at the back of the circular scale. The other end of the wire is bent back, and attached to the extremity of a slight spring, which keeps the wire in a state of extension. The axis of this wheel is 0·062 of an inch in diameter, and the wheel toothed; playing in a smaller wheel, whose diameter, and number of teeth, are one-third of the larger. An index, on the axis of the smaller wheel, indicates the temperature on a circular scale, divided into 360°. Instead of passing the platinum wire round the axis of the larger wheel, it has been found better to attach a short silken thread to its extremity; which, passing round, fixes to the spring. It is plain that the expansion of the pyrometer bar must make the larger wheel revolve, and, with it, the smaller indicating wheel, that indicates the temperature on the graduated scale.

By this instrument, Mr. Daniells has made repeated experiments, that he thinks justify the following table. The fusing point of silver is said to be *most* correct, as by three different trials, the variation did not exceed a degree from one another. Therefore, even by this instrument, we are not to expect absolute accuracy.

	Daniells' Scale.	Fahrenheit's Thermom.	Wedgewood's Results.
Boiling point of Mercury	92°	644°	600°
Fusing point of Tin	63	441	
Bismuth	66	462	
Lead	87	609	
Zinc	94	648	
Brass	267	1869	3807
Pure Silver ..	319	2233	4717
Copper	364	2548	4587
Gold	370	2590	5237
Cast Iron....	497	3479	17977
Red heat, just visible in day light	140	980	
Heat of a common parlour fire	163	1141	

It will be seen, by the above table, that there is very considerable difference between the results obtained from Mr.

Daniells' and Mr. Wedgewood's pyrometers. Mr. D. states that at its boiling temperature, mercury amalgamates with platinum. When the mercury be volatilized by a strong red heat, it acts on platinum powerfully, leaving it in a honey-comb-like condition. Also, that cast iron, strongly heated, and cooled slowly in a muffle, becomes covered with small, distinct, octohedral and tetrahedral crystals, and black oxyd of iron; the facets perfect, and brilliant.

Description of a Hydrostatic Balance, by which the specific gravities of Minerals may be ascertained without calculation. By BENJ. H. COATES, M. D.

This is the substance of a paper read before the Academy of Natural Sciences, Philadelphia. The instrument described was suggested by the presentation to the Academy of another, wherein the common steelyard was employed for the purpose.

The intention of Dr. Coates was to improve on this steelyard, by saving the trouble of calculation: *i. e.* by making the balance itself express the result; so that by the aid of a mere cup of water, the specific gravity of the mineral may be ascertained immediately. The lever resembles that of a common steelyard, and is made to balance correctly by adding to the mass of the shorter arm. The upper edge of both arms is made smooth, instead of being notched, in the usual manner, on the longer arm; so that the minutest possible subdivision may be had, from the accuracy in adjustment. The longer arm has a scale on its face; each division of which is numbered with a quotient of the length of the whole scale divided by the distance of the division, and commencing from the extremity of the arm. Thus, at half the length, is number 2—at one-third, 3—at one-fourth, 4, &c. Also at two-thirds is marked $1\frac{1}{2}$—two-fifths, $2\frac{1}{2}$, &c.: and all the other fractions minutely. These numbers extend as high as the specific gravity of platinum.

The balance is used thus:—Any convenient weight is suspended by a hook from the notch at the end of the scale.

The matter to be weighed is to be suspended by a horsehair on the other arm, sliding it along towards the extremity, until the weight and the matter be in equilibrio. Then the matter kept steady at the point of suspension, is to be plunged, as it suspends, into water, and again balanced by sliding the weight along the scale. The point of the balance, where the weight now is, will indicate the weight of the matter, as required.

The explanation is simple. The body to be weighed, and the weight at the farther end of the other beam, hold each other respectively in equilibrio, in air. On plunging the body into water, it loses as much in counteracting gravity on the weight arm, as is equal to a body of water occupying similar space with itself. Then, to equipoise them, the weight is slided from the extremity, towards the centre of motion of the balance beam, until the two arms are again in equilibrio. The distance passed over by the moving weight, of course, determines the shortened lever, and the consequent specific gravity of the body, as required.

In short, this is precisely the old hydrostatic balance, but with steelyard instead of equal arms in beam; to which is attached, a simple means of determining the relative gravity. But although it may be justly ceded to Dr. Coates, as the suggestion of his own mind; yet it is by no means an original plan: for we saw a balance, similarly constructed, in use by a watchmaker at Derby, more than thirty years ago.

Shower of Snails.

A Bristol paper says—" The inhabitants of this city have lately been amused with the exhibition and sale in our streets of a collection of snail-shells, which are reported to have fallen, or, we should more accurately say, made their sudden appearance, in a field of about three acres, belonging to a farmer at Tockington. 'An Observer of Nature' has obligingly directed our attention to the natural history of this snail in Montagu's *Testacea Britannica*. Its name is *Limax virguta*, or Zoned Snail Shell. 'It may be considered,' he says, 'as a local species; but is found in prodigious abundance in some sandy or barren stony situations, most plentifully near the coast, especially about Whitsand Bay, Cornwall, and in the south of Devonshire, where it is believed they contribute not a little to fatten the sheep, the ground being covered with them.' This snail occurs also abundantly in the neighbourhood of Bristol, and county of Somerset. We witnessed ourselves in a field belonging to Capt. Parish, at Timsbury, a few years since, an innumerable accumulation of them. On approaching heat they are observed to leave their hiding-place near the roots of grass, crawling upon the leaves and plants near it, and thus become visible to the superficial observer. From this remark of Montagu, and the well-known fact that snails furnish much nourishing matter, it would be perhaps best for the farmer belonging to the field at Tockington to turn into it a flock of sheep, which would soon crush the snails in eating them with the grass, and would doubtless improve thereby. In this phenomenon, the philosophic mind will easily trace the provision of Nature, to render these snails (fattened near the roots of the succulent grass) a pasture, when parched by the rays of the sun, of a most nourishing nature to herbaceous animals. Common rumour says, 'that the snails fell in a great shower, which continued upwards of an hour, and that the earth's surface was covered, nearly six acres, three inches deep!!'"

The Gloucester Herald says—"When we first heard the report of a shower of snails having fallen on Thursday week, near Tockington, in this county, we must confess we suspected the tale to be intended as the test of our credulity; but the fact has been subsequently authenticated by so many respectable persons, and having seen from different sources so considerable a number of those little curled light-coloured shells, with a streak of brown, and containing a living fish inside, we feel confident of the truth of the assertion. They fell like a shower of hail, and covered, nearly an inch deep, a surface of about three acres, and great numbers were distributed to a much greater extent; shortly after this, a storm swept so large a quantity into an adjoining ditch, that they were taken up in shovels-full, and travellers were furnished with what quantity they chose to take, and they were soon carried into the principal towns of this and the surrounding counties!!!"

Third Report of Commissioners of Weights and Measures,

The gentlemen selected by the Government for the performance of this important duty, are well known in the scientific world; and it would have been difficult to find parties more competent to its proper discharge. The commissioners were, Sir George Clerk, Bart.—Davis Gilbert, Esq.—Dr. Wollaston—Dr. Young, and Captain Kater.

It was resolved by them,—

1st. That the Parliamentary standard-yard, made by Bird, 1760, be henceforward considered as the authentic legal standard of the British empire, and that it be identified by declaring that 39·1393 inches of this standard, at the temperature of 62° of Fahrenheit, have been found equal to the length of a pendulum, supposed to vibrate seconds in London, on the level of the sea, and on a vacuum.

2d. That the Parliamentary standard troy pound, according to the two pound weight made in 1758, remain unaltered; and that 7000 troy grains be declared to constitute an avoirdupois pound; the cubic inch of distilled water being found to weigh 62°, in a vacuum, 252·72 Parliamentary grains.

3d. That the ale and corn gallon be restored to their original equality, by taking for the statutable common gallon of the British empire, a mean value; such that a gallon of common water may weigh ten pounds, avoirdupois, in ordinary circumstances; its content being nearly 227·3 cubic inches; and that correct standards of this imperial gallon, and of the bushel, peck, quart, and pint, derived from it, and of their parts, be procured without delay, for the exchequer.

We think that the subjoined table, in one of our early numbers, may be useful for the reader to have at command for occasional reference; as we shall frequently express measures as we find them in French authorities.

Weights and Measures.

Table of French Weights and Measures.

1st. Measures of Length: the Metre being at 32°, and the Foot at 62°.

	English Inches.	Mile.	Furl.	Yds.	Feet.	In.
Millimetre ..	·03937					
Centimetre ..	·39371					
Decimetre ..	3·93710					
Metre	39·37100					
Decametre ..	393·71000	0	0	10	2	9·7
Hecatometre	3937·10000	0	0	109	1	1
Kilometre ..	39371·00000	0	4	213	1	10·2
Miriometre..	393710·00000	6	1	156	0	6

2d. Measures of Capacity.

	English Cubic Inches.	Tons.	Hhds.	Wine G.	Pints.
Millilitre ..	·06103				
Centilitre ..	·61028			English.	
Decilitre ..	6·10280				
Litre	61·02800	0	0	0·	2·1133
Decalitre ..	610·28000	0	0	2·	5·1352
Hecatolitre..	6102·80000	0	0	26·419	
Kilolitre	61028·00000	1	0	12·19	
Miriolitre ..	610280·00000	10	1	58·9	

3d. Measures of Weight.

	English Grains.	Pound.	Ounce.	Dram.
Milligramme ..	·0154			
Centigramme ..	·1544			
Decigramme ..	1·5444		Avoirdupois.	
Gramme	15·4440			
Decagramme ..	154·4402	0	0	5·65
Hecatogramme	1544·4023	0	3	8·5
Kilogramme ..	15444·0234	2	3	5
Miriogramme..	154440·2344	22	1	2

THE FOCUS

OF

PHILOSOPHY, SCIENCE, AND ART.

No. IV.]   Saturday, December 22, 1821.   [Vol. I.

On Water Cements, Mortar, and Lime.
(Continued from page 78.)

M. VICAT having gone through the detail of experiments as heretofore expressed, we now proceed to the inferences he draws from them. He considers we may conclude,—

1st. That by the admixture of water with very fat white limes, and without any other ingredient, we may form bodies equally hard as many varieties of natural lime-stones presenting to the geologist: but it is then to be understood that the lime be slacked in the common manner; that not any mechanical, or chemical, agent shall oppose its duly shrinking, while in progress to set; and that it be so worked as to have a due pasty consistence. These, we may observe, are requisites, even in the composition of common mortar, as well as in the setting of plaster of Paris.

2d. That the action of the air, and lengthened time of exposure, increase the hardness of the slacked limes. By the action of the air, he, of course, means the combination of its diffused carbonic acid with the lime paste; for we have not any reason to presume that the paste can decompose the atmospheric air itself.

3d. That the hydraulic limes and water being commixed, especially the coloured hydraulic, yield but soft compounds; if there be not any other ingredient. These limes seem to require additional matter, either to aid the process of crystallization, or to bring the aqueous particles more immediately into contact with those of the lime, by mechanically separating the latter. In this, though, we shall be seen to differ from M. Vicat's further remarks.

4th. That the hardness of the hydraulic limes is increased by the action of the air. That is, as we suppose, not by any atmospherical decomposition, but by the presentation of carbonic acid. But M. Vicat observes, that the hydrates of fat limes are hardened in a far greater degree by exposure to atmospheric air, than the hydraulic limes are.

5th. That the resistances of these compounds do not bear regular proportions to their respective hardness. Their resistances we would presume to be governed by their comparative perfection of crystallization. Their hardness, perhaps, more dependant on the forms of arrangement assumed by the crystals.

In a subsequent page the reader will be shown by M. Vicat, that the commonly received opinion of the necessity for sand, to cause the limes to indurate, is by no means well founded.

The benefit to be derived to art from the common fat limes, will be estimated from some of their properties, as now to be shown. We are not to expect that large, and compact, masses of regenerated calcareous stone, can be formed by art; or at least not within such a period of time as would render it available for purposes of common fabric; the entire life of the longest liver would not enable him to witness the desired effect. For M. Vicat tells us that, in ten years the regeneration will not exceed one-twentieth of an inch in depth, from the exposed surface. It is then the firmness and texture of a composition, containing only lime and water, that we have to look to; and these, under the most favourable circumstances, will not exceed from 2·745 to 3·690; a good brick being 5·690;—nearly twice as compact as the best result to be hoped from water and lime.

This, however, is not the sole difficulty we have to encounter (though it is so apparently insuperable, as to be more than enough to limit our art); for we have another presenting in such compound of lime and water, namely, that, in drying, this hydrate of lime shrinks to a great excess. M. Vicat found that when he formed prisms of it, not exceeding the magnitude of a small brick, and set them on a dry floor, to which they would not adhere, they shrunk without cracking; and dried into solid masses, covered with a slight efflorescence, which rounded off the angles and corners. If the moulds were filled with the compound of lime and water, and left in them to dry, they would do so; but very irregularly; adhering to the moulds, and exhibiting an abundance of cracks; so as to be totally useless. M. Vicat ascertained that kneading the mass well, previously to filling the moulds with it, did not at all improve the result.

The fat limes were observed to shrink the most, as indeed we should have expected; and that, too, in a higher degree, the more thoroughly they had been divided in the slacking. We do not here exactly understand M. Vicat, as to whether he means that it was in proportion to the abundance of the water used, by converting it into a milk of lime; or by the augmented bulk assumed by the lime on its union with the water. Be this as it may, the shrinking property will always debar its use as a mortar, unless in works under water; or in stucco, where the coatings are thin. But it must, for such a purpose, undergo a thorough kneading. The authority of Vitruvius would lead us to infer that the Romans used simple combinations of lime and water, in works of light character, called albaria opera. In the East Indies, it is a common practice to coat walls with a fine stucco made of quick-lime, mixed up with milk, oil, and other ingredients. This Indian compound differs widely, in its nature, from that of a mere mixture of lime and water: the former being a chemical union of the albumen of the milk with the lime; the oil only renders it less assailable by atmospheric moisture. M. Vicat goes on to say that "it would not be difficult to make thin slabs of mere hydrate of lime, which, when smoothed and polished on sand-stone, would imitate fine marble, and might be employed in mosaic works." Now, either the conclusion come to by M. Vicat, as to the length of time necessary to indurate hydrate of lime one-twentieth of an inch deep, must be erroneous; or these slabs would have been better designated as films. What workman can wait ten years for the result of his labours?

When the hydrates are fully formed, water can act only on one species; that is, the hydrate of fat lime. On the hydrate of hydraulic lime it has not any influence. To show that fat hydrates are so affected, make up some of the slacked fat lime into balls with water, and, when dry, expose them to the air. In a few months their surfaces will be indurated by their regeneration of carbonate of lime; and if the tongue be applied, they will be found perfectly insipid. But on breaking one, and again applying the tongue, the well known acrid causticity of the lime will be perceived. And if the central portion be exposed to water, it will all wash out, leaving a spherical shell of carbonate of lime.

M. Descotils supposed that during the burning of the limestone, the silex which may be commixed undergoes such a change as to render it soluble in acids, and that this siliceous matter contracting an intimate union with the lime, makes it less easily acted on by the atmosphere or water. M. Vicat considers this to be a very good explanation of the resistance made by the hydrates of hydraulic lime, to the solvent action of water; but not reconcilable to the weak consistence acquired by their exposure to the atmosphere. For our own parts, we must differ in toto from M. Descotils; for, first, it is against all reasonable conjecture that the siliceous matter should meet with fluoric acid, the only acid with which it has any chemical affinity: and secondly, that its increased solubility would render it less fitted for the required purpose. In our sixth number, this subject shall be diligently pursued.

Electro-Magnetism.

(Continued from page 85.)

We will not here repeat the conjecture with which we closed our last notice of Mr. Faraday's experimental inquiry, further, than to say, that we attach the same qualifying presumption to the result of the paragraph that we now recommence our observations upon, as we did to the concluding one of the preceding. Mr. F. informs us that, if we form a cylinder of rings, by placing them one above another; or if a helix be made; the same kind of accumulative effect, in the extreme lines of wire, will be produced. If the wires be placed cylindrically, we do not understand wherein the analogy with concentric circles, or parallel wires, consists; without the cylinder be presented in the line of its axis. Mr. F. then proceeds to consider the probable motions produced by a set of ring cylinders, or spirals, placed within each other, so as to nearly fill up the hollow of the primary cylinder, or 'spiral, and having currents in the same direction. He concludes that a greater intensity of effect would result in the cylindrical axis. Also, that it would have those two imaginary points, (we crave Mr. F.'s pardon for so terming them,) presumed to exist near the centre of the simple ring, removed to the two extremities of the cylindrical axis; one attractive, and the other repulsive. And, he contends that the phenomena of the cylinder and helix arise from a precisely similar magnetical current as that which takes place round the connecting wire of a battery. Filings of iron, says Mr. F., strewed on paper, and held over the cylinder, arranged themselves in curved lines, as when acted on by a magnet. The ends, too, of the cylinder attract, and repel, like those of the magnet. But, although the analogies between the magnet, helix, and cylinder, are impressive, there are some discordancies; and these he goes on to show.

But we cannot pass over two beautiful experiments narrated by Mr. F. When a flat spiral, whose rings were not continued to the centre, was laid on a heap of iron filings, " they arranged themselves in lines, passing through the ring, parallel to its axis; and then folding up on either side, as radii round to the edge, where they met; so that they represented, exactly, the lines which a pole would have described round the sides of the rings: and those filings which were in the axis of the rings, stood up in perpendicular filaments, *half an inch long*; and so as to form an actual axis to the ring; tending neither one way nor the other; but according, in their form and arrangement, with what has been described: whilst the intermediate portions also formed long threads, bending this way and that, from the centre, more or less, according as they were further from, or nearer, to it." The other experiment was as follows: A helix of silked copper wire, three inches long, round a glass tube, an inch in diameter, was connected with the apparatus, and put into the water, wherein a magnetic needle, about three inches long, was floated with cork. If the end that attracted one of the poles of the needle was brought near that pole, when it entered the tube, the whole needle passed up it to the opposite pole of the helix; or the one that would have repelled it on the outside. The other pole of the magnet was similarly influenced by the other, or corresponding pole of the helix.

These two experiments show a close analogy between the iron filings, and the magnet, as influenced by the voltaic current. The discordancies in action between the helix and magnet are stated to be:—

1st. One pole of a magnet attracts the opposite pole of a magnetic needle, in all directions, and positions; but when the helix be held parallel to the needle, and with opposite poles, which ought to attract, and then the helix be moved on, so that the pole of the needle gradually comes nearer to the middle of the helix, repulsion generally takes place, before the pole gets to the middle of the helix, where, with a magnet, it would be attracted.

2d. The intensity of polarity in the helix, or that point where the needle would, at right angles to its axis, be attracted, is at the end of the helical axis. But in an early part of the paper, Mr. F. showed that, in the magnet, this polar intensity was at a point some little distance from its extremity.

3d. Similar poles of magnets repel each other, when within certain distances; and, on being brought nearly into contact, they are mutually attracted. And when similar poles of a helix are brought near contact, they still repel.

Mr. Faraday proceeds to inform us, that we may not hope to construct magnets resembling the helix, and flat spiral, for that no success has attended his trials to do so. A magnetized steel cylinder was, at one end, north all round; at the other, south; but the outside and inside presented the same effects: for no pole of the needle would have passed up the axis, and down the sides, as with the helix; it would have stopped at the dissimilar pole of the needle. Hence, he infers the certainty that the rings of a ring-cylinder are not in the same state as those which compose the helix. This confirms a previous remark of our own, made in our third number. It was found impossible to magnetize a circular plate of steel, so as to have the polar centres at the centres of opposite sides of the plates, as they are pointed in the flat spiral. Mr. F. could only effect a very irregular distribution.

Mr. F., without committing himself by any doctrinal pledge, thinks it probable that, in the bar magnet, the metal is in the same state as the copper wire of the helix magnet, and perhaps, as M. Ampere thinks, by currents of electricity; but he does not allow that the mere magnetic effects of the copper helix, as hitherto shown, are sufficient to establish the identity of electrical with magnetical power. He says, he has spoken of opposite sides of the connecting wire as two; merely to distinguish one set of effects from the other. Dr. Wollaston considers that the electro-magnetic current, passing round the axis of the wire, in a direction determined by the position of the voltaic poles, is sufficient to explain all the phenomena.

M. Ampere's conjecture that a circular wire, connected with the voltaic poles, would be influenced, by the earth's magnetism, to assume a position of a plane at right angles to the magnetic meridian and dip, is combated by Mr F., as not sustained by experiment. The magnet directing a curved wire, and the curved wire a needle, led him to recur to these experiments successfully.

He floated a galvanic pair of plates, from whose poles emanated a circular wire, in a glass vessel, containing acidulated water. It arranged itself so that the circular plane was perpendicular to the magnetic meridian; and, when disturbed, would resume its position. On examining that side of the plane towards the north, it was found to be that which was attracted by a south pole. A voltaic circle, with a curved wire, floating in a silver capsule, as well as M. de la Rive's small ring apparatus, afforded similar results. The straight connecting wire, being directed by a magnet, leads Mr. F. to conjecture that it will act similarly with the earth, and stand perpendicular to the magnetic meridian. It ought, also, to endeavour to circulate round the magnetic pole of the earth. Mr. F. concludes with remarking that, "theoretically, therefore, a horizontal wire, perpendicular to the magnetic meridian, if connected first one way with a voltaic battery, and then in the opposite way, should have its weight altered; for, in the one case, it would tend to pass in a circle downwards; and, in the other, upwards. This alteration should take place in different parts of the world. The effect is actually produced by the pole of a magnet; but I have not succeeded in obtaining it, employing only the polarity of the earth."

Mr. Faraday disclaims all intention of sustaining any particular theory of electro-magnetism, in his explanatory remarks on the respective experiments he has favoured the world with. He seems to have done just what all experimentalists should do; that is, he has sought for facts by diligent inquiry. Doctrine will arise early enough out of knowledge properly established. We hope that this philosophical spirit may spread, to the honour and benefit of general science.

Mr. Faraday's new Electro-Magnetic Apparatus, made by Mr. Newman, of Lisle Street.

Mr. Faraday in the same number of the Journal of Science, Literature, and the Arts, from whence we have the preceding paper, tells us that since his paper had been printed, he caused an apparatus to be made for the purpose of effecting revolutions of the wire round the pole, and of the pole round the wire. When Hare's Calorimeter was used, with it, he says the wire revolved so rapidly round the pole, that the eye could scarcely follow the motion. And a single galvanic trough, containing ten pair of plates, on Dr. Wollaston's construction, had power enough to move the wire and the pole with considerable rapidity. It consists of a stand, from one end of which a brass pillar rises about six inches high, and is then continued horizontally by a copper rod over the stand; at the other end of the stand, a copper plate is fixed, with a wire for communication, brought out to one side; in the middle is a similar plate and wire; these are both fixed. A small shallow glass cup, supported on a hollow foot of glass, has a plate of metal cemented to the bottom, so as to close the aperture, and form a connexion with the plate on the stand; the hollow foot is a socket, into which a small cylindrical bar magnet can be placed, so that the upper pole shall be a little above the edge of the glass; mercury is then poured in until the glass is nearly full; a rod of metal descends from the horizontal arm perpendicularly over this cup; a little cavity is hollowed at the end and amalgamated, and a piece of stiff copper wire is also amalgamated, and placed in it as described in the paper, except that it is attached by a piece of thread, in the manner of a ligament, passing from the end of the wire to the inner surface of the cup; the lower end of the wire is amalgamated, and furnished with a small roller, which dips so, as to be under the surface of the mercury in the cup beneath it.

The other plate on the stand has also its cup, which is nearly cylindrical; a metal pin passes through the bottom of it, to connect by contact with the plate below; and to the inner end of the pin, a small round bar magnet is attached at one pole by thread, so as to allow the other to be above the surface of the mercury when the cup is filled, and have freedom of motion there; a thick wire passes from the rod above, down perpendicularly, so as to dip a little way into the mercury of the cup; it forms the connecting wire, and the pole can move in any direction round it. When the connexions are made with the pillar, and either of the wires from the stand plates, the revolution of the wire, or pole above, takes place; or if the wires be connected with the two coming from the plates, motion takes place in both cups at once, and in accordance with the law stated in the paper. This apparatus may be much reduced in size, and made very much more delicate and sensible.

The above described seems to make a very compact and effective instrument, for the ascertaining of many facts in electro-magnetism, that remain to be proved and explained.

M. M. Ampere and Arago's Experiments on Electro-Magnetism. London Journal of Arts and Science.

It might be considered a very culpable remissness in us, were we to totally overlook the labours of Messrs. Ampere and Arago, as reported in the public sittings of the Royal Academy of Sciences at Paris; because the results of their judgments must have some doctrinal influence, and especially with all those who have not the opportunities of reducing reputed facts to experimental tests. At the commencement of the ensuing year, we shall be enabled, by a regular supply of the French periodical works on Science, to lay before our readers an early treat on those matters, which it is our object to collect for them. And we shall do so with the more satisfaction to ourselves; because we can then select, and translate, at our own pleasure. On the subject before us, we are indebted to the London Journal of Arts and Sciences for a short notice of Messrs. Ampere and Arago's conclusions. M. Oersted, of Copenhagen, having discovered that electrical conductors generally, and those of the metallic class particularly, were capable of being acted on with magnetical phenomena, when a current of electricity was sent through them, led the above mentioned gentlemen to undertake a series of experiments, from which we have the following results.

They found that, on transmitting electrical currents through two metallic wires, (parallel and separate we presume,) they assumed attractive and repulsive forces; and that when the current was transmitted through both, in the same direction, they were mutually attractive: when the currents passed in contrary directions, they were mutually repulsive. We do not perceive any thing surprising, though we do something useful, in this fact. It may lead us to further discoveries. The next point hinted at, is, however, of a very unexpected character; or rather, was so to the discoverer; namely, M. Arago having ascertained that, by winding a conducting wire round a bar of steel, he could produce as many poles, and consequently, as many separate electrical magnets, as he pleased, in the same bar; and, further, that these effects were producible by both common and voltaic electricity.

Of all the facts elicited by experiment in electro-magnetism, we think this the most remarkable; for who could have anticipated the division of a steel bar, or wire, into multiplied needles, at pleasure; each having its respective poles and powers, as distinct magnets? M. Arago's discovery will signalize him among his brethren pursuing electro-magnetism; and we trust that both he, and M. Ampere, will not relax their efforts.

M. Ampere, in allusion to terrestrial magnetism, asserts that he has constructed an apparatus of brass wire alone, which will obey the magnetic meridian, when influenced by currents of either the common, or the voltaic electricity.

M. Ampere affirms that he has also imitated the natural dip of the magnet, by an analogous combination. And, moreover, that the magnetic, as well as voltaic conductors, are posited by terrestrial action, just as they would be by electrical currents directed according to the apparent motion of the sun, perpendicularly to the magnetic meridian: with an intensity increasing as approaching the equator. On this point, we have merely to observe, that M. Ampere is not, perhaps, quite so correct in his inferences as he may hope. Experiments made with a view of verifying his positions, are said to have been attended by some qualifying, if not hostile, results. In so far as relates to the dip of the needle, M. Ampere's conclusion must be erroneous, if we understand him aright; or our tables of the magnetic dip, said to be constructed from practical observations, in different latitudes, must be false; for we find from them, that the dip decreases towards the equator; and then, from the equator, southerly, increases again. M. A. then taking for granted that the terrestrial directing force is produced by such currents, asks whether the influence of one magnet on another, or on a voltaic conductor, may not, also, be owing to electrical currents, directed in planes perpendicular to the axis, and relatively to the poles, "as the apparent motion of the sun to the poles of the earth, corresponding to those of the magnet?"

From the apparent analogies that respective influences of magnetic, voltaic, and electrical, forces display, M. Ampere adopts a decided opinion of their identity. He is, too, tolerably confident he shall eventually show us that the terrestrial directing force emanates from the equatorial zone, where the heat, and light, act most intensely. He concludes by observing, that M. Arago's experiments point to the electrophorous, or Leyden phial, as an inexhaustible source of magnetic power, for the remagnetizing impaired needles.

The tone of this paper is more positive, and generalizing, than becomes the cautious philosopher. We do not presume to say that M. Ampere will never be able to realize his fond hopes; but we apprehend that he is dangerously premature in dealing forth conjectures, that are rather wide of his own experimental results. Still his labours have a very important value with us: we only quarrel with his anticipations. In our next number we shall give the spirit of a paper lately sent forth by M. Oersted, and another by Mr. Christie, on the subject of electro-galvanism.

Account of the Native Copper on the Southern Shore of Lake Superior, with historical Citations and miscellaneous Remarks, in a Report to the Department of War. By HENRY R. SCHOOLCRAFT.

American Journal of Science.

We consider this a very interesting description of the Native Copper masses, found in the course mentioned; not simply as relates to their magnitude, though, in this respect, they are objects unrivalled; but as additional proofs of the grand resources possessed by the American States. Some years since we had in our care a mass of native copper from Cornwall, weighing near 100lbs.; which excited the admiration of mineralogists. A part of its surface was as clear as if just cast; so much so indeed, that some cautious persons were doubtful whether the proprietor of it had not been using a little of that deceptive art for which the Cornish Miners are distinguished; but the other portions, both superficially and substantially, bore indubitable evidence of its native character. Yet large as this was, it was but a trifle compared with the mass described by Mr. S. as lying on the Ontonagon river.

The account given by Mr. Schoolcraft is contained in a letter to the American Secretary at War; and, after the introductory paragraph, runs thus—

" The first striking change in the mineral aspect of the country north of Lake Huron, is presented near the head of the island of St. Joseph in the river St. Mary, where the calcareous strata of secondary rocks are succeeded by a formation of red sand-stone, which extends northward to the head of that river at Point Iroquois, producing the falls called the *Sault de St. Marie* fifteen miles below, and thence stretching northwest along the whole southern shore of Lake Superior to the Fond du Lac, and into the regions beyond. This extensive stratum is perforated at various points by up-heaved masses of granite and hornblende, which appear in elevated banks on the margin of the lake between Dead river and Presque Isle, and from the Porcupine mountains ten leagues to the west of the Ontonagon river. It is overlayed in other parts by a stratum of grey sand-stone, resembling certain varieties of grauwacke, of uncommon thickness, which appears in various promontories along the shore, and, at the distance of ninety miles from point Iroquois, constitutes a lofty perpendicular wall upon the water's edge called the Pictured Rocks, which is one of the most commanding objects in nature. So obvious a change in the geological character of the rock strata, in passing from Lake Huron to Lake Superior, prepares us to expect a corresponding one in the imbedded minerals and other natural associations—an expectation which is realized during the first eighty leagues, in the discovery of red hematite, prehnite, opal, jasper, sardonyx, carnelian, agate, and zeolite.

" The first appearances of copper are seen on the head of the portage across Keweena point, two hundred and seventy miles beyond the Sault de St. Marie, where the pebbles along the shore of the lake contain native copper disseminated in particles varying in size from a grain of sand to a lump of two pounds weight. Many of the detached stones at this place are also coloured green by the carbonate of copper, and the rock strata in the vicinity exhibit traces of the same ore. These indications continue to the river Ontonagon, which has long been noted for the large masses of native copper found upon its banks, and about the contiguous country. This river (called Donagon on Mellish's Map) is one of the largest of thirty tributaries which flow into the lake between Point Iroquois and the Fond du Lac. It originates in a district of mountainous country intermediate between the Mississippi river and the Lakes Huron and Superior, and, after running in a northern direction for one hundred and twenty miles, enters the latter at the distance of fifty-one miles west of Point Keweena, in north latitude 46° 52′ 2″ according to the observations of Captain Douglass. It is connected by portages with the Menomonie river of Green Bay, and with the Chippeway river of the Mississippi, routes of communication occasionally travelled by the Indians in canoes. At its mouth there is a village of Chippeway Indians of sixteen families, who subsist chiefly on the fish (sturgeon) taken in the river; and whose location, independently of that circumstance, does not appear to unite the ordinary advantages of Indian villages in that region. A strip of alluvial land of a sandy character extends from the lake up the river three or four leagues, where it is succeeded by high broken hills of a sterile aspect, and covered chiefly by a growth of pine, hemlock, and spruce. Among these hills, which may be considered as lateral spurs of the Porcupine mountains, the Copper Mines, so called, are situated at the distance of thirty-two miles from the lake, and in the centre of a region characterized by its wild, rugged, and forbidding appearance. The large mass of native copper reposes on the west bank of the river, at the water's edge, and at the foot of a very elevated bank of alluvion, the face of which appears at some former period to have slipped into the river, carrying with it the mass of copper, together with detached blocks of granite, hornblende, and other bodies peculiar to the soil of that place. The copper, which is in a pure and malleable state, lies in connexion with serpentine rock, the face of which it almost completely overlays, and is also disseminated in masses and grains throughout the substance of the rock. The serpentine rock is not *in situ*, nor is it so found in any part of the regions visited. To account for its appearance in a section of country to which it is geologically foreign, it would be necessary to enter into the inquiry ' by what means have the loose masses of primitive rocks been transported into secondary countries?'—an inquiry which is incompatible with the limits of this Report, and which moreover would, in itself, furnish the subject of a very interesting memoir. I will however suggest, what has struck me in passing through that country—that the Porcupine mountains, which are situated thirty miles west, are the seat of extinguished volcanoes that have thrown forth the masses of native copper which are found (as will be mentioned in the sequel) so abundantly throughout the region of the Ontonagon. This opinion is supported by the fact that those mountains are composed (so far as observed) of granite, which is probably associated with other primary rocks, and among them serpentine,—that the red sand-stone rock at their base is highly inclined towards the mountains, so as to be almost vertical, and apparently thrown into this position by the up-heaving of the granite—and also, that their elevation, which has been calculated by Capt. Douglass and myself at 1800 feet above the level of Lake Superior, their conical and rugged peaks, and other appearances, are such as frequently characterize volcanic mountains.

" The surface of the metal, unlike most oxidable metals which have suffered a long exposure to the atmosphere, presents a metallic brilliancy; which is attributable either to alloy of the precious metals, or to the action of the river, which, during its semi-annual floods, carries down large quantities of sand and other alluvial matter, that may serve to abrade its surface, and kept it bright. The shape of the rock is very irregular—its greatest length is three feet eight inches—its greatest breadth three feet four inches, and it may altogether contain eleven cubic feet. In size, it considerably exceeds the great mass of native iron found some years ago upon the banks of Red River in Louisiana, and now deposited among the collections of the New York Historical Society, but, on account of the admixture of rocky matter, is inferior in weight. Henry, who visited it in 1766, estimated its weight at five tons. But after examining it with scrupulous attention, I have computed the weight of *metallic copper* in the rock at twenty-two hundred pounds. The quantity may, however, have been much diminished since its first discovery, and the marks of chisels and axes upon it, with the broken tools lying around, prove that portions have been cut off and carried away. The author just quoted observes, 'that such was its pure and malleable state, that with an axe he was able to cut off a portion weighing a hundred pounds.' Notwithstanding this reduction, it may still be considered one of the largest and most remarkable bodies of native copper upon the globe, and is, so far as my reading extends, exceeded only by a specimen found in a valley in Brasil, weighing 2666 Portuguese pounds. Viewed only as a subject for scientific speculation, it presents the most interesting considerations, and must be regarded by the geologist as affording illustrative proofs of an important character. Its connexion with a rock which is foreign to the immediate section of country where it lies, indicates a removal from its original bed; while the intimate connexion of the metal and matrix, and the complete envelopement of individual masses of the copper by the rock, point to a common and contemporaneous origin, whether that be referable to the agency of caloric or water. This conclusion admits of an obvious and important application to the extensive strata of serpentine and other magnesian rocks found in various parts of the globe! The Ontonagon river at this place is broad, rapid, and shallow, and filled with detached masses of rock out of place, which project above the water, and render the navigation extremely difficult during the summer season. The bed of the river is upon sand-stone similar to that which supports the Palisadoe rocks upon the Hudson. There is an island nearly in the centre of the river, which serves to throw the current against the west bank where the copper reposes, and which, as it is the only wooded island noticed in the river, may serve to indicate the locality of this mineral treasure to the future inquirer.

"Several other masses of native copper have been found on this river at various periods since it has been known to Europeans, and taken into different parts of the United States and of Europe, and a recent analysis of one of these specimens, at the University of Leyden, proves it to be native copper in a state of uncommon purity, and uncombined with any notable portion either of gold or silver."

(To be continued.)

On the Combination of Chromic with Sulphuric Acid. By Gay-Lussac. (From the Annales de Chemie et de Physique.) Repertory of Arts. No. 234.

If dilute sulphuric acid, in great excess, be boiled on chromate of lead or barytes, the chromic acid never is pure; but always retains a portion of the sulphuric; even should the latter be in ten times the quantity requisite to the decomposition of the chromate. On evaporating the liquid containing the two acids, we have deep red crystals, of quadrangular prismatic form. At a highly concentrated evaporation, the chromic acid is decomposed; yielding a sulphate of green oxyd of chrome. The crystals are soluble, deliquescent, and consist of chromic and sulphuric acid, each one atom. To analyze them, boil them with a mixture of muriatic acid and alcohol, whereby the chromic acid will be decomposed into green oxyd. Divide the liquid, and precipitate one portion with muriate of barytes, to estimate sulphuric acid; the other with ammonia, to estimate oxyd of chrome, and consequent chromic acid. Or the two concentrated acids may be mixed, from which results a red precipitate. Nitric acid has but little action with chromic.

Alcohol dissolves the compound of chromic with sulphuric acid; and, if the solution be concentrated, the mutual action of the acids is almost explosive; the chromic passing into the green oxyd, and the liquid assuming an ethereous smell.

On distilling either of these mixtures, and rectifying over muriate of lime, to keep down undecomposed alcohol, an ethereous mixture is produced, giving a penetrating smell and acid taste like that of acetic ether. On mixture with water, two strata are afforded; one of sulphuric ether, the other of oil of wine. On addition of either chromic acid, or peroxyd of manganese, to sulphuric acid, when distilled with alcohol, the same results present; the oxygen of the chromic acid, or of the manganese, forming sulphuric ether and oil of wine. The sulphuric acid is not changed; but its presence is necessary to the decomposition of the alcohol, and the partial disoxygenation of the chromic acid, or of the oxyd of manganese, by its affinity with chromic and manganesian oxyds. Scheele observed that, on leaving peroxyd of manganese, sulphuric acid, and alcohol, mixed for a few days, and then distilling gently, the alcohol passed with a nitrous ethereal scent. Dobreiner also noticed the same in a mixture of chromate of potash, sulphuric acid, and alcohol, which he considered as an ethereal product, by the action of chromic acid on the alcohol.

On the Combination of Silicium with Platinum, and on its Presence in Steel. By J. B. BOUSSINGAULT. (From the Annales de Chemie et de Physique.)

Repertory of Arts. No. 234.

M. Boussingault was led to a course of experiments on this subject, by M. Pretchel, of Vienna, having announced that he had succeeded in melting platinum, in very refractory crucibles, by an intense fire.

M. B. had access to the wind furnace of the laboratory of the School of Mines; and which, being heated by coke, gave him hope that he, also, might succeed. First, he tried the metal in a plain crucible, and then in a crucible with charcoal; they were both exposed to intense heat for three hours. That without charcoal was unaltered; the other was melted into a button. Similar experiments repeated, gave uniformly similar results. The melted platinum gained weight; which was imputed to its union with a minute portion of the carbon. The properties of the button were, a grey aspect; barely yielding to the file; specific gravity 20·5. In the cold, flattened under the hammer; but soon cracked, with granulated fracture. Forged at a cherry-red heat, became grained; at a low red, slightly flattened and cracked. Temper not changed by heating, and gradually cooling. Not even softened by a blast-forge furnace. To drive off its supposed combined carbon, it was cemented for an hour with oxyd of manganese; but all its properties remained unaltered. M. B.

beginning to doubt whether carbon were really combined with the metal, subjected it to cementation, by stratifying platinum with wood charcoal, in a crucible. After four hours of strong ignition, short of the melting point, he found it had lost its lustre, and presented superficial inequalities, resembling the blistering of steel. The specific gravity from 17 to 18. It became hard; so as to scratch pure platinum and iron; but not steel. The hardness was not increased by quenching in cold water. It had gained a small increase in weight.

In order to discover the quantity, and quality, of the matter with which the platinum had combined, he subjected it to chemical process, whereby he discovered that there was not any carbonaceous component whatever; but from the gelatinous appearance of the solution, he followed up his inquiry to the result of assuring himself that it was silicium, which had combined with the platinum; and which had been derived from about two or three per cent. of ashes, chiefly siliceous, in the charcoal. He adds, that if more than a certain quantity of charcoal be used, the fusion will be imperfect; or perhaps not at all: but he does not specify the due proportions. He estimates that the proportion of combined silicium is about ·005 in its proper purity; but that it gave, by process, ·010.

ON SILICIUM IN STEEL.

Granting a confidence in M. B., we shall deduce from his labours new views of the character of steel. Hitherto, carbon has been considered an essential ingredient in the formation of steel. It will now be seen that, although carbon may always be present, in a sensible degree, in steel; yet there is another ingredient equally requisite; perhaps more so; for, by one process, steel is made without *carbon*; but not, by any, without *silicium*.

M. B. experimented, as follows, on four different kinds of steel; for such we understand iron de rive to be:—namely, 1st. iron de rive—2d. cemented steel—3d. cast steel—4th. steel from Monkland, near Glasgow, made with Dannemora Swedish iron. The steel was dissolved in sulphuric acid, diluted with six times its weight of water; the insoluble residue dried, weighed, and burned. The proportion of carbon was deduced from the loss in weight. This matter, presumed to be carbon, takes fire long before the platinum crucible becomes red hot. After this combination, the residue was digested with dilute muriatic acid, which, by dissolving out the metallic oxyds, left the silex pure. This again was calcined, and weighed when warm.

M. Boussingault does not intimate that his estimate of carbon, by these processes, is rigorously correct; for, he confesses that his main object was the proportion of silicium. The products were—

	Iron.	Carbon.	Silicium.	Manganese and Copper.
No. 1	99·825	A trace	0·175	A trace
2	99·325	0·450	0·225	ditto
3	99·442	0·333	0·225	ditto
4	99·375	0·500	0·125	ditto

M. B. states, doubtfully, that iron, during cementation, combines with a quantity of silicium as well as carbon.

Clouet had long since hinted that iron combines with glass. His process was, to melt soft iron with clay and chalk, which afforded good steel; but the prejudice of the time operated to make him infer that the carbonic acid of the chalk was decomposed by the iron, and the carbon became fixed in the metal. All this he took for granted, for he never subjected the steel to analysis.

M. Boussingault repeated Clouet's process, exactly as he had described it in his Report to the Institute (Journal des Mines 18), with iron, a portion of which did not yield any residue on solution with dilute sulphuric acid. After an hour's exposure to the forge, the fusion was complete, and yielded a specimen of Clouet's steel. It gave way under the file, and forged with more difficulty than the steel of La Berardiere. Nitric acid gave no stain to its polished surface;—dissolved with difficulty in dilute sulphuric acid; preserving its metallic brightness. The residue was bulky, and proved to be silex, pure and white; being in the proportion of 99·2 iron, and 0·8 silicium; without a particle of carbon.

As this metal has all the properties of steel, it ought to

be acknowledged as such; yet it seems that Clouet's steel is never used, and, therefore, in order to render it more capable of being wrought, steel may require some proportion of carbon.

Of Cast Iron,

M. Boussingault questions whether iron fused in a hessian crucible be pure metal. Having tested iron by solution in dilute sulphuric acid, and found no residue, he melted a portion of the same metal in a hessian crucible, and obtained a well fused and brilliant button. It was more difficult to forge than the iron which furnished it; and, like Clouet's steel, remained brilliant during solution in dilute acid, leaving a bulky and white residue; which was silicium. The compound being 99·46 iron and 0·54 of silicium. In this case the fused metal had taken its silex from the crucible; and, in all its properties resembled Clouet's steel. The fusing point of iron in a hessian crucible cannot be strictly estimated, because the union of silicium with it, renders it more easily fused, than alone. Platinum not having so strong an affinity for oxygen as iron has, does not decompose a hessian crucible.

M. Boussingault concludes with observing that, although we cannot strictly determine the exact fusing points in temperature of platinum, iron, and manganese; we may their relative fusibilities, when in contact with carbon, or silicium, or both, as thus—iron, platinum, and manganese; therefore manganese will be found the most refractory.

This view of the components forming steel, will probably lead to some improvements in its manufacture, or the correction of occasional defects. At all events, the more information we have of the nature of the matter with, or upon, which we operate, the better are we qualified to counteract difficulty, or to aid a purpose. So universal is the use of iron, modified in a thousand ways, in all the arts of life, that the acquisition of any new fact respecting it, will diffuse an influence beyond calculation.

On a new Determination of the Constituents of Water. By MM. Berzelius and Dulong.

Monthly Magazine. No. 360.

Water, whether insensible, and its vapour, whether insensible or sensible, as steam, has such an enlarged influence on most of our chemical operations, that a correct knowledge of its component parts, both in quantity and quality, is essential to accuracy. We therefore give this new determination, by chemists of eminent character, which, if correct, will soon be established: if not so, its errors will be detected, and we shall have the truth; which is all we seek.

The results of specific gravity of gaseous bodies, differ widely from some of Dr. Ure's, noted in his table. Nitric acid, for instance, Messrs. B. and D. determine at 3·1812; Dr. Ure, at 2·638. From the mean of three experiments, it appears, that 100 parts, by weight, of oxygen unite with 11·488 of hydrogen, to produce water; which is equivalent to 88·9 per cent. of oxygen with 11·1 of hydrogen. Whereas the number formerly assumed as the proportion of hydrogen to 100 of oxygen, is 13·27, instead of 12·488, which makes a difference of nearly a twelfth part.

The following are the results of the specific gravities of the gases, according to these experiments; the gases being perfectly dry, and atmospheric air being 1·000.

Oxygen................1·1026
Hydrogen..............0·0688
Carbonic acid ....1·524
Azote ....0·976

The gravities of the same gases, as determined by Messrs. Biot and Arrago, are as follow:—

Oxygen................1·10359
Hydrogen..............0·07321
Carbonic acid ....1·519
Azote ....0·969

If we take the above proportions in weight of the elements of water, and take the density of oxygen, as obtained by our experiments, at 1·1026, the specific gravity of the hydrogen will turn out to be 0·0688; but by direct experiment, it gave us 0·0687.

Specific gravity of atmospheric air = 1.

Oxygen ....1·1026
Hydrogen ....0·0688
Azote ....0·976
Vapour of carbon ....0·4214
Carbonic acid.................1·524
Oxide of carbon...............0·9727
Olefiant gas ....0·9804
Carburetted hydrogen gas......0·5590
Vapour of water...............0·620
Oxide of azote ....1·5273
Nitrous gas ....1·001
Hypernitric acid ....0·
Nitrous acid ....3·1812
Dry nitric acid ....0·
Concentrated nitric acid .....0·
Ammonia ....0·5912
Sub-carbonate of ammonia .....0·
Cyanogen ....1·8188
Hydro-cyanic acid.............0·9438
Vapour of alcohol ....1·6004
Vapour of ether...............2·5808

On Refraction of Light. By J. READE, M.D.
Philosophical Magazine. No. 282.

The philosophical world has so long yielded a reverential obedience to the authority of Sir Isaac Newton, that we almost recoil from any investigation that professes to show him somewhat less than infallible. We must confess, however, that these are not the legimate feelings of that sterner judgment, which, in the search after truth, cannot pay respect to time or name. Still our prejudices (if they be such) cling so closely to us in all that regards this presumedly great man, that we must demand from his assailants more than the assertion of probabilities or analogies.—We must have mathematical demonstration of his errors. Dr. R. is not the only gentleman who would show us that Sir Isaac was a mere mortal: for we have another modern authority, of no slight weight, to bring forward, (Dr. Herschell,) who disputes some of the minor points with Sir Isaac Newton, respecting the effect of refraction, not of refraction itself, for that the Doctor accords with; therefore, we feel aware of the necessity of keeping a guard over our determinations.

Dr. Reade speaks out boldly and honestly; telling us that he strikes at the very root of the doctrine of refraction. He does not assail the minutiæ of inference in the detail; but attempts to over-turn the whole of the system, as founded in error.

He commences with considering the common introductory experiment of viewing an object at the bottom of a glass or basin, as varying in apparent position, according as the vessel may contain air or water. He denies that refraction has any thing to do with the effect, for he rejects refraction in toto. He seems to have fallen on a most unhappy explanation of the matter, that is, Mr. Harris', on optics, page 25, who says, " Hence the piece of money appears one quarter nearer the eye than it really is; and on the same principle, a river is one quarter deeper than it appears."

Now we take the liberty to deny that the refracted figure of the piece of money, does appear at all nearer to the eye; and, therefore, partly answer the query of Dr. Reade, who asks, how " the bending of the rays can bring the object nearer." He says, that " if we bend a piece of iron wire, we shorten the length it extended." Surely we do, from point to point; but the line joining these, is not, we humbly infer, the whole extent of that between the figure and the eye, for we see the figure *beyond,* not *from,* the surface; and this constitutes our difference with Dr. Reade, relative to the presumed refraction of the rays. Also, he says, " if the rays were bent in passing from the water into air, a tube, bent in the same direction, should enable us to see the object." Does Dr. R. know that such might not be really the case, were it possible to apply the tube free from exception. He will be pleased to recollect, that to give the axis of the tube such a position as the refracted ray is supposed to take, its angle must be at *the surface of the water;* and this would obscure vision, if the tube were opake; if transparent, the result would be rendered dubious by the light passing through its substance.

The Doctor considers it unnecessary to bring more objections against common explanation of the above-mentioned experiment than the following: "Having placed a piece of money at the bottom of a wine-glass, I made the edge intercept my view; on pouring in a small quantity of water, the shilling seemed to rise; I now perceived two images of the object; one at the bottom; the other floating at the top of the water; very apparent when the glass was a little inclined to the eye. This floating image was agitated by every movement of the water. To ascertain whether this image were the real cause of vision, I held the glass above my eye, and saw the image floating by reflection on the surface of the water, as well defined as if reflected from the face of a mirror. Further, to convince myself that it is this floating image we see, and not the shilling at the bottom of the vessel, I brought my eye on a line with the image, and then gently lowering the glass, at the same time keeping my eye intently fixed on it, I saw the image by transmitted rays. Thus the floating image was seen by the eye above, on a line with, and below, the water."

Observing on this, we must acknowledge that, although we have tried most assiduously, to see the reflected image of the object from the surface of the water when held above the eye; and varied it every way we could, both by candle and day-light; yet we have not been so fortunate as to a catch a sight of the image: nevertheless, we do not dispute the fact as related by Dr. Reade, and shall take it as granted. But admitting it to be so, we respectfully decline receiving it as demonstration of the erroneous principles on which this presumed refraction has hitherto been explained. That it might form an image on the surface, by rays flowing from the object to the surface, and visible to the eye under the level of the surface, by the reflection of those rays downwards, through the water and sides of the glass, obliquely to the eye, is what we will not absolutely dispute; but we hold, that the plate of air, resting on the surface of the water, is, in such a case, a looking glass as to reflecting power; and that reflected images are perceptible only by the apposition of a plane cutting through the rays flowing from the object. If rays from the upper surface of the money, lying at the bottom of the glass, necessarily form an image on the surface; how is it that we do not see that image in all points, when we view the surface of the water, over the margin of the vessel; which we do not. Fill the glass to the brim, and remove the eye backwards, until the surface of the water no longer yields the piece visible. How, we ask, is this? Why do we not see that image, which should be invariably formed on the surface? We answer, on the plain Newtonian principle, that the emergent rays are refracted between our eye and the perpendicular. Approach the glass, and the piece is seen; because the eye, being placed nearer the perpendicular, intercepts the refracted emergent rays. As to the tremulous appearance of the image, as the motion of the surface fluctuated, it is of no value in the argument; because it would equally apply to both doctrines. Standing between the window and the goblet, with the eye at a little distance, so that we can see freely over the margin, we may observe three forms of the money. First, we see the magnified form through the glass at the bottom; secondly, through the surface, we see the refracted form apparently deep in the water; and thirdly, we see an enlarged and concave form, at the further cylindrical, or conical interior surface of the glass. Pass the hand, or a piece of paper, so as to intercept the view of the refracted form, (which Dr. R. calls the image at the surface,) and you will still see the concave form, rising and diminishing, or falling and enlarging, as you elevate or depress the surface of the water before the eye. Now, whether we consider this concave form to be caused by the real piece, or by Dr. Reade's reflected image, again reflected from the side, we beg leave to inquire, how the apparent *enlargement* or *diminution* is to be accounted for, but by refraction? An object reflected by a plain mirror, appears as far behind the reflecting plane, as it really is before it; but it is not changed in apparent magnitude.

Again, we object against the presumed formation of the image on the surface, which image it is that Dr. R. says we see, and not the money itself by the refracted rays; first, because such image should be visible to the eye, looking obliquely on the surface of the water from all points, which we have shown it is not; secondly, because the rays flowing from the money, cannot form an image on the surface of the water: for, as to the water, they are *emergent*; and thirdly, the image could only be seen on the lower surface, or plate of the air in contact with the water, as by the reflection of which the Doctor has spoken, and which we have not been able to verify: for as to the eye, in the air above the surface, the rays are transmittent. Consequently, we infer, that the supposed image cannot exist.

In our next number, we shall pursue the consideration of Dr. Reade's paper, with all the respectful feeling due to a respectable gentleman; and beg leave to assure our readers, that we will impartially state the Doctor's own positions, in justice to his cause. He promises to produce Leibnitz as a counteracting authority against the refractive doctrine.

(To be continued.)

Mr. Whidbey on the Organic Remains found at Plymouth.
Vide Transactions of the Royal Academy.

Much has been said on the subject of these remains; more, indeed, than we think it merited: and we should have declined noticing it altogether, were we not apprehensive that some attention to a matter of philosophical notoriety, like this, would be expected from us, as a duty. We have, then, to state that, Mr. Whidbey discovered fossil bones of the bear; another animal, of the same size; the deer; and the rhinoceros, in a cavern, formed in the bed of lime-stone rock, near Plymouth: about 55 feet below the surface of the rock; 8 feet above high-water mark; 174 yards from the original face of the quarries; and about 120 yards, in that direction, from the spot where the former bones were found in 1816. It seems that the bones were not encrusted with calcareous stalactite. There have been several of these caverns discovered; some showing stalactical depositions, others not. This lime-stone rock contains very little of organic remains in its general mass; and reclines upon clay slate.

We should consider the rock as an alluvial deposit, and the fact of the remains differing, only in modification of their bed, from those found so abundantly, a few years since, close in our own neighbourhood. It will be well remembered, by geologists, that Mr. Kirby Trimmer discovered, near Brentford, at a considerable depth from the surface, a profuse abundance of remains of the ox, the deer, the elephant, and the rhinoceros. Some of the horns and tusks were very large. These were, beyond all doubt, covered by alluvial and regularly stratified depositions. We cannot immediately refer to the account given of them; but we remember that the matter of Mr. Trimmer's paper was very interesting, as leading to some conjecture of the age of old Father Thames.

On Meteorolites. By M. FLEURIAN DE BELLEVUE.
(Read to the Academy of Sciences, Paris.)
Journal of Science,

This paper ought to have preceded that of M. Emer on the Laws of the Propagation of Heat, inserted in our Second Number, page 54, because the latter gentleman founds his doctrine partly on the facts presented by M. de B. The meteorolites to be spoken of, fell in 1820, near Jonzac, in the Department of the Churente; and the following is the spirit of M. de B's remarks on them.

1. The appearances presented by the crust of meteorolites seem to prove that their surface has been fused whilst rapidly traversing the flame of the meteor, and rapidly solidified into a vitreous state on leaving that flame.

2. They prove that in the first moments the movement of the meteorolites was simple, that is, they did not turn round on their own axis whilst those two effects took place.

3. That the impulse each meteorolite has received has almost always been perpendicular to its largest face.

4. That the largest face is almost always more or less convex.

5. Our meteorolites (those of Jonzac) offer new proofs of the pre-existence of a solid nucleus to bolides or meteors.

6. This nucleus could not contain the combustible matter which produces the inflammation of the meteor.

7. It cannot have suffered fusion during the appearance of the phenomena.

8. The gaseous matter which surrounds this nucleus is dissipated without producing any solid residuum. No trace of this matter appears ever to exist in the crust of the meteorolites.

9. Meteorolites are fragments of those nuclei which have not been altered in their nature, but simply vitrified at their surfaces.

10. Many of the appearances which these fragments present, may be referred to determine geometric forms.

11. These latter forms are the consequence of the rapid action of a violent fire, according to a law of the movement of heat in solid bodies, discovered by M. Emer.

Process for correcting and preventing an imperfection in Wines, known by the name of Ropiness. By M. HERPIN.
Bulletin de la Societe d'Encouragement.

Wines occasionally assume this ropiness, by some chemical changes, not yet well understood. We should venture to impute it, in part, to the particular condition of the fruit, from whence it was made; as, either under or above the due degree of maturity; the relative quantities of saccharine and mucilaginous matter; the imperfect fermentation; or, possibly, to some electrical influence previously to its being racked off.

Ropy wine has an oily consistence; becomes flat and insipid; turns yellow when poured out; runs in a thread when poured gently from a phial; will not froth by agitation; and disagrees with the stomach. This change takes place during the insensible fermentation; and by the assumed decomposition, is preventive of the formation of alcohol; or destructive of it when formed, by the new combination of elements. Ropy wine, therefore, yields but little brandy, and that bad in quality; having an empyreumatic flavour, in proportion to the mucilaginous character of the wine distilled.

White wines seldom turn ropy, while in cask; but frequently when in bottle. We presume that, in such case, the fermentative process must have been incomplete, and that the liquid required to be in mass for the perfection of its requisite changes.

Whatever may be the cause, is but of secondary importance, provided we have really a preventive or corrective, and M. Herpin professes to furnish us with one, as follows:—

Dissolve from six to twelve ounces of acidulated tartrate of potash, (cream of tartar) and an equal quantity of coarse sugar, in a gallon of wine, heated to boiling. Pour this mixture, warm, into the ropy wine, and having bunged the cask, shake it well for five or six minutes; then put it in its place, with the bung turned downwards. Having left it at rest in that position, for a day or two, the cask must be turned up again, and the wine fined in the usual way. But instead of stirring it through the bung-hole, as is customary, the cask should be again shaken for a few minutes, and placed with the bung upwards. In four or five days the wine will be clear, limpid, and free from ropiness; but as it cannot safely remain on the sediment, it must be drawn off; when it will be secure from future ropiness. If the ropy wine be in bottle, it must be emptied into a cask, and processed as above mentioned.

All this may be correct; but we confess that we should have been better satisfied if M. Herpin had more distinctly stated how the requisite quantity of super-tartrate of potash is indicated; for he speaks very vaguely when he recommends from six to twelve ounces for use. We wish, too, to learn what theoretical or practical principle led him to adopt this means as a remedy?

Mr. Johnson on an Apparatus for the Consumption of Smoke. (In a Letter to the Editor of the London Journal of Arts and Sciences.) Vide London Journal. No. 12.

Mr. Johnson, actuated by a spirit of disinterested justice, sent, to the above-mentioned Editor, a description of an apparatus, made by a Mr. Johnston, brewer, of Manchester, which is, briefly, this: The steam-boiler is constructed of an oblong form, with the usual appendages of valves, &c.; and the intention of the artist is to throw back the smoke, immediately as it evolves, upon the ignited fuel; whereby it is completely consumed. The body of the fire rests on a grating, whose plane is inclined rather downwards; and, when the door of the fire-place be shut, the fuel is fed with air, through the ash-pit, in the usual way; but farther on in the ash-pit, and beyond the grating supporting the fire, there runs up a perpendicular air-way, which again bending in a return angle, issues directly over the back of the fire. There is, also, a valve, regulating the aperture of the air-way. When the fire-place door be open, or the air-way valve be closed, the smoke passes off under, or around, the boiler, unconsumed; but when the aperture of the air-way be rendered free, by pulling the valve-rod, and the fire-place door be shut, the atmospheric air rushes along, and issues immediately over the burning fuel; where, acting like a blower, it causes the fire to consume the smoke as fast as it is evolved from the fuel.

We have the additional testimony of the Editor above-mentioned, as to the perfect efficacy of this construction; who says, that " the smoke is so completely consumed, that no particle whatever passes through the flues, the whole being converted into vapour."

Working Chain Pumps by the Capstan.

We take the following as we find it, in a weekly journal, hoping that it expresses nothing beyond the fact; and then it cannot need any panegyric from us; for all men may infer its great value, as detailed in the stated effect; but they only, who are accustomed to the dangers of a sea-faring life, can justly appreciate the importance of a means that may be eventually a salvation, in the moment of peril.

" Amidst the vast improvements of late years in mechanical powers, and in their application in particular, there is none of more maritime importance than Mr. Edwards's invention of working chain pumps by the capstan, which is highly approved by nautical men. The following is a comparative statement of its experiment, that was made by order of the Lords Commissioners of the Admiralty at Deptford, on board his Majesty's Ship Narcissus, of 32 guns, in November 1820, when four feet water was let into her clear hold for that purpose.

Men	Water	Min.	Men	Water	Min.
36	pumped out 2 feet in	36	36	pumped out 2 feet in	40
44	.... 2	30			
60 {	.... 2	25			
	.... 2	12			

"Thus sixty men pumped out four feet water in thirty-seven minutes. The men were not fatigued, and preferred working at the capstan: whilst the men were much exhausted at the winches. By having twenty-four capstan bars of the same length, instead of twelve, the men will lay one-fifth farther out, or forty-eight men will be equal to sixty; and they will discharge the same quantity of water in the same time as sixty are shown to have discharged in the experiment. The watch of a frigate consists, on an average, of one hundred men; and when it is necessary to work the pumps, ninety-six of them are required, seventy-two at the chain pumps, their half relieving each other every ten minutes, and twenty-four at the hand pumps, their half doing so likewise; the remaining four of the hundred certainly are not sufficient for the other duties of the ship, consequently, more men must be called up for that purpose, thereby breaking the sleep and rest of the men. At the capstan, thirty-six men can work through the whole watch, (four hours), without ten minute spells, or any relief; twelve more can, of course, be spared, making forty-eight men, who will discharge one-half more water than the double thirty-six, or seventy-two, would, at the same time, at the winches; the remaining part of the hundred will be sufficient for the other duties of the ship. From this comparison it is evident, the capstan method has a great and decided superiority over the winches. The chain pumps can be worked while heaving up the anchor, when they cannot by the winches. As ships of the line have two sets of chain pumps, and more men, the labour in them is in the same proportion as in frigates. The quantity of water pumped out by the new method, is at the rate of two hundred and fifty-eight tons per hour. The apparatus of the plan, and the expense of fitting, do not exceed £100. for each ship.

"The great object in working chain pumps by the capstan, is to reduce the labour of the men; and by this method, forty-eight men (for which power it is constructed) will continue to work four hours, or a whole watch, without intermission, with but little fatigue, and pump out one-half more water than seventy-two men in four hours at the winches.

"Many men have been known to expire from the violent exertion and fatigue in working the winches. Instances also have been known of his Majesty's ships and crews being totally lost in consequence of their inability to continue any considerable time working the winches. By a review of the experiment, it will be seen that, from the vast power of the capstan, and little fatigue of the men, it will be next to an impossibility for any ship to be lost by the ordinary springing of leaks, excepting when she is stranded. By this method, a saving of lives and public property is rendered to the country; and amidst the casualties at sea, the British seaman hereafter may have reason to commend the practical utility of working chain pumps by the capstan."

If we mistake not, Mr. Perkins, who is so well known for his ingeniously applying talent to the purposes of art, has some claim on the credit of working the pump by the capstan instead of the winch.

An Egyptian Obelisk.

This obelisk is the property of Mr. Bankes, jun., and now lies (or did lie) on the deck of the sheer hulk, at Deptford, preparatory to its removal to the seat of Mr. Bankes, in Dorsetshire. Artists are said to have already made drawings from it, preparatory for the engraver. It is of red granite: and had been removed from the island of Philoe, on the borders of Nubia, down the Nile, for freight to England, by the Dispatch. It is particularly interesting; not only as being the first ever brought to England, but as supposed to furnish a key to the interpretation of the hieroglyphical character: since the Greek upon the pedestal, which records its first erection under Ptolemy and Cleopatra, nearly 2000 years ago, is, very probably, a translation of the hieroglyphics, with which all the four sides of the obelisk itself are richly covered.

When gentlemen of fortune expend their wealth thus, in adorning their country with the relics of ancient art, they do honour to themselves and the State to which they belong. Should the conjecture as to the Greek interpretation of the hieroglyphical character be realized, this obelisk will indeed be a treasure.

Egyptian Sarcophagus.

Could a mummy but start into life again, although he might mourn the fallen greatness of his country, yet he would feel an honourable pride in the tribute paid to Egyptian genius, by the refined taste of modern Europe. We, too, take a pleasure in living at a time when our own State is contending with rival Powers, in the noble ambition of possessing the remains of elegant art, that the feuds of men, and the great destroyer of all things, have yet spared, to form models for our improvement or admiration. We may thank the brutal stupidity of the Turks, for those precious monuments of skill and power, that have happily reached our shores. How strange that men generated, and living under the same balmy skies; with the products of nature so profusely abundant as to render toil nothing, compared with that of the western States; where all their faculties might be turned to the contemplation of nature in its purest charms; and where examples of the most exquisite skill abound on every side; should be insensible to the common incitements that have influence on human character! That a few generations of men may be rude, and ferocious, is but natural; but that ages shall pass away in succession, without softening and polishing a horde, in constant communication with enlightened nations, is indeed a melancholy paradox:—but, such are the Turks!

On the 28th of September, says the Editor of the Philosophical Magazine, the celebrated alabaster sarcophagus, which lately arrived from Alexandria, was uncased, and deposited in the British Museum. It is, for the present, in one of the apartments not open to the public, where probably it will be until a place is prepared for it in the Egyptian gallery. This antique is said to be a very extraordinary and admirable specimen of the arts of Egypt. The sarcophagus is nine feet long, and about four feet high, apparently of a single piece, and that of a very fine alabaster; it is shaped like a modern coffin, and more than large enough to hold the mummy with its envelopes; which is presumed to have been deposited within this costly repository. But its chief value is in the innumerable hieroglyphics which cover the sides, interior, and exterior, from top to bottom; they are small. The human figures, of which there are long processions, in various circumstances and attitudes, erect, linked together, towing galleys, bending as if in worship, &c., are from an inch to an inch and a half high. Between these are compartments of symbols, the Eye, the Ibis, and Lotus, &c.—The Serpent occurs frequently; and, in some instances, at considerable size, and with much exactness of detail. This noble work is supposed to be the coffin of Psammis: conjecture, however, has an extensive range in Egyptian antiquity; and some probabilities have been suggested of its being no tomb, but a temple—a small shrine imitative of the original Cymba, or great Diluvian Vessel, to which so many of the Indian emblems refer.

The Ark seems to have formed a vast source of Pagan allegoric sculpture. The pecuniary value of this sarcophagus has been estimated at a very large sum. It was the property of Mr. Salt, the British Consul, and was, we understand, the subject of competition by the Agents of some foreign Powers.

We would stop here, one moment, to ask if these hieroglyphics be decypherable? If not, we really are barbarous enough to consider them as very pretty things to look at, and admire, perhaps, for the skill with which they may have been executed, but nothing more. If, however, they can afford us only one additional ray of light, as to the characters, manners, or powers, of the most extraordinary people that ever figured their little time on this transient stage, we shall hail their arrival as an event of no small moment to the contemplative philosopher.—What an ocean of antiquarian ink will be shed!

M. Humboldt on Shirt Trees.

To speak of trees affording nearly ready-made shirts, does certainly bear a little of the appearance of a hoax; but M. Humboldt describes them particularly, and explains their adaptation. He says, "We saw on the slope of the Cerra Dnida, *shirt trees*, fifty feet high. The Indians cut off cylindrical pieces, two feet in diameter, from which they peel the red and fibrous bark, without making any longitudinal incision. This bark affords them a sort of garment, which resembles sacks, of a very coarse texture, and without a seam. The upper opening serves for the head, and two lateral holes are cut to admit the arms. The natives wear these shirts of marima, in the rainy season. They have the form of the *ponchos* and *ruanos* of cotton, which are so common in New Granada, at Quito, and in Peru. As, in these climates, the riches and beneficence of Nature are regarded as the primary causes of the indolence of the inhabitants, the Missionaries do not fail to say, in showing the shirts of marima, that 'in the forests of the Oroonoko, garments are found ready made on the trees.' We may add to this tale of the shirts, the pointed caps, which the spathes of certain palm trees furnish, and which resemble coarse net-work."

There is a curious coincidence of fashion between the Granadians, the Quitans, the Peruvians, and those idle creatures, on the Cerra Dnida, as to the *form* of garment. We will not conjecture which may have the honour of originating the costume; but we should hold sackcloth and ashes as downright velvet, compared with these inflexible tubes.

Singular Species of Strawberry.

We are informed in the Annals of Philosophy, on the authority of a correspondent of the Editor's, that the singular species of strawberry lately remarked on in the public papers, as found in Scotland, and which blooms in winter, like the celebrated Glastonbury thorn, is not confined to a part of our island, but has flourished more than fifty years in the garden of Tintern Abbey, the seat of Cæsar Colclough, Esq. It was transplanted from Holland by a Mr. Simon, who presented it to an ancestor of Mr. Colclough.

THE FOCUS

OF

PHILOSOPHY, SCIENCE, AND ART.

No. V.] SATURDAY, DECEMBER 29, 1821. [Vol. I.

Native Copper on Lake Superior.

(Continued from p. 125.)

"A MASS of copper discovered by the aborigines on an island in Lake Superior, at Point Chegoimegon, eighty miles west of the Ontonagon, weighed twenty-eight pounds, and was taken to the island of Michilimackinac, some years ago, by M. Cadotte, and disposed of. It was from this mass that the War Department was formerly supplied with a specimen, and from which the analysis alluded to, is also understood to have been made. About eleven years ago, a trader by the name of Campbell, procured from the Indians a piece of copper weighing twelve pounds, which they found on an island in Winnebago lake, about a hundred miles, in a direct line, east of the copper rock on the Ontonagon. This was also taken to the island of Michilimackinac, and there disposed of. Other discoveries of this metal in masses, varying from one to ten pounds, are stated to have been made on the shores of Lake Superior,—the Fox river,—the Chippeway,—the St. Croix, and the Mississippi about Prarie du Chien; but the statements do not rest on sufficient authority to justify any particular enumeration. The existence of copper in the region of Lake Superior, appears to have been known to the earliest travellers and voyagers. As early as 1689, the Baron la Honton, in concluding a description of that lake, adds, 'that upon it we also find copper mines, the metal of which is so fine and plentiful, that there is not a seventh part loss from the ore.' In 1721, Charleroix passed through the lakes on his way to the Gulph of Mexico, and did not allow the mineralogy of the country to escape his observations. 'Large pieces of copper,' he says, in speaking of Lake Superior, 'are found in some places on its banks, and around some of the islands, which are still the objects of a superstitious worship among the Indians. They look upon them with veneration, as if they were the presents of those gods who dwell under the waters; they collect their smallest fragments, which they carefully preserve, without, however, making any use of them. They say that formerly a huge rock of this metal was to be seen elevated a considerable height above the surface of the water, and as it has now disappeared, they pretend that the gods have carried it elsewhere; but there is great reason to believe, that in process of time, the waves of the lake have covered it entirely with sand and slime; and it is certain that in several places, pretty large quantities of this metal have been discovered, without being obliged to dig very deep. During the course of my first voyage to this country, I was acquainted with one of our order, (Jesuits,) who had been formerly a goldsmith, and, who, while he was at the mission of Sault de St. Marie, used to search for this metal, and make candlesticks, crosses, and censers of it, for this copper is often to be met with almost entirely pure.'

"In 1766, Capt. Carver procured several pieces of native copper upon the shores of Lake Superior, and about the sources of the Chippeway and St. Croix rivers, and published an account of his discoveries in his book of travels, which has served to give notoriety to the existence of that metal in the region alluded to, without, however, furnishing any very precise information as to its locality or abundance. He did not, from his own account, traverse the southern shore of the lake, but states that virgin copper is found in great plenty on the Ontonagon, or Copper Mine River, and about other parts of Lake Superior, and adds, that 'he observed many of the small islands, particularly those on the *eastern shores*, were covered with copper ore, which appeared like beds of copperas, (sulphat of iron) of which many tons lay in a small space.'

" Five years after Carver's visit, (A. D. 1771), a considerable body of native copper was dug out of the alluvial earth, on the banks of the Ontonagon river, by two adventurers, of the name of Henry and Bostwick, and, together with a lump of silver ore, of eight pounds weight, of a blue colour, and semi-transparent, transported to Montreal, and from thence shipped to England, where the latter was deposited in the British Museum, after an analysis of a portion of it, by which it was determined to contain 60 per cent. of silver. These individuals were connected with a company which had been formed in England, for the purpose of working the copper mines of Lake Superior, among whom were the Duke of Gloucester, Sir William Johnson, and several other gentlemen of rank. They built a small vessel at Point aux Puis, six miles above the Sault de St. Marie. To facilitate their operations upon the lake, a considerable sum of money was expended; first, in exploring the northern shore of the lake, and the island of Maripeaux, and afterwards, in the mining operations, which were authorized upon the banks of the Ontonagon. These transactions will be best illustrated by a quotation from the narrative account which Henry has himself published. After returning from the Canadian shore of the lake, and passing point Iroquois, where the silver ore was found, he observes, 'hence we coasted westward, but found nothing till we reached the Ontonagon, where, besides the detached masses of copper formerly mentioned, we saw much of the same metal *imbedded in stone*. Proposing to ourselves to make a trial on the hill, till we were better able to go to work upon the solid rock, we built a house, and sent to the Sault de St. Marie for provisions. At the spot pitched upon for the commencement of our preparations, a green coloured water, which tinges iron of a copper colour, issued from the hill, and this the miners called a *leader*. In digging, they found frequent masses of copper, some of which were of three pounds weight. Having arranged every thing for the accommodation of the miners, during the winter, we returned to the Sault,

"'Early in the spring of 1772, we sent a boat-load of provisions, but it came back on the 20th day of June, bringing with it, to our surprise, the whole establishment of miners. They reported that, in the course of the winter, they had penetrated *forty* feet into the face of the hill, but on the arrival of the thaw, the clay, on which, on account of its stiffness, they had relied, and neglected to secure by supporters, had fallen in; that, from the detached masses of metal, which to the last had daily presented themselves, they supposed there might be ultimately reached a body of the same, but could form no conjecture of its distance, except that it was probably so far off as not to be pursued without sinking an air-shaft; and lastly, that the work would require the hands of more men than could be fed in the actual situation of the country. Here our operations in this quarter ended. The metal was probably within our reach; but if we had found it, the expense of carrying it to Montreal must have exceeded its marketable value. It was never for the exportation of copper that our company was formed, but always with a view to the silver, which it was hoped the ores, whether of copper or lead, might in sufficient quantity contain.'

"Eighteen years after the failure of this attempt, (1789,) Mackenzie passed through Lake Superior, in his first voyage of discovery to the north west; and in his description of Lake Superior, says, 'On the same side, (the south) at the river Tennagon, is found a quantity of virgin copper. The Americans, soon after they got possession of that country, sent an agent thither; and I should not be surprised to hear of their employing people to work the mine. Indeed, it might be well worthy the attention of the British subjects to work the mines on the north coast, though they are not supposed to be so rich as those on the south.'

"The attention of the United States government appears first to have been turned toward the subject during the administration of President Adams, when the sudden augmentation of the navy rendered the employment of domestic copper, in the equipment of ships, an object of political, as well as pecuniary moment; and a mission was authorised to proceed to Lake Superior. Of the success of this mission, as it has not been communicated to the public, nothing can with certainty be stated; but from the inquiries which have been instituted during the recent expedition, it is rendered probable, that the actual state of our Indian relations at that period arrested the advance of the commissioners into the regions where the most valuable beds of copper were supposed to be; and that the specimens transmitted to government, were procured through the instrumentality of some friendly Indians, employed for that purpose.

" Such are the lights which those who have preceded me in this inquiry have thrown upon the subject; all of which have operated in producing public belief in the existence of extensive copper mines upon Lake Superior; while travellers have generally argued, that the southern shore of the lake is most metalliferous, and that the Ontonagon river may be considered as the seat of the principal mines. Mr. Gallatin, in his report on the state of American manufactures, in 1810, countenances the prevalent opinion; while it has been reiterated in some of our literary journals, and in the numerous ephemeral publications of the times, until the public expectation has been considerably raised in regard to them.

" Under these circumstances the recent expedition, under Governor Cass, entered the mouth of the Ontonagon river on the 27th of June, having coasted along the southern shore of the lake from the head of the river St. Mary; and after spending four days upon the banks of that stream, in the examination of its mineralogy, proceeded on the first of July, towards the Fou du Lac. While there, the principal part of our force was encamped at the mouth of the river, and the Governor, accompanied only by such persons as were necessary in the exploration, proceeded in two light canoes to the large mass of copper which has already been described. We found the river broad, deep, and gentle, for a distance and serpentine in its course; then becoming narrower, with an increased velocity of current, and, before reaching the copper rock, full of rapids and difficult of ascent. At the distance of three or four leagues from the lake, it is skirted on either side by a chain of hills, whose extreme elevation above the bed of the Ontonagon may be estimated at from three to four hundred feet. These hills appear to be composed of nucleus of granite, arising through a stratum of red sand-stone, and covered by a very heavy deposit of alluvial soil, full of water-worn fragments of stones and pebbles, and imbedding occasional masses of native copper. Such is the character of the country in the immediate vicinity of the copper rock; and the latter is manifestly one of those imbedded substances, which have been fortuitously exposed to the powerful action of the river, against an alluvial bank.

"During our continuance upon this stream, we found, or rather procured from the Indians, another mass of native copper, weighing nine pounds (troy) nearly; which will be forwarded to the War Department. This specimen is partially enveloped by a crust of green carbonate of copper, which is in some places *fibrous*, and on the other side mixed with a small portion of adhering sand, and some angular fragments of quartz, upon which it appears to have fallen into a liquid state. There is also an appearance of crystallization upon one side of it, and a portion of adhering black oxide, the nature of which it is difficult to determine by ocular inspection. Several smaller pieces, generally weighing less than a pound, were also procured during our excursion up the Ontonagon, and in the regions east of it; but all, excepting those cut from the large mass, are somewhat oxidated, or otherwise encrusted upon the surface. The geological structure of the country in detail, and the mineral appearances of the shore about the copper rock, and at other points along the river between that and the lake, are also of highly interesting character; but do not appear to me to demand a more particular consideration in this report."

(To be continued.)

Dr. Reade on Refraction of Light.
(Continued from p. 135.)

We resume the task of considering Dr. R.'s paper, as promised in our last, and shall just state the inferences drawn by the Doctor from the experiment before alluded to; which are,

1st. That in viewing objects through refracting media, we take our ideas from images formed in the refracting media themselves; and not from rays flowing direct from the object, nor from images formed by those rays at imaginary foci.

2d. That in this experiment there is no bending of rays; for rays flowing from the object, form the image on the surface; and we see that image by straight lines, flowing from it to the eye.

These two inferences display the doctrine proposed to be substituted for that of Newton. We cannot agree with Dr. R. on these points, as deduced by him; for the reasons we have shown to prove them not satisfactory; nor do we think he maintains his principle with a better effect as he advances. But although we cannot anticipate our conversion, we will promise to divest ourselves, as much as possible, of mental inveteracies.

Experiment 2d.—Placing a solid globe of glass, 2 inches in diameter, between his eye and a window, he could not perceive the window-frame; all appeared one confused light; but on withdrawing the eye a few inches, he saw distinctly the inverted window frame, and a small fly. He then asks, " Could any person, in this experiment, venture to say that we take our ideas immediately from the object, and not from the inverted image of that object, seeming to float on the posterior surface of the solid sphere? the object being as invisible as if it were placed behind our backs." Not having a globe at hand, we cannot repeat this experiment; but we will grant its accuracy, and yet we really are among those persons who will venture to say that they consider it as not only unsatisfactory to Dr. Reade's purpose, but as bearing completely in proof of the Newtonian principles. We, in our turn, beg leave to ask Dr. Reade, why, if the image be formed at the posterior surface of the globe, and his view of it be independent of refraction of the rays, he does not see it with the eye nearer to the globe, as well as at a little distance? for if there be not any refractive bending of rays, he must have seen the objects by right-lined rays; and these being equally producible, at all imaginary distances, should necessarily render the object clearly visible within the common range of vision; and that, whether the rays flowed from the object direct, or from the image contended for. The distinction attempted to be made between the object and its presumed image, cannot at all affect the question as to refraction of the rays; because, in both cases, the rays must traverse the transparent matter of the globe; and if they do not come to the eye in parallel, they must in bent, or refracted, lines.

We must think, at least yet, that the invisibility of an object at certain distances, when globular or convex transparent bodies intervene between it and the eye, is explainable only by the Newtonian principles of refraction; and that the result of this second experiment is an illustration. That, part of the rays falling on the surface of the globe, would be intercepted, and would form a figure there, to be seen, reflected, by an eye at the back of the globe, or between it and the window, is what we fully admit; as well as that such reflected image would arise from straight rays falling on the globe, and reflected in straight lines from it to the eye: but it is, as we apprehend, quite another case, when that image (supposing it there) be seen *through* the transparent medium. The reflected image we can see at all distances, merely because the rays flowing from it, come in straight lines: but we cannot see the transmitted image through the globe, but at certain distances or points; because the emergent rays are bent, and admit of visual effect at such points only. Were not this the fact, we cannot comprehend why we do not see at all distances through convex or concave transparent media, equally well as through parallel surfaces.

Experiment 3d.—" When we hold a black-lead pencil, or any other substance, behind a cylindrical tumbler of clear water, when the pencil is close behind the glass, we perceive a magnified image. On withdrawing the pencil to a yet greater distance, this image becomes more and more magnified, and two other images, laterally everted, are seen at the sides of the tumbler. At a yet greater distance, we lose sight of the anterior or magnified image; the two lateral ones floating towards each other, at last form one well defined everted image, at the posterior surface; from which, and not immediately from the object, we take our ideas; the object itself being perfectly invisible." The appearances as stated to result from the above experiment, are decidedly influenced by the relative distances of the eye, and the object, on opposite sides of the glass; for if the eye be placed close to the glass, the pencil, on being removed from the glass, diminishes in apparent magnitude; becomes obscured; and is not accompanied by any duplicate of figure. But if the eye be further from the side of the glass, than the focal distance of its cylindrical convexity, the appearances are similar to the Doctor's description. If this trial be made with the back towards the light, the side of the pencil, on the opposite side of the glass, will be enlightened, and the result will be more distinct. Suppose then the pencil perpendicular, and parallel, to the axis of the glass; and that it touch the glass, or nearly so; the rays reflected from it must be more refracted than when it be made to recede from the glass, and of course approach the nearer parallelism; provided the eye be *within* the cylindrical focus. Now bring the eye to a distance from the glass, greater than, and *without*, its focal distance, and on withdrawing the pencil on the opposite side, we observe the magnifying effect much more than when the eye were close to the glass; the reason of which is, as we humbly apprehend, that the refracted rays, on the visual side of the glass, have crossed at the focus, and entering the eye, give an enlarged angular appearance.

Next, as to the lateral and parallel images that are seen to advance from the sides of the cylinder, towards the pencil, as it is withdrawn, receding from the glass, when the eye be farther from the glass than its cylindrical focus, we would presume to be caused thus;—while the pencil be near the glass, the rays reflected from its surface towards the glass, can impinge on but a small portion of that surface laterally; the retiring curvature of the glass falling under and beyond their contact as tangents to the cylindrical convexity. But when the pencil be made to recede sufficiently, the reflected rays impinge on that convexity from one side to the other, until the object or pencil be so far removed as to reflect rays falling parallel on the glass, and of course on all points of one half of the cylinder. On the first recedence of the pencil, we observe these parallel, and lateral, images advancing from the sides; and the original image disappearing in distance; but this is only while the angular incidence of the rays from the object, falling on the cylindrical surface of the glass, are diminishing; for when the pencil be removed distant from the glass, the rays from the former become parallel, and the lateral images become again condensed into one magnified representation. How then is it that there can be any apparent change in the *magnitude* of the object, or its image, if the visual angle at the eye be not enlarged; and if it be so, how can it have been produced but by the refraction of the rays that have been emitted, or reflected, from its surface? Whether the rays flowing from the object be continued, and refracted, so as to arrive at the eye from it, as the primary cause; or whether there be an image of the object painted on the posterior surface of the glass, which image is conveyed through the transparent medium, altered in apparent magnitude, cannot at all affect the question at issue; for in either case, the object, or the image, cannot have been rendered sensible to the eye, but by refracted rays.

We must defer the further consideration of this interesting subject to our next number, when we shall have to meet the Doctor on what he terms the " Experimentum Crucis."

(To be continued.)

On Electro-Magnetism. By Professor OERSTED. (Communicated by the Author to the Editor of the Annals of Philosophy.) Vide New Series. No. 11.

The Professor having traced the steps that led to the results presented in this paper, proceeds to explain his first law of electro-magnetic effects, and which he details as follows:—

" When opposite electrical powers meet, under circumstances which offer resistance, they are subjected to a new form of action. And, in this state, they act upon the magnetic needle in such a manner that positive electricity repels the south, and attracts the north pole of the compass; and negative electricity repels the north, and attracts the south pole; but the direction followed by the electrical powers, in this state, is not a right line, but a spiral one turning from the left hand to the right."

However improbable some philosophers may have thought the spiral direction of electrical power, Professor Oersted flatters himself that he shall prove such to be the fact; and further considers that, on the admission of the principle, many phenomena may be satisfactorily explained, that were before mysterious. And, also, that it will lead us on to anticipate, with correctness, the result of future experiment. The Professor, then, by reference to diagrams, attempts to show, what he acknowledges is rather difficult to comprehend; that is, the spiral course of electro-magnetic power; and we must say that we do not think him at all happier than some of his predecessors in this effort; indeed his manner is rather prolix; but we will endeavour to analyze his subject as well as we can.

It is to be understood that the present conception of the course of electro-magnetic power, is that of a spiral, round the conductor: and that the positive and negative powers are presumed to pass in opposite directions; so that two sides of the conductor may present the different powers. That part of a wire connected with the positive pole of a galvanic pile, will be positive; and the other end the negative. This done, it will always be found, says the Professor, that the south pole of the suspended needle is repelled by negative electricity. We cannot pass this stated fact without requesting our readers to revert to Professor Bockman's paper, in our second number, p. 45, where it is shown, by clear experiment, that repulsion on both north and south poles of the magnet, was almost uniformly produced by electrical discharge of various intensities: and also, that the southern repulsions were as uniformly greater than the northern. Professor Oersted goes on to remark on M. Berzelius's idea of the course of the current; which the latter supposes to be acting round a parallelopiped, having a north magnetic pole at one of its angles, and a south pole at the next adjoining; so that poles of the same denomination are diagonally opposite each other. He thought this conjecture of Berzelius very aptly explained some of the electro-magnetic phenomena; but having observed the regular action of cylindrical conductors, where this superficial distribution of poles could not exist; and having subjected a square conductor to a decisive experiment; he was convinced that the hypothesis was false. Next, he states that when a light magnetic needle be placed upon a large conductor, through which a strong discharge be passed, its direction will be almost entirely determined by the electro-magnetic effect; and the magnetism of the earth will cause but a very slight direction: by which, we presume him to mean, that electro-magnetic force supersedes terrestrial force for a time: but we think that this ought to be taken in a qualified sense. M. O. then notices the spiral wire of M. Pretchel, of Vienna, wherein he represents the galvanic conductor by such spiral, magnetized, as a common cylinder; whereby it acquires transverse poles, but no sensible polarity from end to end. More than two poles being impartable to each coil of spiral, it will affect the magnetic needle like the electro-magnetic conductor produced by the voltaic battery. We now come to M. Oersted's explanation of the attractions and repulsions which galvanic conductors excite among each other.

M. Oersted's apparatus, by which he performed his experiments, consisted of a brass wire bent into a parellelogram, terminating in points that worked in small cups of mercury, which were suspended by attached, or conducting, wires, in communication with the poles of the voltaic battery. So that the parallelogram, and suspending wires, might be considered one continued line of conductive agency: the parallelogram revolving freely round the suspensors, on the pivots in the mercury, in a horizontal direction. When the apparatus be adjusted, and the battery in action, the parallelogram moves with its longitudinal line due east and west; as discovered by M. Ampere. M. O. says, "the only supposition, then, by which the electrical forces can produce the described effects is, that they proceed from every point, in such a manner, that the directions of the opposite forces are separated by the lengthened radius." Or, in other words, we would desire the reader to imagine the section of a cylinder, whose radius is extended onwards out of the circle; also a tangent crossing the radius at the point of the circumference, where the radius issues. Now the whole tangent, and consequently the two halves of the tangent, must necessarily be at right angles with the extended radius; and, within each right angle, formed between the upper and lower half of the tangent, and the extended radius, M. Oersted conceives the positive and negative electro-magnetic forces to project: the positive on one side of the radius; the negative on the other. The Professor then proceeds to explain his view of the force, as applicable to

The Magnetic Needle.

He considers that as fresh electricity is perpetually evolving in the galvanic column, its discharge must be regarded as perpetual addition and subtraction; and that this force, as passing through the conductor, must be perpetually fluctuating. But, in the magnet, the motive force is nearly in a state of repose; forming no close circle. Pursuing this, he says that, to produce the greatest effect, one positive magnetic pole must be presented to another positive, or one negative to another negative. He speaks of points in the respective poles, and not of whole halves of each magnet; for says he, " this (that is, with a whole half) must take place only opposite the end." Our readers, however, will have seen that Mr. Faraday finds the pole of a magnet, not at the extremity; but at a point some little distance therefrom. To a certain degree, he thinks M. Ampere's supposition, of the electro-magnetic force, passing in circles, whose planes are at right angles to the axis of the magnet, and not in the line of the axis, as perfectly compatible with, and explanatory of, some effects produced; but he endeavours to show that, although two cylindrical conductors, with their axes parallel, one fixed, and the other moveable, ought, by their mutual action, to have a tendency to make the moveable one revolve; yet that, in such presumed revolution, different powers must reciprocally present, and be destructive of the effect. He judges that M. Ampere's experiments of a magnetic needle, properly suspended, being either totally repelled or attracted by the conducting wire, is as applicable in confirmation of his own, as of M. Ampere's doctrine. We must think otherwise. M. Oersted cannot account, on M. Ampere's principles, for the magnetic power imparted to steel, by touching or rubbing its sides; and concludes the consideration of the needle, by observing that theory has, hitherto, been insufficient to explain why iron, nickel, and cobalt, are so highly susceptible of magnetism, and all other metals so but in a very small comparative degree. M. Oersted concludes his paper with remarking on the—

MAGNETISM OF THE EARTH.

He supposes that the light and heat of the Sun daily produces changes by the alternate destruction and renovation of electrical equilibrium; which must resemble a galvanic circle, or belt, round the earth. The width of this belt extending nearly to the vicissitudes of day and night; and varying every day as the latitude, or declination of the Sun may govern.

The mean width of this circle will not extend much farther than the polar circle, on account of the violent changes which impede the regular course of the weather; and the regular effect of solar influence, exerting great controul in the countries near the poles. We rather think, on the contrary, that the weather near the poles is more uniform than at intermediate latitudes; and, also, that this presumed electrical belt would rather govern, than be governed by, local electrical changes occurring in its course.

(To be continued.)

Observations on Magnetic Attraction. By S. H. CHRISTIE, (In a Letter to Dr. Brewster.)
Edinburgh Philosophical Journal. No. 10.

Dr. Brewster having requested of Mr. Christie to furnish him with an abstract of a paper, on the above subject, that Mr. C. read before the Cambridge Philosophical Society; the latter complied by transmitting that which is presented to us in the Edinburgh Journal, and whose spirit we shall endeavour to lay before our readers.

Mr. Christie commences by observing, it does not appear to him necessary, in a doctrinal point of view, that any part of a mass of soft iron should possess the power of repulsion; but that it is almost a necessary distinction between unpolarized and polarized iron, for the former to possess attractive power alone; while the latter should possess both attractive and repulsive. Also that several phenomena seemed to indicate that the iron did not act upon the needle, in a horizontal plane; but as if the needle were inclined to the horizon, at an angle equal to the dip. So that when the centre of a sphere of iron be in a plane passing through the centre of the needle, perpendicular to the line of the dip, the upper and lower branches of the needle, being equally acted upon by the iron, the horizontal needle will not be affected by it. And that when the centre of the sphere of iron be *above* this plane, that is, in a plane parallel to the other, but nearer to the pole of the southern polar arm of the magnet; the south end of the magnet will deviate towards the sphere. And that when the sphere be *below* the plane passing through the centre of the magnet, that is, in a plane parallel to the last mentioned, but now cutting the axis of the northern polar arm of the magnet; the deviation will be through the magnetic attraction of the north pole to the sphere. Mr. Christie was then led to infer that this action of the iron, in producing the horizontal deviation, arose from the magnetic particles passing in a line through its centre, in the direction of the dip; and the iron acting on these particles, governed the horizontal deviation.

To put this opinion to the test of experiment, Mr. C. devised the following means. He suspended an iron sphere over a hole in the centre of a table, and having ascertained the magnetic meridian, he divided the table off into angles, of 10° each, for eastern or western horizontal deviation. The compass needle was placed on one of the divisions, so that its north and south line coincided, exactly, with that division; and its centre was at the distance of 12 inches from the centre of the table. Now, by the elevation or depression of the sphere, it is palpable that Mr. C. could render the deviation of the needle at will. When the sphere was opposite to the centre of the magnet, the influence was null; when above that point, the north end of the magnet deviated from the ball; when below it, the deviation was towards the ball. Now, if the deviation were resolvable on mere attraction or repulsion on the horizontal plane, the effect of the iron mass would have been similar on both ends of the needle; that is, either both attractive, or both repulsive. The following table shows the results of actual experiment, and what they ought to be by calculation: and the differences will be found so small, as to warrant a confidence in the principle Mr. C. adopts:—

Angle from the Meridian.	Calculated height at which the deviation should = 0.	Observed height at which deviation = 0. North towards West.	Difference between the observed and calculated heights.	Observed height at which deviation = 0. South towards East.	Difference between the observed and calculated heights.
10°	+ 4·185	− 3·95	− ·235	+ 4·35	+ ·165
20	+ 3·993	− 3·90	− ·093	+ 4·20	+ ·207
30	+ 3·680	− 3·70	+ ·020	+ 3·65	+ ·030
40	+ 3·255	− 3·30	+ ·045	+ 3·25	+ ·005
50	+ 2·732	− 2·80	+ ·068	+ 2·90	+ ·168
60	+ 2·125	− 2·15	+ ·025	+ 2·10	− ·025
70	+ 1·453	− 1.50	+ ·047	+ 1·40	− ·053
80	+ 0·738	− 0.90	+ ·162	+ 0·80	+ ·062

Mr. C. repeated his observations with the needle at 14, 16, and 18 inches from the centre of the table. At angles of 40 and 50°, the deviations were most sensible. Vide the following table:—

Angle from the Meridian.	Distance of needle from centre of table.	Calculated height at which deviation should = 0.	Observed height at which deviation should = 0.	Difference between their observed and calculated heights.
40°	14	3·797	3·75	− ·047
	16	4·340	4·33	− ·010
	18	4·882	4·90	+ ·018
50°	14	3·187	·20	+ ·013
	16	3·642	3·70	+ ·058
	18	4·097	15	+ ·053

This table also shows a very close coincidence between calculation and experiment. Mr. C. observes that, in the observations made from the *south*, towards the *east*, the deviations of the north end of the needle were first *easterly*; that is, *from* the ball; in which direction they gradually increased, as the ball descended, and attained a *maximum*; they then decreased to zero; became *westerly*; attained a *maximum* in this direction; and then decreased, until the needle resumed its original position. In the observations made from the north, towards the west, the deviations were exactly in a contrary order.

The *quality* of the deviations anticipated by Mr. C. being thus proved, he next sought the *quantity*, by carrying the ball round the axis of the dip, at different distances from, and parallel to, the equatorial plane of the dip. Having mathematically illustrated this measure of the cause of deviation, he proceeded to observe the deviations of the horizontal needle, when the sphere was at different points of its circle of revolution; but as this revolution could not be actually accomplished by the ball round the needle, he substituted the revolution of the needle round the ball. Under varied experiments, the deviations of the horizontal needle were observed, at every 10° of longitude, for the several latitudes of 30°, 45°, and 60°: the ball being 18 inches from the centre of the needle; the results were as follow:—

Distance of centre of ball from centre of needle = 18 inches; diameter of ball = 12·78; weight = 288 lbs.

Latitude of the Ball.	Deviations of Axis of Dip computed from the Horizontal Deviations.		
	Mean.	Greatest.	Least.
30°	3° 36'	3° 51'	3° 51'
45	3 55	4 00	3 47
60	3 18	3 25	3 15

Mr. C. seems firmly convinced, and we fully concur with him in the feeling, that the near agreement of the several values of deviation of the axis of dip at the respective latitudes, justify his previous anticipations; and prove, that as the ball was carried round the magnetic axis, or line of dip, the horizontal deviations were such as would arise from the deviations of that axis, or line, under the influence of the sphere, at the various points of its revolutions, and respective latitudes.

Again Mr. C. placed a dipping needle due west, 18 inches from the centre of the table; and the mean of the deviations, when its face was north and south, were taken for different heights of the ball. A horizontal compass was likewise placed 18 inches from the centre of the table; having its centre at the same height as the centre of the dipping needle. The following results were obtained:—

Height of Centre of Ball above Centres of Needles.	Mean Deviation of Dipping Needle.	Horizontal Needle.	
		Mean observed Deviation.	Deviation computed from Deviation of Dipping Needle.
10 inches	2° 05′	6° 10′	6° 13′
5 inches	1 36	5 00	4 47
0	0 05¼	0 10	0 17

The close accordance of observation with calculation, as marked in all the tables; and the several deviations of the dipping needle, and of the horizontal needle, in all positions, being the necessary consequences of his hypothesis, Mr. C. concludes that when a mass of iron be removed a few inches from the ends of a magnetic needle, so that they are beyond the influence of any accidental magnetism in the iron, the deviation in the needle arises from the action of the iron on magnetic particles, in a line passing through the centre of the needle, in the direction of the dip.

(To be continued.)

Meteorological Observations. By F. DANIELL, Esq. F.R.S. M.R.I. Journal of Science and Literature.

This is a very valuable paper, but extremely difficult to abridge, because every paragraph contains what is worthy of distinct remark. We have condensed the three tables that Mr. D. gives; and we trust, with tolerable accuracy. We cannot but lament, that gentlemen so capable, and so industrious, as Mr. D., should neglect to notice the changes occurring in atmospheric electricity; for we presume to judge all meteorological tables imperfect, without a column denoting electrical measure.

Mr. D., after complimenting Mr. Howard as the great meteorological oracle, proceeds to say that, his commencing his tables with the autumnal quarter, was purely accidental. He remarks that particular hours of observation are of importance: they should be nine in the morning, five in the afternoon, and eleven at night. Respecting deposition of vapour, he says, that he does not doubt but it takes place always in the night; though not always sensible in the day. The register thermometer gives us a very exact means of measuring temperature. The degrees of dryness are given as comparable with the thermometer, as well as those of vapour. The same applies as to evaporation. Mr. D. finds the results of the barometer and thermometer closely corresponding with Mr. Howard's observations, for a long series of years. As to Table 3, on Temperature, he apologises for classing within it what may be novel; but he thought himself warranted, as showing additional correspondencies. He notices that the barometer in the last half quarter of winter, averages considerably higher than in the last half quarter of summer. There are great fluctuations in the atmosphere from vapour or moisture; in the winter being least; in the summer, greatest, being nearly double, and much influences temperature. As to evaporation, its rate is in compound proportion to the heat of the water yielding the vapour, the degree of dryness, and the velocity of the wind. But here Mr. D. remarks, very justly, on the capacities of bodies for retention of moisture; thus, after a shower of rain, the atmosphere being at 66°, he has found vapour 60°—running stream 62°—wet glass in sunshine 69°—wet sand 76°—stagnant water 67°—garden mould 84°. He considers that there are wider variations in result in the quantity of rain falling, than in any other department of observation. By consulting his tables, it appears that temperature has a decided influence on this matter; for the barometer was lower, and the force of vapour higher, in the two half quarters of 1821 than of 1820; yet the quantity of rain in the latter was double that of the former: and the average mean temperature 5°¼ lower.

Respecting radiation of heat from the earth, he says he was induced to remark on it, because of its value as relates to vegetation. The medium at night was 4°—the maximum observed was 13°. It may appear extraordinary that there is but a period of about six weeks in the year (in this latitude) in which vegetation, particularly situate, is not exposed to a freezing temperature: and only a quarter of a year wherein the thermometer, so situate, is not subject to a fall of six or seven degrees below the freezing point. If the ground, when covered by mist, be examined, it will constantly be found 5° or 6° below the air of the clearer region.

Respecting dew, he presumes that its average deposition on a circular surface, of 2 inches diameter, for every night in the year, may be about six grains per night. As to radiation of the sun, he considers experimental result but imperfect yet: the average for the half year, from March to August, was 27° above the mean highest in the shade: the maximum 144°.

Mr. D. then proceeds to remark on the period included within observation. As to the autumns, 1819 was 1°¼ dryer, and 2°¼ warmer, than 1820: the depth of rain was, however, greater; for the barometer was lower, and the vapour denser: 1819 was the clearest, driest, and warmest, known for many years. The winters differed more than the autumns; 1819 being very severe; 1820 was mild: the respective mean temperatures were 33 and 38°. In this quarter, the latter regained the dryness which it was behind during the preceding; and the means for the two half years were exactly alike. In the first half quarter of spring,

1820, was backward; and was 1° dryer, and 2°¼ colder, than 1821: which was open and fine. In the second half quarter, the advantage was regained by 1820; but in 1821 the season was cold, with north winds, checking vegetation. At the beginning of summer, 1820, the change to heat was sudden, and intense: The summer of 1821 backward; the temperature low; but at the latter part there were several hot days, so as to raise the average temperature above the corresponding period of 1820. The last summer must be termed wet and cold. Mr. D. concludes with observing that the great characteristic features of the two years were, in the first, a cold winter, and a hot summer; and in the second, a very mild winter, and a backward cold summer.

We have here, including the tables, laid before our readers a mass of information to which, if they think as we do, they will attach a particular value. It has been remarked on the very tables published in the Transactions of the Royal Society, that they are worse than useless; as being in error, and stamped with the seal of authority. It is only from a long series of observations, in all circumstances of climate, soil, and locality, that a collection of facts can be adduced, affording us a practical benefit. However accurately a twelvemonth's observation may have been conducted, it is, as it were, but a moment of time, in which to witness the great, the general, or the apparently anomalous fluctuating states, and conditions, of the atmosphere and the earth. Nor could satisfactory conclusions be derived from any lengthened period, as confined to the same place. And we cannot close this subject without repeating the important value we attach to observations on electrical phenomena, as influencing atmospherical changes: for changes in the relative quantities of free electricity may be a critical measure of all the varieties presenting in the common objects of meteorological regard.

Table I.

TABLE I.

Mean from September, 1820, to August, 1821, both inclusive.

		Half Quarter.	Quarter.	Half Year.	Year.
Pressure of Atmosphere and extremes	Inches	30·49 29·88 28·17	32·52 29·88 29·16	30·58 29·88 28·98	30·82 29·88 28·74
Pressure of Vapour and extremes.	Inches	·501 ·300 ·199	·559 ·325 ·173	·666 ·324 ·147	·628 ·324 ·120
Pressure of Vapour corrected for 24 hours	Inches	·292	·315	·313	·313
Weight of Vapour	Grains	5·471 3·625 2·293	6·076 3·625 2·459	7·044 3·625 1·391	7·366 3·625 1·391
Dryness and extremes	Degrees	$4\frac{3}{4}$	$4\frac{1}{2}$	$4\frac{1}{2}$	$4\frac{3}{4}$
Dryness corrected for 24 hours	Degrees	$4\frac{1}{4}$	$4\frac{1}{2}$	$4\frac{3}{4}$	$4\frac{3}{4}$
Evaporation and extremes	Grains	·29	·29	·29	·29
Quantity of Rain	Inches	2·98	4·91	9·82	19·64
Temperature and extremes	Degrees	66 54 42 38	71 52 42 28	79 52 42 22	82 $51\frac{1}{4}$ 42 24

TABLE II.

Mean from Autumn, 1819, to Summer, 1821, both inclusive.

		Half Quarter.	Quarter.	Half Year.	Year.
Pressure of Atmosphere and extremes	Inches	30·09 29·74 29·63	29·88 29·91 29·86	29·88 29·87 29·84	29·88 29·87 29·86
Pressure of Vapour and extremes	Inches	·352 ·328	·341 ·327 ·325	·331 ·327 ·324	·331 ·327 ·324
Weight of Vapour and extremes	Grains	3·692 3·652 3.625	3·655 3·652 3·625	3·680 3·652 3·625	3·680 3·652 3·625
Dryness and extremes	Degrees	5 $4\frac{3}{4}$ $4\frac{1}{4}$	$5\frac{1}{2}$ $5\frac{1}{4}$ $4\frac{1}{2}$	$5\frac{1}{2}$ 5 $4\frac{3}{4}$	$5\frac{1}{2}$ 5 $4\frac{1}{4}$
Evaporation and extremes	Grains	·37 ·32 ·29	·37 ·33 ·32	·65 ·50 ·45	·37 ·33 .29
Quantity of Rain	Inches	2·45 2·37 2·33	4·99 4·79 4·41	10.32 9·59 9.36	18·72 19·18 19·14
Temperature and extremes	Degrees	$48\frac{3}{4}$ $47\frac{3}{4}$ $42\frac{1}{2}$	54 $48\frac{1}{4}$ $47\frac{1}{4}$	$48\frac{3}{4}$ $48\frac{1}{2}$ $47\frac{3}{4}$	$48\frac{3}{4}$ $48\frac{1}{4}$ 48

Table III.

Table III.

Mean Extremes from Autumn, 1819, to Summer, 1821, both inclusive.

	Autumn.	Winter.	Spring.	Summer.
Temperature in Shade — highest	63	48¼	63	71¼
Temperature in Shade — lowest	34	28½	38	41
Temperature highest in Sun — Degrees	....	50¼	88½	105
Lowest Radiation of Heat — Degrees	30½	23¼	30¼	41
Constituent Temperature of Vapour — highest	54	42¼	46½	58
Constituent Temperature of Vapour — lowest	40	35	42	45¼
Ditto corrected for 24 hours — highest	53	40¼	46	57½
Ditto corrected for 24 hours — lowest	38¼	33¼	41	50
Mean Temperature — highest	56	38½	54	63¼
Mean Temperature — lowest	38	32	43	59
Sun in Summer highest specific — Degrees	....	....	....	144
In Shade in Winter lowest — Degrees	....	11	....	....

On certain Remarkable Instances of Deviation from Newton's Scale, in the Tints developed by Crystals with one Axis of double Refraction on exposure to Polarized Light. By J. W. HERSCHEL, A. M. &c.

Edin. Philosophical Journal. No. 10.

In our last number, when commenting on Dr. Reade's paper on Refraction, we by mistake intimated that Dr. Herschel had controverted some of the refractive detail of Newton, we should have said Mr. Herschel, as will be seen by the heading hereof.

On experiments being made with apophyllite it was found that three remarkable deviations from the refractive results, as laid down by Newton, occurred. Mr. H. would have subjected the matter of the mineral presenting these anomalies to chemical analysis; but, he was deterred by a modest diffidence of his own abilities for the task:—so it cannot yet be determined whether these peculiarities have arisen from chemical composition, or from a modified aggregation.

The best and most transparent portion being insulated, the plate was inclosed in an oil apparatus; when the tints developed on inclining it in a plane making an angle of 45° with that of primitive polarization, were as follows.

TABLE I.

Apophyllite—Third variety. Thickness $= .94499$.

Incidence.	Ordinary Pencil.	Extraordinary Pencil.
0° 0′	White	Black
	Yellowish-white	Sombre Indigo
17 0	Pale yellow	Indigo inclining to purple
	Pale greenish yellow	Pale lilac purple
28 15	White, slightly greenish	Very pale reddish purple
39 14	Very pale green	Pale rose red
47 36	White	White
	White, scarcely perceptibly tinged with pink ?	White scarcely perceptible greenish ?

Mr. Herschel remarks, that, this table of tints indicates a more energetic action on the red and violet ends of the spectrum, than on the intermediate colours, especially yellow; fully corroborated by observations in homogeneous light, which gave the values of minimum lengths.

Table II.

Scale of the Minimum Lengths of the Periods of the different simple Rays in the third variety of Apophyllite, and their reciprocals.

Name of Colour.	Minimum length of period value of L.	Polarizing Power or Value of $\frac{1000000}{1}$	Number of Observations.
Extreme red	43634	22.918	10
Mean orange	101238	9.878	10
——— yellow	366620+	2.728—	10
——— green	88646	11.155	10
——— blue	32211	31·040	10
——— indigo	21947	45.565	10
Extreme violet	13704	72.970	10

Mr. H. says, it is evident from a moment's consideration of the forms of the three curves representing the polarizing powers of the three varieties of apophyllite, that no one of them can be produced by any other two; and we must admit each as a distinct variety, or composed of not fewer than three kinds of laminæ.

Hyposulphate of lime affords another instance of deviation from Newton's scale in crystals of double refraction. The salt crystallizes in bevelled hexagonal tables, which have no distinct cleavage; the axis being perpendicular to their broad surfaces. The following is a scale of tints developed by a plate of this salt exposed to polarized light.

Table III.

Table III.

Hyposulphate of Lime,—Thickness = 35701. The Axis was inclined 5° 12′ to the Surface in the Plane of Incidence.

Incidence.	Ordinary Pencil	Extraordinary Pencil.
0° 0′	White	Black
	White	Very faint sky blue
10° 32′	Very pale yellow	Pretty strong sky blue
	Sombre yellow	Very light bluish white
	Sombre purple crimson	White
15° 1′	Beautiful rich dark purple	White
	Beautiful deep blue	White, a little yellowish
	Bright blue	Bright straw colour
	Bright blue	Yellow
	Fine light blue	Yellow, verging strongly to orange pink
	Light greenish blue	Fine pink
	Light yellow green	Sombre pink
21° 27′	Light greenish yellow	Purple
	Ruddy but pale yellow	Blue
	Pink, light and approaching to brick red	Bright greenish blue
25° 3′	Fine pink	Splendid green
	Pink	Light green
26° 7′	Pale purple	Greenish white
	Dull blue	Ruddy white
	Bright greenish blue	Tolerable pink red
29° 32′	Blue green	Fine rose red
31° 35′	White	Dull pale purple
	Ruddy white	Blue, rather pale
	Good pink red	Green blue
25° 27′	Dull pale purple	White
	Light blue green	Pink red
39° 32′	White	Very pale purple
	Light pink	Very light blue
	White	White
	Extremely pale blue	A most imperceptible pink
	White	White

After the fourth order the colours cease to be perceptible, and the degradation of the tints is much more rapid than in

Newton's scale; thus the blue of the first order, which in that scale is scarcely visible, is here strong enough to influence its complementary tint, depressing it to pale yellow. The green and its complementary pink of the second order, in this table, are fully equal in brilliancy to those of the third in Newton's scale. Accordingly by a fifth series of measures, carefully made, Mr. H. found the values for the several simple colours as follows:—

TABLE IV.

Scale of the Minimum lengths of the Periods in Hyposulphate of Lime, and their Reciprocals.

Name of Colour.	Minimum length of its period.	Polarizing Power or value of $\frac{1000000}{1}$	
Extreme red	3241	308.54	38 very exact
Mean orange	2454	407.45	26
——— yellow	2129	469.65	28
——— green	1861	537.32	20
——— blue	1658	603.21	20
——— indigo	1480	675.83	20
Extreme violet	1129	885.77	29

Mr. Herschel considers these experiments as evincing the wide scale of action of a single axis on different coloured rays, and that either the single apparent axis of either of the above crystals, as resultant of two others of equal energy, but of opposite character, according to Dr. Brewster, or as being itself the real axis of polarization. But be this as it may, he thinks that his experiments fortify Dr. B.'s theory, as applied to crystals with two axes; because they establish the existence of that diversity in the scales of action of the simple or elementary axes, without which their points of compensation (or the poles of the lenmiscates they exhibit in polarized light) must be coincident for all the simple colours; which seldom or never takes place.

We cannot refrain from wishing that gentlemen engaged in experiments on the refraction of light, would endeavour to ascertain what the influence of electric matter may be, as cause or effect; for there is abundant reason to presume it is connected with the results obtained.

On Alloys of Chromium, Iron, and Steel. By M. Berthier. Journal of Science.

We consider the following as containing some experimental deductions that may be acceptable to the chemical class of our readers, and therefore present it to them.

Chromium has so strong an affinity for iron, that the presence of the latter metal very much facilitates the reduction of the former; and the combinations which result, are, according to M. Berthier, more analogous to sulphurets and phosphurets, than to alloys. The oxide of chrome also, has so strong an affinity for the oxide of iron, as frequently to prevent its reduction,—an effect that is not observed with any other substance.

Oxide of chromium, heated very intensely, in a crucible lined with charcoal, was completely reduced, and gave a button that had suffered hasty fusion, was brittle, hard, grey in some places, grey-black in others, perhaps containing carbon in combination.

Mixtures of oxide of iron and oxide of chromium, in various proportions, were heated in crucibles lined with charcoal, and reduced, giving perfect combinations of the two metals. These alloys are generally hard, brittle, crystalline, of a whiter grey than iron, and very bright; less fusible, much less magnetic, and much less acted on by acids than iron; and these characters are marked in proportion as more chromium is present. An alloy, resulting from an equal mixture of per-oxides of iron and oxide of chromium, gave a rounded button, full of cavities, lined with prismatic crystals,— its fracture crystalline,— its colour whiter than platinum, and hard enough to scratch glass like a diamond. It was easily reducible to powder in a mortar, and its powder was metallic. Strong acids, and nitro-muriatic acid, scarcely acted upon it.

Chromate of iron, being heated in a crucible lined with charcoal, the iron was only reduced into a minor state of oxidation, and acted on the magnet. Without the presence of the oxide of chrome, the iron would have been reduced.

On heating chromate of iron with an equal quantity of glass, containing 16 per cent. soda, there was reduction of parts of metals, and a loss of 10 per cent., which M. Berthier thinks is iron and chrome volatilized; because a metallic scoria appeared on the surface of the crucible: and this loss was greater on adding borax, and increased with its quantity.

The best method of obtaining alloy from chromate of iron, is to fuse it in a crucible lined with charcoal, with 30. of lime, and 70. of silica; or with 1. of alkaline glass; or better still, with 40. of borax; and to obtain as much chromium as possible, a portion of oxide of iron should be added.

In consequence of former experiments, M. Berthier was induced to try the effect obtained by adding a portion of this alloy to steel. Two alloys of cast steel and chromium were made, one with 0·01, the other with 0·015 of chromium. These both forged well, the first better than cast steel. A knife and a razor were made from them, and both proved very good; their edges were hard and solid; but their most remarkable character, was the fine damask they took, when washed over with sulphuric acid. This damask was composed of white silvery veins, and nearly resembled that given by the alloy of steel and silver. The white parts are probably pure chromium, on which, acids have no action. There is room to suppose that chromic steel will be found proper for the manufacture of damask blades, which will be solid, hard, and have a fine appearance; and also for many other instruments. It was prepared by fusing together cast steel and the alloy of chromium and iron.

Should further trials confirm these results, the Arts will have made an acquisition of no small importance.

On the Analysis of Alkaline Minerals. By M. BERTHIER.
Journal of Science.

It being requisite to repeatedly heat barytes with the mineral to be analyzed, in order to render its action complete, makes it a very inconvenient agent, and also uncertain; for at high temperatures a portion of alkali is volatilized, when an alkaline glass be added to a sufficient portion of silica. As to boracic acid, it complicates the process, on account of the alkali.

M. Berthier has found oxide of lead a very useful agent; has operated with it more than a year at l'Ecole des Mines, and prefers the nitrate; it not being subject to some inconvenience that the carbonate, which he tried, has given. The process is this: One part of the mineral, two of nitrate of lead, and one of cerusse, are to be well powdered and mixed. Put it into a covered platinum crucible; within another, also covered. Subject to a red heat for a quarter of an hour. It will fuse slowly without swelling, and yielding a yellow or brown transparent glass. Then pour, or force out, as much as may be from the crucible into water: afterwards plunging the crucible in also. The glass splits into small fragments, readily acted on by acids. Boil with nitric acid; crushing the portions of silica from time to time with an agate or porcelain pestle. The silica remains in a gelatinous state. Precipitate the silica by sulphuric acid; testing by sulphuretted hydrogen, that no portion may remain. Boil the solution with carbonate of ammonia, and analyze the precipitate by the ordinary means. Finally, evaporate the liquid to dryness; calcine the saline matter in a platinum crucible; and collect and weigh the residuum. This residuum contains the alkali in the state of sulphate; usually mixed with sulphate of magnesia. Then proceed thus:—

1st. Precipitate sulphuric acid by acetate of barytes—collect and weigh precipitate—precipitate barytes by carbonate or oxalate of ammonia—evaporate clear solution to dryness; and collect salt left. It will be a mixture of alkaline carbonate and caustic magnesia, weight it, and expose it to the air. If it contain potassa, it will deliquesce. Wash off the alkali from the magnesia, and weigh latter; then ascertain whether the alkaline carbonate be of potassa, soda, or lithia. When the sulphates first obtained are neutral, it is sufficient to determine, very exactly, the quantity of sulphuric acid and magnesia, to learn the nature of the alkali.

Or 2d. Precipitate the magnesia and sulphuric acid by barytes water, and the excess of barytes by carbonate of ammonia—evaporate, calcine, and the alkaline sub-carbonate is left pure. Separate the magnesia from the sulphate of barytes, by means of an acid.

Or 3d. Precipitate the magnesia by lime-water, the lime by carbonate or oxalate of ammonia—evaporate and calcine, when you have the magnesia and the alkaline sulphate.

In examining a mineral for alkali; powder, and mix one part with three of cerusse. Half fill a crucible with it—place within another crucible—heat to whiteness, or until perfectly fluid—remove inner crucible—when cold, collect the glass and those parts to which it adheres—pulverize and boil in common muriatic acid—when action is finished, evaporate to dryness—then wash repeatedly with boiling water. The silica will be left with most of the lead, in the state of muriate. Precipitate solution by lime-water, which throws down all the other earths and oxides. Precipitate lime by carbonate of ammonia, boiling them together. Evaporate to dryness — add a little sulphuric acid to the residue, and heat it; the alkaline will remain as a sulphate. If there be no magnesia present, the lime-water may be spared, and the precipitation made at once with carbonate of ammonia.—*Annales de Chimie.*

The Crucible.

In the Edinburgh Philosophical Journal we have a new method described of forming crucibles, by Mr. Charles Cameron of Glasgow, who too justly remarks that the Dutch have long enjoyed an almost exclusive monopoly in the manufacture of the small melting pot, or clay crucible, used by the jeweller and silversmith. The English potter has hitherto failed in imitating those imported from Holland, either in point of shape, quality, or sustaining the sudden transitions of temperature to which they are subjected. In consequence of their superiority, they were an article of great interest to the jeweller during the period of the late war; sometimes they could not be procured, and at other times they sold at five or six times their present price. The English melting pot was then in request from necessity; it is now entirely out of the market. About two years ago, Mr. C. was led, by a curious train of reasoning, to conceive the practicability of forming crucibles similar to the Dutch, by a simple method, that of moulds made of sulphate of lime, or stucco, which would easily give any required form.

He established a small manufactory of them, and carried it on for some time; but owing to particular circumstances, he was obliged to relinquish it, after it had arrived at a state of perfection. Having found it to be the opinion of his friends that the process should not be lost, he was induced to draw up the following account of it, for the Edinburgh Philosophical Journal.

For each of the different sizes of the crucibles, he formed ten or twelve dozen of moulds of stucco, burnt, and powdered, in the usual manner. For the first mould of each size, he formed a piece of soft pipe-clay, into the shape of the intended crucible; and laid it with its mouth downwards, on a flat surface, and inclosed it with a flat cylinder of white iron, distant about half an inch from the angular points of the crucible, and about an inch and a half higher than its bottom; then mixing the stucco with water, poured it into the cylinder. When the stucco was sufficiently set, he removed the white iron cylinder, picked out the clay, and dried the mould; he then squeezed soft clay into the moulds, which, on standing a few minutes, easily came out again. It was enclosed in the cylinder, and stucco poured round it, which formed a second mould; continuing to do so until he had procured the number wanted. They were then all put into a stove, and completely dried ready for use.

In the preparation of the fine clay for the crucibles, he followed precisely the same process as that used at the potteries, by mixing it with a very large quantity of water, and putting the whole through No. 9 silk searce. On allowing the whole to stand a few hours, the clay subsided, and on pouring off the clear water, he procured the clay or slip of the consistence of thick cream. On weighing a gallon of it, he found the portion of clay it contained, and added sand to the whole, in the proportion of seven of sand to seventeen of clay; he then stirred and mixed the whole completely, when it was ready for use. He next took his moulds, previously dried, and arranged them in parallel rows on a table, and successively filled them with the prepared slip. By the time he had filled four or five dozen, he returned to the one first filled, and began alternately to pour the slip out of them, leaving a small quantity unpoured out, which subsided, and gave the requisite thickness to the bottom. In each of the moulds so filled, a crucible is completely formed by the abstraction of the water of the slip, in contact with, and adjoining to, the porous substance of the stucco mould. The crucible will be either thicker or thinner in proportion to the time the slip has remained in it. Five or six dozen will not require more than fifteen minutes in being formed. The moulds, with their contents, are then removed to a stove, placed on their side, and built one above the other. In a short time, from the contraction of the clay, the crucibles easily part from the moulds, and are removed, by introducing the finger into them. The moulds are allowed to remain in their situation until the water they had absorbed is completely evaporated, when they are again ready for refilling. The crucibles remain in the stove until dry, after which they are burned in a kiln in the usual manner. They will last for years.

The process is simple, and combines the advantages of forming them with great facility, and giving the acquired shape, which cannot be accomplished at once on the potter's wheel. One man and a boy are capable of making from ten to twelve hundred per day. The principle is particularly adapted for the formation of a variety of chemical apparatuses, as muffles, retorts, tubes, &c.

It is to be regretted that any circumstances should have prevented Mr. Cameron from pursuing this useful occupation; and the public must stand indebted to him for his liberal disclosure. We hope that some other person may adopt his mode of manufacture, if the crucibles shall be found to answer the desires of the chemist and general artist; and thereby render us independent of the foreign market.

On Comets.

On the authority of the Annals of Philosophy, No. 12, p. 469, New Series; we have information that "the late Mr. Cusac has left some unpublished papers on comets. He supposes them to be globes of water; that on return to perihelion, the solar rays (after sunset) strike on the mass of water, and enter converging to the centre; where, after decussation, they emerge from the globe, diverging; and form the phænomenon in the heavens called the comet's tail. As to the use of these watery bodies, he thinks they were formed by nature to assist in giving a due temperature to our system."

Our knowledge of the nature of comets is so limited, that almost any conjectural opinion may be excusable. We cannot concur with Mr. C., either as to the matter or purpose of them. Without enumerating a great number of objections, to which this supposition is liable, we would merely intimate that, as to influence on the temperature, it is totally untenable; for how should a mere fluid globe retain its coherency, and form, when moving with the velocity of a comet in perihelion? That they may be transparent, is more probable, but then their composition should be solidified. Even Mr. Herschel, with his great powers of observation, has determined that the comet of 1807, shone by its own light; but that of 1811 by reflected light. Now, it is not very probable that the qualities of these bodies should differ so essentially as they must, to warrant these different inferences; but if we suppose them to be transparent, and at the same time solid, many of the difficulties in accounting for apparatus anomalies may be solved.

New Species of Apple.

He who produces to society an improved fruit or grain, throws the glory of the mere hero into comparative shade; and the least we can do for him is, to bestow the meed of grateful praise.—We have, then, to thank a gardener, of Barnwell, near Cambridge, (whose name ought to have been mentioned,) for persevering several years, in an endeavour to bring an entire new species of apple to great perfection. This, it appears, by the Annals of Philosophy, he has accomplished to an admirable degree. The fruit keeps extremely well. In magnitude and weight it far exceeds any other species known in this country; the diameter measuring twelve inches, and the weight being more than a pound. We think there must be a little error here; for surely, with a diameter of one foot, the weight must exceed what is stated. Should the trees producing this fine fruit, bear well, when planted in orchards, we shall have gained a most important acquisition in horticulture: for doubtless the apple ranks first, in use, as a fruit.

Caoutchonc.

Mr. Bringier informs us that trees producing this matter, are now found near the rivers Mississippi, Arkansas, and Red River, in America; and that in a most abundant degree. When incisions are made through the bark, a milky fluid exudes, which coagulates, and becomes the substance we have long been indebted to India for, called Indian Rubber. A single tree will sometimes yield from 150 to 200 pounds of Caoutchonc. This is an enormous produce, and must eventually lower the market price of caoutchonc, so as to make it applicable to many useful purposes, that its high charge has hitherto excluded it from. The bark of the tree is said to be smooth, and the wood very elastic, when dry. If, when the weather is cold, it be rubbed on an electric body, the latter will adhere to a wall: or, a quill will be attracted six inches from a wall, and adhere to the caoutchonc wood, until the electricity be dissipated. There has either been some mistake in the account of the process, whereby the Indian caoutchonc is prepared; or the juices exuded in India must differ from those in America; because we have been told that the elastic rubber of the former, is only the juice exsiccated; while it appears by Mr. B. that the American juice is coagulated.

THE FOCUS

OF

PHILOSOPHY, SCIENCE, AND ART.

Native Copper on Lake Superior.

(Continued from p. 150.)

"The discovery of masses of native copper, is generally considered indicative of the existence of mines in the neighbourhood. The practised miner looks upon them as signs which point to larger bodies of the same metal in the earth, and is often determined, by discoveries of this nature, in the choice of the spot for commencing his labours. The predictions drawn from such evidence, are also more sanguine in proportion to the extent of the discovery. It is not, however, an unerring indication, and appears liable to many exceptions. A detached mass of copper is sometimes found at a great distance from any body of the metal, or its ores; and these, on the contrary, often occur in the earth, or imbedded in rock strata, where there has been no external discovery of metallic copper to indicate it. So far as the opinions of mineralogical writers can be collected on this point, they teach,—that large veins of native copper are seldom found, but that it is frequently disseminated in masses of various size in the rocks, and among the spars and ores of copper and other mines; and when found in scattered masses upon the surface, is rather to be considered as a token of the existence of the sulphuret, the carbonate, and other ores of copper, within the circle of country where it occurs, than as the precursor to contiguous bodies of the same metal.

'Native copper,' says Cleveland, 'is found chiefly in primitive rocks, through which it is sometimes disseminated, or more frequently it enters into the composition of metallic veins, which traverse these rocks. It is thus connected with granite, gneiss, micaceous and argillaceous slates, granular limestone, chlorite, serpentine, porphyry, &c. It also occurs in transition and secondary rocks. It accompanies other ores of copper, as the red oxide, the carbonate and sulphuret of copper, pyritous and gray copper, also the red and brown oxides of iron, oxide of tin, &c. Its usual gangues are quartz, the fluate and carbonate of lime, and sulphate of barytes. At Oberstein it occurs in prehnite; and in the Faroe islands it accompanies zeolite.

"'Native copper is not rare, nor is it found in sufficient quantity to be explored by itself. It sometimes occurs in loose, insulated masses of considerable size.'

"From all the facts which I have been able to collect on Lake Superior, and after a deliberation upon them since my return, I have drawn the following conclusions:—

"1st. That the alluvial soil along the banks of the Ontonagon river, extending to its source, and embracing the contiguous region which gives origin to the Menomonie river of Green Bay, and to the Ousconsing, Chippeway, and St. Croix rivers of the Mississippi, contains very frequent, and some most extraordinary imbedded masses of native copper; but that no body of it, which is sufficiently extensive to become the object of profitable mining operations, is to be found at any particular place. This conclusion is supported by the facts already adduced; and, so far as theoretical aids can be relied upon, by an application of those facts to the theories of mining. A further extent of country might have been embraced along the shore of Lake Superior, but the same remark appears applicable to it.

"2d. That a mineralogical survey of the rock formations skirting the Ontonagon, including the district of country above alluded to, would result in the discovery of very valuable mines of the sulphuret, the carbonate, and other profitable ores of copper; in the working of which, the ordinary advantages of mining would be greatly enhanced by occasional masses and veins of native metal. This deduction is rendered probable by the general appearance of the country, and the concurrent discoveries of travellers,—by the green-coloured waters which issue in several places from the earth,—by the bodies of native copper found,—by the cupreous tinge which is presented in the crevices of rocks and loose stones,—by the geological character of the country, and by other analogous considerations.

"These deductions embrace all I have to submit on the mineral geography of the country, so far as regards the copper mines. Other considerations arise from the facilities which that section of country may present for mining operations,—its adaptation to the purposes of agriculture,—the state and dispositions of the Indian tribes, and other topics, which a design to commence metallurgical operations at the present period would suggest. But I am not aware that any such views are entertained by government, and have not considered it incumbent upon me in this communication to enter into details on these subjects. It may be proper, however, to remark, that the remote situation of the country containing the most valuable mines, does not, at the present period, favour the pursuit of mining. It would require the employment not only of the artificers and labourers necessary to conduct the working of mines, but also of a military force to protect their operations,—first, while engaged in exploring the country, and afterwards, in their regular labours. For, whatever may be their professions, the Indian tribes of the north possess strong natural jealousies, and, in situations so remote, are to be restrained from an indulgence in the most malignant passions, only by the fear of a prompt military chastisement. In looking upon the southern shore of Lake Superior, the period appears distant, when the advantages flowing from a military post upon that frontier will be produced by the ordinary progress of our settlement; for it presents few enticements to the agriculturist. A considerable portion of the shore is rocky; and its alluvions are in general of too sandy and light a texture for profitable husbandry. With an elevation of six hundred and forty-one feet above the Atlantic Ocean, and drawing its waters from territories all situated north of the forty-fourth degree of north latitude, Lake Superior cannot be represented as enjoying a climate very favourable to the productions of the vegetable kingdom. Its forest trees are chiefly those of the fir kind, mixed with white birch, (*Betula papyracea*, the bark of which is so much employed for canoes by the northern Indians,) and with some varieties of poplar, oak, and maple. The meteorological observations which I have made, indicate, however, a warm summer, the average heat of the month of June being 69°; but the climate is subject to a long and severe winter, and to storms, and sudden transitions of temperature, during the summer months. We saw no Indian corn among the savages upon this lake; whether the climate is unfavourable to its growth, or the wild rice (*Zezania aquatica*) furnishes an adequate substitute, is not certain. A country lacking the advantages of a fertile soil, may still become a very rich mining country, like the county of Cornwall in England, the Hartz mountains in Germany, and a portion of Missouri in our own country; but this deficiency must be compensated by the advantages of geographical position, contiguous, or redundant population, and the facilities of a ready commercial intercourse. To these, the mineral district of Lake Superior can advance but a feeble claim; while it lies upwards of three hundred miles beyond the utmost point of our settlements on the north-western frontier, and in the occupation of savage tribes, whose hostility has been so recently manifested. Concerning the variety, importance, and extent of its mineral productions, little doubt can remain. Every fact which has been noticed, tends to strengthen the belief, that there are extensive copper mines upon its shores; while the information that has been gathered in the course of the late mission, renders it certain that not only copper, but iron, lead, plumbago, and sulphur, are productions of that region, together with several of the *precious siliceous* and *crystallized minerals*. The carnelian is first found on approaching the Pictured Rocks on Lake Superior, and afterwards becomes very abundant along the shore extending to the Fond du Lac. Sandy Lake on the head of the Mississippi is a good locality of this mineral, and it is found around the shores of the numerous little lakes in that region. In descending the Mississippi it is constantly met with in the alluvial soil. At the foot of the Falls of St. Anthony it is sparingly found; around the shores of Lake Sepin it is very abundant, and it may be traced below Prairie du Chien, and even as low as St. Genevieve, as I have mentioned in my view of the mines. According to the classification of Werner, which is founded on 'alternate bands of red and white,' many of these specimens may be considered as sardonyx. They are often associated with common chalcedony, with cacholong, and with certain varieties of agate and flinty jasper. In a few instances the common opal, in small fragments, is met with. It is rendered propable also, that silver ore is imbedded in the transition rocks of the region; and whenever it shall become an object with the American government, or people, to institute mineralogical surveys of the country, no doubt can be entertained but such researches will eventuate in discoveries of a highly interesting character, and such as cannot fail both to augment our sources of profitable industry, and to promote our commercial independence. In the event of such operations, the facilities of a ready transportation, either in vessels or barges, of the crude ore to the Sault de St. Marie, will point out that place as uniting, with a commanding geographical position, superior advantages for the reduction of the ores, and for the subsequent conversion of the metal either into ordnance or other articles. At this place a fall of twenty-two feet in the river, in the distance of half a mile, creates a sufficient power to drive hydraulic works to any extent; while the surrounding country is such as to admit of an agricultural settlement.

"I accompany this report with a geological chart of a vertical section of the left bank of the Mississippi at St. Peter's, embracing a formation of native copper, and in which the superposition of the layers of rock, and the several subdeposites forming the alluvial stratum, exhibit a remarkable order. The curvatures in the lines of the alluvial stratum, represent a natural mound or hillock recumbent upon the brink of the river, which has partially fallen in, thus exposing its internal tinued.) The formation was first noticed by the garrison, who quarried stone for quicklime, and for the purpose of building chimneys, at this spot. The masses of copper found are all small, none exceeding a pound in weight."

M. OERSTED on Electro-Magnetism.
(Continued from No. IV. p. 158.)

M. O. next comments on the hypothesis of M. Ampere, as presuming on electro-magnetic force operating round the earth, from east to west; and arising, partly from the revolving surface, and partly from the very structure of the mass: and that there is no other magnetism of the earth, besides the immediate effect of electro-magnetism. M. Oersted differs from him, and contends that a body, capable of becoming magnetic, cannot be surrounded by an electrical current without receiving a magnetic charge. We must remark that whether or not M. Ampere be here wrong, we are not clear that M. Oersted be right; for we think it not sufficient for a bar of iron to be merely in an electrical current, in order to insure its becoming magnetic; but that such bar must be the sole conductor of that current; or part of a mass acting as such conductor; otherwise its mere immersion in electrical fluid will be nugatory, as to magnetic influence. Perhaps the sole difference between simple electrical and magnetical effect, may consist, in the former, as being in a quiescent state, and in the latter, as in active and directive motion, of electric matter. The simple insulation of a wire, however highly the atmosphere may be charged with electricity, would never, as we conjecture, impart to it a magnetic power; but the same portion of electric matter, passed through the wire, as a conducter, acts on it with an intensity comparatively infinite, and produces magnetic effect. "All bodies (says M. Oersted) are susceptible of magnetism, to a certain extent; although generally it is very slight when compared with iron. It follows then, necessarily, from the electrical circulation round the earth, that the earth itself becomes magnetic." We cannot omit observing on this passage that, susceptibility to magnetism, and magnetic power, are two distinct conditions. We can conceive the mass of the earth as magnetically susceptible, without necessarily inferring it to have the power, by any mere motion to which it is subjected, of generating a current, which shall impart magnetic effect to a particular body. And that the earth may be as a conductive wire, that is, susceptible of an electrical influence, not inherently its own; and therefore deriving electrical or magnetical influence from that reservoir of electric matter which permeates circumambient space, and which may, by motions not yet discovered, govern earthly magnetism, as an electrical current does that of a conductive wire. The grand question, then, of earthly magnetic influence, as we understand it, is, whether the globe be a large magnet, generating these motions by a power *per se*; or, that it, in common with all things attached to it, derives this power primarily from the active instrumentality of diffused electricity.

M. Oersted proceeds to show, that there must be a magnetic nucleus in the earth: but this has to encounter some difficulties: such as the varying degrees of both dip and declination of the needle, at different times, in the same place; which cannot be easily reconciled with the idea of a fixed centre of magnetic power in the earth. Besides, M. O. allows that "the intensity of action cannot be equal in the whole of the electro-magnetic belt of the earth; just as the effect of the sun is not the same upon the earth and the sea, and differs according to the elevation of the country above the level of the sea." He then adds, "It appears then that the new discoveries do not, as yet, furnish us with new facts, sufficiently developed, to be useful in mathematical researches upon the situation of the magnetic poles of the earth." Again, "We have hitherto supposed that the limits of the electro-magnetic belt were, throughout, equally distant from the poles of the earth: but there is reason to suppose that the electro-magnetic effect of the sun is but weak in those places which are covered with ice and snow during a great part of the year. It is, then, very likely that the electro-magnetic belt is very needle parallel with the isothermal line of 0°. The form of the electro-magnetic belt determines also the form of the curve in which the greatest intensity of magnetism occurs round the poles of the globe. But the points of this line which are nearest to us, would act most strongly upon our magnetic needles, and would appear as magnetic poles." M. Oersted acknowledges "that he cannot always support his conclusions on evident principles; but he cites, as a confirmation, that the two magnetic poles, indicated by M. Hansteen in the northern hemisphere, are under the same meridian as the celebrated Humboldt places the greatest concavity, that is, the greatest polar distance from his isothermal line of 0°." He " remembers hearing M. Hansteen remark, several years since, that the magnetic poles are distinguished by extreme cold: that is, the northern magnetic poles; for as to the southern, we are in possession of too small a collection of facts to fix the isothermal line." We confess ourselves to be totally ignorant of the data from whence M. Hansteen deduced the existence of two magnetic poles in the northern hemisphere; and wish M. Oersted had enlarged on that point. He considers the " annual and daily variations of the magnetic needle as intimately connected with the relation of the earth to the sun; but not depending on any variation in the intensity of the magnetism of the interior of the earth, by the electro-magnetism which the sun produces; for these variations do not occur upon different parts of our globe, at the same time, in such manner as they must do, if the variation depended upon the increase or decrease of the magnetic powers of the poles. But he thinks it more probable that the electro-magnetic state of the surface of the earth determines these changes." M. Oersted says he has " framed and examined many hypotheses as to the cause of the variations of the needle, without satisfying himself. The different direction which the electro-magnetic belt receives by the united action of the annual and diurnal motions of the earth; the yearly and daily variations which occur in the figure of the electro-magnetic belt; the discharges which may occur when the electro-magnetic effect is at its maximum; the inequalities which may be produced by the different effects of the sun upon the land and the sea;" are considerations that have not yet given him sufficient agreement with the phenomena which have been observed in different parts of the earth; the frequent and unforeseen variations of the magnetic needle seeming to depend on electro-magnetic discharges, of which we have not at present any experimental knowledge. Among such electrical discharges, he particularly reckons polar light, or aurora borealis. He thinks, too, such discharges may occur in certain clouds. Tempests having a well known influence on the magnetic needle, may be accounted for by our now knowing that electrical discharges produce magnetism. Perhaps, too, he adds, electro-magnetic discharges may occur in the air. He suggests that the magnetic needle should form part of a meteorological apparatus: and, touching on some points not immediately worthy of detail, he concludes by informing us as follows:—" In another memoir I shall endeavour to show, that the circular movement of electrical forces in the conductor, which I have admitted as an hypothesis, results from the nature of electrical forces. And I shall also endeavour to give a new explanation to the opinion which I expressed several years since, upon the production of light and heat by the conflict of electrical forces."

Such is the spirit, and partly the substance, of M. Oersted's paper; wherein we perceive some trifling discrepancies of opinion, but no great fund of novelty: still, he is an indefatigable labourer in the cause; and we would not by any means detract from the merit of his former services; nor allay hope of benefit from his future exertions.

Mr. CHRISTIE *on Magnetic Attraction.*
(Continued from p. 162.)

Mr. C. then informs Dr. Brewster that, in the conclusion of his paper, he pointed out the application of his theory to the determination of the deviation of ships' compasses;—and that his computations formed on that theory, agreed to within less than half a degree, with those observed in the variation and dip, as observed in London, during a period of more than two hundred years. Similar computations of the changes for Paris, for the same period, have also given results equally near. We cannot conceive Mr. Christie to be wrong in principle, when he accords so closely with facts, observed during the long period of two centuries. He, now, proposes to apply the same principles to the observations made in different latitudes; and selects those of Mr. Lecount, made at St. Helena, and during the voyage home, on board H. M. S. Conqueror; because they seem to have been very carefully made. Mr. C. makes some passing remarks on the experiments, instituted by Mr. Lecount, on the needle with iron bars, in various positions, and at various angles, at the several dips of 12° S. 23° N. and 61° N. and finds that, when the compass was at the neutral point, the centre of the bar was in the plane of the magnetic equator of the compass; according with Mr. C.'s hypothesis. He then proceeds to consider those experiments on the needle, with iron rings, whereby Mr. Lecount appears to have obtained results still further confirming Mr. C.'s doctrine. These experiments were made in latitude 32° N. longitude 38° W. with an iron ring, 10·2 inches in diameter, and 5·5 inches thick, with the ring vertical. In order to meet Mr. Christie's views, we must suppose this ring to represent the section of a sphere, described about the centre of the needle; and its plane as posited parallel with, or angular to, the equatorial plane of the compass in the several changes to which Mr. Lecount subjected them, relatively; and the centre of the ring, carried in the circumference of the circle; the planes of the circle and ring coinciding.

1st. East and West of magnetic axis.—Rings' plane from vertical to horizontal, southerly, on the south side of magnetic equatorial plane, produced very slight changes; but with an inclination of 45°. top to the northward, the south face attracted all round the north end of the needle; and the north face attracted the south end of the needle all round: edges were nearly neutral.

2d. North East and South West of magnetic axis.—Inclined 55° northward, north side attracted nearly all south; and south side nearly all north: bottom faintly inclined to attract south.

3d. North and South or magnetic axis.—Inclined either way: caused very little alteration.

4th. At North West and South East of magnetic axis.— Inclined 60° East, made east face, nearly all south, west face nearly all north.

5th. West and East of magnetic axis.—Compass placed at bottom of south face, had its south end attracted; but by inclining ring 25° or 30° north, had its north end attracted, and at bottom of north face attracted south, with the ring at all southerly inclinations,—in shifting from N. W. and S. E. to W. and East., west face of ring becomes south.

Mr. Christie then proceeds to apply Mr. Lecount's experiments as confirmatory of his own doctrine, and having done that, considers the aggregate effect of a ship's iron on her compass. He would refer the disturbing forces to a single point, which might be determined experimentally: then as the position of the ship's head changed, this point would revolve round the compass; and its position, with regard to the magnetic equator of the needle, which would depend on the dip, the position of the head, and roll of the ship, would always point out the nature of the deviation; the quantity of which might be accurately computed from the proper data.

The next remarks on Mr. Lecount's recommendation of certain instructions for ascertaining the dip of the needle, which consists of an iron bar that can be adjusted to any angle, with the horizon; and is to be placed in the magnetic meridian. A compass is then to be carried along, parallel to the bar, both above and below it; and the bar adjusted, so that the deviations above the bar, are, for instance, all of the north, and of the needle towards it; and those below, of the south end, throughout the whole length. The inclination of the bar to the horizon, will be the complement of the dip of the same name, as the elevated end of the bar; in the present instance, north. Now (says Mr. C.) when the bar has this position, it will be parallel to the magnetic equator of the needle, and therefore wholly below that equator, in one case;

when consequently the dip end of the needle ought, according to the theory, to deviate towards it; and wholly above in the other; when the contrary end of the needle should deviate. When the compass is at the ends of the bar, this being in the equator, the needle would not be affected. From all these considerations, Mr. C. is satisfied of the coincidence of Mr. Lecount's practice with his own (Mr. C.'s) theory.

The experiments of Oersted and Ampere, are judged by Mr. Christie to sanction his doctrine; and that Ampere's conclusions more especially assimilate. Ampere, in his experiments on the relative actions of the earth, the needle, and the voltaic pile, infers that, electric currents exist in the earth, in planes perpendicular to the axis of the dipping needle; and that the correspondent electrical currents in the horizontal needle, perpendicular to its axis, are guided by these; so that the needle places itself in such a position that the planes of these currents are as nearly parallel as the force of gravity, which acts on the needle, to retain it in a horizontal position, will admit; that is, the axis of the horizontal needle will be in a plane perpendicular to the planes of the electrical current, in the earth. Mr. C. then argues that, if the imaginary needle, or column of magnetic particles, which he has supposed to be influenced by the ball, and to guide the horizontal needle, consist of circular currents perpendicular to its axis; and the ball act principally on these; urging each of them to assume a position parallel to the tangent plane, at the nearest point of the sphere, or perpendicular to the line joining the centres of the sphere and circular current; so that by the joint action of the ball and earth, they assume an intermediate position; then a needle, freely suspended by its centre of gravity, would assume such a position, that the tendencies of the currents perpendicular to its axis, to become parallel to the terrestrial electric currents in the imaginary needle, should be equal on each side of the centre of suspension. And these terrestrial electric currents, towards the imaginary needle, nearest to the ball, being more affected than those at the other end of the suspended needle, would be urged towards the ball; and consequently the terrestrial electric currents would also guide the correcting end of the horizontal needle towards the ball; the respective deviations being estimated precisely in the manner which he had stated in the preceding abstract. He concludes by observing, that the nature of this action of the ball, on all the terrestrial electric currents, would not be inaptly represented by its action on one of them, that which passes through the centre of the needle; or, which is the same thing, on the equator of the dipping needle. And its deviation, arising from this action, or the deviation of its axis, which is equal to it, would represent the deviation of the imaginary needle towards the ball.

Such is Mr. Christie's paper, which we have endeavoured to do full justice to. He appears to have taken a clear view of his subject; and his experimental results coinciding with his calculated, so very nearly, impress a confidence in the soundness of his principles.

Dr. Reade *on Refraction of Light.*
(Continued from p. 154.)

Dr. Reade pursues his subject, (in experiment four,) by declaring that " rays of light instead of converging, in a glass lens, neither do they cross to *form pictures* of objects, as generally believed." He is sanguine enough, he says, to believe that he shall establish these facts, and thereby overturn the present doctrine of optics, in which he predicts as great an eventual revolution as has taken place in chemistry.

He considers that, philosophers, having early observed emergent rays form a cone, and cross each other, hastily inferred that they also converged in the glass medium; and goes on to ridicule their mathematical admeasurements of angular sines, which were totally imaginary, as relative to refraction: with an additional hint that the Newtonian theory may fall like that of Pythagoras. We think this rather an unfortunate simile; because the Pythagorean system of the universe is the established one of this day; nominally the Copernican, it is true: but Pythagoras maintained it more than 500 years before the christian era; besides having left us some incontrovertible mathematical theorems. The other simile of the fall of the Aristotelian Organon, before that of Bacon, is more correct, in fact; but whether applicable as a just prophetic illustration of the downfal of the Newtonian optics, remains to be determined.

Dr. Reade's fourth experiment is this, " Having formed the letter T, on a white sheet of paper, I held the plano-convex lens immediately over it; when it appeared considerably enlarged in all its dimensions: on raising the lens about two inches from the paper, two inverted images appeared nearer to the eye, and floating on the posterior surface; forming a kind of circular appearance, in the centre of which the erect image appeared very much enlarged. At a yet greater distance, the erect image became so diverging, and confused, as to be nearly invisible; and the two inverted images coalesced, and formed into one very distinct, inverted, image; which diminished in size with every increase of distance. It immediately occurred to me that, this union of the inverted images was the focus of the lens; and, consequently, that the rays never cross to form pictures. To prove this, in the most satisfactory manner, we have only to give a circular movement to the lens, held over the letter T, and we find the image will become inverted at the top and bottom; erect when at the sides. I next looked through the lens at a lighted candle. When close to my eye, it appeared magnified; and on slowly withdrawing my eye to about two inches, I perceived two inverted images around the erect one, which formed a brilliant and luminous circle, margined on the outside by bright orange rays, such exactly as we see in the circle of light before the rays are brought to a focus, on a sheet of white paper. On now withdrawing my eye to a yet greater distance, I found this luminous circle, formed by these two inverted images, to diminish or contract; and when coalesced, they formed at about two inches and a half from the eye, a beautiful inverted image of the candle. As the eye was further removed, this image diminished in size. Here were two sets of images, perfectly distinct from one another, and obeying different laws; the erect images magnified, and the inverted images diminished by every increase of distance. I now held the lens opposite the lighted candle, and before a sheet of white paper; at the distance of an inch, I perceived a luminous circle, margined with orange rays, exactly similar to that I saw when looking through the lens at the candle, and formed by the lateral images. On repeating these experiments, (says the Doctor,) any person may be convinced that there is no crossing of rays to form these images, as in fact the inverted image is distinctly seen before the apex of the cone is formed."

In commencing to remark on the above, we must affirm, that although we have followed the Doctor in the above experiments, as nearly as we could, yet we have not had the good fortune to see the inverted images, forming at the circumference of the lens. Whether there be any peculiar facility with lenses of certain foci, and diameters, for such experimental research, we cannot well take upon ourselves to determine; and to what cause the difference of this gentleman's results from our own may be attributed, we are equally at a loss to say; but we do very respectfully assure him, and our readers, that we have been desirous to follow him through his experimental stages, as perfectly as our implements and time would permit. Nor should we have been alarmed for our long cherished Newtonian opinions, even if these fairy spectres had appeared. But to cut the matter short, we will grant the Doctor's positions. He says, at the commencement of the fourth experiment, that on raising the lens from the letter T, the object not only appeared enlarged, but two lateral inverted images were visible at the circumference of the lens, nearer to the eye, and floating on the posterior surface, forming a kind of circular appearance, in the centre of which the erect image appeared very much enlarged. Unhappily, the Doctor is silent as to the focal distance, and diameter of his lens. Ours is about $1\frac{1}{4}$ inch diameter, and about 5 inches focal power. Now, respecting the inverted images, we judge that there are two ways of accounting for them: one is, that as the lens be withdrawn, pencils of rays from the object impinge farther on the lateral convexity, that is, nearer the circumference of the lens; which rays partly reflected would form these images to the eye, situate on the back side of the lens; but of course diminished. Other part of the rays of the same pencil, pass through the lens; and by their being refracted at a shorter angle, form foci, and cross much nearer the lens; consequently, more diverging than the pencil passing through the lens nearer the centre, and therefore under a less angular appearance to the eye, when far from the focal point. Another solution is, that the focal image of the object formed by the rays, when passed through the lens, is reflected from that surface of the lens which is towards the eye; and which reflected objects must be visible, or invisible, as the focal image shall be nearer or more distant from the object. The inversion of the object, when the relative distances of it, and the eye, are increased, is, we presume, too well understood to need a comment.

Next, and fifth, is Dr. R.'s Experimentum Crucis. "Having held a glass globe filled with water, opposite a lighted candle, we shall find a well defined erect image, formed. On placing the plano-convex lens immediately over it, the erect image becomes considerably magnified, and the inverted images are seen forming a luminous circle around; and as the lens is distanced, they contract or coalesce into one inverted image, forming the focus. This may be esteemed an Experimentum Crucis." He then proceeds, by a figure, leaving out the globe, to illustrate even his Experimentum Crucis. We really cannot perceive any special force of argument to be derived from the use of the globe in the fifth experiment, or Experimentum Crucis; and we presume, that as the Doctor omits it in the illustration, he thinks with ourselves. He places a plano-convex lens between a candle and the eye; and says, that a small erect image formed on the convex side of the lens, by reflection, transmits the rays to form the magnified image, seen by the eye, on the plane side of the lens. We argue that it is not the image formed by *reflection* that causes the magnified image between the eye and the glass,—for the image formed by *reflected* rays on the convex side, is absolutely null; nay, more, in so far as it diminishes the body of light that might pass through the lens, is inimical to the formation of a focal image at all. The Doctor, we presume, errs in toto, in supposing this small reflected image to be the image which is magnified by the lens. In short, it is absolutely a negative quantity, if we may so express it. The plain fact is, that, as we said before, part of the pencil flowing from the object, impinging on the convex surface, is reflected; and is so much positive loss of light; the remainder passes through the lens refracted, as universally understood; and the magnified image there, is but the refracted pencil flowing from the object itself. As to the small marginal images, which we have not been so fortunate as to see, we judge that they are resolvable as before mentioned. We shall anxiously look forward for Dr. Reade's further labours, which we shall, with every respectful feeling towards himself, take the liberty to freely analyze.

On a new Salifiable Base. By Dr. G. BRUNATELLI.
Giornale de Fisica, t. iii. p. 444.

The researches of chemists are daily demonstrating to us how various and complicated are the constituents of bodies. When the older schools of chemistry had but the four imaginary elements to study, they had less to load the memory with than we in our time, who are adding to forms, and discovering essences, though not quite so occult as those of our forefathers.

The new substance is produced by the action of liquid acids on uric acid. Those that have been used are the sulphuric, nitric, muriatic, and acetic; and the uric acid may be either that of calculi, or of birds or snakes. It is formed by adding concentrated sulphuric acid, for instance, in small quantities at a time, to uric acid, until a thick paste is formed: it will occasion swelling, the liberation of gas, and a particular odour. When these signs have ceased, add water; the mass will become very white; and, on standing, will separate into two parts. The solid portion is a neutral combination of the new base with sulphuric acid. The fluid is a portion of this compound dissolved in the excess of acid, and containing impurities. The sulphate is but little soluble in water; but the solution, decomposed by alkaline subcarbonates, yields a white, light, flocculent substance, which is the base in question. Muriatic is, perhaps, better than the sulphuric, for the preparation of this substance; inasmuch as the muriate is more soluble. Acetic acid requires boiling to form it, and nitric acid produces it, among other products, at the time of its violent action.

The flocculent matter collected on a filter, appears like gelatine; in drying it contracts and splits, and when pulverized has the appearance of an earth. It has no taste or smell. It is slightly soluble in water, alcohol, acids, and alkalies. The impure acid solution is eminently distinguished by its property of giving a very fine azure precipitate with triple prussiate of potassa, and which may readily be distinguished, after a few experiments, from that caused by iron. It may, perhaps, be applicable to dyeing or painting. The neutral combination of the substance with acids does not give the blue precipitate; it requires, for this purpose, excess of acids.

This substance combines with various simple bodies. With iodine it forms a compound at common temperatures, of a dull yellow colour, resolved by heat into its own principles. When fused with a sulphur, they unite together. Its compound with phosphorus is of a fine red colour, and when dissolved in water, occasions the formation of phosphuretted hydrogen, and a phosphate.

This substance has extraordinary powers of resisting heat. It might be taken for an earth or metallic oxide, in this respect. The following are given as experimental demonstrations of its properties. An acid solution, put on a plate of zinc, gave a yellow spot, with metallic splendour. This well washed, dissolved in an acid, and tested by triple prussiate of potassa, gave a blue white precipitate; the blue colour being attributed to the new substance. The solution that had acted on the zinc gave no blue colour with the test, but only a white.

A portion of it mixed with lamp black and oil, and heated violently in a crucible for half an hour, left a reddish crust, the solution of which, in acids, gave an azure precipitate with the triple prussiate.

The azure matter burnt in the fire with facility, and left a residuum of a bright red colour, if the heat had been intense, but if moderate, and continued, the residuum is scarcely red, and when placed in water produces flocculi of the substance, and bubbles of the gas.

Ammonia dissolves the substance, making it first yellow, then green. When heated moderately, a residuum is obtained of a yellow metallic colour. If more heated, it becomes white, and does not seem to differ from the substance first dissolved. The yellow matter dissolved in dilute acid gives a red tint to ferro-prussiate of potassa, which exposed to the air becomes green. Other changes take place.

Nitric acid appears to alter the nature of the new substance. When it is added in a concentrated state to the substance or its salt, the prussiate does not then produce a blue precipitate, but a yellow tinge. Sulphuric acid, when assisted by heat, offers similar phenomena.

The blue precipitates thrown down, certainly might generate a suspicion that iron were present and combined with the triple prussiate; but we should not too hastily infer, as though only one specific combination could produce a particular colour.

On Pulverized Manure, and its application to general Agricultural Purposes.

Agriculture being the basis of all national wealth and power, we cannot pass unnoticed any principle or practice, that may influence its prosperity; and under this feeling we present some remarks on the subject of pulverized manure, as appearing in the last Farmer's Journal.

The great loss that has been hitherto sustained by the common farmer, from the drainage of his fold and dunghill yards, has been often referred to in speeches and books; but still nothing has been done in the way of economical improvement; with perhaps a few exceptions among experimental agriculturists, whose deep purses have enabled them to accomplish any practicable object. Not so with the general tiller of the soil; whose condition, we all know, has for some time past been so wretched, and almost hopeless, that he has not had either the spirit, or the power, to avail himself of those little means that might afford a beneficial aid to his industry. As to the subject of pulverized manure, it may be considered intrinsically similar to that of saving the drainage in pits or tanks, wherein is imbedded the common dunghill of the farm yard; but in our judgment, the former has its advantages over the latter; and, as we go on, we shall make this appear. What is proposed by the writer in the Farmer's Journal is, to dry and powder soil, ashes, chalk, &c., as may be most conveniently had, separate or combined. During the winter, the drainage should be collected from every possible source, affording animal matter, and, indeed, at all times; but this of course will be the most productive period, on account of the cattle being more housed. A pit, or tank, is recommended to be sunk, at some low spot, in, or as near as possible to, the yard. This pit should be well bricked, or cased, so as to prevent the fluid filtering away. Having constructed it, all the drainage from the stable, cowhouse, piggeries, &c. should be led into it; and all soap suds, blood, animal offal, domestic urine; and, indeed, all the animalized matter that can be procured, must be added. About the early part of May, the sifted soil, sand, or ashes, before directed, should be well saturated with some of this liquor, by mixing some of the latter along with the former. Then form the mass up into conical heaps, which may shortly be broken down again, dried a little, and sifted, previous to its being mingled with the seed, and sown together with a drill. The whole of this process ought to be conducted under a shed; or rain may wash all the fertilizing matter from the soil, with which it had been mixed.

It is also recommended to add green vegetable refuse; but we think this would much deteriorate the quality and strength of the fluid; besides it would certainly have a tendency to promote fermentation, which the writer appears anxious to prevent. It is observed that, although drilling must be the most commodious method of applying the compost; yet, they who use the ribbing machine may sow it broadcast before the wheat. This subject being novel to the general farmer, he must have to learn the proper quantity for use by experience. We cannot overlook one obvious convenience of this plan, and that is, the mingling of manuring principle with any kind of soil dressing which may be required; as sand, chalk, ashes, &c. for clay loam; thus improving the texture of the land at the same time that the fertilizing principle is imparted. There is both good practical sense, and sound philosophy, combined in such a system. We scarcely need enforce the propriety of preventing the access of rain, or the draining of spouts, to the contents of the tank; because the liquor would be diluted, weakened, and wasted by overflow. The covering ought to be sufficient to protect it from frost. As a simpler method of constructing the tank, we would recommend a pit to be dug, of the necessary depth and width; and to be lined with well tempered clay, a small quantity of chalk, and a very little quicklime, mixed together; and, if convenient, burned: if not so, to be applied raw, with a spade, and the surface covered over with a thin coating of slacked, and finely sifted, lime. But be the pit constructed how it may, it should be kept well covered, to prevent evaporation on the one hand, or access of rain on the other; as well as to guard against accidents. Perhaps, too, there may be another and still more important reason, with some apprehensive persons, for excluding its open contact with the air; we mean that, in hot summers, the exhalations from it *might* be thought extremely pernicious. We would not lay a very great stress on this point; witnessing, as we do, the animalized matter of privies perpetually exhaling vapours, especially when the weather be hot, without inflicting any other evil than that of annoying our sense of smell. We consider the mixing of soil with the manuring fluid, as far better than the watering of the land with it in its simple state; because it will be more tenaciously retained in, and combined with, the surface soil of the land: and less likely to drain, or be washed, downwards by early showers. It is to be observed, too, that the plan here proposed, does not deteriorate from the due application of the common dung manure: it merely saves that (and the best part too) which if not absolutely lost by drainage, through the bed of the dunghill, would be much injured by union with vegetable matter; whereby both would be rendered the less productive, as having, by their mutual action, undergone a partial decomposition, that ought to take place only in contact with the soil to be fertilized. Perhaps it may prove a superior advantage to mingle the seed with the pulverized manure, and deposit them together on the land, in direct contact, as this mode enjoins; especially as relates to early vegetation. We have adopted the term " pulverized manure," from the projector of the proposed method, not because we overlook, or are ignorant of its being a misnomer; but because we considered it but due to the proposer to remark on it, under the appellation that he has thought proper to adopt.

On the Geographical Distribution of Insects. By M. LATREILLE. Abridged. Edinburgh Philosophical Journal.

However deserving of the naturalist's attention this subject may be, it has, until lately, been but obscurely and incidentally noticed. It is not, however, the mere curiosity that such a matter might be reasonably expected to call forth; but the real utility of it, in a practical view, that should stamp the study with a value; for, by teaching us where we may expect to meet with a particular class of animated nature, we are, in some degree, taught its habitudes of life, and means of subsistence. On the other hand, knowing those habitudes, we infer its geographical residence.

Of all the qualifying influences, temperature is, probably, the most decided; for though in countries varying greatly in this respect, as to general condition, there will be found local resemblances, rather confirming, than excepting against, the proposition. Thus similar temperature of the elevated regions of the Alps and Andes, may afford similar descriptions of insect character as some of those found on the borders of the frigid zone—each grade of elevation affording some peculiarity common to it alone. The climate governing the produce of the soil; or the rocky formations of the earthy character, bearing some kind of analogy; will form the refuge, the limit, or the restraint of particular modes of insect life. Indeed temperature and quality of soil must form the law of nature with a large portion of animated creation, whose instincts and susceptibilities of existence or action, are calculated only for local means of gratification. Thus insects, especially with articulated feet, abound where there is the most luxuriant vegetation to be met with—such as strong soil, with warmth and moisture. These requisites, of course, are not attainable in the higher latitudes; and there, these insects can never be known. The existence of the insect is necessarily the more localized by its inability to wander far from the spot of its origin. It cannot, like the migratory classes of birds, remove from climate to climate, as its appetites might suggest; nor has it the necessity; for where it comes into existence, Providence kindly spreads a banquet of enjoyment during life; but adapted to its wants and preservation. Herein the insect and the vegetable bear close analogy. In the warmer climates, the insects are numerous, and various; but approaching the high latitudes, they become scarcer, until they totally disappear. Otho Fabricius, in his Fauna of Greenland, mentions only 468 species of animals; and the number of insects included in that class, after the manner of Linnæus; both the crustaceous animals and the arachnides, amount to but 110.

The *prionus depsarius*, supposed to be confined to Sweden, has been found in the mountains of Switzerland. M. Latreille has taken at Cantal, the *lycus minutus*, presumed to belong exclusively to the north of Europe. The *Apollo butterfly*, so beautiful at Upsal, in Sweden, is found in France, only at an elevation of 600 or 700 toises above the level of the sea. Again, the *carabus auratus, acridium grossum*, and many species of the butterfly, viper, &c. existing on the plains near Paris, require a more elevated level in the South of France. In the *Philosophia Entomologica* of Fabricius, climate has rather a geographical than a thermometrical meaning. Indeed, as relates to the insect habitude, many points are necessary to be considered as influencing temperature or moisture; but to terminate all in one expression, we would say that, similar conditions of locality will generally yield similar forms of insect life. M. Latreille proceeds to consider the *genera* of arachnides and of insects peculiar to determinate spaces on the surface of the earth. M. L. reproaches travelling naturalists for inattention to qualities of soil, which he holds to be essential, as indicative of insect character. The *genus licinus*, the *papilio cleopatra*, many of the genus *dasytes (dermestes, Lin.)* some species of *lamia*, &c. are found on calcareous soils only. The *pimelia bipunctuata*, common about Marseilles, scarcely extends to the sea coast. Syria, Barbary, and Egypt, present other species of the same genus; but always on a saline soil, or abounding with salsola. The borders of the Mediterranean, Black and Caspian seas, present the creeping insects; and are, also, the principal seats of the second section of Coleoptera, (the *heteromeres,*) and the genera *lixus, brachyoerus, buprestis,*) the conical formed species,) &c. The distant Cape of Good Hope affords similar description of insect tribe. The aquatic insects of resembling quality, also, show the same resemblances in local residence. M. L. now proceeds to show, as the result of his study in the first Museums of Paris; from perusal of eminent naturalists; his own researches; and extensive correspondence; that—

1st. A great proportion of the arachnides and insects which may be widely dispersed, on similar soil, and under similar temperature, even under the same parallel, is usually of different species; as the arachnides of China, differ from those of parts of Africa, where the soil, latitude, and temperature of the latter, may resemble those of the former.

2d. Specific differences among the arachnides will be observed, as seas, or other natural barriers, intervene; thus, the insects, &c. of America, and New Holland, vary from similar classes of the ancient continent. Those of New Granada, and Peru, differ from those of Guiana; though only separated by the Cordilleras. So the Col de Tende, separates, and designates, those of Piedmont and France. Exceptions may occur with the aquatic insects. Some insects are widely extended; as the *la belle dame*, or painted butterfly, occurring with us, in Sweden, the Cape, and New Holland. The *sphinx du nerion*, and *sphinx celerio*, limited only between France, and the Isle of France. The aquatic *dytiscus friseus* lives in the waters of Piedmont, Provence, and Bengal.

3d. Many *genera* of insects, particularly those which feed

on vegetables, are spread over numerous points in the principal divisions of the globe.

4th. Some are exclusively localized on one or the other of the continents; as the following *genera* are never found on the new. *Anthia, graphypterus, erodius, pimalia, scaurus, cossyphus, mylabris, brachycerus, nemoptera, abeille, (apis of Lat.) anthophora*, and many of the *scarabeides*, &c. While the new continent bears, exclusively, the *agra, galerita, nilio, tetraonyx, rutelia, doryphora, alurnus, erotylus, cupes, corydalis, labidus, pelecinus, centris, euglossa, heliconius, erycina, castina*, &c.; and our bees are, there, replaced by the genera *milipona*, and *trigona*. The genera *manticora, grapluptera, pneumora, masaris*, &c., are peculiar to Africa: the first, and third, confined to the Cape. The *colliuris* in the East Indies. The *lamprima, heleus, paropsis*, and *panops* in New Holland, and its islands.

5th. Many species are governed by locality and altitude; as certain Alpine butterflies, near the regions of perpetual snow. So, in lower elevations, or low grounds, the distributions are preserved, as northerly or southerly; or as temperature may qualify. Thus, too, the northern departments of the Seine, assimilate more in insect character with the colder climate of Germany; and on the warm sandy soils, south of Paris, are found species similar to those of a lower latitude.

6th. Dividing the old and new continents into zones, measured by circles parallel to the equator, it will be found that the respective portions obtain qualifying, or distinct, insect characters. In Swedish Lapland, the insect species differ from those of south Sweden; the latter bearing an affinity with those of Germany: and France, above the latitude of 44° and 45°, affords some resemblances to them. In the southern course of the Seine, where the vine begins to flourish naturally, the species of warmer countries present. As the *ateuchus flagellatus*, the *mylabris chichorii*, the *mantis religiosa*, the *ascalaphus italicus*, &c.; and more especially at Fontainbleau, and about Orleans, where we have *phasma rossii, mantis pagana*, and *sphinx celeris*, &c. Then succeed *cicada, mantis, zonitis, akis, scaurus, termes*, &c.; and particularly *scorpio europæus*, and *ateucus sacer*. The cultivated olive, the spontaneous strawberry, pomegranate, and lavender, mark more distinctly gradations of temperature which will influence the insect species. Advancing to the Mediterranean, species of *mygale, onitis, cebrio, brentus,* and *scarites* first present. Entering eastern Spain, the orange and palm denoting still more warmth; we have the *erodius, sepidium, zygia, nemoptera, galeodes,* and many insects analogous with those of the Levant and Barbary. On the southern shores of Africa to the line of Atlas, we gradually approximate with the Tropics through *anthia, graphipterus, siagona,* &c.

We have but an imperfect knowledge of the insects of the south-east of Europe. The *papilio crysippus* (Lin.) common in Egypt, and the East Indies, begins to appear in the kingdom of Naples.

(To be continued.)

On Water Cements, Mortar, and Lime.

(Continued from p. 112.)

Having the continuation of M. Vicat's paper now before us, we resume our remarks, conformably with our promises given in the fourth number. M. V. proceeds by observing, that lime is an essential ingredient in all hydraulic mortars, or cements for masonry, immersed in water; the lime to be mixed with sand and puozzolana, or the latter singly. The name of puozzolana is applied by M. V. not only to the direct volcanic products of Italy and France; but, also, to any analogous composition, that by being subjected to combination, affords a subaqueous cement. Whether the compounds be formed by nature or art, he considers their aggregate proportions of compositions, to be about 38 silex, 41 of alumine, 6 of lime, and 15 of oxyd of iron. In some, the silex predominates; and it is not uncommon to meet with magnesia and manganese. He infers that all ferruginous clays, ochres, bluish schists, basaltes, lavas, ferruginous sand-stones, &c. may be converted into puozzolana, by calcination; and, therefore, that hydraulic mortars are only combinations of metallic oxyds. We do not understand how this is to be justly infered; for we are not authorized in believing that any other oxyd than that of iron be present or necessary, in the cementing compounds. M. Vicat proposes to limit his remarks to such only of these compositions, as are likely to be in use; and even within these, he thinks there is a very wide field of inquiry.

The puozzolanas, experimented on by M. V., were powdered, sifted, and well beaten into a firm and ductile paste, with lime, of the same consistence as the hydrates notified in a former section. He hesitated as to the best mode of applying the compound. He objected to adopt Mr. Smeaton's method of making the mass up into balls, and partially drying them; because it would not be applied in such a state of consistence, as to the actual masonry; nor does he consider the objections made by M. Sage, as to the sinking of water cement contained in cases, being liable to partial setting, before it comes into contact with the masonry, as well founded: but, even if so, they may be obviated by permitting the cementing fluid to flow through holes in the bottom of the case. We really do not think that M. Sage's objection is here fully set aside. M. V. makes a passing remark that, the extractive matter in new wood prevents the hardening of the cement on its surface. This smells a little too much of theory; for does not old wood also contain extractive matter? M. Vicat says, that although experiments, made on a small scale, have been objected against; as probably yielding but a deceptive result; yet he has always found the trials, on a large scale, to correspond in effect with those on a smaller: indeed, he considers accuracy of more importance than mass. Not any unobjectionable method has yet been adopted to determine the relative hardness of specimens. Some subject the indurated substance to the hammer; some to the wedge; but he holds both to be delusive. His experiments have a two-fold view; that of ascertaining the relative periods, and degrees, of induration. For the former purpose he noted the number of days elapsing before the surface would bear a square steel rod, with a weight at its summit, without impressing a mark. For the latter, by the comparative depth to which a perforation penetrated, when forced by a constant and regular percussion.

M. Vicat urges that, in common buildings the water cements are subjected to dead pressure only; but, that in his experiments the compound undergoes the severer test of pressure by percussion. He found that the squares of percussive pressure were reciprocally proportioned to the resistances of dead weight. Some small differences exist between actual result and calculation; but not more than is common to experiments of such a nature.

Comparison of the Resistances of different Compounds, expressed by the action of a dead Weight, and the force of an uniform Percussion.

Substances employed, each being a quadrangular prism, 0·04 met. in base, by 0·25 m. in height.	Weight required to break it, being suspended at the extremity; the distance of the axis of rupture being 0·03 from the point of suspension.	Depth to which the steel point penetrates, by a given percussion.
	Kil. Hect.	
1. Plaster, a year old	61 · 20	0·00575
2. Fine, prepared, ochreous earth, a year old	17 · 00	0·01060
3. Unburnt brick, two years old	16 · 65	0·01150
4. Brick, once burnt	54 · 36	0·00500
5. Lime of Souillac, a year old	22 · 26	0·00700
6. Lime of Calviac	16 · 13	0·01100
7. Mortar of hydraulic lime, and granite sand, a year old	32 · 00	0·00760
8. Another specimen of the same, 21 months old	47 · 00	0·00550
9. Mortar of common lime, and granitic sand, 21 months old	16 · 34	0·00870

On the Effect which the degrees of Calcination of Puozzolana produce on the Resistance of the Water Cements.

M. Vicat, after remarking that this point has never been examined accurately: goes on to say, that the general rule has been to use well *burnt earth*, in the composition of water cements; but this is manifestly too vague to build a criterion upon. Brick, says he, is said to be burned, when the fire has brought out the proper red, or brown colour: when it is sonorous, and does not fall to pieces in water, like clay. Now, we cannot admit the mere colour to be a means of judging by; for that must be governed by the quantity, and quality of the iron oxyd. Next, when burned again, the colour is deeper; the mass harder; less water is absorbed; and it better resists the action of atmospheric influence. Lastly, it is overburned, or calcined, when it is semi-vitrified; the colour iron-grey; the fracture vitreous; does not adhere to the tongue; and scratches glass. We again reject colour as a test; for we have seen the brick a full and deep red, although vitrified.

Pit coal, strongly heated, forms hard, heavy, cellular scoriæ; but if moderately heated, yields black, light, carbonaceous masses; and reddish ashes.

Blue schist, when heated to redness, and kept so for several hours, becomes yellowish brown; if the heat have been urged to whiteness, the lamellæ swell, and fall into light, friable, porous masses, of a pale green colour.

Basalt is but little altered by long continued red heat; but on augmenting the heat, the matter melts.

Ferruginous sand is similarly affected.

These substances have been considered as constituents of water cements, in the different degrees of calcination, when combined with common limes; not with eminently hydraulic, in themselves. The general results are—

1st. That the first degree of calcination is most proper for clay, and ferruginous sandstone; their cementive powers diminishing, as approaching vitrification.

2d. Pit coal reduced to ashes, by a slow fire, are preferable to scoriæ; whether hard, friable, light, or heavy.

3d. That blue schist requires such heat as will swell it.

4th. That basalt should be fused.

It is, particularly, when these substances are combined with a common, and very fat lime, which, of itself, scarcely resists water, that their efficacy, as water cements, is seen to depend on the degree of their calcination.

(To be continued.)

On Supercarbonate of Lime. By Mr. MURRAY.
Philosophical Magazine, No. 283.

Mr. Murray here confirms what we stated from Mr. Dalton, in our first number, as to the acidulous efficacy of these compounds on the usual tests, and shows, as we apprehended, that foreign matter in water may be eventually injurious: Mr. M. says, he had frequently noticed the interesting fact, that Mr. Dalton has adverted to, in the action of waters containing supercarbonate of lime, on vegetable blue colours; but, "devotion to established authority," induced him to attribute the phoenomenon to the presence of *alkaline carbonate*. Mr. M. observed this first in his analysis of the mineral spring adjacent to the Temple of Serapis, near Puzzouli.

"In analyzing some rain water, from a rain gauge, fixed apart from buildings, I detected a minute portion of *lime:* and as I find that tincture of cabbage, exposed to the atmosphere, soon exhibits a film of a *green* colour, I am disposed to attribute the change to the presence of *supercarbonate of lime*.

"I may be permitted to add, that I have invariably found calculous diseases most prevalent in districts where the water contained *sulphate of lime*; and an almost total absence of the disease where the springs exhibit *supercarbonate* of *lime* on analysis. The county of Norfolk is an example of the former, and Holderness an instance of the latter."

Magnetic Chemistry. By Mr. MURRAY.
Philosophical Magazine, No. 283.

Experiment is daily furnishing us with new proofs of the chemical agency of magnetism, especially in the hands of Mr. Murray.

A small bar magnet being allowed to remain immersed in tincture of cabbage for two or three days, completely *destroyed* the blue colour; and the same thing occurred with that of litmus.

The two legs of a horse-shoe magnet, (about 3-4ths of an inch apart) were placed *separately* in small cylinders, each containing solution of nitrate of silver—around one of the poles thus separated, a dark cloud collected, and a few solitary crystals studded the other on the side nearest to that of its adjunct.— Little alteration was exhibited after a lapse of two days. But both poles being placed together in a vessel, with the same metallic solution, soon effected a complete decomposition, which was exhibited by both the poles becoming completely clothed in brilliant metallic silver, while sparkling minute crystals of the same floated through the liquid, which, from being previously colourless, had become *coloured*.

Phosphorus in Ether.
Mr. MURRAY, in Philosophical Mag. No. 283.

"I had thrown a number of chips of phosphorus into ether, in order to form phosphorized ether. After a considerable lapse of time, I found these chips curiously encrusted with transparent acicular crystals, bearing a remarkable resemblance to the incipient germination of the barley-corn in the process of malting. Incidental agitation unfortunately destroyed them."

On Steam Drying Rooms. By Mr. MURRAY.
Philosophical Magazine, No. 283.

We are not disposed to concur with Mr. Murray in the supposition that the high temperature of the iron acts on the atmosphere of the room, if that be what he means; but rather that a partial decomposition of the atmospheric air may take place where it passes through the ignited tubes, or the interior of a stove. Perhaps, too, a certain portion of moisture may be necessary to respiration. Mr. M. remarks that Dr. Ure has stated, in his "Nicholson's Dictionary of Chemistry," that "the people who work in steam drying rooms are healthy; those who were formerly employed in stove-heated apartments, became soon sickly and emaciated. These injurious effects must be ascribed to the action of cast-iron, at a high temperature, on the atmosphere.

"I remarked that among the Appenines, the Italians place a *shallow earthen vessel, supplied with water*, on the head of the stove, the pipe of which traverses the apartment; and on inquiring the reason, have been repeatedly assured, that without it, they should be subject to the head-ache and other ills—while, with this simple precaution, they experience no inconvenience whatever."

We have lately seen an announcement of a patent obtained by Mr. Perkins, for an apparatus adapted to this very object, and we cannot but wish it success; for the warming of apartments by heated air has such recommendation on the ground of economy; and the comfort of excluding cold currents of air from our persons in the changeable temperature of our season, are objects most desirable of attainment. There is, however, a very simple means of obviating these cold currents, which we wonder has not been generally adopted; and that is, to carry a tube, or air-way, from the outside of the house, or from the passage, under the floor of the room to the hearth, before the fire; which would constantly supply the fuel with its pabulum; and prevent the rush of air from doors and crevices to fill up the vacuum (as it is falsely termed) caused by the rarefaction of the fire.

Gas from Cocoa Nut Oil.

London Journal of Arts, No. 11.

A large quantity of this oil has been lately imported into this country. It has rather a pleasant smell, and is about the consistence of butter. Messrs. Taylor and Martineau have lately used it for the production of gas, which gives an extremely brilliant, and white light, by combustion. It is said that it may be employed economically for this purpose, and on account of its solid form, and pleasant smell, it is very preferable to the oil commonly used, especially in private houses.

Giant Lizard, or Dragon.

The bones of an animal have been found imbedded in rocks near Maestricht and Ricenza, which it is said have hitherto puzzled Cuvier and other eminent naturalists, but have been determined by Sommering to belong to a species of lizard. It is now unknown; but he conjectures that it is the Dragon of antiquity, so universally (though if he be right) falsely reputed fabulous. This enormous lizard is twenty-three feet in length.

On two Antique Canoes found in Ireland.
Annals of Philosophy, No. 12.

The following account affords us not the least satisfaction, further than the bare fact. We are not told whether the canoes were sunk beneath the surface of the soil, or were at all petrified; nor how far they were from the sea shore. We dare not trifle with Irish honour, so far as to hint at these canoes having brought over from the South Sea the stock from whence the Irish race has been derived:—

"Two oak canoes, of great antiquity, have lately been discovered in Loughisland Ravey, near Castlewellan, Ireland. They were each 21 feet in length, and excavated from the tree; the whole of the wood being perfectly sound, and in a high state of preservation. It appears they were intended, when lashed together, to form a double boat, such as is now employed in the South Seas, the right side of the one, and the left side of the other being convex in form, while the two opposite sides were perfectly strait, so that they could very readily be joined together. Unfortunately the finders of these primeval relics in a few hours destroyed what the lapse of ages had failed to effect."

Statuary Marble.
Journal of Science and Literature, No. 23.

Some remarkably fine statuary and other marble quarries have lately been discovered at Seravazza, in Tuscany, much superior to any thing of the kind at Coanara, which threaten to rival and lower the pride of the latter mentioned place. His Royal Highness the Grand Duke of Tuscany gives great encouragement, and protection, both to commerce and the fine arts within his dominions.

Lithography.

Annals of Philosophy, No. 11.

An experiment has lately been made to take off impressions from the leaves of plants by lithographic printing. It appears to have been attempted by merely pressing the leaves against the stone. This process does not, however, appear the most advisable, the better way being to cover the plant with the prepared ink, and after bringing a sheet of clean paper in contact with its entire surface, transfer the impression thus procured to the lithographic stone. We notice this from the great advantage which botanists are likely to derive from this simple mode of preserving and multiplying impressions from rare plants, which otherwise would only be seen in the cabinets of a few collectors.

Fish Flour.

"The Indians in all the Upper Oroonoko, fry fish, dry them in the sun, and reduce them into powder, without separating the bones. I have seen masses of fifty or sixty pounds of this flour, which resembles that of cassava. When it is wanted for eating, it is mixed with water and reduced to a paste. In every climate the abundance of fish has led to the invention of the same means of preserving them. Pliny, and Diodorus Siculus have described the fish bread of the Ichthyopagous nations that dwelt on the Persian Gulf, and the shores of the red sea."—*Humboldt.*

Fig Trees.

Phillips' Pomarium Britannicum.

At Tarring, near Worthing, there is an orchard of fig trees, where the fruit grows on standard trees, and ripens as well as in any part of Spain. The trees are so regularly pro ductive as to form the principal support of a large family. Although the orchard does not exceed three quarters of an acre, it contains upwards of 100 trees, from which the proprietors gather about 100 dozen per day during the season, estimating each tree to produce about 20 dozen.

On the Cultivation of Onions. By Mr. MACDONALD.
Communicated to the Caledonian Horticultural Society.

Mr. Macdonald, gardener to the Duke of Buccleugh, has communicated to the Society the following process for cultivating this vegetable. As soon as the produce of the seed-beds attain the proper size, choose a moist clay, take up the plants, and after immersing them in a puddle, composed of one part soot, and three parts of the earth, transplant them (by drilling), about four inches asunder, in rows, and afterwards carefully hoe them when required. This process answers with any kind of onion, makes it heavier, firmer, and more pungent.

Qu. As soot yields ammonia, or carbonate of ammonia, by sublimation; and as the onion sends forth a strong acrid vapour; may not the chemical affinities of the soot manure form this matter, so essential to the good quality of the vegetable?

Life Preserver.
Annals of Philosophy, No. 11.

An experiment for saving lives from shipwreck, on Mr. Tregrouse's principle, which promises to be of great utility, has been tried with success in Yarmouth Roads, by Rear-Admiral Spranger. It consists in throwing, by a rocket, a line from the ship to the shore, and when the communication is established, binding to that a deep sea line, or any of the running rigging. When these reach the shore, a larger rope, sufficiently strong to bear four men in a chair, is conveyed to the vessel, and the chair pulled on shore by means of a small rope, from whence it returns empty to the ship for a fresh cargo. On one occasion, the chair was on shore in five minutes after the firing of the rocket.

Racing Pedometer.

Annals of Philosophy, No. 11.

An instrument has lately been invented in France, which precisely marks the time that not only the winning, but every other horse takes in running the course, even if there should be thirty of them, and the interval between each only a quarter of a second. The "Jury of the Races," in the arondissements of Paris, have expressed their full approbation of the instrument.

Musical Permutation.

Annals of Philosophy, No. 12.

A very curious invention has been made in the art of musical composition. It consists in the use of prepared cards, on each of which a bar of an air is arranged according to a certain rhythm and key. Four packs of these cards, marked A, B, C, and D, are mingled together, and as the cards are drawn and arranged before a performer in the order of that series, it will be found that an original air is obtained. The cards hitherto made are as waltzes, and succeed perfectly.

Magnetism. Philosophical Mag. No. 284.

The Prussian State Gazette mentions a highly important discovery which Dr. Seebeck had communicated to the Academy of Sciences, at Berlin, in the different sittings. It was on the magnetic properties inherent in all metals and many earths, (and not in iron only, as was supposed, according to the difference of the degrees of heat. This discovery, it is added, opens an entirely new field in this department of natural philosophy, which may lead to interesting results with respect to hot springs, connected with the observations made by the Inspector of the Mines (M. Von Trebra) and others, relative to the progressive increase of warmth in mines in proportion to their depths. According to M. Von Trebra's observations, the heat at the depth of 150 feet below the surface of the earth is one degree; at 300 feet, two degrees; at 600 feet, four degrees, &c. Our readers need not be informed that Dr. S. has been anticipated as to the metallic magnetism.

THE FOCUS

OF

PHILOSOPHY, SCIENCE, AND ART.

No. VII.] SATURDAY, JANUARY 12, 1822. [Vol. I.

M. VICAT on *Water Cements, Mortar, and Lime.*
(Continued from p. 210.)

WE resume M. V.'s observations on this practical subject, by stating that, the comparative powers of resistance in water cements, composed with very fat lime, and the before mentioned puozzolanas, variously calcined, are expressed by him to thus result from experiment.

Water Cements, a year old, composed of the same lime, and ferruginous clay, in the first state of calcination, give a resistance equal to	1·00
Ditto, twice calcined, or as biscuit	0·30
Ditto, semivitrified	0·17
Coal Ashes	1·00
Ditto, hard, and heavy	0·62
Ditto, light, and friable	0·10
Basalt, heated to fusion	1·00
Ditto, heated only to redness	0·16
Schist, heated to swelling	1·00
Ditto, in the lowest degree of calcination	0·12
Ferruginous Schist, in the lowest degree of calcination	1·00
Ditto, fused	0·48

These numerical resistances are not to be compared as one species with another; but only as components of each set; because the elementary proportions of each species are variable, some schists being superior, others inferior, to clays. Choice of material is of importance; for different bricks, belonging to the same clamp, for instance, will undergo different degrees of calcination.

On the effect of different proportions of Lime, relatively to the other materials in the composition of Water Cements.

Suppose experience to have shown that, to form an equally fluid water cement with the same puozzolana, very different quantities of fat common, and lean hydraulic, limes would be requisite; again, the same lime would require varied proportions of puozzolana, according to the character of the latter; therefore, it would be infinitely complex to lay down specific rules for all possible combinary proportions. Some experimental results here follow, in correction of the errors under old authorities.

Suppose 100 measures of sand, and the same quantity of brick cement; or 200 of brick cement alone; mixed with lime, in varied proportions, from 270 to 50 (the lime being slacked by immersion, and measured in powder); the resistances of the cements, thus composed, will range between the above limits, with both common and hydraulic limes.

The *maximum* of resistance, in a water cement, made with a very fat lime, containing of sand and brick cement each 100, will correspond to a quantity of lime somewhere between 100 and 50, but nearer to 100. If the whole 200 parts be brick cement, the maximum will lie between 100 and 50, but nearer to 100. So that about 100 of lime is the average proportion to be used with 200 of the other materials, when the lime be of a fat quality. If moderately hydraulic, nearly the same proportions would be best; but as the hydraulic, or setting, property increases, the proportion of lime must be increased.

It has been remarked before that, one volume of powder of lime, obtained by immersion, yields barely 0·60 when reduced to paste; but 0·60 of lime, with 200 of sand, or brick cement, affords a very lean mortar. A less proportion of lime has scarcely any binding quality.

These facts prove, therefore, contrary to the generally received opinion, that, in water cements, it is better to err on the side of deficiency, in lime, than in abundance: so that, within moderate bounds, there is but little to fear from excess.

The following Table will give the results of the actual experiments on the subject:—

Lime slacked by immersion, and powdered.		Granite Sand	Brick Cement.	Days required by the mortars to stiffen so as to support a steel point with a certain weight.	Relative resistance of each mortar expressed in numbers after a year's immersion.
Common and very fat.	Middling and hydraulic				
2·70	....	1·00	1·00	19	100
2·00	....	1·00	1·00	16	510
1·50	....	1·00	1·00	18	570
1·00	....	1·00	1·00	8	1000
0·50	....	1·00	1·00	9	826
2·70	....	....	2·00	8	1000
2·00	....	....	2·00	8	1000
1·50	....	....	2·00	7	2366
1·00	....	....	2·00	6	2777
0·50	....	....	2·00	6	1108
....	2·70	1·00	1·00	17	390
....	2·00	1·00	1·00	16	693
....	1·50	1·00	1·00	12	693
....	1·00	1·00	1·00	8	907
....	0·50	1·00	1·00	12	615
....	2·70	....	2·00	12	1150
....	2·00	....	2·00	12	1200
....	1·50	....	2·00	10	1234
....	1·00	....	2·00	8	1384
....	0·50	....	2·00	10	1234

Here, then, it will be seen, that within very moderate variations, in proportion, and quality, the eventual resistance of the water cement may be governed, in the result, as nearly ten to one. In general, these influences will operate most, where the lime and puozzolana have least energy in action.

On the mutual Influence of the Qualities of the Lime, and the Puozzolana, in Water Cements.

In regulating the best proportions to be used, between the puozzolana and the lime, it should be borne in mind that, the lime may already contain a greater, or less, quantity of the earths, and oxyds, of which the puozzolana is composed. Hence, if all the known limes are arranged in the direct order of their activity, the puozzolana should be put on the opposite column, in an inversed order; thus, for example, the limes which are, of themselves, eminently hydraulic, will be on the same parallel with the most silicious sand; and the common fat limes will join with the most active puozzolanas.

(To be continued.)

M. LATREILLE on *the Geographical Distribution of Insects*.
(Continued from p. 206.)

M. Latreille proceeds by observing that, many particular groups of lepidopterous insects, and other species, will remain long unknown: all successively spreading, gradually, from east to west, and reciprocally. Many found in the south of Britain, are also met with in Normandy, Brittany, the left bank of the Rhine; and contiguous provinces of Germany. Some of the Levant species have travelled westerly to Austria; as the *cantharis, orientalis, mylabris crassicornis*, and a beautiful variety of *melolontha occidentalis*, brought by Olivier. M. L. considers that, the insects of Asia Minor, Syria, Persia, southern Russia, and the Crimea, though nearly allied to those of southern Europe, are yet specifically distinct. So, also, those of the coasts of Coromandel, of Bengal, of southern China, and even Thibet, have many points of resemblance; but yet are specifically distinct from those of Europe, as well as from those of Africa; although they may be classed in the same genera. The species of *graphiptera, akis, scaurus, pimelia, lepidium*, or *erodius*, appear to be confined to the southern and western parts of Europe. The genus *anthia* occurs in Bengal.

The natural families of the insect tribes of Madagascar, bear analogy with those of Africa; but the species are distinct. The Isles of France and Bourbon afford greater similitudes with India.

The entomologic species of New Holland are analogous to those of south-eastern India, and the Moluccas. The European, African, and Asiatic genus of *mylabris*, does not pass the island of Timor. In New Holland is the genus *papalus*, an inhabitant of the new world.

New Zealand, New Caledonia, the circumjacent islands, and probably the southern archipelagos of the great southern ocean, appear to hold some affinity.

The new continent seems to be marked by its peculiarity of species, in the respective latitudes and longitudes. Carolina affords what Pennsylvania, and New York, do not. The lepidoptera of Georgia, hold their principal seat in the Antilles. The banks of the Missouri, for 20° west of Philadelphia, maintain a peculiarity of entomological character. So, also, in Louisiana. The Antilles may be contrasted with the United States. Trinidad, 10° north, yields the equatorial species; such as butterflies of the divisions called *menelaus*, *teucer*, &c.; which are not found in St. Domingo. The Brazils present some affinities with Cayenne; but the former are likewise abundant in their own peculiarities. The southern insects of America, are not to be found above 43° north latitude; but, in Europe, they appear as high as the 49th°; the genera *scorpio*, *cicada*, and *mantis*, being always our guides. Certain genera requiring a dry, warm soil, and atmosphere, exist with us, that could not bear the colder, and irrigated, country of northern America, of similar latitude; such as *anthia*, *pimelia*, *erodius*, *brachicerus*, &c. Also the carnivorous coleoptera, are few in number, and smaller in size on the new continent, than on the old. The equinoctial scorpions, being less than the *occitanus* of southern Europe: and these latter again, far inferior to the African *afer*. But in the tribes living on vegetables, America is rich: especially the lepidopterous order: and in the genera *scarabæus*, *chrysomela*, *cerambyx*, &c. Also, abundant in the wasp and ant tribes; in orthopterous insects and spiders. But inferior to southern China in the *papilio priamus, bombyx atlas*, &c. Europe, Africa, and western Asia, are almost destitute of the genus *phasma*, or spectres; but the Moluccas, and South America afford them, very large and abundantly. The narrow prolonged form of the new world, its immense rivers, and contiguous oceans, contribute to give it a humidity that may explain, in part, the distinct or modified forms of insect life, as differing from those of the old world. M. Latreille proceeds to show that, the distinction of climates given by Fabricius was arbitrary, and injudicious. And, he endeavours to confirm his position, by reference to the localities of the genera *arachnidea*. Greenland has limited the researches of naturalists in entomology. Among its insects, Fabricius did not enumerate more than 81 species of arachnides. They resemble those of Denmark, Sweden, and the lower latitudes of Swedish Lapland. Perhaps at 81° north, we may consider vegetation as terminating; but M. L. will allow 3° higher, or 84°. We have seen that Lapland had its fauna. That the insects of southern Sweden, down, through Germany, to the latitude of Paris, bore some affinity; but below Paris southerly, and exactly where the natural vine begins to appear, the southern insects first present. The locality of the natural olive, at about 45° in France, gave the domain of the southern species. Where the orange and palm flourish, still more southerly species appeared; and in Barbary, where the date grows, the equatorial kinds presented. Lastly, we approach the equator, through the species of Egypt and Senegal. M. Latreille then goes on to make an imaginary division of twelve sections, from the 84th° of latitude north, to the parallel of Sandwich islands, in 60° south. He argues that, a zone equal to one of these sections of latitude, comprizes a marked distinction of insect character: and at the extremes of two contiguous zones, the resemblances shall almost, or totally, cease: always allowing for local peculiarities. As regards longitude too, an influential character may be noticed; but the temperatures, measuring by longitude, being more congenial, will show less distinct variations.

The insects of northern America, as far as Canada, differ from ours; while those of Greenland are in some degree

European. M. Latreille would consider Greenland the entomological meridian for the old world. This makes the Canaries, Cape de Verd islands, and Madeira, of African insect character; leaving the western Azores, and the island of Ascension, to the westward of the Sandwich land. Comparing the insects collected by Olivier in Persia, with those of southern Europe, and northern Africa; and the marked distinction as compared with those of the East Indies; he thinks that the greatest changes occur southerly, towards the frontiers of Persia and India; and northerly, from the eastern side of the Wralian chain, and sea of Azal, a little beyond the meridian, which is under 60°, to the east of Paris. We will take the limit at 62°; a little to the west of Balk, and Candahar, &c. M. Latreille then divides the surface into four great divisions of longitude; taking the meridian of Paris as the principal. Speaking in latitude measure, he would include, under the polar zone of insect character, Greenland, Iceland, and Spitzbergen. The sub-polar, Norway, northern Sweden, and northern European Russia. Next, the superior zone to contain Britain, south Sweden, northern France to the Loire, Prussia, Germany, and southern Russia to the Crimea. The intermediate to comprehend the south of Europe, and western portion of Asia. From northern Africa, to the equator, will include super-tropical, tropical, and equatorial. The western to be divided by a meridian, separating two parts of 48° each; that is, 14° east of Paris, and near Vienna; leaving to the east, southern Italy, European Turkey, and Egypt. Here he goes on to subdivide, and run his doctrine into a detail too troublesome to follow, and in some degree subversive of its first principles.

We may then conclude, for M. Latreille, that he means to show the insect character as being governed by temperature, moisture, quality of soil, herbage, elevation of habitation, &c.: and we think he proves his case the better, in proportion as he generalizes; for as he descends to particulars, without a due knowledge of local properties, he only bewilders himself, and his readers. Indeed, the localities can be fully understood only by an actual observer; and whatever the personal industry of an individual may be, he must take much on the report of others, as relates to the essentials of his doctrine, when it includes the whole globe within its contemplation.

On the Magnetic Phænomena produced by Electricity. By Sir Humphry Davy, Bart. P. R. S.

The following results of a series of experiments, by Sir H. Davy, we have much satisfaction in laying before our readers, verbatim, as they appear. At present, we shall not remark on them; but, at the close of the paper, we shall presume to add a word or two.

"1st. In my letter to Dr. Wollaston, on the new facts discovered by M. Oersted, which the Society has done me the honour to publish, I mentioned, that I was not able to render a bar of steel magnetic, by transmitting the electrical discharge across it, through a tube filled with sulphuric acid; and I have likewise mentioned that the electrical discharge passed across a piece of steel, through air, rendered it less magnetic, than when passed through a metallic wire; and I attributed the first circumstance to the sulphuric acid being too bad a conductor to transmit a sufficient quantity of electricity for the effect; and the second, to the electricity passing through air in a more diffused state than through metals.

"To gain some distinct knowledge of the relations of the different conductors to the magnetism produced by electricity, I instituted a series of experiments, which led to very decisive results, and confirmed my first views.

"2d. I found that the magnetic phenomena were precisely the same, whether the electricity was small in quantity, and passing through good conductors, of considerable magnitude; or, whether the conductors were so imperfect as to convey only a small quantity of electricity; and, in both cases, they were neither attractive of each other, nor of iron filings; and not affected by the magnet; and the only proof of their being magnetic, was their occasioning a small deviation of the magnetized needle.

"Thus, a large piece of charcoal, placed in the circuit of a very powerful battery, being a very bad conductor, compared with the metals, would not affect the compass needle at all, unless it had a very large contact with the metallic part of the circuit; and if a small wire was made to touch it, in the circuit only, in a few points, that wire did not gain the power of attracting iron filings; though when it was made to touch a surface of platinum foil, coiled round the end of the charcoal, a slight effect of this kind was produced. And in a similar manner fused hydrate of potassa, one of the best of the imperfect conductors, could never be made to exert any attractive force on iron filings; nor could the smallest filaments of cotton, moistened by solution of hydrate of potassa, placed in the circuit, be made to move by the magnet; nor did steel needles, floating on cork on an electrified solution of this kind, placed in the voltaic circuit, gain any polarity; and the only proof of the magnetic power of electricity passing through such a fluid, was afforded by its effect upon the magnetized needle; when the metallic surfaces, plunged in the fluid, were of considerable extent. That the mobility of the parts of fluids did not interfere with their magnetic powers, as developed by electricity, I proved by electrifying mercury, and Newton's metal fused, in small tubes. These tubes, placed in a proper voltaic circuit, attracted iron filings, and gave magnetic powers to needles; nor did any agitation of the mercury, or metal, within, either in consequence of mechanical motion, or heat, alter or suspend their polarity.

"3d. Imperfect, conducting fluids, do not give polarity to steel, when electricity is passed through them; but electricity passed through air, produces this effect. Reasoning on this phenomenon, and on the extreme mobility of the particles of air, I concluded, as M. Arago had likewise done from other considerations, that the voltaic current, in air, would be affected by the magnet. I failed in my first trial, which I have referred to in a note to my former paper, and in other trials, made since, by using too weak a magnet; but I have lately had complete success; and the experiment exhibits a very striking phenomenon.

"Mr. Pepys having had the goodness to charge the great battery of the London Institution, consisting of 2000 double plates of zinc and copper, with a mixture of 1168 parts of water, 108 parts of nitrous acid, and 25 parts of sulphuric acid, the poles were connected by charcoal, so as to make an arc, or column of electrical light, varying in length from one to four inches, according to the state of rarefaction of the atmosphere in which it was produced; and a powerful magnet being presented to this arc or column, having its pole at a very acute angle to it, the arc, or column, was attracted, or repelled, with a rotatory motion; or made to revolve, by placing the poles in different positions, according to the same law as the electrified cylinders of platinum, described in my last paper, being repelled when the negative pole was on the right hand, by the north pole of the magnet, and attracted by the south pole, and *vice versa.*

"It was proved, by several experiments, that the motion depended entirely upon the magnetism, and not upon the electrical inductive power of the magnet; for masses of soft iron, or of other metals, produced no effect.

"The electrical arc, or column of flame, was more easily affected by the magnet; and its motion was more rapid when it passed through dense than through rarefied air; and, in this case, the conducting medium or chain of aëriform particles, was much shorter.

"I tried to gain similar results with currents of common electricity, sent through flame, and in vacuo. They were always affected by the magnet; but it was not possible to obtain so decided a result, as with voltaic electricity; because the magnet itself became electrical by induction; and that, whether it was insulated, or connected with the ground.

"4th. Metals, it is well known, readily transmit large quantities of electricity; and the obvious limit to the quantity which they are capable of transmitting, seems to be their fusibility, or volatilization, by the heat which electricity produces in its passage through bodies.

"Now, I had found in several experiments, that the intensity of this heat was connected with the nature of the medium by which the body was surrounded; thus, a wire of platinum, which was readily fused by transmitting the charge from a voltaic battery, in the exhausted receiver of an air pump, acquired, in air, a much lower degree of temperature. Reasoning on this circumstance, it occurred to me, that by placing wires in a medium much denser than air, such as ether, alcohol, oils, or water, I might enable them to transmit a much higher charge of electricity than they could convey without being destroyed in air; and thus not only gain some new results as to the magnetic states of such wires; but likewise, perhaps, determine the actual limits to the powers of different bodies to conduct electricity, and the relations of these powers.

" A wire of platinum of $\frac{1}{320}$, of three inches in length, was fused, in air, by being made to transmit the electricity of two batteries of ten zinc plates of four inches, with double copper, strongly charged: a similar wire was placed in sulphuric ether, and the charge transmitted through it. It became surrounded by globules of gas; but no other change took place; and in this situation it bore the discharge from twelve batteries of the same kind, exhibiting the same phenomena. When only about an inch of it was heated by this high power in ether, it made the ether boil, and became white hot under the globules of vapour, and then rapidly decomposed the ether, but it did not fuse. When oil or water was substituted for the ether, the length of the wire remaining the same, it was partially covered with small globules of gas, but did not become red hot.

" On trying the magnetic powers of this wire in water, they were found to be very great, and the quantity of iron filings that it attracted was such, as to form a cylinder round it, of nearly the tenth of an inch in diameter.

" To ascertain whether short lengths of fine wire, prevented from fusing by being kept cool, transmitted the whole electricity of powerful voltaic batteries, I made a second independent circuit, from the ends of the battery, with silver wires, in water, so that the chemical decomposition of the water indicated a residuum of electricity in the battery. Operating in this way, I found that an inch of wire of platinum of $\frac{1}{320}$, kept cool by water, left a great residual charge of electricity in a combination of twelve batteries of the same kind as those above mentioned; and after making several trials, I found that it was barely adequate to discharge six batteries.

"5th. Having determined that there was a *limit* to the quantity of electricity which wires were capable of transmitting, it became easy to institute experiments on the different conducting powers of different metallic substances; and on the relation of this power to the temperature, mass, surface, or length, of the conducting body, and to the conditions of electro-magnetic action.

"These experiments were made as nearly as possible under the same circumstances; the same connecting copper wires being used in all cases, their diameter being more than one-tenth of an inch, and the contact being always preserved perfect; and parts of the same solutions of acid and water were employed in the different batteries, and the same silver wires and broken circuit with water, were employed in the different trials; and when no globules of gas were observed upon the negative silver wire of the second circuit, it was concluded that the metallic conducting chain, or the primary circuit, was adequate to the discharge of the combination. To describe more minutely all the precautions observed, would be tedious to those persons who are accustomed to experiments with the voltaic apparatus; and unintelligible to others; and after all, in researches of this nature, it is impossible to gain more than approximations to true results; for the gas disengaged upon the plates, the different distances of the connecting plates, and the slight difference of time in making the connections, all interfere with their perfect accuracy."

(To be continued.)

On New Electro-Magnetic Motions. By Mr. FARADAY.
Journal of Science, No. 24.

On referring to our earlier numbers, the reader will find Mr. Faraday's expressed confidence in making the conductive wire of a voltaic circuit, obey the magnetic poles of the earth; as it does those of a bar magnet. After some unsuccessful attempts, Mr. F. effected his purpose, in the manner, and to the extent, following.

Mr. F. has shown us, in his former paper, that the electromagnetic wire would rotate round the pole, without reference to the position of the axis—joining it with the opposite pole in the same bar; for, whether the axis were horizontal, or vertical, the rotation continued the same. Also, that the wire acted on by the pole, moved laterally, describing circles, in planes nearly perpendicular to the wire, so that when the wire was straight and suspended from above, its revolution described a cone; when in the form of a crank, a cylinder. In all cases, then, it was evident that the plane of the described circle was perpendicular to the electrical current in the wire.

Founded on the above, Mr. F. proceeded to try whether the conductive wire would not revolve round the magnetic pole of the earth, to which we are guided by the dip; describing a circle in the plane perpendicular to the axis of the dip; or, in other words, in a plane parallel with the plane of the magnetic equator. Now, as the dip, with us, is about $72° 30'$, such circle, described by the wire, would be in a plane forming an angle with the horizon of $17° 30'$, measured on the magnetic meridian. A piece of copper wire, about ·045 of an inch thick, and 14 long, had an inch at each extremity bent into right angles, in the same direction; and the extremities amalgamated—the wire being suspended, horizontally, by a long silk thread. A basin of pure mercury was placed under each extremity of the wire; and raised, till the points of the wire became immersed in the mercury, which was, in each basin, covered with a stratum of dilute nitric acid, to dissolve any film; and thereby diminish friction. On connecting the two basins with the extremities of Hare's calorimotor, the suspended wire, instantly, moved sideways, across the basins, till stopped by their sides. On breaking the electrical connection, the wire resumed its former position. On restoring the connection, the motion of the wire was renewed. And, however the wire might be posited, the direction of its motion was always at right angles to its electrical current. Thus, when the wire was E. and W., the E. end to the zinc, the W. end to the copper plate, the motion was towards the North—when the connection was reversed, the motion was towards the south. When the wire hung N. and S., the north end to the zinc plate, and of course the south end to the copper, the motion was towards the west—when the connections were reversed, towards the east,—and the intermediate portions had intermediate motions.

The tendency of the wire to revolve round the magnetic pole of the earth, was, as Mr. F. infers, rendered perfectly evident; and is analogous to M. Ampere's wire ring, made to conduct a current of electricity; which, on turning on a vertical axis, moves in a plane east, and west, of the magnetic meridian: if on an east, and west, horizontal axis, moves in a plane perpendicular to the dip. Mr. F. urges, that, if the curve be considered as a polygon of an infinite number of sides; and each of these sides be compared, in succession, to the straight wire just described; it will be seen that, the motions given to them by the terrestrial pole, or poles, are such as would necessarily bring the polygon, they form, into a plane perpendicular to the dipping needle: so that the traversing of the ring, may be reduced to the simple rotation of a wire round a pole.

Mr. F. then remarks, that, when the wire revolves round the pole of the magnet, the latter is perpendicular to but a small portion of the former; and, more or less, oblique with the remainder. He thought that a wire, delicately hung, and connected, might be made to rotate round the dip of the needle, by the earth's magnetism alone; the upper part being restrained to a point in the line of the dip; the lower being made to move in a circle, round it. And the following was the experiment made to ascertain the matter. "A piece of copper wire, about 0·018 of an inch in diameter, and 6 inches long, was well amalgamated all over; and hung, by a loop, to another piece of the same wire, so as to allow very free motion: and its lower end was thrust through a small piece of cork, to make it buoyant on mercury. The upper piece was connected with a thick wire, that went away to one pole of the voltaic apparatus. A glass basin, 10 inches in diameter, was filled with pure mercury; and a little dilute acid poured on its surface, as before. The thick wire was then hung over the centre of the glass basin, and depressed so low, that the thin moveable wire, having its lower end resting on the surface of the mercury, made an angle of about 40° with the horizon. Immediately the circuit through the mercury was completed, this wire began to move and rotate; and continued to describe a cone, while the connections were preserved; which, though its axis was perpendicular, evidently, from the varying rapidity of its motion, regarded a line parallel to the dipping needle, as that in which the power acted that formed it."

The direction of the motion was, as expected, the same as that given by the pole of a magnet pointing to the south. If the centre, from which the wire hung, was elevated until the inclination of the wire was equal to that of the dip, no motion took place while the wire was parallel to the dip. If the wire was not so much inclined as the dip, the motion, in one part of the circle, capable of being described by the lower end, was reversed: results that necessarily follow from the relation of the dip and the moving wire; and which may be easily extended.

The above effects are attributed by Mr. F. to the north pole of the earth, considering that pole as a centre of action, and acting in a line represented by the dip of the needle: and these experiments have been effected with a view to compare the phenomena with those produced by the pole of a magnet. M. Biot, having shown, by calculation, that the magnetic pole of the earth may be considered as two points in the magnetic axis, very near to each other, in the centre of the globe; M. Ampere, too, having aimed to prove that the earthly magnetism is but electric current, flowing round the earth's axis, parallel to the equator; Mr. F. is disposed to infer that, both these points are in corroboration of his general deductions; and, concur, precisely, with his own experiments, given in one of our former numbers, wherein he states the effect produced on the needle by the north and south planes of the electrical current passing through a wire ring. At all events, Mr. F. judges that, the experiments he has described bear him out in presuming, that, on every part of the terrestrial globe, an electro-magnetic wire, if left to the free action of terrestrial magnetism, will move in a plane perpendicular to the dip of the needle; and in a direction perpendicular to the current of electricity passing along it.

Mr. F. next tried to verify his idea that the apparent weight of a wire, revolving round the needle, would be altered—moving north it must rise; moving south, must descend—because the plane of its circular motion would be partly above, and partly below, the needle's axis. Having adapted the suspended wire to this object, he was surprised to find that, it was lighter in both ascent and descent; but most so, when the motion was northerly. Whatever the position, it would ascend, when the contacts were made. This, however, was discovered to arise from the action of the amalgamated points with the mercury. But on correcting the apparatus, it was found that, on contact, the wires would rise an inch; and fall again, on breaking the voltaic current.

Whether these results will be confirmed, in all, or other, latitudes, as Mr. Faraday confidently anticipates, we would, as yet, be cautious to absolutely decide upon; but we really think them very probable.

On the Nerves; giving an Account of some Experiments on their Structure, and Functions; which lead to a new Arrangement of the System. By CHARLES BELL, Esq.
Philosophical Transactions.

Of the nature of the nervous system we are almost totally in the dark; for, although anatomists have traced its minute ramifications; and we have had some analogies shown in the voltaic electricity with resulting actions of nervous fibrils, operating on muscular fibre; yet we, really, may be said to be in our infancy as to our knowledge of the modus operandi of nervous influence. We see the end produced, and that is almost all we do see. If, then, Mr. Bell can give us a glimpse further, we shall be truly thankful; and that he will, we the rather hope because he is, we think, too philosophically cautious to commit himself wantonly.

Mr. Bell's experiments lead him to propose a distinct arrangement of the nervous system, into two classes. One of them, he supposes to be intended to supply the organs of sense, and locomotion; in animals having nerves, down to the lowest link in the chain of sensibility. The existence of the other system, which he supposes to supply particular organs; as the heart, stomach, and lungs, is governed, in its degree and perfection, by the number and importance of the functions to be performed. Thus, in animals, without hearts, the nervous system is less complex than in those wherein all the varied functions of animal life are combined. So, if the heart be double, and, of course, possess additional power of function, it will have a more complicated nervous appendage than if it were simple. The same with the lungs. Where simple breathing exist, the distribution, and connection, of the pulmonary nerves will be simple; but, where they aid the voice, and occasionally associate in action, as expressive of emotion, &c., they will have peculiar connections with those of the face; which is the index of all emotion.

There are two distinct classes, or sets, of nerves in the face, and head, of man, passing to the same parts in man and the superior brutes. These nerves have all, hitherto, been understood to bear a similarity of character in form and function; as a double provision for associative influence, and augmentation of power. But Mr. Bell aims to prove them to be totally different in functionary quality; and not bearing any analogy as to proposed end of formation.

Mr. Bell, by dividing a particular nerve, distributed to the face, deprived the muscles of active power, especially of the nostril, in consent with respiration; and more; for all that expression, or form of feature, indicating passion, was departed. Yet, although the muscles had lost their emotive power, they retained their contractile; for mechanical purposes; such as the movement of the jaw, in eating.

Again, by dividing the other class of nerves, that govern

mere muscular contractility, the facial actions connected with respiration were not injured; but the contractile power of the masticating muscles, and the sensibility of the skin, were destroyed.

Although these experiments were necessarily restricted to the brute creation; yet we shall derive most important practical knowledge from the facts; because the animal analogy between brutes, and the human race, holds so strongly, that we can confide in a physiological fact of identity in structure, where there is an established similarity of habit, or expression, in character. This discovery of Mr. Bell's, if eventually it shall be confirmed as such, will lay the world under the greatest obligation to him; and hand down his name, with high honour, to the remotest posterity. Mr. B. has promised an additional paper, on the nerves of the neck and throat. We shall look anxiously for it; and not fail to record its spirit within our own pages.

On the Difference of the Functions in certain Nerves of the Face; illustrated by their Anatomy in the inferior Animals, and by a Comparison of their Uses in Man and Brutes. By JOHN SHAW, Esq.

Journal of Science, No. 24.

The gentleman who favours the public with this paper is well known in the anatomical world as having long been aiding, &c. in Mr. Bell's school of anatomy and surgery. His opinions, therefore, may be expected to assimilate with the latter gentleman's; and, indeed, we may consider Mr. Shaw's paper as an able commentary on Mr. Bell's doctrine.

Mr. Shaw commences by remarking that, he was engaged in assisting Mr. Bell in the experiments on which he founded the new system, observed on in the last paper; and, therefore, he must be the more competent to appreciate their value, as having witnessed their progressive stages, and final results. He says that, during these operations, he was naturally led to observe further on the paralytic conditions of the facial muscles, and flatters our hopes of eventually deriving very valuable practical information as to paralysis of the face, by pursuing the train of reasoning now laid down.

In one man, Mr. S. could not observe any symptom of palsy, until he laughed, or sneezed. In another, the paralytic features resumed their natural expression, only when laughter or sneezing was excited. In a third, the paralysis was apparent when the muscles were quiescent; and the facial distortion augmented, on an attempt to laugh or sneeze. We are sorry that Mr. S. has omitted to state what was the condition of the masticatory muscles, and the sensibility of the skin, in these cases, respectively.

Previous to entering into any explanation of these symptoms, Mr. S. proceeds to describe the facial nerves, and the changes produced by division of either set of them.

The one set, hitherto called *portio dura* of the 7th, belongs to the system of additional, or superadded nerves; and passes to every muscle connected with respiration, or expression. The other, called the 5th, or *trigeminus*, is one of the original, or symmetrical, system; and goes, not only to the same muscles, but also to the skin, and the deeper muscles; and principally those of mastication.

The proportion of the facial respiratory is greater to that of the *fifth*, in man, than in any other animal. In the next link of the chain, (the monkey,) the respiratory is diminished, and the *fifth* increased. The distribution is more complicated in the monkey, than in the dog; because the muscles of expression are more numerous in the former, than in the latter. We descend through the lion, dog, and cat, to the horse, ass, and cow. In all these, there is a difference of nervous distribution, from that of the monkey and dog; for, excepting a few twigs to the external ear and eyelid, the respiratory is restricted to the muscles of the nostrils, and side of the mouth; while, in the carnivorous tribes, it is profusely spread over the cheeks, and side of the neck.

In the graminivorous tribes, as the gazelle, sheep, and deer, the nervous distinction is still more simple, than in the horse; while, in the camel, it is more profuse; and intermediate between that of the graminivorous and carnivorous classes. The expression of the enraged, or dying, camel, is ferocious; showing his tusks like a carnivorous animal. The anatomy of the camel is peculiar. In dissecting a courier camel, or maherry, from the interior of Africa, Mr. Shaw remarked many facts, overlooked by preceding anatomists: especially that, the distribution of the nerves of the neck and stomach differed from those of the horse, the ass, and a number of ruminating animals. The distribution of the nerves of the neck resembled those of a large bird, as the swan, &c., more than those of a horse, or bullock: particularly in the spinal accessory, or superior respiratory of the trunk; being either deficient altogether, as in birds; or differing from the greater number of quadrupeds. Mr. Shaw considers this fact as confirmatory of Mr. Bell's idea of the use of this nerve.

The elephant is said to assume a sublime and terrific expression, when in a rage; but this expression, Mr. S. infers, from the anatomy of the *portio dura*, must be very different from the ferocious snarl of the lion. The respiratory, and expressive nerve, is nearly confined to the proboscis; with slight branches to the eyelid; therefore, Mr. S. presumes that, the facial expression would be confined to those parts.

Mr. S. familiarized himself with an elephant, at Exeter 'Change; and judged, from the perfect mobility of the proboscis, that there must be an abundant supply of nervous power to the part, as in the human fingers; but as the proboscis forms so important a part of the respiratory system, in this animal, he thought that a dissection of one, would afford decided proof of the correctness or the fallacy of Mr. Bell's doctrine. This animal died, and Mr. Shaw found the trunk supplied, not only by branches of the *fifth* pair, as described by Cuvier; but, also, by a very large branch from the *portio dura*, which was found emerging from the parotid gland, as in other mammalia. Some ascending branches went to the neck; but the main nerve passed behind the jaw to the proboscis, almost entire; and of the size of the human sciatic. Small twigs had been given off to the muscles of the eye and ear; and to a muscle analogous with the platysma myoides. Before it passed into the substance of the proboscis, it united with the second division of the *fifth* pair, which comes from the infra orbital hole, in two large branches. The two nerves, then closely united, passed between the layers of the muscles, forming the mass of the trunk. The *portio dura* diminished rapidly in size, as it sent off muscular branches profusely; but the *fifth* continued very large, to near the extremity of the trunk: in this respect resembling the human digital nerves. On making a section of the proboscis, near the extremity, the nerves were seen abundantly.

A few branches of the *portio dura* went to the valvular apparatus in the upper part of the trunk; but this part was principally supplied by a branch of the *fifth* pair, winding round, under the orbit.

On comparing the facial respiratory nerve of the various classes of birds, with the distribution of that of different quadruped tribes, we shall perceive an analogy. In the game cock, nervous branches pass to the loose skin under the jaw; which is dilated in crowing; the principal branches going to the neck, whereby the feathers are ruffled, as in combat. But in the duck, which, when enraged, has but little power of expression, the similar nerve passing to the jaw, is not larger than a cambric thread. The effect of dividing the facial respiratory nerve, as we might expect, is measured by the intricacy of its distribution; and as it is the trunk or the branch. Mr. S. has never witnessed its section in man, with a view to such effect; but he recollects, and will, further on, detail the consequences of its injury, by accident or disease.

Some time back, he divided the left facial respiratory of the most expressive monkey he could select at Exeter 'Change; and immediately power of expression, on that side, was lost. When the animal was irritated, he snarled; but showed the teeth of the right side only. During a month, he could not shut the left eye; and though, of late, able to do it, yet, when attacked, the orbicularis muscle is so convulsed, as to render the eye useless. He then keeps guard with the other eye; not winking it.

The effect of injury to this nerve, in the human subject, will be particularly shown, by Mr. S., in a future paper, on the case of a little girl; who, when she laughs heartily, has the right cheek, and side of the mouth, quiescent; while the muscles of the left, are convulsed with emotion. On making effort to laugh, with the right side, she raises the angle of the mouth; but evidently through influence of the *fifth* pair, and the countenance assumes a singularly droll expression, which Mr. S. thought bore strong affinity with that of the popular mimick, who invites the public to see him *at home*. Having made experiments on the *portio dura* of several animals, he was so much impressed with the similarity of some of the facial muscular actions to those of the actor alluded to, that he was impelled to visit the Theatre, and observe him again. Mr. S. found, as he says, evident marks of paralysis of the *portio dura*; but yet there was much expression displayed on the same side; for which he could not then account. He, however, thinks it now explainable by reference to the little girl's cheek; for when she attempts to laugh with the right side, the expression is so similar, that it is almost a proof of this actor's having gained such an habitual power of command over the muscles influenced by the *fifth*, as to be able to bring them into a state similar to that in natural laughter. But, as this is done through the *fifth*, instead of the *portio dura* of the seventh, it makes the expression on one side totally different from that on the other, and, consequently, renders the countenance peculiarly ludicrous. We understand Mr. S. to mean that the ludicrous expression consists principally in the want of correspondence of muscular action on the two sides of the face.

Now, what would be the appearance, if the actor possessed such a command over both sides of the face at once, (which perhaps he may) that is, if he can command the nervous influence of the *fifth*, and that of the *portio dura*, at pleasure, and distinctly? We conjecture, that in the case of voluntary excitement on both sides of the *fifth* only, the expression would scarcely resemble laughter. But, should it be eventually shown that, the *portio dura*, and the *fifth*, can be excited, on one, or both, sides; and in pairs, or singly, at pleasure; it will certainly be an additional fact demonstrating that a nerve can be dissevered from its habitual associates; but it will not prove further than that each individual nervous distribution may be occasionally influenced at will, independent, and unconnected with, other portions of nervous ramification. It must not be overlooked that, from our earliest infancy, we are habitually using the facial muscles, not only in single pairs, but also congregated pairs; and, therefore, the respective nerves, supplying such pairs, may be greatly influenced by such habitual actions; so as that, in a long life, and where no effort has ever been made to dissever the muscular actions, and consequently the nervous excitements, the individual nerves of pairs may be as inseparable in voluntary excitement, as those of the pairs, or the pairs themselves, that go to organs over which the will has not any controul.

(To be continued.)

Some Observations, and Experiments, on the Papyri, found in the Ruins of Herculaneum. By Sir H. DAVY, P.R.S.
Transactions of Royal Society.

We consider this too interesting a subject to pass over without notice; and, therefore, present it to our readers; as likely to be acceptable to their literary tastes. Sir H. D. addresses the Royal Society as follows:—

" In a paper, intended for private circulation only, on the MSS. found in the excavations made at Herculaneum, but which was published, by mistake, in the Journal of Science and the Arts, I have described, in a general manner, the circumstances which led me to make experiments on those remains, and mentioned some of my first observations on the subject. Mr. Hamilton, to whom this communication was sent, entered into my views with all that ardour for promoting the progress of useful knowledge, which so peculiarly belongs to his character; and, on his representation of them, the Earl of Liverpool, and Viscount Castlereagh, with the greatest liberality, placed at my disposal such funds as were requisite for paying the persons whom it was necessary to employ, in trying new chemical methods of unrolling the MSS. Secondly, a description of the rolls in the Museum of Naples, and of some analytical experiments I made upon them. Thirdly, a detail of the various chemical processes carried on in the Museum at Naples, on the MSS., and of the reasons which induced me to renounce my undertaking before it was completed. And, lastly, some general observations on the MSS. of the ancients.

"I trust these matters will not be found wholly devoid of interest, by the Society; and that they will excuse some repetitions of what I have stated in the report before referred to, as they are necessary for a complete elucidation of the subject.

1st. An account of some Experiments, made in England, on Fragments of Papyri, in 1818.

"In examining, chemically, some fragments of a roll of papyrus, found at Herculaneum, the leaves of which adhered very strongly together, I found that it afforded by exposure to heat, a considerable quantity of gaseous matter; which was principally inflammable gas: and when acted on by muriatic, or nitric, ether, it coloured them; and when it was exposed to heat, after the action of those fluids, there was an evident separation of the leaves of the MSS.

"Chlorine and iodine, it is well known, have no action upon pure carbonaceous substances, and a strong attraction for hydrogen; and it occurred to me that, these bodies might, with propriety, be used in attempting to destroy the matter which caused the adhesion of the leaves; without the possibility of injuring the letters on the papyri: the ink of the ancients, as it is well known, being composed of charcoal.

"Having, through the polite assistance of Sir Thomas Tyrwhytt, procured some fragments of papyri, on which Dr. Sickler, and some on which Dr. Young, had operated; and by the kindness of Dr. Young, a small portion of a manuscript which he had himself unsuccessfully tried to unrol, I made some experiments upon them, by exposing them to the action of chlorine, and the vapour of iodine; heating them gently after the process. These trials all afforded more or less hopes of success. When a fragment of a brown MS., in which the layers were strongly adherent, was placed in an atmosphere of chlorine, there was an immediate action: the papyrus smoked, and became yellow, and the letters appeared much more distinct; and by the application of heat, the layers separated from each other, giving off fumes of the muriatic acid. The vapour of iodine had a less distinct action; but still a sensible one; and it was found that by applying heat alone to a fragment in a close vessel, filled with carbonic acid, or the vapour of ether, so as to raise the heat very gradually, and as gradually to lower it, there was a marked improvement in its texture; and it was much more easily unrolled.

"Even in these preliminary trials, I found that it was necessary to employ only a limited, and small, quantity of chlorine; too large a quantity injuring the texture of the layer, and decomposing the earths which it contained; and that the action of heat was much more efficacious when the MS. had previously been exposed to chlorine, as the muriatic acid vapour formed greatly assisted the separation of the leaves, and a smaller degree of heat was required. But in all the trials, I found the success depended upon the manner in which the temperature was regulated. When the fragment was too rapidly heated, the elastic fluid disengaged usually burst the folds of the MS.: and when the heat was lowered too suddenly, the layers sometimes split in irregular parts, probably from the sudden contraction consequent on quick cooling.

"From the products of the distillation of these fragments, which were water, acetous acid, ammonia, carbonic acid, and much inflammable gas, I inferred—that, the papyri, to which they belonged, must contain much undecomposed vegetable matter. But, as there were great differences in the appearances even of the few papyri in England, which had been presented to His Majesty George IV., when Prince of Wales, an opinion on this subject was more likely to be correct, when formed after an examination, not only of all the MSS. found at Herculaneum, but likewise of the circumstances of the excavations made there. And I had an opportunity, during the time I remained at Naples, in two successive winters, to satisfy my mind on this subject, and to obtain the information which will be given in the next section.

2. On the State of the MSS. found at Herculaneum.

"The persons who have the care of the MSS. found at Herculaneum state that, their original number was 1696, and that 431 have been operated upon, or presented to foreign governments, so that 1265 ought to remain: but among these, by far the larger proportion are small fragments, or specimens so injured and mutilated, that there is not the least chance of recovering any portion of their contents. And when I first examined the rolls in detail, in January, 1819, it did not appear to me that more than from 80 to 120 offered proper subjects for experiments. And this estimate, as my researches proceeded, appeared much too high. These MSS. had been objects of interest for more than 70 years; the best had, long ago been operated upon; and those remaining had not only undergone injuries from time, but likewise from other causes: such as transport, rude examination, and mutilations, for the purpose of determining if they contained characters.

"The appearances of different rolls were extremely various. They were of all shades of colours, from a chesnut brown to a deep black: some, externally, were of a glossy black, like jet; which the superintendants called "varnished." Several contained the umbilicus, or rolling stick in the middle, converted into dense charcoal. I saw two or three specimens of papyri found which had the remains of characters on both sides; but, in general, one side only was written upon. In their texture they were as various as in their colours; the pale brown ones, in general, presented only a kind of skeleton of a leaf, in which the earthy matter was nearly in as large a proportion as the vegetable matter; and they were light, and the layers easily separated from each other. A number of darker brown ones, which, from a few characters discovered in opening them, appeared to be Latin manuscripts, were agglutinated, as it were, into one mass; and when they were opened, by introducing a needle between the layers, spots, or lines of charcoal appeared, where the folds had been, as if the letters had been washed out by water, and the matter of which they were composed deposited on the folds. Amongst the black MSS., a very few fragments presented leaves, which separated from each other with considerable facility; and such had been for the most part operated upon; but in general, the MSS. of this class were hard, heavy, and coherent; and contained fine volcanic dust within their folds. Some few of the black, and darker brown MSS., which were loose in their texture, were almost entirely decayed, and exhibited, on their surface, a quantity of brown powder. The persons to whom the care of these MSS. is confided, or who have worked upon them, have always attributed these different appearances to the action of fire, more or less intense, according to the proximity of the lava which has been imagined to have covered part of the city in which they were found; but this idea is entirely erroneous, that part of Herculaneum being, as I satisfied myself by repeated examinations, under a bed of tufa, formed of sand, volcanic ashes, stones, and dust, cemented by the operation of water (probably at the time of its action in a boiling state). And there is great reason to conclude, that the different states of the MSS. depend upon a gradual process of decomposition: the loose chesnut ones probably not having been wetted, but merely changed by the re-action of their elements, assisted by the operation of a small quantity of air; the black ones, which easily unrol, probably remained in a moist state, without any percolation of water; and the dense ones, containing earthy matter, had probably been acted on by warm water, which not only carried into the folds earthy matter, suspended in it, but likewise dissolved the starch and gluten used in preparing the papyrus, and the glue of the ink, and distributed them through the substance of the MSS. And some of these rolls had probably been strongly compressed, when moist, in different positions."

(To be continued.)

Nitrogen in Sulphureous Waters.

Annales de Chimie.

If M. Anglada's experiments and observations should be found correct, by future inquirers, we shall have some new views of the character of sulphureous waters, and their medicinal action.

The existence of nitrogen in mineral waters has been frequently ascertained; and its quantity stated; but no very precise ideas have hitherto been published, on the cause of its existence in the waters. The attempt of M. Anglada is, perhaps, the first made, to show its source, and the situations in which it may be expected. Having observed, from the experience of others, and himself, that nitrogen occurred in waters, containing sulphuretted hydrogen, he was induced to search whether it was not constantly present in such waters; and finding that to be the case, reasoned and experimented upon its production. In many sulphureous springs, the sources of which were easily arrived at, it was readily observed, that nitrogen either arose from the sides of the spring, or could be obtained without difficulty from the water; but in others, which were confined by pipes or conduits, it was necessary to open up the works, and get to the source. In all cases, however, sulphureous waters were found to contain nitrogen; and it was remarked, that though the water contained abundance of sulphuretted hydrogen, the gas contained none.

M. Anglada expected, by heat, to obtain sulphuretted hydrogen and carbonic acid gas from sulphureous gas. Guided by this result, he concluded that, in all the suphureous waters that had thus yielded him nitrogen, that gas came from the air which the waters had taken up in their subterraneous course, and from which the oxygen had been separated by the sulphur, &c. In order, as it were, to prove this opinion, a portion of a sulphureous water was treated with acetate of lead, to separate all the sulphuretted hydrogen from it, and then boiled: it gave out more gas than before, and the gas was a mixture of oxygen and hydrogen.

The air thus furnished to waters, is given to them, M. Anglada thinks, in the bowels of the earth, by currents of air, of which we know little or nothing.

In consequence of this action of the air on waters of this kind, it happens, sometimes, that a water, decidedly sulphureous at its source, ceases to be so at a little distance from it; dependant on the strength of the water, and the means it has of getting air. In these cases, the previous sulphureous state of the water may be deduced from the disengagement of pure nitrogen, or containing very little oxygen, and from certain glairy appearances which are exhibited by those waters.

M. Anglada also remarks, that in many waters containing carbonic acid, abundance of nitrogen is found; and he suggests, that probably the air may act in them on some carbonaceous matters, giving rise to carbonic acid and nitrogen at the same time. It is also remarked in the conclusions attached to this paper, and which being given above, need not be repeated, that the change takes place at all temperatures, and that if nitrogen is not found in every sulphureous water, it is in all those containing a hydro-sulphuretted alkali.

British Mechanical Powers.
Journal of Science, No. 24.

We present the following extract, as not only being the flattering tribute of a foreigner's admiration; but, also, as in proof of our national resources in mechanical efficacy; to an extent perhaps very imperfectly understood by ourselves, generally; and as infinitely surpassing that of the proudest empire which ever existed. M. Dupin, whilst speaking of the immense mechanical force set in action by the steam engines of England, gives the following illustration of its amount:—The great pyramid of Egypt required for its erection the labour of above 100,000 men, for twenty years; but if it were required again to raise the stones from the quarries, and place them at their present height, the action of the steam engines of England, which are managed at most by 36,000 men, would be sufficient to produce the effect in eighteen hours. And M. Dupin says, that if it were required to know how long a time they would take to cut the stones, and move them from the quarries to the pyramid, a very few days would be found sufficient.

The calculation of M. Dupin is as follows: the volume of the great pyramid is 4,000,000 cubic metres, its weight is about 10,400,000 tons, or 10,400,000,000 kilogrammes. The centre of gravity of the pyramid is elevated 49 metres from the base; and taking 11 metres as the mean depth of the quarries, the total height of elevation is 60 metres, which, multiplied by 10,400,000 tons, gives 624,000,000 tons raised one metre. Then, the total of the steam engines in England represents a power of 320,000 horses. These engines moved for 24 hours, would raise 862,800,000 tons, one meter high, and consequently 647,100,000 tons in eighteen hours, which surpasses the produce of labour spent in raising the materials of the great pyramid.

Tests for Arsenic.

It is indeed desirable to have a never failing test of this deleterious drug; for in our Courts of Justice we have had so many instances of poisoning by aid of it; and have read such defective evidence, given by medical attendants, on these criminal trials; that we should be happy to know any means of specifically identifying arsenic, so as to leave the mind destitute of anxious doubt.

Dr. Porter, of the University of South Carolina, in observing on the tests for the detection of arsenic, remarks that, an appearance, similar to Scheele's green, is produced by carbonate of potash, added to a solution of copper, containing coffee, but without arsenic, more striking than if a weak solution of arsenic be used. He also states that, in the production of Scheele's green by arsenic, sulphate of copper, and carbonate of potash, chromate of potash might be substituted for the arsenic; and that the precipitate produced could not be distinguished by the eye from Scheele's green. Also, that Mr. Hume's test of the nitrate of silver (as modified in its application by Dr. Marcet) gave, with chromate of potash, a yellow precipitate, which, when placed side by side with one produced by arsenic, could not be distinguished by colour or appearance from it.

It seems, then, that Mr. Hume's arsenical test, with Dr. Marcet's modification, cannot be relied on. We sincerely hope that, Dr. Porter's discovery of the use of coffee in the testing, may be found more exclusively identifying arsenic when present. At least, we have a new method pointed out, of obtaining the pigment, called Scheele's green.

Rapacious Whale.

This must be a dreadful enemy to meet with in a distant sea and a small vessel: may it not be probable that these fish are furious during particular periods only?

The Aleutians count seven species of whales, the most of which are probably unknown to natural history. One of these species is a rapacious animal, which is well known not to be the case with other whales, as they have no teeth. It devours every thing it can catch, and often pursues the Aleutians, whose little baydaus, if it is able to overtake them, it upsets with one blow of its tail. It is said that a baydau, with 24 oars and 30 men, were lately destroyed by the blow of such a monster, near Onalashka. The Russians and Aleutians relate, that if a piece of the blubber of this animal is swallowed, it has the property of immediately passing through the body undigested.

A Red Sea Serpent.

If faith may be allowed to the repeated accounts we have had of sea serpents, some of the species must greatly surpass our very largest on land; of which the following is a specimen. But we ought to make ample allowance for the exaggeration of terror.

M. Kriukof's description of a sea animal which pursued him at Behring's Island, where he had gone for the purpose of hunting, is very remarkable. Several Aleutians affirm they have often seen this animal. It is of the shape of the red serpent, and immensely long; the head resembles that of the sea lion, and two disproportionately large eyes, give it a frightful appearance. "It was fortunate for us," said Kriukof, "that we were so near land, or else the monster would have swallowed us: it stretched its head far above the water, looked about for prey, and vanished. The head soon appeared again, and that considerably nearer: we rowed with all our might, and were very happy to have reached the shore before the serpent. The sea lions were so terrified at the sight, that some rushed into the water, and others hid themselves on the shore. The sea often throws up pieces of flesh, which, according to opinion, is that of this serpent, which no animal, not even the raven, will touch. Some Aleutians, who had once tasted some of it, suddenly died. If a sea serpent really has been seen on the coast of North America, it may have been one of this frightful species."

Superb Mummy.

Philosophical Magazine.

We can estimate the propriety of a national taste for these human remains, as matter illustrative of historical character, and for exhibition in public museums; but that a domestic passion should prompt a family to dispatch agents into the interior of a distant country, to collect dry bones, is somewhat more than amusing.

A Danish family, desirous of purchasing a beautiful mummy for one of the museums in Copenhagen, wrote to M. Dumrecher, Danish Consul at Alexandria; who, assisted by M. Tedenat, the French Consul, procured an intelligent man to set out for Upper Egypt, with a firman from the Pasha, to search the tombs of the ancient kings. For the greater dispatch, they employed two different parties of the natives, from Lougsor and from Karnack. The former were the most fortunate, discovering a tomb that had never been opened, and where they found on the third day, a mummy with five cases; they asked for this 6000 piastres of Egypt, (£133.,) which was paid them. The fellahs of Karnack, thus disappointed, and having had three days' toil for nothing, had warm disputes with those of Lougsor; and mischievous consequences might have ensued, as their villagers took a part in the quarrel, if the possessor of the mummy had not given 1000 piastres (£22.) extra to the Arabs of Karnack, to whom also some participation was made by those of Lougsor. This mummy is the most superb and beautiful of all that have hitherto been discovered. To judge of it from the ornaments in relief, which decorate the cases, and especially one, whereon gold has been lavished, from the rich style of the amulets, from the largeness of the papyrus, and all the hieroglyphical enbellishments about the body, it must have been that of some Egyptian king or prince. This conjecture is corroborated by the number of cases, as the mummies of the greatest persons in general have only three.

South American Potato.

The produce of this potato was certainly large; but, probably, not larger than any other tolerably productive kind would yield, if allowed space in well dug soil of good quality. We have witnessed a greater produce, some time last year. Mr. Thomas Lorimer, residing near Rockhall, the seat of Sir Robert Griesan, Bart., received from an acquaintance, a single potato which had been brought from Spanish Town, South America. This potato he kept till spring, when cutting it in two, he planted the pieces at a trifling distance from one another in a corner of his garden. These plants, or slips, speedily sprung up, and in due time put forth blooms and apples like any other potato; and there was nothing either in the colour or luxuriance of the shaws, that excited particular notice; but on raising the said exotics, Mr. Lorimer found, to his surprise, that they had produced no fewer than 41 potatoes, 30 of which are of an uncommon size. Two of the largest of these were brought to this office a few days ago, one of which weighed 2 lb. 2 oz., and the other 1 lb. 4 oz., while both measured nearly eighteen inches in circumference. From the size and appearance of *thumping* roots, we were inclined to set them down as a species of yam; but on this point Mr. L. completely undeceived us, by declaring that the residue of the produce, which cannot weigh much less than 30 lbs., is rather of a round shape, and in other respects, bears a pretty close resemblance to the common potato.

Spade and Plough Husbandry.

In this comparative trial, the superior efficacy of the spade in produce is decidedly marked. But which is eventually the most economical?

In the neighbourhood of Hamilton, an experiment was made this year, to try the difference between the spade and the plough. A field was taken, which was in beans last year, and oats the year before; two ridges were dug and two ploughed alternately, and the whole was sown on the same day; a part both on the ploughed and the dug being drilled with the garden hoe; the whole was reaped the same day; and being thrashed out, the result was, that the dug, sown broad cast, was, to the ploughed, cast, as 52 to 42. The dug and drilled was as $20\frac{1}{4}$ to $12\frac{1}{4}$, upon the ploughed and drilled. The additional grain is not the only beneficial result gained by digging, as in this instance there was also a great deal more straw. The land is free of weeds, and will be more easily fallowed next year.

Animal Temperature in Chlorine.

We do not feel satisfied with the explanation given by Dr. Hare of the following fact: for when chlorine be mingled with the atmospheric air of a fumigated apartment, the animal temperature is not sensibly changed.

Dr. Hare, of Philadelphia, has found that, when the temperature of the air is about 60°, the hand, when immersed in chlorine, experiences a sensation of heat equal to 90° or 100°, even though the common thermometer should not be affected when immersed. Dr. Hare conjectures, " that a sort of chemical action may take place between the gas and the insensible perspiration of the skin, as the power of chlorine in dissolving animal effluvia is well known."

Fossil Giant Lizards.
Philosophical Magazine.

It is remarkable that this animal is opening to our view, as it were suddenly; but we are not yet satisfied as to the correctness of its presumed character.

In the beginning of November, Mr. Mantell discovered in the chalk, Lewes, three vertebræ of the celebrated fossil animal of Maestricht. This is the first instance of the remains of that oviparous quadruped being found in this country, or in any part of the continent, except in St. Peter's Mountain near Maestricht.

Gigantic Polypus.

The following is extracted from Kotzebue's voyage, and should the narrative be founded in fact, this aquatic animal must be a very formidable enemy to encounter.

"The Aleutians also relate stories of a gigantic polypus. It has happened, that a polypus has thrown its long arms, which are twice as thick as a strong man's arm, round the baydau of an Aleutian, and would have carried it into the abyss, if the Aleutian had not had the presence of mind to cut through with his knife, the fleshy arm of the polypus, which was furnished with large suckers. The polypus remains with his body fast at the bottom of the sea, and generally chooses a place from which it can reach the surface with its arms. The last accident happened in the passage which is found by the southern point of the island of Oomnack, and the little island lying near it."

Earthquake.

Probably this was not what it is represented to be, that is, a real earthquake; but an aërial commotion; for the latter often affords analogous phenomena.

An earthquake was distinctly felt at Inverary, on the morning of 22d Oct. Several persons in the town felt the shock, and others heard a noise like that of several carriages in motion. About 13 miles further down Lochfine, some of the peasantry were much alarmed at seeing the furniture violently shaken. The day was rainy and lowering; and about four o'clock there was a loud and continued peal of thunder, with some vivid flashes of lightning.

Prolific Shark.

Philosophical Journal.

Here we have a proof of fecundity, that we would hope far exceeds the general issue of this voracious fish.

The ship Brailsford, on her passage from Bombay to England, in latitude 29° 26′ south, longitude 40° 2′ east, caught a large blue female shark, 12 feet long, on opening which, there were found no less than 77 young ones alive, each about a foot long, and weighing from one-half to three-quarters of a pound.

Red Snow.

The following is not a solitary instance of snow being tinged red; for independent of the Highland coloured snow, similarly coloured falls have occurred on the Alps, and in western Italy.

Snow of a *reddish tint*, was found in this region, as in the Arctic countries described by Captain Ross. It appears to owe its colour to some cryptogamic vegetable, probably of the same general nature as that described by Brown and Bauer, in their account of the red snow of the Arctic highlands.

THE FOCUS

OF

PHILOSOPHY, SCIENCE, AND ART.

M. VICAT *on Water Cements, Mortar, and Lime.*
(Continued from p. 220.)

M. VICAT considers the conflicting results of experiments made by others, as principally attributable to the difference in the quality of the limes that have been made use of by the parties respectively subjecting them to trial. The experiments of Chaptal were repeated by the Commissioners of the port of Cette; and the result would seem to justify an opinion that the puozzolanas of the Vivarais are very inferior to those of Italy. But, those of M. Faujas would prove the contrary. Again, M. Gauthey concludes that fat lime will not set under water, because, by mixing it even with puozzolana, we cannot combine enough with metallic oxyds. The lime of Rome is made from pure Travertino marble, and consequently very fat; yet with such, and puozzolana, the cements of the aqueduct, the hot baths, &c. have been made; now so hard as to be worked into snuff-boxes, and bear a high polish. The fact is, that too much lime is frequently used; sometimes amounting to one half; which is, by half, too much. Descotils will have it that the hydraulic effect is dependant on the state of the silex in the puozzolanas; and M. V. considers the opinion strengthened by the fact that silex shows itself in a semi-gelatinous state when ochre is treated with muriatic acid; proving, according to Berzelius, a chemical combination between the silex and the oxyd of iron.

We combated this conjecture before; and would again inquire whence the acid is derived in these cementing compounds? Let us suppose it possible for muriatic acid to be present; its union with the silex must be destroyed by the lime; and we know that muriate of lime is so deliquescent that it must be totally subversive of all setting property in the compound: therefore we infer, not only from the improbability of the presence of muriatic acid, but also from its counteracting efficacy if present, that M. Descotils must conjecture erroneously. When the pottery biscuit be baked, and immersed in a solution of muriate of soda, and again subjected to the oven, superficial vitrification, or glazing, takes place; but this is totally independant of the muriatic acid, the effect being produced by the union of the alkali of the muriate of soda with the silicious matter of the biscuit. Lastly, can, and has, chemical analysis ever traced the smallest vestige of muriatic acid in puozzolanous earths?

Chaptal says that clays free from iron cannot be successfully employed in water cements. This is more probably just than the opinion of Descotils. Aluminous earth is thought by M. Vicat to not contribute to cementing efficacy by a peculiar affinity; but yet necessary to promote it. He urges also, that in making good water cement, it is not the duly proportioning of the ingredients only that will insure the effect, for the mode of manipulating will have its influence. Thus, if we mix together water with 100 of pure lime, 100 of silex, 80 of alumine, and 1 of peroxyd of iron, we shall obtain a bad cement. But if we mix 100 of lime, 20 of silex, 10 of alumine, and 5 of peroxyd of iron; and make a paste with the remainder of the ingredients; then calcine each separately; and lastly, combine all with water; we shall have a good and durable cement.

In aquatic constructions, we should consider a distinction between that part of the cement in contact with the water, and as indurating before the deeper substance. Cements made with common limes, after a time become superficially hardened; of a deeper colour; and instead of progressively hardening, will progressively retrograde, so as to be less consistent than at first immersion. This applies to fat cements of lime with sand. That is, the cement forms only by superficial crust, which, on gentle removal, may be repeatedly renewed; but it never solidifies through the body, and therefore when accident remove the crust, and a violent appulse of water occur, the whole will be puddled, or washed away,—which M. V. imputes to the water *dissolving* the lime out of the compound. Now, we hold that the water cannot *dissolve* the lime so totally as to produce the effect; the fact is, that the cement is imperfect; and so it is destroyed by the water mechanically.

With lean hydraulic limes such effects do not occur; because, says M. V., when combined with the puozzolana, they resist the dissolving action of the water. He should say that the composition setting more effectually resists the mechanical action of the water. It may be thought, perhaps, that this distinction is useless in a practical sense; but we take the liberty to urge, that correct scientific principles are what we sought M. Vicat's paper for, and we are unwilling that his authority should go to enforce any erroneous presumption that may (as principles ever must) influence future practice.

Common Limes, with Sand alone, will not form Water Cement, unless exposed to the Air; and scarcely then. Whereas good Hydraulic Lime sets better with Sand than with Puozzolana.

M. Vicat proceeds to remark on (what he erroneously persists in terming) the dissolving of the lime out of the cement, by the action of the water. He says that this action slackens, and finally ceases, when the excess of lime in the mortar has disappeared. And this, he says, may teach us how to determine the best proportions of lime with puozzolana. Were we to make a ball, with rather an excess of lime, of about two-thirds of an inch diameter, and expose it for a year under running water, then the proportion of lime remaining, found by subtracting the entire loss of weight during submersion, will be the proper quantity for the puozzolana employed. Water, then, will have but little action on well constituted cements, excepting always those containing only fat lime and sand; for those possessing scarcely any of the character of cement, will not resist the mechanical operation of water, whatever their constituent proportions may be.

On the influence of Time, in hardening Cements.

The next point of consideration is, the lapse of time requisite for the induration of cements; that is, the passing from the pasty consistence of their first formation, to the compactness called setting; as well as their progressive state to positive hardness.

After the due relative proportions of the constituting ingredients, perhaps, the next essential is, the due working into a mass, as stiff as can be well applied, with a trowel, in order to promote a rapid setting. If the mass be too soft, it either sets very slowly, or, by admitting a too free union with the water, does not set at all. But if either excess of consistence be preferable, it is on the side of softness; for if the mass be suffered to indurate, or set, before application, it is spoiled for the intended purpose. We consider it in this case to bear an analogy with plaster of Paris; which, if partially set before casting, will never be compact in the cast.

If the cement be made by mixing the quicklime with the puozzolana, before slacking the former; and then the lime be slacked in this mixture, by sprinkling; it will harden rapidly, provided it be compressed by surrounding matter; but if left free to expand, it will mingle with water, so largely, as to injure its mechanical and setting texture: so that it will be best to slack the lime a few days before mixture with the puozzolana. Indeed, the first setting depends greatly on the due management of the extinction of the lime. It will be found extremely difficult to bring to the same consistence mixtures that require very different quantities of water for this purpose; for a little more or less will probably retard or hasten the setting process. The season of the year, too, will have its influence; the cement setting more rapidly in summer than in winter. Cement in water, at 40° of Reaumur, will set in a few hours; but the same in a stream, at 7°, will require several days.

(To be continued.)

Sir H. Davy *on the Magnetic Phenomena produced by Electricity.* (Continued from p. 228.)

"The most remarkable general result that I obtained by these researches, and which I shall mention first, as it influences all the others, was, that *the conducting power of metallic bodies varied with the temperature, and was lower in some inverse ratio as the temperature was higher.*

"Thus a wire of platinum of $\frac{1}{220}$, and three inches in length, when kept cool by oil, discharged the electricity of two batteries, or of twenty double plates; but when suffered to be heated by exposure in the air, it barely discharged one battery.

"Whether the heat was occasioned by the electricity, applied to it from some other source, the effect was the same. Thus a wire of platinum, of such length and diameter as to discharge a combination without being considerably heated, when a flame of a spirit-lamp was applied to it, so as to make a part of it red hot, lost its power of discharging the whole electricity of the battery; as was shown by the disengagement of abundance of gas in the secondary circuit; which disengagement ceased as soon as the source of heat was withdrawn.

"There are several modes of exhibiting the fact, so as to produce effects which, till they are witnessed, must almost appear impossible. Thus, let a fine wire of platinum, of four or five inches in length, be placed in a voltaic circuit, so that the electricity passing through it may heat the whole of it to redness, and let the flame of a spirit-lamp be applied to any part of it, so as to heat that part to whiteness, the rest of the wire will instantly become cooled below the point of visible ignition. For the converse of the experiment, let a piece of ice, or a stream of cold air be applied to a part of the wire; the other parts will immediately become much hotter, and from a red, will rise to a white heat. The quantity of electricity that can pass through that part of the wire submitted to the changes of temperature, is so much smaller when it is hot than when it is cold, that the absolute temperature of the whole wire is diminished by heating a part of it.

"In comparing the conducting powers of different metals, I found much greater differences than I had expected. Thus six inches of silver wire, of $\frac{1}{220}$, discharged the whole of the electricity of 65 pair of plates of zinc and double copper, made active by a mixture of about one part of nitric acid of commerce, and fifteen parts of water. Six inches of copper wire, of the same diameter, discharged the electricity of 56 pairs, of the same combination. Six inches of tin, of the same diameter, carried off that of 12 only; the same quantity of wire of platinum, that of 11; and of iron, that of 9. Six inches of wire of lead, of $\frac{1}{200}$, seemed equal, in their conducting powers, to the same length of copper wire of $\frac{1}{220}$. All the wires were kept as cool as possible by immersion in a basin of water.

"I made a number of experiments of the same kind, but the results were never precisely alike, though they sometimes approached very near each other. When the batteries were highly charged, so that the intensity of the electricity was higher, the differences were less between the best and worst conductors; and they were greater when the charge was extremely feeble. Thus, with a fresh charge of about one part of nitric acid, and nine parts of water, wires of $\frac{1}{220}$ of silver and platinum, five inches long, discharged respectively the electricity of 30, and seven double plates.

"Finding that when different portions of the same wire, plunged in a non-conducting fluid, were connected with different parts of the same battery, equally charged, their conducting powers appeared in the inverse ratio of their lengths: so, when six inches of wire of platinum, of $\frac{1}{220}$, discharged the electricity of 10 double plates; three inches discharged that of 20; an inch and a half that of 40; and one inch that of 60; it occurred to me that, the conducting powers of the different metals might be more easily compared in this way, as it would be possible to make the contacts in less time than when the batteries were changed, and consequently with less variation in the charge.

"Operating in this way, I ascertained that in discharging the electricity of 60 pair of plates, one inch of platinum was equal to about six inches of silver; to five and a half inches of copper; to four of gold; to 8·8 of lead; to about $\frac{9}{10}$ of pallidium; and $\frac{8}{10}$ of iron; all the metals being in a cooling fluid medium.

"I found, as might be expected, that the conducting power of a wire for electricity, in batteries of the size and number of plates just described, was nearly directly as the mass; thus, when a certain length of wire of platinum discharged one battery, the same length of wire, of six times the weight, discharged six batteries; and the effect was exactly the same, provided the wires were kept cool, whether the mass was a single wire, or composed of six of the smaller wires in contact with each other. This result alone showed, that surface had no relation to conducting power, at least for electricity of this kind, and it was more distinctly proved by a direct experiment. Equal lengths and equal weights of wire of platinum, one round, and one flattened by being passed transversely through rollers, so as to have six or seven times the surface, were compared as to conducting powers: the flattened wire was the best conductor in air, from its greater cooling powers; but in water, no difference could be perceived between them.

"I tried to make a comparison between the conducting powers of fluid menstrua and charcoal, and those of metals. Six inches of platinum foil, an inch and one-fifth broad, were placed in a vessel which could be filled with any saline solution; and a similar piece of platinum placed opposite, at an inch distance; the whole was then made part of a voltaic circuit, which had likewise another termination by silver wires in water; and solution of salts added, till gas ceased to be liberated from the negative silver wire. In several trials of this kind, it was found that the whole of the surface of six inches, even with the strongest solutions of common salt, was insufficient to carry off the electricity even of two pair of plates; and a strong solution of potassa carried off the electricity of three pair of plates only; whereas an inch of wire of platinum of $\frac{1}{220}$ (as has been stated) carried off all the electricity of 60 pair of plates. The gas liberated upon the surface of the metals, when they are placed in fluids, renders it impossible to gain accurate results; but the conducting power of the best fluid conductors, it seems probable from these experiments, must be some hundreds of thousand times less than of the worst metallic conductors. A piece of well burnt compact box wood charcoal was placed in the circuit, being $\frac{3}{10}$ of an inch wide, by $\frac{1}{10}$ thick, and connected with large surfaces of platinum. It was found that one inch $\frac{2}{10}$ carried off the same quantity of electricity as six inches of wire of platinum of $\frac{1}{220}$.

"I made some experiments with the hope of ascertaining the exact change of ratio of the conducting powers dependant upon the change of the intensity and quantity of electricity; but I did not succeed in gaining any other than the general result, that the higher the intensity of the electricity, the less difficulty it had in passing through bad conductors; and several remarkable phenomena depend upon this circumstance.

"Thus, a battery where the quantity of the electricity is very great, and the intensity very low, such as one composed of plates of zinc and copper, so arranged as to act only as single plates of from twenty to thirty feet of surface each, and charged by a weak mixture of acid and water: charcoal made to touch only in a few points, is almost as much insulating as water, and cannot be ignited; nor can wires of platinum be heated when their diameter is less than $\frac{1}{80}$ of an inch, and their length three or four feet; and a foot of platinum wire of $\frac{1}{30}$ is scarcely heated by such a battery; whilst the same length of silver wire, of the same diameter, is made red hot; and the same lengths of thicker wires of platinum or iron are intensely hot.

"The heat produced where electricity of considerable intensity is passed through conductors, must always interfere with the exact knowledge of the changes of their conducting powers, as is proved by the following experiment. A battery of 20 pair of plates of zinc, and copper plates, ten inches by six, was very highly charged with a mixture of nitric acid and water, so as to exhibit a considerable intensity of electrical action, and the relative conducting powers of silver and platinum in air and water ascertained by means of it. In air, six inches of wire of platinum of $\frac{1}{80}$, discharged only four double plates; whilst six inches of silver wire, of the same diameter, discharged the whole combination: the platinum was strongly ignited in this experiment, whilst the silver was scarcely warm to the touch. On cooling the platinum wire by placing it in water, it was found to discharge 10 double plates. When the intensity of the electricity is very high, however, even the cooling powers of fluid media are of little avail: thus I found that fine wire of platinum was fused by the discharge of a common electrical battery under water; so that the conducting power must always be diminished by the heat generated, in a greater proportion as the intensity of the electricity is higher."

(To be continued.)

Mr. Shaw on the Facial Nerves.

(Continued from p. 239.)

Mr. Shaw next details the particulars of division of the facial respiratory nerve of a dog. He suffered but little inconvenience from the operation, and is now well. When he fawns, the right side of his face is motionless (the nerve of the right was cut). When threatened with a blow, there is a tremulous expression of fear on the left side of the face. He cannot close the eyelid; and when in alarm, the eye-ball itself is turned up. When excited, there is an alacrity of expression in the muscles of the left side of the face, and a brilliancy in the left eye; while the right is inanimate: this is particularly visible when fighting. There is not any remarkable difference in the ears; but this Mr. S. says is accountable for by the principal nerves going to the ear lying so deep as to render their section dangerous to the animal. Nor was the effect on the respiratory muscles so marked as in the case of the ass (to be detailed presently); but the power of twisting the nose, so distinct in a setting pointer, was destroyed. In two months, this dog perfectly recovered from the paralysis of the affected muscles.

The experiment was repeated in another dog; at the same time cutting the infra orbital nerve of the opposite side. He is now in very good health, and remarkably displays the effect of dividing the respiratory on one side, and a branch of the *fifth*. Mr. S. cut the same nerve in a cat, as near its exit from the stylo mastoid foramen as he could. When she was irritated, the paralysis of the muscles supplied by this respiratory was fully exhibited. She spat with that side only where the nerve was entire. The ear, too, was paralyzed; for when she spat, the ear on the defective side stood erect and motionless; on the other, was laid down. These experiments are easily performed on an ass, or an ox previous to death in a slaughter-house. The effect on the nostril is the most obvious symptom when the nerve is cut in the ass. This is rather remarkable; and we wish Mr. Shaw had stated whether there is any peculiarity in the distribution of the facial respiratory of that animal, which will account for an effect more decided in degree, than that witnessed in the dog; whose sense of smell is so acute. But, perhaps, the nervous section had been more extended in the ass. However, he goes on to report that, after having cut the right nerve, and closed the whole nose for a period, to suppress breathing, the ass, when freed, will snort with the left nostril only; and carbonate of ammonia will not affect the right nostril: but if applied to the left, he will curl it up as if about to sneeze, while he remains quiescent. Mr. Shaw failed in an experiment on a horse, when in Paris, but it was demonstrated to be owing to a large branch of the *fifth* pair, which runs for a short way parallel with the *portio dura*, and then unites with it. And this branch of the *fifth*, which being mistaken for the *portio dura* itself, was divided without the expected effect. When the latter was cut, the effect was complete.

Mr. Shaw then cut the plexus of the *portio dura* on one side of a game cock's neck, and the ruffling of his neck feathers when provoked was much diminished. On cutting the nerves on both sides, he presumed that it would wholly be prevented; but an unfortunate violence committed on the branches of the par vagum, killed him instantly.

Mr. S. remarks that, though he has generally followed the old nomenclature, *portio dura* of the *fifth*, yet he believes it to be erroneous to consider this nerve as at all connected with the auditory nerve. In the duck, there is not the slightest connection between them. Comparative anatomy would rather teach the connection of the *portio dura* with the *eighth*, than with the *portio mollis*. Perhaps the name of " respiratory nerve to the muscles of the face," as given by Mr. Bell, is the most appropriate, because indicative of its principal function.

Comparative Anatomy of the Fifth Pair.

This is, in all respects, different from the facial respiratory nerve. Comparative anatomy of its minute division in man, and in the lower classes of animals, justify Mr. Bell's conclusion, that the *fifth* pair is similar to those nerves which rise from the spinal marrow; and which, in their origin and distribution, are so essentially different from the class of respiratory nerves.

The rudiments of the *fifth* are discoverable in the very lowest classes of animals; for whether it be a feeler, the antenna of a lobster, the *moustache* of a phoca, or the trunk of an elephant, still it is the branch of the *fifth* which supplies sensibility and muscular power to the part; similar to the digital nerves of man passing from those of the arms to the tips of the fingers.

The facial respiratory is, in many animals, connected with the organ of taste, and large in proportion to its delicacy and power of taste and mastication; in the lower animals larger than in man. Mr S. says that this relative magnitude of the *fifth*, compared with that of the *portio dura*, may give us a better estimate of the comparative degree in power of expression than can be deduced from any other anatomical fact. The goose and duck are good instances in illustration.—In the latter, the six branches of the *fifth*, when laid together, form a mass equal in size to that of the largest nerve in a man's arm; while all the combined branches of the *portio dura* would not exceed a common sewing thread.

In the cat and hare, the branches of the *fifth* pass not only to the muscles, but also to the whiskers; while those of the facial respiratory go past the hairs, and enter into the muscles moving the tip of the nostril. The nerves going into the bulb of the hair of these small animals are difficult to demonstrate; but not so in the phoca. A M. Andral shows this fact in the Journal de Physiologie Experimentale, by M. Magendie; and it is further demonstrated by dissection of animals having tufts of hair over the eyes, as in the American squirrel, where Mr. S. has traced the first division of the *fifth* into such bulb. Mr. S. now proceeds further to show that the uses of the *fifth* and the *portio dura* are distinct.

In the same ass, of which the facial respiratory had been cut on the right side, the infra orbital on the left had also been divided. On cutting this nerve, no change was produced in the action of the muscles moving the left nostril in respiration; the other nostril was paralyzed by the division of the *portio dura* of the right side. The muscles of the lip, during feeding, were peculiarly affected; for though they were not paralyzed in the act of respiration, yet they were rendered incapable of mastication and voluntary motion. The sensibility on this side was destroyed, for the puncture of a needle did not rouse the animal. When quiescent, the nose is twisted to the side on which the *fifth* is entire, and the *portio dura* deficient: but the moment he is excited the nose is pulled to the other side.

Mr. Shaw promises another communication, wherein he will describe the different kinds of palsy, and prove their dependance on the particular systems of nerves dissected. Also that the two systems (the *portio dura* and *fifth*) are seldom or never affected at the same time. Likewise, that by exciting the actions of the one, the distortions arising from the paralysis of the other will disappear.—Query. If the respective excitements of these nerves can be made productive of their mutual corrections, will not this rather militate against the doctrine sought to be established?

Mr. Shaw concludes by observing on the practical advantages to be derived from the pursuit of this interesting subject, and we shall wait impatiently for his further developement.

On the Papyri found at Herculaneum.
(Continued from p. 243.)

Sir Humphry Davy proceeds in his detail as follows:—

"The operation of fire is not at all necessary for producing such an imperfect carbonization of vegetable matter as that displayed by the MSS.; thus, at Pompeii, which was covered by a shower of ashes that must have been cold, as they fell at a distance of seven or eight miles from the crater of Vesuvius, the wood of the houses is uniformly found converted into charcoal; yet the colours on the walls, most of which would have been destroyed or altered by heat, are perfectly fresh; and where papyri have been found in these houses, they have appeared in the form of white ashes, as of burnt paper; an effect produced by the slow action of the air penetrating through the loose ashes, and which has been impeded or prevented in Herculaneum by the tufa, which, as it were, has hermetically sealed up the town, and prevented any decay, except such as occurs in the spontaneous decomposition of vegetable substances exposed to the limited operation of water and air; for intance, peat and Bovey coal.

"The result of the action of heat upon the different specimens of the papyri, proved likewise, that they had never before been exposed to any considerable degree of temperature.

"Various specimens of papyri were heated to dull redness in a small covered crucible of platinum, to which air had no access. Some of the chesnut, and most perfect, specimens lost nearly half their weight; and the very black ones, and those containing the largest quantity of white ashes, all lost more than one-third, as the following results, selected from a number, will show:—

No. 1. 100 parts of a pale chesnut papyrus, lost .. 45 parts
No. 2. 100 parts of a decomposed papyrus, chesnut-coloured, but darker, lost 43
No. 3. 100 parts of a very black papyrus, lost 42
No. 4. 100 parts of a pale papyrus, extremely loose in texture, and partly converted into white ashes, lost 41
No 5. 100 parts of another, of the same kind, lost.. 38

" When the whole of the carbonaceous and vegetable matter was destroyed by slow combustion, the white ashes remaining, which were principally carbonate of lime and lime, proved to be from $\frac{1}{10}$ to $\frac{1}{20}$ of the original weight of the papyrus; and in those specimens which were most dense, and that contained a white powder, the proportion of ashes was greater, and a larger quantity was insoluble in acids.

" Ammonia was found in the products of all the papyri that I distilled, but least in those which contained no distinct characters; from which it is probable that it arose principally from decomposed glue, used in the manufacture of the ink, and which had been principally dissolved and carried off in those papyri which had been most exposed to the action of water.

" I ascertained, that what the Neapolitans called varnish, was decomposed skin, that had been used to unfold some of the papyri, and which, by chemical changes, had produced a brilliant animal carbonaceous substance; this substance afforded abundance of ammonia by distillation, and left ashes containing much phosphate of lime.

" Only one method, and that a very simple mechanical one, has been adopted for unrolling the MSS. It was invented by Padre Piaggi, a Roman, and consists in attaching thin animal membrane, by a solution of glue, to the back of the MSS. and carefully elevating the layers by silk threads when the glue is dry.

" In considering this method in its general application, some circumstances occurred to me which afforded an immediate improvement. A liquid solution of glue had been used, which, when the texture of the MSS. was loose or broken, penetrated through three or four layers, and these, when the glue dried, separated together. To obviate this objection, I mixed the solution of glue with a sufficient quantity of alcohol, to gelatinize it; and a mixture of the jelly and the fluid being made, and applied by a camel's hair brush, a film of jelly remained on the exterior of the surface of the leaf, which attached itself to the membrane.

" The effect of the solution of glue, applied in the ancient method, was always likewise to separate the layers, by expanding the imperfectly carbonized fibres. In the improvement I have mentioned, the alcohol, from its greater lightness, penetrated further into the papyrus, but produced its greatest effect immediately on the first layers.

"I adopted in some cases ether, as an agent for assisting the separation of the layers; and it was always found very efficacious, whether it was necessary to remove a single layer, or several layers at a time, in order to discover if a roll contained characters. The ether was applied, by a camel's hair brush, lightly to the surface of the leaf, when its operation was intended to be merely on that leaf; and it was suffered to sink deeper according as more layers were to be separated; the mere circumstances of its evaporation, which in some cases I assisted by heat, tended to detach the layers. For the black MSS. I employed sulphuric ether; and for the brown ones, muriatic or nitric ether, in their impure states, *i. e.* mixed with much alcohol.

"No artificial means had been employed by the Neapolitans for drying the papyrus in the operation of attaching the membrane, and no means, except mechanical ones, of detaching it after it was dried.

"By throwing a stream of air, gradually warmed, till it attained a temperature above that of boiling water, upon the surface of the leaf, I succeeded not only in drying the layers with much greater rapidity, but likewise in separating them with more delicacy.

"I tried different modes of heating the air to be thrown upon the papyrus, such as passing it, in a spiral metallic tube, through warm water, or oil, by a double bellows; and from a large bladder through a straight tube, having a very fine orifice, and heated by a copper ball, surrounding the body of the tube, and exposed to burning charcoal; which last method, from its simplicity, I found the one best fitted to the Neapolitan operators. By sending the stream of air from a greater or smaller distance, so that it mixed with more or less cold air, the degree of temperature applied was regulated at pleasure. It was always found necessary to suffer a few minutes to elapse after the membrane was attached, and then to begin with a very slight increase of temperature; as otherwise, by too sudden an application of heat, the membrane became shrivelled before it became adherent, and the vapour suddenly raised destroyed its union with the papyrus; whereas, when the moisture was suffered to drain from the gelatinized glue, and the temperature was gradually raised, the expansion of the skin and the upper layer separated them perfectly from the lower layers, so that the unrolling was performed, as it were, by chemical means: and an operation, which hitherto had required some hours for its completion, was easily effected in from 30 to 40 minutes.

"I tried several experiments, by substituting solution of resins in alcohol, and of gums in water, for the gelatinized solution; but none of them answered so well; the resins would not adhere with any tenacity to the membrane, and the gums, when dried, had not that flexibility which is an important character in the glue.

"The alterations in the mode of applying and drying the membrane used to detach and preserve the leaves of MSS. capable of being unrolled, were applied generally. I shall now mention the plans I adopted for the preparation of the MSS. for this operation.

"MSS. in different states required a treatment of a directly opposite kind, which was to be modified according to circumstances. The pale chesnut coloured MSS., covered partially with white ashes, were generally of a texture so loose, and had their layers so destroyed, that there was considerable danger of their falling into pieces by mere touching. The characters that remained in many of them were extremely distinct; and when a number of layers were taken up at once, it appeared as if they presented perfect columns of writing; but the fact is, the papyrus was full of holes, and each line was made up of letters from several different folds of the MSS. When the process of unrolling these papyri was performed in the common way, the result obtained, appeared, till it was examined minutely, a perfect column; but was, in fact, made up of the letters of different words. I endeavoured to obtain the fragments of a single leaf attached to a layer of membrane, by applying a solution of caoutchonc in ether to the surface of a MS., so as to supply the parts of the leaf destroyed. But operating in this way, I obtained only a few characters, and never an entire word; so that after various unsuccessful trials, I was obliged to give up the MSS. of this description as hopeless; more than 5-6ths of their contents probably being always destroyed, and even that in so irregular a way as to leave no entire sentences, or even words." (To be continued.)

Observations on the Production of Electricity by Contact. By C. G. GMELIN, Professor of Chemistry in the University of Tubingen. Edinburgh Phil. Journal, No. 11.

Professor Gmelin states that he distrusted the propriety of the conclusions come to by Sir H. Davy on an experimental research into this subject, in the year 1806; where Sir H. D. seemed to prove unequivocally the electrical opposition between alkalies and acids, as well established by galvanic action on their compounds. Sir H. showed that, if the solid acids, as the oxalic, succinic, benzoic, boracic, phosphoric, &c., were touched on extensive surfaces by an insulated copper plate, they were negatively electrified, while the plate was positive; and that the alkalies and earths, as lime, strontia, magnesia, &c., were positively electrified, and the copper negatively. A zinc, or tin plate, showed similar results with that of copper: the intensity of the positive charge being the same, whether the plate were insulated or not. The Professor doubted:—

1st. Because Sir H. D. himself had found that if the temperature changed a little, as, for instance, if the earths were touched during their cooling, the opposite electricity often appeared.

2d. Because, in those experiments, the condenser was employed; an instrument which may so easily be a source of errors; and which, at any rate, unnecessarily prolongs the experiment.

3d. Because it appeared to Prof. G. very improbable that those pulverulent bodies should turn out so very different in their electrical relations towards the metals, considering that the opposition between acids and bases is not an absolute, but only a co-relative one; and that it might be impossible to anticipate the relation of silica, for instance, and of those bodies in general which are possessed neither of a marked acid, nor basic, character.

Having touched magnesia with a plate of zinc, 7¼ Paris inches in diameter, and with all the precautions suggested by Sir H. D., the zinc was found to be positively, and the magnesia, negatively electrified. The electrometer of Volta, with its condenser, was used. This result conflicting with Sir H. D.'s, the Professor was induced to repeat many of the experiments of the former.

To obviate repetitions, Prof. G. states that, in the following experiments, he used the new electrometer, with two zambonic piles; whose superior sensibility immediately indicated the electrical quality, and superseded the necessity of a condenser. The substances were heated in a covered platinum crucible, and ignited when their natures admitted it. The crucible, while hot, was put on a bath of dry mercury, and covered with a perfectly dry glass. Thus, the substance in the crucible assumed the temperature of the surrounding atmosphere, without having been in contact with the air. Twenty-four hours passed; it was touched, still confined in the crucible, with round plates of zinc, or copper, of two Paris inches in diameter, insulated by a glass handle. No difference was perceived, whether the substance was insulated, or not.

The experiments (if not otherwise noticed) must be understood to have been under insulation, and the season dry, temperature varying from $+ 12°$ to $+ 16°$ of Reaumur; but he found no difference in this respect, if the substances had been protected from moisture, and had assumed the atmospheric temperature. The evolved electricity was always more intense on strong pressure in contact: thereby generating an idea of friction being influential; but on the other hand, rough substances, whose friction is the greatest, gave little or no electricity.

The first substance subjected to experiment was magnesia. It was ignited; and while hot, the metallic contact was made: yielding an intense electricity. In the lapse of time, it became indifferent, and then null. But afterwards yielded the opposite, or positive electricity. And the experiment could be repeated several days with similar result.

Perfectly pure magnesia, prepared by precipitating it from sulphate of magnesia, by aid of a boiling solution of subcarbonate of potash.—This magnesia, under all circumstances, gave the positive electricity; whether hot or cold; itself being in the negative state. The intensity was so great, that the gold leaf touched the pile after a single contact. The Professor adds that this experiment was often repeated; and seemed so completely to refute Sir H. D.'s, that he almost considered further trial requisite.

Burned Carrara marble, perfectly freed from carbonic acid, by slacking in a platinum crucible, and strongly ignited again, after cooling, commonly imparted negative electricity to the plate: in some trials, intense; in others, weak. The same results proceeded from the lime, when it was hotter than the surrounding atmosphere. In one instance it imparted positive electricity; that is, when it had been closely confined for 24 hours in a dry bottle, and then poured out on a glass plate. And, also, when the contents of the crucible had been emptied into a porphyry mortar and were become cooled down to the atmosphere, so that the lower surface of the lime in the crucible became the upper in the mortar, it imparted moderately positive electricity. Friction always rendered the plate intensely negative.

With calcined oyster-shells, under similar process of experiment, and while the crucible was hot, he always had positive on the plate; and down to the temperature of the atmosphere, though less intense. This was the case when the lime was touched while in the crucible; as well as when the plate was rubbed against the lime. Whilst, therefore, the lime from Carrara marble becomes positively electrified by its contact with zinc; that from oyster-shells becomes negative under similar contact.

The Carrara marble was found to contain magnesia; and that from oyster-shells sulphuret of lime, phosphate of lime, magnesia, and oxide of iron. Therefore the Professor prepared a perfectly pure lime, by dissolving Carrara marble in nitric acid, and digesting the solution with burned and slacked Carrara marble, so that the iron and magnesia were precipitated; the solution was precipitated by carbonate of ammonia, then thoroughly washed, and burned in a platinum crucible, and made perfectly caustic. Pure as this was, it still had a rough surface, and rendered the plate moderately negative. When powdered in a hot porphyry mortar, again heated in a platinum crucible, and then cooled, the plate acquired intense positive electricity. And after several weeks' confinement in a closely stopped bottle, it imparted positively to the plate. Professor G. then infers that the quality of the electricity imparted is governed, rather by the physical constitution, than by the temperature of the matter.

Caustic strontia, obtained by igniting nitrate of strontia, imparted weakly positive when finely powdered. Caustic potash and soda did not afford any satisfactory result.

Uria, purified from oxide of cerium, gave intensely positive even when a small surface was touched.

Beryllia imparted intensely negative; the more remarkable because its external characters resemble magnesia.

Silica gave positive to the plate; but ceased on exposure to the air.

Oxide of zinc, by a single contact, imparted intensely positive.

Oxide of cerium gave similar result.

Crystallized and fused boracic acid imparted positively.

Phosphoric acid vitrified, prepared from phosphorus by nitric acid, was null. Ignited red, and cooled, was also null. The same, even at a white heat and an evaporation of white acid.

Oxalic acid constantly imparted positively when crystallized; when in powder (hydrate) very weak.

Next Professor G. tried saline compounds:—

Pure carbonate of barytes constantly imparted intensely positive.

Carbonate of soda, fused, and hot, imparted intensely negative. When cooled down to the atmosphere, was sometimes positive, sometimes negative.

Carbonate of soda, effloresced, constantly positive at atmospheric temperature, and even higher; but rarely negative.

Crystals of sulphate of potash, ignited, powdered, and hot, imparted weakly positive; when cooled, was increased to intensity.

Sulphate of soda, freed from water of crystallization, imparted positively.

The Professor concludes by observing, that though the electrical opposition between acids and bases be well established by other means; yet it cannot be deduced from the electrical relation between these bodies and metals.

On Artificial Mineral Waters; with some Remarks on Light. By SAMUEL MOREY.
Silliman's American Journal.

We think that American philosophy has one general advantage over our own; that is, it is of a more practical nature: and philosophical research has but little comparative value, which is not directed to some special purpose of human benefit.

Mr. Morey addresses Dr. Silliman, stating that his object is to furnish, at a cheap rate, an abundant supply of light; and, by the same process, to afford the means of making artificial waters resembling those of Seltzer and Saratoga. This compound effect he would produce, by passing aqueous vapour over ignited charcoal; the result of which would be, as is well known, a generation of hydrogen, and a formation of carbonic acid; estimating the product, from one pound of charcoal and about four of water, to be about two hundred and fifty gallons of carbonic acid gas, and five hundred gallons of hydrogen gas, equal in combustive illumination to about twenty-five pounds, or six wax candles, during twenty-five hours. But there is an error in Mr. Morey's estimate of the hydrogen, by his not adverting to the modern correction of the constituents of water. He says, some very trifling addition of spirit of turpentine should be made, to render the flame white. We think there will be no little difficulty in effecting this point. Mr. M. proposes to force the carbonic acid gas, with currents of water, along pipes, to issue at pleasure. In this way, he thinks, cities may be supplied with a pleasant and wholesome beverage; and by the same channels also have their supply of combustible gas for light. He says, there must be an addition of some kinds of fuel, to preserve the red heat of the charcoal, and vaporize the water. This is a matter of course, and scarcely worthy of mention, as we think, if the ultimate objects be really practicable; of which we should give a very guarded opinion.

For the purpose of furnishing these waters, Mr. M. had a cool spring of water brought through wooden pipes, about one hundred and fifty yards, on a descent of fifty feet, so that the water should not fill the bore, and thereby retard the gases, if turned into the aquæduct with the water; or forced in at the bottom. A pressure equal to one hundred and thirty feet, or one hundred and forty feet, was easily obtained. Very fine streams, issuing from this fall, and meeting a plane surface at right angles, were dashed into a mist, which being forced into a strongly compressed atmosphere of carbonic acid gas, became powerfully impregnated. To aid the impregnation, and detain any loose sulphuric acid, he filled a vessel (a three-gallon stone jar will answer the purpose) about two-thirds, with fragments of marble, the size of peas. In this way, water under a pressure of twenty or thirty feet, issuing about a pint per minute, flows in, pure, at the top, and flows out, nearly saturated, at the bottom. By increasing the pressure at once, or by a succession of falls, any strength of water may be obtained. And, when impregnated with carbonic acid, if it percolate iron in the pipes of transmission, a chalybeate will be formed. Or, carbonate (subcarbonate?) of soda may be added. How easy then, says Mr. M. to produce, at one establishment, from a single spring of pure water, our choice of any number of mineral waters; and these as good as any to be found in nature, or probably better!

He next proposes to avail ourselves of the extrication of carbonic acid gas from breweries; which might be impelled, by forcing pumps, at pleasure, through tubes, with a sufficient quantity of water, and conveyed as the demand may require. Should greater pressure be necessary, a valve may be loaded accordingly.

When the gas be generated by the decomposition of marble, occasional agitation of the ingredients is necessary; and the best means Mr. M. has tried is, that of making a stone jug revolve on its axis, and end over end, at the same time having the marble very coarse. We do not well understand this as practicable, for purposes of magnitude, without the aid of machinery; though he speaks of effecting it by weights, springs, or a parapet of water, or occasionally by the hand; these are clumsy methods, and very ill adapted for an enlarged scale of production. We will here give another mode recommended by Mr. M. He says, "A very cheap, quick, and agreeable mode of preparing the water, where we have (or have not) an aquæduct, or head, to resort to, is to take four, or five, or more decanters, say of the capacity of a quart; fill them with fragments of marble; set them in a row, or other form, each with a good cork; let a tin tube screw upon the axis to receive the gas, and press pieces of cork or other stuffing to the vessel, to make it tight round the axis. This tube, near the other end, is of a conical form, and turned down at a right angle, far enough to be inserted through the cork of the first bottle; another tube, turned down at each end, so that one leg shall pass through the cork, also to the bottom of the first decanter; and the other through the cork of the second decanter; and so on, with as many as are to be used. A small reservoir is to be placed as many feet above as convenient; and the first vessel, with a small pipe leading down, and through, the first cork, with an opening at the lower end, about one thirtieth of an inch in diameter; a quantity of pulverized lime, and water, may be put into the revolving vessels; then more water, containing a small quantity of clay or sulphate of lime; this will be deposited on the lime, so as to prevent the action of the acid when poured in; which may now be added; and this vessel corked. It is now ready for use. Put cool water into the reservoir, turn the vessel moderately, if the gas is not already forming fast enough; the water strikes on the first fragments of stone, is thrown over them, and passes over the surface, from the one to the other, to the bottom, where it is continually taken up by the tube, with a portion of the gas, and discharged just below the cork of the second vessel; or thrown out in a spray, by, and with, the gas; or else discharged at the lower end of the tube in bubbles: thereby furnishing a carbonic acid gas within and without, with an almost infinitely thin film of water between, to absorb it on each side."

This is a very troublesome, operose, and bungling method of doing a most simple thing; and the description given is extremely tedious, as well as indistinct. The principle is plain; and the following will be found a cheap and equally effectual method of making the waters:—Bring water, finely divided, as in spray, into contact with carbonic acid gas; and it will become saturated. Or, previously dissolve subcarbonate of soda in the water, and you will have a soda water, after having subjected the spray, as above mentioned, to the combination with carbonic acid.

Into a strong eighteen-gallon cask, put some rough fragments of stone, and from the top of this cask carry up a tube to your reservoir of water above (the higher the reservoir may be placed, the better). A stop-cock should close or open this pipe, near its entry into the cask, to regulate the fall of water according to the rapidity of the generation of carbonic acid. In another small cask should be put the fragments of marble, or chalk, with the diluted sulphuric acid. Then, by a tube joining the two casks, the gas generated in the small one would pass into the large one, where it would meet the water passed down from the reservoir and dashed on the stones at the bottom into spray, and, uniting with it, might issue out near the bottom, by a tube or cock. The contents of the small cask might be agitated, either by an occasional shake of the cask itself, or by an axis running down to the bottom, with cross staves; and the upper part of the axis projecting out at the top, might, with a winch affixed to it, be made to revolve, and stir up the ingredients at pleasure.

Mr. Morey is so wedded to his project, partly from the personal benefit he has derived from drinking the carbonic acid with water, that he will not willingly suffer an atom of the gas to be lost; and having before proposed applying the carbonic acid, generated during fermentation in breweries, to the manufacture of Seltzer and soda water, he goes on to suggest the natural gaseous extrication being arrested in its progress; as that of the Grotto del Cani; wherewith he would cool the whole population of the city of Naples. We have not any doubt that these waters may be obtained largely, and cheaply, by every private family; but we are not, like Mr. Morey, mounted on a hobby.

A geographical and commercial View of Northern Central Africa, cantaining a particular Account of the course and termination of the great River Niger, in the Atlantic Ocean. By JAMES M'QUEEN.

North American Review.

The above work was published at Edinburgh in 1821; and sets out, in its very title, with an assumption that cannot be conceded. It is denominated "A particular Account," &c., which implies a detail or narrative of facts, or circumstances; whereas it is nothing more than an *Essay to account for*; or a body of conjecture; supported by a little known, and much reported. The Editors of the above Review make some comments, that are not altogether unworthy of notice; and as the question of the Niger has long interested the inquiring world, we think it may be acceptable to our readers that we give them an outline of the matter.

The reviewers commence with showing that, Mr. M'Queen has but little merit as to the novelty of his conjectures; for he has been anticipated by others. Mr. M'Q.'s hypothesis is, that the Niger, after flowing in an easterly course, a few degrees beyond the longitude of Tombuctoo, turns towards the south; and discharges itself into the Gulph of Guinea, by several mouths, at the Bights of Benin and Biafra. Reichard, in 1808, maintained the same opinion, in the Ephemerides Geographiques de Weimar. And Malte-Brun has adopted it from him, in his Geographie Universelle.

Reichard says, "At the west of Wangara, the Niger flows to the south; and the Misselad, after passing the Lake of Fittree, and that of Semegonda, in flowing from the latter, divides into two principal branches, which surround the Wangara, and fall into the Niger. This last named river afterwards continues to flow towards the south west, until it discharges itself into the corner of the Gulph of Guinea, where it forms a delta; the western branch of which is the river Benin, or Formoso; and the eastern branch, the Rio del Rey." M. Reichard then goes on, by varied calculation, to show that Major Rennel's opinion of the waters of the Niger, El Gazel, and Misselad being dissipated by evaporation, is utterly untenable: for M. R. contends, on the authority of Edresi, that the Nile of the Negroes surrounds the Wangara, during the entire year. The Niger coming from the west, is divided into two branches above Ghana; the northern flows directly to the east; the southern, forming a curve equal to the extent of Wangara, returns towards the north, and both flow into the Lake Semegonda. At least this must be supposed. But is this correct? How can a navigable river, from one to two English miles wide, fall into a lake which is hardly twenty or twenty-five miles square in extent, without making it overflow? To contain the waters of the Niger alone, a lake equal to Lake Aral would be necessary. But the Lake of Semegonda receives, besides, all the rivers from Bornou, Kagou, Begarme, Bergou, Four, and Misselad; the latter especially never being dry. All these rivers meet in Lake Fittree, and are discharged from it. It is only thus that the rivers mentioned by Edresi can be explained. He gives to his Nile, which surrounds Wangara, a general direction toward the west. This can be only the Misselad. Horneman says that this river flows from the Lake of Fittree; the communication of the waters of the Kagou with the Lake Semegonda alleged by Edresi, is confirmed. But the Lake of Semegonda being too small to receive and evaporate the waters of all these rivers, the two branches which flow from it, must run, one to the west, and the other to the south west, and discharge into the Niger, at a considerable distance from each other; the true Niger, then, only washing the western part of Wangara in its course to the south west. But the nature of the soil of Benin and Biafra, with the character of the rivers, constitute the most impressive proofs; thus urged by Edresi:—

"The countries of Benin, Oware, New Calabar, and Calbango, are the Delta of a large river, which comes a great distance from the north west. From accounts given by Nyendal, Bosmann, Dapper, and the two Barbots, we learn that the Rio Formoso is eight miles wide at the mouth; higher up, it is only four; and higher still, it is wider, and narrower. It divides into an infinite number of branches, which spread into all the neighbouring country. It is possible to pass in a boat from one branch to the other. There is also, in the interior, a passage by water to Calabar, and it is quite easy to reach that place in a canoe. From Rio Formoso to the western shore of the river of the Cameroons, the coast is very low, and marshy. It preserves the same character further up into the country. The whole of this country forms an immense plain, crossed by large and navigable rivers; such as the Forcados, Ramos, Dodos, Sangama, near Cape Formoso, Non, Oddi, Filana, St. Nicholas, Meas, St. Barthelemy, New Calabar, Bandi, Old Calabar, and Del Rey. This last is from seven to eight marine miles wide at its mouth. It preserves its width far into the country; and comes a great distance from the north. All these rivers belong to the same principal river: for the Rio del Rey, coming from the north, and the Rio Formoso from the north east, the two lines which they follow must meet, at forty or fifty geographical miles, higher north. Both must have one course, for, at least, two hundred miles. Then why not grant that their courses unite for three or four hundred miles? What an extent indeed must it have, since the Delta, including Cape Formoso, occupies a length of ninety (geographical) miles along the coast, and contains so many branches! It much surpasses, in size, the Delta of the Ganges." In aid of these arguments it is urged (and we think forcibly) that the Delta, composed of mere slime, without any stones, must have been formed by the periodical inundation of one or more large rivers; that, according to the testimony of Jaques Barbot and Grasilheir, who inspected all the country about Calabar and Bandi, and witnessed its overflow every year, in the months of July, August, and September, this inundation corresponds with that in Wangara; and that pimento, which is abundant at Benin, is equally so at Darkulla. To these, M. Malte-Brun adds, the coincidence of the name of the island of *Oulil*, which, according to the Arabs, is situate at the mouth of the Nile of the Negroes, and is the only country of Nigritia where salt is obtained, with that of an island on the coast of Guinea, at the mouth of the old Calabar, called, on the Portuguese maps, *Olil*, which is covered with a bed of marine salt.

In the preface to the narrative of Robert Adams, we have a statement, derived from a gentleman who had resided for a considerable period at the settlement of Lagos, and at other stations on the coast of the Bight of Benin, which strongly corroborates this hypothesis. It is there asserted, that traders from Houssa (a town on the Niger, near the spot where Mr. Park is supposed to have been killed,) previously to the abolition of the slave trade, were continually to be met with at Lagos, and that they still come down to that mart, though in smaller bodies. These traders stated their journey to the coast as occupying three or four months, and as retarded, not by mountains, but by rivers, morasses, and large lakes, which intersect the country between Houssa and the coast. They crossed them on large rafts, capable of transporting many passengers and much merchandize. The traders were often detained by waiting for a sufficient freight for the rafts. This informant was fully persuaded, from his frequent communications with the traders, that it would be practicable to penetrate safely from Benin to Houssa. Add to all this, that Mr. Park, in his last letter to Sir J. Banks, mentioned his having met with a guide who was one of the greatest travellers in that part of Africa; who stated that the Niger, after passing Kashna, runs directly to the right hand on the south; and that he was sure it did not end near Kashna or Bornou, as he had resided in both of those kingdoms; and Park speaks with confidence of following the river until it reaches the sea coast.

Although the course of the Niger be not of any direct importance, as a matter of pure scientific research, yet it has caused so much disquisition, and the sacrifice of so much valuable life, that we cannot but consider it as worthy the consideration of the disciples of philosophy, and have therefore introduced it to our readers. We need not, either here, or in a future number, follow Mr. M'Queen into detail; we shall only state his general reasons, in proof that the Niger falls into the Gulf of Guinea.

(To be continued.)

On Mr. MURRAY's *Decomposition of Metallic Salts by the Magnet.*

In a former number we gave a series of experiments, made by Mr. Murray, on the decomposition of several of the metallic salts by the magnet; whereby he made it appear that the decomposition was specifically effected by magnetic action. We now have this position controverted by an anonymous writer, in the Annals of Philosophy, who attributes the effects produced in Mr. Murray's experiments as due to the iron alone of the magnet. As the indicators of truth, we must state impartially on both sides, and therefore give this writer's stated results.

He placed a perfectly unmagnetized steel bar in a dilute solution of permuriate of mercury: pure mercury was immediately precipitated.

He placed an unmagnetic steel bar in a solution of nitromuriate of platinum; and the platinum was precipitated with all the phenomena exhibited in Mr. M.'s experiment.

Mr. Murray stated that fine Dutch steel wire, non magnetic, was immersed in nitrate of silver for fourteen hours, and remained unaffected. But on making this wire part of the circuit between the north and south poles of two bar magnets, it became speedily plumed with crystals of silver. Again (says Mr. M.) a portion of the same wire was snapped in twain, and the magnet passed over one of the fragments, and both projected into solution of nitrate of silver. The magnetized portion reduced the silver; the other did not.

Our anonymous experimentalist observes on the above, that he divided a dilute solution of nitrate of silver into three portions. In one he placed a steel bar, hardened at the ends, but not having any effect on iron filings. Into the two other solutions he put magnets, formed of similar bars; the north pole of the one, and the south pole of the other, being immersed, their opposite poles projecting above the edges of the glasses containing the solutions, the poles were then connected by an unmagnetized steel wire. Many hours elapsed before fine brilliant flakes of metallic silver appeared in all of them slowly; and, afterwards, rapidly: but there was not any perceptible difference between the solutions containing the magnetized or the unmagnetized bars. The writer next imitated Mr. Murray's experiment with platinum wire: wherein he (Mr. M.) stated that platinum wire, which was not affected by a solution of nitrate of silver; when united with the two poles of a powerful magnet, became discoloured and was acted on. To disprove this, Mr. M.'s opponent immersed a platinum wire, in contact with the two ends of a strong horse-shoe magnet, into a solution of nitrate of silver. It remained immersed for thirty hours; but wholly untarnished.

Mr. Murray's experiment on the immersion of magnetic bars in phosphorous acid, the acid being said to be decomposed; the north pole of one of the bars being scarcely affected, but that of the other being corroded half an inch deep, affording a fasciculated structure, as described by Mr. Daniell. On the other hand, the secret experimentalist declares that he arranged magnetic, and unmagnetic, bars in phosphoric acid; in the form he had before stated in the solutions of nitrate of silver; but the action of the phosphoric acid on the magnets, was not, in the slightest degree, increased by contact.

He reproaches Mr. Murray for not adverting to the fact of simple iron precipitating silver from its nitrate; which is distinctly recorded by Newmann, Murray, and Thenard.

The results obtained by these gentlemen differ so totally, that we think Mr. Murray bound in honour to refute his antagonist, on points implicating matter of fact. But we cannot think it quite fair for a party to shield himself under the protection of secrecy, when he assails the veracity of an experimentalist. If Mr. Murray have been wrong, we cannot discover what there is to be apprehended in telling him so, with gentlemanly urbanity.

American Lime for Water Cement.

In Silliman's Journal, we have the subjoined copy of a Letter from B. Wright, Esq. Engineer of the Erie Canal, dated Rome, June, 24, 1821.

"The specimen of argillo-ferruginous lime-stone, herewith presented, is found in great abundance in the counties of Malison, Onondaga, and Cayuga, in the State of New York. When found *in place*, it is always under the blue lime, which is uniformly overlaid with grey lime. The grey is the upper stratum, and is found in large heavy blocks; the whole six or eight feet in thickness. The blue, which next occurs, is various in thickness; and from it is made the beautiful white lime. Under the blue lies the first described, which is found to be a superior water cement, and is used very successfully in the stone work of the Erie canal, and believed to be equal to any of the kind found in any other country. I cannot give you the analysis:—if convenient to give a sample to Mr. Silliman, for his examination, it might be useful to the community to have its properties fully understood; and if he thinks it merits a place in his useful publication, I presume he will give it. I do not know that it is found in the countries west of Cayuga, but presume, from the geological character of that country, it may be found in all the country west to Niagara, and, probably, further west. It is pulverized, (as it will not slack,) and then used by mixing two parts of lime and one part sand. It hardens but under water; and it is believed its properties are partially lost, if permitted to dry suddenly, or if not used soon after mixing.

"Mr. Canvass White, a friend of mine, has obtained a patent for it when used for *hydraulic purposes:* and it is believed it will answer an excellent purpose for rough casting, &c. For cisterns it will be much used, no doubt; and for all the principal erections of stone work for canals, it is indispensable. I am, &c."

The editor of the journal then goes on to say:—

"We are informed by Mr. Woolsey that, the price of this lime, pulverized and burnt, and delivered at Utica, is twenty per cent. the bushel. Mr. W. remarks that, 'Mr. Wright is a gentleman, equally distinguished for respectability of character and high attainments as a civil engineer, and that his accuracy may be relied on.'

"In February we had an interview with Mr. White, from whom we obtained the following result of the analysis of the hydraulic lime, by Dr. Hadley:—

Carbonic acid	35·05
Zinc	25·
Silex	15·05
Alumine	16·05
Water	5·03
Oxide of iron	2·02
	98·20."

We have taken the above from a new journal, called the Technical Repository, edited by Mr. Gill, a gentleman well known to the Society of Arts, being, as we think, at the head of one of its departments. We cannot think the name of lime appropriate; for the matter is a true puozzolanous compound; and lime only a constituent.

The following testimony is added by one of the Commissioners of the great canal, addressed to Dr. Silliman: and it shows distinctly that our opinion of its character as puozzolanous earth is correct:—

"Mr. White, one of our engineers on the Erie canal, and a man of good character and useful attainments, especially on subjects connected with his profession, discovered in the course of the season before last, the material for making an excellent water-proof cement, existing in great abundance in the western district of this State. And we have made extensive and profitable use of his discovery, in the locks and other mason-work of the Erie canal. It is probably superior to Parker's Roman Cement in quality, and may be afforded at less than half the expense of that. It will therefore, probably soon come into general use throughout our country, wherever such cement is required. Mr. White has some specimens of the stone which constitutes the principal material of his discovery, which he intends presenting to you."

Much valuable information, as to the principles of composition in the water cements, may be derived from M. Vicat's paper on Water Cements, Mortar, and Lime; which we have partly presented our readers with in this, and some former numbers; and which we shall pursue to the end of his essay.

Account of an improved Method of planting Vines for forcing. By Mr. DANIEL JUDD, F. H. S.

London Horticultural Society.

That the vine can be cultivated in our latitude, and with profitable effect, cannot be doubted; for, some centuries back, the banks of the Thames yielded a vinous produce, from its vineyards, that had no small repute. The following is Mr. Judd's proposed improvement in its propagation:—

" Herewith I send an account of my management of the vines in the garden of Charles Campbell, Esq., of Edmonton, of which I have the charge.

" My compost was formed as follows: In the winter of 1817, I procured a quantity of top spit of soil from a common in the neighbourhood, which consisted of a rich loam, rather inclined to be gritty; which property I prefer, because it gives a porousness to the compost, thereby allowing the water to pass freely through it. At the same time, I collected some lime rubbish, well broken to pieces, and sifted; some old tan; some leaf mould; and a quantity of the richest old dung I could select from the forcing beds and elsewhere.

" These materials, having been kept separate and frequently turned over in the summer, were mixed together in the autumn of 1818, in the following proportions: one-fourth of the dung, and one-fourth of the lime rubbish, united with the tan, and leaf mould. They were well mixed, by frequent turnings (but were not sifted) during the winter, when the weather was frosty or dry; for this operation should never be performed in wet weather.

"It may be noticed, that I did not use so much dung in my compost, as is sometimes done; for I have observed that an excess of it retards the growth of the vine, notwithstanding it is considered to be a plant which will bear an extraordinary quantity of manure. The addition of old tan to the compost, which is not usual, I recommend; because I know, from experience, that the vines will root in that more freely than in any other substance.

"In March last, the border, in front of the vinery, was cleared to the depth of upwards of three feet; below which it was drained; and then filled up with the new compost, to the level of the bottom plate of the house; this was done in fine weather, and the new mould had full two months' time to settle well before the young vines were planted in it.

"My vine plants were raised from single eyes, in March 1818; they were treated in the usual way through the summer, and kept from the frost during the winter, until March last; when they were cut down to one eye, and placed in the pine pit, in order to produce young shoots of sufficient length to draw into the house, at the time of planting. After they had made shoots about two feet long, they were removed to the green-house (which was at that time kept at a temperature of about 60°, for some other purposes); here they continued growing till they had attained to the length of three or four feet. By this treatment the whole plant was rendered more hardy, and consequently more fit for its final removal into the open border.

"Early in May, having made good the height of the border quite to the level of the holes where the plants were to be carried into the house, so that no part of their stem should be exposed to the external air, I opened the holes for the reception of the plants, leaving them open upwards of a week, to remove any noxious quality in that part of the compost which would first receive the roots.

"My planting was executed on the 13th of May; but I consider any period between the 10th of May and 10th of June, will be equally successful, provided the work be done in seasonable weather, that is, when it is neither wet nor cold.

"At the time of planting, I turned into each hole a common wheel-barrow full of very old tan from the pine house, in the middle of which tan the roots of my vine plants remained after the plants had been treated as I shall now describe. I first cut off the leaves from the lower part of the plant, about two feet and a half of its length, leaving about an inch of the foot stalk of each on the plant, the end of which was then drawn very carefully through the hole, under the plate, without injuring the tender part of the shoot. The pot being removed, the ball or root of the plant was placed two feet distant from the front of the house, upon its side, so that the stem lay in a horizontal position, about six inches below the level of the surface of the border. When thus placed, the whole of the stem which was to be covered, was slit, or tongued, at each eye, like a carnation layer, by passing a sharp knife at three quarters of an inch below each eye, and on the side of the eye, about one-third of the thickness into the wood, and then upwards to the centre of the joint. This being done, the stem was covered with about four inches of old tan, and the other two inches were filled up with the mould of the border. It is essential to the safety of the plant that the slitting be done the last thing, and whilst it is laid in its position, lest the skin should be broken.

"The effect of the operation of slitting the stem is the production of abundance of roots from every eye. The progress is not very great until the roots begin to push out; after these shoot, it is surprising how fast the vines grow.

"I gave a little fire in the house for the first month after planting, though sparingly, and air was admitted into it continually, until the plants had got sufficient hold of the border; air was then admitted in the day, but the house was shut up at night. Under this treatment the shoots of the present season of these young plants, are from twenty-five to thirty feet long, and their strength is fully proportionate to their length.

"It is not my intention to grow any thing on the border, which will exhaust it, or deprive the vines of their full nourishment. To protect their roots in the winter, I shall use a covering of old tan, about six inches thick; which I prefer to dung, or muck of any description.

"I have this season planted vines in the same way, in other houses besides the one I have now mentioned, and with equal success."

Premature Florescence.

We have read several statements, in the public papers, of the effect produced by the singularly mild temperature of the season, on the vegetable kingdom; but certainly not any thing equal to the following: for the goddess Flora seems to have yielded herself up to her feelings, rather than consulted the wisdom of Jove, in exposing her charming offspring to the rude hand of Boreas; who, we fear, will sadly punish her inconsiderate confidence. In the garden of Lieut. Col. Graham, near Edinburgh, there is, in full flower, the sweet william, mignionette, purple stock, clove gilliflower, branching larkspur, larkspur, xeranthemum lucidum, honey flower, wall flower, white stock, heart's ease, curled mallow, yellow lupin, hepatica, red xeranthemum, double primrose, sweet pea, frog's mouth, double daisy, holly oak, marygold, yellow hawkweed, strawberry plant, and adonis. This is the gay parterre of June. In our own garden, we had, a fortnight ago, the African marygold put forth a flower; and we have now also the heart's ease, but rather diminutive; our lilacs, and all those around us, seemed a few days back to be bursting their leaf buds; and some few have put forth the leaf; but the air, having been rather cooler again, has checked them. Our nasturtium, of last summer, has never ceased renewing its leaves until within these ten days.

THE FOCUS

OF

PHILOSOPHY, SCIENCE, AND ART.

No. IX.]   SATURDAY, JANUARY 26, 1822.   [Vol. I.

Sir H. Davy *on the Magnetic Phenomena produced by Electricity.* (Continued from p. 261.)

"It might, at first view, be supposed, that when a conductor placed in the circuit left a residuum of electricity in any battery, increase of the power of the battery, or of its surface, would not enable it to carry through any additional quantity. This, however, is far from being the case.

"When saline solutions were placed in the circuit of a battery of 20 plates, though they discharged a very small quantity only of the electricity when the troughs were only one quarter full, yet their chemical decomposition exhibited the fact of a much larger quantity passing through them, when the cells where filled with fluid.

"And a similar circumstance occurred with respect to a wire of platinum, of such a length as to leave a considerable residuum in a battery when only half its surface was used; yet when the whole surface was employed, it became much hotter, and nevertheless left a still more considerable residuum.

"I found long ago, that in increasing the number of alternations of similar plates, the quantity of electricity seemed to increase as the number, at least as far as it could be judged of by the effects of heat upon wires; but only within certain limits; beyond which the number appeared to diminish, rather than increase the quantity. Thus the 2000 double plates of the London Institution, when arranged as one battery, would not ignite so much wire as a single battery of 10 plates with double copper.

"It is not easy to explain this result. Does the intensity mark the rapidity of the motion of the electricity? Or merely its diminished attraction for the matter on which it acts? And does this attraction become less in proportion as the circuit through which it passes, or in which it is generated, contains a great number of alternations of bad conductors?

"Mr. Children, in his account of the experiments made with his battery of large plates, has ingeniously referred the heat produced by the passage of electricity through conductors, to the resistance it meets with, and has supposed, what proves to be the fact, that the heat is in some inverse ratio to the conducting power. The greatest heat, however, is produced in air, where there is reason to suppose the least resistance; and as the presence of heat renders bodies worse conductors, another view may be taken, namely, that the excitation of heat occasions the imperfection of the conducting power. But till the causes of heat and electricity are known, and of that peculiar constitution of matter which excites the one, and transmits or propagates the other, our reasoning on this subject must be inconclusive.

"I found that when equal portions of wires of the same diameter, but of different metals, were connected together in the circuit of a powerful voltaic battery, acting as two surfaces, the metals were heated in the following order: iron most, then palladium, then platinum, then tin, then zinc, then gold, then lead, then copper, and silver least of all. And from one experiment, in which similar wires of platinum and silver, joined in the same circuit, were placed in equal portions of oil, it appeared that the generation of heat was nearly inversely as their conducting powers; thus the silver raised the temperature of the oil only four degrees, whilst the platinum raised it twenty-two. The same relations to heat seem to exist, whatever is the intensity of the electricity; thus circuits of wires placed under water, and acted on by the common electrical discharge, were heated in the same order as by the voltaic battery, as was shown by their relative fusion; thus iron fusing before platinum, platinum before gold, and so on.

"If a chain be made of wire of platinum and silver, in alternate links, soldered together, the silver wire being four or five times the diameter of the platinum, and placed in a powerful voltaic circuit, the silver links are not sensibly heated, whilst all those of the platinum become intensely and equally ignited. This is an important experiment for investigating the nature of heat. If heat be supposed a substance, it cannot be imagined to be expelled from the platinum; because an unlimited quantity may be generated from the same platinum, i. e. as long as the electricity is excited, or as often as it is renewed. Or if it be supposed to be identical with, or an element of, electricity, it ought to bear some relation to its quantity, and might be expected to be the same in *every* part of the chain, or greatest in those parts nearest the battery.

"The magnetism produced by electricity, though with the same conductors it increases with the heat, as I mentioned in my last paper; yet with different conductors I found it follows a very different law. Thus, when a chain is made of different conducting wires, and they are placed in the same circuit, they all exhibit equal magnetic powers, and take up equal quantities of iron filings. So that the magnetism seems directly as the quantity of electricity which they transmit. And when in a highly powerful voltaic battery, wires of the same diameters and lengths, but of which the best conducting is capable of wholly discharging the battery, are made, separately and successively, to form the circuit, they take up different quantities of iron filings in some direct proportion to their conducting powers.

"Thus, in one experiment, two inches of wire of $\frac{1}{30}$ of an inch being used, silver took up 32 grains, copper 24, platinum 11, and iron $8\frac{1}{15}$."

It may assist the reader if we recapitulate the foregoing observations in a contracted form. Thus, Sir Humphry Davy concludes,—

That the magnetic influence imparted to steel will be as the perfection of the conducting electrical chain.

That magnetic phenomena were precisely similar where a small quantity of electricity was passed through large and good conductors, and where the imperfection of the conductors transmitted only a small quantity.

That imperfect fluid conductors do not yield any polarity; but air does.

That the magnet acts on the charcoal conductor when the latter passes through air.

That the quantity of electric matter conducted by metals is not limited only by their fusibility or volatility, as produced by the electrical current; for a platinum wire $\frac{1}{220}$ inch, kept cool by water, was incapable of discharging more than six batteries of certain powers.

That the conducting power varied with the temperature in some inverse proportion as the heat was augmented, whether the heat were excited by the electric current, or by the extraneous source of a lamp.

That the conducting powers of wires of the same metal were in inverse proportions to their lengths.

That the relative conducting powers of different wires were in these proportions,—1 inch platinum; 6 silver; $5\frac{1}{2}$ copper; 4 gold; $3\frac{8}{10}$ lead; $\frac{9}{10}$ palladium; $\frac{8}{10}$ iron; all in a cooling fluid medium. That the conducting power of each metal respectively is as the mass, in a cooling medium; but in air, surface will have an influence.

That the best fluid conductors are some hundreds of thousands of times inferior in conducting power to the worst metallic conductors.

That the greater the electrical intensity, the more easily does it pass through bad conductors.

That the heating effect of alternating plates is limited within a few series numerically: 2000 double plates ignited less wire than 10 only with double copper.

That the order of fusibility of different metals, by the same battery, were, as most so, iron, then palladium, platinum, tin, zinc, gold, lead, copper, and silver.

That with alternate links of thin platinum wire; and silver, but thicker; the former will ignite, the latter remain cool.

That with alternate links of several metals, all will be

equally magnetic, or attract equal portions of iron filings. But

That separately applied as conductors to the same battery, their magnetic powers will be, by the taking up of iron filings, in a proportion thus—silver 32 grains; copper 24; platinum 11; and iron $8\frac{2}{10}$.

The foregoing results open a wide field for speculation; and, we conjecture, will be the cause of much extended experiment. Some of the facts, as contrasted, are very remarkable; for instance, metallic wires cannot be made to transmit more than certain quantities of electric matter, whether ignited by the current, or kept cool. We may also note changes of heating effect in the same wire, when extraneous caloric be applied to it during its transmission of the electrical current.

On the Papyri found at Herculaneum.
(Continued from p. 269.)

"On two brown MSS., which were firm in their texture, and had the appearance of peat, and the leaves of which would not separate by common means, I tried the experiment of heating, after they had absorbed a small quantity of chlorine; and I found that in both cases the leaves detached themselves from each other, and were easily unrolled. But these MSS. had been so penetrated by water, that there were only a few folds which contained words, and the letters were generally erased; and the charcoal which had composed them was deposited on the folds of the MSS.

"Of the black MSS., of which the layers were perfect, and easily separated, all the best specimens had been unrolled or operated upon; so that fragments only of this description remained. By assisting the operation of detaching the layers, by muriatic ether and other processes before mentioned, many parts of columns were obtained from several of the fragments; by which some idea of their contents may be formed.

"On the black, compact, and heavy MSS., which contained white earthy matter in their folds, I tried several experiments, with the hopes of separating them into single layers, both by the action of muriatic and nitric ether, and by the operation of chlorine and of weak hydro-fluoric acid, assisted by heat; but generally the fibres of the papyrus had been so firmly cemented together, and so much earthy matter had penetrated them, that only a very imperfect separation could be obtained, and in parts where vestiges only of letters appeared, so that from MSS. of this kind only a few remains of sentences could be gained.

"During the two months that I was actively employed on the papyri at Naples, I had succeeded, with the assistance of six of the persons attached to the Museum, and whom I had engaged for the purpose, in partially unrolling twenty-three MSS., from which fragments of writing were obtained, and in examining about 120 others, which afforded no hopes of success; and I should gladly have gone on with the undertaking, for the mere prospect of possibility of discovering some better results, had not the labour, in itself difficult and unpleasant, been made more so by the conduct of the persons at the head of this department in the Museum. At first, every disposition was shown to promote my researches; for the papyri remaining unrolled were considered by them as incapable of affording any thing legible by the former methods, or, to use their own word, *disperati*; and the efficacy and use of the new processes were fully allowed by the Svolgatori, or unrollers of the Museum; and I was for some time permitted to choose, and operate upon the specimens, at my own pleasure. When, however, the Rev. Peter Elmsley, whose zeal for the promotion of ancient literature brought him to Naples for the purpose of assisting in the undertaking, began to examine the fragments unrolled, a jealousy, with regard to his assistance, was immediately manifested; and obstacles, which the kind interference of Sir William A'Court was not always capable of removing, were soon opposed to the progress of our inquiries; and these obstacles were so multiplied, and made so vaxatious towards the end of February, that we conceived it would be both a waste of the public money, and a compromise of our own characters, to proceed.

Some General Observations.

"The Roman MSS. found in the Museum, are in general composed of papyrus of a much thicker texture than the Greek ones, and the Roman characters are usually larger; the rolls much more voluminous; the characters of the Greek MSS., likewise, with a few exceptions, are more perfect than those of the Latin ones.

"From the mixture of Greek characters in several fragments of Latin MSS., and from the form of the letters, and the state of decomposition in which they are found, it is extremely probable that they were of a very ancient date when buried.

"I looked in vain amongst the MSS., and on the animal charcoal surrounding them, for vestiges of letters in oxide of iron: and it would seem, from these circumstances, as well as from the omission of any mention of such a substance by Pliny, that the Romans, up to his period, never used the *ink of galls and iron* for writing: and it is very probable, that the adoption of this ink, and the use of parchment, took place at the same time; for the ink composed of charcoal and solution of glue can scarcely be made to adhere to skin, whereas the free acid of the chemical ink partly dissolves the gelatine of the MSS., and the whole substance adheres as a mordant; and in some old parchments, the ink of which must have contained much free acid, the letters have, as it were, eaten through the skin, the effect being always most violent on the side of the parchment containing no animal oil.

"The earliest MSS. probably in existence on parchment, are those codices rescripti, discovered by Monsignore Mai, in the libraries of Milan and Rome. Through his politeness I have examined these MSS., particularly that containing some of the books of *Cicero de Republica,* and which he refers to the second or third century. From the form of the columns, it is very probable that they were copied from a papyrus. The vegetable matter which rendered the oxide of iron black is entirely destroyed, but the peroxide of iron remains; and where it is not covered by the modern MSS., the form of the letter is sufficiently distinct. Monsignore Mai uses solution of galls for reviving the blackness. I have tried several substances for restoring colour to the letters in ancient MSS. The triple prussiate of potash, used in the manner recommended by the late Sir Charles Blagden, with the alternation of acid, I have found successful; but by making a weak solution of it with a small quantity of muriatic acid, and by applying it to the letters, in their state of mixture, with a camel's hair pencil, the results are still better.

"It is remarkable, that no fragments of Greek, and very few only of Latin poetry, have been found in the whole collection of the MSS. of Herculaneum; and the sentences in the specimens we unrolled, in which Mr. Elmsley was able to find a sufficient number of words to infer their meaning, show that the works of which they are the remains, were of the same kind as those before examined, and belonged to the schools of the Greek Epicurean philosophers and sophists.

"Nearly 1000 columns of different works, a great part unrolled under the superintendance of Mr. Hayter, and at the expense of his present Majesty George IV., have been copied and engraved by the artists employed in the Museum; but from the characters of the persons charged with their publication, there is very little probability of their being, for many years, offered to the world; which is much to be regretted; for, though not interesting, from their perfection, as literary works, they would unquestionably throw much light upon the state of civilization, letters, and science, of the age and country to which they belonged.

"Should discoveries of MSS. at any future time be made at Herculaneum, it is to be hoped that the papyri will be immediately excluded from the atmosphere, by being put into air-tight cases, filled with carbonic acid after their introduction. There can be no doubt that the specimens now in the Museum were in a much better state when they were first discovered: and the most perfect even, and those the coarsest in their texture, must have been greatly injured during the 69 years that they have been exposed to the atmosphere. I have found that a fragment of a brown MS., kept for a few weeks in a portion of air confined by mercury, had caused the disappearance of a considerable part of the oxygen, and the formation of much carbonic acid."

On the Course of the Niger. By Mr. M'QUEEN.
(Continued from p. 281.)

In our last number, we brought the observations and opinions of others down to the time of Mr. M'Queen's publication as to the presumed fact of the Niger flowing into the Atlantic Ocean in the Gulf of Guinea, and it will be seen that the conjecture had been distinctly urged previous to that gentleman's favouring the world with his conjectures too; for we are not furnished by him with more than merely conjectural matter. We now proceed to state Mr. M'Q.'s reasons in confirmation of this presumed course and egress of the Niger.

Mr. M'Q. takes notice of the various opinions that prevail, and divides them into—1st, That the Niger flows eastward to beyond the parallel of the 18th degree of north latitude; then in about 20° east longitude, flowing south east; and is the parent stream of the Bakr el Abiad, or Nile of Egypt—2d, That it terminates in a large lake in the interior, which also receives the waters of the Gir and the Nile of Soudan, coming from the eastward—3d, That the waters of both rivers are lost in swamps, and sandy desarts, in a country called Wangara—And 4th, that the Niger, from its middle course, flows south, and joins the great river Congo, or Zaire.

All these hypotheses, he considers to be false; as opposed to the general principles of geography, as well as to the direct information obtained by the late Congo expedition; which proves that the Niger and Congo are different rivers. That the lake into which the Gir and Niger are said to disembogue themselves has not an existence. That Wangara is not a swampy country. And, lastly, that the Niger flows to form the Bakr el Abiad, is confuted by the best ancient and modern authorities.

Mr. M'Q. appeals to Ptolemy, who describes the Caphas, or Kong Mountains, as between the sources of the Niger and the Gulf of Guinea; and that eastward, in the same parallel, is an opening; and then comes Mount Thala, at 10° north and 12° east. From Ptolemy's description of the country, and the course of the Gir, it is inferred that the Niger flowed through that opening. From many Arabian authors also, Mr. M'Q. draws such information as may fortify his opinions.

He then proceeds to describe the course of the Niger, with its tributary streams, beginning at its source in the Kong Mountains; flowing north easterly, and navigable more than 400 miles before arriving at Bammakoo; the point where Park in his first travels left the river; considering it as the head of navigation: but here it was a mile wide, and with a rapid current. From Bammakoo to Silla, more than 300 miles, the course is well known; being a little northward of east. Silla is in 14° north; a few miles east of Greenwich. From Silla, it goes north easterly 200 or 300 miles, and afterwards, at Tombuctoo, it curves south easterly. After a course of more than 700 miles south east and south, it receives the Gir, and, turning south west, flows onwards to the Atlantic, as before stated, by the complicated mouths or Delta at the Bights of Benin and Biafra; having traversed more than twenty-six hundred miles of surface.

Mr. M'Q. takes into consideration the vast reticulated channels of water, that ramify into each other, as they approach the ocean by the Delta. Also the immense volumes that the respective estuaries comprise; each of which may bear comparison with the mouths of some of the greatest rivers known, as the Ganges, the Mississippi, the Oronoco, and Wolga. Perhaps the African Delta may really exceed any of them in the masses it rolls to the ocean; for independent of the great breadth of its estuaries, they surpass all others in their depths, so that the moving volume is comparatively greater than it would show from its superficies. The countries through which this great African network of waters flows, are described, by some travellers, as transcendantly beautiful, and abounding in produce; cotton and indigo being plentifully yielded to the labour of a very large population. The very name of Rio Formoso implies the rich and picturesque scenes presenting from the banks of that river.

The wealth of the country is indicated in some degree by its towns; Benin being described as large, with broad streets, and houses of clay—formerly the capital of an extensive empire. The trade is said to be extensive, especially in slaves.—So much for the humane exertions, and sacrifice of interests, made by the feeling policy of Great Britain. The salt works afford large supplies for the interior; and may perhaps be considered as the mines for African currency: salt being the instrument in measure of general value among many tribes. When prepared for consumption, the salt is freighted in canoes and large vessels on the banks of the Bonny, &c.; some of them, it is said, are capable of carrying two hundred people. Boussa, on the Niger, is a great emporium for this traffic. The Delta is flooded from May to December; but, principally, during July and August. The inundation extends over a wide surface of country, and brings down such depositions of mud as to cause a perpetual encroachment of the land on the sea. The periods of inundation are worthy of remark, as demonstrating that these rivers have not any communication with the Congo; for the latter does not begin to rise until September. Besides, the flood of the Congo does not correspond with the time of the annual rise of the known Niger; but the floods of the Delta do; and therefore we have not only a positive proof that the Congo and Niger can neither be the same river, nor can they communicate; but we have very strong presumptive evidence by the coincidence of the periods of inundation, that the Delta and the Niger are but different portions of the same mighty stream. That the flooding of the Delta does not arise from the rains falling on the countries approaching the coast, is also clear; because the greatest rains there, are in May and June, but the height of inundation is not until August, when the waters of the contiguous surface must have passed away; and the subsequent inundation of the Delta must arise from the increased volume accumulated and flowing from the higher body of the Niger, or some river of equal magnitude.

We will suppose, however, that the Niger have other termination than the Delta, and that it discharge its volume into the Soudan Sea, as urged by some; but have we not a difficulty as great presenting itself, to ascertain what river does really feed the Delta with its immense flow of waters, as we have hitherto had in coursing the Niger? Can any known river be pointed out to us, which has been traced from the ocean upwards to its source, at all equal to the supply of the Delta? The vast body of water falling into the ocean from the coast of Guinea must have been collected from a commensurate surface of drainage, and consequently that drainage must have been extremely great, both as to width and length, of course.

It is certainly possible, as suggested by some, that Africa may contain a great Mediterranean Sea; but it is scarcely possible that the waters of the Niger, and others of various magnitudes also, falling into it, should be disposed of by evaporation; though under a tropical sun that process would approach its maximum; governed, however, by the direction of the periodical winds, if any, as well as by the relative degrees of moisture of the air. Besides, the temperature of this sea would probably be low; because, from the conjecture of its magnitude, we must presume it to be deep; and this alone would powerfully retard evaporation.

Taking then all the points urged by Mr. M'Queen into due consideration, we are inclined to think that, of the various hypotheses espoused by the moderns respecting the course of the Niger, his presents, at least, as many imposing correspondencies and analogies as the best of the others. Still we are fully aware that it is one thing to prove, from the immense waters of the African Delta, that there must exist some immense primary river to afford the supply; and another to prove the identity of such river with the Niger of the ancients. Mr. M'Queen's question we consider to be simply this—There is in Africa a river, better known to the ancients perhaps than ourselves, called the Niger; a portion of this is known also to the moderns, as growing into a magnificent stream, that we have not any recorded trace of to its mouth. There is, also, on the coast of Guinea, a vastly congregated mass of water, flowing, by great ramifying channels, into the Atlantic; the parent streams being directed upwards to a probable point of the known Niger, whose period of inundation corresponds with that of the Delta. Therefore, Mr. M'Q. would ask, if we are not warranted in considering the Niger as the parent river, collecting the waters of north western Africa; and the Delta as the multiplied channel of its discharge into the ocean?

An Account of Electro-Magnetic Experiments, made by MM. VAN BECK; Professor VAN REES, of Liege; and Professor MOLL, of Utrecht. In a Letter to Doctor Brewster. Edinburgh Philosophical Journal, No. 11.

Professor Moll makes this communication to Dr. Brewster, modestly attributing whatever merit there may have been in the experiments instituted, to MM. Van Beck and Van Rees; as he says they had the principal share in devising and constructing the apparatus. This consisted of an electrical machine of two plates of 70 centimetres (about $20\frac{1}{4}$ inches) in diameter. The battery consisted of seven Leyden phials, containing a coating of 5962 square centimetres, or $2346\frac{1}{4}$ inches. Steel needles were employed, as free from magnetism as possible, $7\frac{1}{2}$ centimetres (or nearly 3 inches) in length; also, a sensible magnetic needle, to measure the magnetism communicated by electricity to the other needles.

1st. A brass wire was twisted so as to form spiral windings from left to right round a glass tube; within which tube was a steel needle. On discharging the battery through the spiral, the steel was found to be magnetic; having the north pole towards the negative end of the spiral.

2d. Repeated; but with the spiral coiled round the tube to the left. The needle became magnetic, with the north pole to the positive of the spiral. It being understood, that the Professor means, by the north pole, that which points to the north, when the needle be freely suspended.

3d. A steel wire, 64 centimetres (nearly $26\frac{1}{4}$ inches) in length, was placed in a glass tube, round which was coiled a spiral wire from right to left, and from left to right, alternately, eight times on the length of the tube; the wire and tube were externally covered with sealing wax, to prevent the electric spark crossing from one winding of the spiral to the next. The electric discharge being sent through the spiral, and the steel taken out, the latter was found to have as many poles as the turns of the spirals changed their directions.

4th. A brass spiral, as in the 1st and 2d experiment; but instead of being placed within a glass tube, the needle was enveloped in paper, and fastened on the *outside* of the spiral, parallel to its axis. When a right hand spiral was used, the needle was rendered magnetic by the electrical discharge, with its north pole to the positive side or pole of the battery.

5th. As before; but with the spiral to the left hand; the north pole now towards the negative.

This reversal of the poles, says the Professor, may be rendered very striking by placing one needle covered with paper, or glass, on the inside, and another, similarly covered, on the outside of the spiral; as the electrical discharge will impart opposite poles to the contiguous ends of the needles. This experiment had been made before by some Italian philosophers with the galvanic pile.

6th. A spiral of soft iron was coiled round a glass tube, within which tube was a brass wire, connected with the electrical battery. On discharging the battery, and removing the tube, with its brass wire, the spiral was found to be magnetic. If the coil were to the right hand, the north pole was to the negative; if to the left, to the positive side of the battery. When the ends of the spiral were brought into contact, the magnetic effect disappeared; but on separation, it was again renewed.

7th. A small glass plate was placed on a straight copper wire; on the glass, at right angles with the wire, was laid a needle. The discharge being thrice passed through the brass wire, rendered the needle strongly magnetic, with its north pole to the left hand, the observer facing the side of the battery.

8th. As above; but with the needle *under* the glass plate, and the brass wire above it. The pole was reversed.

9th. A brass wire was bent into the form of the letter V; over this was a glass plate, and on the plate a needle, in a transverse direction, or at right angles across the wire. The end of the needle projecting to the left hand we will call A;

that to the right, B: A being connected with the positive end of the battery, and B with the negative end. After making the discharge, the transverse needle was found to have three poles; that is, from the extremity A to the wire on one side, and from the extremity B to the wire on the other side, the poles were found to be both south; while that portion of the needle which passed over the space between the legs of the angle V was north.

10th. Repeated; but with the needle *under*, and the brass wire *above* the glass. Each extremity of the needle was now north, and the middle south.

11th. A brass wire was bent into a series of regular angles, or, plainer, into a zigzag form, and placed under a glass plate, and over this a straight steel wire, across the angles, and extending beyond at the ends. We will call one end of the brass zigzag A, connected with the positive end of the battery, and the other B, connected with the negative end. Having made three discharges of the battery, the needle was found to have a separate north and south pole for each leg of each angle: the north poles at each of those extremities of the zigzags which pointed towards the positive end of the battery, the south poles towards the negative end of the battery.

12th. Repeated; but now with the steel wire *under* the glass, and the brass zigzag above it. The poles of the brass wire were now reversed, but equally numerous as before.

13th. A needle was placed on one side of a glass plate, and a connecting wire on the other, but parallel to the needle. After repeated discharges of the battery, the needle had not acquired any magnetism.

14th. A steel *magnetic* wire was placed under a glass plate, and a parallel conducting wire above it. After repeated discharges the needle was found to have lost its magnetism.

15th. Repeated discharges through a magnetic needle destroyed its magnetism.

We have not much novelty of result from these experiments; but they have the merit of simplicity, and, in so far as they confirm what has gone before, have their value; for we hold, that a fact cannot be established on too wide a basis;

and therefore are pleased when we observe a consonance resulting in experiments instituted widely apart; and perhaps with various views. The third experiment was well imagined for its purpose; so was the fifth. The ninth also, as well as the tenth, proves what had been before known: namely, that a wire might be converted into as many distinct magnetic needles as we should please. We likewise see that when the wire was placed *parallel* to the electrical current, it had not magnetic power imparted; and that when the magnetic needle was subjected to the electrical discharges, its magnetism was destroyed. We confess that we have always been at a loss to comprehend this last fact, for it is not a new one; nor have we met with any thing like a satisfactory explanation. Why an electrical discharge shall impart magnetism to a single needle, and destroy magnetism, whether by discharge from an electrical machine, or lightning, in a magnetic one, is a fact requiring more investigation than has hitherto been equal to a proper solution.

The influence of present caloric, as we shall show hereafter, is not to be overlooked; and in strong discharges the needle may be heated so as to affect the result: indeed, we have long known that great heat will destroy the magnetic powers of a magnetic needle.

On Chromic Compounds.

"The acid chromate of potash is anhydrous: I obtained it by digesting the neutral chromate of potash with nitric acid, separating from the first crop of crystals all those of nitre, and then re-dissolving and again crystallizing the chromate.

"When this salt is strongly calcined it melts, and passes to the state of neutral chromate, giving up half its acid, which is decomposed, and leaving an oxyd of chrome crystallized in brilliant greenish scales. The neutral chromate thus obtained was analyzed by a solution of sulphureous acid, which changed it instantaneously into sulphate of potash, sulphate and sulphite of chrome. The metallic oxyd was precipitated by ammonia, and the sulphate of potash evaporated. The super-chromate, therefore, contains twice as much acid as the neutral chromate, and is coposed of

 Chromic acid (two atoms)............ 68·846
 Potash (one atom) .... 31·154
               100·000

CARBONATE OF CHROME.

"M. Vauquelin, on pouring sulphureous acid and potash into liquid chromic acid, obtained a brown precipitate, which he thinks is an oxyd, more oxygenated than the green oxyd of chrome. This, however, is not an oxyd, but a carbonate of chrome. It dissolves without effervescence in diluted acids. When boiled in distilled water it is decomposed, and the green oxyd and carbonic acid gas are obtained; on which account care should be taken not to wash it with hot water. This salt may also be procured in another way, that is, by passing a current of nitrous gas and air through chromate of potash, mixed with an alkaline carbonate. Carbonate of chrome then falls down on boiling the mixture; but, if it contains too much nitrous acid, the whole will pass to the state of nitrate of chrome. This method, however, often fails: it is evidently the nitrous acid which reduces the chromic, and the oxyd thus produced attracts to itself the carbonic acid driven from the carbonate by an excess of acid. A better method of obtaining this carbonate is, to evaporate to dryness a mixture of nitrate of ammonia, chromate, and carbonate of potash; or of muriate of ammonia, with a nitrate, carbonate, and chromate of alkali. This mixture, when gently dried, blackens; it is then to be re-dissolved in water, and a drop or two of ammonia, which has the effect, I believe, of separating a small quantity of carbonate of chrome, which the nitrate of ammonia had retained in solution.

"If too great heat were applied, the excess of nitrate would re-produce the chromate. Here it is the protoxyd of azote (nitrous oxyd), in its nascent state, which decomposes the chromic acid; for, when once become gaseous, it has no longer this property. If, on the other hand, the chromate of potash and the nitrate of ammonia are acidified with nitric acid, and dried and heated in a tube protected from the contact of air, no carbonate of chrome whatever is obtained.

"A mixture of nitrate and muriate of ammonia acts in the same manner as nitrate of ammonia, because a double decomposition takes place, on account of the facility with which the nitrate of ammonia assumes the gaseous form. This double decomposition always occurs when these salts are heated with the nitrate of any metal capable of forming a fixed chloruret with muriate of ammonia.

"Therefore, to obtain nitrous oxyd, instead of employing caustic nitrate of ammonia, we may use nitrate of potash and muriate of ammonia, in the proportions suited to complete decomposition, leaving, however, an excess of nitrate, to avoid any sublimation of the sal-ammoniac. The proportions may be about three parts of nitre to one of sal-ammoniac."

ON THE CHROMITES,

"The existence of these salts is still doubtful, and Berzelius has not yet ventured to admit them positively in his *System of Mineralogy*. However, Vauquelin obtained a precipitate by pouring chromate of potash into proto-sulphate of iron, which he has found to be composed of oxyd of iron and oxyd of chrome, and is analogous to the chromic ore of the Var, particularly when the latter is calcined. Other chromites may be obtained with the muriates of manganese and of tin with oxyd of chrome. That with tin is green; with manganese, chesnut brown. They have all very similar properties; they dissolve in acids, and are precipitable from them without decomposition; the chlorate and nitrate of potash change them into alkaline chromates, and metallic oxyds. I have tried, but without success, several methods of separating them by analysis. With chlorate of potash they undergo a combustion similar to that of nitre and cream of tartar. A soluble chromate is indeed obtained, but the oxyds of iron, of manganese, or of tin, retain much of the chromic oxyd. Muriate of chrome renders muriate of manganese very soluble in alcohol: caustic alkalies cannot separate the whole of the oxyd of tin from the oxyd of chrome. These compounds deserve a fuller examination."

On Chromate of Lead.

"It is well known that a reddish chromate of lead is obtained by precipitating acetite of lead with an alkaline chromate of potash; but if the sub-acetite of lead and neutral chromate are used, both boiling hot, a yellow precipitate falls down, which in a few moments passes into a most brilliant orange red. This tint may be heightened by boiling a little alkali with the red, or even the yellow chromate with lead. I have made a comparative analysis of the yellow and the red artificial chromate, and the native red lead of Siberia: all of them give exactly the same proportion between the acid and the oxyd. They are neutral chromates, only the red chromate contains a small quantity of alkali, apparently from 1 to $1\frac{1}{4}$ *per cent*. The method which I used in these analyses was to dissolve the chromate in muriatic acid, which, in a boiling heat, becomes muriate of chrome; then to precipitate the lead by sulphuretted hydrogen, the oxyd of chrome by ammonia, and lastly, to evaporate, to obtain the muriate of potash. All the alkalies will change the fine yellow of the chromate of lead, and also of bismuth, into red.

"It remains to inquire whether the alkali is combined with the chromic acid, the oxyd of lead, or the chromate of lead. For this purpose, I treated a very pure chromate of lead and bismuth in excess with a small quantity of alkali, assisting the action by heat. After some instants the liquid had ceased to redden turmeric; and had assumed a yellow tint. Sometimes the turmeric test showed the absence of free alkali before the liquid changed colour, at which time the chromate contained free oxyd of lead. Indeed, if a little litharge is added to the chromate along with the alkali, it will become red without losing chromic acid. One may even obtain red chromate by boiling together chromate of potash and litharge.

"It follows from these facts, that the alkali appears to be combined with the oxyd of lead; and that this compound, united to chromate of lead, gives rise to the red chromate, which thus contains a little more oxyd of lead than the neutral chromate. A few drops of dilute nitric acid take away from it immediately its red colour, by dissolving the alkali with a little of the oxyd of lead. I examined whether the red lead of Siberia, which is also yellow when reduced to powder, might contain a portion of alkali: I found in it, after taking every precaution, a little lime, but I am ignorant whether or not it is accidental."

On the best method of Warming and Ventilating Houses and other Buildings. By CHARLES SYLVESTER.

Repertory, No. 236.

Mr. Sylvester commences with remarking on the various circumstances qualifying atmospheric temperature; such as the opacity of the earth; its limited power of conducting heat; the modifying effect of specific soils; and the comparative obliquity of incident solar rays. He then considers the heated volume of air ascending from over the heated surface perpendicularly, and the colder volume from the surrounding level rushing horizontally to that surface, as two distinct simultaneous volumes. We would rather be disposed to consider them as but different portions of the same volume, in a mechanical sense. And he goes on to say that "by this beautiful provision of natural economy, the heated air of the torrid zone, and the chilling currents from the polar regions, mutually contribute to the prevention of those extremes of heat and cold, which would otherwise be fatal to every class of animated beings."

We must beg leave to enter a caveat against this doctrine of qualifying temperature by the admixture of equatorial, and polar currents; for we do not think the imputed cause as uniform with the effect. We humbly apprehend that atmospheric temperature is by no means solely, and indeed but slightly, modified by mere currents; and we would beg leave to intimate the fact of our suffering under excessive extremes of heat, or cold, when the atmosphere shall be perfectly quiescent. We are not so absurd as to contend that a northerly, and a southerly wind, will at all times equally affect the thermometer; but we presume that either the one, or the other, or both, have but a limited influence in the general production of temperature. Except a wind have continued to blow for a protracted time, it perhaps may be doubted whether it have not its origin from but a small horizontal distance; and, consequently, not capable, by the extent of its traverse, to bring particles much influenced by difference of climate. Again, we experience a marked difference of effect produced on the thermometer, by opposite winds blowing from points in the *same parallel of latitude*: thus, *cæteris paribus*, a westerly, is warmer than an easterly wind, and that, at all periods of the earth's rotation. The inclination of the surface, as to, or from, the sun, will also have an effect; but where all the circumstances of exposure be similar, we contend that the existence, or non-existence of currents, can influence the temperature but in a modified degree. We have frequently intense frosts under easterly winds, blowing from our own parallel; or even a little southerly: and to prove that this cannot arise from the eastern current of the European continent being cooled by passing to us over the German ocean, we may observe that, the same wind shall augment the intensity of cold over that part of the continent which it has traversed before it arrive at the ocean. Also, that the temperature of the surface of the sea does not vary in any proportion with the extremes experienced on land at the summer and winter solstices; and certainly, if possible, less, as compared with our diurnal fluctuations in degree of heat. If horizontal winds were always dependant on perpendicular volumes, and the former but currents rushing toward the heated surface from whence such volumes arose above their level, how could we ever experience a current of air *from* the south, or equatorial zone? Does not the disputed doctrine say that, the cold dense current rushes over and in contact with the surface of the earth to the ascending heated column? And how are we to reconcile this, with the fact that, on almost every exposed point of the earth, winds may blow from every quarter of the compass? and where they do not but uniformly in one direction, as the trade winds, &c. still they are very imperfectly accountable for under this system. In order to the consistency of such a doctrine, there ought to be but two currents on the earth's surface; that is, one sweep of atmosphere from each pole to the equator: and not any exception should be admitted locally, but in the case of existing combustion. Besides, are not the cross currents, over the same point of the earth, and at the same time, directly in refutation of such a doctrine? For how shall an eastern and western, or a northern and southern wind blow over our heads at the same moment, and that too at no great difference perpendicularly, if wind be only air pressing to fill up the space of local rarefaction? Our opinion of the nature of wind, is rather electrical, than mechanical; and of atmospheric temperature, rather as dependant on radiation and absorption of caloric. But we would speak most guardedly: because, although electro-magnetism is gradually evolving important analogies, we are yet very deficient in data; and dare not hazard a judgment so dogmatical, as that which has been almost hitherto maintained, and which, we suspect, has little more than antiquity and universality to recommend it. But, whatever may be the cause of all the diversity in course, and strength, of currents of air; we have not any hesitation in declaring that, such changes have but a very limited influence on the atmospheric temperature; and therefore, that, although every " provision of natural economy" is *beautiful*, we would combat the fallacious views this doctrine, sustained by Mr. Sylvester, presents of the *modus operandi*, in this particular instance.

Mr. S. proceeds to explain that the temperature of enclosed spaces, as a hot-house, &c. is partly occasioned by the warm air within not being allowed to escape upwards, as its intermixture with caloric, and consequent rarefaction, would dispose it to. Also, that where bodies require an uniform heat, they should be immersed in a bath of caloric: therefore, the warming of rooms, by open fires, cannot have the effect of keeping us comfortable; because, on different sides, we have different temperatures. This is a very just view of the matter; for in a small room, and with a fire-place containing a large fire, we find it impossible to keep clear of the cold current rushing towards the warm column of the chimney: so we are scorched on one side and chilled on the other, and that exactly in proportion to the intensity of the combustion. Mr. S. next remarks on what he considers the erroneous practice of making the doors and windows of the room air-tight; and supplying the air by a channel from without, carried under the floor, to the fire hearth, and opening before, or under the fire: because, he says, " the air entering the room so near the fire, supplies the current up the chimney, without changing the air of the room." We agree with him, that if the aperture be nearly under the stove, the effect will be as he states; but there is not any necessity for its approximating so closely to the fire. All that is requisite being, for the aperture to pour forth its current at any reasonable distance from the fire, so that it be between the latter and ourselves: say one foot and a half, or two feet, from the perpendicular line of the front of the stove. Here will be ample space for a part of the air to warm, rarefy, and ascend into the room, before it can come under the line of the chimney-piece; and we think that a large portion of the warm air so ascending, instead of passing up the chimney, is usually at the horizontal distance, from the fire, of about two feet to a yard. The exit of the rarefied and vitiated air may be, by a very small aperture outwards, near the ceiling. By this simple contrivance, all the advantage of a moderate warmth, with circulation of air, may be obtained; and the inconvenience of a stagnant atmosphere, which is so distressingly felt when the apartment be warmed by radiation from a stove, is completely obviated. Still we confess, that an open fire-place is not so governable in the regularity of its temperature, as flues are.

Respecting close stoves, Mr. S. says they should be metal, and under the temperature of 300°; otherwise the animal and vegetable matter mingled with the air, will be decomposed, and become offensive. The surface should be kept clean, but not polished. We would recommend a coating of charcoal powder, mixed with lime and white of egg, to increase the radiation. A certain degree of moisture is also necessary in the warm air of the apartment; for where rooms be heated by close stoves, it is observed that the unpleasant sensations are relieved by a vessel containing water, which is imperceptibly evaporated by contact with the stove. Air may be made to pass over the external surface of a metallic body heated internally: that is, between an outer tube and an inner tube; the latter exposed to the operation of fire or heated air. And Mr. Sylvester says that at Mr. Strutt's (of Derby) cotton works, it was considered a great improvement to place the wall at a distance, to admit of a sufficient quantity of air; and make a number of apertures in the wall, about two inches and a half square, with a view to compel the air to blow upon the heated surface. Mr. Strutt has improved on this method, by carrying tubes through the wall, projecting inwardly and close to the heated body; so that the air could not ascend before it was fully brought into contact with that body. And further by bringing such tubes close to the cockle (or stove) itself. And still further, by compelling the air to traverse both up and down the tube. This method has been adopted, Mr. Stevenson tells us, at the Derby Infirmary, and elsewhere, successfully; but it has also failed in some places, when attempted by persons ignorant of the principles on which it is founded.

On Olefiant Gas. By an Anonymous Correspondent with the Editor of the Annals of Philosophy.

The letter to be here observed on, is addressed to Mr. Phillips, by a writer who aims to prove the preference of one of two dubious propositions, offered by Dr. Henry, on the constitution of the new gas presenting in his experiments on the aëriform compounds of charcoal and hydrogen.

Dr. Henry described a new gas, obtained by heat, from oil and pit coal; which was condensed to a liquid form by chlorine, without the agency of light; and analogous with olefiant gas; but not according with it in specific gravity, illuminating power, or combustion with oxygen. Dr. H. determined this gas to be either a mixture of olefiant gas with a heavier, or more combustible gas, or vapour; or, a new gas, *sui generis*, consisting of hydrogen and charcoal, in proportions yet remaining to be ascertained. The writer considers the former supposition to be the fact, but modified. Speaking of Dr. H.'s experiment, he says " the specific gravity of this specimen was ·906, common air being 1, and it yielded in 100 parts, 38 volumes of a gas, condensible by chlorine; and 62 volumes of mixed gases, not possessing that property, being of the specific gravity of ·606. Now ·906 × 100 − 606 × 62 ÷ 38 = ·1395; which is the specific gravity required by the 38 volumes of condensible gas, to give an aggregate weight of ·906 to the mixture: but the specific gravity of the olefiant gas is ·972. It is evident, therefore, that the greater part, at least, of the above 38 volumes could not be olefiant gas; but that it consisted of some other compound, the elements of which exist in a much closer state of condensation."

He considers the proportionate combination with oxygen as an additional proof: for four volumes and a half of oxygen are required to one of the gas, in combustion, the result being three of carbonic acid; while for one of olefiant, only three of oxygen are requisite; the result being a difference of a volume and a half of the latter, and the produce being two of carbonic acid. Therefore, as we have with the new gas one and a half more oxygen consumed, and one volume more of carbonic acid produced, he infers that the new gas contains an atom each of carbon and hydrogen more than exists in an equal bulk of olefiant gas, and that its specific gravity will be increased by the amount of that of those elements. The specific gravity of olefiant gas being ·972, and formed of carbon and hydrogen, each one atom. The specific gravity of vapour of carbon is ·4166, hydrogen ·0694: but ·4166 + ·0694 = 486, which is half the specific gravity assigned. Hence the writer infers that, in the constitution of olefiant gas, two volumes of gaseous carbon, and two of hydrogen, are condensed into one volume; as confirmed by the explosion of this gas with oxygen.

To explain the consumption of the three volumes of oxygen, and production of two of carbonic acid gas, it is presumed that two of gaseous carbon saturating two of oxygen, produce two of carbonic acid; and also, that there are two of hydrogen uniting with the remaining oxygen, and forming water. Thus, the new gas will be compounded of three volumes of gaseous carbon and three of hydrogen, condensed into one volume, and its specific gravity will be that of olefiant gas, augmented by that of each of the additional component elements; or, $\cdot 972 + \cdot 4166 + \cdot 0694 = 1\cdot 458$.

Supposing, then, the 38 volumes of condensible gas forming the subject of Dr. Henry's experiments, to be " a mixture of olefiant with a heavier and more combustible gas," and that this heavier is the one above described; the proportion of the two, requisite to produce a specific gravity of $1\cdot 395$, will be 100 volumes of heavy olefiant gas, if it may be so called, and 1·49 volume nearly of olefiant gas: for $\frac{\cdot 972\, x + 1\cdot 458}{x+1} = 1\cdot 395$; from whence $x = \frac{063}{423} = .14893$. Here, then, it is concluded that the new gas is not " *sui generis*, consisting of hydrogen and charcoal in proportions which remain to be determined," but a modification of olefiant gas; with *triple*, instead of *double*, compound atoms. And it is surmised that there may be a yet simpler form of carburetted hydrogen, consisting of one atom of each of the component elements.

On the Means of giving Strength to the Stems of Plants growing under Glass. By T. A. KNIGHT, Esq.

Transactions of London Horticultural Society.

Mr. Knight presents to the Society the results of some experiments directed to a very useful object in that department of art which contributes much to our gratification; and as whatever that gentleman may even conjecture, must be in some degree impressive with the lovers of horticulture, we shall lay the paper before our readers. Mr. K. then, states that,—

" The forms of the stems of trees and shrubs which grow under glass, are generally found much more slender and weak than those of other plants of the same species which grow in the open air,—often to such an extent as to render necessary the unsightly appendage of supports or props; and, in many of those species which are cultivated for ornament only, to destroy the relative proportions requisite to constitute beauty. These defects may be traced to a concurrence of causes: to the shade necessarily given by the roof of the house; to the injudicious application of high temperature at periods when light cannot be obtained; and to the too close contiguity of plants to each other; but chiefly to the total absence of the motion which is naturally given by the winds.

"I have stated the results of experiments, in the Philosophical Transactions of 1803, and 1811, which, I believe, satisfactorily prove, that if the stems, or branches, or roots, of a tree, be in any part bent by the action of the winds, an increased quantity of alburnum will be in such parts generated, by which means additional strength will be given, wherever it is requisite to preserve the tree, in any situation where art or accident might have placed it. Hence the insulated tree upon the mountain necessarily acquires the short and sturdy form best adapted to enable it to brave, with impunity, the fury of the storm; and long and slender stems are as necessarily confined to more sheltered situations.

"I have subsequently ascertained, that the hand of the gardener can readily do, with the forcing house, all that is beneficially done by winds out of it; and, I am perfectly confident, that not only the beauty, but the health also of the tree is improved by being given the form and proportion which nature intended it to receive. To effect this, the stem should be bent in every direction, nearly as far as can be done without breaking it: but how frequently this must be done, to produce the requisite effect, I am not at present prepared to say; having, in all my experiments, been rather endeavouring to discover the utmost degree of strength which could be given, than the degree which would simply prove beneficial to the plant. I have, however, some reason to believe, that the operation need not be, in any case, repeated more often than once in eight or ten days, and that, only during the periods in which the stems and branches are increasing in bulk.

"The extent to which the diameter of the stem of a plant, comparatively with its length, may be increased by the means above mentioned, is probably much greater than will easily be credited. A dahlia plant, of a year old, and growing in a pot in the forcing house which I usually devote to experiments, presented, in the spring of 1817, a stem, which, at half its height from the mould, exceeded an inch in diameter, when it was only twenty-two inches high; though the experiment was made in April and May, and of course before the sun had nearly acquired its full powers, and under glass of by no means good quality. But both myself and my gardener had frequent occasion to enter the house; and neither of us, I believe, ever passed the plant without bending it; which ultimately became an operation which required very considerable force. The dahlia is not, however, one of those plants which can receive benefit by this mode of treatment; for the excessive strength of the stem would only expose the soft and succulent branches to more certain destruction upon the plant being removed into the open air; and I mention the result of the experiment, merely to illustrate the effects of the process I have recommended."

Account of some Vegetable Remains found in a quarry near Bath. By Mr. H. Woods.

Annals of Philosophy.

Mr. Woods informs the respectable Editor of the Annals, of one more instance in proof of the doctrine that our island has been submerged in the ocean. Indeed, the facts are so multiplying on our observation, that he must be a very sceptic by formation, who can resist the evidence, of not merely our little spot of habitation, but the whole of the present visible surface of the globe, having some time formed the bed of the ocean.

In a quarry of white and blue lias, at Tiverton, near Bath, Mr. W. found wood in different stages of petrifaction. The quarry consists of a thin stratum of vegetable mould, followed by fragments of stone; next, a bed of white lias, two feet thick; which, with its substratum of clay, abounds in cornua ammonis, gryphoid oysters, and several species of anomia; under these, lie six feet of lias, partly blue, with its substratum of clay, containing a few cornua ammonis, but the mass almost consisting of venuses, muscles, gryphoid oysters, agglutinated by media of sand and clay. In the clay was a fragment of compact iron ore; and several trochitæ of the stem of the pentacrinite. Under these, was a bed of white and blue stone, containing some petrifactions. The quarrymen stated, that mundic was occasionally found. The quarry is about 20 feet deep. Near the wall of the quarry, and among a heap of blue paving-stones, he observed a cavity, lined with small brown crystals; within which, and partly attached, lay a roundish mass of similar crystals, arranged longitudinally in grooves, and divided by transverse septa of white crystals: the channels were filled up with a crumbling substance resembling charcoal; combustible, without flame.

By this Mr. W. was induced to again examine the strata; and, in an interstice, between two large blocks of stone, near the bottom of the third stratum, he found a larger quantity of similar matter, but unconnected with the blocks themselves, though the former had been imbedded in the central substance of the rock. The matter, between the blocks, is heavier than the first specimen; has a carbonized appearance, but is less crystallized, and scarcely combustible, having a larger portion of earthy matter intermixed. Mr. W. remarks on the Rev. Mr. Townsend having found charcoal in the great oolite, and forest marble; but that neither he, nor other observers, have duly noticed the depth, and quality, of strata accompanying this charcoal; nor whether it were organic or inorganic: Mr. W. considering his specimens to be wood, indisputably.

Mr. W. concludes with stating his anxiety to have this fact accounted for; that is, how should carbon be deposited beneath three strata of stone, 20 feet thick, and formed of oceanic remains? The deluge being presumed to be one single convulsion; whereas the rock, wherein this matter was found, bears not any mark of disturbance; and therefore this deposition must have occurred by some convulsion or change, prior to those which have piled successive strata of oceanic remains above it.

We must express our surprise that Mr. Woods should not fully comprehend the current doctrine of the day, respecting oceanic depositions, and the probable successive superficial formations, or changes, so well explained by Cuvier and others. The fact Mr. W. gives us, is but one of a thousand, wherein is displayed a proof of terrestrial changes, long, very long, antecedent to the creation of man.

New Analyses of Meteoric Iron. By Dr. JOHN.
Annales de Chimie.

Dr. John, of Berlin, has lately submitted to analysis, specimens of meteoric iron which is disseminated in the aërolites of Chatonnay, of l'Aigle, and of Sienna. The following are the results of his experiments:

Iron of the Aërolites.

	Of Chatonnay.	Of l'Aigle.	Of Sienna.
Iron	92·72	92·72	92·72
Nickel	5·50	5·50	5·10
Sulphur	1·00	} Minute quantities which were not weighed.	
Cobalt	·78		
Chrome, a trace			

Dr. John states, that by comparing these results with those of the analyses of the great masses of malleable iron to which a meteoric origin is usually attributed, it is found—

1st. That the iron of the aërolites, and the malleable iron in large masses, contain the same substances; that is, iron, nickel, cobalt, chrome, and, perhaps, a trace of manganese, which Dr. J. discovered in the iron of Ellbogen.

2d. It appears, that the iron of aërolites does not contain quite so much nickel as the great malleable masses.

3d. The iron of the aërolites evidently contains sulphur; but as it is at the same time very malleable, it is probable that the sulphur is not combined with the whole of the iron, but only with a small portion; and arising from the magnetic pyrites disseminated through the whole mass. The great masses of iron prove this assertion; for when they are very malleable and ductile, as the iron of Pallas, that of Humboldt, that from Ellbogen, &c., they do not contain any trace of sulphur. It has been said that the iron discovered in Siberia, by Pallas, does contain a portion of this substance; but Dr. John could not discover any in it.

Nubian Antiquities.

M. Jomard, of the French Institute, has just received a letter from M. Caillaud, dated the 5th of May, from Assour, a village about a day's journey from Chendy, in Nubia, in the kingdom of Sennaar, in which that traveller communicates his latest discoveries. At a short distance to the south of the confluence of the Atbara, the ancient Astatoras, and four days' journey from Barbas, he found the ruins of a great town, with a temple and 40 pyramids still standing, and 40 others in ruins. The bases of the largest of the pyramids are about 62 feet, and their height 77; and on one of the sides of each, is a small temple, ornamented inside and outside with hieroglyphic emblems, and with key stones and ribs like ours. This traveller has ascertained that those temples are of the same age as the pyramids. The antiquities of Mount Barkal, near a place called Merawe, are about 70 leagues below, and very far from the confluence of the Atbara, which formed the Isle of Meroe. All the materials are of freestone, like the rock on which they are built. Ismael Pasha, who commands the military expedition into Abyssinia, permitted M. Caillaud to open one of these pyramids; some Greek letters were found in another of them. The site of the temple and the ruined town is about a league and a half from the Nile, and most of the pyramids are a league further, the same as at Memphis. Bruce must have passed two leagues only to the east, without suspecting their existence. An avenue of sphinxes, in the shape of rams, 262 feet long, leads to the temple; and the wall which encloses it, is 426 feet round. The island of Curgos, mentioned by Bruce, is to the south of Assour, and contains no monuments. M. Jomard is of opinion that the great ruins near Assour are those of Meroe; their latitude, about 16° 50', agrees with that of Meroe, as is given by Strabo and Eratosthenes. The positions laid down by Bruce, in his map, are tolerably accurate; but he has traced the limits of the ruins too much to the south. M. Caillaud proposed to remain during the rainy season at Sennaar, with the expedition; to take up his residence at the Fazuelo; and to proceed afterwards up the *Bahr-el-Abiad*, or the White River, which he will ascend to a certain distance, in order to procure information respecting the source of the Niger. The thermometer was constantly, during the month of April, as high as 45° and upwards, and even as high as 48° (43° of Reaumer, exposed, no doubt, to the sun). M. Caillaud could not discover any remains of the tradition of Queen Candace, whose dynasty, according to Bruce, were in his time still on the throne of Chendy. For a long time our traveller had not taken the meridian altitudes of the sun, which is too close to the zenith, and he can only determine the latitudes of places by means of the moon and stars.

M. Caillaud is proceeding on his African expedition with no little success, if we may rely on his reported progress; and we do not see much reason to doubt. But we are sorry that he should direct his attention to the discovery of the *source* of the Niger, as he states to be his object, instead of pursuing its line downwards; for we have as much knowledge of it upwards, as can interest us commercially; that is, we know it has been coursed up to what was considered to be the head of its navigation. Now, we are more anxious to have it explored with the stream; and the glory to be acquired from tracing it to its mouth, wherever it may be, would far surpass that of determining the spot from whence its earliest spring may be covered with a basin.

We hold that the tracing a river up to its source, from the head of its navigation, is of very secondary, and often, of very frivolous, importance.—It is little better than childish curiosity. But the same time and talent, spent in tracing its navigable course, and connections, to the place of its final discharge, may not only impart equal gratification as a pursuit, but also confer the highest benefit on mankind, as well as imperishable honour on the discoverer. The misfortune is, that one traveller goes forth as a geologist; another, as a botanist; a third, as an ornithologist; a fourth, as a zoologist; a fifth, as a mere trading agent; and a sixth, as a dilettanti wanderer: and it is very rarely indeed that the same individual unites all, or even several, of these characters within his own. So we have to search them collectively for our general information; at any enormous charge they may be pleased to put upon their paper and print.

Aërolite at Juvinas.

A large aërolite fell in June last at a village in the department de l'Ardèche, of which some very curious details have been preserved. The time it fell was about four o'clock, p. m. The atmosphere being perfectly clear, a loud rumbling noise was heard for a few minutes, in the course of which, four distinct detonations took place. The report was heard at Nismes, and still further off. Several individuals at Nismes, St. Thome, &c., observed a brilliant fire in the air; and they all agree in saying it appeared like a burning star, and slowly descended in the N. W.; and on its disappearing, it left behind a long train of smoke. Several foolish reports were propagated concerning the noise and fire. However, in the course of a few days, two peasants, of the village of Juvinas, some distance to the N. W. of Viviers, (who were working within a few yards from the spot where the aërolite descended,) said they heard a most dreadful noise, and turning round, observed an enormous ball of fire fall about five yards distant from them, tearing up the ground, and emitting a great smoke. Being rather disconcerted at the circumstance, they retreated; and would not, in the first instance, mention the circumstance. Shortly afterwards, however, several persons became acquainted with the fact, and on examining the place where the fire descended, they found, at the depth of five feet, a great stone, weighing very little short of 200 cwt. The countrymen having by this time recovered from their fright, supposing, from its bulk and size, that it contained gold, could not be prevented, either by arguments or promises, from breaking it into pieces. A few of the fragments have been preserved by several gentlemen at the place. From the appearance of the stone, we should be inclined to believe it was composed of two substances. The outside is covered with a thin coating, somewhat like the glaze the common brown earthenware is coated with. It is rather hard, but does not strike fire with steel; nor is it acted upon by nitric acid.

In another account, given by M. L. A. D. Firman, it is stated, that a stone of much smaller dimensions fell within a short distance of the spot where the former one descended. A gentleman who was looking towards the place where the fire first appeared, showed it to some of his workmen; and comparing the time it took in its descent, with the motion of his pulse, found it occupied about five seconds. He also observed a misty train left in the air after the fall of the meteorolite. It separated before the stone reached the ground, and was not emitted afterwards.—*Journal de Physique.*

Aurora at Belleville, Inverness-shire.
Edinburgh Philosophical Journal.

"On the evening of the 23d August, about half past nine o'clock, p. m., when there was not a breath of wind, and when the thermometer stood at 63°, the noise of very distant thunder was heard towards the south. Sheets of very brilliant lightning illuminated the sky, issuing, in general, from a small black cloud near the horizon. I was surprised, however, to observe, that, with the exception of a few thin black clouds, which were rendered visible by the lightning, the greater part of the sky was covered with shining masses, like those which form the aurora borealis. The stars were easily seen through this luminous matter, which was arranged in irregular masses, separated by clear intervals, but having a tendency to assume the appearance of irradiations diverging from the cloud whence the lightning appeared to issue. When the lightning flashed, it was propagated in a particular manner along these masses of light; but what was very singular, the luminous patches were constantly in a tremulous or undulating motion. During the intervals of the flashes of lightning they shifted their place, and changed their form, exactly like the light which appears in many of the varieties of the aurora borealis. As the luminous clouds now described did not appear in the northern part of the horizon, and were distinctly related, in their position and form, to the thunder cloud from which the lightning emanated, we are entitled to refer the two classes of phenomena to the peculiar electrical condition of the atmosphere, and to suppose that the phenomena of the aurora borealis may have an analogous origin."

Earthquake in Joyce County.

Journal of Science.

Nearly one hundred acres of land in this county, belonging to the Provost of Trinity College, principally pasture and mountain, and rather populously inhabited, was observed moving, and carrying with it large quantities of earth and rocks, destroying the whole produce of the land, and forcing the entire mass into the sea. Before its motion a loud noise was heard for a short time, with a motion in the earth. A day or two after, a tract of land in the same neighbourhood suffered in a like manner; but, if any thing, in a more violent degree; the inhabitants not being able to save a single article, all being swallowed up by this dreadful visitation of nature.

Rein Deer.

Mr. Bullock has succeeded in bringing specimens of the rein deer to this country, and hopes are entertained that they may lead to the colonization of our mountain forests by this animal. While on a tour in Norway, he procured a herd of twenty, which were destroyed by eating a poisonous plant that grew on a small island on which they were kept. He then bought a second herd of twelve, and succeeded in bringing them alive, and well, into the Thames. Here, however, in consequence of the custom-house officer not feeling authorized to allow the deer to be landed, eight died on board the vessel before permission could be obtained from the authorities in London. The remnant saved consists of a male and female, a fawn, (since dead,) and a male which has been cut: the latter is about ten hands high, and proportionally stout; the others are a hand or two lower. Their fur is very thick and fine, and delicately warm and soft. The horns branch beautifully, and are covered with a short fur. The antlers of the largest animal are three feet in length. Their hoofs are very broad, and flexible between the divisions, enabling them to clamber up precipices, and hang on rocks inaccessible to other animals. They are very swift. They seem reconciled to hay, as food; and like brandy, which is administered to them as medicine.

With the deer, Mr. Bullock has brought a native Laplander, his wife, and child. These beings are about four feet eight inches in height; the man being of the common size, the woman rather tall. The child is about five years old.

Preservative against Scarlet Fever.

It is announced in the *Journal de Medicina pratique* of Berlin, that the belladonna is a preservative against this fever. The fact was first discovered at Leipsig, but it has lately been confirmed by several experiments.

We have not any great faith in German specifics or doctrines; and shall be equally surprised and gratified if experience prove the above means as efficacious as stated.

Mud Volcanoes.   Journal of Science.

A small bog, not far from Mountmellick, in rather a north east direction from Kilmaleady bog, has been greatly agitated for several days. It rises upwards, to a great height, and falls again on the same spot from whence it rose. It is, as yet, confined to the place from whence it issues, but the inhabitants are in the greatest alarm, expecting every moment a sudden overflow.

The Boa Constrictor.

A very singular discovery took place in the island of St. Vincent, a short time since, which might have been attended with more serious consequences than it fortunately was. A party of negroes, who were engaged in labour at Sandy Bay, came unexpectedly upon an enormous serpent, which, in the moment, was fired at by one of the party and killed. It cannot be discovered in what manner a snake of this description could have reached the shores of St. Vincent. Its extreme length was just fifteen feet, and the circumference of the body was nearly four feet. When found, it was lying in a coil, but raised itself on being disturbed.

THE FOCUS

OF

PHILOSOPHY, SCIENCE, AND ART.

Method of Ventilating Coal Mines. By Mr. JAMES RYAN, for which the Gold Medal and One Hundred Guineas were awarded by the Society of Arts, &c.

THE sense of the Society for the encouragement of Arts, &c. on the merits of Mr. Ryan's proposed mode of ventilation, must have been high indeed; or so munificent a mark of its favour would not have been conferred on that gentleman. And we think that there can scarcely be an object found of superior importance, whether as involving considerations of policy or humanity. The lamentable destruction of human life, among a class of society whose industry, and privations, we are so greatly indebted to, for comfort and wealth, is, or ought to be, a matter of sincere sorrow to us all. Perpetually immured within the bowels of the earth; abandoning all the gratifications of visual sense; and in momentary danger of being involved in sudden destruction; they surely must have such irresistible claims on our sympathy as to make even selfishness itself ready to sacrifice to their security. We shall participate, most sincerely, in the satisfaction all humane hearts must feel in a conviction that some certain method of ventilation has been discovered, and we will hope Mr. Ryan's plan may supply the desideratum. Many gentlemen, high in the scale of scientific fame; and many more, who, being personally partakers in the dangers of a mining life, and practical observers; have, within these few years, devoted attention to the object of ventilating mines; or devising ingenious means to prevent fatal effects from the deleterious gases, where largely accumulated; yet still we have had to seek further powers, or new applications. In Sir H. Davy's, and Dr. Clanny's safety lamps, we had a strong confidence; but we now fear that the security to be expected from them is not so entire as to divest us of apprehension. And we may truly add that, in these cases, the slightest error in principles, or defect in art, may lead to a fatal confidence on the part of the miner; for he will be led into augmented dangers by his unlearned presumption of security. This consideration should induce every mining proprietor, and superintendant, to most cautiously weigh suggestions of improvement in modes of ventilation, or construction of lamps, &c. before he put them to the test of experience; and even then, gradually, as well as on a limited scale: above all, to fortify himself against the delusion of a high sounding name.—We beg to be distinctly understood as not hinting at any applications, personally; for none can entertain a more profound respect for the parties named, than we do; and certainly there is a large debt of gratitude due to them, by the mining interests, for their persevering efforts to accomplish the object sought.—We cannot, however, hesitate one moment as to a preference of the means whereby this security is to be obtained. The drawing, or the driving off the gases, as they become generated, has a value superior to the partial convenience of approaching them with diminished danger; inasmuch as that the former is preventive, the latter mitigative, of the evil.

But Mr. Ryan's plan involves further practical benefit than its paramount object in protection of the miner; for it enables the proprietor to draw more wealth from his coal beds, by diminishing the requisite magnitude of the pillars left unwrought to sustain the superincumbent strata. The reader who may be ignorant of the common mode by which the mines are worked, will perhaps be surprised to learn that three-fourths, or thereabout, of the seam of coal is left standing, in massive pillars; and so much of that mass left, as exceeds the quantity absolutely necessary for sustaining the earth above, is dead loss to the proprietor.

By the firing process, to be explained, slenderer columns might be shattered in the explosion, and the roof be thereby let down. Mr. R.'s workings not being subjected to these explosive concussions, there is not any necessity for wasting more coal in the remaining pillars than may be equal to the mere mechanical support of the superincumbent surface. Nor is it necessary that these pillars be left in mathematical arrangement for the purpose of forming regular transverse lines of head-way; consequently a mine may be made to yield a produce, augmented in proportion with this improved principle of working; always, of course, governed by the quality of the strata above.

Mr. R. proposes to illustrate the proper idea of a coal seam by supposing it to resemble a large thin book, placed in a slanting position, on a bed of clay or stone, and covered with another bed, or stratum, equally impervious to gas; the laminæ of the coal to be represented by the leaves of the book:—"This," says he, "is precisely the case in those mines where the seam of coal runs out to the surface, uninterrupted by faults. In such mines explosions are never known. But when the seam is separated by a fault, which, to pursue the illustration, may be imitated by cutting the book into two, with its supporting, and superincumbent strata; raising or depressing one portion, until the leaves of the book, no longer touching each other, rest against the clay; and vice versa; such a fault, it is evident, will no longer permit the free transmission of the noxious gases into the atmosphere from the portion of leaves situate below the fault; whilst that part which still presents its higher edge to the surface, continues as safe as before. In this case, I bore a sufficient quantity of holes from the seam below the fault, or downcast, to the seam above it, or upcast, in order to let the gas pursue its course."

We will pursue this figure of illustration; and desire our readers to imagine that the two portions of the book may constitute planes lying, relatively, at every degree of angular inclination; so that by possibility, the one may be perpendicular to, or at right angles, with the other. This extreme, however, is seldom or never met with. But it will be readily comprehended that the respective and relative inclinations must greatly modify the adoption of means for ventilation; and some instances may be conceived wherein Mr. Ryan's principle could not well apply, as thus:—suppose the book to be nearly horizontal, and the divided portions to be greatly but equally depressed; this would throw the superior portion nearer perpendicularity with the horizon, and bring the divided edge of the inferior portion below the horizontal level. Or rather, suppose the line of stratum to be broken, and each portion of the book to take an inclination upwards; this would resemble the letter $_aV^b$, either supposed erect or slanting but with the break at the angular point downwards; it is obvious that Mr. R's leading a bore from one upward leg, as a, of the letter V to the other, as b, could only affect the portion of a below the point of connection, and all the superior part of a would be subject to gaseous accumulation.

What we have here supposed to be the case with the seam, as presumed to be divided into two portions only, like the division of the book, is not a common occurrence, or, at least, not in the degree of angular divergence that the letter V would represent; but the book, or seam of coal, may be very properly supposed as divided into several transverse portions, lying successively in varied angular deviations from the general plane, forming a zigzag line of successive angles at each break, the superior end of each portion will meet with a bar to the ascent of the generated gases; consequently they will accumulate there in a dangerous degree. If the upper plane or roof of the seam be not worked even; or if fallings-in take place from the roof, and excavations of it present; they will contain the gases, dangerous in a degree proportioned to their magnitude and relative situation as to distance from the obstruction at the superior end.

We now proceed to show what the old mode of practice has been; and shall afterwards explain that proposed by Mr. Ryan. The beds of coal excavated, are called boards; and are aptly illustrated, as above, by supposing them of a book-like form—about four yards wide, twenty yards long, and not exceeding eight feet in depth or thickness.

Now, suppose these excavations running parallel, and at the distance of eight yards from each other, then the masses of coal, left to support the roof, are twenty yards by eight; and consequently twice the amount worked out for use. Here is an immense loss of fuel. The cross lines, at twenty yards apart, as above mentioned, are called head-ways; and are carried into lines, running longitudinally, from one extremity of the mine to the other. These latter lines are the main channels for atmospheric circulation. At the distance of two-thirds, or one-half, of the length of these longitudinal channels of circulation, are two pits, or shafts, running upwards to the earth's surface: the one called the downcast shaft; the other, the upcast; in reference to their uses: or one shaft only, bratticed or boarded off, so as to serve the double purpose of both downcast and upcast. It will be easily conceived that, where the downcast shaft run into the lowest level of the workings, and the upcast rise from the highest level; where there be no break, or angular horizontal deviation; and where the roof be not excavated, so as to form inverted basins, accumulating the lighter gases; the combustible vapours must necessarily pass up the inclined plane, and in contact with the roof, to the opening of the upcast shaft, and thereby be completely discharged, as fast as generated. In this case the mine will be exempt from the usual dangers of working. But, as almost every mine is subject to occasional fallings-in of the roof, or excavations of its surface; and as the transverse lines, or head-ways, terminate abruptly in the coal vein; there are large and destructive volumes of gas perpetually accumulating, to the terror of the miner, and the loss of the proprietor. Thus a large mine is but an immense labyrinth [of right angular cuttings; presenting probable destruction at every point.

The present mode of ventilation consists in carrying currents of atmospheric air through every possible cutting, and of directing the profuse issue of gas into the line of draft, by what are called stoppings; that is, by turning the gaseous course by doors, or brick work, so as to facilitate its passage by the most easy, and least dangerous, channel, towards its aperture of issue, the upcast shaft. The course of an atmospheric current through the windings of a working, about 600 yards square, is estimated at 27 miles.

The Sunderland Society for preventing accidents in coal mines, in their first Report, say, "The only method we are at present acquainted with, for preventing accidents by fire, is a mechanical application of the atmospheric air to the removing, or sweeping away, the inflammable gas, as it issues from the several fissures which the workings intersect in their progress."

One method is, that of forcing air down the shaft, and along the courses; but this is deficient in power for the removal of so large a volume as they contain.

A second is, by falls of water, carrying with them a current of air. This is not only subject to the objection against the former, but also to that of the expense and labour in again raising the water out of the mine.

A third is, the use of the air pump; which is not only unequal to the desired effect, but also, while acting, renders the upcast shaft useless to the miner.

A fourth is, that of a furnace, near the bottom of the upcast shaft; in order to rarify the current passing up it, and draw, along with it, the air of the courses. This method is highly dangerous; for, if an extraordinary issue of gas should rush from a line of working, and come in contact with the fire, destruction would be certain.

A fifth is, the diluting method; whereby so much air is carried, or forced, through the workings, as shall dilute the generated gases below the point of combustion. This means will succeed, where the coal seam be thin, and the gases not abundant: and has been effectually adopted in some of the Staffordshire collieries.

The last method to be mentioned is, that of the firing line, as it is termed. This is done by men accustomed to the process, who, having prepared a light, under the gaseous accumulation, or as near to it as possible, retire into a stable, well secured; and, by pulling a properly directed wire, bring the light into contact with the gas, when an immediate combustion and explosion take place. In some mines, where the accumulations are profuse, it is necessary to fire them three times daily; and as the miners are all obliged to retire, during each firing, there is a great loss of time. Besides, there must be immense pillars of coal left uncut, or the firing process would tear them down, and involve the whole works in destruction. Sometimes, too, the ignited gases set fire to the coal seam itself, and it becomes necessary to stop up the shafts, until the extinction be accomplished.

Having thus laid before the reader the various methods of preventing the destructive consequences that may ensue from combustion of carburetted hydrogen, issuing from the coal seams, we will proceed to explain the peculiar advantages of Mr. Ryan's plan.

He considers that the carrying a traverse all round the working is essential to security, so that the head-ways may all terminate in this surrounding channel, and therein pour the collections of the respective cuttings and head-ways; these are, in course of current, from the inferior to the superior level of the mine, and terminating in an enclosure, from which is carried a gas-way, running upwards, like a chimney, into the upcast shaft, a few yards above its bottom, so as to secure the gaseous current from contact with the lights necessary in use near to the floor of the shaft.

When the horizontal line of the seam be broken by perpendicular fissures, filled with foreign matter, and the angular inclinations of the bed be reversed; he would carry a boring from the upper part of the lower leg of the angle to a point of the superior leg, on a higher level than that from whence the boring commenced; and render the whole as effectually drained of gas, as if the stratum were one unbroken and oblong plane of working. By carrying collateral cuttings from gaseous accumulations, whether produced by basins in the roof, or fallings-in of earth, into the surrounding head-way, or gas channel, he provides against local evils. And, in some instances, where the gas issued from vents, not easily connected with the head-way, he closed the cavity in, leaving only a small aperture for its egress, to which he set fire as a jet, and thereby converted into a useful light, for the miners without to work by, what, if lighted when freely expansible, would have exploded, to their destruction. Perhaps this is as beautiful an instance of skilful application in science, as can be produced: the very instrument of terror being converted into an auxiliary of operation.

It is not the lighter gases only, that are objects of alarm to the miner; for the choke-damp, as it is called, is also as certainly destructive. This consists principally of carbonic acid gas, or fixed air, which being of greater specific gravity than atmospheric air, necessarily lies in a stratum on the floor of the mine; and, if accumulated to such a depth as to equal the greatest possible height of the miner's head, must be inhaled by him; when almost instant death would ensue. In order, then, to draw off this ponderous gas, Mr. Ryan bores apertures level with the floor of the workings, and carried into the surrounding head-way, so that both that on the floor level, and the carburetted hydrogen in contact with the line of roof, are carried off by the same general outlet.

We lament to learn from Mr. R. that he met with all the malignity of prejudice, and perhaps too of envy, in his attempts to carry so valuable an object into effect; for after having sought in vain for opportunities of proving the efficacy of his plan, even in mines where great destruction of life had just previously been sustained, he could not prevail over ignorance, or interest, or perhaps both.—But, at length, through the powerful medium of Sir J. Sinclair, to whom he in a kind of despair resorted, he obtained the active patronage of the Hon. Washington Shirley; who recommended Mr. R. to Messrs. Fereday and Smith, coal owners in Staffordshire: these gentlemen selected a very dangerous working, which Mr. Ryan cleared shortly; in spite of the jealousy of the neighbouring directors. So that this pit became securely workable, while the surrounding works could not be carried on, without firing, at least once daily. In one instance, he effectually discharged the gases from workings in six hours; that other practical men declared he could not effect under some months.

The Sunderland Society at length opened its eyes; and wrote to Mr. Fereday; who, in return, spoke highly to the Secretary of Mr. R.'s success. They then wrote to Mr. Ryan, who left Ireland, and went to Sunderland; where he conferred with Drs. Gray, Pemberton, and Clanny; and afterwards went on to Newcastle; where he could not prevail on the owners, or directors, to permit his trial; although a Mr. Buddle had been urged by Dr. Gray. Mr. R. then goes on to complain of rather partial injustice which he received from the northern Directors; and which, if not mistaken, or overdrawn, reflects no little disgrace on the parties alluded to. But this is their business, and we must leave the matter with their consciences, to settle how they may.

We think Mr. Ryan's plan well entitled to the approbation so judiciously, and liberally, stamped upon it by the Society of Arts; and shall be gratified to hear of its further adoption with success.

Experimental Researches on Water Cements, Mortar, and Lime. By L. J. VICAT.

(Continued from page 256.)

We have to apologize to our readers for the repeated continuations on this head; but as we take the subject from a periodical work, whose issue of matter we of course cannot controul; and as we were not aware at first of the great length to which it would run; we have deceived ourselves in the expectation and hope that each number of the work alluded to, would bring the subject to a close: but that is not the case, even with the one before us. We will not fail, however, to cut it as short as we can, without injury to the matter under consideration.

Making allowance for common errors, the following inferences seem justifiable:

1st. Excess of lime, in water cements, retards the setting; which bears a direct proportion with the hardness.

2d. Active puozzolanas set better with fat, than with hydraulic, limes; but hydraulic limes are most active of all with middling puozzolanas.

3d. Slacking by immersion, and by atmospherical exposure, are preferable to that by affusion, for speedy setting.

Tracing the relative induration by age, we shall find that:

1st. Water cements, with common lime, harden quicker during the third year than the second.

2d. With highly hydraulic limes, acquire their maximum of hardness by the end of the second year.

Cements made with common lime, sometimes, do not fully indurate within ten years. And with such lime and sand, they have been found soft at the end of 25 years. We should doubt whether such cements (if they can deserve the name) ever would indurate at all.

On Common Mortars.

We come now to a still more important stage of M. Vicat's essay. M. V. commences with observing that, the common mortars are exposed to many injurious influences, from which the water cements are exempted: such as changes in temperature; in degrees of moisture and dryness; the varied qualities of the matter with which they are brought into contact; action of light and vapour, &c. &c.; all of which tend to diminish the cohesive effect. Here M. Vicat examines some theoretical opinions, as to the principle on which mortar solidifies. First, he shows that M. Faujas St. Fond's idea of the water, in time, seizing the carbonic acid that remains in the lime, unexpelled by the burning, and that it again forms calcareous crystals, having an affinity for, or adhesive union with, the other matter, as the sand, is absurd; for agreeably with it, chalk or limestone would be more efficacious unburned, than burned.

M. V. says that when we fracture old and good mortar, the brilliant particles are not calcareous crystals; because, on exposure to air, they become white; that is, opaque, from their efflorescing, as we understand it; for we cannot agree with him, until he prove the fact by analysis, that they are not really calcareous crystals. Their opacity, on exposure, is not a proof that they are otherwise. Nor do we think M. Duret's having found that the ancient mortars do not contain more than half the carbonic acid of their lime of composition, as militating against our opinion. M. V. does not accord with those who think that the mortar derives carbonic acid from the atmosphere, presuming that it cannot penetrate much beyond the surface; especially where it have been smoothened down by the trowel. Nor does he concur with Loriot, that the lime is a simple matrix; and the sand a mere foreign body. These different opinions have led to much practical diversity: as the slow drying; the exclusion of light; the occasional watering; the converse, in preservation from wet; the slacking with boiling water; or, lastly, the addition of quick-lime in powder, to hasten setting.

On the Qualities of the Sand.—M. Rondelet has contended that we ought to be more governed, in this respect, by the nature of the material with which it is to be mixed, than by that of the sand itself. This M. Vicat will not allow; for he says that some sands, as those of the rivers Isere and Drac, are blackish, and give a very bad mortar; but that some yellow veins at Souillac yield sand of an almost cementing quality. In his own experiments he has used the sand of the Dordogne, principally quartz; but containing mica, feldspar, schorl, and basalt: the relative magnitude of whose particles has been the particular object of his studies.

The comparative hardness of mortars at the end of a year have been thus—First, Limes that when wetted would alone form the most solid bodies, with sand produced the weakest mortar—Secondly, Quartzose sand may increase, diminish, or nullify cohesion, according to the quality of the lime, as exemplified by these facts:

1st. Hydraulic limes, with quartzose sand, increase the cohesion, and form harder under water than the lime would alone.

2d. That limes, with quartzose sand, will scarcely set at all, under moist soils.

3d. Middling limes, have intermediate qualities, governed by those of the sands, as to character and grossness.

The second inference is especially sustained, by the facts that Paris plaster (a matrix not shrinking in setting) has a resistance of the matrix, to that of a compound plaster and sand, as 1·00 to 0·58. That clay (a matrix shrinking) has a resistance of that matrix, to a compound of clay and sand, as 1·00 to 0·21. Fat lime, slacked in the common way (a shrinking matrix) has a resistance of the matrix, to that of the mortar, as 1·00 to 0·25.

Hence, fat lime, with quartzose sand, resembles plaster and clay; that is, the action is limited to the mere mechanical involution of the silicious and other bodies, contained in the mass: so that fat lime, and fine silicious sand, cannot yield mortars indurating in the air. Yet sand cannot be dispensed with; for its presence subdivides the contractions of the lime infinitely, and thereby facilitates combination with carbonic acid. Still M. V. thinks that, although the carbonic acid must have this effect of regenerating limestone, it does so only with the individual dry particles; but they have not a cementing union within themselves. Now we think, on the contrary, that the congregated crystals will acquire a firmness, by affinity and composition, and thereby the whole mass of crystals be embodied together. And, also, we dissent from his idea, that the particles of lime will be too dry for such aggregation: for if the carbonic acid can penetrate the interior of the mortar mass, so may atmospheric moisture, in sufficient abundance; and if individual crystals can be formed, why not the calcareous stone be regenerated? No difficulty can present to our view, as arising out of the impenetrability of the mass; for when we recollect that, even the interior substance of thick brass rods will assume new forms of arrangement of particles, by exposure to muriatic and nitrous acid vapours, we cannot hesitate to believe it possible that chemical affinity may force its way for effect into matter comparatively soft.

The hydraulic limes appear to be better adapted for exposure to air, than as water cements. How the silicious and aluminous matter, combined in these limes, may be modified, during calcination, cannot perhaps be satisfactorily explained; but they do set, and that well, with an additional portion of one of the components in a gross form; that is, sand. Even a compound of clay and lime, in equal proportions, when calcined together, will set as mortar; though of an inferior quality. We would suggest that these may not be the just proportions to produce the greatest effect; and that experiment may determine from them a product not inferior to the compound with sand.

On the Size of the Grains of Sand.—For highly hydraulic limes, the order of merit is fine sand; coarse and fine sand and gravel; and coarse sand. For moderately hydraulic, mixed sand; fine; and coarse. For common fat, coarse sand; mixed; fine. The difference of quality resulting from the various sands, is, in the common fat lime, as a fifth; but in the hydraulic limes, with the sand relatively, it is more than one-third.

The mortars of the Romans have been the admiration and envy of the moderns. The magnificent structures with which they adorned Rome and its provinces, doubtless led their architects to study the composition of cements, as a means essential to their reputation. We find silicious matter, in fragments of varied magnitude, throughout their works; and they probably had learned the art of best adapting fine or coarse sand, gravel, or shingle, to the particular qualities of particular limes. That they have made studious selections is plain, from their having preferred one quality, in places where both presented. Yet be it found where it may, and compounded with such relative proportion in silicious grain as it may; it is always of such hardness as must lead us to conclude that the quality and proportion of ingredients have been the best possible. But we may observe, as lessons, that where the limestone is of middling character, they used only gravel. And, again, in Syria, where the lime-stone is grey, and probably highly hydraulic, they used fine sand.

We may, then, infer that the more intimately quartz be divided, the better it is adapted for hydraulic limes; and that the common limes require a coarser grain.

On the best Method of warming and ventilating Houses and other Buildings. By CHARLES SYLVESTER.

(Continued from p. 312.)

Although we differed a little from Mr. Stevenson as to the theoretic principle whereby he would account for aërial currents, we have the pleasure to observe that his practical details are such as meet with our decided approbation; and as we feel them to be worthy of public attention, shall recite them fully.

By reference to p. 312, it will be seen that Mr. S. gives a description of a stove used by Mr. Strutt; where the air current was brought into contact with the stove itself; and afterwards, compelled to traverse both up and down the tube. This stove, being perfect in principle, only required the due adaptation of relative proportions. By bringing an increased volume of air in contact with the heating body, less intensity of heat, and consumption of fuel, were requisite; the quantity of volume was increased; and what with us is, at least, equal, the air would have less of a burned character; which latter is perhaps the cause of heated air being so unpleasant. We do not mean that the air itself is burned, but that the dusty particles, floating in it, become scorched, and yield an unpleasant scent. The temperature, too, by this latter improvement of Mr. Strutt's, would be more uniform, and the apparatus be rendered capable of equal effect, at a less expense of wear.

Mr. Sylvester is entitled to our thanks for accomplishing what had been strangely neglected; namely, a measure of the heating effects, and sums, of circulating volumes. For this purpose, he constructed an apparatus, thus—"A very light brass wheel, like the first of the smoke jack, with an endless screw upon the same axis, gives motion to a wheel of 50 teeth; on the axis of which is an index, which is watched by the eye, when the instrument is exposed to the current. The wheel acted on by the current, is about $2\frac{1}{4}$ inches in diameter, and the vanes, or sails, are eight in number, and fill up the whole circle, when their faces are parallel to the planes of their motion; and they are adjusted to an angle of 45°." Fifty revolutions of the first movement were found to take place while the current causing those revolutions moved through forty-six feet.

The duration of each experiment was 12 hours, with a uniformly good fire; the velocity and temperature, in the main flue, taken every half hour, and the average; also, the quantity of fuel consumed: the excess of the average temperature of the flue over that of the outward air, forms the required datum; and the average velocity denotes the aërial current, in cubical feet.

Put A = the number of pounds of air heated in 12 hours, allowing 14 feet of cubic air to 1lb.

T = the excess of temperature above that of the atmosphere.

W = the weight, in lbs. of coal consumed in the same time.

E = the effect of the above, which in stoves of all sizes, on the same construction, should be generally a constant quantity: since A, the quantity, and T, the excess of temperature, are advantages to be produced by W, the weight of coal.

E, the effect, will be, directly, as A and T; and, inversely, as W. Therefore $E = \frac{AT}{W}$. For instance:

A stove warming 100,000 cubic feet of space, to 60°, in the coldest season, and placed at 9 feet below the level of discharge of warm air, will furnish about 45 cubic feet per second, at 60° above atmospheric temperature. At 12 hours, this will require 3 bushels, or 252 lbs. of coal. This will be at the rate of 1,944,000 cubic feet in 12 hours; equal to 138,857 lbs. Thence E will $= \frac{138,857 + 60}{252} = 32,930$, which may be taken nearly as a constant quantity expressive of the power of any stove; as well as the lbs. weight of air heated 1° of Fahrenheit, by 1 lb. of Newcastle coal.

The magnitude of the stove, and the facility of issue of the foul air, will have an influence. The force and direction of the wind will also be of consequence. When the air be calm, the rush of horizontal current towards the stove will be measured by the power of perpendicular ascent given to the air within the tube, by the existing intensity of the fire; and this power of ascent and current is usually quite sufficient. But, when the horizontal current be strengthened by the wind blowing towards the entrance aperture of the tube, the circulation will be proportionally augmented, and the heat of the stopple less wasted. In order to gain as much of this extrinsic power as possible, Mr. S. affixes to the entrance aperture a turn-cap, or cowl; whereby he can regulate the counter current of the atmosphere: although unequal quantities may enter, when different winds occur, there does not seem to be any injurious effect beyond, perhaps, an occasional augmentation of temperature, which can be corrected by the command over the aperture of exit of foul air.

The turn-cap for the escape of foul air, is at the top of the building, and in common with the roof; every room having a separate foul-air flue, all terminating in the turn-cap. This arrangement is followed at the Derby Infirmary, and the Wakefield Lunatic Asylum. When the stove is not in action, as in summer, the current may not be equal to the ventilation; in which case, the turn-cap is affixed to the top of a cylindrical cavity, and all the foul-air flues are led into it, as well as the flue of the stove and other fire-flues of the building: whereby the rarefaction in the foul-air line of exit is augmented. By uniting all the fire-flues with the foul-air flues, Mr. S. suggests that there could not be any downward currents, in any individual chimney; because of the increased ascending impetus in the exit current, in which every flue would participate: besides, such plan would render one chimney aperture equal to the discharge of all the smoke, &c. of the whole building; and thereby contribute to the external symmetry of the structure, so generally deformed by a multitude of projecting tubes.

A cold-air flue, 50 yards, has been found by Mr. S. to have a cooling effect in summer, about equal to the arithmetical mean between the temperature of the air and earth; and the converse may be advantageously enjoyed in the winter, when the earth is warmer than the atmosphere. Such flue should (contrary to the heating tubes exposed to fire) present the greatest surface possible.

This is the sum of Mr. Sylvester's remarks: and as they are probably the result of a judicious experience, we attach a greater importance to them, than to many of those conjectures which have scarcely consistency enough to even amuse us. The great expense of fuel, and the inconveniences we suffer from under the old mode of warming our apartments, with the superior efficacy of the flue process, will, jointly, have the ultimate effect of establishing the latter, to the advantage of our persons and our pockets.

On the Macquarrie River, New Holland.

The Surveyor General, Mr. Oxley, having explored the Macquarrie as far as then practicable, reported to the Governor of the Colony that he had arrived at the Port of Stephens; and circumstances rendering it necessary that Mr. Evans should proceed to Newcastle, he embraced the opportunity to make to his Excellency a brief report of the route pursued by the western expedition entrusted to his direction.

His previous letter, dated the 22d of June, acquainted the Governor with the sanguine hopes he entertained from the appearance of the river, that its termination would be either in interior waters, or coast-ways. When he wrote that letter to the Governor he did not anticipate the probability that a few days' further travelling would lead him to its termination as an accessible river.

On the 29th of June, having traced its course, without the smallest diminution or addition, about seventy miles further to the N. N. W., there being a slight fresh in the river, it overflowed its banks; and, although they were at the distance of nearly three miles from it, the country was so perfectly level that the waters soon spread over the ground on which they were. They had been, for some days before, travelling over such very low grounds, that the people in the boats, finding the country flooded, proceeded slowly; a circumstance which enabled him to send them directions to return to the station they had quitted in the morning, where the ground was a little more elevated. This spot being by no means secure, it was arranged that the horses, with the provisions, should return to the last high land they had quitted, a distance of 16 miles; and, as it appeared to him that the body of water in the river was too important to be much affected by the mere overflowing of its banks, he determined to take the large boat, and in her to endeavour to discover their point of discharge.

On the 2d of July he proceeded in the boat down the river, nearly thirty miles, on a N.N.W. course, the first ten miles of which was covered with water; the stream continued twenty-four miles distance. He was sanguine in his expectations of soon entering the long desired lake, when, to his surprise, it suddenly spread over the surrounding country, running with the same rapidity as when confined within its proper banks. This point of junction with the interior waters is in latitude 30° 45′ south, and longitude 147° 10′ east.

If an opinion might be hazarded from actual appearances, he felt confident he was in the immediate vicinity of an inland sea. There is not a single eminence on this apparently boundless space, except those points on which he remained until the 28th of July.

The south west side of the river was found to be a wet and barren marsh, without a single dry spot to which their course might be directed.

On the 18th of July, Mr. Evans returned from the country to the north east, not being able to continue in that direction above two days' journey. And he afterwards proceeded in a more easterly direction, and at fifty miles distant from Macquarrie River, crossed another, wider; and nearly arrived at the Mountains (80 miles distance) seen from the tent.

The party quitted their station on the 30th of July, being in latitude 31° 18′ S. and longitude 147° 31′ E., and, on proceeding to the coast, arrived at the mountains to which their course had been directed; from the summit of which they had the most extended prospect. From south by the west to north, it was one vast level, resembling the ocean in extent, but yet without water being discerned; the range of high land extending to the N. E. by N., elevated points of which were distinguished upwards of one hundred and twenty miles.

From this point, Mr. Oxley pursued a N. E. course; when, finding himself surrounded by bogs, he was compelled to take a more easterly direction; having practically proved that the country could not be traversed on any point deviating from the main range of hills which bound the interior.

On proceeding more easterly, numerous fine streams watered a rich and beautiful country. On the 7th of September they crossed the meridian of Sidney, as also the most elevated point known in New South Wales, being then in latitude 31° 30′ S. On the 20th of September they had a view of the ocean at a distance of fifty miles. On descending the mountain, they fell in with a river, which carried them to the entrance of the port which received it; having passed over, since the 8th of July, a tract of country nearly five hundred miles in extent from east to west.

This inlet is situated in latitude 31° 23′ 30″ S., and longitude 152° 50′ 18″ E., and had been previously noticed by Capt. Flinders, but he did not discover that it had a navigable entrance. The depth was estimated at about three fathoms, with a safe, though narrow entrance, through the *sand rollers*.

On the 12th Oct. they quitted this port for Sidney, and soon discovered how little the best marine charts can be depended upon; as the distance of Capt. F. from the coast did not allow him to perceive openings, which, though of little consequence to shipping, presented the most formidable obstacles to travellers by land.

Mr. Oxley hoped to have had the satisfaction of returning without any accident, but such is the ferocious disposition of the natives to the northward, that notwithstanding the greatest care and attention, they could not save themselves from having one man severely wounded by them.

Mr. C. Frazer, the colonial Botanist, has added nearly *seven hundred* new specimens to the already extended catalogue of Australasian plants.

The termination of the Macquarrie river, as narrated by

Mr. Oxley, is of a rather singular nature: for the extended spread of water could not be properly denominated an inland sea. Indeed it is probable that the waters again collect within a narrow channel, and form a magnificent river. Should the neighbouring country be eventually cultivated, as is highly probable, human art may at some remote period effect the draining off of this immense lake. A lower or a shorter fall through some mountainous passage, may lead the surplus into junction with another river beyond the Alpine chain. We think that the enterprizing spirit of the colony will not rest here, nor should it; for the Macquarrie river must be of great importance to the settlements on the eastern coasts of Australasia.

On the Properties of Peroxide of Hydrogen, or Oxygenated Water. By M. THENARD.

Traité de Chimie.

A knowledge of the action of oxygen and hydrogen under every possible form, is so desirable, that we cannot omit presenting the following experiments by a well known chemist, to our chemical readers.

"Water is combined with a large quantity of oxygen, by dissolving peroxide of barium in muriatic acid, and adding sulphuric acid to the solution. These two operations are to be several times repeated with the same liquor; then adding sulphate of silver, and at last barytes, and separating the precipitates successively by the filter. Muriatic acid readily dissolves the peroxide, and there result muriate of barytes and weakly oxygenated water. The sulphuric acid precipitates the barytes, and liberates the muriatic acid, which then acts upon a fresh quantity of peroxide of barium, so that there is no difficulty in repeating the process several times, and there remains at length water, holding more or less oxygen in solution. The mode in which the sulphate of silver acts is evident; the use of it is to separate the muriatic acid, and replace it by sulphuric; the barytes combines with the sulphuric acid, and precipitates it. When the operation is performed with pure materials, and in proper proportions, it is evident that the last result is entirely oxygenated water: it is then to be put into a glass vessel with a foot, and this placed in a large capsule, two-thirds filled with concentrated sulphuric acid; the apparatus is to be put under the receiver of an air-pump, and the air exhausted. The pure water evaporates much more readily than the oxygenated water, so that in two days it will contain 250 times its volume of oxygen; and when the solution contains 475 times its volume of oxygen at the temperature of 57°, no further concentration takes place by keeping it longer in vacuo."

PROPERTIES OF PEROXIDE OF HYDROGEN.

"The peroxide of hydrogen is fluid and colourless as water. It is inodorous, or at least it is so nearly so, that few persons can discover any smell. It gradually destroys the colour of litmus and turmeric paper, and makes them quite white. It acts upon the epidermis very readily, sometimes suddenly whitens it, and occasions prickings, which continue for a longer or shorter period, according to the nature of the individual, and the thickness of the portion of liquor applied; if it be too thick, or be renewed, the skin itself is attacked and destroyed. Applied to the tongue, it whitens and pricks it, thickens the saliva, and produces a sensation which it is difficult to describe, but which resembles that of certain metallic solutions. Its tension is extremely weak, much weaker than that of water: this is the reason why oxygenated water, at common temperatures, is concentrated in vacuo by the intervention of an absorbing body, such as sulphuric acid. This also is the reason why the evaporation in this case becomes gradually slower, so that at the end it is extremely slow; still, however, it always takes place, for it finishes by the whole of the liquor disappearing; and this occurs without the production of any gas; which shows that the peroxide of hydrogen is vaporized without decomposition.

"I tried, but ineffectually, to solidify the peroxide of hydrogen. Exposed to a low temperature for three quarters of an hour, it remained liquid; when also water, which contains only 30 or 40 times its volume of oxygen, is subjected to a temperature of 12°, the part which remains fluid is much more oxygenated than that which freezes. It is even probable that if the latter contains any oxygen, that it is derived from a certain quantity of interposed water.

"I thought at first that I might employ this process to concentrate the oxygenated water, especially by taking care to break the ice and to press it strongly in linen: it did not succeed; the ice, even after compression, retained too much oxygen to be rejected.

"One of the properties of peroxide of hydrogen which I endeavoured more particularly to establish, is its density; this I found to be 1·452. It is, therefore, evident, that the peroxide is much more dense than water, and it is not necessary to take its specific gravity to be convinced of this; it is sufficient to pour it into water, for although it is very soluble, it flows through it like a syrup."

Action of Bodies on Peroxide of Hydrogen.

"There are some bodies which have no action upon peroxide of hydrogen; others render it more fixed; whilst some decompose it, and combine with a part of its oxygen; but it is particularly worthy of remark, that a considerable number decompose it at common temperatures, without uniting either to the water or to the oxygen gas which results; sometimes even this decomposition occurs with a sort of detonation, owing to the sudden disengagement of the gas. In this case, the temperature is so far from being reduced, as might be supposed on account of the oxygen passing to the gaseous state, that it is so much raised as to produce light. Sometimes also the body, during its decomposition of the peroxide, is itself decomposed; such is, for example, the oxide of silver, which immediately upon coming into contact with the peroxide, even largely diluted with water, disengages all the oxygen, and is itself reduced."

Action of Imponderable Bodies.

"Heat quickly decomposes the peroxide of hydrogen; but the decomposition takes place more slowly as it proceeds. The water, in proportion as it is liberated, undoubtedly combines with the undecomposed portion, and renders it more fixed. This may be learned by the following experiments:—

"Put some peroxide of hydrogen into a small glass tube, heat it gradually from 55° to 212°; by placing the tube in water, it will be seen that the decomposition will be quite sensible at 68°; it occurs with greater ebullition, if the peroxide is subjected immediately to 212°. The experiment would be dangerous in a vessel with a narrow neck, with eight grains of the peroxide; nevertheless, when thrown upon a red hot metal plate, it does not detonate.

"Let this experiment be repeated, after having so diluted the peroxide, that it shall contain only seven or eight times its volume of oxygen; the disengagement of the gas will not be perceptible even at 120°; but it becomes so, soon afterwards, and goes on increasing until it ceases; from this period, the liquor contains no gas, and consequently will not effervesce with oxide of manganese.

"All other circumstances being equal, peroxide of hydrogen suffers no more alteration by exposure to light than in darkness. In both cases, small bubbles are disengaged from time to time, and it finishes at the expiration of some months, even at common temperatures, being for the most part deoxidized. This deoxidizement, which probably depends upon many causes, appears to me to be principally produced by some particles of matter which the peroxide retains. To preserve it as much as possible, it must be surrounded with ice.

"When the peroxide is subjected to the action of the voltaic pile in the same way that water usually is, similar results are in both cases produced, excepting that with the peroxide, the disengagement of oxygen gas is much greater. I ought to observe, however, that I have not collected the gases, to examine them."

ACTION OF METALS AT COMMON TEMPERATURE.

"In general the metals tend to decompose the peroxide of hydrogen, and to restore it to the state of protoxide, or water. I know only four which do not sensibly possess this property; iron, tin, antimony, and tellurium. The most oxidizable are oxidized, and at the same time produce a disengagement of oxygen. The others, on the contrary, retain their metallic states, so that all the oxygen with which the water combines to become peroxide is liberated.

"In order to effect the decomposition readily, it is indispensably necessary that the metallic matter should be finely divided. Any metal which, in the state of fine powder, readily disengages the oxygen of the peroxide, effects it very slowly if the powder be coarse, and still more so if it be in a mass.

"The same phenomena occur even when the peroxide is diluted with water, excepting that they are less distinct, and continue longer. This will appear from the examination which I am going to state, with respect to the action of metals upon the diluted peroxide.

"The experiments were all performed in the same way. The liquid was first put, with a small pipe, into a glass tube closed at one end, after which, the metal was introduced. The quantity of peroxide employed in each experiment amounted only to a few drops; when diluted with water a larger quantity was employed. The action was considered as complete, when no more gas was evolved; and this was rendered certain by the addition of a small quantity of oxide of manganese. All the metals were tried in this manner, excepting uranium, titanium, cerium, barium, strontium, calcium, lithium, and the metals of the earths."

METALS DECOMPOSING PEROXIDE OF HYDROGEN AND DISENGAGING OXYGEN, WITHOUT CHANGE.

"*Silver*, finely divided, procured by the recent decomposition of nitrate of silver by copper, and pure peroxide of hydrogen. Sudden and violent action, the extrication of heat so great, that the tube became burning hot; the silver retained its metallic state, and all the oxygen was instantly disengaged.

"*Silver*, finely divided, and peroxide containing nine times its volume of oxygen. Sudden and brisk effervescence, no sensible heat: the silver was not oxidized; the action was soon over, and all the oxygen was disengaged. The tube is not heated unless the peroxide contains at least thirty times its volume of oxygen.

"*Silver*, precipitated from the solution of nitrate of silver by copper, but the parts of which were become less finely divided by drying. Action upon the peroxide much weaker than with the finely divided silver of the two preceding experiments.

"*Silver* in filings. Action much weaker than the last.

"*Silver* in mass. Action extremely weak compared to that with divided silver.

"*Platinum* in fine powder prepared from the ammoniaco-muriate, calcined with common salt and pure peroxide of hydrogen. Phenomena similar to those with silver; the action, perhaps, a little stronger. I do not conclude from this, that the platina itself acts more upon the peroxide than silver; for in order to ascertain this, the state of division of the metallic particles, which so much influences their action, must be equal.

"*Platinum* in fine powder, and peroxide containing nine times its volume of oxygen. Phenomena similar to those with silver.

"*Platinum* in filings and in mass. The same action upon the peroxide as with silver in filings and in mass.

"*Gold*, finely divided, procured from the decomposition of muriate of gold by sulphate of iron. The same action upon the pure and diluted peroxide as with silver and platina, provided the liquid be not sensibly acid.

"*Gold* in filings and in mass. The same action upon the peroxide as with silver in filings and in mass.

"*Osmium* in black powder and pure peroxide. Action more violent than with the preceding metals, which may depend upon the metal being more finely divided; in other respects, the phenomena were similar; the same effects, except as to intensity, with osmium and diluted peroxide, as with platina and silver.

Palladium in powder, prepared by calcining ammoniaco-muriate of palladium, and pure oxide. Ready and very lively action, but less so than that of platina, silver, gold, and osmium; great extrication of heat. All the oxygen was disengaged almost as soon as the action occurred, the metal did not appear to be oxidized. If the peroxide was sensibly acid, it acted much less readily.

"*Palladium* in powder, and peroxide containing only nine volumes of oxygen. The same phenomena as with silver, excepting that the disengagement of oxygen was rather less rapid.

"*Rhodium* in powder, prepared by calcining the ammoniaco-muriate of rhodium with pure and diluted peroxide. The action of this metal is nearly the same as that of palladium, excepting that the presence of a little acid did not retard it so much.

"*Lead* reduced to fine filings and pure peroxide. Action at first slow, but which gradually increases and finishes in a few minutes, becoming extremely strong, and exciting much heat. All the oxygen is disengaged, and I do not think that the lead is oxidized.

"*Lead* reduced to fine filings, and peroxide containing nine volumes of oxygen. Action at first weak, gradually becoming stronger, and then the bubbles of oxygen are rapidly liberated, and raise the metallic particles. Is there not a little oxide formed, which, it will be hereafter seen, readily decomposes oxygenated water? It is certain, at the expiration of an hour, no oxygen remains in the liquor.

"*Bismuth*, well powdered, and pure peroxide. The same phenomena as with lead.

"*Bismuth*, well powered, and liquor containing only nine volumes of oxygen. The action is extremely slow. Bubbles are only occasionally given out; but at the end of some hours the liquor was always deoxidized. The metal did not appear to be oxygenated.

"*Mercury* and pure peroxide. The same phenomena as with lead and bismuth, provided the solution be not acid; when it contains a little sulphuric acid, there is also formed a red substance, which is probably a subsulphate.

"*Mercury* and peroxide containing only nine volumes of oxygen. Very evident disengagement of gas, especially when the solution is rather alkaline than acid: the mercury is not oxidized: one drop of a very weak acid is sufficient to stop the disengagement.

"*Cobalt, nickel, cadmium, copper.* Very weak action."

Considering this to be a very valuable practical paper, and that it will be more acceptable to our readers to have it presented to them at full length, than in a mere abridgment, we feel obliged to defer the conclusion till our next number.

On Napthaline, or an apparently concrete essential Oil obtained by Distillation of Coal-Tar at a Red Heat. By J. KIDD, Professor of Chemistry, Oxford.

Transactions of the Royal Society.

This is not presented by Dr. Kidd as an absolutely new product; for it had been previously remarked on in the Annals of Philosophy and the Journal of Science, Literature, and the Arts. This process consists in passing the vapour of coal-tar through red hot iron tubes, with which was connected a vessel to receive any undecomposed vapour, or other products elicited by distillation.

At the end of each experiment, this condensing vessel was found to contain an aqueous fluid, having an ammoniacal odour; and a dark coloured liquid, resembling tar.

The latter was black in the mass, but reddish brown when extended; thinner than tar, so as to partly pass the paper filter and leave a tarry deposit.

Odour slightly aromatic and ammoniacal; specific gravity 1050; that of the original tar being 1109.

Entirely soluble in ether; partially, in alcohol; and milky on addition of water; not mixible with water, but tinging it brown, and giving it a sweet and aromatic flavour, as well as becoming alkaline; burning with, first, a clear, and ending in a smoky flame.

Distilling a pint of this dark coloured matter, slowly, for forty hours, there was obtained, half a pint of a liquid of two qualities, that had come over together uniformly. The upper like pale olive-oil; the latter, and rather larger, portion resembling water; and this relative quantity, greater, under rapid distillation.

After these, there passed a white flocculent substance. At the end of sixty hours, the heat was increased, which produced a dark thicker oil; congealing into the consistence of butter.

Lastly, there arose a yellow vapour, condensing in the neck of the retort, into a yellowish farine. When the retort cooled, the residuum was found to resemble pitch.

Properties of the aqueous product.—Taste alkaline, with ammoniacal, aromatic, odour. Specific gravity 1023. Blue on addition of prussiate of potash.

On evaporating 700 grs. under an exhausted receiver, with dry muriate of lime, the residuum was not more than half a grain, consisting of a brown oil, and soluble saline matter containing sulphuric and muriatic acid.

Properties of the oily fluid.—Taste and scent pungent, bithuminous, aromatic, and ammoniacal. Specific gravity 0·9204. Boiling at 210° F.; perfectly fluid at 32°.

Evaporated at atmospheric temperature, leaves about $\frac{1}{6}$ of a peculiar concrete substance, which is again dissolved by $\frac{2}{3}$ of the oily fluid.

Inflammable, and emitting much smoke.

Mingles with water on agitation, but again separating; and when boiled with it, is transparent; but on cooling, milky.

Unites with alcohol and ether at all temperatures. With alkaline solutions, slightly turbid and white. Absorbs ammoniacal gas without sensible change. But thickened by absorption of several times its volume of muriatic acid gas.

With solution of acetate of lead forms a white curdy mass, by the intervention of potash or ammonia; but with the metallic solution alone, soon separating unchanged.

Properties of the white concrete substance.—Taste, pungent and aromatic.

Scent, narcissus like, diffusive, and durable.

In powder, smooth and unctuous, of a silvery lustre. Specific gravity greater than that of water.

Camphor evaporated in atmosphere within eighteen hours, but this concrete required four days.

On exposure to heat, did not boil under 410° F., congealing partially, and suddenly, when down to 180°, and entirely solid at 170°, in crystalline and slightly flexible laminæ. Difficultly inflamed; but then burning rapidly, with copious and dense smoke.

Affects neither litmus nor turmeric.

Insoluble in cold, and sparingly soluble in hot, water; and separating milky; when the water be filtered, some minute crystals are formed. Readily soluble in alcohol, more so in ether, especially in both when warm.

Dissolved in four times its weight of boiling alcohol, becomes, when cool, a solid crystalline mass.

Soluble in oil, and oil of turpentine.

Not combining with solution of potash, ammonia, or with ammoniacal gas.

Soluble in acetic, and oxalic acids, giving a pink tinge; and in hot acetic, cools to a crystalline solid.

It blackens boiling sulphuric acid, and is not precipitated on adding water or ammonia.

Sparingly soluble in hot muriatic acid, with a pink tinge. In boiling nitric acid, and cooled, yields acicular crystals, grouped stelliform; which when dried, by pressure or blotting paper, easily melted by heat. In cooling the mass, gave traces of a yellow acicular crystallization; which readily inflamed, burning with a bright flame, emitting much smoke, and leaving a carbonaceous residuum.

Thrown into a red hot crucible, a white dense vapour arises; which when received into a bell-glass, condenses at the lower part, in a white powdery form, but at the upper, of a beautiful silvery lustre. Similar sublimed results, on boiling the concrete in water, in a mattrass with a long neck.

Just melted under a bell-glass, the vapour rises like flakes of snow.

Boiled cotton, dipped in this melted substance, fired, and then blown out, gives a vapour condensing again round the wick in thin transparent crystals.

The usual form of crystallization of this substance is that of a rhombic plate, the greater angle from 100° to 105°; or an hexagonal plate.

To illustrate the crystallization, dissolve 25 grains of the concrete in a fluid ounce of alcohol; cool slowly, place the vessel between the eye and the light, when rhombic crystals will be visible, refracting the light variously.

Dr. K. acknowledges himself at a loss to state the elementary constitution of this concrete mass, farther than that it has a very large proportion of carbon. He adds, as relevant to the matter, that he has twice observed a similar concrete substance, forming minute crystals, refracting the light prismatically, on subjecting animal matter to the destructive distillation.

Properties of the yellow Farina.—There was but a small portion of this to operate upon; therefore its qualities could not be fully ascertained; but it was found to be soluble in alcohol, forming a bright yellow solution, and from which it was precipitable by water, remaining permanently suspended as a yellowish powder.

When heated, it melts into a soft, tough, gummy consistence, of a deep reddish brown colour.

We shall conclude this paper with the following inferences deduced by Dr. Kidd:—

"Of the four several substances which result from the distillation of the black liquid described in the former part of this paper, it is probable that the water and the yellow farina are the only real products; and that the others are mere educts of that distillation; for with respect to the water, its proportion is variable according to the greater or less degree of rapidity with which the distillation is conducted; and if it were present as water, in the black liquid, there is reason to believe it would be found supernatant on its surface, after having remained still for some time. The essential liquid oil, and the white concrete substance, which pass over during the distillation, are probably contained, originally, in that thin portion of the black liquid, which may be filtered through unsized paper; for the odour of this filtered portion closely resembles that of the oil; and the oil by exposure to light frequently becomes of a darker and darker shade, so as at last to be nearly of a deep brown colour. With respect to the white concrete substance, this was not only found crystallized in that part of the original apparatus where the black liquid was condensed, but has been obtained from that liquid by simple evaporation of it at the common temperature of the atmosphere.

"The yellow farina is probably produced from the tar, which is contained in the proportion of about $\frac{1}{4}$ in the black liquid; for it does not make its appearance until towards the end of the distillation, when the more volatile substances have ceased to pass over, and the heat has been increased to the utmost.

"And if common coal-tar be exposed to a low red heat, it will be found that when the tar has been nearly evaporated, this yellow farina will begin to pass off."

On a new Method of supplying Gas for Family Use.

If the above can be effected at a moderately cheap rate, we think it may be esteemed as a convenience of no small moment. The expense of laying on gas-pipes from the main, is so chargeable, that we have been rather surprised in witnessing the adoption of gas-lights so generally, for persons are not very willing to sacrifice a sum, however small, for an eventual good. And we are rather inclined to think that, in abundant instances, parties have had gas laid on, not so much from inclination and preference, as from the necessity of following the fashion of their neighbours; just as we see the foolish expenditure of elegant brass work in the front of dashing shops. We are, however, sure of this, and we appeal to our readers in proof, that the generated gases are not now nearly so pure as they were when first exhibited; and we can daily perceive them becoming worse. This is usually the case with public works, which, when established, become too powerful for individual controul. What redress would a party obtain, who should state that his gas flame was yellow; and the roof of his shop blackened by the carbonic vapours? We can well remember, when the lights in Parliament Street and Pall Mall displayed a brilliancy of clear electric-like light; but how do they appear now? The flame is frequently as yellow as that of an indifferent oil lamp; and the lamp glasses are obscured by a filthy coating of carbonic vapour; so that the effulgence by which this species of illumination first attracted the public attention, is looked for in vain, now the Companies have involved individuals in expense for laying on the pipes, that each is unwilling to sacrifice by relinquishing what he no longer approves. We would turn the notice of the reader to those streets lighted by the new reflecting lamps; which burn the volatile oil obtained from the coal tar. They are really beautiful. The light is pure, clear, and steady; forming a strong contrast with the yellow, flickering flame of the gas. Compare them, as they are exhibited in Howland Street, with the gas lamps in Tottenham Court Road, and the former will show a manifest superiority, in the fine silvery glow of combustion. Coal tar oil is burnt in many parts of the town; but the lamps are constructed in so despicable a manner; and the glasses are suffered by the parish protectors to be so shamefully neglected; that it were better to be without such twinkling lights than to have vision distracted by their obtrusion. If the person who lights Howland Street can afford to extend his contract, at an expense little exceeding that of gas, and he would engage to keep his lamps in similar condition to those in that street, we do not hesitate in saying that, we should gladly see them substituted instead of the coal gas lamps every where. If this be not practicable, we should wish that the oil gas were used instead of coal gas. It is far purer, and burns more brilliant. But in any case, we would urge the public to make reiterated complaints, when not duly served with that pure article which the Companies are bound to afford; and if redress cannot be had, as we apprehend, we would strenuously urge the establishment of a fund, to carry proper grievances into a Court of Law. One chastisement from a Jury would make the Companies respect their supporters. We do not know a more galling oppression than that of legalized companies; whose pecuniary means of defence set them above the controul of the parties from whom they derive their profits. And indignation is still more keen, if possible, against the persons who, having large sums of parish money in their hands, shall so visibly, and shamefully, connive at the jobbing defaults of contractors. We have gone at large into the abuses of illumination, because we think it high time that some check were put to them.

Mr. Caslon, the proprietor of the North London coal gas works, carried on, we believe, in Cromer Street, Gray's Inn Lane, has devised a means of accommodating the public with gas for domestic use, where there are not any gas-pipes laid down, or where parties may prefer to have it delivered in portions, as they may want. Mr. Caslon's proposal is to condense 12 or 15 atmospheres of oil gas, into cylindrical iron, or copper vessels, by means of powerful condensing instruments, at the gas works. These vessels, or reservoirs, will be conveyed to private houses, manufactories, &c. in such quantities as may be required: and by proper stopcocks to communicate with the line of tube within the apartments; so that one or more rooms may be illuminated at pleasure. If the gas were to issue from the reservoir direct into the tube, it would have too great an impetus; therefore Mr. C. has contrived an intermediate means, whereby he modifies the pressure up the tube, after the gas issues from the reservoir; and it flows from the last aperture, for combustion, with a governable velocity. To use the gas, a stopcock is turned; and re-turned for extinction.

Oil gas is very properly preferred; as not only being purer, and giving a superior light to coal gas; but also because from similar volumes, the former will yield three or four times as much illuminating effect as the latter.

The reservoir has an appendage, whereby the quantity of its gaseous contents can be measured; and of course the quantity that may be consumed; and by which the charge is regulated. The expense will be one penny per gallon of gas; which, if consumed within the hour, may be equal in illuminating effect to about twelve tallow candles.

We would recommend to Mr. Caslon that he should accompany his reservoir with printed directions; for if servants can do wrong, we all know that they will. It may not perhaps be superfluous to hint, that there would be some danger in placing the highly charged reservoir near a fire; for its contents might expand, and produce dreadful consequences, by bursting like a bomb-shell.

We do not yet despair of human ingenuity devising a secure means of generating these gases by a stove; that shall answer the double purpose of warming our apartments and supplying us with illuminating material;—for never was the intellect of man so active in combining, or modifying, the elements of nature, to purposes of practical value, as in the present age. Indeed, we might almost fancy ourselves on the eve of that perfection, of which we have been declared capable by certain metaphysicians.

Account of Experiments to determine the Acceleration of the Pendulum, in different Latitudes. By Capt. EDWARD SABINE, of the Royal Artillery, F. R. S. F. L. S., &c.

Captain Sabine's devotion to science cannot be better shown than by the voluntary privations he has submitted to for its promotion; and with an effect also that will attach to his character no moderate portion of celebrity. In 1818 he accompanied Captain Ross; and, in 1819 and 1820, Captain Parry; in their respective arctic expeditions. The clocks and pendulums, by which he experimented, belonged to the Royal Society, and had been previously prepared by Captain Kater.

In the first voyage, the number of variations was ascertained at two stations only, viz. Gardie-house, on the Island of Brassa; and on Waygate, or Hare Island, on the West Coast of Greenland;—the latitude of the first, 60° 9′ 42″ N., and that of the second, 70° 26′ 17″ N. The vibrations in a mean solar day, at London, being 86497·4—at Brassa, 86530·507—at Hare Island, 86562·6386; or an acceleration of 33·107 between Brassa and London; and 32·1316 between Brassa and Hare Island; or 65.2386 between London and Hare Island.

In the second voyage, by experiment on Melville Island, in the Polar Sea, the latitude 74° 47′ 12″ 4‴ N., the mean diurnal acceleration was found to be 74·734 vibrations.

Captain Sabine gives a very interesting description of the preparatory measures taken at this station, for the commencement of his scientific operations. The difficulty of procuring a sound basis of soil for the clocks, &c. to rest on; and the intensity of cold, surpassing expectation; rendered it impossible to proceed in the experiments, before the return of warmer weather. All that could be done was, to erect an observatory house, of such materials as were at command; namely, store plank, with the seams lined with moss, and a tarpaulin cover—the interior being lined with russia matting. The latter, unfortunately, caught fire; and the whole structure, with all the instruments, escaped ruin only by the active exertions of the officers and crews of the ships. One poor artillery man, who accompanied Captain Sabine, by an incautious exposure of his hands to the air, was so frost bitten, as to render necessary the amputation of three fingers of the left hand, and two of the right.

It was not until the end of April that the Sun had sufficient power to raise the thermometer a few degrees above zero; and when the boxes, containing those thermometers which accompanied the clocks, were opened, the mercury was observed to be retired into the bulbs, and frozen; although the atmospheric temperature had not for several weeks, been so low as the freezing point. The thermometer boxes were inclosed, each, with the pendulum to which it belonged, in a stout case of oak; and these again were contained in chests, holding each one clock, with its complete apparatus. During the winter, the cold had penetrated to the very interior of these cases, so as to cool down the thermometer to, or below, the freezing point of mercury; but the increasing temperature of returning spring had not yet been intense enough to impart caloric necessary for the liquefaction of the metal. "It may be mentioned, in proof of the slowness with which such a mass of solid brass, as constituted the bob of the pendulums, conforms to the temperature of the surrounding atmosphere, compared with the mercury in the thermometer tube, that several hours had elapsed, after the pendulums were taken out of their cases, (when it is presumed they also may have been at 40°) before they ceased to cause a deposit of moisture from the air of the room, which was about the same number of degrees above zero: the mercury in the thermometers, on the other hand, took up the temperature of the room within half an hour after their exposure. The clocks were put in motion on the 30th of April, and the account taken up on the 4th of May, the room having been kept at about the temperature of 45° for the preceding three days and nights."

About the end of May, the weather became so warm as to have permitted Captain S.'s commencement of operations; but he had numerous difficulties to encounter: for not only the strong winds had drifted the snow, so as to bury the observatory, and render it necessary to dig down, in order to come at the room where the clocks were deposited; the temperature being then 6°; but in a fortnight more, the temperature rose to 25°, and the thaw became so troublesome as to make a total abandonment of the house necessary, before any satisfactory observations had been effected.

In the middle of June, the clocks were set in order, in a tent, where the fire of a stove might be occasionally had; and the result of the experimental series, then instituted, goes to show that, the length of the seconds pendulum being at London (as ascertained by Captain Kater) = 39·13929 inches—at Brassa, is 39·16929—at Hare Island, 39.1084—and at Melville Island, 39·207.

Lastly, Captain Sabine shows the diminution of gravity from the pole to the equator, and the ellipticity of the earth, as deduced from his observations; and by the method described by Captain Kater in the Philosophical Transactions for 1819, to be thus: Between London and Brassa diminution of gravity is ·005506—ellipticity $\frac{1}{314\cdot3}$; London and Hare Island ·0055082 and $\frac{1}{314\cdot2}$; Brassa and Hare Island ·0055139 and $\frac{1}{313\cdot6}$; London and Melville Island ·0055258 and $\frac{1}{312\cdot6}$.

Instead of paying that tribute which is due from us, in common with all parties engaged in science, to the merit of Captain Sabine, by any formal expressions of our own, we will transcribe the more important approbation of Sir H. Davy, on his delivery of the Copleyan medal to that gentleman, through the hands of his brother; Captain S. being now on an expedition to the torrid zone, and to which the President alludes, thus: " Having braved the long night, and almost perpetual winter, of the Polar Regions, he is gone, with the laudable object, to expose himself to the burning sun, and constant summer of the equator." And concludes with this injunction to the brother: "Assure him how strongly we feel his disinterestedness, and genuine love of science; and that our ardent wishes are expressed for his safe return; and for the successful accomplishment of all the objects of his voyage; which will ensure to him additional claims upon the gratitude of all lovers of science."

On the Formation of the Prussiate of Potash. By M. DIVE.
Journal of Science, from Journ. de Pharm.

This gentleman formed the prussiate, by calcining a mixture of sixty-four grammes of the dry powder of crude tartar, with eight grammes of pulverized sal ammoniac, in a covered crucible. He explains the rationale of the process by considering that the nascent carbon of the tartar being presented to the nascent ammonia, disengaged from the muriate by the potash, acts so as to form cyanogen: and that this action is favoured by the temperature, which weakens the combination of the hydrogen and azote in the ammonia. The latter element being, in every point of the mass, in immediate contact with the particles of carbon, easily unites with it in the requisite proportions for forming cyanogen; this latter being immediately fixed by the potash.

He also states that, a current of carbonic acid partially decomposes the neutral tartrate of potash; and he ascribes to this cause the formation of the bitartrate in the juice of the grape, during its fermentation. Accordingly, on mixing neutral tartrate with fermentable materials, he found cream of tartar in the fermented liquor.

Should the above process for the formation of prussiate of potash be found correct and effectual, it will supersede the present disgusting mode of forming it, by the combustion of animal matter with potash: for, as is well known by manipulists, the vapours arising from the blood or horn, generally used, are of a most intolerable scent.

Respecting M. Dive's opinion as to the decomposition of the tartrate of potash by the generated carbonic acid in fermentation, thereby converting the former into supertartrate, by the abstraction of a portion of its alkali; we would observe that, the carbonate of potash necessarily resulting, has not been hitherto found in the fermented mass, in so far as we know; nor does he intimate that he has detected it himself. In the acidulous wines, we should think that the carbonate cannot so exist, for it would neutralize the nascent acid. Although fermentation may be generated in fermentable matter, by the addition of a mixture of supertartrate of potash, and carbonate of potash, yet there is a distinction to be observed between the excitement of fermentation by means of these compounds, ready formed, and the formation of them, as the result of the fermentative process itself.

On the Uniformity of Terrestrial Magnetism, at any given Place on the Earth's Surface. By Professor HANSTEEN.

Annales de Chimie.

M. Hansteen adopted the law of magnetic attractions, determined by M. Coulomb, in order to discover whether local magnetic force be uniform or variable; that is, he took the fundamental admeasurement as inversely to the square of the distance. He suspended a magnetized rod, $2\frac{1}{4}$ inches in length, and $\frac{3}{40}$ of an inch in diameter, by a thread of a silk bocoon, depending from the top of a brass tube, fixed in the centre of the lid of a brass box. On the other side of this vertical tube, the lid of the box was formed of glass, so that the graduated arcs at the bottom might be visible. This is considered superior to suspension on a point, as not likely to be changed by friction; and M. Arago has adopted it at the Royal Parisian Observatory. The Professor H. puts the needle in motion by presenting a piece of iron to one of its poles, for a moment. He then counts, by a chronometer, the period of every ten vibrations, up to 360; and then takes the mean thus—namely, the difference between the end of the 1st, and the end of the 300th: the end of the 2d, and that of the 310th, and so on to that of the 60th and 360th. The longest period of 300 vibrations was 813′ 6″; which he denominates his minimum, or zero, of force. But the force of the magnetic power is inversely proportioned to the squares of the times of similar vibrations of the same magnetic needle. We draw the following results from the table exhibited:

1st. A daily variation in magnetic power; the minimum from 10 to 11, A. M., the maximum from 4 to 5, P. M.

2d. The yearly variation from the mean of each month, is greatest in winter.

3d. The greatest monthly variations are in December and June.

4th. The minimum variations occur in the two months of spring and autumn when the sun is at the mean distance from the earth.

5th. The greatest daily variation is in summer; the least in winter.

6th. The maximum of annual variation is 0·0359.

M. Hansteen imagined there was a variation of dip also, as indicated by one of Dollond's dipping needles of 15' excess in winter; and from 4 to 5 in the forenoon; but from the observations of others, this is perhaps not correct.

He observed a singular difference in result of horizontal variation, as obtained in an observatory, and its contiguous garden. In the former, which was a round tower, he found that for 300 vibrations 836' 57" were requisite—in the garden only 779". The tower is 126 feet high, with thick walls, with a staircase winding round its axis, as a hollow cylinder. Having repeated his observations below, and found the mean to be 787", he then proceeded to the top of the tower, and noted the duration downwards, of 300 oscillations, as follow:

At the top was denoted 842·37—first platform, 836·57—third, 837·3—four and a half, 834·43—six and a half, 804·07—bottom, 813·0.

From continued observations he deduced, that all perpendicular bodies, of whatever matter, become magnetical: the upper extremity having a south pole, and the lower end a north pole; and that at the under end the needle oscillated quicker on the north side than on the south: but at the upper end, quicker on the south side, and slowest on the north.

M. Hansteen made observations from noon to noon, during an aurora borealis, and found it to rather enfeeble the magnet.

We ought to remark that M. Hansteen's experiments on magnetic variation are reported as only including the year from December, 1819, to October, 1820; therefore we must not implicitly rely on the monthly mean, and still less on the annual; but wait for more lengthened observations.

ON THE VARIATIONS OBSERVED AT PARIS.

Since April, 1819, M. Arago has observed the variation of the needle to be retrograde—the total between 1818 and 1820, being, by a comparative effect, in the mornings, 3′ 22″—noon, 4′ 22″—evenings, 4′ 0″.

At the Observatory of the Board of Longitude of Paris, there is a needle exclusively used to determine horizontal deviation, which, having been deranged in 1819, was re-mounted last February; since which it has retrograded easterly. The mean westerly deviation of February, 1821, is less than that of 1820, by the amount of 2′ 15″.

Annales de Chimie.

CAPT. KOTZEBUE'S OBSERVATIONS OF MAGNETIC DIP.

The only observations, relating to the dip of the needle, that Captain K. records, are as follow—In longitude 122° 12′ 30″ W., latitude 37° 48′ 33″, the dip was found to be 62° 46′. In longitude 157° 52′, latitude 21° 7′ 57″, was 43° 39′—longitude 190° 6′ 50″, latitude 9° 32′ 36″, was 17° 55′,—longitude 166° 31′ 53″ W., latitude 53° 52′ 25″ was 69° 45′.

We cannot help reproaching Captain Kotzebue for the little attention he appears to have paid to this department of his professional duty.

On the Flower Buds of Trees passing through Wood, as noticed by Cicero and Pliny. By Mrs. AGNES IBBETSON.

To the honour of the tender sex, we have here to present some philosophical observations of a lady, not only in corroboration of the testimony given by the illustrious characters, Cicero and Pliny, but also in direct opposition to some modern authorities, to whom we look up with habitual respect. The lady commences thus: " Some late dissections of wood have enabled me to notice the curious manner in which the flower-buds pass, *layer* by *layer*, through the wood, even to the root; and have shown me that each mark is peculiar to the sort of wood to which it belongs;" for instance, " in the oak, the buds being sessile, or without stalk, and in large numbers together, they generally appear grouped in a circle, and it is hardly possible to pass through the wood, and then take fibre from fibre, without encountering innumerable buds, thus passing up from the root perpendicularly; or crossing the stem at right angles to its former direction. As it is in old wood, torn down, not cut, the gastric juice (which always precedes the bud) is rarely seen, though its effects are most visible, and remain permanently so; for if a set of buds have to cross a knot, many holes are perceived in the knot, through which they have passed, and in which the gastric juice has formed them a passage; but which do not close again, as the wood usually does, because of the hardness of the parts around the knot. In the beech, where the buds follow each other in a sort of laxus racemi, it presents a very different picture. Here the buds being small, they will run up between the layers of the wood; and are not so conspicuous as in the oak; though when the wood is *torn up, not cut*, the whole number show with peculiar grace, as forming a sort of stripe of apparent flowers, which the figure of the bud produces; thus passing up perpendicularly. In the yew, they are an assemblage which show buds of all ages; many peeping just through the wood; others more advanced towards the bark; but all, generally, surrounding an old one, an innumerable assemblage that are hastening on to the bark. What should cause some buds to proceed all the way up the wood, perpendicularly, and others to cross at once to the bark, I cannot conceive, and have never been able to guess; but so it is. The olive shows like one large peaked bud, appearing at some little distance from each other; but I suspect that it is a collection, since it carries that divided appearance when it is followed into the interior. It is certain that woodlines diverge in a manner that proves that innumerable buds are hourly passing, for the yearly lines never move out of the circle, but to effect this purpose: a most striking circumstance."

Whether the bud be formed in the alburnum, or arise from the root, and pass through the wood, is, as we think, of but little importance, as determining the matter of original sustenance; for we cannot but believe that the pabulum of the bud must be, in either case, derived from the radical juices. It is, however, another question whether the bud be, as it were, of a parasitic quality; growing out of the body of the parent tree, or as rising through the ligneous matter from the root, a distinct portion of the tree; or a secondary tree in itself. There is one rather staggering occurrence, that we do not well know how to reconcile; namely, that if every bud originate from the root, how can such an immense assemblage be at once carried up the trunk, and appear eventually bursting forth at every point of every branch? Were the process of vegetable budding one of long succession, we could the better comprehend them individually arising through their course to the extremities; but as their evolution is almost simultaneous, we cannot but pause, to satisfy our reason a little, before we assent to this lady's presumed demonstrations. It would give us pleasure to see the specimens that she assures us have astonished and convinced many botanists; and we should gladly be convinced too, for we only doubt, because our senses have not yet informed us to the extent that Mrs. Ibbetson's collection might possibly afford the means of gratifying. This lady assures us that, " she can show the bud evidently passing through the woody fibre; proving that it is not formed in the alburnum, but even passing through old knots in its upward progress. She, however, acknowledges, that she finds some of them passing transversely, towards the outer bark, without any traceable vestige of the upward progress: whence do these originate, we would ask; or are there two descriptions of flower buds; the one cortical, and the other radical?

Mrs. Ibbetson endeavours to prove, on the authority of Cicero and Pliny, that some of the Romans knew the proper period to cut the timber so as to have the section of the flower-buds on the plane of the polished wood; showing peculiarly beautiful configurations; and for which they paid enormous prices. By taking sections of timber, a short time previous to the bursting forth of the flower-buds, we should, says Mrs. I. have similar configurations displayed; but the budding period, or the time of the ascent of the buds through the trunk of the tree being so limited, we are very likely to permit their transmission unnoticed: therefore, to ensure the favourable result, we must know, and act in, the moment of passing upward from the root. Mrs. I. quotes Grew, as authority to prove her correctness; for he says that he has seen the bud pass up through the middle of the plant in the interior, full six months before it shows itself in the exterior of the plant; " consequently," says she, " he must therefore have seen it in the root; for the new shoot, at the top of which they afterwards appear, could not at that time be formed: how, then, should the bud be protruded there? 'Tis plain, therefore, it appears, even at the exterior, at the first, in the lower part of the plant."

The trees which have the property, more decidedly, of exhibiting these configurations are the yew, the citron, and the maple; both the Italian and the French. Pliny's description is, " Acer, operum elegantia et subtilitate citro secundum, Gallicum in transpadana Italia transque Alpes nascens. Alterum genus, crispo macularum discursu, qui cum excellentior fuit, à similitudine caudæ pavonum nomen accepit."

She tells us that she has some of this curled wood, so exactly described by Pliny, in many foreign woods, as well as the maples. The molluscum was most prized by the Romans; of which Mrs. I. has, by her, some beautiful specimens of Indian woods. The bruscum is more intricately crisped and curled than the molluscum; and Cicero remarks, that had we trees to make, or saw, into broader planks, they would be preferred to citron. Of the ash this lady has specimens, with perfect polish, with configurations like a crab or spider; also of beech, in regular stripes of green, brown, or pale yellow; arising, as she supposes, from ferreous or cupreous matter at the root.

Mrs. I. says she never should have discovered the proper period, but from so often cutting the buds on the outward bark or rind to find out the season at which the nucleus of the bud entered under the scales of the bark. When the nucleus were not found, but the scales appeared on the bark, she was sure that the buds were rising from the root, and that the proper period for cutting the wood had arrived. In the lime tree she found a beautifully arranged figure, bearing a distant resemblance to the peacock's tail. In some Indian woods, the bud is partially concealed by the flourishes round it.

After enumerating a few more instances to justify her doctrinal conjectures, Mrs. I. concludes; and we cannot avoid complimenting her on her devotion to philosophical pursuits; as well as on her spirit in contending against our Goliahs in science. But this is not the first occasion of the fair lady's presenting herself before the learned public; and we trust it will not be the last.

On a Substitute for Flax and Hemp. By GEO. and WM. SHOOBRIDGE.

This is taken from the specification of Messrs. Shoobridge's patent, as given in the first number of the Technical Repository. The material recommended is the hop-bind or stalk, which contains a fibrous substance between the pith and the bark. First, they are cut into convenient lengths; as of a few feet, immediately after the hops are gathered, and before the binds become dry. Next, they are immersed in boiling water, until the fibres become easily separable. Or, they are immersed in soft cold water, until the fibrous matter can be stripped from the pith: but this immersion is tedious. After steeping the binds, the fibrous substance, along with the bark, is stripped off from the pith, by a simple mechanical process, which need not be detailed; but which may be understood in principle, by supposing the power of the finger and thumb, of one hand, capable of pinching hard enough on the bind, while it is drawn through by the other hand; the fibrous part, and the outer bark, of the bind, would then be a confused mass stripped off, and lying before the thumb and finger. This mass is next unravelled; washed, to separate the cortical fibres; laid in longitudinal order, and dried in the air, or by stoves, as quickly as possible. The fibrous matter, when dry, is beaten with mallets, and hackled.

This process it appears, then, scarcely differs from the old, and objectionable one, adopted with the flax and hemp plants. But it accords with the principle governing the instructions laid down by the Society of Arts, in their offer of premium in the year 1760, for making cloth from hop-stalks or binds. No proper claim was made for this premium; for although the practice had been common in Sweden, it had not been known, or not adopted, here. However, a Mr. Cooksey, in 1761, had presented some specimen resulting from his experiments on the subject; but, as he confesses, in a subsequent letter, he could not justly lay claim to the reward. In 1791, a Mr. Lockett, of Donnington, Berks, obtained the Society's premium of twenty pounds. He states his process to be this: having cut the binds into about four feet lengths, he boiled them in a copper, with some ley, that had previously boiled linen for bleaching. The bind separated easily. He next worked the fibres as flax; but found them so united by some cementing matter, that they could not be minutely separated. Some was hackled while wet, but still it would not do. Carding succeeded better, and gave it the appearance of cotton; but it was deeply coloured, as was the ley water in which it had been boiled.

We must remark on the foregoing account of Messrs. Shoobridge's, and Mr. Lockett's, means to render the fibrous matter of the hop-bind useful, as a substitute for flax and hemp, that although they have deserved the thanks of the public for pursuing so praiseworthy an object; yet we cannot applaud the means adopted by process to effect it. Indeed, we think that the Society has rather led operators astray, by the very directions they have given as a guide. To immerse a substance so hard as the hop bind, in water, with a view of breaking down its texture by incipient putrefaction, is by no means an elegant mode of extricating the fibrous matter; and certainly must take a long time to fully accomplish. It seems that Mr. Lockett approached very nearly to the attainment of his wish; much nearer indeed than either the Society or himself appear to have understood. Had he used the pure ley, instead of the bleaching and partly spent refuse; then washed the fibre clean in alkaline water, after having stripped off the bark; and again subjected the fibre to a boiling, in renewed ley; we suspect that the cementing matter would have been dissolved, the fibre divested of its dyed tinge, and that it would have worked well under the hackle.

We trust that we shall not be considered presumptuous if we lay before the reader our idea of the most rational method of proceeding, to obtain the fibrous part separate from the ligneous and cortical, of those plants which afford the material sought. We have ever been of opinion that the process, whereby this result should be effected, ought to partake of a joint chemical, and mechanical, character. We would propose that the raw material should be gently bruised by grooved rollers; then be washed, and afterwards be boiled in weak caustic ley, to extract the colouring and cementing matter; then again washed in soft water, or a very weak alkaline solution; then dried, and subjected to the gentle action of the roller; after which, it should be delivered to the hackler to be combed clear for use.

This is the process we would recommend when the material be used green; but when used dry, we cannot but think that Mr. Lee's mode of operating deserves a preference over all others; and we have seen specimens produced by his machinery, which differed, in appearance, but little from the silken cocoon.

As to the immersion of the vegetable in water, until the putrefactive fermentation have broken down its external texture, there are many serious objections. First, as to time; secondly, as to the deleterious quality of the extricated gases; thirdly, as to the uncertainty when the cortical matter be fully decomposed, and the fibrous not injured; and lastly, as to the tinged or dyed state, in which the fibre is left, rendering a subsequent bleaching process necessary.

On Matting made from the Typha latifolia, or greater Cat's Tail. By WM. SALISBURY.

Transactions of the Society of Arts.

As bearing some distant analogy with the foregoing article, we present this to our readers. We will not assert that this object is of equal importance; because the material with which we cover and protect our persons, must necessarily rank before that upon which we trample; but still we hold ourselves greatly indebted to any enterprizing individual who converts raw refuse into useful manufacture. The efforts made by Mr. Salisbury, in the very teeth of many discouraging circumstances; and his triumphant success; stamp an additional value on the perseverance that surmounts such formidable obstacles. We ever have, and ever shall, hold an individual in higher esteem, who confers on society but a partial practical benefit, than him, who shall give us nothing but essences and doctrines. Whatever does not contribute to the solid comfort and happiness of mankind, although deemed very pretty or very fine, deserves the contempt of every rational being.

Mr. Salisbury has long laboured to bring into use many materials of fabric, &c. that have either not been known to be applicable to human purposes, or have been unjustly measured below their value. The greater cat's-tail has not had justice done to it; for it really is capable of supplying some desiderata that are seriously felt, though it is not totally neglected. The woolly down, surrounding the seed, is used in Prussia, mixed with feathers, for stuffing bolsters. Blotting paper is also made of the same down, mixed with woollen rags. We have, occasionally, used it for rush bottomed chairs, and for caulking the joints of coopers' casks.

The cat's-tail may be made an article for industrious operation by the country poor: they may convert it into coverlids, carpets, and many other tissues of a serviceable nature; for as it grows on swampy grounds, and is not held in any worth, it may be largely and cheaply obtained. But it is not for the domestic use of lower life only, that it may be sought; for there would be a wide market opened in the supply of all classes. We think that in this double capacity of contributing to their own personal comfort, in multiplied ways, and as a means of working up a profit, especially during the inclemency of winter, when human labour is in but little demand in the country, that it may be a valuable resource for the industrious poor.

The article which has been long in use for chair-bottoming, is the scirpus lacustris, or common bull-rush, growing in deep, slow, streams; and particularly abounding in the vicinity of Newport Pagnel, Bucks. The demand, however, has far exceeded the possible supply of this, and other districts; so that we have been obliged to have recourse to the Dutch market, at a very considerable annual sacrifice of national capital. And, in time of war, the price has necessarily been exorbitant.

Previous to the winter of 1818, Mr. S. was actuated by the praiseworthy motive of giving profitable employment to the industrious poor, and presented the typha as a substitute for the scirpus. The overseers of the parish of St. George, Hanover-square, yielded the labour of some of their paupers, to collect $2\frac{1}{2}$ tons of it, from the marshes of Little Chelsea and Clapham; part of which they afterwards manufactured into mats, baskets, hassocks, and chair bottoms. Specimens of this manufacture were presented to the Society of Arts, in December, 1817; and it appeared, that, with equal skill in the process, the typha might give an article as good as the scirpus. The test of experience was resorted to—a piece of the best Dutch matting, at 2s. 6d. per yard, was laid by the side of another, made of the typha, in the premises of the Society; and in order to equalize the exposure, they from time to time had their relative positions changed. They were laid down in December, 1817, and taken up in March, 1821, for examination by the Committee. They were found to be, each, about equally half worn out; the typha matting being in as good a condition as the Dutch.

As to the relative expense of the two kinds, a very accurate judgment cannot well be formed; because Mr. Salisbury's tissue was worked by the parish poor, who had nothing else to do. He paid two guineas for as much of the typha as he might think proper to cut, from about 10 acres of marsh. From 1000 to 1500 yards of the matting have been sold within the last three years, at from nine-pence to fifteen-pence per yard.

The scirpus, or bull-rush, does not grow abundantly, being confined to particular districts; and, in the gross, too limited for general demand. But the typha, or cat's-tail, may be collected from almost every swamp; and is therefore so universally attainable, as to come within the easy gathering or purchase of the industrious poor, every where residing on the low lands throughout the kingdom. If the Society of Arts were to address the parochial Clergy generally; and point out the value of the typha, now treated as mere refuse; and give some concise directions for the process in use; they might be more effectually instrumental in diffusing such acceptable knowledge to the industrious and distressed peasantry.

Experiments on Saline Manures. By R. G.

The Farmer's Journal, February 11th.

That saline matter has been found to promote vegetation abundantly, on some soils, we cannot doubt; without we impute direct falsehood, where there not only were not any special interest to promote; but also where the high characters of the experimentalists must stand above all suspicion. In the trials to be mentioned, it will, however, be seen that saline manure is of limited efficacy.

The writer did not expect any practical good to result from the use of nitrate of potash as a manure, yet he determined to try its effects as such, and at the same time to try other similar substances. Upon beds, each a yard square, he, last spring, sowed a row each of Talavera wheat, barley, and oats; some of the beds were spread over with the nitre, in fine powder, in different quantities; the smallest quantity 84 pounds, and the largest 336 lbs. an acre. He says that other beds were spread over with nitrate of potash, potash, and nitrate of lime, in similar proportions to the nitre. But we do not understand him here; for nitre and nitrate of potash are similar. Upon other beds he had salt (as sold at the salt works for manure) spread at the rate of from 5 cwt. to 27 cwt. an acre. The salt was put on the beds six weeks before they were sown; the other salts were put on the beds when the grain was up, in distinct rows. Soon as a growth of weeds had taken place, he had the intervals between the grain hoed, and sown with clover-seed. One bed was sown with clover, in the same way as the rest; but without any dressing whatever.

He was convinced that no benefit whatever was derived from any of the applications; for, at no period of the growth of the crops, did any of them discover superior luxuriance to the bed sown without any manure; and he was equally satisfied, that salt compost, and all the rest of the salts experimented upon, are useless upon his land. He did not come to this conclusion from the above experiments only; for he had used it in considerable quantities, by having it spread upon his land, at the rate of from six to 20 hundred weight per acre. If intended for wheat, it was put on a month before sowing the land; if for turnips, six weeks before sowing. He has also had salt compost put to stable manure, a month before putting it into turnip, and potato drills; but from none of these methods of using the salt, has he experienced good or harm, except in the instances of its being mixed with the manure; the turnips manured with which made a very poor figure for a considerable time, and had not the season turned out unusually wet, and kept mild to so late a period, he thinks the crop would have been miserably bad. But owing to these favourable circumstances, it ultimately became nearly as good as the rest of the field. The potatoes manured with the salt and manure, were only about two thirds the quantity, and much smaller in size than those produced in other drills, where stable manure only was used.

Wheat so dressed will, in a short time, become of a darker green, than other parts of the field; but this colour gradually disappears, and no increased growth arises from the nitre. He does not think it arises from increased vigour, but the contrary: his reason for thinking so is, having observed that the blades of wheat growing from grain that has been steeped in lime water, or a solution of sulphate of copper, being in the early stages of its growth of a darker green colour than from wheat sown without any such preparation; and says he, "it is well known that the vegetative powers of grain are weaker in proportion to the time it remains in such steeps as the above."

There is one great defect in this communication, viz. the writer does not describe the quality of the soils to which he applied these different saline dressings. Unfortunately, too, he is so little of a chemist as to be ignorant of the components of the respective neutral salts used: thus he implies a distinction between nitre and nitrate of potash. We cannot but think that it is vain to expect great vegetative exciting power in mere salt: the quality of the salt, and its chemical action on the soil, must ever govern the resulting effect. It is also of importance that the saline matter be applied either in a state of solution; or that it be soon dissolved by falling rains; or, in a dry season, it may never come into activity at all. From the comparative observations that, in our limited way, we recollect having made, its application to pasture land has been the most beneficial. Nevertheless, the experiments instituted by this writer have their value, crude as they are; for we may deduce the practical knowledge of wheat, barley, and turnips, not being more productive when these dressings are used; as well as that potatoes may be injured by them. Qu. Were not the quantities, as 27 cwt. of salt to the acre, rather large? We cannot pass over a remark at the conclusion of the paper; that is, he says, "the vegetative powers of grain are weaker in proportion to the time it remains in such steeps." We have repeatedly, in our previous numbers, urged the presumed dangers to be apprehended from immersing seed grain in cupreous solutions too hot, or for too long a duration: and we cannot but urge the matter again: it is unphilosophical; and can only be excusable where the party practising it be totally ignorant of all chemical effect: therefore, we have been the more surprised at the recommendation coming from some gentlemen whose general knowledge of science should have led to better results.

On the Baltic Air in Asthma.

It having been reported to M. Vogel of Munich, when visiting the Baltic shore, that asthmatic invalids found relief when at sea, he determined on an analysis of the atmosphere impending over the land, as comparative with that over the sea. By admitting portions of them respectively into an exhausted globe, filled with a solution of barytes, it was found that sea air, taken a league from the shore, did not produce any change in the solution; but the land air gave an immediate turbidity. Solution of nitrate of silver, in contact with sea air, formed some chloride.

M. V. then infers that the Baltic air, at a league from the shore, contains less carbonic acid than that over the land: and also that the former contains muriates in greater or lesser proportions.

On the above, we may observe that the data are too sparing for us to found any curative doctrine. Besides, we know that asthma is produced by a great variety of causes, some of which cannot be influenced by the quality of the inspired air: and therefore, but a very limited proportion of asthmatic invalids could reasonably expect advantage from a marine atmosphere. In some cases, indeed, such might be positively injurious. Many persons labouring under this distressing disease, can breathe best in a crowded atmosphere or populous city. Others require a purer air. Some prefer it moist, if warm; others, dry and cold. In short, in so far as regards the air to be respired, we have not any criterion to indicate remedial effect. What may be the local peculiarities of soil or manufacture, on the spot where M. Vogel made his inquiry, we are not informed; and therefore are left at a loss to judge from what would have constituted our surest means of decision.

On the Organic Remains found near Brentford. By Mr. KIRBY TRIMMER.

In consequence of our having, in a former number, alluded to the fact of organic remains having been discovered so near the metropolis, we have been requested, by two of our readers, who were not apprized of the matter, to relate the particulars. Fortunately, we noted what will be given below, at the time of our reading the account in the Philosophical Transactions, of (we think) 1813. We do not recollect what circumstance led Mr. Trimmer to make his researches under the earth's surface; but his success, as will be seen, amply justified his attempt.

In the first field, about half a mile from Kew Bridge, and twenty-five feet above the Thames, at low water, the strata were found to lie in the order, and their containing remains, as thus:—

1st. Sandy Loam; six to seven feet in thickness. This was free from all vestige of remains.

2d. Sandy Gravel; a few inches. This contained small shells, and a few bones of land animals; but so mutilated that the class to which they belonged could not be ascertained.

3d. Loam, slightly calcareous; one to five feet. This contained the horns and bones of the ox; the horns, bones, and teeth of the deer; besides snail shells and shells of river fish.

4th. Peat in small detached particles; a few inches. This presented the teeth and horns of both the African and Asiatic elephants; the teeth of the hippopotamus; and the bones, horns, and teeth of the ox.

5th. Gravel containing water; thickest under the peat; two to ten inches. This stratum is not noticed as containing any remains.

6th. London Clay; two hundred feet. In this, the animal remains were all marine; but there were some specimens of fruit, and petrified wood. The other fossils were nautili, oysters, prima marina, crabs' teeth, and bones of fish, and a great variety of small shells.

The second field, about a mile west from the first, and a quarter of a mile from the River Brent, is forty feet above the Thames, at low water: and the deposition of the strata is as thus:—

1st. Sandy Loam; eight to nine feet: No animal remains.

2d. Sand; coarser towards the lower part; three to eight

feet: In this stratum, but always within two feet of the next beneath, were found bones and teeth of the hippopotamus, and the elephant. The horns, bones, and teeth, of the deer, and ox; together with the shells of snails, and river fish. One tusk of an elephant, as it lay on the ground, measured nine feet, three inches; but it broke on an attempt being made to remove it. The remains of hippopotami were so abundant, that in turning over an area of 120 feet, in this second field, parts of six tusks of the hippopotamus were found.

3d. Stratum; loam highly calcareous: one inch, to nine feet.

4th. Gravel; containing water; depth unknown.

5th. London Clay; depth unknown.

Of the three last strata we have not any account recorded of remains, and therefore suppose that the paper from whence we took our notes must have been silent as to their containing what might have been worthy of notice.

This paper affords some interesting matter for reflection: partly in a pure philosophical sense, and partly as to a spot in our own immediate neighbourhood, that has evidently been the scene of wild rendezvous in ages preceding the present race of man. The first point to be noticed is, that although these two fields are a mile apart; and at a difference in level of about 15 feet, on the banks of separate rivers; yet their strata and contents are respectively the same, or nearly so. Thus, in both, the first consists of sandy loam, and destitute of remains. The second stratum of the first field has small shells; the second of the second field has also snail, and river shells; besides the remains of the large land animals: and probably the mutilated bones found in the second of the first field, were of a similar character. The third of the first field, contained in part (as of the deer and ox) similar remains as the second of the second field; as well as the shells of snails and river fish. But the fourth of the first field, assimilates more directly with the second of the second. It seems that below the second stratum in the second field, there were not any remains whatever found; but it was far different in the first, for under the fourth stratum, containing the animal remains, there was merely a thin bed of peat, separating it from the deep mass of London clay, containing a variety of *marine* fossils.

We may infer from the bed of peat existing in the order of stratification, in the first field, and its non-existence in the second, that there had been a forest on the former ground; but not on the latter: and with this single difference excepted, we may perceive that there was such a resemblance in the qualities of the respective strata of the two fields, wherein the organic remains of the land animals were discovered, as to justify a belief that the creatures of whom they were parts, were co-existent on those points, after a given time. For we may infer too, that they lived on the banks of the Thames earlier than on those of the Brent; because, in the latter case, the remains are limited to the sandy or gravelly stratum, near the surface; whereas, in the first field, remains are found in the calcareous, and peaty strata, below the corresponding sandy and gravelly of the respective fields. Perhaps the river Brent did not exist, when the animals whose remains are found in the calcareous, and peaty strata, were living; and we may suppose, then, that when it became a stream, the beasts would frequent it as well as the Thames; being in the immediate vicinity of each other.

But we have a remarkable difference in the respective beds of London clay: that in the first field containing marine remains only; and that in the second not any remains whatever. These beds of clay, of course, have no relation either to remains found above them, or to the rivers Thames and Brent; for the clay, with its contents, was necessarily deposited before the existence of either of these rivers. It is, also, worthy of remark, that *fruit* was found in the clay stratum, among *marine* remains.

What a scope is here given to philosophical conjecture! Perhaps Cuvier's Theory of the Earth and Man, approaches nearer to the satisfaction of our minds, than any other; as it better accords with those facts which have been established, partly by the industry of research, and partly by chance. We are aided to a conclusion, respecting the above discoveries, by taking M. C.'s principles for our guide; as he teaches that the surface of the earth has several times been covered by the sea: that several successive races of inhabitants have been destroyed: and that all these revolutions took place before the continents, which we at present know, were inhabited by the present race. He judges from a combination of natural facts, that our race cannot have existed previous to the period assigned by the Old Testament to the deluge: that the date given by all the primary nations, Egyptians, Assyrians, Chinese, and Indians, points to the period of the flood as according with the sacred authority; which catastrophe must have involved not only the human race in destruction, but also have annihilated all records of institutions, monuments, and learning. Although the discoveries made at Brentford are not very magnificent as to extent; they are not less impressive as to the principles they would sustain; and, we think, add but another instance to the large stock of facts, now within the cognizance of man, in proof of his probable existence in successive races.

We cannot conclude without adverting to a circumstance made known to the public some time since: namely, that the celebrated terrestrial theorist, Woodward, had left behind him at Cambridge a rich treasure of geological specimens, and of organic remains, which had lain in one of the colleges unknown, or as lumber; but which accident had shown the value of. Since the bare announcement of this matter, we have not been fortunate enough to meet with any further notice of it. But we trust that the University will do justice to that learned and industrious philosopher as well as to the public, by publishing a full account of whatever may remain yet unknown as the result of Dr. Woodward's philosophical zeal.

Description of the Trinity Pier of Suspension at Newhaven, near Edinburgh. By Captain SAMUEL BROWN, R. N. addressed to Dr. Brewster.

Edinburgh Philosophical Journal, No. 11.

Captain B. commences by remarking that the Union-bridge of suspension carried over the Tweed in 1820, has been in continued use; has fully answered every purpose intended, as well as if constructed of iron or stone; and has, within the first year, more than paid interest on the capital expended, so that the redemption of that sum may be reasonably anticipated.

The intercourse with that part of the coast which this structure is intended to facilitate, being so increased as to render the improvement of landing requisite, the Trinity Pier Company, and the owners of the steam vessels, preferred, at once, constructing this suspension pier, to litigation with the trustees of Newhaven pier; and to Lieut. Crichton, R. N., who proposed the matter to those interested, the public is indebted for the convenience. Besides, the Edinburgh magistrates honoured the plan with their sanction.

The length of the pier is 700 feet from high water mark; 4 feet wide; consists of three equal divisions of 209 feet, without any central support; and is 10 feet above high water. The pier head 60 feet by 50, supported by 46 piles driven about 8 feet into stiff blue clay: the heads of the piles secured by beams at right angles; and by diagonal trusses and warping, which form a secure frame for the deck of two-inch plank. Such is Captain B.'s description of its dimensions.

Without entering more minutely into the mode of its construction, we will proceed to just state that Captain B. intimates the only improvement he has attempted is, that of using strong bolts over the points of suspension, where the stress is greatest; and diminishing them towards the centre, where it is least; proportioning each bolt to the strain which it has to bear in the curve.

Captain B. after numerous experiments, found that a round bolt, $1\frac{1}{4}$ inch in diameter, can sustain nearly the enormous weight of 147,000 lbs., applied in the direction of its length; but begins to stretch with $\frac{3}{15}$ of this weight, when uniformly supported. He has proved the main connecting bars to be equal to about 40 tons, and since the erection they have borne more than 21; which he conjectures to be nearly equal to the greatest weight they are likely to be subjected to. Founding on piles, for marine exposure, has many advantages, such as admitting the ready flow of the sea, and being less dangerous for a vessel to dash against: besides, experience proves them to be extremely durable; as at Yarmouth, Ostend, and Cronstadt.

Captain Brown conjectures that those suspension piers might be thrown out seawards, on points where the surfs render our coast dangerous; and he notices some appendant means, that would contribute to the benevolent purpose of saving human life, when boats could not put off from shore, but might from the extremity of a suspension pier.

The more we consider these bridges, and piers, of suspension, the more we are satisfied of their public utility; and the peculiar advantages they, in many respects, possess, over the more solid structures of stone. It cannot be long before the good sense of the south shall catch a ray of this wisdom from the north, and present us with suspension bridges over the Thames, in lieu of some uncouth structures now disfiguring its noble stream.

On Improvements in Setting Razors and other cutting Instruments. By G. REVELEY, Esq. In a letter to Arthur Aikin, Esq., Secretary to the Society of Arts, &c.

We consider this subject as worthy of some notice, and intended giving it insertion in one of our early numbers, but it was forgotten. Mr. Reveley writes as follows:

" Sir,   Queen-square, Bloomsbury, Jan. 8, 1821.

" I beg to communicate to the Society of Arts, for the benefit of the public, a new method of setting razors, by substituting soap instead of oil. Not having any oil to set my razor, it occurred to me to try the soap I was washing with, called palm soap; and I found it so completely to answer my purpose, that I have constantly used it ever since, instead of oil, both for razors and penknives. It sets quicker, gives a good edge, and removes notches with great facility: it is a more cleanly material, oil being liable to drop on and soil any thing it comes in contact with: dust will frequently get into oil, which will spoil the edge, and in such case it must be changed. It is as cheap or cheaper than oil; a small square of palm soap costing only three pence, which will last for a great length of time. The operation is performed as follows: Having first cleaned your hone with a sponge, soap, and water, wipe it dry; then dip the soap in some clean soft water; and, wetting also the hone, rub the square of soap lightly over it, until the surface is thinly covered all over; then proceed to set in the usual way, keeping the soap sufficiently moist, and adding from time to time a little more soap and water, if it should be necessary. Observe the soap is clean and free from dust, before you rub it on the hone; if it should not be so, it is easily washed clean: strap the razor after setting, and also again when you put it by, and sponge the hone when you have done with it.

"I am, Sir, &c. &c.
"GEO. REVELEY."

Mr. Reveley exhibited to the Society the testimonies of several gentlemen, who expressed their decided approbation of his plan.

Method of smoothing the Edge of Razors, by means of the crystallized Tritoxide of Iron called, by Mineralogists, Specular Iron Ore. By M. MERIMEE.

Bulletin de la Societe d'Encouragement.

We lay this paper before our readers in immediate succession to Mr. Reveley's account of the use of soap, with the hone; because it describes the next process after honing. We would just make a passing remark as to the imparting of an edge to a razor, that there is more manual dexterity required for success, than many are willing to allow. We think that the result of strapping is as much governed by the manner in which it is performed, as by the material which covers the strap.

M. Merimee says that he had "determined on making known a preparation which appeared to him, as well as to those who have used it, particularly adapted to make the razors sharp." He prefers the flat form for the strap; the leather of which should be thick, fine grained, and of close texture, or two layers of thinner, well glued together. The strap, as usual, to have two faces. On the first, the grinding material to be finely powdered emery, hone, whetstone, pumice stone, slate, calcined clay, iron cinders or scales, &c., sifted through silk, and mixed with a small quantity of charcoal, which makes the razor pass more smoothly over it: these are to be mixed, with grease, into a paste. This is the first bed to sharpen on, by taking off the roundness of the edge.

To finish, by imparting a fine smooth edge, we must discard the powders hitherto used, such a colcothar, fine emery, black lead, &c. and substitute this crystallized tritoxide of iron, called by the French, *fer oligiste spéculaire*, either as found naturally, or as prepared thus:—

Rub together equal parts of sulphate of iron, green vitriol, and hydrochlorate of soda (common salt), with which fill a crucible, and heat to redness; vapour will be disengaged; the matter will be saline, and have a metallic appearance, in brilliant spangles; and the powder be of a purple brown, that is a colcothar, the nearer this colour (not black) the better. Wash the mass in water, when the spangles will fall to the bottom; and are to be preserved, as the material sought, for giving the required edge to the instrument. The red portion, or colcothar, if well washed, and dried, will make good polishing powder.

The spangled powder to be applied to the strap, previously greased, in a very slight degree, so as to retain the powder on the surface, but not to mingle with it, and form a paste. When the razor seems to adhere to the surface, more of the powder must be applied.

This is the substance of M. Merimee's paper; and as such we present it to the public, without a comment. If any gentleman should be induced to try the process, we should be thankful to learn the result.

As relates to our own experience in straps, we would recommend a metallic one, made by Mr. Still, Surgeons' Instrument maker, Leicester Street, Leicester Square. It has an excellent effect in imparting a smooth edge, which is of more consequence to the instrument, as aiding its action on the beard, than what is called a sharp one. A good butcher's steel, having its surface polished, is also an excellent implement for the use proposed; but it requires a nice dexterity in applying the razor to its surface. With Mr. Still's straps, however, there is not any difficulty to be encountered.

On Natural Phenomena, as resolved by JOHN HERAPATH, Esq., and confirmed by other Writers.

Annals of Philosophy, No. 13.

Through a succession of very long papers, that have appeared in the above Journal, Mr. Herapath has traced the principles of the following phenomena by analytic process; and we think that the recapitulation, though rather prolix, may be well worthy a place in our journal, as displaying the elementary constitution of matters perpetually presenting to the philosophical reader. Mr. H. generally adds to each of the laws, if they may be so named, the authorities sanctioning them, as he lays them down.

PHENOMENA.

The elasticity of a given portion of gas is the same, whatever may be the figure of the vessel in which it is contained; provided capacity and temperature be the same.

Authority—Generally admitted, rather than the result of direct experiment.

Cæteris paribus, elasticity of gas directly as compression; or reciprocally as space.

Boyle on Air; and other Gases by others.

Elasticity, as square of temperature directly; and simple of space inversely. Boyle, De Luc, and Herapath.

Elasticities being, equal spaces as squares of temperatures.

De Luc and Herapath.

Equal changes of temperature affect equal volumes of all gases, cæteris paribus.

Elasticities of two gases, having an invariable ratio, and temperatures an invariable ratio, their volumes will have an invariable ratio. De Luc and Herapath.

Temperature of water, freezing to that of boiling as $\sqrt{8}$ to $\sqrt{11}$ De Luc and Herapath.

Same results had from measuring temperatures by elasticities, under invariable volume; as from volumes under invariable compression.   Mariotte, Dulong, and Petit.

Sudden gaseous condensation produces heat; sudden rarefaction, cold; but, either, slowly made, no change in temperature.   Mollet and Dalton.

Gases transmit caloric rapidly; but feebly in right lines.
      Leslie.

Gases abstract temperature (under certain circumstances) in proportion to their levity.
      Leslie, Davy, Dulong, and Petit.

Barometrin of hydrogen, four times greater than that of oxygen.   Crawford nearly confirming.

Two particles of oxygen, with one of hydrogen, form water.
      Crawford.

Absolute cold, 448 Fahrenheit below 32 Fahrenheit.
      De Luc and Herapath.

Methegmerin of mercury to water, as 1 to 2—masses of particles, as 27 to 1.
      Calculations and Comparisons, with Experiments of
      H. Dalton.

Phenomena of "capacity for caloric" due to methegmerin.
      Dalton in variis.

Phenomena of "latent heat" due to aggregation, and decomposition of particles.
      Black, Watt, Rumford, Kirwan, Irvine, Lavoisier
      and La Place, Ure, Crawford, Southern, &c.

Attraction in small bodies, sensibly distant, inversely as square of central distance; directly, as mass of attracted body; and, temperature being same, as mass of central body.
      Newton.

Particles attracted by distant sphere, as masses of particles and sphere; (temperature invariable) and square of central distance inversely.   Newton.

Law of attraction, on a perfectly solid imperviable cylinder.
      Cannot be confirmed, but by induction.

Two homogeneous spheres of same temperature, attract each other as their quantities of matter directly; and square of central distances inversely.   Newton.

Present theory of gravitation would not produce the least sensible effect on the system of the universe, in a period of

many million times 285779606767610 years.
Newton and Laplace.

Activity of attraction so great as to act equally on matter with, or against it, with a velocity, at least many million million times faster than motion of light.   Laplace, who has proved that the activity must be at least six million times greater than that of light.

Resistance of gravific fluid cannot produce sensible effect within many million years.   Newton and Laplace.

Attraction directly proportional to temperature of attracting body.   Euler, Laplace, diminution of planetary attraction in receding from the sun, and in the small action of the comets.

Ellipticity of the earth by old theory, of uniform attraction, should be too little by pendulum; by Newton's calculation, too great.

By pendulum, $\frac{1}{336}$; most of the admeasurements, $\frac{1}{310}$; Newton, $\frac{1}{230}$.

Attraction between particles nearly touching, increases faster than squares of distances diminish.
   Many chemical phenomena; Newton, Desaguliers, Laplace, &c.

Affinity and phenomena of chemical action, arise from figures of component particles.
   General idea, but not proved.

Bodies expanding by heat, have greatest barometrin, or "capacity."   Davy.

Barometrin of gaseous bodies and air, usually greater than that of solids.   Crawford, &c.

During liquefaction, temperature is stationary (as of ice).   Qu. Fahrenheit?

Given weight and temperature of a fluid, just dissolving a solid mass, will just dissolve same in powder.   Qu. Black?

Temperature of ebullition in fluids, constant.   Hooke.

Liquefaction of solids, and vaporization of fluids, usually of apparent diminished temperature; solidification the reverse.   Black?

During solidification, temperature constant.   Black?

Water may cool below 32° without freezing; but if agitated, rises to 38°, and congeals.   Blagden.

Water, with opaque bodies floating, freezes at a little below 32°.   Blagden.

Gently cooled below 32°, will not freeze: suddenly, will freeze.   Blagden.

Water, as it cools below 40°, expands   Biot.

Fluidity results from sphericity of particles; or extent of aberration overcoming influence of irregularity of figure: therefore solidity results from irregularity of figure, and smallness of extent of corpuscular vibration. Carbonic oxide and oxygen, unite into carbonic acid, with a less barometrin, and with a greater specific gravity, than either alone.
    Berard and Delaroche.

Solids may be converted into airs, with increase of temperature.   Gunpowder.

An augmentation of particles, from same matter, causes diminished temperature; diminution of particles augmented temperature.

Chemical changes, generally, but not universally, change temperature.

Aërial particles generally less than those of fluids. Hence, in equal weights, particles most numerous in air.

Barometrin of airs usually exceeds that of fluids or solids.

Condensation of vapours caused by irregularity in figure of particles; therefore produced by diminished temperature.

Difference between vapours and gases, is merely in figure of particles.   Dalton and Herapath.

Vapours, unconnected with their fluids, at all higher temperatures than that of their condensation, are perfect gases; and follow same laws.   Dalton.

Mixture of different vapours; or of vapours and gases, where no chemical action; has same law as mixture of gases.
    Dalton, Gay-Lussac.

Pressure aids condensation of vapours; but diminishes, as temperature increases.   Dalton.

Gases, separately incondensible; on admixture, may condense.   Sulphureous gas, and hydrogen.

Temperature of ebullition, in all fluids, increases and diminishes with increase and diminution of pressure.

Robinson.

Fahrenheit temperature of ebullition increases and decreases more rapidly than compression.

De Luc, Betancourt, Shuckburg.

Temperature of liquefaction, not influenced by pressure.

Ebullition, caused by violent decomposition within the interior, not at the surface, of fluids. Hamilton.

Evaporation, is decomposition of superficial particles, arising from mutual collisions, or temperature of matter.

Presumed to be admitted.

In equal, or unequal, but great, depths; evaporation, at same temperature, proportional to exposed surface.

Dalton, Leslie.

Two portions of same fluid, cooled from any common, to any common temperature, by evaporation alone, lose quantities proportional to original quantities; and conversely.

Two portions, at equal temperatures, losing, by evaporation, quantities proportional to their weights, are equally reduced in temperature.

Incremental condensation of a vapour, at same temperature, in vacuo, is, cæteris paribus, as its elasticity.

Dalton, Gay-Lussac, De Luc.

Increment of condensation, is as cube of temperature; methegmerin being same. Same authorities.

Incremental condensation as elasticity and temperature conjointly. Same.

Incremental condensation in same vapour, as specific gravity, and cube of temperature, conjointly. Same.

Cæteris paribus, mixture of any quantity of gas with vapour, in a given space, has no effect on celerity of condensation, however much it may increase elasticity. Same.

With sufficient fluid, and at same temperature, tension of vapour will be same; whatever be the occupied space.

Dalton.

Pressure, no effect in augmenting or diminishing absolute evaporation; temperature being same. General theory.

Vapours, in vacuo, only support given pressure, according to temperature; but mixed with sufficient gas, can support indefinitely. Dalton.

Rarefaction of air promotes desiccation. Leslie.

Apparent evaporation, proportional to velocity of current of air passing over surface. Leslie.

Current, or agitation of air, increases apparent evaporation, and diminishes temperature. Leslie and Dalton.

Water or ice, in a current or agitation of air, may lose more in weight in a given time, than at a higher temperature, and in still air. Clare, Rowning, or Hamilton?

Water commonly colder than atmosphere.
Wells and Herapath.

Temperature of no evaporation is 130°. Ure.

Temperature of ebullition, higher than that of tension.
Robinson, Dalton, and De Luc.

Baromerin of ice, to that of water, as 19 to 22.
Black, Kirwan, Irvine, Thompson, &c.

"Capacity" of water being 1, that of ice, is 86.
Mean of Irvine and Kirwan.

Theory of calorimeter.
Calculation of capacity of iron plate 116.
Lavoisier and Laplace, 111.

Theoretical calculation of water, frozen by agitation, in two experiments, differed in one instance $\frac{1}{182}$ part; the other $\frac{1}{420}$. Thompson.

Baromerin of vapour, to that of water, as 11 to 6.
Mean difference from four experiments by Thompson, Ure, and Rumford, $\frac{7}{40}$ of a degree of Fah.

Theoretical "capacity" of aqueous vapour, 1·83; that of water 1. Crawford 1·55.

Specific heats of lighter airs, exceed those of heavier.
Crawford, De Laroche, and Berard.

Mean capacity of water between 32° and 122° Fahrenheit, to that between 122° and 212°, as 15·1 to 14.
De Luc and Herapath, as 15 to 14.

Capacities of water and mercury, decrease with ascent of temperature; and vice versa.
De Luc, Dalton, Ure, and Herapath.

The greater the ratio of water to vapour, the less the numerical value of latent heat.   Ure and Rumford.

The higher, also, either or both temperatures, the greater the value of latent heat.

Combining calorific with formula, temperature has less influence; calculation giving 11° under certain circumstances.
            Southern's experiments give 8°.

On English and Foreign Copper, Zinc, and Brass. By Mr. GILL, Editor of the Technical Repository, vide No. 2.—With an account of Mr. Sheffield's Patent.

Mr. Gill presents his paper with a view to show the causes producing the inferiority of the English brass, so well known, and so injurious, to the British artist; as well as to offer some means remedial of the defects.

Leaf copper, commonly called Dutch leaf, not being manufactured in this country, is imported from the continent, and in war-time is, necessarily, at an exhorbitant price. It is not generally known what process the metal may have undergone during the manufacture of the leaf; but Mr. G. proposes to give information on this point hereafter. He merely mentions now, that copper must be brought into that lamellated state, before it can be united with pure zinc, to form brass, equally malleable.

English brass is commonly made, in the large, by cementing copper, in a divided state, with calamine, or other ore of zinc. The copper which has not been previously treated in a proper manner, as by the above mentioned lamellating process, is, in our manufacture of brass, made to unite with the *crude* zinc; thereby partaking of lead, or other deteriorating metals, combined in the blendes, or ores. Therefore the compound called brass, which ought to be a union of pure copper with pure zinc, is deficient in its ductile and malleable properties, for the purposes to which it is, or might be, applied. Besides, it is the more likely to become decomposed, in particular conditions of the atmosphere; as that of combined moisture and cold, during a thaw: when the brass, of English make, will become black and rotten; while the continental will remain uninjured.

Mr. G. says, that the best brass wire strings, for pianofortes, are made of foreign brass; as also the wire studs with which glass drops for lustres are hung together, paying a price to the German manufacturers of the wire, of half a a guinea per pound. And watchmakers pay even a guinea per pound, for the Flemish brass wherewith they construct their delicate wheel-work. The tinsel for theatrical decorations is, also, of a similar quality; and, indeed, all the fine leaf metal of this kind is foreign.

Mr. Sheffield, a gentleman lately deceased, obtained a patent previous to his death, and commenced preparations for the establishment of a brass manufacture, in Derbyshire. Prospectuses were circulated, of which the following is a copy:

" Improved apparatus for extracting zinc or spelter, from its ores. A patent, which was taken out by W. E. Sheffield, who wishes to have it carried into effect, either by forming a company for that purpose; disposing of the patent to a company already formed; or by granting privileges to those who wish to avail themselves of the patent improvements.

" Zinc, or spelter, is used in the composition of brass, in the proportion of one-third; and notwithstanding the immense consumption, and importance of the subject, the ores of zinc or spelter are less understood than those of any other metal.

" Mr. Sheffield has been employed in this pursuit, many years; and from the success which has already attended the investigation of these ores, he is convinced it deserves the greatest encouragement, both in a commercial view, and as a source from whence much profit might be expected, with very little risk indeed. The makers of brass purchase only the richest and purest ores of zinc or spelter. It will, therefore, not answer their purposes, unless it contain 30 per cent. of zinc, or more. These rich and pure calamines having been in request for several centuries, are now become scarce and dear. Calamines, less rich, or pure, do not find a market at all, even at an inferior price; to the great loss of the miners, who are compelled to relinquish all those mines which do not produce a calamine sufficiently rich and pure for the makers of brass. The distress occasioned in a mining country, where the poorer calamines abound, and cannot find a sale, has occasioned Mr. S. to consider the subject, and endeavour to find a remedy; which, with much expense of time and money, he has, in some degree, acccomplished, by inventing an apparatus; with which the greater part of the calamines, rejected by the brass makers, may be rendered useful; and zinc be extracted from them, with advantage: the operation requiring less time and fuel than in the usual way. By which a profit of 40 per cent. per annum, on the capital employed, may be reasonably expected. And, according to experiment, actually made, may be more.

"Mr. S. has also obtained another patent for preparing copper, in a fit state for being beat out into leaves; in order to compose, with a due proportion of zinc, a very fine brass; either for plates or wire. And also an improved apparatus for dividing the plates of copper, brass, &c. to fit them for drawing. From the metals thus prepared, wire will be obtained much sounder and stronger than by any other method.

"In order to derive the greatest advantages from the above mentioned improvements, the same company should possess both patents; and have a copper and brass work, as well as a zinc work. The whole united would form a regular and connected business, of great consequence; capable of employing a very large capital, which might be increased to any amount; and possessing, and affording, advantages, much superior to any other company manufacturing similar articles in this kingdom."

Mr. S. has left relatives, and, among others, a son; whom he made thoroughly acquainted with his superior processes; and capable of carrying them into effect, when an opportunity shall offer of so doing.

Wire, drawn from metals, which have been slit into rods, by the usual operations in the large, is constantly unsound, throughout its whole length: arising from the shape given to the rods in the act of slitting them, by the cutters; which cause one edge of each rod to be rounded, while the opposite edge is hollowed. The edges of this hollow side, by the operation of the wire-drawing, are gradually brought nearer together, until at length, they meet and close, and thus form, as it were, a sort of tube or hollow, along one side of the wire. In Mr. S.'s improved process, this evil is completely avoided.

We will now advert to the patent, and the spirit of its specification.—First, " The one part is called an air conductor; and to be applied to, or constructed in, and along with, a furnace, or furnaces, and to be therewith used, for the purpose of introducing into direct contact with the ores, or other materials to be exposed to the action of heat in the said furnace, or furnaces; atmospheric air, or any other gas, or elastic fluid, which may be found or considered to be useful in, or as to the treatment of the the said ores or materials. And also, one other part or portion thereof, which is a m●●●l pot or vessel, for the beneficial separation of ●●● in the metallic state, from the ore. And the said furnaces are constructed, for the like purpose, of beneficial ●●●rating, &●●● The improvement in the melting pots, ●●●●●e as well as we can; they consist of this: that is, thro●● bottom of the pot there runs up perpendicularly a tub●●●●n at the lower end, and minutely perforated, which admits the passage off of the sublimed zinc downwards, into a condensing vessel, that would otherwise have been lost in its traverse through the body of heated ore. This melting pot has an aperture at the top, through which it is charged, and closed by a cover; also it has a tube branching off, like a retort, for the escape of generated vapours, and the remainder of the sublimed zinc, that could not pass down the perpendicular tube before mentioned.

Next as to the furnace: There arises, in the fore part, a blast or air tube, which augments the intensity and heat; but the principal improvement consists in enlarging the exposed surface of the ore to the action of the fire. This is accomplished by spreading the ore over the ground plane of the furnace; and the introduction of shelves within its cavity; or otherwise, by close, but separate, compartments; so as to give the convenience of reducing more than one quality of ore at the same time, as well as effecting the extension of surface. By the air passage, gas of any desired quality, as oxygen, &c. may be passed over the surface of the exposed ore.

These constitute the principal points of excellence, in the proposed mode. They who are conversant in such manipulations will be best able to judge of the peculiar advantages, if any, and what; for ourselves, we can merely intimate that, the means seem well adapted to the end; and if the adoption of the plan should eventually be crowned with success, it will be a great national benefit gained, as well as a convenience to those concerned in the manufacture of brazen articles.

On the Preparation of Carbonate of White Lead and Verdigris. By Mr. HAGNER, as detailed in the Specification of his Patent.

Technical Repository, No. 1.

The following is the method pointed out in the specification, but which presents no novelty of principle to us:

"Mr. Hagner's improvements in the art of making the pigment, commonly known by the name of white lead, consist in the use of a machine, or machines, for granulating lead; and which said machine may be a revolving cylinder, or other proper vessel, turning upon axles, and having an opening at one end of it, into which melted lead may be poured: and after being granulated by the rotary action of the machine, may be readily discharged, by causing the vessel to be inverted, or the opening at the end of it to be turned downwards; this may be effected in various ways, not necessary to be particularly described; and the lead, so granulated, may be afterwards used with advantage in the manufacture of white lead.

"Mr. Hagner's improvement in the art of making verdigris, consists in the use of a machine, or machines, which may be a revolving vessel, or vessels, turning upon axles; or other proper vessels capable of receiving an alternating motion, or of being agitated; as also of fixed vessels, in which agitators may be put into motion. Into any or either of these vessels Mr. Hagner puts copper, in a state of division; the more minute the better; and adds to the copper, pyroligneous acid, vinegar, or other acetic or acetous acid; and either mixed with water, or not, so as that the copper shall only be partially covered by the liquid; and causes the same to be put into continual agitation, by any proper first mover, so as to present fresh surfaces of the metal to the acid; and to abrade or rub off those parts of it which may be sufficiently oxided.

"In case the vessel or vessels be wholly or in part closed; Mr. Hagner introduces carbonic acid gas, during the operation of the machine; and continues the process for a greater or lesser period, or until the verdigris be formed; when it may be withdrawn from the vessel or vessels, and finished for use."

It will be seen that the only advantage in the above, consists in the increased renewal of surfaces that the acting bodies present to each other; and thereby accelerating the progress of the manufacture: but as time is money to the manufacturer, this advantage has its value.

On a new Carriage to be moved by Steam. By Mr. GRIFFITHS, of Brompton.

From the commencement of the late trials, made to propel light vehicles on the public roads, we have been confident that a spirit was raised which would not be allayed short of the accomplishment of its object; and we feel the same anticipation yet; although the bungling specimens exhibited hitherto, have fallen far short of our expectation; and indeed have been unworthy of the mechanical character of our country.

Mr. Griffiths, of Brompton, is a gentleman not unknown in the literary world, by his Travels in Asia Minor, and other works. Mr. G., in connection with a professor of mechanics on the continent, has at length solved the long considered problem of propelling, by steam, carriages capable of transporting merchandize, and also passengers, upon common roads, without the aid of horses. The actual construction of such a carriage is now proceeding in, at the manufactory of Messrs. Bramah; and its appearance in action may be expected to take place in the course of the spring. We shall endeavour to obtain a drawing of this carriage when completed, and furnish our readers with such other particulars as may merit their attention.

The power to be applied in this machine is equal to that of six horses, and the carriage altogether will be twenty-eight feet in length, running upon three-inch wheels, and equal to the conveyance of three and a half tons, with a velocity of from 3 to 7 miles per hour, varied at pleasure. All our intelligent readers will be sensible of the vast importance, in a political and social sense, of the introduction of such machines on all our great roads. The saving in carriage of goods, will be fifty per cent.; and for passengers, inside fares will be taken at outside prices. The universal importance of this great triumph of the mechanical arts, has led Mr. Griffiths to take out patents in Austria and France, where the governments have honoured themselves by their liberal attention and special patronage: and one carriage has actually been launched at Vienna, and operates with success. By availing himself of various improvements, in the transfer, regulation, and economy of force, all the usual objections are removed, such as the ascent of hills; securing a supply of fuel and water; and in fine, the danger of explosion is prevented, not only by the safety valve, but by the distribution of the steam into tubes, so as to render any possible explosion wholly unimportant. Every carriage will be provided with a director of the fore wheels, sitting in front; and with a director of the steam apparatus, sitting in the rear; and the body of the vehicle will be situated between the fore wheels and the machinery.

In contemplating the probable event of some such carriages as the above being found equal to the wants or wishes of the public, we ought to look a little deeper than the surface, as to the national advantages and disadvantages: nay, start not, reader; for *disadvantages* would assuredly arise. We admit that men who must in the present state of things be contented with such power of locomotion as their legs may afford them, might, with one of these carriages, move more rapidly; or might, if infirm in the lower extremities, gain, by the entire power of moving at all. Also for the lighter kind of carriage, as carriers, market gardeners, &c., and various other descriptions of persons, engaged in occupations consisting in light transits of commodities, it would be beneficial, in a small degree; also, for purposes of pleasure, and travelling in a limited degree, such a convenience might be desirable. These, then, we will call the advantages. We will now turn to the other side of the consideration, and ask What would be the consequence to the agricultural interests? What must the farmer do with the capital employed in the growth of that portion of grain, hay, straw, &c. consumed by horses; as well as the saddlers, smiths, leather traders, &c.; all of whom employ capitals profitably on breeding, feeding, harnessing, &c. of these valuable animals? To agriculture, especially, such a change in the mode of moving persons and property, as now meditated, would be ruinous. The farmers could not plough by steam, nor sow by steam; they would be almost the only class deprived of the benefit specifically enjoyed. But they constitute a class requiring more of propulsive power than any other description of men. To say, that by the reduction in the number of horses generally, the consumption of grain would be proportionably diminished, would be insufficient; for grain is now so abundant, that the cultivator has a distressing surplus on hand; and no artisan can reasonably complain that the loaf is dear, if he have the wages of labour to purchase with at all. We then anticipate, as a matter of course, that so soon as these, or any other carriages, propelled by mechanism, shall attain a certain practical perfection, they will be subjected to a very heavy tax. This, the inventors must look too, as what we will presume to declare a very natural and very fair consequence.

On the good effects of Watering the Frozen Branches of the Peach and Nectarine Trees, very early in the Morning. By G. H. Nochden, L. L. D., F. L. S., &c.

Transactions of the London Horticultural Society.

The gentleman, in whose garden the experiment of watering the peach and nectarine trees has been tried, as a preservative of the blossoms against the spring frosts, is James Stuart Wortley, Esq. M. P., of Wortley Hall, near Sheffield. His garden lies uncommonly high, perhaps as high as any garden in Great Britain, above the level of the sea. It consequently has not the advantage of a sheltered situation; but the local position seems, on the contrary, to be rather unfavourable. To the eastward, it slopes a little down the right side of a very high hill. The quantity of fruit alleged to have been produced, Mr. Wortley found, upon minute investigation, had been very much exaggerated by common report. He lays great stress upon the method of pruning and training the trees, practised by the gardener; and he attributes to it, a considerable portion of the success which has attended the gardener's labours. The man seems to excel in that part of his business. Mr. Wortley says, he can hardly do him justice in describing it, for he never saw trees so beautifully trained, and upon such good principles. The chief rule which he follows is, as Mr. Wortley states, never to allow the shoots that are left for bearing fruit, to run to any length from the strong wood; for which reason, when the trees are pruned in autumn, the gardener shortens the bearing branches for the next year, as much as he can, by taking care not to leave more fruiting buds than he thinks will come to perfection. The peach and nectarine blossoms upon the open walls, in other gardens in Mr. Wortley's neighbourhood, were almost entirely destroyed by the frosts last year and the year before; but in both years Mr. Wortley was equally fortunate in the preservation of his produce. I will now subjoin Mr. Wortley's answers to several queries, which I took the liberty of proposing.

"*Query* 1.—What is the exact method which the gardener practises, to which he ascribes his success with the fruit trees? Is it exclusively the operation of watering the blossoms and the branches, or has he any accessary means?

"*Answer*.—The peach and nectarine trees are pruned and nailed in December and January; when the gardener always takes two-thirds of the young shoots away; and in two hand dressings in May and July, leaves the lowest and weakest shoots for a succession in the year following, pinching off the leading and other shoots.

"This answer implies, that a great deal is supposed to depend upon the pruning and dressing, and not every thing upon the watering, to which point the query was directed.

"*Query* 2.—At what time does he apply the water, and in what manner?

"*Answer*.—The gardener applies cold water at the time of the blooming, and setting of the fruit, in the following manner: viz. if upon visiting the trees, before the sun is up, in the morning, after a frosty night, he finds that there is any appearance of frost in the bloom or young fruit, he waters the *bloom* or *young fruit* thoroughly with cold water, from the garden engine, and he assures me, (says Mr. Wortley) that even if the blossoms or young fruit are discoloured, this operation recovers them, *provided it be done before the sun comes upon them*. He farther says, that he has sometimes had occasion to water particular parts of the trees more than once in the same morning, before he could get entirely rid of the effects of the frost.

"I think this information extremely interesting, and I wish to recommend it to the investigation of every member of this Society, who may have an opportunity of examining it; but especially to the acuteness of our worthy President. It is singular, that according to the testimony of the gardener, the operation of watering, in counteracting the frost, produces its effects only if it be done before the sun comes upon the blossoms or young fruit. This seems to be analogous to the condition of a frost-bitten joint or limb, which is recovered by the application of cold water; but injured, and sometimes destroyed, by being brought near a fire, or the influence of sudden warmth.

"*Query* 3.—What led the gardener to the discovery of that method?

"*Answer*.—The gardener says, that he first discovered this method by the following accident. In planting some cabbage plants, among the rows of some kidney-beans, very early in the morning, after a frosty night, in spring, before the sun was high enough to come upon the frosted leaves, he spilt some of the water upon them which he used in planting the cabbage plants; and to his surprise he found that the leaves began immediately to recover.

"It is impossible not to applaud the sagacity and reflection of the man, in not suffering this fact to pass by unheeded;

I think it an honour, well merited by him, that his name should be mentioned to the Society—it is Charles Harrison.

"*Query* 4.—Were the trees sheltered from the frost by any sort of covering?

"*Answer.*—The trees are protected from the frost in the month of January by branches of broom; these are previously steeped in soap-suds, mixed with one-third of urine, for forty-eight hours, in order to clear them from insects, and when dry, dispersed thinly over the whole tree, letting them remain on only until the trees begin to break into leaf.

"*Query* 5.—What was the quantity of fruit that was ripened, as near as can be ascertained?

"*Answer.*—I have good reason to believe, that the number consumed in the house, and given away in presents, was 5,850 peaches and nectarines, exclusive of all waste, from decay and other means.

"*Query* 6.—Was the fruit thinned?

"*Answer.*—The fruit was twice thinned in the course of the spring and summer.

"*Query* 7.—Did it grow to a good size, and ripen well?

"*Answer.*—The fruit ripened well, was exceedingly well flavoured, and was uncommonly large; some of the peaches measuring nine and ten inches in circumference, and some were as much as eleven inches.

"*Query* 8.—What was the number of trees upon which it was produced; and their age?

"*Answer.*—The number of trees upon which this crop was produced, was thirty-three. They were planted in the border about nine years ago.

"*Query* 9.—What is the extent of the wall?

"*Answer.*—The extent of the wall is about 172 feet, which are flued.

"By the facts which have been stated, the efficacy of cold water upon the vegetable organization, in repelling the injuries of frost, seems to be established; and this practice may possibly throw some light upon certain points in the theory of vegetable life, which were hitherto unnoticed, or it may open a new path of inquiry to the attentive and philosophical observer.

We cannot omit calling the attention of the reader to the striking analogy that the above practical results on vegetable life show with the laws governing animal vitality. The gardener adopted precisely similar means for restoring his frost-bitten plants, that a surgeon would use in a case of frost-bitten limb. This curious and useful fact may lead to further experiments on vegetable life; wherefrom some new, and interesting points of similitude between the laws of vitality governing both the animal and vegetable kingdoms, may be elicited, to the advantage of mankind.

On the Culture of the Pear Tree. By T. A. KNIGHT, Esq. F. R. S. &c.

Transactions of Horticultural Society.

Such papers as the following are what we seek most anxiously for, as really worthy of perusal; and we should be happy were we able to select more practical matter than presents to us, in the periodical works of the time. In some of our counties, the pear is, or might be, a very valuable fruit; and therefore a knowledge of the means of augmenting the produce cannot be too widely diffused. Under this impression, we lay Mr. K.'s paper before the public.

" The pear tree exercises the patience of the planter, during a larger period, before it affords fruit, than any other grafted tree which finds a place in our gardens; and though it is subsequently very long lived, it generally, when trained to a wall, becomes in a few years unproductive of fruit, except at the extremities of its lateral branches. Both these defects are, however, I have a good reason to believe, the result of improper management; for I have lately succeeded most perfectly in rendering my *old* trees very productive in every part, and my *young* trees have almost always afforded fruit the second year after being grafted; and none have remained barren beyond the third year.

" In detailing the mode of pruning and culture I have adopted, I shall probably more easily render myself intelligible, by describing accurately, the management of a single tree of each.

"An *old* St. Germain pear tree, of the spurious kind, had been trained, in the fan form, against a northwest wall in my garden, and the central branches, as usually happens in old trees thus trained, had long reached the top of the wall, and had become wholly unproductive. The other branches afforded but very little fruit, and that never acquiring maturity, was consequently of no value; so that it was necessary to change the variety, as well as to render the tree productive.

"To attain these purposes, every branch which did not want, at least, twenty degrees of being perpendicular, was taken out at its base; and the spurs upon every other branch, which I intended to retain, were taken off, closely, with the saw and chisel. In these branches, at their subdivisions, grafts were inserted at different distances from the root, and some so near the extremities of the branches, that the tree extended as widely in the autumn, after it was grafted, as it did in the preceding year. The grafts were also so disposed, that every part of the space the tree previously covered, was equally well supplied with young wood.

"As soon, in the succeeding summer, as the young shoots had attained sufficient length, they were trained almost perpendicularly downwards, between the larger branches and the wall, to which they were nailed. The most perpendicular remaining branch upon each side, was grafted about four feet below the top of the wall, which is twelve feet high; and the young shoots, which the grafts upon these afforded, were trained inwards, and bent down to occupy the space from which the old central branches had been taken away, and therefore very little vacant space any where remained, in the end of the first autumn. A few blossoms, but not any fruit, were produced by several of these grafts in the succeeding spring; but in the following year, and subsequently, I have had abundant crops, equally dispersed over every part of the tree; and I have scarcely ever seen such an exuberance of blossoms as this tree presents in the present spring (1813). Grafts of eight different kinds of pears had been inserted, and all afforded fruit, and almost in equal abundance. By this mode of training, the bearing branches, being small and short, may be changed every three or four years, till the tree is a century old, without the loss of a single crop; and the central part, which is unproductive in every other mode of training, becomes the most fruitful. When a tree, thus trained, has perfectly covered the wall, it will have taken very nearly the form recommended by me in the Horticultural Transactions of 1808, except that the small branches necessarily pass down behind the large. I proceed to the management of young trees.

"A young pear-stock which had two lateral branches upon each side, and was about six feet high, was planted against a wall early in the spring of 1810; and it was grafted in each of its lateral branches; two of which sprang out of the stem about four feet from the ground, and the other at its summit, in the following year. The shoots these grafts produced, when about a foot long, were trained downwards, as in the preceding experiment, the undermost nearly perpendicular, and the uppermost just below the horizontal line, placing them at such distances, that the leaves of one shoot did not at all shade those of another. In the next year, the same mode of training was continued; and in the following, that is the last year, I obtained an abundant crop of fruit, and the tree is again heavily loaded with blossoms.

"This mode of training was first applied to the Aston town pear, which rarely produces fruit till six or seven years after the trees have been grafted; and from this variety, and the Colmar, I have not obtained fruit till the grafts have been three years old."

On scraping and clearing Apple Trees from Incrustations of Bark, Moss, &c. Monthly Magazine, No. 364.

How far the following process may be beneficial, beyond the mere clearing away parasitic or mossy vegetations from the surface of the tree, we cannot well determine: but we apprehend that the practice of scraping off any portion of the real bark ought to be very cautiously adopted.

"In my instruction in the way I manage my very *old trees*, I thought the mode I gave was perfectly clear, but your correspondent thought otherwise, therefore I shall endeavour to make my method more clear. In my address, your correspondent, on reading my instruction, will find I was only observing upon very *old trees*; 1 shall now endeavour to explain myself more clearly. It is observable in very old trees the greater part of the outward rind is mostly loose, so that it will easily peel off, and what will not come off, I take a bill and cut away, taking care to injure the middle rind as little as possible, though not to be prevented in a small degree. I took a small hoe, and scraped every branch, to clear away the moss, in doing which you will scrape a little of the thin coat of the outward rind, which will rather be of service than an injury; and all cankered parts I cut out, as my former instructions directed. My young trees I scrape in the same manner as the branches of the old, where there is any moss or unhealthy appearance by being much cracked and hide bound. I found it of great use; and if there is a want of wood, I take my knife and score through the rinds from the branches to the bottom of the stock, which will give a quantity of young wood: but if there is plenty to score, I would check these bearing. I found the scraping beneficial to most trees. I have proved it with a mulberry tree that was very much cracked (though a young tree); I scraped it to the bottom of the crack, but not to injure the middle rind, and found it greatly improved the following year. Some very old myrtle trees had a great deal of loose outward rind and moss; I scraped them on the same principle, with the same advantage. In stone fruit trees great care is required, as they are very much subject to gum, but scraping the bough does good, without going too deep. My soil of earth is a very strong clay, which is a great cause of some of my young trees not thriving well, and cankering; others do well and flourish. I have observed on the gravelly soil the same injury, and it would be a great benefit to the public, if the nurserymen would make it their duty to find out a stock that would thrive best on these soils, and give information through your magazine."

Detail of the Successful Result of an Experiment on Draining. By J. C. CURWEN, Esq.

Transactions of Society of Arts.

The authority of Mr. Curwen, in all agricultural matters, is so highly respected, that we cannot but oblige the public by aiding the promulgation of any doctrine or practice adopted by him. And with the view of still further effecting publicity we respectfully present his paper to our readers; premising that the thanks of the Society were voted to Mr. C. for the communication.

"The encouragement given by the Society of Arts for the improvement of agriculture, and every useful undertaking, emboldens me to submit to them the details of a work recently executed.

"In the present state of the country, more important service cannot be rendered it, than suggestions for the profitable application of capital to labour.

"Draining has universally been allowed to be the first and most essential step towards the permanent improvement of land. Fully as all writers are agreed upon this point, the cost that may profitably be expended in accomplishing this desirable object, is by no means ascertained; nor, till a few months ago, should I have ventured to have estimated its advantages, as I feel myself now justified in doing. A recent occurrence brought this point strongly under my observation.

"It may appear strange, that after twenty years' assiduous attention to agriculture, I should not have formed a pretty correct estimate of the injury sustained from the want of a proper drainage of spring and surface water on any one crop; but so in truth was the case.

"A field of forty acres, on the Schoose farm, was last year cropped with Swedish turnips; the land was winter-fallowed, and in the highest state of tillage, so as to admit of the turnips being sown in the latter end of April, previous to the long-continued wet, which proved so destructive to the turnip-crop in the north of England: it had thirty tons of good dung per acre. The crop averaged, on thirty-eight acres, thirty-two tons and a quarter per acre; that is, twenty-six of bulbs, and six and a quarter of tops: the produce of two other acres scarcely reached twenty tons. The soil and management was the same throughout. It is a strong clay, by no means applicable to the growth of turnips; but the farm afforded no other soil more proper for the purpose. These two acres had by some means been overlooked, when the rest of the field had been drained. The injury arose partly from springs, and partly from the surface-wet resting upon the land. The value of Swedes, in common years, is 10s. a ton for the bulbs; in the present year they would have sold at 15s. The loss, therefore, on twelve ton of bulbs, was eighteen pounds, besides the tops, which, at 2s. 6d. a ton, would have amounted to 1l. 10s., making a total of 19l. 10s.

"Seventy-two rods of drains (seven yards to the rod) were immediately cut, the cost of which was 5s. a rod, or 18l.

"Had the drainage been executed previous to putting in the crop, it would have been more than paid for by the produce of the present year.

"That good often results out of evil, was never more fully exemplified; and, with such a striking instance before me, of the advantages resulting from completely freeing the land from water, I was powerfully stimulated to undertake the re-drainage of a field of eighty acres, adjoining the Schoose farm buildings, and within less than half a mile of the town of Workington.

"I was still further excited by the daily and hourly applications for labour, arising, I fear, from the decreased and decreasing capital of the farmer.

"The scale of labour has annually been declining, which cannot but be a matter of deep regret to every friend to the country.

"The nation has witnessed scenes of great distress during the years of scarcity; but these bore no comparison to the present times.

"The hope of the privations being temporary, gave courage to bear up against them: but now the future has nothing to invigorate exertion, or inspire fortitude. Numbers are daily forced into the ranks of pauperism against their will. Industrious habits are destroyed, and with them that providence and forethought which is the basis of the happiness and respectability of the working classes. In order, not only to continue in employment the usual hands, but to extend it to the employing of others, at a season when the active labours of the year are nearly closed, I determined on undertaking the re-drainage of Walriggs, a field of eighty acres, which had been drained about eighteen years before, in a manner then considered to be effectual.

"The main drains, as far as they go, were well done; and these have been made available, in many instances, in the present drainage. They all run into the ditches which surround the whole, from which there is a considerable fall on every side of the field. The collateral drains were only twenty inches deep, set with three stones, in the form of a triangle, having about eight inches of cover upon the top. A drain of twenty inches was then thought to be sufficient; and all that was aimed at, was to cut off the springs, no regard being paid to carry off the rain water, which is so injurious to clay land.

"Subsequent experience has shown, that, in most instances the stratum which holds the water is at so great a depth, as to be below the bottom of such shallow drains; that, to do the work effectually, the drain must reach the stratum where the wet rests.

"The importance of deep ploughing was not heretofore known or provided for.

"Five years ago this field was deep ploughed: it had been foreseen, that in many instances the plough was likely to come in contact with the head of the drains: this did happen, and the consequence has been, to render the land as wet, or nearly so, as it was before any thing was done to it.

"Fifty out of the eighty acres were greatly injured by water. The work was commenced in November, and was finished the second week in January.

"The cutting was let, as it requires practice to keep the drain the exact width. Bad hands are apt to increase the dimensions, and thereby greatly augment the expense of filling, which is the expensive part of draining. Gathering and getting stones was done by the day, and employed a number of women and children, besides the persons occupied in the quarries, which were fortunately near at hand. The depth of the drains is from three feet and a half to four feet; the breadth, twenty inches at the top, and twelve inches at the bottom. The drains have a cavity at the bottom of six inches, being set with two side stones and a cover, and then filled with stones to the top, the six inches next the top being filled with small stones, that in case the plough should strike into them no injury is done to the drain. The drains are thus filled to within ten inches of the surface. It required a solid yard of stone to fill a rod of seven yards; in weight above two tons.

"To furnish such an enormous quantity of stones as eight hundred and fifty-nine rods required, was an undertaking of no small difficulty, and could not have been executed in the time, had not other substitutes been found. In coal countries there are strata known by the name of sill or schistus, and rattler, which is a mixture of coal and schistus. Sill is a substance that will not bear exposure to the atmosphere, but rattler does not fall, and is very light in comparison to its bulk.

"Recourse was had to these substances, and many hundred cart-loads of both were collected from the coal banks; the remainder was gathered from the ground, and obtained from the quarries.

	s.	d.
The cutting, filling, and setting, was	1	3 a rod.
Collecting stones, supposing two gathered to each rod	0	8
Two carts from the quarries	1	0
Loading	2	0
Cutting the drains by the plough	0	1
	5	0

"The distance the sill and rattler had to be led so increased the cost of the cartage as to make their cost equal to that of stones.

	£.	s.	d.
Cutting and filling 859 rods of seven yards, at 1s. 3d	53	13	9
3,436 cart loads of stones for filling, at 10d. a cart	143	3	4
Carting the above at 6d.	85	18	0
Filling, at 1d.	14	10	6
	£.297	5	7

"Fifty acres of the field have been benefited by this drainage. The general quality of land deciding the value at which it would be estimated to let, it was considered as worth 40s. an acre; from its locality, I conceive I am within bounds, when I rate it as worth from 50s. to 55s. The expenditure of 297l. has added 60l. to the value of the field, which is obtained at five years' purchase, or a little less for interest. It is to be observed, the horse-work is valued as if it had been hired; the real cost of that part, done at such a season, is not, to a farmer, one-half. My object was to put the cost at the highest point, more strongly to enforce the advantage resulting from the practice, as it thus leaves nothing to object to.

"This field had in the last course thirty tons of manure; it is strong clay. First crop potatoes, product twenty-six hundred stone *per* acre: sown with wheat and clover: both these crops were admirable. The oats this last year are calculated to produce sixty Winchester bushels *per* acre; it is now preparing for green crop again, and to have fifty tons of manure *per* acre. Admitting the green crop to profit 3l. *per* acre by the drainage, which is only half what was lost at average prices this year on the Swede crop, this, on the fifty acres, would be 150l.; calculating it to yield three Winchester bushels *per* acre more of wheat, at 7s. *per* bushel, this would be 52l. 10s. 10d. *per* acre; for the clover for two years 50l. more, making a probable increase of produce, without any extra expense, of 252l. 10s. Thus, in five years' course, the whole expense will, in all probability, be repaid, and an annual permanent increase of rent, to the amount of sixty *per cent.* gained.

"Wet is more destructive to pasture than it is to grain and green crops; and as pasture is the most material object near to towns, draining, in such situations, is a more profitable improvement than in any other situation, and will consequently justify a greater expense.

"When once dry land is well laid down to pasture, the improvement is permanent. If flooded with water, it cannot remain for any length of time in pasture, but must be again brought under tillage. On wet soils, improvement is almost labour in vain—costly at all times, but now ruinous."

On the Geology of Ceylon.

Dr. Davy's Travels in Ceylon.

"In Ceylon, nothing is to be observed of that order and succession of rocks that occur in Saxony and in England, and in many parts of Europe. Uniformity of formation is the most remarkable feature in the geological character of the island. As far as my information extends, the whole of Ceylon, with very few exceptions, consists of primitive rock. Another remarkable geological circumstance is, that though the varieties of primitive rock are extremely numerous, and indeed almost infinite, the species are very few, and seldom well defined. The most prevailing species is granite, or gneiss; the most limited are quartz rock, hornblende rock, and dolomite rock, and a few others, which may be considered, perhaps, with advantage under the head of imbedded minerals.

"The varieties of granite and gneiss are innumerable, passing from one to another, and occasionally changing their character altogether, and assuming appearances, for which, in small masses, it would be extremely difficult to find appropriate names. Regular granite is not of very common occurrence. One of the best instances I know of it, is in the neighbourhood of Point de Galle, where it is of a grey colour, and fine grained. Graphic granite is still rarer. The only good example of it with which I am acquainted is at Trincomalee, where it occurs of a beautiful quality, on the sea shore, about half a mile beyond Chapel Point, imbedded in a granite rock. The quartz in this instance is black or grey rock crystal, and the feldspar highly crystalline, and of a bright flesh colour. The quartz envelopes the feldspar in very thin hexagonal or triagonal cases, so that nothing can be more different in the appearance than the longitudinal and transverse fracture of the rock. Neither is sienite common. It occurs, rather forming a part of rocks of a different kind, than in great mountain masses. Well formed gneiss is more abundant than granite. Its peculiar structure may be seen in many places, but no where more beautiful than at Amanapoora, in the Kandyan provinces, where it consists of white feldspar and quartz, in a finely crystalline state, with layers of black mica, containing, disseminated through it, numerous crystals of a light coloured garnet. The more limited varieties of primitive rock, as quartz, hornblende, and dolomite rock, seldom occur in the form of mountain masses.

" Quartz in large veins and imbedded masses, is abundant in the granite rocks. It is in general milk-white, translucent, full of rents, and so very friable as to remind one of unannealed glass.

" Pure hornblende and primitive greenstone are far from uncommon. They constitute no entire mountain or hill that I am aware of, but they form a part of many, particularly of Adam's Peak, and of the hills and mountains adjoining Kandy.

" The varieties of dolomite are almost as numerous as those of granite. When purest, it is snow-white, generally crystalline, often highly crystalline, composed of rhombs that are easily separated by a smart blow, but rarely finely granular. I found a specimen of the highly crystalline kind, of specific gravity 1·93, composed of

Carbonate of magnesia	56·0
Carbonate of lime	36·9
Alumina	4·1
Silica	1·0
Water	2·0
	100·0

" A very fine granular kind, of a beautiful whiteness, well adapted for statuary purposes, is found in the neighbourhood of Port Macdonald. A specimen of it that I tried was of specific gravity 2·74, and contained only a very small proportion of carbonate of magnesia. The varieties of most importance are mixtures of dolomite with feldspar and mica, and even quartz. It is in rocks of this kind that the nitre caves of the interior are found.

" In external character and general structure, the varieties of primitive rock exhibit fewer marked differences than might be expected à priori.

" The recent formation is highly deserving of investigation, both as a partial exception to the comprehensive idea, that the whole island is composed of primitive rock, and on account of its own interesting nature. The rock that occurs in this formation, is of two kinds, limestone and sandstone; both of these may become very useful. Very good lime may be made of the former, and serviceable mill-stones may perhaps be made of the latter, if it can be found, as is very probable, of a coarse quality."

On the Saline Productions of Ceylon.

"The saline productions of Ceylon are far from numerous. The only salts, the existence of which I have ascertained in a satisfactory manner, are the following; viz. nitre, nitrate of lime, sulphate of magnesia, alum, and common salt. These salts, with the exception of common salt, have been found hitherto in the interior only, and in certain caves, where, not being liable to be washed away by the heavy tropical rains, they admit of being detected.

"Nitre and nitrate of lime are of frequent occurrence. Judging from four nitre caves that I have visited, and from the specimens of rocks of several more that I have examined, I believe that they are all very similar; and that the rock in which they occur, in every instance, contains at least feldspar and carbonate of lime; from the decomposition of the former of which, the alkaline base of the salt is generally derived, and by the peculiar influence of the latter (yet not at all understood) on the oxygen and azote of the atmosphere, the acid principle is generated.

"*Nitre Cave of Memoora.*—The first view of the place was exceedingly striking. A large cave appeared in a perpendicular face of rock, about 300 feet high, crowned with forest, at the base of which was a stage, or platform, of rubbish, that seemed in danger of sliding into a deep, wooded, valley, closed in by mountains of considerable elevation and remarkable boldness. The cave was 200 feet deep; and at its mouth, which was nearly semicircular, about 80 feet high, and 100 wide. Its floor was rocky and steep, rapidly ascending inward, and its extremity was narrow and dark. To facilitate the ascent, ladders were placed in the most difficult situations. The nature of the rock of which the walls of the cave are formed, has already been described. The workmen, whom I found at their labours, sixteen in number, were the rudest set of artificers I ever witnessed; their bodies, almost naked, were soiled with dirt, and their bushy beards and hair were matted, and powdered, with brown dust. When I arrived, they were occupied, not in the cave, but on the platform before it, attending to the operations that were then going on in the open air, of filtration, evaporation, and crystallization. The apparatus employed was curious, from its simplicity and rudeness. A small stream of water was led from a distance to the place by a pipe of bamboos; the filters were of matting, in the shape of square boxes, supported by sticks; and the evaporating vessels, and indeed all the vessels used, were the common chatties of the country; of which a great many were assembled, of various sizes. The cave may be considered partly natural and partly artificial. I was informed that, during the last fifty years, for six months in the dry season, it has been annually worked; and that each man was required to furnish a load of nitre, which is about 60 pounds, to the royal stores."

Saltpetre.—The preparing of saltpetre, and the manufacture of gunpowder, are arts which the Singalese, for many years, have practised. The process of preparing the salt, in many parts of the country, was very similar. When the salt occurred impregnating the surface of the rock, as in the cave near Memoora, the surface was chipped off with small strong axes; and the chippings, by pounding, were reduced to a state of powder. This powder, or the loose fine earth, which, in most of the caves, contained the saline impregnations, was well mixed with an equal quantity of wood-ash. The mixture was thrown on a filter, formed of matting, and washed with cold water. The washings of the earth were collected in an earthen vessel, and evaporated at a boiling temperature till concentrated to that degree that a drop let fall on a leaf became a soft solid. The concentrated solution was set aside; and when it had crystallized, the whole was put on a filter of mat. The mother lye that passed through, still rich in saltpetre, was added to a fresh weak solution, to be evaporated again: and the crystals, after having been examined, and freed from any other crystals of a different form, were either immediately dried, or, if not sufficiently pure, redissolved and crystallized afresh. The operations just described were generally carried on at the nitre caves. In the province of the Seven Korles, besides extracting the salt at the caves, the workmen brought a quantity of the earth to their houses; where, keeping it under shed, protected from the wind and rain, without any addition excepting a little wood-ash, they obtain from it, every third year, a fresh quantity of salt.

Common Salt.—Dr. Davy says that common salt forms in great quantities in certain lakes on the sea shore; but of rare occurrence indeed in the interior, except in very minute quantity. The Doctor has given a detailed account of the manner in which salt is procured, and is decidedly of opinion that the sea is the source from which the salt is derived, and that evaporation is the cause of its production or formation. He observes, that the importance of the subject is greater than may be presumed by a casual reader, the monopoly of salt of the Megam-pattoo yielding Government a revenue of at least 10,000*l*. a year, and the whole island being almost entirely dependant on that district for the supply of this necessary of life. He adds: " Were the salt lakes scientifically managed, they might be made to yield not only any quantity of common salt to supply all India, but almost any quantity of magnesia might be extracted from the residual brine."

On the Chinese Method of Printing. By Mr. MILNE.

We consider the following as a very interesting subject; and as such, beg leave to present it to our readers. It will show that the Chinese were far before us in the adoption of particular modes of impressing characteristic signs, on the stereotype principle; and that the art of printing, generally, has been studied by them in a particular degree, is evinced in the diversified methods occasionally resorted to.

"The Chinese have three methods of printing. The first invented, and that which almost universally prevails, is called '*Moh-pan*, or *wooden plates*.' It is a species of stereotype, and answers all the ends thereof, as the letters do not require to be distributed and re-composed; but, being once clearly cut, they remain, till either the block be destroyed, or till the characters be so worn down by the ink-brush, as to be illegible.

"The second is called Lah-pan, i. e. '*wax-plates*,' and consists in spreading a coat of wax on a wooden frame, after which, with a graving tool, they cut the characters thereon. This method is rarely adopted, except in cases of haste and urgency; and it differs from the former only in the kind of plate on which the words are engraved. This sort of printing I have not seen practised by the Chinese, nor observed it noticed in any book. The printers employed at Malacca, say, that when an urgent affair occurs, a number of workmen are called in, and a small slip of wood, with space for one, two, or more lines, is given to each, which they cut with great expedition, and when all is finished, join together by small wooden pins; by this means, a page, or a sheet, is got up very speedily, like an extra gazette in an English printing-office. This method, they say, is, from its expeditiousness, called *Lah-pan*, and they know nothing of the other.

"The third is denominated Hwo-pan, '*living plates*,' so called from the circumstance of the characters being single, and moveable, as the types used in European printing. *Kang-he*, in 1722, had a great number of these moveable types made of copper, whether *cut* or *cast*, it is not said. The Chinese are not, however, entirely ignorant of *casting*, though they do not use it to any extent. The Imperial seals on the Calendar, are cast with the Chinese character on one half of the face, and the Manchow-Tartar on the other. Copper vessels used in the temples, and bells, have frequently ancient characters, and inscriptions, cast with them. Whether they have ever attempted to cast single characters, or to frame matrices, similar to those which are used in casting types for alphabetic languages, does not appear.

These Hwo-pan, or moveable types, are commonly made of *wood*. The Canton daily paper, called *Yuen-mun-pao* (i. e. A report from the outer gate of the palace,) containing about 500 words, or monosyllables, is printed with these wooden types, but in so clumsy a manner as to be scarcely legible.

"At Macao, in the Missionary department of the College of St. Joseph, I have seen several large cases full of this description of type, with which they print such Roman Catholic books as are wanted for the Missions. In the Anglo-Chinese College Library at Malacca, there is *a Life of the Blessed Virgin* in two, and *the Lives of the Saints* in 26 volumes, 18mo. printed with the wooden type, at the College of St. Joseph; but all that can be said of the printing is, that it is barely legible—a vast difference between it and the other Catholic books, which were executed in the common way,—those of them that were cut at Pekin, in blocks, are elegantly printed. On asking the priests at St. Joseph's, the reason why they used the moveable type, seeing it was so much inferior in beauty to the other method, they answered, that the persecutions in China had obliged them to adopt this method, as blocks were more cumbersome, and not so easily carried off, or hidden, in cases where the Missionaries were obliged to flee, or where they expected a search to be made by the Mandarines. The copper types look better on the paper than the wooden ones; but the impression is inferior in beauty to that from moderately well executed blocks. A history of the *Loo-choo* Islands, in 4 vols. octavo, compiled by the authority of *Keen-lung*, was printed with copper types; and may be given as an instance of this inferiority, though its execution is by no means bad. The Chinese have no press; but whether the forms are of wooden blocks, waxen plates, or moveable types, they have the same method of printing, or casting off, that is, by means of a dry brush rubbed over the sheet.

"The Chinese have six different kinds, or rather six different forms, of the character, each of which has its appropriate name, and all of which are occasionally used in printing. That which, like our *Roman*, prevails most generally, is called *Sung-te*. To write this form of the character, is of itself an employment in China. There are men who learn it on purpose, and devote themselves entirely to the labour of transcribing for the press. Few of the learned can write it: indeed, they rather think it below them to do the work of a mere transcriber. With respect to moveable types, the body of the type being prepared, the character is written *inverted*, on the top: this is a more difficult work than to write for blocks. After this, the type is fixed in a mortise, by means of two small pieces of wood, joined together by a wedge, and then engraved; after which it is taken out, and the face lightly drawn across a whetstone, to take off any rough edge that the carving instrument may have left.

"The process of preparing for and printing with the blocks, or in the stereotype way, is as follows: The block or wooden plate, ought to be of the *Lee*, or *Tsaou* tree, which they describe thus:—'The *Lee* and *Tsaou* are of a fine grain, hard, oily, and shining; of a sourish taste; and what vermin do not soon touch, hence used in printing.' The plate is first squared to the size of pages, with the margin at top and bottom; and is in thickness generally about half an inch. They then smooth it on both sides with a joiner's plane; each side contains two pages, or rather, indeed, but one page, according to the Chinese method of reckoning; for they number the *leaves*, not the pages of a book. The surface is then rubbed over with rice, boiled to a paste, or some glutinous substance, which fills up any little indentments, not taken out by the plane; and softens and moistens the face of the board, so that it more easily receives the impression of the character.

"The transcriber's work is, first to ascertain the exact size of the page, the number of lines, and of characters in each line; and then to make what they call a Kih, or form of lines, horizontal and perpendicular, crossing each other at right angles, and thus leaving a small square for each character—the squares for the same sort of character, are all of equal size, whether the letter be complicated as to strokes, or simple: a letter or character with fifty strokes of the pencil, has no larger space assigned to it than one with barely a single stroke. This makes the page regular and uniform in its appearance, though rather crowded, where many complicated characters follow each other in the same part of the line. The margin is commonly at the top of the page, though not always so.—Marginal notes are written, as with us, in a smaller letter. This form of lines, being regularly drawn out, is sent to the printer, who cuts out all the squares, leaving the lines prominent; and then prints off as many sheets, commonly in *red ink*, as are wanted. The transcriber then, with black ink, writes in the squares from his copy; fills up the sheet; points it: and sends it to the block-cutter, who, before the glutinous matter is dried up from the board, puts the sheet on inverted, rubs it with a brush and with his hand, till it sticks very close to the board. He next sets the board in the sun, or before the fire, for a little, after which he rubs off the sheet entirely with his fingers: but not before a clear impression of each character has been communicated. The graving tools are then employed, and all the white part of the board is cut out, while the black, which shows the character, is carefully left. The block being cut, with edged tools of various kinds, the process of printing follows. The block is laid on a table; and a brush made of hair, being dipped in ink, is lightly drawn over the face. The sheets being already prepared, each one is laid on the block, and gently pressed down by the rubbing of a kind of brush, made of the hair of the Tsung tree. The sheet is then thrown off; one man will throw off 2000 copies in a day. Chinese paper is very thin, and not generally printed on both sides, though in some particular cases that is also done. In binding, the Chinese fold up the sheet, turning inward that side on which there is no impression. On the middle of the sheet, just where it is folded, the title of the book, the number of the leaves, and of the sections, and also sometimes the subject treated of, are printed, the same as in European books, except that in the latter, they are at the top of the page, whereas here, they are on the front-edge of the leaf; and generally cut so exactly on the place where it is folded, that one, in turning the leaves, sees one half of each character on one side, and the other half on the other. The number of sheets destined to constitute the volume, being laid down and pressed between two boards, on the upper one of which a heavy stone is laid, they are then covered with a sort of coarse paper—not with boards as in Europe; the back is then cut, after which the volume is stitched, not in our way, but through the whole volume at once, from side to side, a hole having been previously made through it with a small pointed iron instrument. The top and the bottom are then cut, and thus the whole process of Chinese type-cutting, printing, and binding, is finished. Though the transcribing, cutting, printing, and binding, form each a distinct occupation, yet they can be all easily united in one person. The first person employed as a Chinese printer by the Mission at Malacca, performed all these himself.

"The Chinese type-cutting, which is called Kih-tzse, is of two different kinds: the one is denominated Yang-wan, i. e. '*masculine letter*.' In this the strokes which form the character are carefully left untouched and prominent on the face of the plate, and all other parts cut out, and after printing, the black or *inked* part exhibits the character. This is the common and prevailing kind of letter. The other is called Yin-wan, i. e. '*feminine letter*;' and is the very reverse of the former: here the strokes which form the character alone are cut out, and all the rest left untouched; hence, after printing, the white or *uninked* part exhibits the character. This kind of letter is very little used. In the *Commentaries* of books, at the head of the first line of a paragraph, one, two, or three Yin-wan characters are sometimes employed, to introduce the subject; or as a head line; or to mark the nature of the paragraph, whether paraphrastic, explanatory, or critical: or to refer to some highly valuable author. This division of the printed character into masculine and feminine, is a further proof of what has already been noticed respecting the powerful hold which the hermaphrodite principle has of the notions of the Chinese.

"The method of printing now described, has existed in China for upwards of 900 *years*; and has been applied to all the various kinds of composition; to books on politics, on history, on ethics, on philosophy, and on science, whether in poetry or in prose. It has likewise been applied to all dimensions of books, from the *elephant folio* down to the *one hundred and twenty-eights*; to all sizes of letter, from the twenty-lines pica to the diamond; to all kinds of character, whether plain or hieroglyphic, whether the manuscript or printed form; to all sorts of ornaments and borders; and in some cases to foreign languages as well as the native. Of this last there is an example in the *Lung-wie-pe shoo*, a miscellaneous work, consisting of eighty duodecimo volumes: the eight last volumes of this book are devoted to the purposes of general geography, giving very brief sketches of the countries bordering on China, and westward through India, Persia, Arabia, Turkey, Europe, Africa, and the Malay Archipelago, round by Formosa and Corea, to Tartary. In these, besides specimens of the coins, and costumes of various nations, there are exhibited also specimens of *seven* different languages, both of the character and sounds, among which the Burman, the Sanscrit, the Pali, and the Arabic, may be particularly mentioned. And two of the volumes contain a copious vocabulary of a foreign language, in which the characters are cut in wood, just as the Chinese, and the sounds imperfectly expressed by Chinese characters. Tartar-Chinese and Chinese-Tartar Dictionaries furnish another example of the application of the Chinese method of printing to foreign languages. In the Tartar-Chinese Dictionaries, the words to be defined are Tartar, and the definition is Chinese: in the Chinese-Tartar the reverse takes place, just as in any of our Latin and Greek, and Greek and Latin Dictionaries.

" With respect to the *advantages and disadvantages* of the Chinese method of printing, as contrasted with the European, it would require a person more fully acquainted with both, than the writer of this can pretend to be. In order to do perfect justice to the subject, three things must be premised:—That *the Chinese language is essentially different from alphabetic languages*—and that though the European mode of printing alphabetic languages, will here be frequently adverted to, yet it is *the European mode as applied to the Chinese language, in which the contrast is chiefly intended*. And finally, *that the Chinese mode of printing must chiefly be viewed as it exists in China, among the Chinese themselves*—and not as cumbered with the extreme disadvantages under which it appears abroad. Let these three things be kept in mind: how they bear on the subject will appear as we go along.

"The *disadvantages* of the Chinese mode of printing with wooden blocks may perhaps be such as the following:—1. It does not seem so well adapted for miscellaneous pieces, and works of an ephemeral kind, (e. g. newspapers, lists of sales, bills, &c.) as the European method, because the expense of preparing a block, say, for an Extra Gazette, which may never be called for after the first impression is struck off, would be just as great as to prepare one for a book of lasting utility, which may be called for in ten or fifteen years hence.

"2. It does not appear so well suited for expedition as the European method is. The characters require considerable time in cutting; a hundred and fifty per day being about the number which a good workman can cut, taking the whole year together.—In regard to casting off impressions, there may perhaps be very little difference, except where a press admits of a large form; in that case, the Chinese method, which admits generally of no more than two pages, will be found the slowest. But suppose an European press to admit a form of four pages only, then I conceive there will be scarce any difference, because the European press requires two men to work it, and the Chinese only one; and two Chinese workmen, each printing from a separate block, will, between them, throw off about as many sheets in a day as the two men at the English press can, supposing both parties equally qualified in regard to skill and strength. But if the European press be wrought by *Europeans*, not by people brought up in India, then in point of speed the advantage will doubtless be in favour of the European method.

"3. When printing is extensively carried on in the Chinese method, blocks greatly accumulate and become cumbersome; because, however many inches of letter press there may be in a book from beginning to end, there must be exactly as many inches of block, so that a book of the size of an octavo

Testament, will require a common trunk to contain the blocks, though closely packed up.—In Chinese printing-offices, the blocks are all laid on their edge, on the shelves of a wooden frame, like a book-case. In the *Hae-chang-sze* printing-office, there is a vast number piled up on such frames. The blocks of a book of 240 large octavo vols. like the *Tatsing-ye-'tung-che*, must require a very large space to contain them. This disadvantage the method has in common with European stereotype. Both sides of the wooden plate are, however, uniformly cut, in order to diminish the number as much as possible.

" 4. When a very large edition is printed off from the blocks; the face of the character wears down, and it loses in some measure its clearness; hence the page is apt to have a blotted appearance. This is naturally to be expected of wooden plates, however fine the grain of the wood may be, and however durable its quality. The Chinese try to modify this disadvantage by repeatedly drying the blocks, and not suffering the face to soften by being kept long wet with the ink. After printing 2000 or 3000 copies, they gently wash the plate and let it dry.

" The permanent clearness of a Chinese impression depends greatly on the quality of the wood of which the plate is made; on the goodness of the type-cutter's work; on the proper tempering of the ink, and on the care of the printer. If, for example, the printer be a clumsy or careless workman, the very first thousand copies will appear blotted, and the blocks will not last any length of time—perhaps they will not bear casting off 6 or 7000 copies without being renewed, or at least repaired. I am not able to say, with certainty, *what number* of copies good blocks will bear to be cast off: our printers there affirm, that *thirty thousand* can be printed from the same plate, if it possess the qualities and advantages above-mentioned. From some that we have used, in the service of the Mission, upwards of *ten thousand* copies have been printed, and they seem perfectly able to bear another edition of the same number, if carefully treated.— Indeed, no printing with moveable metal types that has been executed here, or that we have yet seen from India, equals in beauty the elegant editions of some valuable books printed with blocks at Pekin; but such elegant books are not intended, nor well fitted, for general dispersion; and, after allowing the very utmost to the block-printing which its most firm supporters could demand, the palm, in regard to a clear and durable legible impression, must undoubtedly be yielded to the metal.

" 5. The necessity of cutting the same character over and over again, if it should occur a thousand, or five thousand times in the same book; and the inapplicability of the blocks to any work but that one for which they were prepared—are to be esteemed great disadvantages.

" 6. The Chinese mode of printing is, like their national policy, very unsociable; it is ill suited to sort with that used in other languages. Attempts have been made at different times to combine blocks and types in the same form; but they do not look well; and they must be exceedingly inconvenient, difficult to fit in, and cannot fail to render the execution very tedious. In some works on the Chinese language published in France, and in Dr. Marshman's Confucius, this combination seems to have been attempted; but, it must have been attended with infinite trouble, and, after all, is very inferior and even awkward in its appearance. Since the casting of the Chinese character in India, and the engraving of moulds at Macao, began, the combination is just as easy and beautiful as that of Greek and English—or Latin and Arabic. Here again, the Chinese mode appears to great [disadvantage, and the palm must be yielded to the moveable metallic types.

" 7. To these we may add, that Chinese blocks are of no service when the characters are worn down; whereas, metal types, however old, furnish the materials of a new font. They can be recast. Other disadvantages may deserve notice, but these are what have occurred to the writer, as the chief ones.

" The *advantages* of the Chinese method of printing with wooden-blocks, when contrasted with the European method as applied to the Chinese language, may be such as the following.

" 1. It seems suited to the nature of the language. The

difference between alphabetic languages, and the language of China, is very great. In the former, the number of letters seldom exceeds *forty*, which being variously combined, can form all the words in the language—while there are more than *forty thousand* in the latter. The preparing of 40,000 matrixes, in which to cast these characters, is a formidable undertaking; while to cut them in wood appears comparatively easy. But as this part of the subject will be more fully discussed, when we come to consider the head of *expense*, I shall dismiss it by remarking, that though a selection of perhaps *ten thousand* characters of most frequent use, may be made, for which to form matrixes, and the herculean task thus greatly abridged; yet the characters in less frequent use must now and then be employed, if a man write extensively; and suppose he requires to use any given character only twice in his life, yet for this character he must be at the same cost to provide a matrix, as for one which may be required 5000 times—suppose such a matrix to cost *twenty shillings;* now, for these *twenty shillings* he can have more than *fifteen hundred* characters cut in wood. In this there appears a vast and manifest advantage in the Chinese method. There are no rules, so far as I know, by observing which a man may avoid the necessity of using such a character, but one, and that is by substituting a synonymous character; this may sometmes be done; but in the greater number of instances, the sense would suffer by such a proceeding; for, as the Chinese themselves observe, respecting their synonymous characters, ' Though they seem alike in meaning, yet there are certain shades of difference; and though in some instances they may be used for each other, yet in very few, with equal justness, clearness, and force.'—The more fully we study Chinese, so much the more will this observation be confirmed.

"2. It possesses all the advantages of European stereotype, except two—durability of the block, and the combining of several pages in a large form for printing. In most other respects the advantages are equal, and in one particular, superior, namely, in the ease with which the Chinese block is prepared—in correcting, also, I imagine the advantage will be in favour of the Chinese mode.

"3. In the Chinese method, all sizes and forms of the character may be cut by the same hand, with nearly equal expedition and cheapness. Suppose a book on science, illustrated by a paraphrase and notes. Here the text would be in a larger letter, the paraphrase in a smaller, and the notes in a third size.—There must be *three* different founts of *types*—to these add the mathematical, astronomical, and physical signs, all of which in the work supposed, would find their place—thus matrixes for three different sorts of signs must be prepared. Here then is a combination of *six* kinds of letters and signs, which require to be cast in *six* different kinds of matrixes, and to be arranged in *six* different cases or departments: so many matrixes must be very expensive—and so many cases must require a good deal of room. Turn now to the Chinese method; and you see the same man combine all the three sizes of letter, and all the three sorts of signs in the same page: cut them all with the same instruments; and for about the same price, as if they were all the common letter. The Chinese do not, indeed, use the same signs in scientific books as we do; but from their simplicity (two or three excepted) it would be an easy matter to introduce them; or to substitute other marks, equally efficient, but more familiar to the Chinese—and to either of which, the reasoning here would apply with equal force. This may be extended not only to characters of all sizes, supposing them so many as *twenty*; but likewise to all their diversified *forms*, to the *Chuen, Le, Tsaou, Hing, Sung, Kae-shoo*, and other forms, with nearly equal facility. I say *nearly* equal, because there would be really *some* difference both in regard to speed and expense. A very large, or very small size of character, and their less frequently recurring forms, will necessarily make some difference; but not so as to affect the argument at all. Now, if it be considered that for all these, no moulds and matrixes for casting, no cases for arranging of them, (the block-frames excepted) and no particular qualification in setting up, beyond skill of hand in tracing the lines on the copy, are required, there will appear an astonishing advantage on the side of the Chinese method. Whether that may not be counterbalanced, by the disadvantages that attend it, must be left to the judgment of the reader.

"4. The apparatus necessary for the whole process of Chinese printing, is exceedingly simple. No foundry for casting; no complicated machines for printing and binding; and no heavy-rented house for a printing-office, are here required. In printing Chinese on a small scale, every instrument necessary for the whole process, (a table and chair excepted) may be carried in the workman's hand, in a tolerably large pocket handkerchief, and all the work performed in the corner of a cellar, or garret, without noise, and by the labour of one person only. And to carry it on an extensive scale, a common trunk of four feet by two and a half, if well packed, will contain the whole requisite apparatus. The disadvantage of the Chinese *press*, (or rather of their way of casting off sheets, for a press it cannot be properly called) in not admitting to print large forms at once, is, in some measure, counterbalanced by the remarkable simplicity and consequent cheapness of its apparatus.

"5. There may be a considerable saving of expense in paper, on the Chinese plan.—Moveable types cannot be kept long standing; an edition of some extent must be printed off at once; if not, the labour of distributing and composing the type several times, must be submitted to. If a large edition be struck off, a considerable sum of money must be at once sunk in paper, and if there be not a rapid demand for the book, the chances are that no small proportion of the copies will be entirely lost. But with the wooden blocks (as with European stereotype,) there need be no more cast off than to serve the immediate demand, and no more paper purchased than the copies require. Thus, neither the out-lay of capital, nor the loss of interest, nor the rent of warehouses, need be incurred. If a hundred copies be wanted, they are cast off. When a second demand for another hundred, or for a thousand, comes, it is served also; and so on through ten or twenty different editions, if the blocks last as long—and at such intervals of time as the circumstances may require, in as much as the blocks once prepared require no further labour.

"6. The Chinese method possesses some advantages for

security against error, and even for progressive improvement in the style of a book, which deserve notice. Chinese books, it is true, are often full of typographical errors; but that is entirely owing to the neglect of those who execute, or superintend the execution of them, and not at all incident to the mode itself. For, if the plates be once correct, they remain so through whatever number of editions may be cast off. Let us suppose good plates, well cut, and corrected, to last for twenty years to come, (and if well cared for, they will perhaps last this length of time,) and that an edition is cast off every year. The care of the author is exerted to the utmost over the first edition, which he renders correct; but through all the subsequent nineteen editions, no farther attention is required from him. Should he go abroad, the printing of his book, through the given twenty years, will not suffer by his absence. Should he die, it will be the same—the blocks may be left as an inheritance to his children, who though they may not know a single character themselves, have only to hire in by the day, the nearest workman, (as ignorant of letters as they are,) and print to supply the present demand, or fifty subsequent ones; and at the distance of twenty years from the author's death, the twentieth edition will be just as correct as the first was. In books of standard value, this is of incalculable importance, as every new edition by moveable types is in danger of superadding a fresh share of errors."

Description of the Glaciers.

Letters from France and Switzerland.

The unparalleled phœnomenon of the Glaciers has been described by many wandering travellers; but it is so sublime a subject for philosophical consideration, that we cannot place it too conspicuously before the mind's eye. And thinking the following is as lively, and as correct, an account as any extant, we transcribe it into the Focus; having omitted some digressive flights of the writer, with which the reader may very well dispense.

" If we may judge from appearances, the far greater part

of this extensive valley of the Arve was formerly a chain of lakes, and one in particular is known to have been near Servoz. In the centre of this lake, stood, on a craggy island, the castle of St. Michel, and a few miles below was the little town of St. Denys, not far, in all probability, from where the *pont des chevres* is placed on the map. Could an inhabitant of those days be called to life again, how great would be his astonishment, at the change which has taken place! The poor dismantled remains of St. Michel are no longer on an island. The lake disappeared by the sudden failure of the mound which supported it, and the waters, in their retreat, swept away the town and all its inhabitants. It must have been a horrible catastrophe, and as unexpected as it was irresistible. For an hour or two from Servoz (for in this country they count by hours and not by miles,) the road has more the appearance of stairs, badly cut in the rock, than of a means of communication in carriages. Evan the *char-a-banc*, of which I send you a drawing, is with difficulty dragged along. To the right is a steep, impending rock; to the left is a precipice, with the Arve bursting his way from one obstacle to another, at the bottom. The opposite side rises abruptly to a very great height, and almost perpendicularly; and yet, not far from the summit, I observed a man mowing. The spot which was to reward his industry, seemed less than a quarter of an acre. It lay, like an island, amid a waste of barren rocks, and was so steep, that had he lost his foot-hold, he must have fallen into a chasm of at least 2000 feet.

" The Arve runs along the middle, and on either side, the banks, which rise by a very rapid slope, are diversified by various sorts of produce, till they become too steep, or too barren, to be cultivated. Houses and villages are thickly scattered, and every thing bespeaks plenty and good husbandry, while the glaciers, which, like enormous icicles, are protruded down the sides of the mountains they belong to, create a contrast with the beauties of vegetation, which exceeds all I ever beheld, in novelty and in magnificence.

" Hitherto, the inhabitants of Savoy, though frequently in possession of a fertile soil, had appeared a poor, dispirited, and miserable race; and the shepherdesses of the Alps had looked more like gypsies, than those elegant rural forms which the genius of painting has bestowed upon them. But in the valley of Chamouny the race of the inhabitants seemed improved; the men are well looking and well behaved, and the women are a great proportion of them pretty; all seemed industrious, and their children were well clothed.

"The moonlight view from Chamouny is extremely sublime. At a small distance appears Mont Blanc, at the perpendicular height, above the valley, of upwards of 12,000 feet, and to the left is a range of lofty eminences, the lowest of which would, in any other situation, command the admiration of travellers.

"The next morning, at an early hour, we proceeded to ascend a mountain, which is on the opposite side of the valley to the Montanvert, each of us mounted on a mule, and each accompanied by a guide on foot. These guides are a race of active, intelligent, good humoured people, who live by attending strangers on such occasions, and know the value of a good character. The ascent was every where rapid, and the road, in some places, was but a narrow shelf, hanging suspended over a frightful declivity; so perfectly surefooted, however, are the mules, and so entirely do they assume the management upon these occasions, that no one seems afraid. After a long ascent, we found ourselves on an eminence, which the calculations of geometers have fixed at 3000 feet above the Priory; and here, upon turning round, we beheld Mont Blanc, in all its sublimity of height and of eternal snow. The other mountains and needles of granite, were like enormous giants upon guard around its base. It seemed as if the curtain of creation had been raised, as if we were arrived at some other world. It is hence that the efforts of those who have attained to the top of Mont Blanc may be conceived, and that the various glaciers may be traced from their origin, in the mountains, to the valley below. We remained here about half an hour, and then descended a little lower, to a a spring, where, as Mr. Coxe expresses himself, we refreshed ourselves with some cold victuals we had brought with us. Plain truth needs, indeed, no flowers of speech, but such a dinner, in such a place, is deserving of a few words more.

A rock, from which the water sprung, served us as a table, and towards the end of our dinner, we were joined by two young women of Chamouny, with baskets of berries, which they had collected from the rocks above us. They were attended by a gothard, who, with a hunting horn slung from his neck, and with a wild yet good natured countenance, was the very emblem of rural simplicity.

"The comfortable accommodation of a good inn enabled us to undertake the ascent of the Montanvert the next day; but the mules which we set out upon could only carry us half-way up, and it was necessary to perform the rest of the expedition on foot. This our ladies prepared themselves for with courage, and each placing herself between two guides, who walked one before and the other behind her, and resting with either hand upon two poles, the extremities of which were held horizontally by the guides, moved slowly forwards, while the others of us walked singly. We ascended in this manner about three miles, from where the mules were left, stopping frequently to take breath, and admiring, at every pause, the beauty of the valley below us, in which the narrow fields of grain, of clover, and of potatoes, seemed spread along like ribbons. We passed below many fragments of rock, which seemed to have been accidentally impeded on their descent towards the foot of the mountain, and over some steep gullies, where a person committing himself to his own weight, would have descended with frightful velocity. We approached, at length, to an open space: it was a small pasturage, and there was a hut and another small building of apparently elegant construction, which seemed ready for our reception; but the sensation of fatigue gave way to that of admiration or surprise, when, on moving across the narrow space which terminated the ascent, we found ourselves on the brink of another valley, broader than that of Chamouny, and filled up to within a few hundred feet with ice, which rose into a variety of forms and inequalities. This is the place described by travellers as the sea of ice, and which, extending for several miles, and bordered by high, inaccessible, and naked rocks of granite, and opening from place to place into frightful chasms, seems the seat of eternal winter.

"If you can suppose, for a moment, the valley which leads through the S. W. mountains from immediately behind the house at Belvoir, filled up with snow blown from the neighbouring heights, and that snow compressed by its own weight, and connected into one mass by the water, which, trickling through from the surface, becomes frozen as it descends, and the extremity of this mighty mass protruded into the old fields, and ending abruptly, and a rapid stream issuing from below it, you may form some idea of what a glacier is. Mr. Coxe gives a very good description of the scene which was now before us, availing himself of those who have gone before him, and particularly of M. de Saussure. We left some of our company at the top of the mountain, and descending with the others to the surface of the sea of ice, advanced upon it with great caution, as you may imagine, for about 150 yards. On all sides there was to be heard a rush of waters; and there were crevices, the very idea of approaching which was painful, and inequalities like the waves of a high sea.

"After surveying the scene about us for some time, and hearing the effects of the large fragments of rock, which our guides rolled into the crevices, we ascended again, and having registered our names in a sort of temple of fame, which the edifice generously erected by a Monsieur Desportes, for the protection of travellers, has been converted into, and on the same pannel with those of Mr. and Mrs. Derby whom you must remember at K——, we commenced our return towards the valley, taking another road for that purpose, and descending towards the source of the Arveiron, which is at the lower extremity of the sea of ice, and 2782 perpendicular feet below the edifice on Montanvert. We were too late in the year to enjoy the sublime beauties of this view, as they are described by travellers. The immense arch of ice of 100 feet in height, and broad in proportion, had lately fallen in; but various tints of colour, from a pale white to a deep green, diversified the surface, which rose abruptly, and ended in pyramidical forms; while the Aiguille de Dru, one of the naked rocks of granite, which I mentioned as appearing to bound the valley of ice, was visible above all, rising like an immense obelisk to the stupendous height of upwards of 9000 feet from the spot we stood on. What added to the singularity of the scene before us, were the forest trees which covered the sides of the Montanvert, and of the opposite mountains, from the bosom of which the glacier descends. It was now late in the day, and we returned to our inn along the meadows and well cultivated fields of the valley.

" The whole of this country has undergone very great alterations, and by very violent means. The glaciers were evidently 1500 feet more elevated, at some distant period, than they are now; and the strata of several of the mountains we had passed on the road to Chamouny are not only vertical, but what is still more difficult to be accounted for, they may be almost said to form segments of circles. Perhaps upon the sudden withdrawing of the great mass of waters, in the depths of which these mountains were formed, by successive accumulations of some soft material, their foundations gave way as the earth became dry, and they thus assumed, by the extension of some parts, and the contraction of others, those singular appearances which we now behold. I have already mentioned the evident marks to be met with, of the sea having covered the tops of very lofty mountains, and it is certain that the extremity of the eminence immediately behind the little village of St. Martin, near Salenche, which rises to the height of upwards of 6000 feet, is entirely composed of marine fossils. As to the former altitude of the glaciers, it is inferred by the immense detached rocks remaining in different places, where no other power we know of but that of the glaciers can have conveyed them, and where they have been left on the slope of the valley, as the ebb tide leaves pebbles on the beach of the ocean.

" Our third and last day in this happy valley was chiefly employed in visiting the Glacier de Buisson, which is of very easy access. The road lay for a little way along the river side, amid small clusters of houses, each of which was generally provided with an oratory, in which the figure of the Virgin, with the holy infant in her arms, appears in a recess, behind a grating of wire, and at the top is a sacred promise made by the Bishop, that so many prayers said in that spot, will operate as a mitigation of so many days in purgatory. But to return to the glacier, we approached by a gentle slope, and halted for a moment in a wood to admire the striking and beautiful contrast which is created by the cones of ice as they rise up at a distance like the minarets of a Moorish town, and glitter through the trees. The ascent became afterwards more rapid, and the cones appeared in all their singular magnificence of height and structure. There seemed to be many of them higher than the tallest trees, while the base of the solid ice they rested upon must be some hundred feet in thickness. As this part of the glacier is uninterruptedly connected with a great mass of ice and snow stretching towards the upper region of Mont Blanc, for an extent of perhaps seven or eight miles, and as the valley it rests upon is, in this place, extremely rapid, the probability is, that immense fragments moving down confusedly together, have been brought to assume their present appearance, by the joint operation of the rain and of the sun. A little higher up, and where the ascent is for a short space much less steep, the glacier may be crossed with safety; and we walked deliberately along, under the direction of our guides, upon the bed of ice. It was a warm day in August, and that circumstance added not a little to the novelty of every thing about us.

"We undertook no distant excursion either here or upon the sea of ice, or on Mont Blanc; but you may form a very good idea of the accidents to which persons who make these perilous attempts are exposed, by reading M. de Saussure, or Mr. Coxe, who has followed him very exactly. That a hunter who had been from his infancy accustomed to the sight of precipices, should be instigated by the desire of providing for his family, by the love of a sort of glory, and by the animation of pursuit, to risk his life amid the frightful wilds ' of covered pits unfathomably deep,' does not surprise me; but I am, I confess, astonished that the desire of novelty, and that the objects even of Monsieur de Saussure's curiosity, should lead any one to incur the danger of putting an end to his existence in this wilderness. The danger arises very much from what Thomson, who seems to have been inspired, calls ' Those precipices huge, smoothed o'er with snow.' It is not long since a person walking upon the surface of a neighbouring mountain, and on a part always covered with snow, suddenly disappeared, to the great horror of his companions. In as short a time as possible ropes were procured, and a resolute mountaineer was let down through the same orifice: at the depth of between two and three hundred feet were found the remains of the unhappy traveller; he had been precipitated between two walls of ice, which approached as they descended, and had been compressed to death by the shock; still, however, the ice immediately before his mouth had the appearance of having been slightly thawed, so that he must have survived his fall for at least three or four minutes.

" A monument by the road side on the way to Chamouny records his name and his misfortune, and gives a wholesome caution to travellers. On our way back to Chamouny, I observed several of the inhabitants gathering elm leaves, which were to be put up and used as fodder during the winter, the length of which induces them to neglect no means of providing for their cattle. It frequently happens, that the snow remains to the thickness of a foot in the month of April, but those who are desirous of sowing their grain as soon as possible, are careful to accelerate the thaw by scattering handfuls of dark earth over the surface of the snow.

" Every one who visits the valley of Chamouny will be made sensible of the greatest obligations to M. de Saussure, if he takes the trouble of looking into the works of that distinguished traveller. He was the third individual who was able to surmount the difficulties and dangers, which attend the ascent of Mont Blanc, and very skilfully availed himself of the few hours which he passed there. Seated upon this noble observatory, and provided with every necessary instrument, he proceeded without a moment's loss of time to accomplish the objects of so perilous an undertaking. The barometer gave him, according to the improved process of M. de Luc, within a few feet of the same height which had been attributed to the mountain by the usual mode of trigonometrical measurement. The hygrometer showed the air to contain six times less humidity than the atmosphere of Geneva, which no doubt contributed, with other causes, to that continued thirst the guides and himself laboured under; and the temperature at which water boiled was found to contain scarcely a twelfth of the heat necessary to create ebullition in the regions below. This last experiment had been suggested by M. de Luc, and is very ingeniously and accurately applied to measurement of height, as I will explain to you hereafter. We may easily suppose, that no one would be tempted to remain long in these regions of eternal winter, even had not nature made it impossible to do so. The extreme rarity of the atmosphere renders an increased operation of the lungs necessary to respiration, this of course affects the circulation; a fever is brought on, and there succeeds a dislike to every sort of sustenance but water, which can only be procured by melting snow. Nothing, in short, but the most ardent curiosity, founded on a knowledge of all the various branches of natural history, could have enabled M. de Saussure to remain four and a half hours on the summit of Mont Blanc. His constitution, which was naturally robust, was thought to have suffered extremely by these annual excursions, and it was his misfortune to outlive, for some time, the faculties of his mind."

On the Respiration of the Whale. By a CORRESPONDENT.

I observe Sir W. Scott in his last work, the Pirate, makes the whale blow up water; and I was, until lately, of the same opinion: but happening to fall into company with a particular friend of mine, who was on the first northern expedition with Captain Ross, I learned that the whale blows up, or breathes, air only. On crossing the Atlantic in the year 1820, I was fully convinced of this; for our vessel being surrounded by a large shoal of whales, and one of them breathing almost close under the bows, while I was sitting on deck, I could distinctly perceive that it was merely the breath of the creature which was blown upwards. I believe it is a generally received opinion that the whale blows up water; and perhaps, if you insert this in your pages, it will elicit some facts from persons engaged in the fisheries, or others to whom it may be a subject worthy of notice.

By the same opportunity I would beg leave to offer a remark or two on a subject of more importance, as connected with the convenience of the human species, and the benefit of commerce.

Having seen, in one of your numbers, an account of a more economical method of generating combustible gas, by decomposing oil, than that which is now practised in the decomposition of coal, may I trouble you by asking, if the palm oil has ever been tried? This oil, which is the staple produce of our colonies on the western coast of Africa, may be procured in such abundance, and at so very low a rate, that I am sure no other oil can come in competition with it. The possible supply would equal any possible demand. Indeed it is now at so low a price, that the merchants scarcely attempt to collect it. I know well, from a long residence in Africa, that, as a lamp oil, it is equal even to spermaceti. When imported into England it is of the consistence of soap, and is very largely used as tallow for making soap; especially a very fine perfumed cosmetic soap, as which I prefer it to all others. It is used abundantly, and exclusively, in Africa, in sauce to food.

I was led into these observations from seeing an article in your Focus of Philosophy, &c. stating, that cocoa nut oil has been used by Messrs. Taylor and Martineau for the production of gas, and which gives an extremely brilliant and white light, more economical, and preferable to the oil commonly used.

Having seen both these oils in use in Africa as lamp oils, and the palm being infinitely better liked, both for its clearer light and finer scent, I shall feel much obliged by your insertion of these facts, which may be beneficial to the colonists of western Africa. AFRICANUS.

We will first notice our correspondent's remark on the respiration of the whale, respecting which we dare not hazard a positive opinion, because we have not had any personal experience on the subject. But we may state, that as all fishes are cool-blooded animals, we should be inclined to infer, that the ejected volume could not be condensed aqueous vapour, combined with expired air; because the atmospheric temperature, in warm climates, would not admit of such condensation; nor would the expired matter exceed the heat of their own bodies. Even in the winter temperature of our higher latitudes, the expired vapours are visible in very cold weather only. If the impelled columns were air alone, they could not be visible at any temperature. But may we not suppose that the ejection is merely part of the natural process of respiration by gills, or analogous structure? Perhaps the animal can eject water in all states of division, from a massive column to a fountain of fine spray. If so, we may easily account for the diversity of presenting appearances. We shall be thankful to any marine naturalist, who has had ample opportunities of observing for himself, for further information on the subject.

Next, as to the recommendation of palm oil, instead of cocoa-nut oil, for the supply of combustible gas, we cannot hesitate one moment. The abundance of the former, and its competency to answer every purpose of combustion, whether as oil or gas, is, with us, beyond the remotest doubt. We feel sure that that the cocoa-nut oil can never be brought into the market in such almost unlimited supply as the palm oil may; and the purity of the latter, as a vegetable product, is, at least, equal to the former. We should be highly pleased to witness the general introduction of palm oil into the gaseous laboratories, in preference to all other combustible matter; because we feel a thorough conviction that it must meet every wish in a superior degree. Its cheapness; its competency; and its being *our own produce*, (for, as colonial, we may call it such,) all conspire to render the mere suggestion of its use quite sufficient to lead to practical conviction and general adoption.

An Account of Oil intended to be applied to Watch-work, and to other delicate Machinery, to diminish the Friction. By M. CADET DE GASSICOURT.

Bulletin de la Societé de Encouragement.

The purification of expressed oils for the purpose of diminishing friction, in slight mechanism, will be a useful art; if practicable, as proposed. And we can fully rely on the authenticity of the following; as well as on the chemical judgment dictating the process successfully adopted by M. Chevreul.

"The sample of oil of olives submitted to our examination, was prepared by M. Maurin, at Aix, in Provence. Its specific gravity is less than that of good common olive oil. Placed for an hour in the midst of melting ice, its transparency was slightly affected, in consequence of the separation of a very small quantity of stearin, so small indeed, that it would have been extremely difficult to separate it from the *elain*. The oil contined fluid.

"We mixed this oil with about two-hundredths of its weight of sulphuric acid, and shook it up with twice its volume of water. The oil became slightly turbid, without giving any precipitate. This oil, therefore, contained no mucilage. We also found that it contained no acid. Hence it is proper for the use of watchmakers, for the oil which they employ should not congeal by cold, nor attack the metals by the acid which forms when the oil turns rancid.

"We shall terminate this report by a very simple remark, which it may be useful to communicate to all watch and clockmakers. According to the properties which they look for in oil, it appears to us that pure *elain* fulfils all the conditions they desire. Now it is easy to extract the elain from all the fine oils, and even from fats, by following the process given by M. Chevreul. It consists in treating the oil in a matras, with seven or eight times its weight of alcohol, nearly boiling, decanting the liquid, and suffering it to cool. The stearin separates in the form of a crystalline precipitate. The alcoholic solution is afterwards to be evaporated to one-fifth of its volume, and the elain will be obtained. It ought to be colourless, with little odour, tasteless, without action or infusion of litmus, having the consistence of white olive oil, and not easily congealable. Watchmakers use so little oil, that the preparation of elain would be an inconsiderable increase of expense to them, and they would also be certain of always using the same matter.

An Account of a remarkable Quadruped, discovered in South Africa. By the Rev. John Campbell, Missionary.

Monthly Mag. No. 362.

As the zeal of the Missionaries is carrying them to points little, or imperfectly explored, we should wish that they were more generally qualified, by their philosophical attainments, to convey to their countrymen at home information which would be thankfully received, and might be beneficially applied.

A remarkable animal has been discovered in South Africa, by the Rev. John Campbell, of the London Missionary Society. The Hottentots who shot the creature, never having seen or heard of an animal with a horn of so great a length, they cut off its head, and brought it bleeding on the back of an ox to Mr Campbell. Mr. C. would gladly have transported the whole of it with him to Europe; but its great weight, and the distance of the spot (the City of Mashow) from Cape Town (about 1200 miles), determined him to reduce it, by cutting off the under jaw. The head measured, from the ears to the nose, three feet; the length of the horn, which is nearly black, is also three feet, projecting from the forehead, about ten inches above the nose. There is a small horny projection of a conical shape, measuring about eight inches, immediately behind the great horn, apparently designed for keeping fast or steady whatever is penetrated by the great horn. This projection is scarcely observed at a little distance. The animal is not carnivorous, but chiefly feeds on grass and bushes. It is well known in the kingdom of Mashow, the natives of which make from the great horn handles for their battle axes. The animal appears to be a species of the rhinoceros; but judging from the size of its head, it must have been much larger than the common rhinoceros of South Africa, which has a large crooked horn, nearly resembling the shape of a cockspur, pointing backward, and a short one of the same form, immediately behind it. Mr. Campbell was very desirous to obtain as adequate an idea as possible of the bulk of the animal killed near Mashow, and with this view questioned his Hottentots, who described it as being much larger than the rhinoceros, and equal in size to three oxen, or four horses.

On Arseniate of Copper with Coffee.

M. Bizio, on repeating the experiment of Brugnatelli, had occasion to observe some new phenomena. When a drop of the infusion or decoction of the grain fell upon a piece of cloth, it formed a yellow spot, surrounded with a beautiful green border. He attributed this green colour to the oxidation of the oil of coffee. In order to fix that colour, he boiled a hectogramme of coffee powder, and reduced the decoction to eight hectogrammes. He added an equal quantity of sulphate of copper, dissolved in water, and used, as a precipitate, a solution of caustic soda. A deposit was formed, weighing 105 grammes, which, on drying in the air, took a green colour; the more it was exposed to the air, while it remained humid, the brighter the colour became. Water, ether, alcohol, and the alkaline subcarbonates, had no effect on the colour. Ammonia indicated the presence of copper; caustic potash changed it to sky blue, and took itself a green colour; caustic soda did not alter it, and received but a slight tinge of the green.

The deposit, which is a true lac, resists acids sufficiently well, and, with the exception of the sulphuric and oxalic, no others destroy the colour totally. Acetic acid, in dissolving this lac, produces a solution of a much finer green.

We noticed, at page 246, the observations of Dr. Porter, on arsenic, as a test and a pigment, when combined with a decoction of coffee; and we have here further authority to show that, as relates to the colouring matter, somewhat may be hoped from its easy preparation. A good permanent green is a desideratum with artists.

Egyptian Obelisk.

The *Journal des Debats* gives the following as the version of the inscription on the Egyptian obelisk lately brought from the island of Philœ, to this country, by Mr. Banks. The translator, M. Letroune, says that it contains a petition from the Priests of Isis in the island of Philœ, to Ptolomæus Euergetus the Second.

"To the King Ptolomæus; to the Queen Cleopatra, his sister; to the Queen Cleopatra, his wife; the Gods of Euergetus, greeting:

"We, the Priests of Isis, who is adored in the Abatum and at Philœ, the most mighty Goddess. Considering that the Strategists, the Epistatists, the Thebarchons, the Royal Registrars, the Commanders of the troops guarding the frontiers, and all others of the King's Officers, who come to Philœ; in short, that the troops which accompany them, and the whole of their suite, compel us to furnish them with abundant supplies belonging to the Temple; the consequence of which is, that the Temple is impoverished, and we run the risk of not having means to defray the regular and fixed expenses, caused by the ceremonies and libations, the object of which is the preservation of yourselves and your children. We supplicate you, most powerful Gods, to authorise your kinsman and epistolographist Numenius, to write to Lorchus, also your kinsman, and the Strategist of the Thebiad, enjoining him not to practise such vexations with regard to us, nor to permit any persons whomsoever to do so; to grant us, moreover, letters testifying your decision on this subject, and granting us permission to erect a *Stele*, on which we will inscribe the beneficence you have displayed to us on this occasion, in order that this *Stele* may transmit to the remotest posterity the eternal memory of the favours you have granted us. This being permitted us, we shall be, and with the Temple of Isis, in this, as in all other things, your grateful servants. May you be ever happy."

According to M. Letroune, the date of this petition must have been previous to the year 126 of our era. The object of this memoir is to extol and explain the various peculiarities which the Greek text presents; to explain the customs to which several passages of the petition refer; and to form from it some idea of the state to which the cast of priests was reduced under the domination of Ptolomey. M. Letroune by no means joins in the expectations which have been conceived of the advantages of comparing the Greek text engraved upon the pedestal with the hieroglyphics on the obelisk itself. He seems to think, both from the sense and the object of the Greek inscription, that, if the obelisk be not of a more ancient date, and afterwards restored by the priests of Isis, and consequently, if the hieroglyphics which cover it were really sculptured on this occasion, which seems to him the more reasonable hypothesis, these hieroglyphics contain, in the terms of the Greek text, a testimonial of the gratitude of the priests to the princes, and not a second copy, in the sacred language, of the petition inscribed on the pedestal.

Explosion of Hydrogen and Chlorine by Light.

It has been long known that a mixture of chlorine and hydrogen explodes when exposed to the direct action of the sun's rays. In order to try if this effect could be produced by the radiation of a common culinary fire, Professor Silliman filled a common Florence oil flask (well cleaned) half full of chlorine gas, and was in the act of introducing the hydrogen in the pneumatic cistern. "There was not only no *direct* emanation from the sun, but even the *diffuse* light was rendered much feebler than common by a thick snow storm, which had covered the sky-light above with a thick mantle, and veiled the heavens in a singular degree from such a storm. Under these circumstances, the hydrogen was scarcely all introduced before the flask exploded, with a distinct flame; portions of the glass stuck in the wood-work of the ceiling of the room, and the face and eyes escaped, by being out of the direction of the explosion: nothing but the neck of the flask remained in hand. This occurrence then proves that a mixture of chlorine and hydrogen gas may explode spontaneously, in a diffuse light, and even in a very dim light." (American Journal of Science, vol. 3, No. 2, page 343.)

Suffocation from Vapours, by Iron Cement.

The following accident is recorded in the Maidstone paper, and shows the necessity of caution in similar cases of descent into vessels where confined vapours may be apprehended. The play of affinities between the components of the cement may easily account for the extrication of a gas that, if anticipated, would certainly not have been encountered.

"A most melancholy accident occurred in this town on Saturday evening: Mr. Cowen, Jobbing Smith, was repairing the inside of the boiler of a steam engine, at the brewery, in the West Borough, belonging to William Baldwin, Esq., and in joining on some pieces of iron, he made use of a cement composed of sal-ammoniac, sulphur, and iron turnings, which produced such a quantity of fume, or gas, that it overpowered Cowen, and he, in a few moments, was suffocated.

"William Pearce, his man, being at work on the outside, and hearing a struggling noise within, got through the aperture at the top, which was but just large enough to admit his body, and was descending to his master's assistance, when he inhaled the fumes, and fell to the bottom.

"An alarm was immediately given, and a man named Oliver attempted twice to descend, but was so powerfully affected by the effluvia, that he was compelled to relinquish the task. A large quantity of water was thrown into the boiler, and, after some minutes had elapsed, the bodies were extricated. Pearce was found quite dead; but some appearance of life was visible in Cowen, who was immediately taken home, and surgical assistance promptly obtained. Every means that could be devised were resorted to; but all the efforts made to restore animation proved unavailing, and he expired about three o'clock on Sunday morning."

List of Patents lately granted.

Owen Griffith, of Tryfan, Carnarvonshire, Gent., for an improvement in making trusses for the cure of rupture or hernia, in whatsoever parts of the body it may be situated. Oct. 18, 1821.

Thomas Martin and Charles Grafton, of Birmingham, printing ink manufacturers, for a method of making fine light black, which they call spirit black; and a new apparatus for producing the same. Oct. 24.

Benjamin Thompson, of Ayton Cottage, Durham, Gent.; for a method of facilitating the conveyance of carriages along iron and wood rail ways, tram ways, and other roads. Oct. 24.

John Frederick Archbold, Esq., of Sergeant's Inn, Fleet Street, London, for a mode of ventilating close carriages. Nov. 1, 1821.

Neil Arnott, of Bedford Square, M. D., for improvements connected with the production, and agency of, heat in furnaces, steam and air engines, distilling, evaporating, and brewing apparatus. Nov. 14.

William Baylis, Junior, of Painswick, Gloucestershire, clothier, for a machine for washing and cleansing clothes. Nov. 27.

John Bates, of Bradford, Yorkshire, machine maker, for certain machinery for the purpose of feeding furnaces of every description, steam engines, and other boilers, with coal, coke, and fuel of every kind. Nov. 9.

John Collinge, of Lambeth, engineer, for an improvement in hinges. Nov. 22.

Franz Areton Egells, of Britannia Terrace, City Road, Middlesex, engineer: for certain improvements in steam engines. Nov. 9.

James Gardner, of Banbury, Oxfordshire, ironmonger, for a machine preparatory to melting, in the manufacture of tallow, soap, and candles; and which machine may be used for other similar purposes. Nov. 9.

Joseph Grout, of Gutter-lane, Cheapside, London, crape manufacturer, for a new manufacture of crape. Nov. 13.

Samuel Hobday, of Birmingham, patent snuffer maker, for a method of manufacturing the furniture of umbrella and parasols, and of uniting the same together. Nov. 1.

Thomas Motley, of the Strand, patent letter maker and brass founder, for certain improvements in the construction of candlesticks or lamps, and in candles to be burnt therein. Nov. 27.

Richard Macnamara, Esq., of Canterbury-buildings, Lambeth, for an improvement in paving, pitching, and covering streets, roads, and other places. Nov. 20.

Thomas Parkin, of Skinner Street, Bishopsgate Street, merchant, for an improvement in printing. Nov. 24.

Henry Robinson Palmer, of Hackney, civil engineer, for an improvement in the construction of rail ways, and tram roads, and of the carriages to be used thereon. Nov. 22.

William Penrose, of Stummorgangs, Yorkshire, miller, for various improvements in machinery for propelling vessels, and in vessels so propelled. Nov. 10.

David Redmund, of Agnus Circus, Old-street-road, Middlesex, engineer, for an improvement in the construction or manufacture of hinges for doors. Nov. 9.

Bowles Symes, of Lincoln's Inn, Esq., for an expanding hydrostatic piston, to resist the pressure of certain fluids, and slide easily in an imperfect cylinder. Nov. 10.

Charles Tueley, senior, of Kenton-street, Brunswick-square, cabinet-maker, for certain improvements applicable to window sashes, either single or double hinge, fixed or sliding sashes, casements, window shutters, and window blinds. Nov. 1.

Richard Wright, of Mount-row, Kent-road, Surrey, engineer, for improvements in the process of distillation. Nov. 9.

Robert Bill, Esq. of Newman-street, Mary-le-bone, for an improvement in the construction of certain descriptions of boats and barges. Dec. 5, 1821.

Charles Broderip, of London, Esq., now of Glasgow, for his improvement in the construction of steam engines. Dec. 5.

Samuel Briarley, of Salford, in the parish of Manchester, and county of Lancaster, for his improved method of preparing raw silk, and cleansing it, for the purpose of dyeing and manufacturing. Dec. 19.

Pierre Erard, of Great Marlborough-street, London, for certain improvements in piano-fortes, &c. Dec. 22.

John Gladstone, engineer, of Castle Douglas, in the county of Galloway, for improvements in the construction of steam vessels. Dec. 22.

Julius Griffith, of Brompton-crescent, in the County of Middlesex, Esq., for certain improvements in steam carriages, without the aid of horses. Dec. 20.

William Horrocks, of Portwood, within Binnington, in the County of Chester, cotton manufacturer, for his improvement in the construction of looms. Dec. 14.

George Linton, of Gloucester-street, Queen-square, in the County of Middlesex, merchant, for a method of impelling machinery, without the aid of fire, air, water, wind, or steam. Dec. 22.

Henry Ricketts, of the Phœnix Glass Works, Bristol, in the County of Somerset, glass manufacturer, for improvements in the making of glass bottles. Dec. 5.

William Warcup, of Dartford, in the County of Kent, engineer, for his improvement upon a machine for washing linen and cotton cloths of every description. Dec. 10.

James Winter, of Stoke-under-Hamdon, in the County of Somerset, Gent., for his improvements in sewing and pointing leather gloves. Dec. 19.

Augustus Applegarth, of Duke-street, Lett's-town, Lambeth, Surrey, printer, for certain improvements in printing machines. Jan. 14.

Sir Wm. Congreve, of Cecil-street, Strand, London, Bart., for certain improved methods of multiplying fac-simile impressions to any extent. Jan. 29.

Peter Ewart, of Manchester, in the County of Lancaster, civil engineer, for his discovery of a new method of making coffer-dams. Jan. 29.

Alexander Gordon, of London, and David Gordon, of Edinburgh, for their improvement in lamps, and of compositions and materials to be burnt in them. Jan. 14.

David Gordon, of Edinburgh, Esq., for an improvement in steam-packets and other vessels. Jan. 14.

Richard Summers Hartford, of Ebbro Vale Iron Works, in the County of Monmouth, iron-master, for his improvement in that department of iron, called Puddling. Jan. 9.

James Harris, of St. Mildred's Cross, in the City of London, tea dealer, for an improvement in the manufacture of shoes for cattle. Jan. 9.

David Loescham, of Newman-street, Oxford-road, London, musical instrument maker; and James Allwright, of Little Newport-street, in the Parish of St. Anne, Soho, cheesemonger, for a new improved keyed musical instrument. Jan. 14.

Richard Ormrod, of Manchester, in the County of Lancaster, iron-founder, for an improvement in the mode of heating liquids in boilers. Jan. 7.

William Ravenscroft, of Searle-street, Lincoln's-inn-fields, peruke maker, for his new-invented forensic wig. Jan. 14.

THE FOCUS

OF

PHILOSOPHY, SCIENCE, AND ART.

On Water Cements, Mortar, and Lime. By M. VICAT.
(Continued from page 337.)

On the Influence of Desiccation according as it is natural, retarded, or accelerated by various Causes.

THE desiccation of mortar may be delayed for many years, by covering it with earth or sand, but so exposed to the weather as to receive the rain that falls, or else kept occasionally watered. On the other hand, the drying may be hastened by artificial warmth, or by the contact of spongy absorbent substances. In walls exposed to the open air, but in the shade, mortar dries gradually; in foundations, and under ground works, slowly; in the higher parts of buildings exposed to the sun, and particularly when the masonry be composed of bricks or porous materials, the mortar dries rapidly.

Mortars composed of hydraulic lime, which can solidify all the water which they contain, should dry slowly. They may lose by common drying three-tenths, and by rapid drying eight-tenths of the force that they would have retained by slow drying.

Common limes, which either do not at all, or not till after many years, solidify the water that enters in excess into the mortar, appear to derive no advantage from a very slow desiccation when carried on for many months, or for a year. On the other hand, a rapid desiccation is equally unfavourable to the setting of common and of hydraulic lime. All masons are agreed on this point.

An examination of the mortar of the quay of Montauban, which gave way in 1812, has afforded a curious example of the influence of rapid drying. The upper parts of the quay were built of bricks, which not being dipped in water before using, greedily sucked up the moisture of the mortar that came in contact with them: the rains, on the other hand, kept the lower parts much longer cool and damp; whence it was observed that there was a gradual diminution of the resistance, from below upwards; and a corresponding one in the quality of the mortar; which was very good at the bottom, and finished by being an incohesive powder as it reached the top of the building.

The influence of slow desiccation in promoting the solidity of mortar made with hydraulic lime, has long been known in Italy. They manufacture at Alexandria in Piedmont artificial stones, to which they give the name of *prisms*, because, as they are chiefly intended for the angles of walls and the starlings of bridges, they are made of a triangular shape. They use in this manufacture an excellent hydraulic lime, obtained from the neighbourhood of Casel; they slack it in the usual way, and when it has been six days liquid they put it in the middle of a basin of sand of unequal grain, from the smallest size to that of coarse gravel; this sand is highly quartzose, and contains some calcareous fragments. The mixture is then made with much care. They previously prepare a triangular prismatic trench of any required length, in a level plot of ground, out of the reach of inundation, and smooth its sides with a wet trowel; they then fill it with the prisms of the prepared mortar in successive layers, mixing up equally with it flint-stones of regular size. They then cover the whole with the earth dug out to make the trench; keeping always a thickness of about a foot over it. The proportions for a cubic metre are 0·14 of lime in paste, 0·90 of sand of unequal grains, and 0·20 of flints.

The prisms are made up of 55 inches in length, to 31¼ inches for the breadth of one of the sides. They commonly remain buried for three years; but two are sufficient when the lime is of the first quality; after which they are withdrawn for use.

It is not always possible for builders to preserve the mortar in that degree of macération which contributes to the greatest degree of solidity; but it should be dried as slowly as possible. Quadrangular prisms of hydraulic mortar of one and a half to two inches diameter acquire nearly the same degree of solidity, when buried under moist earth for six months as for a year, provided they are afterwards exposed very gradually to the air.

A square of mortar, made of common sand and lime slacked spontaneously in the air, was enclosed in a covering of water-cement, and immersed under water for a year; after which the external covering of cement was pulled off, and the enclosed square of lime placed on the floor of a damp cellar, intending to bring it forwards by degrees to a drier and more exposed situation. At the end of a few months, finding the outer part of the square appeared very hard, it was brought up suddenly to a dry granary to hasten the desiccation, and some time after subjected to the usual proof trial of its resistance. When it broke, the inner part separated from the outer, nearly as the yolk of a hard-boiled egg separates from the white, and the inner portion was still so soft as to be friable under the finger, though the outer was quite firm. The broken portion was exposed anew to the air for a considerable time, but it never acquired the hardness of the outer, a well-marked line of separation always existing between the two portions.

On the Influence of the Seasons.

The common vicissitudes of the seasons, where the temperature does not descend below the freezing point, far from being prejudicial to mortars, rather increase their hardness; particularly those that are rather lean than fat. Walls beaten by the wind and the rain for centuries afford a convincing proof of this, when compared to the texture of the mortar of in-door masonry; and persons who have examined ancient ruins with this view, constantly observe that the parts the most exposed to the inclemencies of the weather are always the firmest. In some cases, the common frosts of our climate do no injury; but in others they cause the mortar to peel off and fall to powder.

The particular texture of mortars and stones in general has a great influence on the manner in which severe cold operates. Some observers have attributed to the expansive force of water when in the act of freezing, the rupture of substances that contain a portion of this fluid; and architects have thence deduced as a consequence, that the fine close-grained stones ought to resist frost better than the more porous. Experience, however, shows the fallacy of this conclusion; for sand-stone, and a number of lime-stones so permeable as to be used for filtering, resist great cold perfectly well; whilst others, whose texture is so hard as to be almost vitreous, will burst asunder.

We may explain what happens in these different circumstances by considering, that it is not so much the absolute quantity of water contained in a solid body, as the mode of its distribution, which determines the fracture by expansion. When it is contained in long continuous threads, however small, they act as wedges in their whole extent when expanded by congelation; but in stones of a porous or cellular texture, the expansion of each interstice may be supposed to act independently of the adjoining ones, or, like key-stones of an arch, one may resist and counteract the other. Near the surface there is besides in the porous stones a slight transudation, so that after a severe cold they are covered with a thin coating of ice. When there is not a free transudation in frost, the surfaces effloresce or fall to powder, exposing fresh surfaces to the same destructive process, till the whole crumbles to pieces; this is often the case with fat mortars, bricks, works in *pisé*, &c., but modified by the tenacity of each body. Fat mortars of hydraulic lime resist the frost extremely well; whilst mortars with common lime, composed of the same proportions, have utterly fallen to pieces.

It would be an interesting inquiry to determine what are the best proportions of sand to be used to particular species of lime, to enable the mortar best to resist exposure to cold.

In general, the greater the quantity of sand, the less readily is the mortar affected by frost.

On the Effect of Time on the Texture of Mortar.

If mortar be still fresh at thirty years old, as masons assert, what can we think of that which has been employed for experiments, the trial pieces of which have generally been examined after twenty to twenty-three months. We shall not attempt to determine at what age mortar acquires its utmost hardness, as the question is complicated with so many circumstances depending on the nature of the mortar, of the brick or stone employed, the exposure, &c. Nevertheless, we may ascertain some limits to the inquiry, which will suffice for our present purpose. M. Rondelet tried, in a machine, the hardness of a specimen of mortar made in 1787 with common lime then eighteen months old, and found it to be 2552. On repeating the same trial in 1802, that is to say, fifteen years after, the hardness was 2864. The increase during these fifteen years, therefore, was only $\frac{12}{100}$, and as it is certain that the law of increase proceeds in a rapidly diminishing ratio, we may reasonably infer that a second period of fifteen years would have produced but little change. This agrees pretty nearly with experiments. We may, therefore, infer that small pieces of mortar, after a short exposure to the air, arrive to a degree of hardness, which, if not exactly the greatest that they are capable of acquiring, at least is sufficient to allow us to infer with certainty what it will amount to in eighteen or twenty months' time. Small pieces thus exposed, though dried very gradually, will in this time be more advanced to their utmost solidity, than they would be for ten years inclosed in the centre of a thick wall. The like may be said of their penetration with the carbonic acid of the atmosphere.

On the ancient Mortars compared with modern.

Our ancestors have left us, in a crowd of monuments, incontestible examples, which show us that if they did not always act upon the best principles of architecture, they well understood that of making cements. A few years ago there existed at Agen the ruins of a bridge, thought to be antique on account of the hardness of the mortar, which was so great that they were obliged to employ blasting to remove the remains of a foundation. This bridge, however, which the lovers of the marvellous were inclined to carry back to the time of the Pelasgi, was built by a charter obtained from Richard I, King of England, who was at that time master of Agen, and a great part of the South of France.

The mortar of the bridge of Valentré, built at Cahors in 1400, resembles, in every respect, both in the quality of the lime and the size and proportions of the sand, that of an ancient theatre whose ruins still remain in the same town, at five or six hundred paces from the river. Its hardness appears from many trials in the machine to be 1839, and that of the bridge 1893. These examples might be infinitely multiplied. Experiments on the hydraulic, natural, or factitious limes, show besides, that one may obtain in very little time, and without the use of puozzolanas, mortars at least equal in hardness to the best of the Roman.

In ascertaining the causes of the duration of the ancient monuments, sufficient distinction has not been made between what is due to the mortar, and what to the thickness of the wall, the disposition of the materials, &c. It is bad reasoning always to infer the goodness of the mortar from the duration of the edifice to which it belongs: we may, on the contrary, say with accuracy, that there are some buildings that have better preserved the mortar, than the mortar has preserved the buildings. Such are all edifices of which the masonry is faced with enormous blocks of hewn stone.

We must not imagine that all the Roman buildings have been made with the same care as those of which portions remain to us; for Pliny says expressly, that the badness of the mortar often causes the ruin of the common houses. We have only one method of making an accurate reasoning on this subject, which is, from the actual measurement of the relative hardness of the different specimens; and the result of experiments is, that these mortars are by no means equally good, as has been pretended; and that, therefore, time is not the only cause of their hardness. We see, besides, that this cannot be attributed exclusively, either to the perfection of the mixture or to the presence of puozzolana.

In taking a general view of all that has been said on this subject, and the results of the experiments, we shall find that the distance which separates the extreme numbers, expressing the respective resistances of different cements, is so great, that we may with convenience divide them into three classes, under one or other of which we may, without much error, include every species of mortar that has come under examination.

The first class includes the relative resistances expressed by the numbers 5000 to 3000, which correspond to an absolute mean resistance of 9·60 kilogrammes on the superficial centimetre. To this class belong all the well-made mortars with common quartzose sand, and eminently hydraulic lime, natural or artificial.

The second class includes the relative resistance of 3000 to 2000, corresponding with a mean absolute resistance of 6·00 kilogrammes. The well-made mortars, with the moderately hydraulic limes and quartzose sand, belong to this class.

The third class has a relative resistance of 2000 to 1000, and a mean absolute resistance of 3·60 kilogrammes. The mortars made of the same sand, and the common middling or fat limes, fall under this class.

The antique mortars almost all come within the second and the third class.

As to the common wet mixtures of lime and sand used by our masons, if they deserve the name of mortars, they will form a fourth class, whose absolute mean resistance does not exceed 1·50 kilogrammes.

The extreme limits of good mortars, therefore, come within 12·00 kilogrammes and 2·40 kilogrammes. On the other hand, the resistance of building-stones, from the basalt of Auvergne, to the common calcareous wrought stones, is from 77·06 to 20·40. We see, therefore, that we must not understand literally what some authors assert, of the possibility of making with lime, puozzolana, and sand, factitious stones as hard as the flint which nature presents to us.

At length, we conclude this paper; which, being of great practical importance, we have been induced to abridge as little as could be consistent with justice to the author, or benefit to the reader.

On the Peroxide of Hydrogen. By M. THENARD.

(Continued from page 351.)

Of the Metals which decompose the Peroxide of Hydrogen, absorbing Part of the Oxygen, and disengaging the remainder.

Arsenic in powder and pure peroxide. Sudden and most violent action; flame produced by the combustion of the arsenic, which, acidifying, prevents the whole of the oxygen from being disengaged or absorbed, at least instantaneously; consequently very great disengagement of heat. When the peroxide is in excess, all the arsenic becomes acid, and is dissolved.

Arsenic in powder and peroxide containing only one-ninth of its volume of oxygen. No effervescence; the liquor becomes immediately acid. This acid rendering the peroxide more fixed, it remains for a long time more or less oxidized.

Molybden reduced to powder and pure peroxide. Very violent action; combustion of the metal with light; great extrication of heat; production of a very soluble acid, the taste of which is rather strong, and gives a yellow colour to the water. All the molybden disappears when the peroxide is in excess.

Molybden reduced to powder, and peroxide containing only nine volumes of oxygen. Sudden brisk effervescence; production of acid; absorption or disengagement of all the oxygen: at the end of 15 hours, the liquor was of a superb blue colour.

Tungsten, chrome, and pure peroxide. The action weak at first; and with the tungsten only, after some time it becomes violent.

Potassium and pure peroxide. Sudden and violent action; vivid combustion; disengagement of oxygen, and formation of alkali: the experiment ought not to be made in a narrow tube, for sometimes explosion occurs.

Sodium and pure peroxide. The same phenomena as with potassium.

Manganese and pure peroxide. The metal, in the form of small globules, produces brisk effervescence, and deoxidizes the liquor readily. May it not be imagined that it is first oxidized, and that it is the oxide which expels the oxygen? Yet the globules did not appear to be altered. In powder it acts still more strongly, becoming very soon violent: at the same time that the oxygen is disengaged, great heat is excited.

Manganese and peroxide containing only nine times its volume of oxygen. Brisk and sudden effervescence; no heat; complete deoxidizement of the liquor in a short time.

(Zinc.) Action very weak.

Iron, tin, antimony, tellurium. No, or scarcely any, action at all, even with the concentrated liquor.

Action of the simple non-metallic Combustibles.

Among the simple non-metallic combustible bodies, there are only selenium and charcoal, which act upon peroxide of hydrogen in a marked manner.

Selenium in powder and pure peroxide. Sudden and very violent action; disengagement of great heat without light; complete acidification of the selenium, which, owing to this, immediately dissolves.

Selenium and peroxide containing only nine times its volume of oxygen. No heat. Occasional bubbles are disengaged; but the liquor is acidified in a few minutes.

Charcoal in fine powder and pure peroxide. Sudden and very brisk action; production of very considerable heat; disengagement of all the oxygen without the formation of any carbonic acid.

Charcoal in fine powder and peroxide containing only nine times its volume of oxygen. Brisk effervescence without heat; all the oxygen is disengaged without the production of carbonic acid. Pass a certain quantity of the liquor up an inverted tube containing mercury, then introduce some well powdered charcoal. It will be found that the gas which is readily evolved from the liquor is merely oxygen, and that it will be deoxidized in a very short time.

Lamp Black. No action; unquestionably because the liquor does not moisten it.

Action upon Metallic Sulphurets at Common Temperatures.

The greater number of the metallic sulphurets which I have tried have a very marked action upon the peroxide of hydrogen. Very often this action is violent, and accompanied with much heat when the liquor is concentrated. Moreover, whether it be diluted with water or concentrated, there almost always results a sulphate, and a more or less sensible disengagement of oxygen. This occurs with the sulphurets of copper, antimony, lead, and iron: they are scarcely brought into contact before they are converted with effervescence into sulphates.

The sulphurets of arsenic and of molybden act with more violence than the preceding upon the concentrated peroxide; heat and light are produced; but no sulphate is formed; the arsenic is acidified, and the sulphur remains almost unacted upon. The sulphurets of bismuth and of tin act very freely, even upon the peroxide in the most concentrated state; the sulphurets of silver and of mercury (cinnabar) have no action at all.

Action of Metallic Oxides at Common Temperatures.

In general, metallic oxides tend to restore the peroxide of hydrogen to the state of protoxide of water. Some of them produce this effect by becoming more oxidized; others without alteration, but disengaging all the oxygen in the gaseous form, which water absorbs to become peroxide. Some again disengage the oxygen, and are themselves reduced; but few exert no action at all.

The decomposing power of the oxides varies much. Several expel the oxygen so suddenly from the liquor, that a kind of explosion occurs, and then much light and heat are evolved. The action of others, on the contrary, is slow, occasioning but slight effervescence, and no sensible heat.

Of the Oxides which absorb the Oxygen of the Peroxide, and restore it to the State of Protoxide or Water.

These oxides are barytes, strontian, lime, oxide of zinc, oxide and peroxide of copper, oxide of nickel, the protoxides of manganese, iron, tin, cobalt, oxide of arsenic, and probably several others. It is requisite that the metallic oxide should be moist or in solution: otherwise the oxygen would be disengaged, or would remain in combination. It is moreover evident, that in proportion as the new oxide is produced, it is possible that it may expel a portion of the oxygen from the liquor, so that the action may become complicated.

Barytes. When barytes water is poured into concentrated or diluted peroxide, a great number of brilliant scales are precipitated; these are merely hydrate of peroxide of barium, but if barytes reduced to powder be used instead of barytes water, with slightly diluted peroxide of barium, a violent extrication of oxygen gas takes place, and much heat is excited. This heat may be derived from the absorption of the water of the peroxide by the barytes. As to the disengagement of the oxygen, it may be attributed to the heat produced by the absorption of water, and the formation of a small quantity of peroxide of barium: hydrate of barytes possesses the power of evolving oxygen from the peroxide of hydrogen in all cases.

Strontian. Strontian presents the same appearances with the peroxide as barytes does.

Lime. This base also produces with the peroxide of hydrogen, phenomena analogous to those which have been mentioned with the two preceding bases.

Hydrate of Copper. This hydrate, when mixed with the peroxide of hydrogen, becomes immediately a new oxide of an ochre-yellow colour, and it rapidly evolves the oxygen of the peroxide which remained undecomposed. When the peroxide is concentrated, the action is vivid, there is disengagement of heat, and it requires much to convert all the oxide of copper into peroxide. In order that the peroxidation may take place, it is not only requisite that the peroxide of hydrogen should be diluted with water, but other circumstances hereafter to be mentioned must be attended to.

Calcined Peroxide of Copper. In this state the oxide of copper cannot of course combine with more oxygen; it produces a very evident effervescence of oxygen gas when put into peroxide of hydrogen.

Hydrate of Zinc. The same as copper: this oxide becomes a peroxide with oxygenated water, so that very little oxygen is evolved.

Oxide of Zinc by Calcination. More converted into peroxide than in the former case; the evolution of oxygen gas is extremely slight.

Hydrate of Nickel. This is another oxide, which, with the peroxide of hydrogen, probably forms a new oxide; it also occasions a slight disengagement of oxygen.

Oxide of Nickel by Calcination. Very evident effervescence of oxygen from the peroxide of hydrogen.

Protoxide of manganese, iron, tin, cobalt. These protoxides, when in the state of hydrates, are converted into peroxides in the same way as those already described. When oxygenated water is poured upon these hydrates recently precipitated by potash from their solution in acids, they are immediately peroxidized. The peroxides of manganese and cobalt will afterwards act upon the undecomposed peroxide, causing the rapid expulsion of its oxygen in the state of gas; the action of the peroxide of iron is not very strong, and that of tin produces no sensible effect.

Oxide of Arsenic becomes acidified.

Of the Oxides which expel Oxygen from the Peroxide of Hydrogen without being Peroxidized or Deoxidized.

There are a considerable number of oxides which possess this property; they will be described as nearly as possible in the order of their power of decomposing.

Native peroxide of manganese in fine powder, with concentrated peroxide of hydrogen. Sudden and very violent action; the heat occasioned so great as to make the tube burning hot; the deoxidation of the peroxide of hydrogen instantaneous and complete.

The same oxide of manganese with peroxide containing only nine volumes of oxygen. Very brisk and sudden effervescence; all the oxygen disengaged in a very short time from the oxygenated water.

Very finely divided peroxide of manganese, obtained by adding oxygenated water to a solution of manganese, and decomposing the solution by potash. The action of this oxide is stronger than that of the native oxide; and when the experiment is performed with the concentrated oxygenated water, it takes place with a kind of explosion.

Peroxide of cobalt in powder. This produces the same effects with the concentrated peroxide of hydrogen as the native peroxide of manganese does.

Massicot in powder and highly concentrated peroxide of hydrogen. Violent action, great heat; disengagement of all the oxygen in a few minutes.

Minium and peroxide of lead. These two oxides act also very strongly upon the peroxide of hydrogen; the action of the peroxide is extremely violent, and it becomes protoxide.

Hydrate of peroxide of iron, and concentrated peroxide of hydrogen. Action soon becoming very strong; great heat, and complete deoxidizement of the liquor in a very short time.

Hydrate of peroxide of iron, and liquor containing only one-ninth of its volume of oxygen. Very sudden effervescence, but not brisk; so that the deoxidizement requires some hours for its completion.

Oxide of iron, from the decomposition of water by hot iron. Weak action upon the peroxide both concentrated and diluted. Fifteen hours were not nearly sufficient to complete the deoxidizement of the liquor; for it was found after this time nearly unaltered.

Oxide of nickel, peroxide of copper, oxide of bismuth. The action of true oxides upon the concentrated liquor is not very strong, but it is sufficient to evolve all the oxygen in the space of a few hours, and in 15 hours they evolve it from the peroxide containing only one-ninth of its volume of oxygen.

Potash, soda. Strong action even when they are dissolved in water upon the concentrated peroxide of hydrogen; rather rapid evolution of oxygen; very soon perfect deoxidizement. When the peroxide of hydrogen is diluted with water, the decomposition takes place less rapidly, but eventually all the oxygen is expelled.

Gelatinous magnesia, and highly concentrated peroxide of hydrogen. Very evident evolution of oxygen gas, which gradually subsides before the total deoxidizement.

Gelatinous magnesia, and liquor containing nine times its volume of oxygen. Rather brisk effervescence, which gradually subsides before the deoxidizement is complete. It appears, however, to evolve proportionally more oxygen when the liquor is dilute than when it is concentrated.

Magnesia in powder. The action is weaker than when in the gelatinous state.

Hydrate of barytes, strontian, and lime. But little action.

Oxide of uranium, procured by decomposing sulphate of uranium with potash. Still less action than the last oxides.

Oxide of titanium in powder, sublimed oxide of zinc, oxide of cerium. Weak effervescence. At the end of 30 hours the liquor was scarcely deoxidized.

Of the Oxides which evolve the Oxygen of the Peroxide of Hydrogen, and which at the same time lose their own either partially or totally.

These oxides are the oxides of silver, mercury, deutoxide and peroxide of lead, of gold, platina, and probably iridium, palladium, and rhodium.

Oxide of silver. Of all oxides, this appears to have most action upon the peroxide of hydrogen; it immediately expels its oxygen, and this occurs so rapidly, that explosion may happen when the peroxide is concentrated: moreover, the heat produced is such that luminous spots are perceived when the experiment is performed in the dark. Under these circumstances, it is not extraordinary that the oxide of silver should be reduced: the experiment should not be made in a narrow tube.

The action is very strong, even when the peroxide of hydrogen is diluted in water. In fact, oxide of silver occasions very evident and sudden effervescence in water which contains only a fiftieth of its volume of oxygen; so that, when a tube is filled with mercury, and inverted, and water containing twelve times its volume of oxygen is passed up into it, oxide of silver afterwards thrown up, sinks the mercury so suddenly that the eye follows it with difficulty. In this case, there is no sensible production of heat, and yet the oxide of silver is reduced. This oxide is reduced even in the most diluted peroxide of hydrogen, so that it must not be conceived that the expulsion of the oxygen from the metal is not the effect of temperature; it may happen that at the moment of the action of the oxide of silver upon the peroxide of hydrogen, the particles which act upon each other are much heated, and that their number being very small, compared with the liquor, they are incapable of raising its temperature half a degree.

Peroxide of lead in powder. The action of this oxide upon the peroxide of hydrogen is nearly as strong as that of the oxide of silver, and the results are similar, excepting that the peroxide of lead is not reduced, but becomes merely yellow protoxide in the concentrated liquor. I doubt whether it undergoes similar deoxidizement in the diluted liquor.

Minium and peroxide of hydrogen. The same phenomena as with the peroxide, excepting that the action, which is less rapid, takes place without the evolution of light, and with less extrication of heat.

Hydrated peroxide of mercury, and peroxide of hydrogen. The hydrate of mercury, previously moistened with water, was put upon blotting paper, and the trial was then made in the usual way. In a moment, the yellow colour of the oxide became red, effervescence occurred, and soon became violent; there was then great extrication of heat, the mercurial oxide was reduced, and the liquor completely deoxidized.

Hydrate of peroxide of mercury, and liquor containing only nine volumes of oxygen. Very moderate effervescence; no sensible heat; the oxide reduced in 24 hours; complete de-oxidizement of the liquor also, provided the peroxide of mercury is in excess.

Peroxide of mercury by heat in fine powder. This oxide in powder was of a greenish ochre yellow colour; when put into the concentrated peroxide of hydrogen, it became red, like the hydrate, and acted like it, but less quickly; the action always finished violently, the disengagement of heat being very great, and the oxide reduced. Its action upon the diluted liquor is weak.

Brown oxide of gold in powder, and highly concentrated peroxide. Action sudden; violent; great extrication of heat; reduction of the gold; complete deoxidizement of the liquor.

Oxide of gold, and liquor containing only nine volumes of oxygen. Sudden, brisk effervescence; no heat; the gold reduced; and the liquor deoxidized in a short time.

Oxide of platina in powder, obtained by boiling muriate of platina with soda. Similar action upon concentrated and diluted peroxide of hydrogen as the oxide of gold.

Oxide of osmium, procured by calcining osmium with chlorate of potash, and highly concentrated peroxide of hydrogen. No sensible action; but as soon as a small quantity of potash is added, great effervescence, much heat; and the clear colourless liquor becomes of a dark brown. It is uncertain whether the oxide of osmium is reduced. The peroxide diluted with water acts similarly, excepting with less intensity.

Of the Oxides which do not act sensibly, if at all, upon the Peroxide of Hydrogen.

These are alumina, silica, oxide of chrome, peroxide of tin, protoxide and peroxide of antimony and tungstic acid.

Several other oxides are undoubtedly similarly circumstanced, but having had no opportunity of trying them, I cannot speak with any certainty.

Description of Mount Etna and its Crater.
Letters from the South of Italy.

If the glaciers, as described in our last number, present an object of admiration and astonishment, Etna excites similar feelings in a still higher degree; accompained also by inexpressible terror; if the visitor be a stranger, and the volcano in an active condition. Perhaps the whole surface of the globe cannot present such specimens of extreme operations of nature as are here exhibited, almost in the vicinity of each other: on the one hand is the intensity of an eternal winter cold; on the other, that of immeasurable heat. We give this account to the reader from motives precisely similar to those urging our presentation of the descriptive outline of the glaciers.

"*Catania, Aug.* 27, 1819.

"We set out at three o'clock, P. M. from this city, and proceeding slowly on my mule, I ruminated on the description which I am about to give you of the most celebrated of volcanoes, of which you have already heard so much, that I have decided simply to relate to you what came under my own observation. We began our march in frightful roads, amidst rocks of lava, which cover the first part of the route. Our mules, habituated to these rough passes, never once stumbled; but an accident happening to mine, embarrassed me greatly. I felt my foot wet, and one side of my pantaloons was covered with blood; I alighted, and perceived that my mule had been recently hurt. With a handkerchief and thong we bound up the wound, and continued our journey in a road covered with lava, but bordered with superb Indian fig trees, (this fruit, which is despised in America, is an article of great consumption in Sicily,) ordinary fig trees, and enormous olives: every where else this tree appeared to me paltry, and of a difficult vegetation; but here it grows to admiration. Some miles further we perceived, and afterwards passed through, another village called Masca-Luscia: it contains two churches; one of which, nearly destroyed by an earthquake, was never very remarkable, and the other is only rendered so, by a steeple fantastically decorated with stones of various colours. We arrived, in fine, at the last village, that of Nicolosi, which appeared poorer than all the rest: this was surely, in former times, the Town of Etna, where the inhabitants of Catania took refuge, on the arrival of the Greeks: the environs abound in olive trees and vineyards, which produce excellent wine. All this part was covered with ashes by the eruption of Monte Rosso, a secondary volcano, which formed itself at the time of the last eruption. Monte Rosso is one of those mountains by which Etna is surrounded. It appears that when an eruption takes place, the lava, making its way on the flanks of the mountains, pierces the ground in the place which offers the least resistance, and there forms a swelling, which it afterwards consolidates by flowing from above. In this village we found the guide, or, as he is called, the Pilot of Etna. After some conversation, he engaged to ascend for three piastres, about twelve shillings and sixpence. From thence to the convent, where we were to rest our beasts, we had no more than a mile to go, which we performed in coasting along Monte Rosso, whose summit was gilded by the sun, and behind which it had already set, when we arrived. This mountain is several miles in circumference. I profited by the last light of the sky, in order to sketch a view of the convent, which, although of the common extent, is nevertheless very picturesque. Built against a small hill, long since become cold, and covered with woods, it seems sheltered from the destructive effects of the volcano; from the other side, between superb fir trees, you perceive the sea, the plains of Catania, and Syracuse. You are received into the convent nearly in the same manner as you would be at an inn; the best situated room for the view is reserved for strangers; but is very indifferently furnished. We were four hours in coming from Catania, which is, notwithstanding, only a distance of twelve miles. Being provided with a fowl, &c. I supped pretty well, slept in my cloak, and we set out at half-past nine by moonlight, the guide, servant, and myself, on our mules, the mule-driver always on foot. We first entered into an immense torrent of lava; the uncertain glimmerings of the moon gave an extraordinary aspect to the huge masses by which I was surrounded. I forgot to tell you, that in this convent, which is very convenient for the traveller visiting Etna, as he there dines and rests himself, you also put on winter clothing; in fact, that season was drawing near when we quitted the monastery. You might have seen me then on the 21st of August, dressed nearly in the same manner as in England in the month of December. Soon after, long shadows scattered here and there, and a trembling of the leaves, announced the approach to the forest of oaks, which formerly encircled Etna to the height of several miles; but which an immense torrent of lava had cruelly ravaged. The light of the moon, the huge and broken rocks, the great oaks, whose vegetation surprises the beholder, in the midst of lavas, the silence of my guides, interrupted only by the rustling of the leaves, and by the trampling of our mules,—every thing led me to reflection. How can we reconcile the evident primitiveness of Etna with what Moses informs us of the creation of the world? It is true he does not say that God created the world in infancy; and if He made Adam at the age of thirty years, He might also well create Etna with an open crater, and its flanks covered with lava.

"While journeying along, I asked my guide if it was true, as I had read, that the mountain subsisted all kinds of game and wild beasts; he begged me not to be afraid: I repeated the question to him, and received the same reply, he being still persuaded that the fear of encountering ferocious animals caused me to speak in that manner. I should, notwithstanding, be led to believe that the mountain, considering its extent and gradual temperature, might well support them; but it seems to me that Mr. Brydone gave too wide a scope to his imagination, when he described Etna as a general botanic garden, an almost universal menagerie. As for the rest, I had not the pleasure of seeing any of these animals, and we arrived without molestation, at the extremity of their domain, the forest, which may be about six miles in width. We then entered into the most fantastical lavas; they have more of a slope, and the crevices which form there, as soon as they become cold, acquire more extent, and present a more rent appearance. It was one o'clock, and already the wind blew piercingly cold.

"I was sorry not to have brought a thermometer, but I had not been able to find one for sale, either at Messina or at Catania. As for a barometer, it would have been almost useless to me; the custom of calculating the elevation with this instrument, is extremely blameable. Some have found the elevation of Etna to be twelve thousand feet, and others twenty-four thousand. Cassini reckons ten fathoms for the falling line of the mercury, by adding one to the first ten, two to the second, &c. but he has never surely made the experiment of his method on very high mountains, where the air is rarefied in a much more rapid progression. Etna might be measured trigonometrically, for it descends as far as the sea, the shore being taken for the base. We may even have an approaching idea of its elevation by the time which the sun's light takes in descending from its summit to the sea.

"In returning from Alexandria to Marseilles in the month of March, I saw Etna covered with snow. A calm having lasted some hours, I profited by it to take the height of this mountain. With the aid of a mariner's compass, I perceived that the Cape Sparti-Vento, in Calabria, reached us by the N.N.E., and Cape Passaro, in Sicily, by the S.W.; I was then sure of the point where I found myself on the chart. (We made use on board of the French charts of the Mediterranean, which are very good.) This point being at a distance of sixty miles from the foot of the axis of Etna, I measured at that time the angle which the summit of the mountain made with the horizon; it was found to be six degrees; which gave me a rectangular triangle of which I knew a side and the three angles, the one right, the other of six degrees, and the third of eighty-four degrees. The base being of sixty miles, there remained for me only to make the following proportion:

$Sin. 84° : 60$ miles :: $Sin. 6° : 4\frac{24}{84}$

"The result is found to be, for the axis side of Etna, four miles and twenty-four eighty-fourths, above four miles and a quarter, or about twenty thousand four hundred feet for the total height. This measure is not perhaps perfectly correct, but, at least, it approximates very near to it. If this height appears surprising, we ought to consider that other great mountains have never been measured but with the barometer, and that Mr. Brydone was surprised to see the mercury here, descending nearly two inches lower than on the summit of the Alps.

" Having arrived near a mass of snow which filled one of the narrow passes of the mountain, a summit which looked black in the sky, made me believe that I was at the end of the journey; an old tower which I took for the *Torre del Filosofo*, confirmed me in my error. I soon after perceived another summit covered with a whitish smoke; I asked if it was much higher than the other: my guide affirmed that it was, and he was in the right, for it seemed to me to surpass the first in the whole height of Vesuvius. The road became more united, and the acclivity gentler, but the wind was very violent, and the cold as sharp as it is with you in winter. We coasted along a torrent of black lava, the more singular, as its elevation was from eight to ten feet, and perpendicular like a wall, which clearly proved to me, that this matter, in flowing, is not in perfect fusion; as a great part of the substances which it drags along, are sufficiently hard to prevent their melting, and that they are like the basalt, detached from the immense vaults which, during many ages, supported this natural forge. The sky began to adorn itself in the east, and we perceived the house called *Les Anglais*. You have generally the key of this hut; but not having sent a shilling, with my request, to the person it belonged to, or rather to his domestic, we entered into the stable, where we kindled the charcoal which we had brought, and I can assure you, that I experienced there a pleasure which I had not for a long time enjoyed, that of being cold, and feeling the beneficent heat of the fire. After a light breakfast I directed my steps towards the place, where, according to custom, the curious go to behold the rising of the sun.

" There is no sight in the world which can equal this: the point of Calabria, the sea which separates it from Sicily, the mountains of Southern Italy, even the clouds which covered them, seemed to be at your feet.

"The horizon was in a blaze: a globe of fire escaped from the floods, it was the sun appearing in the midst of the fog: it was of a greyish red, and its horizontal diameter was much greater than the perpendicular. The colour became more vivid: a rapid flash of lightning, which glided along the surface of the sea, announces the presence of the star of day; its diameter enlarged, and it rose in the heavens. I profited by the moment in which the shadows still lengthened on the plains, to climb up the last summit, at a distance of two miles.

"I do not exactly know how it can be explained, why the sun appears lengthened in the fog, if it is not by the pressure which each bed of the latter produces on the one under it; the stars appeared brilliant and numerous, and the moon was small but bright. I have already more than once remarked this effect in the most elevated places, which I attribute to the rarefaction of the air diverging a little the luminous rays.

"The mule-driver remaining with our beasts, I bent my steps towards the last summit, which, covered with a light white smoke, seemed to move away from the impatient traveller. We walked near a mile on an almost horizontal lava, or, to speak more correctly, on striated scoriæ, or dross, which made a cracking noise under our feet, and soon after on a large swamp of snow, where we found a large round stone, three feet in diameter, of the species of those called volcanic balls, which the mountain throws up in great eruptions: but it is only a grain of metal in comparison with the volcano, which ejected it from its bosom. In fine, we mounted the last cone which supports the crater; the ashes and the stones slipping under our feet. The cold was excessive, but exercise kept us warm; I quitted my cloak, and rolling up in it some pieces of lava, I left it on the mountain. My guide, in order to repose himself, invited me at every moment to enjoy the view which presented itself. At last we arrived on the borders of the crater; but the wind was so violent, that I could scarcely cast a glance over it. I was thrown down, and had it not been for my *ciceroni*, I might have rolled to the foot of the declivity which had given us so much trouble to ascend.

Fastened and lying down on the ridge of the crater, I considered it at my ease, and braved the fury of Æolus and Vulcan.

"It is a vast aperture, having four summits of different heights, rather more than a mile in width, and, on account of its inequalities, I should think it about four in circumference. It is divided into two craters, by a cone rising from its centre, and which forms a crater itself, the slope of which is not very rapid. The ancient aperture is united to this cone by a gentle declivity, where has probably been formed, within a recent period, a small crater, a partial volcano, a perfect truncated cone, from whence issues a great quantity of smoke. The general aspect of the crater is much less dreary than that of Vesuvius; the substances surrounding it are not so black, but have rather the colour of potter's earth. It is now six years since Etna has made an eruption, but it has given concussions which have alarmed the inhabitants of Catania and overthrown some houses.

"How can I describe to you the immense panorama which developed itself before my eyes! The whole of Sicily was encircled round Etna, which its own grandeur insulates from every thing that surrounds it,—the other mountains, rivers, woods, and plains, are simply traced on a map extended at my feet. Calabria, from which a small canal alone separates us, is only a point of land, which is almost lost between the two seas. Farther off is Greece, but I could not see it. The point which is distinguished to the south, in the midst of the immensity of waters, is Malta, that bulwark of Christianity, that rock on which split the glory of the Ottoman arms.

"I was assured that we might see the coast of Africa; but the weather was very foggy, and I could not perceive it. One thing struck me, although it was only a very simple effect of the perspective, and this was the inclined plane which the sea presented towards me.

"In that moment, when the sun rises to render life to so many creatures, so many towns which are only a point in the extent embraced by the eye, I was truly enraptured to find myself in the centre of so vast a panorama. Of how many successive beds of lava and ashes is this mountain formed?

How many generations has it seen? With how many eruptions has it alarmed the various inhabitants, of which we have not even an idea?

"I could not make the entire tour of the crater, on account of the violence of the wind, which prevented me also from descending into the interior, which appeared to me less rapid than that of Vesuvius.

"It is when seated on the borders of the crater, that we may look down from one side into the rugged flanks of the mountain, and from the other, on an immense horizon: it is then, I say, that one is tempted to reason on the nature of volcanoes. I passed in review the various systems with which I was conversant, and I am forced to confess that each of them presents difficulties.

"It was with great regret that I quitted a spot where I breathed, I thought, with more freedom than in any other part of the world. Having arrived at the *Maison des Anglais*, I there finished my breakfast and amused myself in designing. You perceive from thence in the south east, a tower which is detached in the sky, and which is called the Philosopher's Tower; it is a small square heap of stones and bricks which have been elevated on the ruins of a more ancient edifice, and which was primitively constructed for the philosopher Empedocles of Agrigentum, who, wishing to retire from the world and give himself up to reflection, established himself there. It is said, that wishing to have it believed that he had been carried away by the gods, he precipitated himself into the crater, and that the latter, an unfaithful depository of the remains of this madman, vomited his brass sandals, which were found on the borders of the crater. Strabo does not believe in this story; he also relates something very extraordinary, which would seem to prove that the ancients knew less of Etna than we do. He says that two travellers wishing to approach the crater, were driven back by the smoke, and were unable to see it.

"In a little time we arrived in the temperate regions: we found some verdure, and saw the goats which are brought to drink of the water flowing from a heap of snow, which is preserved by being covered with ashes. It is from thence that the people draw the water which they carry away and sell at Catania. The road became difficult, I toiled, and the fatigue became overwhelming for my beast and for myself. Having arrived at the forest, I set foot on the ground and walked, profiting by the shade of the foliage, for by this time the sun became troublesome. Near the middle of the forest is the cavern of goats; it is a vacant space under an ancient torrent of lava; it is twenty feet wide, but very few in depth. I don't know why travellers have spoken so much about it; the names of a number of the curious, inscribed on the surrounding trees, is the only remarkable thing which I saw there; I added my own; the proverb only bears, I believe, against those who write on the walls. This forest which belongs to Prince * * * *, contains oaks from twenty to thirty feet round, but their exportation is very difficult; I should have even thought it impossible if I had not met with a square piece which was transported on rollers, gliding on two rafters, successively placed on the lava. We afterwards entered into the vast torrent of lava which flowed from Monte Rosso: the heat became insupportable. Having reached the convent, I dined there with a good appetite, but having been charged somewhat exorbitantly, I took my leave rather discontented. I entered into the torrid zone, and again put on my summer clothing. This Etna is truly an image of the earth; it may be compared to one of the two hemispheres, of the north or of the south; its icy summit resembles the pole, and is not susceptible of culture; its temperate zone, on the contrary, presents the finest vegetation. The superb forest which surrounds it like a covering of verdure, and its base, where the torrents of lava, finding less declivity, extend the more, resemble the countries situated between the two tropics; some plants are even found there, such as the date tree, which are peculiar to them."

Considerations on the Passage round North America. By A CORRESPONDENT.

As the pages of a work devoted to objects of practical science, can scarcely be occupied with more interesting matter of reflection than the discovery of a passage north about, or north western to Asia, I take the liberty to address you with a few remarks on the voyage of Kotzebue, and if you agree with me, that the subject can merit a place in the "Focus," I shall feel favoured by your insertion of my crude notions thereon. Perhaps I need not add that I am a fond believer in the possibility of such a passage. I shall not intrude on your space, by observing on points foreign to the particular object proposed, and therefore come at once to the navigator, when making through Behring's Strait, on the American side, and in latitude little more than 66° north. M. K. says that, "We saw a great quantity of drifted wood on Saritscheff Island, and among these, trees of a considerable size. Upon our anchorage, which is astronomically determined, we observed that the current constantly ran to N. E. along the coast: thus it is probable that the wood is drifted into Behring's Strait from the south. The longitude of our anchorage, by the chronometers, was 166° 24′, and observed latitude 66° 14′. On the 1st of August we observed that the coast took a direction to the east, the land continuing to be low. At eleven o'clock we were at the entrance of a large inlet: we lost the coast we had hitherto pursued; and whilst in E. and N. we saw a lofty ridge of hills. Here the wind suddenly declined, and we were obliged to come to anchor, upon a clayey ground, in a depth of seven fathoms. The nearest land from us lay in S. E. at a distance of four miles; the current running strongly toward the entrance." M. K. goes on to say, that "I cannot describe my feelings when I thought that I might be opposite the long sought for N. E. passage, and that fate had destined me to be its discoverer. In order to get some idea of the direction of the land, I went on shore with two boats. The depth was gradually decreasing, and half a mile from shore we found only four fathoms water. We landed without difficulty at the foot of a hill, which I immediately ascended. From this I could see no land in any part of the Strait. The high hills in the north were either islands, or a distinct coast; for that both coasts could not be connected, appeared evident, from this being very low, and the other very high land. From my hill I had a distinct view of the land, which continued in a large plain, occasionally interrupted by morasses, small lakes, and a river; which, meandering in various directions, had its rise near us. As far as the eye could reach, every thing was green; here and there were flowers, and snow could only be seen, at a great distance, on the tops of the hills: yet, by digging six inches into the ground, all under this sward was icy and frozen. It was my intention to have examined the coast in the boats; which, however, was prevented by several baydares coming along the shore, from the east, towards us."

I omit the interview with Americans, and resume in the Captain's words. " On the shore we perceived a round tower, built of stone, from 24 to 30 feet high, and six feet in diameter." Again. "At seven o'clock I took my course, with a gentle south breeze, towards the inlet. The Americans followed us in their baydares, showing us their skins, and pointing out, by signs, that we should find a great many of them in the direction we were sailing. At the same time one of them frequently repeated the words, ' Iannieæ eæ,' while he was repeatedly pointing, first to the ship, and then to the inlet. The latitude of our anchorage, by the ship account, was 60° 42′ 30″; longitude, by the chronometers, 164° 12′ 30″. While we were at anchor, the current constantly ran to N. E., one mile and a quarter in an hour. At sun-set the Americans left us, and we sailed, during the night, in an eastern direction; the increasing depth adding fresh vigour to our hopes. On the 2d of August, at day-break, the man whom I sent to the mast head still saw an open sea to the east. In the north we saw high land, taking its direction to the east; being a continuation of that which we had seen the day before from our anchorage. Discovering in the south a low land, taking its direction to the east, we could not doubt but that we were in a broad channel; and our joy was increased by still seeing an open sea in the east. The wind turning round to S. E., we were obliged to tack. The weather was fine; the latitude at noon was 66° 35′ 18″; the longitude 162° 19′. At five P. M. we saw land at various points, and our hope, as yet, only rested upon an open space between high hills. On the 3d, during the night, we reached this spot, but were obliged, on account of the dull weather, to anchor over a clayey ground, in a depth of eight fathoms. When the weather cleared up, at noon, we found ourselves before an inlet, five miles broad, the shores of which consisted of a high rocky land; the passage remaining open as far as the eye could reach. At the same time the tide regularly changed; and the current ran out with a greater rapidity than it entered. We heaved anchor, and sailed towards the inlet; but having passed the Strait, dropped again over a clayey ground, in seven fathoms of water. The land which, in sailing in, lay on our right hand, was an island of seven miles in circumference. In the north the sea was still open; but I somewhat despaired, when the sounding boat that I had sent out could no where find above five or six fathoms of depth. I resolved to let my people rest to-day, in order to prosecute the examination with renewed alacrity on the following day. In the mean time we made an excursion to the island, which I called after our naturalist, Chamisso. On the 4th, at six o'clock, A. M., I left the ship, in a boat, accompanied by the lieutenant, and our scientific gentlemen, provided with arms and provisions for some days; before starting we took several altitudes, and found the longitude of our anchorage 161° 42′ 20″, the latitude, after several observations, 66° 13′ 25.″ The land was high and rocky, and from the summit of a hill, which we ascended, we discovered we were upon a small rock of ground, and that the land, in the north, seemed to join that in the east,—a very disagreeable surprise to us; yet the total junction not being visible, we still entertained some hope, and took our course easterly, towards the opposite coast. In the middle of the navigable tract, we had from five to six fathoms depth; which, however, so decreased, on approaching the shore, that, for fear of running aground, I turned to the north, straight towards the land which we had seen at noon, from the top of the hill; and when we had approached within 100 fathoms, we again had only one fathom of water left. On the 7th we set out again for the examination of the eastern part of the bay, and at noon we had penetrated far enough to see that the land met every where: within a mile from the end, the depth had already decreased to five feet, and we gave up even the hope of finding a river."

Now, I must presume so far as to state, that I think Captain Kotzebue's conclusion, as to all easterly passage from Schismariff's Bay, rather too hasty; nothing short of passing on to the point where he supposes the land closed, should have satisfied him. The mere shallowing in depth of water is frequently fallacious. But the matter to which I think navigators should principally direct their attention, is the stated fact of there being a constant current, northerly, through Behring's Strait. Where can this current set to, if not round the northern extremity of America, and down again, southerly, to Baffin's Bay? where the current is known to set from north again to south, along the western coast of extreme northern America. If there really be such a current as this, of which Kotzebue seems to be fully impressed, there may very probably be a passage for shipping; though, indeed, it must run very high north; perhaps near the pole. Still I feel so impressed with an idea of the possibility of such a passage, that I cannot abandon a hope of its accomplishment. In a future paper I will trouble you with a summary of all the published arguments that I have been able to collect on this subject; and I assure you that I have been rather industrious in the pursuit. AMICUS.

Our Correspondent is very sanguine in his expectations of this long-tried object: but we would inquire what may be the utility of such repeated and expensive expeditions? Suppose a passage made in very high northern latitudes; (and we now know that they must be truly high, if made at all) what market do we open for merchandize? Why, we obtain furs at a more moderate price; an article that nine-tenths of Europe have not any occasion for. And what would the exchangeable value in manufactured produce, exported from Europe to the northern shores of America and Asia, amount to? Why, absolutely nothing, in the grand scale of commercial enterprize. We will venture to predict, that let such passage be discovered, at what point of latitude it may, the severity of the winter seasons, and the consequent icy accumulations, will ever render trading so precarious, and so dangerous, and, often, so much prolonged, as to secure the Hudson's Bay

Company from any very dangerous competition. In so far as regards the employment of commercial capital, it is then a mere delusion: nor need Great Britain, as we trust, be ferreting out such holes and corners as these for national prosperity: let her look to the improving means of old and new Spain; where she may hereafter gather far more abundant wealth than a thousand worlds of such Quixotic commerce as the north western passage could produce. With respect to science, these expeditions have a value, and it is only in that view which we can be reconciled to them: for all the rest is but a random pursuit after vain glory; a bubble to amuse a prince; or a secret delusion *ad captandum vulgus*. Were the expenses incurred in these expeditions but applied to the improvement of harbours, the clearing of lands, and the rendering of commercial facilities with New Holland, &c., the country would reap something more than a limited and speculative uncertainty. Besides, the contiguity of British with Russian settlements, would be a perpetual source of misunderstanding between the two countries. Even Spain, we may remember, has contested rights and profits with us there.

The reproaches that our Correspondent casts on Kotzebue, may be partly just; but we think that even if he had pursued the inlet in Schismariff's Bay, easterly, it would have led him into the Bay of Good Hope, in Kotzebue's Sound, and not into any eastern sea, communicating with the northern Atlantic; Schismariff's Bay, and the Bay of Good Hope, lying in the same parallel. As to the flow of the Pacific, northerly, through Behring's Strait; and north easterly, along the north western coast, from Cape Prince of Wales to Kotzebue's Sound; we think it very far from being conclusive, that a vessel should be carried round the northern extremity of America by such current; or that the higher northern sea should necessarily be open. The north-eastern current to Kotzebue's Sound, ", setting," as the commander states, " strongly towards the entrance," goes, as we think, to supply that Sound: and perhaps there is an under current, outwards, from the Sound to the ocean; as at the entrance to the Mediterranean, from the Atlantic. The great body of the Pacific passing northerly through Behring's Strait, must be largely diffused round Kamschatka, into the northern Asiatic sea, as well as north and north westerly. Whether there be any continued line of ocean round the extreme point of America, as presumed by some, from the current setting northerly, on the western side; and southerly, on the eastern side; can be of but little importance, in a commercial view: for such passage must be so near the pole, and consequently so replete with inclement difficulties, as to place it out of the speculation of probable accomplishment.

On the Circle, Sphere, Square, and Equilateral Triangle. By Mr. JAMES UTTING.

Philosophical Mag. No. 286.

The relative proportions of the circle, sphere, square, and equilateral triangle are determined by Mr. Utting to twenty places of decimal figures and upwards; but as, for all common purposes, the first five decimals may be amply sufficient, we shall not trouble our readers by detailing beyond that number.

Diameter of a circle, being 1, the circumference is 3·14159, &c.

Diameter of circle being 1, the area = 1·78539. &c.

Diameter of sphere being 1, solidity = 1·52359, &c.

Diameter of circle being 1, side of the circumscribed equilateral triangle = 1·73205, &c.

Diameter of circle being 1, side of inscribed equilateral triangle = ·86602.

Diameter of circle being 1, side of an equilateral triangle of equal area = 1·34677.

Diameter of circle being 1, side of a square of similar area = ·88622.

Diameter of circle being 1, side of inscribed square = ·70710

Side of a square equalling 1, diameter of circumscribed circle = 1·41421.

Side of square equalling 1, side of circumscribed equilateral triangle = 2·15470.

Side of square equalling 1, side of equilateral triangle of similar area = 1·51967.

Side of equilateral triangle equalling 1, diameter of its inscribed circle = ·57735.

Side of equilateral triangle equalling 1, diameter of its circumscribed circle = 1·15470.

Side of equilateral triangle equalling 1, diameter of a circle of similar area = ·74251.

Side of equilateral triangle equalling 1, side of inscribed square = ·46530.

Side of equilateral triangle equalling 1, side of square of similar area = ·65803.

Side of equilateral triangle being given, to find its area; multiply square of side by ·43301.

Lines circumscribing a square and a circle of similar areas are in proportion as 3·54490 to 3·14159. Or as 1, to ·88622, &c.

Lines circumscribing a square and an equilateral triangle of similar areas are in proportion as 1, to 1·51967, &c.

Lines circumscribing an equilateral triangle and a circle of similar areas are in proportion as 1, to ·77756, &c.

Area of a hexagon to that of circumscribing circle as 1, to 1·20919. Or as ·82699, &c. to 1.

Remeasurement of the Cube, Cylinder, and Sphere, used by the late Sir George Shuckburgh Evelyn, in his Inquiries respecting a Standard for Weights and Measures. By Capt. H. KATER.

Philosophical Transactions.

As bearing a mathematical analogy with the preceding paper, we present this concise determination of the relative proportions of the cube, cylinder, and sphere, by Captain Kater. When Sir George Evelyn made his experiments in 1798, his attention was directed rather to the *weight* than the *measurement*. And as Captain K. was one of the Commissioners of Weights and Measures, lately sitting, to correct and determine for final standards, he instituted a series of careful experiments, wherefrom he deduces thus:

The mean result of measurement of three sides of the cube gives for contents 124·1969 inches.

The length of cylinder, deduced from three means, is 5·9960 inches.

To measure the sphere Sir G. used a brass square; the sides of the latter rather exceeding the diameter of the former. The sphere being placed within the square, a micrometer screw, passing through one side of the square, was brought into contact with the sphere, and the index of the micrometer noted. On removing the sphere, and substituting a brass ruler of known length, the micrometer screw was brought into contact with the extremity of the ruler, the difference between whose length, and that of the diameter of the sphere was of course found; and by Captain Kater's re-measurement, determined to be 0·0012281 inches excess of that diameter above the length of the rules. Captain K. then found the brass ruler, by measurement, to = 6·006309 inches, and therefrom deduced the diameter of the sphere, which denoted for solid contents 113·5264 inches.

Lastly, the Captain deduced as the result of experiment that a cubic inch of distilled water, in a vacuum, at 62° = 252·888 grains of Sir George's standard; or 252·722 grains parliamentary standard.

Volcano de Taal, on Lucon, one of the Philippine Islands. By Dr. A. Von Chamisso.

Dr. Von C. was the Naturalist who accompanied M. Kotzebue in his voyage to discover a North East passage from the Pacific to the Atlantic Ocean.

"We had an opportunity to make only one excursion, of eight days, into the interior, to Taal, and the volcano of the same name, in the Laguna de Boudborig. The military escort accompanying us, which was a mark of Spanish pomp, was very troublesome, and increased the expenses of a journey where only a guide would have been requisite, among the mild and hospitable Tagalese. The island of Lucon is every where high and mountainous; the highest summits do not seem, however, to exceed the woody region. Three volcanoes rise from it: first, in the north, the Aringuay, in the territory of the Ygorrotes, in the province of Ilocos, which, on the fourth of January, 1641, broke out at the same time with the volcano of Iolo, and the Sanguil, in the south of Magindanao, on which occasion this island presented one of the most terrible scenes recorded in history; the noise was heard on the continent of Cochin China; secondly, the volcano de Taal, which particularly threatens the capital, from which it is distant a day's journey; and lastly, the far seen Mayon, near the Embocadera de San Bernardino, between Albay and Camarines.

"Gold, iron, and copper mines, which are very rich, but neglected, show that there are other mountains as well as volcanic ones. On the way we went, we saw no other than volcanic tuff, consisting of ashes, pumice-stones, and dross; and, in Manilla, Cavite, Taal, Balayan, &c., no other stone for building but this same tuff and calcareous reef-stone, procured from the sea. The granite used in Manilla for building is brought here as ballast from the coast of China.

"As you go from Cavite, southward towards Taal, the land insensibly and gradually rises till you reach the eminences on the other side, which are rugged and steep, and from which you may overlook, at your feet, the Laguna de Boudborig, and the large smoking crater, which forms in it a dreary naked island.

"The lake (the Laguna) is about six German miles in circumference; it empties itself into the Chinese sea by an outlet navigable now only for small boats, though formerly it could carry larger vessels; it runs with great rapidity, and the length of its course is about a German mile. Since the devastation in 1754, Taal has been removed to its mouth.

"The water in the Laguna is brackish; but it is, however, drinkable. In the middle it is reported to be unfathomable. It is said to be full of sharks and caymans, of which, however, we saw none.

"As we were embarking from the Laguna for the island, the Tagalese exhorted us to look round us in this haunted place, but to keep silence, and not to irritate the spirit by any incautious, or inconsiderate word. The volcano, they said, showed symptoms of displeasure whenever a Spaniard visited it, and was indifferent only to the natives.

"The island is nothing but a mass of ashes and scoriæ, which has fallen in itself, and formed the wild irregular crater, which creates so much terror. It does not appear that the lava has ever flowed out of it. From the bank, where a little grass grows in scanty spots, and where some cattle are kept to pasture, you climb, on the east side, up a bare and steep ascent, and in about a quarter of an hour, reach the edge, from which you look down into the abyss as into the area of an extensive circus. A pool of yellow sulphureous water occupies about two-thirds of the bottom. Its level seems to be the same as that of the Laguna. On the southern edge of this pool are several hills of sulphur, which are slowly burning. Towards the south and east of it, a narrower crater is beginning to form itself in the interior of the great crater. The arch which it makes, surrounds, like the *moraine* of a glacier, the burning hills by which it is produced, and rests with both its ends on the pool. The pool boils, from time to time, at the foot of the burning hills.

" You can clearly distinguish, in the internal wall of the crater, the situations of the differently coloured scoriæ of which it consists. Smoke ascends from some points of it.

" We observed from the place where we made a drawing of the crater, a place on the opposite side of it, where a fall into the interior seemed to afford a slope from which it might be possible to descend to the bottom. It cost us much time and trouble to gain this point, as we found the sharp and pointed edge on which we walked, in many places impassable, and were frequently obliged to descend on the outside almost to the bank. Being under the wind of the fire, we were but slightly incommoded by the sulphureous exhalations.

" The place just mentioned is that on which, during the last eruptions, the water poured that was thrown up. We attempted to descend into several clefts, but where ultimately obliged to abandon our intention, after we had reached about two-thirds of the depth. We were not provided in Taal with the cords we required, and by the assistance of which we might have descended the perpendicular wall, of several fathoms high, which first presented itself to us, without being able to reach the bottom, as the precipice became always steeper the farther we descended. We found, in this neighbourhood, the ground covered with plumose alum.

" The time was too short to permit us to visit the other hills.

" The other craters are at the pool of the principal crater.

" The most terrible eruption of the Volcano de Taal was in the year 1754. Its desolating progress is circumstantially related in the twelfth chapter of the thirteenth part of the history by Fr. Juan de la Conception. The mountain was tranquil after the former eruptions, (the last took place in the year 1716,) and sulphur was obtained from the apparently extinguished crater. It began to smoke anew in the beginning of August; and, on the 7th, flames were seen, and the earth trembled. The consternation increased from the 3d of November to the 12th of December; ashes, sand, mud, fire, and water were thrown up. Darkness, hurricanes, thunder and lightning, subterraneous roarings, and long protracted, violent, and repeated earthquakes, alternated in frightful succession. Taal, lying at that time on the banks of the Laguna, and several villages, were totally ruined and overthrown. The mouth of the volcano was too confined for such eruptions; it widened considerably, and a second opened, which likewise threw up fire and mud. Nay, even more, the fire broke out in several places in the Laguna, at a considerable depth below the surface of the water, which boiled up. The earth opened in many places, and a deep gulph yawned particularly wide, extending far in the direction to Calambourg. The mountain continued to smoke a long time. There have since been eruptions, though with decreasing violence."

Extraordinary Cave in Indiana. Described by Mr. BENJAMIN ADAMS, *Proprietor of the Cave, in a Letter addressed to H. Farnham, Esq. Frankfort, Ohio.*

Archæologia Americana.

This is, indeed, a very extraordinary cave, and well worthy to be particularly described. The date of its existence cannot, of course, be known; but it appears that the aborigines were not ignorant of its natural wealth; and doubtless drew from its walls much of an article which they might convert to useful purposes.

"The cave is situated in the north-west quarter of section 27, in township No. 3, of the second easterly range in the district of lands offered for sale at Jeffersonville. The precise time of its discovery is difficult to ascertain. I have conversed with several men who had made transient visits to the interior of the cave, about eleven years ago, at which time it must have exhibited a very interesting appearance, being, to use their own phraseology, *covered like snow*, with the salts. At this period, some describe the salts to have been from six to nine inches deep, on the bottom of the cave, on which lumps of an enormous size were interspersed; while the sides presented the same impressive spectacle with the bottom, being covered with the same production. Making liberal allowances for the hyperbole of discoverers and visitors, I cannot help thinking that the scenery of the interior, at this time, was highly interesting, and extremely picturesque. I found this opinion upon conversations with Generals Harrison and Floyd, who visited the cave at an early period, and whose intelligence would render them less liable to be deceived by novel appearances.

"The hill, in which the cave is situated, is about four hundred feet high from the base to the most elevated point, and the prospect from the south east, in a clear day, is exceedingly fine, commanding an extensive view of the hills and vallies bordering on Big Blue River. The top of the hill is covered principally with oak and chesnut. The side to the south east is mantled with cedar. The entrance is about midway from the base to the summit, and the surface of the cave preserves, in general, about that elevation; although I must acknowledge this to be conjectural, as no experiments have been made with a view to ascertain the fact. It is probably owing to this middle situation of the cave, that it is much drier than in common.

" After entering the cave, by an aperture of twelve or fifteen wide, and in height, in one place, three or four feet, you descend, with easy and gradual steps, into a large and spacious room, which continues about a quarter of a mile pretty nearly the same in appearance, varying in height, from eight to thirty feet, and in breadth, from ten to twenty. In this distance the roof is, in some places, arched, and in others a plane; and in one place, particularly, it resembles an inside view of the roof of a house. At the distance above named the cave forks; but the right hand fork soon terminates, while the left rises by a flight of rocky stairs, nearly ten feet high, into another story, and pursues a course, at this place, nearly south east. Here the roof commences a regular arch, the height of which, from the floor, varies from five to eight feet, and the width of the cave from six to twelve feet; which continues to what is called the *creeping place*, from the circumstance of having to crawl ten or twelve feet into the next large room. From this place to the 'pillar,' a distance of about one mile and a quarter, the visitor finds an alternate succession of large and small rooms, variously decorated; sometimes mounting elevated points, by gradual or difficult ascents, and again descending as far below; sometimes travelling on a pavement, or climbing over huge piles of rocks detached from the roof by some convulsion of nature.

"The appearance of the pillar, as it comes in sight, from the reflection of the torches, is grand and impressive. Visitors have seldom pushed their inquiries farther than two or three hundred yards beyond this pillar. This column is about fifteen feet in diameter; from twenty to thirty in height, and regularly reeded from the top to the bottom. In the vicinity of this spot, are some inferior pillars, of the same appearance and texture. Chemically speaking, it is difficult for me to say what are the constituent parts of these columns, but lime appears to be the base. Major Warren, who is certainly a competent judge, is of opinion that they are satin spar.

"I have thus given you an imperfect sketch of the mechanical structure and appearance of the cave. It only remains to mention its productions.

"The first in importance is the sulphate of magnesia, or Epsom salts, which, as has been previously remarked, abounds throughout this cave, in almost its whole extent, and which, I believe has no parallel in the history of that article. This neutral salt is found in a great variety of forms, and in many different stages of formation. Sometimes in lumps, varying from one to ten pounds in weight. The earth exhibits a shining appearance, from the numerous particles interspersed throughout the huge piles of dirt collected in different parts of the cave. The walls are covered, in different places, with the same article, and re-production goes on rapidly. With a view to ascertain this fact, I removed, from a particular place, every vestige of salt, and in four or five weeks the place was covered with small needle-shaped crystals, exhibiting the appearance of frost.

"The quality of the salt in this cave is inferior to none; and when it takes its proper stand in regular and domestic practice, must be of national utility. With respect to the resources of this cave, I will venture to say, that every competent judge must pronounce them inexhaustible. The worst earth that has been tried, will yield four pounds of salt to the bushel; and the best from twenty to twenty-five pounds.

"The next production is the nitrate of lime, or saltpetre earth. There are vast quantities of this earth, and equal in strength to any that I have ever seen. There are also large quantities of the nitrate of alumina, or nitrate of argil, which will yield as much nitrate of potash, or saltpetre, in proportion to the quantities of earth, as the nitrate of lime.

"The three articles above enumerated are first in quantity and importance; but there are several others which deserve notice, as subjects of philosophical curiosity. The sulphate of lime, or plaster of Paris, is to be seen variously formed, ponderous, crystallized, and impalpable or soft, light, and rather spongy. Vestiges of the sulphate of iron are also to be seen, in one or two places. Small specimens of the carbonate, and also the nitrate of magnesia, have been found. The rocks in the cave principally consist of carbonate of lime, or common lime-stone.

"I had almost forgotten to state that, near the forks of the cave are two specimens of painting, probably of Indian origin. The one appears to be a savage, with something like a bow in his hand, and furnishes the hint, that it was done when that instrument of death was in use. The other is so much defaced, that it is impossible to say what it was intended to represent."

We do not comprehend Mr. Adams's assertion, that there is an abundance of nitrate of alumina, which will yield as much nitrate of potash, as a similar quantity of nitrate of lime; except he may mean, by the addition of potash to the aluminous and calcareous nitrates, the making a new saltpetre formation. This cave seems to be a natural magazine of saline manufacture, with the exception of the cave of Memoora, in the island of Ceylon, seldom equalled, in so far as is yet known, for the quantity and varied quality of its productions.

The Ear of Dionysius.

We all recollect the story of the Syracusan tyrant confining the miserable objects of his wrath in dungeons; so constructed, that by a reverberation of sound, he could place his ear to an aperture, and learn, from their secret exclamations, what might be the real condition of their minds. The cave here described is said to have been the scene of this refined cruelty; and that the form of it really resembles an ass's ear.

"The interior is a corridor turning to the right, to return afterwards to the left, which suddenly stops, as if it had not been finished. It is 252 feet long, eighteen in width at the entrance, and thirty in the middle. The height is eighty feet, and the vault becoming narrower at the top, carried the sounds into a small square room, where Dionysius placed himself to hear the conversation of the prisoners. You mount into this chamber in a basket, to which a rope is attached. The acoustic properties of this cavern induced me to carry away some powder, which I inclosed in a piece of paper, squeezed it hard, and having set fire to it, it caused a detonation, a frightful rolling in the vaults. You see along the walls the chains, preserved in the rock itself, with which they bound the prisoners.

"The vast quarry, or garden, is really very curious; it is called Latomia, and is covered with lemon, orange, pomegranate, and olive trees, which proves how much the climate is favourable to vegetation; often deprived of the sun, they would soon perish in any other country. Were I to choose a hermitage, it would certainly be Latomia."

Account of an Assemblage of Fossil Teeth and Bones belonging to extinct Species of Elephant, Rhinoceros, Hippopotamus, Hyæna, and other Animals, discovered in a Cave at Kirkdale, near Kirby Moorside, Yorkshire. By the Rev. W. BUCKLAND, F.R.S.

Read before the Royal Society.

The following paper gives a succinct account of another interesting fact respecting animal remains; the deluge having left them on the spot where it found them.

The den is a natural fissure, or cavern, in oolitic limestone; extending 300 feet into the body of the solid rock; and varying from two to five feet in height and breadth. Its mouth was closed with rubbish, and overgrown with grass and bushes; and was accidentally intersected by the working of a stone quarry. It is on the slope of a hill, about 100 feet above the level of a small river; which, during great part of the year, is engulphed. The bottom of the cavern is nearly horizontal, and is entirely covered, to the depth of about a foot, with a sediment of mud; deposited by the diluvian waters. The surface of this mud was, in some parts entirely covered with a crust of stalagmite: on the greater part of it, there was no stalagmite. At the bottom of this mud, the floor of the cave was covered, from one end to the other, with teeth, and fragments of bone of the following animals, hyæna, elephant, rhinoceros, hippopotamus, horse, ox, two or three species of deer, bear, fox, water-rat, and birds.

The bones are, for the most part, broken, and gnawed to pieces; and the teeth lie loose among the fragments of the bones; a very few teeth remain still fixed in broken fragments of the jaws. The hyæna bones are broken to pieces, as much as those of the other animals. No bone or tooth has been rolled, or in the least acted on by water; nor are there any pebbles mixed with them. The bones are not at all mineralized; retaining nearly the whole of their animal gelatine; and owing their high state of preservation to the mud in which they have been imbedded.

The teeth of hyænas are most abundant; and of these the greater part are worn down almost to the stumps, as if by the operation of gnawing bones. Some of the bones have marks of the teeth on them; and portions of fæcal matter of the hyænas are found also, in the den. These have been analyzed by Dr. Wollaston, and found to be composed of the same ingredients as the album græcum, or white fæces of dogs that are fed on bones; viz. carbonate of lime, phosphate of lime, and triple phosphate of ammonia and magnesia. And on being shown to the Keeper of the beasts at Exeter 'Change, were immediately recognized by him as the dung of the hyæna. The new, and curious, fact of the preservation of this substance is explained by affinity to bone.

The animals found in the cave agree in species with those that occur in the diluvian gravel of England, and of great part of the northern hemisphere; four of them, the hyæna, elephant, rhinoceros, and hippopotamus, belonging to species that are now extinct; and to genera that live exclusively in warm climates; and which are found associated together only in the southern portions of Africa, near the Cape. It is certain, from the evidence afforded by the interior of the den, (which is of the same kind with that afforded by the ruins of Herculaneum and Pompeii) that all these animals lived and died in Yorkshire, in the period immediately preceding the deluge; and a similar conclusion may be drawn with respect to England, generally; and to those other extensive regions of the northern hemisphere, where the diluvian gravel contains the remains of similar species of animals. The extinct fossil hyæna most nearly resembles the species which now inhabit the Cape, whose teeth are adapted, beyond those of any other animal, to the purpose of cracking bones; and whose habit it is to carry home part of its prey to devour them in the caves of rocks which it inhabits. This analogy explains the accumulation of bones in the den at Kirkdale. They were carried in for food by the hyænas; the smaller animals, perhaps, entire; the larger animals piece-meal; for by no other means could the bones of such large animals as the elephant and rhinoceros have arrived at the inmost recesses of so small a hole, unless rolled thither by water, in which case, the angles would have been worn off, by attrition, but they are not.

Judging from the proportions of the remains now found in

the den, the ordinary food of the hyænas seems to have been oxen, deer, and water-rats. The bones of the larger animals are more rare; and the fact of the bones of the hyænas being broken up, equally with the rest, added to the known preference they have for putrid flesh and bones, renders it probable that they devoured the dead carcases of their own species. Some of the bones and teeth appear to have undergone various stages of decay, by lying at the bottom of the den while it was inhabited; but little, or none, since the introduction of the diluvian sediment in which they have been imbedded. The circumstances of the cave, and its contents, are altogether inconsistent with the hypothesis of all the various animals of such dissimilar habits having entered it spontaneously, or having fallen in, or having been drifted in by water, or with any other than that of their having been dragged in, either entire, or piece-meal, by the beasts of prey whose den it was.

Five examples are adduced of bones of the same animals discovered, in similar caverns, in other parts of this country; viz. at Crawley Rocks, near Swansea; in the Mendip Hills; at Clifton; at Wirksworth, in Derbyshire; and at Oreston, near Plymouth. In some of these, there is evidence of the bones having been introduced by beasts of prey; but in that of Hutton Hill in the Mendips, which contains rolled pebbles, it is probable they were washed in. In the case of open fissures, some may have fallen in.

A comparison is then instituted between these caverns in England, and those in Germany, described by Rosenmuller, Esher, and Leibnitz, as extending over a tract of 200 leagues, and containing analogous deposits of the bones of two extinct species of bear, and the same extinct species of hyæna that occurs at Kirkdale.

In the German caves, the bones are in nearly the same state of preservation as in the English, and are not in entire skeletons; but dispersed, as in a charnel house. They are scattered all over the caves, sometimes loose, sometimes adhering together by stalagmite, and forming beds of many feet in thickness. They are of all parts of the body, and of animals of all ages; but are never rolled. With them is found a quantity of black earth, derived from the decay of animal flesh; and also in the newly discovered caverns, we find descriptions of a bed of mud. The latter is probably the same diluvial sediment which we find at Kirkdale. The unbroken condition of the bones, and presence of black animal earth, are consistent with the habit of bears; as being rather addicted to vegetable than animal food: and in this case, not devouring the dead individuals of their own species. In the hyæna's cave, on the other hand, where both flesh and bones were devoured, we have no black earth, but instead of it we find, in the album græcum, evidence of the fate that has attended the carcases, and lost portions of the bones, whose fragments still remain.

Three fourths of the total number of bones, in the German caves, belong to two extinct species of bear, and two thirds of the remainder to the extinct hyæna of Kirkdale. There are also bones of an animal of the cat kind (resembling the jaguar or spotted panther of South America) and of the wolf, fox, and pole cat, and rarely of the elephant and rhinoceros.

M. Rosenmuller shows that the bears not only lived and died, but were also born, in the same caverns in which their bones have been thus accumulated; and the same conclusion follows from the facts observed in the cave in Yorkshire.

The bears and hyænas of all the caverns, as well as the elephant, rhinoceros, and hippopotamus, belong to the same extinct species that occur, also fossil, in the diluvian gravel, whence it follows that the period in which they inhabited these regions, was that immediately preceding the formation of this gravel by that transient and universal inundation which has left traces of its ravages committed at no very distant period over the surface of the whole globe; and since which, no important, or general, physical changes appear to have affected it.

Both in the case of the English and German caverns, the bones under consideration are never included in the solid rock; they occur in cavities of limestone rocks of various ages and formations; but have no further connection with the rocks themselves, than that arising from the accident of their being lodged in cavities produced in them, by causes wholly unconnected with the animals that appear for a certain time to have taken possession of them as their habitation

On the Clarification of Sugar. By Major Rohde.

We presumed that this process had been lately brought to the very acme of practical perfection; but if this gentleman's idea of the impurities being merely superficial on the saccharine crystal, be correct, his process must, by its simplicity, surpass all others. To avoid the possibility of the patentee's being misunderstood, we present his own description of the process, as detailed in the specification:—

"It being ascertained that a considerable proportion of the discoloured matter and other substance which constitute molasses, or syrup, is formed on the surface of the crystal of the purer sugar, the method I employ for separating or extracting the molasses, or syrup, from such crystals, is to absorb the molasses or syrup by using linen, or some other substance of absorbing quality, assisted by mechanical or manual motion, and friction, in manner following; that is to say: I break any lumps that may be in the sugar, so as to admit of its passing through a sieve of sufficient texture and size, without breaking the grains or crystals. I then spread the sugar, so reduced, in thin layers on linen, or some other substance of absorbing quality; and having folded it, place it in bags or other packages, and apply manual or other mechanical power to put it in motion, so as to afford the friction necessary to separate the molasses or syrup from the sugar. By these means the molasses or syrup is absorbed by the linen or other absorbing substance, and the purer crystals remain on the surface, and are separated by brushing, shaking, or scraping them off. The molasses or syrup is afterwards extracted from the linen, or other absorbing substance, by means of water or steam. Or I employ any means by which an absorbing substance comes in contact with the sugar, so as to allow of its absorbing the molasses or syrup, whilst it leaves the crystals on its surface."

On the Analysis of Black and Green Tea. By Mr. Brande.
Annals of Philosophy.

Mr. Brande has lately made a comparative analysis of black and green tea, from which he finds that the quantity of astringent matter precipitable by gelatine, is somewhat greater in green than in black tea, though the excess is by no means so great as the comparative flavours of the two would lead one to expect. It also appears that the entire quantity of soluble matter is greater in green than in black tea, and that the proportion of extractive matter not precipitable by gelatine, is greater than the latter.

Sulphuric, muriatic, and acetic acids (but especially the first) occasion precipitates in infusions both of black and green tea, which have the properties of combinations of those acids with tan. Both infusions also yield, as might be expected, abundant black precipitates with solutions of iron; and when mixed with acetate, or more especially with subacetate of lead, a bulky buff coloured matter is separated, leaving the remaining fluid entirely tasteless and colourless. This precipitate was diffused through water, and decomposed by sulphuretted hydrogen; it afforded a solution of tan and extract, but not any traces of any peculiar principle to which certain medical effects of tea, especially of green tea, could be attributed.

Mr. Brande observes, that there is one property of strong infusions of tea, belonging especially to black and green, which seems to announce the presence of a distinct vegetable principle; namely, that they deposit, as they cool, a brown pulverulent precipitate, which passes through ordinary filters, and can only be collected by deposition and decantation. This precipitate is very slightly soluble in cold water, of the temperature of from 50° downwards, but it dissolves with the utmost facility in water of 100° and upwards, forming a pale brown transparent liquid, which furnished abundant precipitate in solutions of isinglass, of sulphate of iron, of muriate of tin, and of acetate of lead; whence it may be inferred to consist of tannin, gallic acid, and extractive matter.

The following table is given by Mr. Brande, as showing the respective quantities of soluble matter in water and alcohol, the weight of the precipitate by isinglass, and the proportion of inert woody fibre in green and black tea of various prices.

ONE HUNDRED PARTS OF TEA,	Soluble in water.	Soluble in alcohol.	Precipitate with jelly.	Inert residue.
Green Hyson, 14s. per lb...	41	44	31	56
Ditto 12s.	34	43	29	57
Ditto 10s.	36	43	26	57
Ditto 8s.	36	42	25	58
Ditto 7s.	31	41	24	59
Black Souchong 12s.	35	36	28	64
Ditto 10s.	34	37	28	63
Ditto 7s.	36	35	24	64
Ditto 6s.	35	31	23	65

We may add the above analysis to the stock of results from experiment on vegetable matter, as one more proof of the general inutility of essays to discover specific principles. Vegetable analyses are seldom to be relied on, even in the hands of such chemists as Mr. Brande: and if he cannot bring us to satisfactory conclusions, we must be of rather sanguine characters in retaining much confident hope. Still we are willing to allow, that, latterly, some little progress has been made in the art. But we are presumptuous enough to think that, although we may often elicit from vegetable matter that portion in which resides the active principle; yet we shall not be able to demonstrate any thing in it of specific chemical composition, so as to be able to reproduce such principle synthetically.

On the Illumination of the Tron Church and Post-Office Steeple Clocks, Glasgow.

The following paper describes a very useful application of the combustible gas. We sincerely wish to witness the adoption of it here in London. Perhaps a sight of the clock-dial is as desirable in the darkness of evening, as it is useful in the day: and as we now have the gas laid on every where, it could not be much additional charge on the parochial rates, were each parish to carry the thing into effect.

Messrs. John and Robert Hart, of Glasgow, who have been long known to the public for their scientific acquirements, as well as their practical ingenuity, have erected a very ingenious apparatus for illuminating with gas the dials of the Tron Church and Post-Office steeples in Glasgow. The apparatus consists of a No. 1 argand burner, placed a few feet out from the top of the dial, and enclosed in a nearly hemispherical lantern, the front of which is glazed; the back forms a parabolic reflector. The dial receives not only the direct, but a conical stream of reflected rays, and is thus so brilliantly illuminated, that the hours and hands can be seen with nearly the same distinctness, at a distance, as through the day. To mask the obtuse appearance of the lantern, its back has been made to assume the form of a spread eagle, above which is placed the city arms, the whole handsomely executed and gilt. The gas-pipe and lantern move on an air-tight joint, so that the lantern may be brought close to the steeple for cleaning, when necessary. The gas is first ignited by means of a train, or flash-pipe, so perforated, that when the gas issuing from the holes at the one end is lighted, the holes along the pipe become so, and thus the gas inside the lantern is kindled, as if by a train of gunpowder. In this way the light might be first communicated either from the street or from the steeple. The effect of the lighted dial is at once cheerful, pleasant, and useful. By a simple contrivance, the clock disengages a small detent, something similar to the larum in the wooden clocks; this shuts the gas-cock, and instantly extinguishes the light.

Observations on Vision through Coloured Glasses, &c. By Dr. BREWSTER.

Edinburgh Phil. Journ. No. 11.

Dr. Brewster may be considered a Colossus in the philosophy of refracted light, and therefore we always expect instruction in the perusal of his papers: but this one is more practical than elementary; and, as such, more valuable to those who are seeking for the useful, rather than the splendid.

The Doctor, after remarking on the capricious selection of green and grey glasses, as fashion has influenced; and on the natural presumption that any homogeneous colour, transmitted through a vitreous medium, should better aid vision, by the compactness of the optical convergency, than compounded coloured rays; proceeds to explain his own error as arising out of the latter. For, he says, " Impressed with this opinion, I was surprised to find that vision, through a piece of blue glass, became so painful to the eye, that it was not able to endure the impression for any length of time." By experiment, he found that the blue glass absorbed the middle rays only of the spectrum, viz. green, yellow, and orange, and transmitted the violet and red; therefore the spectrum " consisted of two separate images, the one red, and the other blue: hence the eye was not able to see distinctly by means of rays of such different refrangibilities." The Doctor informs us that, if the eye be so adjusted as to see the blue image, it will be surrounded with a red circle; and *vice versa*.

Having subjected coloured glasses, of every tinge, to experiment, the Doctor found that, as homogeneous coloured glasses will not transmit homogeneous light, without obscuring the visual image, we must seek that colour " which produces the shortest spectrum, with the greatest illumination;" and he found it in the yellowish green tint. He says " it almost entirely absorbs the extreme red rays, and extinguishes a very great proportion of the blue extremity of the spectrum. Hence, it not only relieves the eye, by attenuating the incident light, but improves the image, by diminishing the error arising from its different refrangibility."

Having imparted to us this important practical fact, the Doctor goes on to show the value of its application to microscopes and telescopes, through which we need not follow him; having said enough to show, that the principle of the discovery is adaptable to the aid of vision, under every form of optical construction.

Remarks on the Insensibility of the Eye to certain Colours. By JOHN BUTTER, M. D. &c. In a Letter to Dr. Brewster.

Edinburgh Physical Journal, No. 11.

Dr. Butter transmits the account of this case to Dr. Brewster, because the latter gentleman is so competent an authority to determine whatever may appertain to the philosophy of vision. The subject is a Mr. Robert Tucker, son of Dr. Tucker, of Ashburton, Devon. His age is 19. About two years ago, his incapacity to distinguish between orange and green, while making an artificial fishing fly, gave rise to the trials which we will relate the result of. Some of the primitive colours, he neither knows, nor remembers when pointed out: he calls orange green; and green orange: brown he terms red, and *vice versa*: blue silk appears to him pink, and the reverse. Indigo, he calls purple. The prismatic colours are thus misnamed:—

1st. Red is mistaken for .... Brown.
2d. Orange .... Green.
3d. Yellow, generally known, but sometimes mistaken for .... Orange.
4th. Green .... Orange.
5th. Blue .... Pink.
6th. Indigo .... Purple.
7th. Violet .... Purple.

Black and white he seldom mistakes.

Supposing the colours to be classed in three divisions, as 1st. Red and brown; 2d. Blue, pink, indigo, violet, and purple; 3d. Green and orange; he will generally say to which of these classes a particular colour may belong, though he may not be individually correct. He does not seem to know the *grades* of some colours: for instance, he does not know a bay from a chesnut or brown colour, as in the horse; yet the scarlet coat of a soldier he terms red: and some shades of green are distinguishable by him: but as not distinguished from orange. He always knows yellow; and, what is remarkable, never mistakes the green of grass for orange, as he does all other greens. Black, white, and yellow coloured bodies, seem to be the only ones whose tint he can be said to distinguish certainly; grass, as before said, excepted. Closing one eye, did not change the effect. His health is stated to be good, and the defect considered natural, not morbid.

Description of Mr. R. Tucker's eyes.—" Apparently well formed; being oblate spheroids, with corneæ neither remarkably convex, nor flat; irides light ash colour. His vision exceedingly acute. It has been frequently exemplified in finding birds' nests; in shooting small birds; and in reading minute print at a short or long distance. Light appears to him as light. He sees the forms of surrounding objects like other people at noon day, in the twilight, and at night. In short, his sight is remarkably good in any light, and at any distance. His grandfather, on his mother's side, seems not to have possessed the faculty of distinguishing colours with accuracy."

Dr. Butter then proceeds to explain the cause of this deviation from the common course of vision: and after tracing the varied colours of the tapeta of animals generally, without satisfying himself that any peculiarity in the tapetum of Mr. R. Tucker can have produced the stated effects; and considering the form of the visual organ itself as apparently perfect; he concludes, that we must seek the solution of the mystery in physiology alone; and that it arises from a want of the " organ of colours."

Dr. Brewster, being no friend to the speculative doctrine of Spurzheim, has omitted Dr. Butter's detail of reasoning on this principle; and states his own opinion on the case to be that, the cause may reside in the visual organ itself; as, " that the insensibility of some eyes to weak impressions of light, requires no other explanation, than that either from original organization, or some accidental cause, the retina of one person may be less delicate, and less susceptible of luminous impressions, than the retina of another; without being accompanied with any diminution of the powers of vision." Also, " I have lately ascertained that, some eyes, which perform all the functions of vision in the most perfect manner, are insensible to certain impressions of highly attenuated light, which are quite perceptible to other eyes." And he refers, analogously, to Dr. Wollaston's Paper on Sounds, as musical notes, &c., inaudible to certain ears.

We are not certain that we understand Dr. Brewster correctly; but if he mean to intimate that relative states of sensibility in the retina, would produce these chromatic deviations from accurate perception, we must beg leave to differ from him, with all the deference due to such an authority; because it would imply a specific sensibility; as requisite for the just perception of a specific colour: a doctrine that must be at variance with the train of facts produced by every case of ophthalmia: wherein, although the *intensity* of colour be apparently heightened by the increased irritability of the retina, yet the colour is not varied *per se*. In short, the varying sensibility of the retina, must, as we humbly presume, govern rather the *quantity*, than the *quality* of perceptive effect.

The subject being of a very interesting nature, we hope to stand excused for dilating a little on it, and to present an idea differing both from Dr. Brewster and Dr. Butter. We cannot agree with the latter gentleman, that the effects existing can be caused by a loss of the "organ of colours;" for we cannot easily comprehend how an "organ" is to be lost, nor how it is to arise, after the original conformation of the embryo.

Our opinion is, in some degree, divided, between the possibility of this aberration from common perception as arising from some change in the cornea, lens, or vitreous humour of the eye; or from some perversion of mental faculty. The former may, perhaps, be most easily explained: for, without meaning to impute, in the remotest degree, against the scrutinizing power of observation by Dr. Butter, we may justly declare that he could know nothing of the mathematical form of the deeper component parts of the eye. He might judge of the comparative convexity of the cornea; but there his visual scrutiny must cease. As to any change in the form of the lens, or the vitreous humour, he could not determine any thing whatever. We need not do more than intimate the possibility of such change. And we would put it to the consideration of Dr. Brewster, especially, whether a change of form might not influence the refractive power of the eye, so as by the derangement, in the mathematical figure, of one or more of the visual constituents, the ultimate effect, in chromatic perception, may not be diversified?

There is one point in Mr. R. Tucker's case, that we cannot omit noticing: and that is, his power of always identifying yellow. Now Dr. Brewster, in his observations on vision through coloured glasses, states, that the *yellowish* green tint is the most favourable medium through which the eye can view objects. Mr. R. T. mistakes green for orange, which latter is composed of red and yellow; and the former, of blue and yellow. And if we trace his perception of the entire colours, as classed in three divisions, we may infer, that a tendency to perceive yellow has some curious influence, wherefrom we may partly account for the peculiarities of susceptibilities. He seems to be defective as to the impression of blue. As relating to this department of optics, there is an ingenious paper in the last No. of Annals of Philosophy, which we shall proceed in our next article to analyze and remark on.

Remarks on a peculiar Imperfection of Vision with regard to Colours. By WHITLOCK NICHOLL, M. D. &c.

Annals of Philosophy, No. 14.

After observing on the cases of defective susceptibility to colours that have been recorded in the Philosophical Transactions; Transactions of the Medical and Chirurgical Society of London, &c.; and on the varied sensibility of the retina to the stimulus of light when presented in varied intensity; the Doctor endeavours to show that alternating spectra of vision arise from the particular states of the retina itself, and argues on the general grounds assumed by the celebrated Darwin, and others,

Having adverted to the visual effect of the prismatic colours, when a long continued impression have been made on the retina, so as to produce a coloured spectrum; as, for instance, after having long observed a green object, which will produce a red spectrum, and *vice versa;* as well as noticed that the continued impression as to *shape* and *extent* of *surface* never is varied to our perception, as the circumstance of colour is; he infers that there is a certain state of the retina necessary in order that the mixed rays of light so affect it as to produce vision: also, that a particular state of the retina is necessary, in order that each separate and distinct set of the rays of light so affect it as to produce a corresponding, peculiar, and distinct kind of vision. That state of the retina wherein all the rays of light, whether blended or distinct, produce correct vision, he would term *general sensibility:* and where the rays, blended or distinct, fail to produce correct vision, he would term the state of the retina that of *general insensibility.* Some of the prismatic colours being in some cases correctly perceived, and others not so; according to the particular state of sensibility of the retina; and therefore such particular state of the retina as may qualify it to correctly receive impression by one prismatic ray, does not necessarily fit it for being so acted on by others, singly or collectively, of the prismatic rays. It appears then, says the Doctor, that whenever light acts upon the retina in such a man neras to produce vision, it produces a certain condition, or state of the retina, which is essential to the existence of that kind of sensation which is termed *seeing:* and in order that each distinct set of the prismatic rays so affect the retina, as to produce a distinct corresponding kind of the sensation *seeing*, it is necessary that it produce a distinct corresponding state of the retina; which state is essential to the existence of such corresponding sensation. Thus, one state of the retina is essential to the seeing of red, another to that of yellow, &c.; so that when we speak of *seeing* a certain number of colours, we imply, that the retina can have that number of distinct states produced in it. These states, which are essential to the presence of sensation, the Doctor would term *sensual* states. He contends, then, that as when the sensation seeing red ceases, the sensation seeing green will or may exist, the sensual states of the retina, under those different impressions, must be contrary or reversed. Consequently, says he, if the retina be incapable of assuming any sensual state, the individual must be blind: and if it be incapable only as to the sensual state requisite for red, he will be blind *quoad* that sensation. These sensual states for seeing colours, may arise from the action of light, or during its absence; and therefore the Doctor infers that the presence of light is not essential to the production of such sensual states; the *colour* which is *seen* being connected with the presence of light only in the relation of effect and cause. Suppose the retina insensible to the colour *red*, it would probably be sensible to its reverse spectrum, *green;* or its components, *yellow* and *blue:* so with the other prismatic colours, and *vice versa* their spectra and components. A retina insensible to *blue* may be sensible to *red* and *yellow*, or their compound, *orange;* if insensible to *orange*, it may be owing to its insensibility to *red* or *yellow*, &c. If a retina be insensible to a primary or a compound ray of light, it can only be affected by light so as to the sensations *seeing three prismatic colours;* two of which colours will be primary, and the third, a colour compounded of these two. If insensible to the *green* ray, still sensibility to its components, *blue* and *yellow*, as well as *red* and *orange*, may exist; or *red, blue,* and *violet,* produced by the action of prismatic rays. These individuals, he says, confound *pink* with *blue, pink* being a faint shade of *red;* and as the Doctor has contended that the red and the green rays cannot each affect the retina of these persons so as to produce *seeing,* but that their retina must be insensible to one of these two prismatic rays; so he deduces that they cannot be sensible to both the *pink* and *blue* rays; but that they must be insensible to either the *pink* or the *blue.* If sensible to the *pink*, he concludes they must be sensible to the *red;* but if sensible to the *pink,* not so to the *blue;* consequently, if sensible to *red* and *pink* rays, they must be insensible to *blue* rays. Thus the retina being sensible in the one case to *yellow, blue,* and *green* rays, in the other to *red, orange,* and *yellow* rays; but in any case to *yellow:* and this correctness as to *yellow* rays is always observable.

Dr. Nicholl proceeds to trace the necessary consequences, as he presumes, to follow from the various modifications of specific coloured vision, arising out of the insensibility of the retina to certain primary, prismatic, or compound rays;

and he lays much stress on the spectra denoting a peculiar state of the retina being produced by the appropriate colours; and concludes by considering (as in the preceding paper it is shown Dr. Brewster has considered), that there is an analogy between these cases of imperfect vision, and those of what is called an unmusical ear.

Before we proceed to trace the principles espoused by Dr. Nicholl, we may just remark on sound, or tone, that a person may have what is called a nice ear to music, without being able to modulate the voice to harmonical concord; and and that, perhaps, arising from the construction of the larynx, or the want of delicate command over the muscles of the arytænoid cartilages. Some persons also will perform in concert with perfect correctness, as to harmonical tone, but be incapable of duly measuring the proper periods of notes or bars; that is, cannot properly measure time.

Our principal objection to Dr. Nicholl's hypothesis, strikes at its very root; for we do not hold with the principle of *specific* sensibility, or particular *sensual* state, as he terms it, of the retina, as requisite for producing effective vision. We do, then, adhere to our opinion, as expressed in the former paper, that in the varying sensibility of the retina, the colour is not varied *per se*, and such variation must govern the *quantity* rather than the *quality* of the perception. We do not meet with any thing in Dr. N.'s essay that ought to make us waver, however elaborate and ingenious it may be.

In viewing that part of his doctrine, wherein he urges the specific, or *sensual*, state of the retina, as being the specific action of a particular primary or compound ray, we are not able to see the matter as he places it. He instances the ability to distinguish shape or form, where there may be a defect in distinguishing colour. Are we, then, to conclude that there are two kinds of sensibility in the retina, one transmitting a perception of colour, and another of form? Without entering into the profundity of abstract and compound perception, we may just infer that this multiplied specific character of sensibility in the retina, leads to a more complex, we might almost say occult, consideration of the nervous sensibility of organs, than, from the simplicity of the works of nature, we are authorized to determine. Or, are we to understand that this *sensual* state of the retina be produced by the specific action of specific rays; so that there is not any change in the mere quantum of retinal sensibility, but the various rays stimulate with various intensities, and so produce specific perceptions?

The latter is the most rational; but still, as we think, rather short of philosophical accuracy: for we maintain that the perception of *colour* depends on the formation of the eye, as a *refractive optical* organ; and that the perceptive effect may be widely varied according to the condition of the respective parts of this compound instrument, the retina always being presumed to be sensibly perfect, in the simple meaning of nervous sensibility. If we look through a convex lens, at a certain distance of the eye, or the glass, or both, from an object, we see the form and colour distinctly; but on varying the relative distances, we shall see the object coloured, or obscured by particular prismatic rays. Now, in this case, the nervous sensibility of the retina is not varied, but the perception is; because the optical medium, through which the object is seen, governs the eventual effect. So we suppose that there is always some peculiar form, or change in form, of the component parts of the organ of vision, *as a mere optical instrument*, when the perception be varied from that of general *chromatic* effect.

Dr. N. states that spectral colours may exist independent of the positive stimulus of light, and even in its absence; but we beg leave to doubt this: for in all the cases we know of existing spectra, there has been, and ever must be supposed to have been, previous excitement by particular prismatic light on the organ of vision. It is no sufficient argument to urge that this is a mere *sensual* state of the retina; for we maintain that previous stimulation, by *specific* rays, must have been produced by the optical component parts of the organ of vision. In fine, we contend that the sensibility of the retina is simple and invariable in its quality; and that coloured perception is caused by the *conformation* of the eye, as an optical instrument.

On Siderography; or, the Art of Engraving upon Cast Steel; of Decarbonating it; Carbonating it; and Hardening and Tempering it. By Messrs. PERKINS, FAIRMAN, and HEATH.

Transactions of Society of Arts, &c.

The Society for the Encouragement of Arts, Manufactures, and Commerce, having devoted so much of their valuable time to investigate the different methods proposed for the prevention of the forgery of Bank Notes, we, the proprietors of the Siderographic art, believe that a full account of our plan (which has been in successful operation many years in America, and is now adopted by many banks in this country) will not be thought unworthy of their attention.

We will, in the first place, state what we consider to be the grand basis of *security* in this plan; and, secondly, the means of executing it. Although it is certainly not a new idea, that the greatest security which could possibly be afforded, in preventing forgery, would be that of employing a combination of the talents of the first-rate artists in fabricating a bank-note plate, and of having the notes always *identically* the same; yet we conceive the following plan, to effect this object, is entirely new: it is the power of re-producing and multiplying the works of the greatest artists, which constitutes the strength of this system; it is the basis on which we build our hopes. The method of multiplying engravings is as follows:—

A steel plate (the method of preparing which will be hereafter described) is engraved or etched in the usual way: it is then hardened. A cylinder of very soft steel, of from 2 to 3 inches in diameter, is made to roll backwards and forwards on the surface of the steel plate, until the whole of the impression of the engraving is seen on the cylinder in alto relievo: after this cylinder has been hardened, it is made to roll backwards and forwards on a copper or soft steel plate, and a perfect fac simile of the original is produced of equal sharpness. The following calculations will show to what extent this system of preventing forgery may be carried.

Suppose 20 of the best historical and other engravers were

employed, each to engrave a vignette, each vignette to occupy four square inches, and each artist to expend six months on his vignette: let these 20 vignettes be transferred to two steel plates, one for the front of the note, and the other for the back; the result will be, that one man (could such a one be found) would be occupied 10 years, or 20 men six months, to produce a note of equal goodness. Is it possible to suppose any thing better can be adopted, than to make it unprofitable to be engaged in such business? If a bank-note plate can be made to cost 10,000l., (which would be the case if 20 artists, whose time would be worth 1000l. per annum, were engaged six months each,) would it not be much less likely to be imitated than one that would cost but 5l. or 10l.? If a bank-plate can be made to contain the work of 20 of the best artists in the world, could another plate of equal goodness be made without employing the same artists? It is hardly to be presumed that 20 such artists would be engaged in making a spurious note; but admitting it possible, it would not be a fac simile, and might be easily distinguished from the true note, by any one acquainted with the original. One of the peculiar features of this invention is, that any one may be furnished with a perfect fac simile of the whole, or of any part of the original note; which will serve to identify the note, if good: this is owing to the infinite number of impressions that may be obtained from the original engraving. Having shown that a plate may be made to cost 10,000l., we will undertake to prove that it is not incompatible with economy. To show the economy of this plan, in its best light, we must be allowed to apply it to the best advantage, which would be by its being adopted by a bank whose daily consumption is not less than 25,000 notes.

Suppose the first steel plate cost 10,000l., the next 999 plates will only cost 10,000l.: then 1000 steel plates will amount to 20,000l. Each steel plate will print at least 150,000 impressions: of course, 1000 plates would furnish 150,000,000 impressions, which is the number that would be wanted in 20 years, at 25,000 impressions per day. Now the cost of impressions, from steel plates, would be (where the above number is wanted) one penny for $31\frac{1}{4}$ impressions, whereas, if copper plates were used, which cost only 3*l.* each plate, the number of impressions for a penny would be but 8⅓, since a copper plate prints but 6000 impressions before it is worn out.

Another very important consideration is, that steel plates admit of an improved method of printing, and, when worked to the greatest advantage, will make a saving of 50 per cent.: this saving, in 20 years, in printing the above number of notes, would be 75,000*l.*, which would not only pay the whole cost of making the plates, but leave a balance of 55,000*l.*

The system of making plates, and of printing, will apply equally well to that of ornamenting standard works, particularly bibles, prayer books, primers, catechisms, spelling books, and works of natural history and philosophy. In proportion to the number wanted, will be the advantage of adopting this plan. It is often the case in this country, that from four to six copper-plates are worn out in one edition, and not half the impressions perfect. A hardened steel plate will print more *proof impressions* than the above number of copper-plates can furnish, even of common impressions. This fact is demonstrated by the two impressions from the same plate, which accompany this communication: of which one is of the first impression taken from it, and the other was printed after 35,000 had been taken from it.

This plate will also show the practicability of identity. The four medallions, by inspection, will be found to be perfectly the same, *line for line and dot for dot*. By examining the machine engraving, particularly the chain; the two *styles* of work, viz. copper-plate and letter-press printing, will be seen beautifully combined. This is effected by the process of transferring and re-transferring. This kind of engraving is extremely difficult to imitate. This machine, which is denominated the geometrical lathe, was invented, in America, by Mr. Asa Spencer. Its powers for producing variety are equalled only by the kaleidoscope; but for beautiful patterns it surpasses every thing of the kind. It has one of the peculiarities of the kaleidoscope, viz. that the turning of a screw, like the turning of the kaleidoscope, produces an entire new pattern, which was never before seen, and perhaps would never be seen again. This pattern, however, may be perpetuated by the transferring process. We are now printing from a plate of the most delicate work, which has already printed above 100,000 impressions, and is yet sound. We cannot yet say how long a well hardened steel plate will last, having never printed more than 500,000 impressions from the same plate: it should, however, be observed, that this plate consisted principally of writing, or work quite as strong. It may also be observed, that the impressions are yet good. The manufacture of printed calicoes, ribbons, &c. as well as of earthenware, may be much improved by adopting this system; and we are happy to say that experiments are soon to be made thereof. This improvement in engraving will apply to about one quarter of the present number of plates used. The others must necessarily be of copper, as a sufficient number of impressions would not be wanted to defray the expense of a steel plate. Not less than a number of impressions which would wear out three copper-plates would warrant the making a steel plate. But such is the number of subjects to which this art will apply, and the great inducement to publishers to embellish their works, where large editions are wanted, which they now can do, in consequence of its economy, that, instead of the demand of engravers being lessened, it will be very much enhanced.

The use of fine and delicate engraving for bank notes has been objected to, in consequence of the difficulty of printing on such highly sized paper. But this objection is entirely got over, by our method of printing in the water-leaf, and sizing after printing. This improvement has a triple advantage,—that of producing beautiful impressions, having on its surface, after printing, a better size, and preventing the ink from being so easily transferred.

In order to describe the method of preparing and hardening the steel plate and dies, the following particulars are necessary.

In order to decarbonate the surfaces of cast steel plates, cylinders, or dies, by which they are rendered much softer and fitter for receiving either transferred or engraved designs, we use pure iron filings, divested of all foreign or extraneous matters.

The stratum of decarbonated steel should not be too thick for transferring fine and delicate engravings; for instance, not more than three times the depth of the engraving: but for other purposes, the surface of the steel may be decarbonated to any required thickness.

To decarbonate it to a proper thickness for fine engravings, it is to be exposed for four hours in a white heat, inclosed in a cast iron box, with a well closed lid. The sides of the cast iron box are made at least three quarters of an inch in thickness; and at least a thickness of half an inch of pure iron filings should cover or surround the cast steel surface to be decarbonated. The box is to be suffered to cool very slowly; which may be effected by shutting off all access of air to the furnace, and covering it with a layer, six or seven inches in thickness, of fine cinders. Each side of the steel plate, cylinder, or die, must be equally decarbonated, to prevent it from springing or warping in hardening. It is also found, that the safest way to heat the plates, cylinders, or dies, is by placing them in a vertical position.

The best cast steel is preferred to any other sort of steel, for the purpose of making plates, cylinders, circular or other dies; and more especially, when such plates, cylinders, or dies are intended to be decarbonated. For the reason given above, the steel is decarbonated, solely for the purpose of rendering it sufficiently soft for receiving any impression intended to be made thereon: it is therefore necessary, that, after any piece of steel has been so decarbonated, whether it be in the shape of a plate, or a cylinder, or a die, it should, previously to being printed from, be again carbonated, or re-converted into steel capable of being hardened. In order, therefore, to effect this carbonization or re-conversion into steel, the following process is employed:—a suitable quantity of leather is to be converted into charcoal, by the well known method of exposing it to a red heat in an iron retort, for a sufficient length of time, or until most of the evaporable matter is driven off from the leather. Having thus prepared the charcoal, it is reduced to a very fine powder; then take a box made of cast iron, of sufficient dimensions to receive the plate, cylinder, or die, which is to be re-converted into steel, so as that the intermediate space between the sides of the said box, and the plate, cylinder, or die, may be about one inch. This box is to be filled with the powdered charcoal, and, having covered it with a well fitted lid, let it be placed in a furnace similar to those used for melting brass; when the heat must be gradually increased, until the box is somewhat above a red heat: it must be suffered to remain in that state till all the evaporable matter is driven off from the charcoal. Then remove the lid from the box, and immerse the plate, cylinder, or die, into the powdered charcoal; taking care to place it as nearly in the middle as possible, so that it may be surrounded on all sides by a stratum of the powder, of nearly an uniform thickness. The lid being replaced, the box, with the plate, cylinder, or die, must remain in the degree of heat before described, from three to five hours, according to the thickness of the plate, cylinder, or die so exposed. Three hours are sufficient for a plate of half an inch in thickness; and five hours when the steel is one inch and a half in thickness. After the plate, cylinder, or die has been thus exposed to the fire for a sufficient length of time, take it from the box, and immediately plunge it into cold water. It is important here to observe, that it is found, by experience, that the plates, or other pieces of steel, when plunged into cold water, are least liable to be warped or bent when they are held in a vertical position, or made to enter the water in the direction of their length. If a piece of steel, heated to a proper degree for hardening, be plunged into water, and suffered to remain there until it becomes cold, it is found by experience to be very liable to crack or break; and, in many cases, it would be found too hard for the operations it was intended to perform. If the steel cracks or breaks, it is spoiled. In order to render it fit for use, should it happen not to be broken in the hardening, it is the common practice to heat the steel again, in order to reduce or lower its temper, as it is technically called. The degree of heat to which it is now exposed determines the future degree of hardness, or the temper; and this is indicated by a change of colour upon the surface of the steel. During this heating, a succession of shades is produced, from a very pale straw colour, to a deep blue. It is found, however, by long experience, that on plunging the heated steel into cold water, and suffering it to remain there no longer than is sufficient for lowering the temperature of the steel to the same degree as that to which a hard piece of steel must have been raised, in order to temper it in the common way; it not only produces the same degree of hardness in the steel, but, what is of much more importance, almost entirely does away the risk or liability of its cracking or breaking.

It is impossible to communicate by words, or to describe the criterion by which we can judge of, or determine, when the steel has arrived at the proper degree of temperature, after being plunged into cold water; it can only be learned by actual observation, as the workman must be guided entirely by the kind of hissing or singing noise which the heated steel produces in the water while cooling. From the moment of its being first plunged into the water, a varying sound will be observed; and it is at a certain tone before the noise ceases that the effect to be produced is known. The only directions which can be given, whereby the experimentalist can be benefited, are as follow; namely, to take a piece of steel which has already been hardened by remaining in the water till cold; and, by the common method of again heating it, to let it be brought to the pale yellow, or straw colour, which indicates the desired temper of the steel plate to be hardened by the above process: as soon as he discovers this colour to be produced, to dip the steel into water, and attend carefully to the hissing, or, as some call it, singing noise, which it occasions: he will then be better able, and with fewer experiments, to judge of the precise time at which the steel should be taken out. It is not meant to be understood that the temper indicated by a straw colour, is that to which the steel plate, cylinder, or die should be ultimately reduced; because it would then be found too hard; but merely that the temperature which would produce that colour, is that by which the peculiar sound would be occasioned when the steel should be withdrawn from the water for the first time. Immediately on withdrawing it from the water, the steel plate, cylinder, or die, must be laid upon or held over a fire, and heated uniformly, until its temperature is raised to that degree at which tallow would be decomposed; or, in other words, until smoke is perceived to arise from the surface of the steel plate, cylinder, or die, after having been rubbed with tallow. The steel plate, cylinder, or die, must then be again plunged into water, and kept there until the sound becomes somewhat weaker than before. It is then to be taken out, and heated a second time to the same degree, by the same rule of smoking tallow as before; and the third time plunged into water, till the sound becomes again weaker than the last. Expose it a third time to the fire as before; and, for the last time, return it into the water and cool it: after it is cooled, clean the surface of the steel plate, cylinder, or die; and by heating it over the fire, the temper must be finally reduced by bringing on a brown, or such other lighter or darker shade of colour, as may best suit the quality of the steel, or the purposes to which it is to be applied.

We, of course, cannot know, nor indeed can we conceive, the motives of the Commissioners who were appointed to investigate the plans presented for executing note-plates to be used by the Bank, for rejecting **Mr. Perkins'** proposed mode. As to an inimitable bank-note, which it was their designated object to effect, nothing could be more absurd; and we are rather surprised that the good sense of the scientific gentlemen composing the committee did not revolt against an elevation to such a ludicrous title. To discover a thing that man could do once, but could not do twice, was, it seems, rather too difficult a problem for these, or any other gentlemen, to solve; and therefore, if they were not allowed to effect any thing short of this folly, they very naturally ended their labours as they began. An inimitable bank-note was not to be made; and, therefore, the best suggested means for preventing the crime of forgery, and the consequent destruction of human life, were not worthy of the high consideration of that unwieldy corporate body, the Bank. In their supreme sagacity, they rejected a protection because a palpable impossibility could not be accomplished. We hope to never more hear any hypocritical canting of certain representatives of the Bank in the House of Commons. The means of preventing successful forgery consists in not merely executing a plate with a masterly hand; but far more in rendering its imitation extremely expensive, and thereby striking at the very root of fraudulent gain.

On Warming and Ventilating Rooms. By JACOB PERKINS, Esq.   Transactions of the Society of Arts.

The large silver medal was voted to Mr. Perkins, for the communication of this plan of imparting warmth to our apartments, with a free circulation of air. It consists in encompassing the whole, or a large part, of the fire stove, by an iron case, running parallel with the former; at such a distance as may allow a free current; but so as to make all the air to be heated to pass over, and in contact with, the stove: which current is supplied through an aperture leading from the outside of the room. In the first instance, Mr. P. directed the construction of the stove in the usual way; wherein the supply of air for the combustion of the fuel, was upwards from the ash-pit: but he has now improved on that form, by directing the volume, feeding the fire, to pass downwards from above the fuel: and by that means he carries the fuliginous matter through the body of burning coal, and so consumes all the smoke. As the stove will not burn well, when the apartment be air-tight, he directs an aperture to be made near the ceiling. The effect is much increased where there is a chimney-draught in the room, opposite to the stove; and more so, if a small fire be kept up in the chimney of the room. Experience teaching that a very dry, and warm air, however frequently renewed, by rapidity of current, is not wholesome; and to obviate this, Mr. P. directs a small water reservoir, on the top of the stove, whereby a gentle, but constant aqueous evaporation may be going on.

There is, also, a very simple, but perfect, application of warmth and ventilation, to each range of flooring; by cutting off the warm air-current, before it pass through the ceiling; but, of course, continuing the fire-flue upwards. In order to give the effect to the second floor, an air-current is let in from without; which circulates upwards, round the fire-flue, and is again cut off near the ceiling, in the same manner as it had been below. And thus, for each flooring, in succession.

If we pronounced on this plan, from a simple consideration of its principle only, we should give it unqualified approbation; but we are much pleased to find that it claims our respect on better grounds than mere theoretical estimate; for it has been carried into effect with the completest success. Mr. Hansard, a printer, is stated to have adopted it in his printing premises, with decided convenience and efficacy, as well as others, who have availed themselves of its competency to meet all the purposes of ventilation and warmth; and there are so many manufactures and trades, to which these joint conveniences are important desiderata, that we anticipate the grateful feeling of the public towards the inventor. We should add, too, that it is not to manufacturers and traders alone, that the objects effected may be of value; but in private houses, also, this mode of ventilating and warming apartments may contribute, in no small degree, to our personal comfort. The most formidable opponent to be encountered, in the general establishment of warming our rooms by close stoves, or by currents, consists in that attachment which we have for the blazing fire, and which perhaps carries some little reason with it, in so far as its sparkling brilliancy elicits our livelier emotions. An Englishman cannot well divest himself of the idea of poverty, where his winter room does not afford him a blazing companion; and rather than be without his long-cherished friend, he would roast his nose, and freeze his shoulders.

On the Difference of Temperature in Apartments, at different Degrees of Elevation. By Mr. MURRAY.

Mr. Murray has noted the difference of temperature observable on the floor, and at $6\frac{1}{4}$ feet high, in a summer apartment, as indicated by good thermometers. He thinks that when the difference exceeds 2¼ degrees, rain may be expected. He gives a table of his observations in a room at Nottingham, which seems to justify his conclusion. If we recollect aright, the difference never exceeded 5°. As to the difference in warmth, at various points of elevation in an apartment, whether in winter or summer, it has been so universally known as to render experiment unnecessary; but it is the presumed fact of the *degree* of this difference constituting an indication of atmospherical condition or change, that renders it interesting. Further trials, however, are necessary, to aid our judgment in determining probable weather from such a means.

Observations on the Impregnation of Wood with Sea Water. By WILLIAM SCORESBY, Esq., F. R. S. E. and M. W. S. Read before the Wernerian Society.

The following paper, by Mr. Scoresby, confirms the fact of immense pressure at depths greatly below the surface of the ocean: which we shall follow with a short extract from Mr. Campbell's second Tour in Southern Africa, wherein will be shown some very remarkable effects produced by pressure on the corks of the sunken bottles.

"It has been my privilege to make a number of experiments on the effect of enormous pressure on wood, sent to great depths in the sea, in augmenting its specific gravity, by impregnation with sea water. In these experiments, however, some of the water was observed to escape out of the wood, on its being removed from pressure, by the expansion of the compressed air contained in its pores; a circumstance that prevented me from ascertaining the highest degree of impregnation of which the wood was susceptible. A mode of obviating this inconvenience occurred to me during my last voyage to the polar seas; and this mode also promised to show to what extent, and under what degrees of pressure, sea water might be forced through the pores of wood. Not having any metallic vessel suited for the purpose, I employed a strong wine-bottle. I ground the inside of the neck (for the cork) perfectly circular, by means of a cone of wood, with sand and water, and reduced it to such a form, that a piece of wood, in the form of a frustrum of a cone, fitted the neck through the extent of an inch in length, and formed a perfectly air-tight plug. This plug was of very dry ash, and two inches in length. It had a square head, of somewhat greater diameter than the rest of the plug, so that the cone terminated by a kind of shoulder, touching the extremity of the neck of the bottle, to prevent the pressure from thrusting it farther in, and bursting the glass. The neck of the bottle being now heated, the plug, first coated with sealing wax, was introduced, and, the heat being sufficient to render the wax fluid, it was worked down to the shoulder. The plug and the glass being thus intimately united by a thin intermediate coat of sealing wax, there could be no doubt that it was perfectly tight.

" In this state, the bottle was sent to the depth of 125 fathoms, and after remaining a quarter of an hour, was handed up. About two ounces of water was found to have penetrated the pores of the wood. The bottle, unopened, was then sunk a second time to the same depth, and a small additional quantity of water was found to have entered within the bottle, at this second sinking.

" Now, by this process, I expected, that on pressure being applied to one end only of the wood, instead of every part, as in my former experiments, the flow of water through the pores would force all the air contained in the wood into the bottle, and not confine it by compression, as had before been the case: and in this way I expected that a much higher degree of impregnation could be obtained.

" Before examining the plug, I sank the bottle to the depth of 2,928 feet; but here the pressure being unfortunately too great for the strength of the glass, the bottle burst, and only the ring of the neck, encompassing the plug, came up. The result was as follows:—

Before immersion the piece of wood weighed .. 207 grains.
After the experiments 315

Quantity of water absorbed 108

Weight in the air, after immersion .... 315 grains.
Weight of the plug, in fresh water (temp. 40°).. 21¼

Weight of an equal bulk of water .... 293¼ grains.

Hence specific gravity of the wood, after immersion .... 1·078.

"As I apprehended that the portion of the plug, through which the water had made its way into the bottle, would be more impregnated than the rest, from the expulsion of the air into the bottle, I cut away the projecting sides and corners, and formed the central part into a cylinder. But the specific gravity of this was less than that of the whole, being only 1·032; and the extremity that was in the bottle was lightest of all. This effect I attributed to the want of expansion in this part, occasioned by the strength of the ring of the bottle, by which it was compressed; thus preventing it, on the lower part, from receiving its due share of moisture. On splitting the wood, it was found to be wet throughout its substance.

"I next attempted the filtration of water through the pores of a cylindrical piece of mahogany, 4¼ inches in length. In this experiment, I employed a strong oblong vessel of copper, kindly furnished me by Captain Manby (who, with his usual public spirit, accompanied me on the voyage, with a view of trying an apparatus for increasing the facilities, and diminishing the dangers of capturing the whale). This vessel, with the mahogany screwed into the neck, was sent to the bottom, where the depth was 5040 feet, and allowed to remain an hour and a half. But the enormous pressure to which it was subjected, being about 50 tons, (a ton per square inch) crushed the vessel, though every part was an arch, into an irregular flat form, and tore the copper in four different places. Thus the particular design of the experiment being frustrated I could only ascertain the quantity of impregnation. The weight of the mahogany, when dry, was 155 grains; the weight gained in the experiment, 90 grains. Increase of bulk equal to three grains of water.

On Sinking Corked Bottles in the Sea.

Vide Mr. Campbell's Second Tour in Southern Africa.

During my former voyage to South Africa, we sunk bottles fifty fathoms into the sea, after they had been secured from the admission of water, in the best manner we could devise, by covering the corks with resin: on that occasion they were brought up full of water, but without any visible alteration in the cork or resin; which led some to imagine that part of the fluid had entered by the pores of the glass; and some persons even supposed the water might thereby have been divested of its saline particles.

To settle these points a friend had presented me with two crystal globular bottles, hermetically sealed, and made on purpose by Messrs. Pellatt and Green, St. Paul's Churchyard.

In latitude 14°. 27'. N. to the westward of the Cape de Verd islands, these and some other bottles were sunk, by permission of Capt. Creery of the Westmorland, bound for Bombay, two hundred perpendicular fathoms, by means of two leads, the one weighing twenty-two and the other twenty-eight pounds. To pull up this great length of rope, and weight of lead, required the exertion of ten men for a quarter of an hour.

On the two globular bottles being brought on deck, they were found empty; but a wine bottle sent down at the same time, corked and plastered over with resin, came up full of water, with the cork inverted. This we could not mistake, as the head was covered with red wax, previous to the application of the resin, and upon its reaching the deck it was indeed still corked, but the waxed end was undermost in the neck of the bottle. Another wine bottle had the pitch remaining entire on its mouth, but the inside was nearly full of water, in which also the cork was swimming. Two other bottles were full of water, but the corks and resins of these were in the same state as when let down. The water in the inside was not fresher than before its entrance.

Observations on the Difference of Level between the East and West Seas. By J. ROBINSON, Esq. F.R.S.E.

Mr. Robinson addresses himself to Dr. Brewster, to show that the assertions of Dr. Thomson respecting a difference in level, between the eastern and western seas, are erroneous; and he institutes very judicious means to determine the matter. He also shows some sources of very easy error. Our readers need not be informed that the Friths of the Forth on the eastern, and of the Clyde on the western sides of Scotland, are not very far apart; and that this short line must be convenient to determine whether there really be, as suggested, any difference in the level of the respective seas. Mr. Robinson instructed the superintendants of the east and west districts of the Forth and Clyde canal, on three particular days, to notice the rise and fall of the tides. Also, he took similar measures to ascertain the difference of level of every lock when full and empty.

		Ft.	In.		Ft.	In. below summit level.
Oct. 13,	Clyde, calm, high water	151	1	low water,	159	8¼
	Forth	144	6		162	6
Nov. 1,	Clyde, west breeze	150	0		157	10¾
	Forth, west gale	152	6		not specified.	
Nov. 3,	Clyde, calm, with river flood	153	10½		157	2¼
	Forth, south breeze	152	6			

The observer on the Forth considers the tide of the 13th October as two feet higher, and those of November to be much lower, than the average tide levels.

Mr. Robinson remarks that a particular wind will influence the amount of tide level, in a very great degree. The observations at the two extremities of the canal, which unite with the respective seas, are to be continued for some time; and if much variation from the above be found to result, Mr. R. purposes to communicate the fact to Dr. Brewster. Although we may anticipate the result, we shall gladly receive it; for the sooner error be set at rest the better.

On the Separation of Iron from other Metals. By J. F. W. HERSCHEL.

An easy and exact method of separating iron from the other metals with which it may happen to be mixed, has always been a desideratum in chemistry. Every one conversant with the analysis of minerals is aware of the difficulty of the problem, which indeed is such, that, in experiments conducted on any thing like a large scale, it might hitherto be regarded as insuperable. In consequence of this, and of the importance of the inquiry, there is hardly a chemist of eminence who has not proposed some process for the purpose; but with the exception of that which depends on the insolubility of the persuccinate of the obnoxious metal, (which I have not tried, and which is too expensive to be resorted to for any but the nicer purposes of analytical research,) they are all of them either inadequate to the end proposed, intolerably tedious, or limited in their application. That which I have now to propose, on the other hand, is liable to none of these objections, being *mathematically* rigorous, of general application, and possessing in the highest degree the advantages of facility, celerity, and cheapness. It is briefly this:—

The solution containing iron is to be brought to the maximum of oxidation, which can be communicated to it by boiling with nitric acid. It is then to be just neutralized *while in a state of ebullition*, by carbonate of ammonia. The whole of the iron, to the last atom, is precipitated, and the whole of the other metals present (which I suppose to be manganese, cerium, nickel, and cobalt,) remain in solution.

The precautions necessary to ensure success in this process are few and simple. In the first place, the solution must contain no oxide of manganese or cerium above the first degree of oxidation, otherwise it will be separated with the iron. It is scarcely probable in ordinary cases that any such should be present, the protoxides only of these metals forming salts of any stability; but should they be suspected, a short ebullition with a little sugar will reduce them to the minimum. If nitric acid be now added, the iron alone is peroxidized, the other oxides remaining at the minimum. Moreover, in performing the precipitation, the metallic solution should not be too concentrated, and must be agitated the whole time, especially towards the end of the process; and when the acid re-action is so far diminished that logwood paper is but feebly affected by it, the alkaline solution must be added cautiously, in small quantities at a time, and in a diluted state. If too much alkali be added, a drop or two of any acid will set all right again; but it should be well observed, as upon this the rigour of the process depends, that no inconvenience can arise from slightly surpassing the point of precise neutralization, as *the newly precipitated carbonates of the above enumerated metals are readily soluble, to a certain extent, in the solutions in which they are formed (though perfectly neutral)*. In the cases of cobalt and cerium, this re-dissolution of the recent precipitate formed by carbonate of ammonia is very considerable, and a solution of either of these metals, thus impregnated with the metallic carbonate, becomes a test of the presence of peroxide of iron, of a delicacy surpassing most of re-agents used in chemistry; the minutest trace of its being instantly thrown down by them forms a boiling solution, provided no marked excess of the acid be present. To be certain, however, that we have not gone too far, it is advisable after separating the ferruginous precipitate, to test the clear liquid, while hot, with a drop of the alkaline carbonate. If the cloud which this produces be clearly re-dissolved on agitation, we may be sure that only iron has been separated. If otherwise, a little acid must be added, the liquor poured again through the filter, so as to wash the precipitate, and the neutralization performed anew.

The precipitation of iron above described, seems at first to result from a double decomposition. Were it so, the principle of the method would be merely a difference of solubility in the carbonates of iron and the other metals, and as such, would have no claim to be regarded as rigorous. Such, however, is not the case. The iron is not separated in the state of a carbonate, but of a sub-salt, or a simple peroxide, the whole of the carbonic acid escaping with effervescence at each addition of the alkali. The phenomenon turns on a peculiarity in the peroxide of this metal, in virtue of which it is incapable of existing in a neutral solution at the boiling temperature. If we add an alkaline, earthy, or metallic carbonate, by little and little to a *cold* solution of peroxide of iron, the precipitate formed is re-dissolved with effervescence, readily at first, but gradually more and more slowly, till at length many hours, or even days, elapse before the liquid becomes quite clear. Meanwhile it deepens in colour, till (unless much diluted) it becomes dark brown or red. If the addition of the carbonate be carried as far as possible without producing a permanent precipitate, the solution is perfectly neutral, and continues clear at a low temperature for any length of time. In this state it may be evaporated to dryness *in vacuo*, and the residue (which *does not effervesce* with acids) is still soluble in water, without letting any iron fall; and so on as often as we please.

The compound thus formed is, however, far from permanent. It is in fact, in a state of tottering equilibrium, which a very slight cause is sufficient to overset. Supposing the point of saturation to have been exactly obtained, the addition of an extremely small quantity *more* of the alkaline solution is sufficient to determine the separation of the whole, or nearly the whole metallic contents; and if the solution operated on be pretty well concentrated, it fixes after a longer or shorter time, into a stiff and almost solid coagulum.

Again, if to the coagulum so formed, a quantity equally inappreciable of the original ferrugineous solution be added, it gradually liquefies, and after some time is completely re-dissolved; forming no inapt representation of the celebrated imposture of St. Januarius's blood.

A similar change is produced by an increase of temperature. If we heat a solution neutralized as above described, it speedily grows turbid, deposits its ferruginous contents in abundance, *and at the same time acquires a very decided acid re-action*. The acid so developed, holds in solution a portion of oxide; but if the neutralization be formed afresh *while hot*, this separates entirely, and the liquid, after filtration, has no more action on gallic acid, ferrocyanate, or sulphocyanate of potash, than so much distilled water.

It is not my object in this paper to enter into a minute detail of the nature of the persalts of iron, a subject not nearly exhausted, and which want of leisure alone has prevented my entering upon, but merely to point out the practical application of this one of their properties, to an important object in analysis. The principle here developed furnishes a ready method of detecting the minutest quantities of other metals in union with iron, and therefore cannot but prove of important service in various cases where this metal constitutes the chief ingredient in the substance examined, as in meteoric iron, the various natural oxides of this metal, &c. &c. I will exemplify this in one or two instances.

36.00 grains of meteoric iron (furnished me by the kindness of Dr. Wollaston) were dissolved in dilute nitro-sulphuric acid, leaving behind a minute quantity of a brilliant black powder, which, however, dissolved by digestion in nitro-muriatic acid, and appeared only to contain an excess of nickel. The solutions were mixed, and being neutralized at a boiling temperature by carbonate of ammonia, and the iron separated, a green solution remained. Into this, when boiling, a drop of persulphate of iron being let fall, was immediately precipitated in the state of subsulphate, which being separated, the solution was boiled with excess of caustic potash, till all smell of ammonia disappeared. Oxide of nickel separated, which collected and strongly ignited, weighing 4·65 grains, or 12·92 on the hundred, which (taking the atom of nickel to weigh 30, and that of oxygen 8, hydrogen being unity) gives 10·20 per cent. for the contents of the specimen analyzed, in metallic nickel.

One hundred grains of titanious iron from North America, being dissolved in muriatic acid (after the requisite ignition with potash), were treated (after separating the titanium) with excess of carbonate of lime, and filtered. The excess of carbonic acid being expelled, ammonia was added, and a small quantity of a white precipitate fell, which speedily blackened in the air, and proved to be mere oxide of manganese, uncontaminated by iron, and amounting to half a grain.

Manganese has been suspected in various species of cast iron; and though Mr. Mushet's experiments seem to prove that it does not usually enter in abundance, they can hardly be regarded as establishing the fact of its absence. It might not be uninteresting to resume the investigation with the aid of a mode of analysis so well adapted to experiments on a large scale; as I have no doubt that, with proper care, one part in a thousand, or even less, of manganese might be insulated from iron.

The separation of iron from uranium cannot be accomplished by the process above described, that metal possessing the property analogous to that which forms the subject of this paper. By inverting the process, however, we shall succeed even here. A mixed solution of iron and uranium being deoxidized by a current of sulphuretted hydrogen, and then treated with an earthy carbonate, the iron passes in solution, while the uranium separates. This difference in the habitudes of the two oxides of iron, presents us in fact with a kind of chemical dilemma, of one or the other of whose horns we may avail ourselves in any proposed place. In studying the habitudes of uranium, however, I have met with some anomalies which require further investigation. Zirconia too, might probably be forced from iron with equal facility, by similar inversion of the process; but this I have not yet had an opportunity of trying satisfactorily.

On Cadmium, and the Habitude of some of its Ores, showing the Means of detecting the Presence of the Metal in English Ores of Zinc. By E. D. CLARKE, LL. D., Professor of Mineralogy in the University of Cambridge, &c.   Annals of Philosophy, No. 14.

We will divide Mr. Clarke's paper into two sections; the first relating to the process of separating cadmium, and the second to the direction for procuring the ores whence it may be most abundantly obtained.

Dr. Clarke, two years ago, first discovered cadmium in the zinc ores of Derbyshire, and has since found it combined with a greater variety of matter than he had anticipated. He describes a specimen of cadmium sent to him by Dr. Wollaston as peculiarly pure and beautiful, having the colour and lustre of silver, with the pliability of tin.

Among the processes for reduction we notice these:

1st. A small quantity of the pure *oxide* of *cadmium* was dissolved in pure muriatic acid, and a piece of paper being steeped in the solution, and dried, was made into a pellet between the fingers, and supported upon a slip of platinum foil before the *blue flame* of the blow-pipe. Here, as the muriate became concentrated by the burning of the paper, and afterwards decomposed, the *oxide* of *cadmium* was reduced by the *carbonaceous* matter both of the paper and of the *blue flame*; and as it began to burn and exhibit its *reddish brown protoxide* upon the platinum foil, a small bead of cadmium remained upon the surface of the platinum; which, being fixed into the end of a deal splinter, admitted the action of the file, and exhibited the silvery aspect of the pure metal.

In this experiment Dr. C. had full confidence, because the oxide of cadmium came from Professor Stromeyer, and the other matters employed were truly pure. Dr. Wollaston, in speaking to Dr. Clarke respecting the oxide of cadmium, says, "fixed at the tip of the blue flame, it is gradually reduced, volatilizes, and is carried along the slip of platinum, coating it with its peculiar reddish brown protoxide, in a way that cannot be mistaken by one who has once seen it."

The other method of trying for the discovery of cadmium is,

2ndly. Triturate a portion of the *silicate* or *carbonate* of zinc, supposed, or not, to contain *cadmium*; and place about the tenth of a grain of the powder upon a slip of *platinum foil*. Then direct the blue flame of a candle towards it, by means of the blow-pipe. If any cadmium be present, its oxide will be reduced, volatilized, and a protoxide will be deposited upon the surface of the *platinum*, with the peculiar reddish brown colour before mentioned.

Dr. Wollaston's process consists in dissolving the *carbonates* of *zinc*, or gelatinizing the *silicates* in *muriatic acid*, getting rid of the excess of *acid*, and adding distilled water: then removing any metals that *iron* will precipitate, and filtering the solution, which is to be received in a platinum capsule containing a piece of zinc. The cadmium, if any be present, will coat over the interior surface of the capsule with a precipitate of a dull leaden hue, and will adhere so firmly as that it may be washed, and thereby be freed from any remaining solution of zinc. Muriatic acid being now poured into the capsule, will dissolve the lead coloured coating with effervescence, and either the carbonate of potass or caustic potass will yield a white precipitate; which, by heat in the *flame* of the blow-pipe, will exhibit the remarkable character already pointed out, as characteristic of *cadmium*.

Next we proceed to mention the places where cadmium may be best obtained from; viz. the Cumberland Cave, near Matlock, contains cadmiferous carbonate and silicate of zinc, generally called calamine. To distinguish the silicate from the carbonate, they must be mixed with acids: the former not effervescing, but, as the solution evaporates in a watch-glass over the fire, becomes gelatinized, the latter will effervesce. Carbonates of zinc, containing cadmium, are to be met with in the Mendip Hills, Somersetshire: these are found investing cavities, stalatitical, of a dark grey colour.

We apprehend that cadmium is rather to be considered as a chemical play-thing, than as a metal obtainable in any quantity rendering it useful to man.

On Facilitating the Conveyance of Carriages along Iron and Wood Rail-ways, Tram-ways, and other Roads. By BENJAMIN THOMPSON, Patentee.

Perhaps the specification of patent, from whence we take the matter of this paper, would have been more correct, had it expressed the object to be the MOVING of, rather than the *conveyance* of, carriages: a verbal error is of so much importance in specifying principles or applications, that we must strongly urge parties in pursuit of patents to be extremely cautious in selecting terms that cannot admit of doubtful interpretation.

This plan, like almost every other mechanical device of modern days, involves the power of that colossal prime mover the steam-engine; an instrument that will eventually affect the condition of society more than any other human means of influence; the printing press perhaps alone excepted. But while we admire its stupendous impulsive force, and the variety in construction of machinery which it puts in motion, we cannot but observe the tendency to limit the demand for human labour, and render the comforts of the artisan more precarious. We will suppose a new species of manufacture to be introduced, working up raw produce by human labour. In order to lower the market price, and extend the consumption, the manufacturer introduces powerful machinery; and thereby diminishes his demand for human labour. No, says he, the extended market will require all we can produce by mechanism, to complete the article; and we shall still want as much human labour, for the preparatory detail, as we formerly did for the whole process. Very good, so far. But in course of experience he finds that he can also accomplish the *detail* by an *extension* of machinery. And human labour is driven into a narrower corner of retreat, until the population cannot find a sufficiency of labour to exchange for the price of bread. Besides, while the manufacturer has been amassing wealth, by an ingenious application of mechanism, the labourer finds his importance, as an instrument of production, rapidly decline. His case becomes hopeless, for time cannot better his condition. He sees that, should new demand arise, it can, and will, be met by the augmentation of mechanical agency; as a far cheaper instrumental means than his labour, at the very lowest charge existence could allow, must cost the manufacturer. It is not one description of manufacture alone, but all, that thus substitutes mechanism for the honest sweat of the brow. Were a new world of consumption opened to us as a market, all would be well; but the evil consists simply, and wholly, in an excessive production by mechanical facilities; a limitation to the consumption; and a demand, unfortunately, not for labour, but for employment, and its wages. Thus we see vast individual opulence amidst general misery. This evil may fluctuate, but must gradually increase; until, like all others, it become corrected by its very excess.

Mr. Thompson's application of the steam-engine, as a substitute for the draught horse, is not likely to stop here; for its efficacy seems to be completely established. He says,—

"In order that my invention, and the use of it, may be the better understood, it may be necessary to state, that there are various modes in use by which animal and mechanical powers are made available for the purpose of conveying carriages upon rail and tram-ways, where the trade or carriage is principally, or altogether, in one direction. Fixed engines are employed to draw loaded carriages up inclined planes, the empty carriages being enabled by their gravity, and the declination of such planes, to run down the same, and take out the rope, from the engine, along with them. Self-acting inclined planes are made use of where it is expedient to pass loaded carriages down declivities sufficiently great to allow their pulling upward an empty set of carriages at the same time. And where neither the acclivity nor the declination of a road is such, as to admit of one or the other of these methods being adopted, then horses are used for the purpose of drawing the carriages, and in some, although very few instances, locomotive engines. Endless chains have also been applied, but owing to the great friction, and consequent waste of power attendant on them, their use has been very circumscribed, and their application limited to comparatively very short distances. These modes, combined or separately, according to circumstances, have hitherto afforded the means by which rail and tram-ways have been travelled. My method might, in most cases, and with considerable advantage, supersede them all. Whether the line of road rises or falls, much or little, is level or undulating, matters not; the carriages, loaden and empty, are made to pass in both directions, with a uniformity of progress, and at the same time with a dispatch not heretofore known. A road on which my invention is about to be applied, must be divided into stages, attention being given in determining their distances, to the nature of the line, in regard to curves or bends, and to the undulation of the surface. The nearer it approaches to a level, and the fewer, as also the easier the bends are, the better will it allow of the stages being extended. On the other hand, should the line prove to be a very uneven one, with frequent and short bends, then the intervals or spaces, between stage and stage, will necessarily be required to be shortened accordingly. I shall probably be able, more clearly to explain my method, by describing a supposed case. Let the supposed road, to which my invention is to be applied, be a rail-way (either already in being, or to be made) from a colliery to a staith, seven and a quarter miles in length. A proper survey being taken, and a plan and section of the line made, I find it to be expedient to divide it into five stages.

"The first stage from the colliery may be formed to a tolerably uniform ascent, by the aid of cuts and batteries, of one and a half inch to the yard, being three-quarters of a mile in length, and terminating at a summit, on which is to be erected a steam-engine, of power sufficient to draw up the plane six loaden coal waggons at once, containing a Newcastle chaldron each, at the rate of seven and a half feet per second. This stage is a regular inclined plane, and is to be wrought according to the first of the modes already described as now in use; for the returning empty waggons will pass downward by their own gravity, and take the rope with them, preparatory to the drawing up of another loaden set. The full set being drawn up in eight minutes and forty-eight seconds, the empty set allowed to pass down in seven minutes and eighteen seconds, and three minutes occupied in the changes at the ends, will cause one operation of the plane to be completed in nineteen minutes and six seconds. The engine, which I call No. 1, is the first station. The second stage lies over a variable or undulating surface, the two extremities of which are distant one mile and three quarters, and stand nearly level with each other, the intermediate country not admitting, but at too great a cost, of the line being rendered level; the ascents and declivities are moderate, neither exceeding one inch in the yard, and the curves or bends are easy and not numerous. A steam engine, No. 2, is erected at the further termination, which is the second station, to be used for drawing twelve loaden waggons along this stage at once, at the rate of eight and three quarters feet per second, and bringing along with them a rope from No. 1 engine, which is allowed to run off a wheel, not connected with No. 1 engine, during their passage to No. 2 engine; upon their arrival at which, twelve empty waggons are substituted, which are drawn back to No. 1, by the re-connection of the rope-wheel with that engine, bringing with them a rope from No. 2 engine, which is, in like manner, suffered to run off a wheel then thrown out of connection with No. 2 engine. The operation of this stage, both from and towards the colliery, is thus carried on by the alternate action of Nos. 1 and 2 engines, standing at its extremities. The passage of a set of waggons takes up seventeen minutes and thirty-six seconds each way, and the changes three minutes, making together, for a completion of the operation, thirty-eight minutes and twelve seconds, or double the time taken by a set of half the number on the first stage. The third stage is also one mile and three quarters long, and very similar in regard to plan and section to the second stage. A steam engine, No. 3, is placed at the third station, which is the further extremity of the stage, to draw the loaden waggons along the same, and the empty ones are to be taken back by No. 2 engine, in the manner which has just been described on the second stage. The speed, and the number of waggons to a set, are the same also. The fourth stage is more favourable than the second and third, extending over a gently undulating country, and being nearly straight. The fourth station, or further extremity of the stage being, in point of level, twenty feet higher than the other end of it. A steam engine, No. 4, is to stand at the fourth station, to be used for drawing the full waggons from the third station. Nos. 3 and 4 engines will thus alternately act to each other on this stage, as Nos. 1 and 2 have been described to reciprocate on the second stage, and also Nos. 2 and 3 on the third stage. The length of this stage is two miles, and twelve waggons are to travel together, at the rate of ten feet per second, which will complete the process of a passage each way, with the changes, in thirty-eight minutes and twelve seconds. The fifth and last stage, which is one mile long, declines regularly, by the help of cuts and batteries, to the staith, averaging three quarters of an inch to the yard. The loaden waggons are made to pass down the same, in connection with the machinery of No. 4 engine, and also during the time of its drawing a set of full waggons along the fourth stage. The waggons along the fifth stage moving with half the velocity of the waggons along the fourth stage, or five feet per second, and consequently performing the journey in the same time. The advantages of this co-operative movement are, that No. 4 engine, being aided by the gravity of the twelve loaden waggons passing down the inclined plane to the staith, requires only about one half the power which otherwise would have been necessary for drawing independently the full waggons from the third station, and the descending waggons themselves are restrained from proceeding too rapidly, and their speed accurately regulated. The engine No. 4 is used to draw the empty waggons back again from the staith. This mode, whereby the gravity of the loaden waggons passing down an inclined plane is applied in aid of an engine for drawing loaden waggons forward upon another stage, is quite new, and has never been used before; but I do not claim it as any part of my said invention. The second, third, and fourth stages are those on which my method is applied. Nos. 1 and 2 engines reciprocate, or act interchangeably with each other on the second stage, No. 2 drawing the loaden waggons from the first to the second station, and No. 1 pulling the empty (or, in case of need, loaden) waggons back again. Engines Nos. 2 and 3 operate alternately in the same manner with each other upon the third stage; and so also do Nos. 3 and 4 on the fourth stage. The engines are severally to be furnished with two rope-wheels, and a rope to each, of a length and strength suitable to the stage upon which they are to be used. The rope-wheels must be so constructed as to allow of a ready connection, or the contrary, with their respective engines, so as to be capable of being acted upon by them, or of turning round, independently, at the will of the engine man. This may be readily accomplished by any one of the modes in use with mill-wrights for throwing machinery into or out of gear, with a moving power, and does not require to be here described. I make use of very light friction wheels, placed vertically, at proper intervals, to bear the ropes from the ground, where the road is straight; and round the curves, or bends, I place similar wheels, in inclined positions, for the same purpose. Although two miles have been mentioned as the longest of the stages upon the supposed road, it is practicable, under the circumstance of a favourable country, to extend the operation to much longer stages. Without the application of my invention to the supposed road, of which a detailed account has been given, horses would be required to draw the waggons upon the second and third stages, because the ascents of one inch to the yard are too great for locomotive engines to be used upon, independent of the question as to their effecting a saving at all, upon horse labour, on those level roads where they are applicable. Upon the fourth, or two-mile stage, they might be adopted; but from the doubt as to an advantage under any circumstances arising by their use, horses would most likely be deemed the more eligible for working it also. Compared with horse labour, my method would, upon these three stages, effect, in all probability, a saving of seventy-five *per centum*.

"In cases of greater inequality of surface, the saving would be in a still greater ratio. A further and very important reduction in the cost of a new road would result from its adoption. In the formation of a road, it is generally necessary to make deep cuts, and raise high batteries, in order to obtain a uniformly rising, falling, or level surface; and it frequently happens, too, that the direct line of way must be materially diverged from to favour that purpose. My plan dispenses with such nice attention to regularity, the engines being capable of surmounting acclivities, and the wheel which gives out the following, or passive rope, affording the means of restraining the too rapid progress of the waggons down a declivity. In short, there is no country, however uneven or variable its surface, but that may, by my method, be traversed. For conveying of minerals underground, where the unevenness of the strata, and their general disposition to undulation, do not allow of a uniformly ascending, descending, or level road, my invention is peculiarly applicable.

Briefly, then, and it will easily be collected from what has been said—'My method of facilitating the conveyance of carriages along iron and wood rail-ways, tram-ways, and other roads,' is the reciprocal action of two engines, standing at the extremities of a stage, or portion of road to be travelled over, one engine drawing the carriages forward in a direction towards itself, and along with them a rope from the other engine; which rope, in its turn, pulls the same or other waggons, by means of the other engine, back again, and also a rope therewith—thus, by the alternately active and passive agency of two ropes, are the powers of fixed engines made to act in opposite directions, thereby causing a road to be traversed both ways, by loaden or empty carriages, and at any desired speed. It is the reciprocal and interchangeable application of power, as hath been described, which I claim to be my invention."

We have presented our readers, thus far, with the Specification of Patent; and as the article, at length, would intrude too much on our space within this number, we shall defer Mr. Thompson's illustration of the practical effect, until the next month.

Description of a Mill-stone of a superior quality in Halkin Mountain, Flintshire. By W. BISHOP and Co.

Transactions of Society of Arts.

The smaller, or Isis gold, medal, was voted to Bishop and Co. by the Society, for their communication on this subject.

Perhaps it may not be generally known to our readers that British mill-stone was an important desideratum; for previous to this discovery, our millers were at the mercy of France for the best material of this valuable implement; and during war-time the stones were enhanced to a very great price; but now we fortunately have a resource in our own quarries.

The Secretary of the Society notices that the qualities fitting a stone for grinding corn; especially wheat, are, hardness, to prevent its wearing down by perpetual friction; a certain degree of tenacity to prevent the surface from scaling or chipping;

and a cellular structure to augment the triturating asperity of the cutting plane, the walls of the cells being firm enough to resist the strain. These united properties are so seldom met with, as to render good mill-stone very scarce. The resulting advantages are, that the flour is but little mixed with the abraded material of the stone; the grinding is performed more expeditiously; the bran more completely disengaged from the flour: and the flour itself less heated by the friction of working. The latter is of most consequence; for heated flour, or, as technically called *killed*, will not duly ferment when made into bread.

In some parts of the valley of the Seine and adjoining districts, in which fresh water lime-stone occurs, is found a siliceous rock, in detached masses or blocks of various size, known on the spot, and in commerce, by the name of *buhr*. It is a substance intermediate between horn-stone and chalcedony; and possesses, in an eminent degree, the qualities which peculiarly fit it for grinding wheat. All the fine flour required for the supply of the metropolis, and of the large towns in this island, is prepared by means of mill-stones of French buhr. The northern shore of the Isle of Wight is the only district in this country in which the fresh water lime-stone had hitherto been found; but it does not appear to contain any buhr-stone. The entrochital chert, or horn-stone, (vulgarly called *screw-stone*) which occurs, interstratified with the mountain lime-stone in Derbyshire, as it resembles buhr-stone in quality and texture, has occasionally been made trial of for grinding-stones, but always unsuccessfully, on account of its fragility and softness. Having given these preliminary remarks, we shall now proceed to the substance of Messrs. Bishop and Co's paper:—

In the year 1816 Mr. Thomas Hooson, of Flint, observed on Halkin mountain a bed of remarkably fine porcelain clay, which, on exposure to the potters' fires, was found to assume a more delicate whiteness than any substance of a similar nature hitherto found in this kingdom; and seeing also other substances, which he thought likely to be useful to the potters, he obtained from Earl Grosvenor a lease of all clays, rocks, and stones (except lime-stone), within his Lordship's liberties;

and subsequently, with a view to an extended trade, formed his present partnership with Mr. Richard Fynney, Mr. William Bishop, and Mr. James Whitehead, established under the firm of the "Welsh Company, at Nant-y-Moch, near Holywell," where they have erected works for preparing the clay, which is called "Cambria," for sale, by separating it from a white siliceous sand and rock, with which the bed is found mixed, to a depth at present unknown, but which has been proved as deep as twenty-six yards. The sand, when separated, is used for glass making; and the white siliceous rock, now called "Rock Cambria," is ground down, and used in the composition of china and earthenware, instead of ground flint, or is mixed with it. For this process of grinding several thousand tons of chert are annually consumed in the Staffordshire potteries, and much is supplied from Halkin mountain. In quarrying this chert, some of it in the state of vesicular entrochital horn-stone was raised, which, when used together with common chert, indicated such a superiority, by its expeditious grinding, and its little wear, and showed such a proximity in appearance (after having been worked) to the French buhr, that its use for grinding wheat was considered probable; and this led to the first application of the vesicular Halkin rock as a buhr-stone.

Halkin mountain (called "Alchene" at the Conquest, according to Pennant) is a range of high uncultivated land, in Flintshire, the mineral property of the Right Hon. Earl Grosvenor. On the inland side it runs parallel to the boundary hills of the vale of Clwyd; and on the north-east stretches from Holywell, for about four miles, till nearly opposite Northop, in an angle of about twelve degrees with the river Dee, and averages about a mile in breadth. It is composed of mountain lime-stone, with the usually accompanying rocks, and abounds with large veins, containing lead-ore, blende, and calamine, with some appearances of copper: it also affords a rock of whitish quartz, well adapted for certain kinds of mill-stones, for which (according to all our old historians) Flintshire has been famous. But these quarries had been neglected for many years, till lately re-opened by the discoverers of the still more valuable buhrs, and promise to regain their celebrity as grey-stones for grinding oats, &c.

The buhr-stone itself, or entrochital horn-stone, is found near the middle of the eastern ridge of Halkin mountain, and on the west side of the ridge, into which it penetrates with a dip of about one yard in six. Its present appearance presents a bed about four yards thick, between two layers, of a compact siliceous slaty chert, covered with a shivery siliceous shale. It dips eastwardly, like all the other strata on the mountain, which consist of lime-stone, rock, and chert. Rotten masses sometimes occur, and blocks are occasionally found of too close a texture for the miller; and some few are quite solid. Still the corallite structure pervades the whole: the entrochites being perfect and entire in some instances, while in the chief parts of the bed the casts alone remain; thus leaving the rock vesicular, and in this respect differing from the nature of the pores in the French buhr, which appear to have been caused by corrosion, their edges being rusty and impure, whereas those in the Halkin buhrs are of pure flint, and exceedingly sharp and hard.

The quarry from which all the buhrs hitherto used have been procured, now presents a fore-breast of forty yards, and is of the same quality and thickness as at first, but has a thicker covering of shale as it dips into the hill. At the distance of a mile to the north-west, a second quarry is now opening, and appears similar in every respect to the former, and from fragments of buhr here and there found, with pieces of shale and of chert, half concealed in the mountain turf, traces of the same stratum may be observed from the one quarry to the other. About half a mile to the south-east of the main quarry, in the same chert formation, the buhr-stone is also seen to crop out; and in the valley at the foot of the ridge, where a thick bed of lime-stone forms the upper stratum, with a sub-stratum of chert, the miners, in their search for lead-ore, have met with the buhr-stone at the depth of 160 yards from the surface.

In order to prove the Halkin buhrs, the discoverers had some made into mill-stones, which they set up in a neighbouring mill in the borough of Flint; some were had by a mill-wright, and afterwards sent to a mill at Dunham-o'-th'-Hill, mixed with French buhrs; and one large buhr was shaped into a mill-stone, and put up at a mill at Ysceifiog.

They considered it would require much time to prove the real character of the buhrs, and that it would be useless to endeavour to make sales till this proof could be satisfactorily made, and therefore they took but little trouble in circulating the object of their discovery for nearly two years, when, finding that the stones at Flint mill were highly approved, and found to be a substitute for the French buhrs, they turned their attention to the subject.

They were advised to lay specimens of the buhrs before the Society of Arts, &c. immediately, lest they might be anticipated by some other person in their pretensions to the premium offered, and they accordingly ventured to do so in February 1820 (under the name of Flint Buhrs); but not having then had sufficient trial made of them, they were not in possession of certificates sufficiently extensive, on which to rest their claims to the notice of the Society.

As, however, they are now able to adduce proofs that the Halkin buhrs are fully equal to the French, and in some cases are declared to be actually superior to them, they trust that the Society, in looking to the national importance of the discovery, will pass over the trouble that was last year so unintentionally occasioned, and again take the matter into their consideration.

They request permission to lay before the Society the accompanying certificates and letters on the subject; and in order to show that they have not been selecting a few, and withholding any less favourable to their hopes, they beg to state the result of every sale made by them up to the end of the last year, and to add a short review of the particular certificate connected with each case; observing, at the same time, that not one unfavourable or unsatisfactory trial has yet occurred.

Some of the buhrs got on the discovery of the quarry were (as before stated) converted into mill-stones, and put up, about three years ago, at Mr. Evans's mill in the borough of Flint, who certifies that " he used them nearly two years, occasionally for wheat, but chiefly as grey-stones, in which they excelled; that at first he used them seldom for wheat, but afterwards more and more frequently, as he found them answer the purpose; and, by way of comparing them with the French stones, he took six measures of wheat, and ground one half on the Halkin stones and one half on the French stones. There was some very slight difference in the flour, which was in favour of the French; but he did not consider it as a fair trial, as the Halkin stones were not at the time properly faced for wheat-grinding; and if the French stones had been faced as rough, the flour from them would not have been better than the other. Bread was made from the two kinds of flour; but no one could distinguish between the two. He then had the Halkin stones regularly faced and cracked as French, and has found them ever since equal to the French stones in every respect whatever."

Others of the buhrs, got about the same time, were used more cautiously by a mill-wright, who made a large pair of mill-stones of Halkin and French buhrs, fixed in alternately; and these were set up more than three years ago, at the Horn Mills, near Dunham-o'-th'-Hill, in Cheshire. Mr. John Peers, the present tenant of this mill, entered on it nearly three years ago; and he states that " the stones were in a rough state, and required six months to get them to a proper face, when they ground wheat as well as the best French stones, and have ever since continued to do so: that he prefers the Halkin and French stones mixed to those of French buhrs entirely, as they grind faster, and as well, and full as cool as the French; that he uses them for all purposes; and considers them equal in every respect, and superior in some respects to the French buhrs."

A large buhr, got about the same time, was sold to Mr. John Edwards, the occupier of a small mill at Ysceifiog, in Flintshire. He states, " that from various causes the buhr was not used till about twelve months ago, when he shaped it into a mill-stone of three feet six inches diameter. That he has no French stones, but used this as a runner over a blue stone for grinding wheat, and found the flour of good colour, and the bran broad and light; that the stone would bear the finest cracking, and continued to improve and harden till he left the mill in November last."

The next sale was to John Dumbell, Esq. of the Mersey Mills, Warrington (said to be the largest establishment in the kingdom, and containing twenty-two pair of mill-stones); and he certifies that " in March 1820 he received a quantity of Halkin buhrs, which he had forthwith made into mill-stones, and these were so much approved, that in May 1820 he had buhrs for a second pair; that the two pair of Halkin mill-stones have been regularly at work ever since, and continue to give great satisfaction to the bakers and flour dealers; that he conceives they are precisely the same kind of stones as the French buhrs, and cut the grain like them, and are like them in respect to oatmeal, in which neither French nor Halkin stones are used to advantage; and he considers the discovery of great national importance."

Messieurs Hurstfield and Passand (now the occupiers of some large mills at Lymm, near Warrington, but who were lately foremen to Mr. Dumbell, and have been practical millers nearly thirty years,) state " that they made the Halkin stones which were set up at the Mersey mills, where there are nine pair of French stones at work; that they made an experiment with some wheat, by grinding some on the best French pair and some on the Halkin stones, in order to compare the flour, in which there was scarcely any perceptible difference; though the preference was given in favour of the Halkin stones by a corn and flour dealer, to whom the samples were shown; that bread was made from each, but no difference could be perceived; that at first they thought the Halkin stones not quite so hard and tough as the French, but they found them continue to improve, and to become as good as French; that they have seen all varieties of mill-stones, and made all sorts of mill-stones, but never saw any buhrs to come in competition with the French except the Halkins, which they are satisfied will answer every purpose."

We decline further pursuing the matter of proof that the buhr-stone of the Halkin mountain is equal to the purposes required: therefore we shall merely intimate, that Messrs. Bishop and Co. produce sufficient certificates to satisfy the

Society. We consider the discovery of this stone as of a national treasure that will be duly appreciated by the miller, when we again contend with our Gallic neighbours.

Description of certain Improvements in the Construction of Pistons. Invented by JOHN BARTON, and for which he obtained a Patent.

This patent is of some standing; and if the piston really possess the advantages stated, it must be extremely valuable, and cannot be too widely announced. The principle on which it is constructed appears theoretically good. It is that of a circular or spiral spring operating laterally from the centre towards the circumference, thus: the piston, if intended to act as a solid or close one, has its body divided into segments, with the spring from the centre forcing the segments outwards, so that the external circumference, or friction face, of the piston will always be in close, but accommodating, contact with the surface of the cylinder in which it works. If the piston be hollow, the circular spring will occupy the internal surface of the aperture.

Mr. Barton represents his object to be that of diminishing friction, and promoting durability. He says his invention is applicable to all kinds of pistons; to prevent the escape of steam, air, water, or any other fluid, and likewise to prevent its escape by the piston rod. The piston may be made of any material suitable for the proposed work; but they are generally made of some metallic substance. As to the body closing the cylinder, and through which the rod works, we ought to observe that its construction is directly the reverse of that of the piston which moves in the cylinder; the operation of the latter being by its outward circumference, requires the spring expansion *from* the centre, but the body through which the piston rod moves, acting by its inner surface, has its spring pressing from the circumference *to* the centre. These pistons are adapted to other forms as well as the cylindrical. But Mr. Barton shall speak for himself:

" The improved metallic pistons will be found inestimable in all concerns where it is an object to avoid delay; mines, water-works, breweries, steam-vessels, draining land, and in all engines and pumps where hard and constant work is required. These facts have been proved by five years' experience; and the patentee can give references to many gentlemen of the first respectability, who have them now in use.

"In mines, the saving of time and expense will be one-third, as it will be a double advantage, not only in the engine, but in the buckets in the shafts, and will not require a tenth of the stoppages for repairs, as on the present system.

"In ships' pumps, water works, breweries, distilleries, and all concerns where there is much pumping, above one-fourth will be saved in time and expense, as they will not require any stoppage for repairs, and the friction is nearly done away; and there is every reason to judge, from experience, that they will last as long as the engine, as they improve by use.

"In draining fen land and irrigation they possess an incalculable advantage over the present system, as they will deliver more water than the present draining mills at any time, and will work with the most moderate wind, when the present mills will not move: they are cheaper in erection, and less expensive in repairs.

"In steam vessels above a fourth of fuel will be saved, with much greater safety to the vessels; and where there are two engines, above a mile an hour will be gained in speed, and the fatal consequences attending explosion, in a great measure obviated.

"In fire and garden engines they will throw the water much higher, and work with less labour, than the present method; and the alteration of the engines now in use will cost but a small sum.

"They are using with every satisfaction in various parts of these kingdoms, and likewise in France and America, of which certificates can be produced by the proprietors, Barton and Co. No. 3, Winsley-street, Oxford-street, who are ready to agree with any person for the use of the invention, by application (post paid).

On the Propagation of the Walnut Tree by Budding. By T. A. KNIGHT, Esq., President of the London Horticultural Society, F. R. S., &c.

From the Society's Transactions.

The ill success of many attempts to *propagate* the *walnut-tree* by grafts, or buds, led me, in a former communication, to discourage all attempts to increase it, except by seeds, or by grafting by approach. I nevertheless continued, annually, to make a few experiments, with the hope of discovering a method of budding which would prove successful in the culture of varieties of this fruit, and of others of equally difficult propagation; and I have found in ultimate success the usual reward of patient perseverance.

The advantages of propagating varieties of the walnut-tree by budding, will, I think be found considerable, provided the buds be taken from young, or even middle-aged healthy trees: for, exclusive of the advantage of obtaining fruit from very young trees, the planter will be enabled to select not only such varieties as afford the best fruit, but also such as endure best, as timber-trees, the vicissitudes of our climate. In this respect some degree of difference is almost always observable in the constitution of each individual seedling tree; and this is invariably transferred with the graft or bud.

The walnut, it is true, as a fruit, contains but little nutriment, and perhaps constitutes, at best, only an unwholesome luxury: but the tree affords timber of much greater strength and elasticity, comparatively with its very low specific gravity, than any other of British growth, and it is consequently applicable to purposes for which no good substitute has hitherto been found; the stocks of the musket of the soldier, and of the gun of the sportsman.

The buds of trees, of almost every species, succeed with most certainty when inverted in the shoots of the same year's growth, but the walnut-tree appears to afford an exception; possibly in some measure because its buds contain, within themselves, in the spring, all the leaves which the tree bears in the following summer; whence its annual shoots wholly cease to elongate soon after its buds unfold. All its buds of each season are also, consequently, very nearly of the same age; and long before any have acquired the proper degree of maturity for being removed, the annual branches have ceased to grow longer, or to produce new foliage.

To obviate the disadvantages arising from the preceding circumstances, I adopted means of retarding the period of the vegetation of the stocks, comparatively with that of the bearing tree; and by these means I became partially successful. There are at the base of the annual shoots of the walnut, and other trees, where those join the year-old wood, many minute buds, which are almost concealed in the bark; and which rarely, or never, vegetate, but in the event of the destruction of the large prominent buds, which occupy the middle, and opposite end of the annual wood. By inserting in each stock one of these minute buds, and one of the large and prominent kind, I had the pleasure to find that the minute buds took freely, whilst the large all failed, without a single exception. This experiment was repeated in the summer of 1815, upon two yearling stocks which grow in pots, and had been placed, during the spring and early part of the summer, in a shady situation under a north-wall, whence they were removed late in July to a forcing house, which I devote to experiments, and instantly budded. These being suffered to remain in the house during the following summer, produced from the small buds shoots nearly three feet long, terminating in large and perfect female blossoms, which necessarily proved abortive, as no male blossoms were procurable at the early period in which the female blossoms appeared: but the early formation of such blossoms sufficiently proves that the habits of a bearing branch of the walnut-tree may be transferred to a young tree by budding, as well as by grafting by approach.

The most eligible situation for the insertion of buds of this species of tree (and probably of others of similar habits) is near the summit of the wood of the preceding year, and of course, very near the base of the annual shoot; and if buds of the small kind above mentioned be skilfully inserted in such parts of branches of rapid growth, they will be found to succeed with nearly as much certainty as those of other fruit trees, provided such buds be in a more mature state than those of the stocks into which they are inserted.

The advantages which may be obtained in the propagation of other species of trees, by procuring buds for insertion in a more mature state than those of the stock, are sufficient to deserve some attention, and are not, I believe, at all known to gardeners and nurserymen. The mature bud takes immediately with more certainty under the same external circumstances: it is much less liable to perish during winter; and it possesses the valuable property of rarely or never vegetating prematurely in the summer, though it be inserted before the usual period, and in the season when the sap of the stock is most abundant. I have, in different years, removed some hundred buds of the peach tree from the forcing-house to luxuriant shoots upon the open wall; and I have never seen an instance in which any of such buds have broken and vegetated during the summer or autumn: but when I have had occasion to reverse this process, and to insert immature buds from the open wall into the branches of trees growing in a peach-house, many of these, and in some seasons all, have broken soon after being inserted, though at the period of their insertion, the trees in the peach-house had nearly ceased to grow. The result was, in both the preceding cases, in opposition to my expectations; but it appears necessarily to have been occasioned by the mature bud having naturally sunk into a state of repose, preparatory to its long winter sleep, previously to its having been removed; and by the more excitable state of the powers of life in the bud taken from the open wall.

If the mature buds of the peach tree, when taken from the forcing-house, contain blossoms, these may be carried a great distance and still afford fruit in the following spring. I have thus readily obtained fruit from blossoms sent me from the vicinity of London; and I entertain no doubt of the practicability of obtaining fruit from blossoms sent from Paris, or even the South of France, if properly packed. In such cases it would be necessary to pare the wood of the bud thin, instead of wholly extracting it: and this will sometimes be found expedient, when buds are to be taken from a peach-house, in which the fruit has been made to ripen early in the summer, to be inserted in the open air.

On the Cultivation of the Under-ground and some other Onions. By JOHN WEDGWOOD, Esq. F.H.S.

Transactions of London Horticultural Society.

I have just now read, in the Horticultural Society's Transactions, Mr. Maher's paper on the cultivation of the underground or potato onion.

I am myself a grower of these onions, but do not entirely agree with Mr. Maher in all particulars; I will state wherein I differ from him. His method of planting is very good, but in the subsequent treatment, I believe he is wrong.

I never use the hoe to the plant, except for clearing the ground from weeds, when the onions have shot out their leaves to their full size, and when they begin to get a little brown at the top. I clear away all the soil from the bulb, down to the ring, from whence proceed the fibres of the roots, and thus form a basin round each bulb, which catches the rain, and serves as a receptacle for the water from the watering-pot. I find that the old bulbs then immediately begin to form new ones, and if they are kept properly moist, and the soil is good, the cluster will be very large and numerous. This is not the only advantage of this mode of treatment, as the bulbs thus grown above ground are much sounder than those formed beneath the surface, and will keep much better; indeed I find them to keep quite as well as any other sort; but this was not the case until I adopted the plan I have described.

Having said thus much on under-ground onions, I am tempted to give the result of three different trials of growing common onions, which I made this year for my own satisfaction; and as my mind has been thoroughly convinced as to the best method, it may be useful to give the particulars. I claim no merit in what I have done; but I think it is of great advantage, repeatedly to call the attention of gardeners to good methods, which had been previously made known, but have been suffered to pass by unheeded.

My first mode was with the small bulbs of Portugal onions, sown in May 1818, and which were of the size of small nuts; the ground was trenched two spades, graft deep, but no dung was put in, and the bulbs were planted on the 10th March last, six inches apart, and the rows were at the same distance asunder: they have produced a very good crop of fine onions.

The second mode was with onions sown in September 1818, and transplanted into rows, the same as in the preceding case, into the same ground, and at the same time. They did not produce bulbs so large as the first.

The third mode was sowing the seed in drills, six inches asunder, and thinning the plants to about four inches distance. These were sown in the same soil, and on the same day that the others were planted, and produced a very good crop; but not to be compared to the first, which had also the advantage of ripening at least a fortnight sooner.

I planted also some small bulbs, of the sowing of the early part of the spring of 1818, but they almost all went to seed, and when the flower bud was pinched off, the bulb produced two new ones.

My own conviction of the value of Mr. Knight's method of sowing the seed in May, to form bulbs for the next year's stock, is so great, that I shall for the future adhere to it, and only sow a little seed in the spring, to supply green onions.

The kinds of onions I have sown are, the Portugal, the James's-keeping, and the two-bladed onion.

I shall merely add, that the soil of my garden is a light sand, and that I have difficulty in procuring dung in sufficient quantities, which will account for my not using any in these experiments.

Account of a Method of conveying Water to Plants in Houses. By Joseph Sabine, Esq. F.R.S. &c. Sec.

Transactions of London Horticultural Society.

I have great pleasure in communicating to the Horticultural Society the particulars of a plan for watering plants in houses, invented by Mr. George Loddiges, one of the partners in the firm of Messrs. Loddiges and Sons of Hackney, whose extensive nursery gardens are well known to every collector of rare and valuable plants.

The plan I am about to describe is most simple in its operation, and not only supplies water to the plant, without labour, but in a way that must be more beneficial than the usual one, by a watering-pot.

A leaden pipe, of half an inch bore, is introduced into one end of the house, in such a situation that the stop-cock, which is fixed in it, and which is used for turning on the supply of water, may be within reach; it is then carried either to the upper part, or the back of the house, or to the inside of the ridge of the glass frame-work, being continued horizontally, and in a straight direction, the whole extent of the house, and fastened to the wall, or rafters, by iron staples, at convenient distances. From the point where the pipe commences its horizontal direction, it is perforated with minute holes, through each of which the water, when turned on, issues in a fine stream, and, in descending, is broken, and falls on the plants, in a manner resembling a gentle summer shower. The holes are perforated in the pipe with a needle, fixed into a handle like that of an awl; it being impossible to have the holes too fine, very small needles are necessarily used for the purpose, and in the operation great numbers are of course broken. The situation of the holes in the pipe must be such as to disperse the water in every direction that may be required, and in this particular the relative position of the pipe and of the stations of the plants to be watered must be considered, in making the perforations. The holes are made, on an average, at about two inches distance from each other, horizontally, but are somewhat more distant near the commencement, and rather closer towards the termination of the pipe, allowing thereby for the relative excess and diminution of pressure, to give an equal supply of water to each end of the house. A single pipe is sufficient for a house of moderate length: one house of Messrs. Loddiges, which is thus watered, is sixty feet long, and the only difference to be made in adapting the plan to a longer range, is to have the pipe larger. The reservoir to supply the pipe must of course be so much above the level as to exert a sufficient force on the water in the pipe, to make it flow with rapidity, as it will otherwise escape only in drops; and as too strong a power may be readily controlled by the stop-cock, the essential point to be attended to in this particular is to secure force enough.

From the above details it will be observed, that some nicety is required in the arrangement and formation of the machinery; but it is only necessary to view the operation in Messrs. Loddiges' house, to be convinced of the extreme advantage and utility of the invention, when it is properly executed.

On the Cultivation of Figs on the back Walls of Vineries. By JOSEPH SABINE, Esq. F. R. S. &c.

Transactions of London Horticultural Society.

In the common method of cultivating grapes under glass, it may always be observed, that the vines trained to the back wall of the houses seldom yield either an abundant or well-flavoured crop: this is caused by the plants being too far removed from the glass, and too much shaded by the vines trained under the rafters. I have always considered fig-trees as better suited to the back wall in a grape-house than vines, and have lately seen them succeed so well in the garden of a friend in Norfolk, that I cannot better describe the plan I recommend, than by detailing the practice I there observed.

The house I allude to is forty-four feet long, by twelve feet and a half wide, in the clear; the back wall is fourteen, and the front wall rather more than four feet high; there is no upright glass in front: the vines are planted on the outside, on a border raised against the front wall, and are brought into the house under the wall plate; the flue is in front only, returning upon itself, the chimney being over the fire-place, which is at one end of the house, the door being at the other end, so that there is no dip in the flue: a paved walk goes along the house, near the flue, leaving a border between the pavement and the back wall. Two fig-trees are planted against the back wall; one is a brown, the other a white fig, kinds which are common in Italy and the south of France, and both bearing fruit of a short and flattened form. These trees have been planted fifteen years, and entirely cover the wall; the border in which they are planted was originally made very rich, and they have grown well in it: the branches are trained to a trellis against the wall, but they are also suffered to project from the wall. The trees are pruned in the autumn, after their wood is well hardened, where it is necessary to prevent them from incumbering the house; but as the object is to get the trees to the largest possible size, in which state they will produce more of the short fruit-bearing shoots, they are cut but little, except it be occasionally necessary to thin them, by taking out a strong limb. It is the practice to begin forcing when the grapes break in the middle of April; the first crop of figs ripens in June, and the second crop in August. The grapes begin to ripen in September, and continue fresh until near Christmas.

Under such treatment both kinds of fruit are of great excellence. It is advisable not to train the vines entirely under the whole of the glass, but to leave a space in the centre of each light, its whole length, for the admission of the sun's rays: the grapes, perhaps, will be as much benefited by this practice as the figs. The height to which the fig-trees are suffered to grow must be regulated by the consideration, whether it be desired to sacrifice part of the crop of grapes to the increase of the produce of figs. If the fig-trees are permitted to reach the glass, the vines must be shortened in consequence; but if it be desired that the vines should bear the whole length of the rafter, it will be necessary to keep the fig-tress shortened, so as not to interfere with the vines.

On the Absurdity of burying Weeds, and turning in young Crops, with the Intention of making them serve as Manure. By Mrs. AGNES IBBETSON.

Philosophical Magazine, 286.

Mrs. Ibbetson endeavours to justify the title of her paper, by presenting cases, wherein the practice of applying recent vegetable matter to the purposes of manure, is evidently at variance with the common processes of nature. We remember having, some time since, read a paper written by this lady, in one of the Philosophical Journals, showing, experimentally, that vegetable matter would long retain its vitality when immersed in earth; and when not so retaining the vital principle, it might be preserved from decay. Mrs. I. makes a very proper distinction between the common dunghill of the farm yard, and the mere mass of vegetable matter accumulated for manuring objects. She enumerates the means we pursue for *preserving* many of our edible vegetables, as exactly resembling such as, for manuring purposes, we have recourse to, with a view to the *decomposition* of vegetable matter. That the argument holds, in so far as relates to the turning in of a green crop, we have no doubt; because the vegetable matter is living and growing; and so the turnip and potato retain vital principle, when we heap them in store, under mounds of earth. But when the vegetable be absolutely dead, as straw, &c., the analogy ceases. Mere moisture and warmth will resolve it into elementary principles. She instances the opinion of Sir H. Davy, that vegetables do not produce manure that can be serviceable to a crop. But surely this is a hasty decision, and directly in the teeth of incontrovertible evidence: and indeed, in the course of the paper, Mrs. I. refutes it herself; by a reference to the rich vegetable mould found in the cleared ground of America. We cannot better state our own ideas than by saying, Ask an American farmer what kind of soil he finds to reward his labours, in clearing away the forest of ages? His answer, we presume, would correct the pride of philosophy. But Mrs. I. shall speak for herself, as to recent and living vegetables. She says:—

"We wish to keep our roots, such as carrots, turnips, potatoes, free from decay till we want them; for this purpose we place them in the earth; cooks and others having experienced that placing venison in the soil will either freshen it, or at least stop its further progress towards decomposition. These various trials, therefore, prove the earth to possess the power of repelling putrefaction. How then can we in the same manner, and at the *same season*, turn in our weeds, and the refuse of our fields and gardens, and expect by *this means to procure* for that crop just put in, manure that will nourish and support it? Is that not pretending that the earth will preserve and at the same time decay? Can it do both? If the crop requires manure, is it not deceiving ourselves to turn in that matter which will not produce it? If the positive proof we have received, both in the animal and vegetable world, of the earth's preserving powers, does not suffice to convince us, *a trough is easily procured*. I tried two for three years. We know that potatoes, &c., are not only preserved, but that their roots *grow*, and that the plants throw up suckers and new shoots: on examining the trough, I found that the grass and weeds had repeatedly spread suckers through the top of the case, which proved that they were still perfectly alive. Sir H. Davy, (that great luminary of the physical and chemical world) has said that vegetables do not produce manure that can be serviceable to a crop; which, when we consider the process the plants must pass through after death, before they can be sufficiently decomposed to serve as manure, is completely exemplified.

"It always appeared to me that there was a strange confusion by botanists and gardeners in comparing fresh vegetables, or plants but just dead, with dung, as if *they both* passed through the same process when replaced in the earth. Dung has already been exposed to a very high temperature, to the effects of the gastric juice in the stomach of the animal; and therefore enters the earth after it has undergone each separate fermentation. No wonder it is of such general use, since it is capable of being directly applied to the service of supporting the plants; but how different is the situation of vegetables just cut or drawn up by the roots, and then replaced in the earth! They are not even dead. After keeping one trough closed for nearly three years, in which I had placed boughs of trees and herbaceous vegetables; and another, in which were weeds and indigenous plants; most of the latter *grew up again*, and many made their way through the top of the trough,—but in the first the bark of the boughs was alone destroyed: no other part was touched, merely dirtied. What is most curious, several of the shoots had formed fresh buds in the earth, but perfectly without scales; which accords with the early decay of the bark.

"It is certain a very great expense would be spared the farmer, and he would soon find his fields by degrees grow clean, when he had three or four times taken out all his weeds without returning them to the earth, to burn them alone (not paring and burning); though they will make but a very few ashes, still that little quantity may be of use: and they would soon find what an expense would be spared. The greater part of pernicious weeds are only to be killed by manuring; drawing them from the earth by *ploughing* often only increases the number. A gentleman in this county had a lawn so overgrown with colt's-foot, that he ploughed four or five times, and each ploughing increased the quantity; at last he was persuaded to give it a thorough dressing of dung, of short muck, but turned in hot from the cart. It completely killed the weeds, and he had as fine a field of *red clover* as I should ever wish to see. *Sonchus palustris*, which had over-run a lawn adjoining the Ex, was entirely destroyed, so as not to appear again, by manuring a few times with rather hot lime.

"Sir H. Davy has informed us of lime, 'that in its passage from quick lime to carbonate of lime it is capable of decomposing vegetables;' but he expresses himself as if not quite certain of the fact. It was, however, on this opinion I have acted, and founded my various trials. I first placed different sorts of meat in a small trough on mild lime, and covered it with the same matter. Its effects were most curious: the lime formed a cake near two inches in thickness around the meat, which appeared to shut out all air, as it was perfectly dry and hard. The manner in which animals and vegetables decay, is very different; the first undoubtedly forms a vacuum, and thus preserves it. In the case of vegetables the lime is always perfectly loose, and not in any manner coagulated; but to my great astonishment they were so much decayed, even in their wood and muscle, (the hardest part) as to promise total decomposition, if lime had been once more applied.

"My weeds were all marked, before they were placed in the trough, with coloured threads, by which means I knew them again when growing up. I cannot think it a fair trial without the matter said to have been weeds is taken out and examined, to show in what state *it is*, whether really capable of manuring plants, or not. A gentleman, after letting his gardener rake out the hole, showed me earth which he declared *had been weeds* two months before; I only insisted on seeing the raked matter, and all the weeds which had not grown up were in it in a half-dying state: but in woody plants the folly is still more complete, and in turning-in young crops of beans or vetches, except the leaves that are eaten by vermin, all the rest remains perfect, take it out when you will."

Mrs. I. next proceeds to detail the results of experiments made on various plants, in various soils, in order to discover which might be best adapted to a profitable cultivation; and she states as follows:—

"There are but few agricultural plants usually made use of by a farmer; of these I selected *twenty*, to try in a variety of soils, to endeavour to ascertain in which ground each would yield the greatest return, looking to profit. The turnip and carrot gave three parts in twenty more in sand than in any other soil. The cabbage two parts more in clay than in any other earth. The immense difference maintained by the saintfoin, in chalk or lime-stone, never proved less than an increase of four in twenty: hops showed a predilection nearly as great. The cow clover was equally decided in its choice of poor sand. The mangel evinced its superiority $2\frac{1}{4}$ in clay. As to the wet and dry clovers, to change their soil is to destroy them. In the wheats, to mistake the soil for which they are intended is to blight them more or less each year. I have been constantly able to banish and bring on the blight by this means." There are several wheats for each sort of land, so that the identical plant may be changed as often as is necessary. The experiment of the farming plants, tried three years successively, and the quantity of manure given them, though differing in quality, was as nearly as possible the same in measure."

We must now take leave of this Lady; and as the best mark of our respect for her talents and assiduity, we shall simply observe that, numerous gentlemen of landed property, may contemplate her superiority with suffused countenances.

On Hare's Galvanic Deflagrator. By the Editor of the American Journal of Science.

This is a letter addressed by Dr. Silliman to Professor Hare, confirming the power of the deflagrator, with some additional remarks. After some complimentary matter, Dr. S. proceeds to say:—

"With your eighty coils of fourteen inches by six, for the copper, and of nine by six for the zinc, I obtained effects which, as to every thing that related to intense heat and light, and brilliant combustion, far surpassed the powers of a battery of the common form of six hundred and twenty pairs of plates—one hundred and fifty pairs of which, of six inches square, are insulated by glass partitions—one hundred pairs of the same size, and three hundred of four inches square, are insulated by resin, and the rest either by Wedgwood's ware or by resin, making in the whole a battery with a surface of thirty-six thousand eight hundred and eighty square inches. Yours has a surface of only twenty-two thousand and eighty square inches, *but even without insulation* it is incomparably more powerful than the other with that advantage. This is the most singular circumstance connected with your new apparatus, and which goes far to shake our previous theoretical opinions, if not to support your own.

"I repeated every important experiment stated in your

memoir; and with results so similar, that it is scarcely necessary to relate them. The combustion of the metals was brilliant beyond every thing which I had witnessed before, and the ignition of the charcoal points was so intense, as to equal the brilliancy of the sun: the light was perfectly intolerable to eyes of only common strength. If I were to name any metallic substance which burned with more than common energy, it would be a common brass pin, which, when held in the forceps of one pole, and touched to the charcoal point on the other, was consumed with such energy, that it might be said literally to vanish in flame.

"The light produced between the charcoal points when immersed beneath acids, oils, alcohol, ether, water, &c. was very intense, and platina melted in air as readily as wax in the blaze of a candle. It is a very great advantage of your Deflagrator, that we can suspend the operation at any moment, with the same facility with which it was commenced. A look, directed to the assistant, is sufficient to raise the coils out of the fluid. All action instantly ceases—neither the metal nor the fluid is wasting any further, and the lecturer is therefore at ease while he illustrates and reasons; and when he is ready, and not before, he proceeds to his next experiment. In the mean time, the instrument, during a certain period, rather gains than loses strength, by the raising of the coils. It seems as if the imponderable fluids, partially exhausted from it by its continued action, had time again to flow in from surrounding objects, and thus to impart new energy. I found the power of the instrument to last for several days, although declining, and charcoal points, prepared by igniting pieces of mahogany beneath sand in a crucible, would also continue to operate for several days. When the coils, after immersion, had been suspended, for some hours, in the air, a coating of green oxide or carbonate of copper always formed on one part of the outside of the copper coils, and on the same part in all, but no where else. If I do not misremember, it collected next to the negative pole, but was, of course, always removed by the next immersion, though it was formed again at the next suspension.

"One circumstance occurred during these experiments, which demands further attention.

"In the hope of uniting the power of your Deflagrator with that of the common galvanic battery, I connected your instrument with the powerful one mentioned above. Both instruments, *when separately used*, acted *at the time*, with great energy, producing both their appropriate and common effects in a very decided manner; but, on connecting by the proper poles, the battery of six hundred and twenty pairs, with the Deflagrator of eighty coils, I was greatly surprised and disappointed, at finding the power of both instruments so completely paralysed, that, at the points where a moment before, and when separate, a stream of light and heat, hardly to be endured by the eye, was poured forth—now, when connected, both instruments could scarcely produce the minutest spark. On separating the instruments, they both resumed their activity; on again connecting them, it was again destroyed, and so on, as often as the experiment was made. While they were in connection, provided the coils were lifted out of the acid, so as to hang in the air merely, then the power of the common galvanic battery would pass through the Deflagrator, which appeared to act simply as a conductor; and, as might have been expected when so extensive a conductor was used, the power of the common battery was, in this case, considerably diminished, while that of the Deflagrator did not act at all.

"If, while things were in this situation, the coils of the Deflagrator, without being plunged, were lowered so far as merely to dip their inferior extremities say only one-fourth of an inch in the acid, the communication was immediately arrested, and all effect destroyed almost as completely as when the coils were wholly immersed. Thus it appears that the inability to act, in connection with the common galvanic battery, depends upon the relation of the fluid and metal, and not upon that of the metals merely. These experiments should be repeated, with the aid of the insulating glasses, placed so as to receive the coils of your machine. I should be very curious to know whether the effects would be the same; and as I now have the glasses, I shall, as soon as possible, try this experiment. We must look to you, Sir, for the explanation of this singular incompatibility between the two instruments. At present, I confess myself unable to explain it. It may, very possibly, lead to important results, and may have a bearing, such as I have not now time to discuss, on your own peculiar theory.

"I would state that the mode of connecting the two batteries was varied in every form which occurred, not only to myself, but to several able scientific gentlemen who were present at these experiments, and who were equally with myself surprised and confounded by their results.

"I remain, &c."

On the Cause of Heat. By Professor HARE.
American Journal of Science.

The Professor in this paper combats the opinion of Sir H. Davy, the late Count Rumford, and others, of heat being caused by corpuscular motion; and having quoted Sir H. D.'s Elements, wherein he supposes the particles of solids to be in a "constant state of vibratory motion; and that the particles of the hottest bodies move with the greatest velocity, and through the greatest space." Also, that " in liquids and elastic fluids, besides the vibratory motion, which must be conceived greatest in the last, the particles have a motion round their own axes with different velocities; the particles of elastic fluid moving with the greatest quickness: and that, in ethereal substances, the particles move round their own axes, and separating from each other, penetrate in right lines through space, &c."—he proceeds thus:—

"These suggestions of Sir H. Davy's are to me unsatisfactory.

"It is fully established in mechanics, that when a body in motion is blended with and thus made to communicate motion to another body, previously at rest, or moving slower, the velocity of the compound mass after the impact will be found, by multiplying the weight of each body by its respective velocity, and dividing the sum of the products by the aggregate weight of both bodies. Of course it will be more than a mean or less than a mean, accordingly as the quicker body was lighter or heavier than the other. Now, according to Sir Humphry Davy, the particles of substances which are unequally heated, are moving with unequal degrees of velocity: of course when they are reduced by contact to a common temperature, the heat, or, what is the same (in his view), the velocity of the movements of their particles, ought to be found by multiplying the heat of each by its weight, and dividing the sum of the product by the aggregate weight. Hence, if equal weights of matter be mixed, the temperature ought to be a mean; and if equal bulks, it ought to be as much nearer the previous temperature of the heavier substance as the weight of the latter is greater; but the opposite is in most instances true. When equiponderant quantities of mercury and water are mixed at different temperatures, the result is such as might be expected from the mixture of the water, were it twenty-six times heavier; so much nearer to the previous heat of the water is the consequent temperature. It may be said that this motion is not measurable upon mechanical principles. How then, I ask, does it produce mechanical effects? These must be produced by the force of the vibrations, which are by the hypothesis mechanical: for whatever laws hold good in relation to moving matter in mass, must operate in regard to each particle of that matter; the effect of the former can only be a multiple of that of the latter. Indeed, one of Sir Humphry Davy's reasons for thinking heat to consist of corpuscular motions is, that mechanical attrition generates it. Surely then a motion produced by mechanical means, and which produces mechanical effects, may be estimated on mechanical principles.

"How inconceivable is it that the iron boiler of a steam engine should give to the particles of water, a motion so totally different from any it can itself possess, and at the same time capable of such wonderful effects, as are produced by the agency of steam! Is it to be imagined that in particles whose weight does not exceed a few ounces, sufficient momentum can be accumulated to move as many tons? There appears to me another very serious obstacle to this explanation of the nature of heat. How are we to account for its radiation *in vacuo*, which the distinguished advocate of the hypothesis has himself shown to ensue? There can be no motion without matter. To surmount this difficulty, he calls up a suggestion of Newton's, that the calorific vibrations of matter may send off radiant particles, which lose their own momentum in communicating vibrations to bodies remote from those whence they emanate. Thus, according to Sir Humphry, there is radiant matter producing heat, and radiant matter producing light. Now, the only serious objection made by him to the doctrine which considers heat as material, will apply equally against the existence of material calorific emanations. That the cannon, heated by friction in the noted experiment of Rumford, would have radiated as well as if heated in any other way, there can, I think, be no doubt; and as well *in vacuo*, as the heat excited by Sir Humphry in a similar situation. That its emission in this way would have been as inexhaustible as by the conducting process, cannot be questioned. Why then is it not as easy to have an inexhaustible supply of heat as a material substance, as to have an inexhaustible supply of radiant matter, communicating the vibrations in which he represents heat to consist?"

We cannot help thinking that Dr. Hare presses Sir H. Davy with much force of argument: and have selected the principal matter of the Professor's paper; not choosing to lead our readers away from more valuable objects by quoting the whole; for we feel that even Sir H. D. may injure his well-earned celebrity, by wandering into the wilds of obscure speculation.

Experiments to determine the Weight of an Atom of Alumina. By THOMAS THOMSON, M.D., F.R.S., &c.

Annals of Philosophy, No. 15.

The Doctor commences by conjecturing that many persons who do not, as he does, attach importance to the atomic weights of bodies, may consider his pursuit of such an object but a frivolous waste of time. He, however, judges that when " this desirable object is gained, the art of analysis, at present so laborious and so uncertain, will be greatly simplified. Besides, alumina being a constituent so generally found in crystallized minerals, an exact knowledge of its atomic weight cannot but throw considerable light upon the constitution of a very numerous and interesting series of crystallized minerals."

" I may observe, before detailing my own experiments, that we have a good many analyses of alum. But the one which appears to have been made with the greatest care, and which approaches nearest the truth, is that of Berzelius, first given to the public in the Annales de Chimie, vol. lxxxii. p. 258. The result of this analysis is as follows:

Sulphuric acid	34·23
Alumina	10·86
Potash	9·81
Water	45·00
	99·90."

By a corrected analysis, Berzelius resolves thus:

Acid	33·82
Alumina	10·86
Potash	9·90
Water	45·00
	99·58

Leaving a deficiency of almost a half per cent.; which Dr. T. says may be attributed to water, not being driven off by a spirit lamp.

Dr. Thomson then enters into a detail of the processes, whereby he ascertained the proportion of the sulphuric acid, water, potash, and alumina, in the composition of alum; and that the true weight of an atom of alumina is 2·25. He concludes his paper thus:

"For this purpose let us take the constituents of 60·875 grains of alum as determined by the preceding experiments.

Sulphuric acid	20·000 or	4 atoms
Water	28·125	25 atoms
Potash	6·000	1 atom
Alumina	6·745	3 atoms
	60·870	
Loss	0·005	
Total	60·875	

"There is obviously a loss amounting to 0·005 of a grain. If we add this to the alumina, it will make the three atoms of it to weigh 6·75; and consequently the weight of 1 atom will be 2·25. Now as the weight of an atom of sulphuric acid, potash, and water, is known with precision, it is obvious that the loss can only fall upon the alumina. Hence there can be no doubt that the true quantity of alumina contained in 60·875 grains of alum is 6·75, and that an atom of alumina weighs exactly 2·25. Alum then is composed of

4 atoms sulphuric acid	= 20·0
3 atoms alumina	6·75
1 atom potash	6·0
25 atoms water	28·125
	60·875

So that the weight of an integral particle of alum is 60·875.

"We may represent the composition of alum in a different way, as follows:

3 atoms sulphate of alumina	21·75
1 atom sulphate of potash	11·0
25 atoms water	28·125
	60·875

"These proportions are more convenient for calculation than the usual mode of representing the constituents of 100 grains of alum. However, for the sake of those who prefer that method, I shall state the centesimal constituents of alum as follows:

  Sulphuric acid 32.8542
  Alumina 11.0882
  Potash 9.8562
  Water 46.2012
              ———
              99.9908

Or it may be stated in this way:

  Sulphate of alumina 35.72885
  Sulphate of potash 18.06975
  Water 46.20123
              ———
              99.99983

"But it is much more convenient in general, because we are not perplexed by a great number of decimal places, to employ in our calculations the weight of an atom of the salt. The atomic weight of an integral particle of any salt never can contain more than three decimal places. When the atoms of water in it are represented by an even number, then the decimal places never can exceed two.

"It has been alleged that alum owes its property of reddening vegetable blues to a quantity of bisulphate of potash which it contains; and this opinion has been supported by the following experiment: Mix together solutions of sulphate of alumina and sulphate of potash—a precipitate, it is said, appears. Hence it is alleged that the sulphate of potash is converted into bisulphate of potash, and that the alumina thus partly deprived of acid becomes insoluble, and occasions the precipitate. I have repeated this experiment with all possible care, and with salts in a state of purity. I never could obtain any immediate precipitate whatever; but when the mixed liquid was allowed to remain for 24 hours, there was always a deposit of alum crystals. We have, therefore, no evidence whatever of the presence of bisulphate of potash in alum; and the preceding experiments are quite incompatible with such a supposition."

Remarks on the Geology of the Cliffs at Brighton.
Annals of Philosophy, No. 15.

Mr. Daniell having published some observations on this subject, the writer addresses a paper to the editor of the Annals, in refutation of what the first named gentleman has stated. It is said that Mr. D., in his account alluded to, describes the very remarkable appearance of a bed of *loose pebbles* in the *solid chalk:* and veins of flint passing from one part of the chalk to another, *through the bed of pebbles*, without suffering any fracture or dislocation: and that these beds lie about half way between Brighton and Rottingdean. "Indigator" (for that is the name assumed by the writer) denies the existence of such beds; and adds, that Mr. Webster omits mentioning them at all, in his paper on the strata lying over the chalk, in the second volume of the Transactions of the Geological Society, though he describes the peculiar structure of the cliff at Brighton.

Mr. Daniell is made to say, "About half a mile between Brighton and Rottingdean, the cliff presents some very curious and important particulars. The upper bed, which has been assuming, by gradual degrees, more and more the characters, is decidedly chalk, and towards the top contains two horizontal veins of thin flint. The bed of shingles suddenly contracts to the width of a few inches; but maintains its situation and characters uninterrupted. The lower bed of chalk is intersected by veins of flint, which here traverse the bed of shingles, and continue their course, through the upper bed, till they reach the horizontal veins before described."

"Indigator" states the strata to be, "From the top to about four feet above the level of the shingle (as it then was) the cliff consists of fractured chalk flints, intermixed with small, mostly rounded, fragments of chalk, cemented together by a very pale ferruginous clay; the cohesion of these materials, though not very firm, is sufficiently strong to make it difficult to pull out a projecting flint by the hand, and also to allow the cliff to be absolutely perpendicular, which is mostly the case: the fragments of flints, though they appear to have been subjected to the action of water, are nevertheless by no means rounded; they are merely deprived of their sharp edges and angles.

"Under this stratum, which, as I have said, occupies the whole of the cliff to within about four feet of the level of the shingle, is a bed or layer of perfectly rounded pebbles; they appear to be mostly chalk flints, are quite loose, and rest upon a thin layer of fine siliceous sand, and this again rests upon the solid chalk. The latter circumstance cannot, however, at present be seen till you have advanced about a mile east from this spot.

"These rounded pebbles are mostly of a large size, and have no intermixture of clay or other substance to bind them together: this may be said generally of the bed. In several spots, however, and particularly a little east of the groin, in the upper part of the bed, the interstices are filled up by calcareous matter, in a state of very distinct crystallization: hence these pebbles, falling from the cliff, form masses of considerable firmness; in other parts, the calcareous matter is in an earthy state: further to the eastward, they are not unfrequently mixed with clay or sand, but still continue loose.

"The stratum which forms the upper and main part of the cliff is tolerably uniform throughout, merely varying in this; that in some parts the flints are more abundant, but always of the angular description above mentioned; in others the fragments of chalk and agglutinating clay are most predominant, sometimes to the total exclusion of the flints. At about one-eighth of a mile from Rottingdean, the solid chalk is seen to form the whole of the cliff, but it is very difficult to say at what exact point the debris ceases, and the chalk begins, owing probably to the washing down of the surface by the rains, which, in many parts, conceals the real structure of the cliff.

"Although I have described this stratum, and the bed of pebbles, as continuing the whole way from Brighton to Rottingdean, yet it must be particularly noticed, that about half way between the two places, for about 100 yards, the cliff is formed entirely, from top to bottom, by the solid chalk. On the west side, the bed of pebbles is seen gradually to cease. On the east, it disappears, under masses which have fallen from the upper parts of the cliff: at this part, therefore, not only the bed of loose pebbles, but the upper and thick stratum of angular flints and clay, are entirely wanting.

"Above the cliff I could not see the slightest indication on the surface of the junction of the debris with the chalk; it certainly does not extend far inland; for at the west end of the town, there is, very near the shore, a clay from whence they make bricks. At the church, the chalk is close to the surface, and on the opposite side of the valley, it is seen at a less elevation; and between the town and Rottingdean, there are several indications of the chalk from within half a quarter of a mile to half that distance from the edge of the cliff.

"It is remarkable that this stratum of debris externally conforms to the various undulations of the chalk surface to which it is united; so that, from external appearances, no alteration of the substratum would be suspected.

"At low water, the solid chalk may be seen forming the shore all the way between Brighton and Rottingdean."

The peculiarities of this reported stratification having been the subject of much remark, "Indigator" was induced to take a critical survey, of which this paper is the result. We have omitted such parts as we think may be dispensed with, without injuring its purport. The matter must be settled by observation.

On Mineral Produce.

Annals of Philosophy, No. 15.

The editor of the Annals, in his review of Mr. Westgarth Foster's Treatise on "A Section of the Strata from Newcastle upon Tyne, to Cross Fell, in Cumberland, with Remarks on Mineral Veins in general, &c.," combats several of Mr. F.'s positions; and especially his estimates of relative quantities of various minerals, produced within the district he surveys, as compared with the entire produce of the island.

"Excluding the iron from our account, although both that and coal are mineral treasures of the very first importance, yet they are not derived from veins such as Mr. Foster had in his view; and, secondly, because we do not know any good estimate of the value of iron in this kingdom.

"We shall confine ourselves, then, to the produce of the true mines of the metals, of which accounts may be procured.

"We will first state the proportion of lead which these mines produce, compared with that of the kingdom at large; and though, from documents before us, we should have ranked them higher in this respect, yet we must of course take Mr. Foster's account to be correct. We wish, that instead of a short average of the quantity of lead ore raised annually, from 1800 to 1821, he had given us tables of each year's produce. Such tables would be very interesting, particularly when compared with prices preceding or succeeding changes of quantity.

"We have, in the following statement, added two columns, one in which the ore is reckoned in pig lead, according to Mr. Foster's rule; and the second, in which the value is stated, taking it at £24. per ton, its probable value, when smelted, and delivered at the usual places of shipment; and we shall reckon the value of the metals from other districts in the same way.

"Mr. Foster states the average annual produce, ending with 1820, p. 420, as under:—

	Bings of ore.	Tons of pig lead.	Value.		
			£.	s.	d.
Teesdale mines	8000 equal to	1778	42672	0	0
Weardale ditto	17000	3777	90648	0	0
Allendale ditto	8000	1778	42672	0	0
Alston Moor and Cross Fell	19000	4223	101352	0	0
Dufton Fell, Dunn Fell, Silver Band and Hilton mines, in Westmoreland	1500	333	7992	0	0
	53500	11889	285336	0	0

"We will next state what we believe, from good authorities, and for some of which we can vouch, to be a near approximation to the quantities of lead produced in other mining districts in the kingdom.

	Tons of pig lead.	Value.
		£. s. d.
Yorkshire	4900	107600 0 0
North Wales and Shropshire	6000	144000 0 0
Scotland	2000	48000 0 0
Derbyshire	5000	120000 0 0
Devon and Cornwall	1200	28800 0 0
	19100	44840 0 0

Thus it stands as under:

Alston Moor, &c. &c.	11889	285336 0 0
Other parts of the kingdom	19100	448400 0 0
	30989	733736 0 0

"Here then we find that the mines in question produce about four-tenths of the *lead* of the kingdom, a large proportion certainly. We have still to estimate the extent of other mineral treasures, limiting ourselves, as we have before mentioned. This can be done from more certain sources; and Mr. Foster would find accounts of the annual produce of copper and tin in Cornwall, to a certain period, in Dr. Price's book on the mines of that county, and he would see it also continued to the year 1810, in Rees's Cyclopedia. The quantity of copper made in England is likewise published every six months, when the East India contracts are made, and may be seen in the Cornwall newspapers.

"From sources of this kind, we are enabled to state, that the produce of copper in the kingdom was, in 1820, as follows:—

		£	£. s. d.
Cornwall	6915 tons fine copper	112	774480 0 0
Devon, Anglesea, Staffordshire, &c.	1788	ditto	200256 0 0
	8703		974736 0 0

"The tin of Cornwall and Devon was reduced in quantity, about this period, by a great depression in price, but it may be estimated at—

3000 tons block and grain at £70. .... 210000 0 0

"The total value of these metals of the kingdom may, therefore, be stated to be:—

	£.	s.	d.
Copper	974736	0	0
Lead	738736	0	0
Tin	210000	0	0
	1918472	0	0

"In comparing individual mines with other lead mines, Mr. Foster unfortunately gives us but few data: he mentions, p. 274, Breconsike, as having formerly produced, in some years, 10,000 bings of ore, which would be 2250 tons of lead; and, p. 232, Hudgill Burn mine, is stated to be yielding 9000 bings, which would be 2000 tons of lead. We have reason to think that the produce of this rich mine has increased, and is now near 3000 tons of lead.

"But even this has been exceeded by other lead mines; one in Halkin mountain, in Flintshire, the property of Earl Grosvenor, produced within the last seven years, 1900 tons of ore in a quarter; which would be at least 5000 tons of pig lead in the year. And, in the same mountain, in the late Earl's time, there was at another mine, at one period, 3000 tons of ore, pressed and washed ready for smelting."

A Description of Specimens collected on a Journey from Delhi to Bombay. By B. FRASER, Esq. The Conclusion read before the Geological Society.

"The distance from Delhi to Bombay is about 720 English miles, but the author's deviations from the immediate route make his course amount to not less than 1000 miles. He apologizes for the incompleteness of his collection, and the accompanying memoir, by stating the difficulties which attended the conveyance of specimens, unfavourable, and other circumstances.

"It is, the author states, generally known, that the central part of India, north of the Nurbuddah, and between that river and the valley of the Jumna and Ganges, rises gradually from north to south, abruptly from the west, and irregularly from the eastward, so as to form a sort of plateau, the southern portion of which, in the province of Matira, is elevated about 1600 or 1700 feet above the Nurbuddah, and about 2000 feet above the sea. The present memoir relates principally to the western and north western portion of this elevated tract.

"The city of Delhi is placed upon a rocky ridge, about 120 feet in height, close to the river Jumna, and on the north-eastern verge of the plateau just described. The most northern point of the hilly region is at Tooham, south of Hansee, about ninety miles north of west from Delhi. This hill, which is about 700 feet in height, is composed of granite. The hilly country is terminated on the north west by a long range of hills, which skirts immediately the great western plain, of which the sandy desert forms the principal portion.

"The northern part of the tract described by the author, is composed entirely of primary rocks, which are succeeded, on the south, by a very extensive trap formation, stretching down the west of the Peninsula, as far south as the neighbourhood of Goah, a distance of more than 500 miles. The extent of the trap formation to the eastward is not yet known; but the author supposes the primary rocks to be continued southward, through the whole of the peninsula, to Cape Cormorin.

"At Delhi, the rock is quartz, and the same substance occupies a very large portion of the surface, to the south and west, constituting, apparently, the upper part of the mountainous tract, and frequently assuming the form of sharp insulated peaks, called by the natives '*dants*,' or teeth, which are described as being, in one place, 'of pure white, and glittering like snow.' Other primary rocks, granite, gneiss, mica slate, and clay slate, and in a few places granular limestone, are occasionally observed.

"Dolomite, of a bluish-grey colour, is commonly used for

building in the vicinity of Ambire and Taypore, and the white marble of Mokranna, about 35 miles north of Ajmere, is remarkable over all this part of India.

"About 14 miles west of Ajmere, the primary tract is succeeded by a country comparatively plain; from within which, the primary range is seen extending to a considerable distance towards the north, and to the west of the south. This plain is diversified by sand hills, with clay in the hollows between them, and occasionally by barren high banks of hard clay, mixed with 'kunken,' a term applied by the author to a peculiar sort of calcareous concretion, which he has not described in detail. The basis of the flat country seems to be sandstone of several varieties; but in general of a dull reddish hue; the beds sometimes rising into hills 300 or 400 feet in height. In several places all the buildings are formed of this reddish stone, and it colours all the water in the tanks. The sand appears to have been formed of the detritus of this rock.

"Within the flat country, north and west of the primary mountains, many salt lakes occur, one of which, that of Sambur, north-west of Jaypore, supplies nearly the whole of Upper India with salt; the waters becoming impregnated during the rainy season to such a degree, that when the lake dries up, the salt is found crystallized in abundance under the mud which it deposits.

"The hills about Joudpoor, the most western point to which the author's course extended, occupy a considerable space to the north, west, and south of that place, and are of very different appearance from those above described. They consist of claystone porphyry, which appears to repose on the sandstone.

"In returning towards the south-east, 'dentated peaks' of quartz were seen about Pahlee, and the country became more fertile; and in crossing the mountainous range already mentioned, about 70 miles south of the neighbourhood of Ajmere, the rocks were still found to be principally quartz, the peaks of which rose to about 2000 to 2500 feet above the plains to the west. The plateau, in general, in this place, being about 700 to 1000 feet above the country immediately on the south.

"About Odeypoor, the quartz lies upon reddish granite, which continues for some miles to the east, and is succeeded by a low range of quartz, extending to 50 or 60 miles from Odeypoor; after which no more primary substances were seen. Beds of compact limestone occur just below this quartz range, and occupy, apparently, a tract of considerable extent in the vicinity of Neymutch.

"In this vicinity also, low hills, like artificial mounds, are observed; the commencement of the extensive basaltic district already mentioned, which, in its progress to the south, rises into numerous summits of remarkable structure and appearance. The upper part of the heights is generally perpendicular, with a rapid slope beneath; and the faces of the hills, which, in some instances, rise to the height of 1500 feet, are divided by parallel and horizontal beds of basalt, alternating with amygdaloid, which abounds in zeolite. In one place, about fifteen or sixteen such beds were distinctly observable.

"A small hill, near the bank of the Nurbuddah, is crowned with basaltic columns, and less distinct appearances of the same kind were seen in other places. In one case, the basaltic rock was traversed by a dyke of very compact texture, resembling lydian stone.

"The immediate bed of the Nurbuddah consists of basalt, but in the valley to the north of the river, a granitic compound, gneiss, and clay slate, were found *in situ*; the last in vertical strata, ranging about N.W. and S.E.

"The town of Baug, at a short distance from the river, is built on horizontal beds of sandstone, and the route, for six or eight miles, was over rocks of the same kind, of various shades and colour, red, yellow, and white, disposed in strata. In several of the hills a bed of compact yellowish-grey limestone, containing caves, was observed above the sandstone, and immediately beneath the soil, resembling the limestone of Neymutch, already mentioned, about 140 miles to the north.

"The trap range, south of the Nurbuddah, is of bolder features, but of the same materials and structure with that above described. Similar rocks were found along the route through the Candeish, a low tract, surrounded on all sides by mountains; and the appearance and geological structure of the heights in all that part of the country, agree precisely with those of the *ghauts* that bound the table land of the Peninsula to the westward, the singular forms of which have frequently attracted the observation of travellers."

On the Height of Himalaya Chain of Mountains and Limitation of its perpetual Snows. By BARON CUVIER.

A skilful English engineer, Mr. Webb, having measured, trigonometrically, the highest peaks of the great chain of the Himalaya, that bounds India on the north, some were found more elevated than any till then known. The height of one is 7,820 metres, which as much surpasses the Chimborasso, as Mont Blanc does Mont Perdu. The exactness of this measurement, however, has been controverted, chiefly because in the northern reverse of the chain, the perpetual snow does not come down as low as might be expected from the latitude. Another objection is, that plants vegetate there at an elevation where they would grow no where else, and to this is added, that the refraction may be taken for something in those calculations.

M. de Humboldt has made observations to show, that to bring down these mountains to the level of the Chimborasso, we must suppose the co-efficient of the refraction to be 0·3 instead of 0·08, a quantity inadmissible in so southerly a zone. It is very true, that in the passages, and at the back of the Himalaya, abutting the plains of Tartary, the snow melts in summer at the height of 5,077 metres; a height where, under the equator itself, it is doubtless eternal. Mr. Webb found none at 300 feet still higher, although he made his observations at the 31st degree of N. latitude. In that very latitude, north of the crest of the Himalaya, are found pastures, wheat, and excellent vegetation, at the height of 4,549 metres, while on the southern point of these same mountains, the phenomena are little different from what has been observed in other countries of the globe.

M. Humboldt remarks on this subject, that the limits of

perpetual snow form one of the most complicated results of physical causes; that they are not so much regulated by isotherm lines (or of a medium and equal heat during the year) as by isotheres, or of equal extreme heat in summer; and that these two kinds of lines are far from being parallel. It is also admitted that in the interior of large continents, the annual heat, and especially the summer heat, in equal latitudes, becomes stronger than on the coasts, by reason of the sun's radiations. We may conceive then that on mountains, whose backs incline towards large plains, perpetual snow may be more retired and nearer the heights; indeed similar effects are witnessed on the chain of Caucasus.

M. Humboldt analyzes and appreciates several other causes that may contribute to the above variations, and introduces some observations made by him on the subject, in different parts of America.

Aurora Borealis.

The following description of this beautiful phenomenon is taken from Anspach's History of Newfoundland.

In Europe, says he, the dry freezing winds proceed from north to east: in North America they are from north to west. When these prevail, the sky is clear and of a dark blue, and the nights transcendantly beautiful. The moon displays far greater radiance than in Europe; and in her absence, her function is not ill supplied by the uncommon and fiery brightness of the stars. The Aurora Borealis frequently tinges the sky with coloured rays of such brilliancy, that their splendour, not effaced even by that of the full moon, is of the utmost magnificence, if the moon does not shine. Sometimes it begins in the form of a scarf, of bright light, with its extremities resting on the horizon, which, with a motion resembling that of a fishing net, and a noise similar to the rustling of silk, glides softly up the sky, when the lights frequently unite in the zenith, and form the top of a crown; at other times the motion is like that of a pair of colours waving in the air, and the different tints of light present the appearance of so many vast streamers of changeable silk; or spreading into vast columns and altering slowly; or by rapid motions into an immense variety of shapes, varying its colours from all the tints of yellow to the most obscure russet; and after having briskly skimmed along the heavens, or majestically spread itself from the horizon to the zenith, on a sudden it disappears, leaving behind an uniform dusky tract; this is again illuminated, and in the same manner suddenly extinguished. Sometimes it begins with some insulated rays from the north and the north-east, which increase by degrees until they fill the whole sky, forming the most splendid sight that can be conceived, crackling, sparkling, hissing, and making a noise similar to that of artificial fire-works. These phenomena, which are generally considered as the effects of electricity, are looked upon as the forerunners of storms; and when these arise from the north-east they spread the most horrid gloom over the island. Immense islands and fields of ice, brought down from the northern regions, fill up and freeze every bay and harbour, and block up the coast to the distance of several leagues into the ocean. The wind blowing over this immense surface, is full of frozen fogs or frost smoke, arising from the ice, in the shape of an infinite number of icy spiculæ, visible to the naked eye, penetrating into every pore and into the smallest apertures of the wooden houses, and rendering exposure to the open air very disagreeable and even painful.

Memoir on a Deposit found in the Waters at Lucca. By Sir H. DAVY, Bart. &c. &c. &c.

The following paper is contained in the Memoirs of the Royal Academy of Sciences at Naples, of which Sir H. Davy is a member.

The waters of the baths at Lucca, at the spot where the temperature is the greatest; that is to say, in what are termed the caldi or hot baths, eject, in a considerable quantity, a substance that produces a deposit of a brownish yellow hue. Having collected various quantities of this deposit, and having submitted it to chemical experiments, I have discovered it to be a compound of oxide of iron and silica. Not having a balance sufficiently accurate, it was impossible for me to ascertain with precision the exact proportions: in the single experiment, however, that I made for this purpose, the oxide of iron was to the silica in the proportion of 4 to 3.

It is extremely probable that the oxide of iron and the silica had been dissolved together in the water, and deposited at the same time; because the silica being separated from the oxide by means of a weak acid, it appears to resemble gelatine; and because the deposit, when examined in its natural state, was found to be uniform in its substance, even when looked at through a lens.

Although the oxide of iron, when first discovered, proves to be peroxide, it is nevertheless very probable that it exists in the water in the form of protoxide, or that it is converted into peroxide by the action of the air which is dissolved in the water. The probability of this opinion is further confirmed by the circumstance, that the colour of the water is not changed by the addition of the triple prussiate of iron, nor by that of gallic acid, it being well known that protoxides generally have a greater disposition than peroxides.

The analogy which I established some time since, during my researches, as to the decomposition of alkalies and earths, between the base of silica and that of boracic acid, and the facts described by MM. Smithson and Berzelius, furnish reasons for classing silica among the acids; and it seems probable that the oxide of iron and the silica undergo a real chemical combination in the warm water, and they separate from it in consequence of its cooling after issuing from the mountain.

When the deposit is obtained from its diffused state in water, it contains no other substances than oxide of iron and silica; when it is taken from the bottom of the waters, carbonate of lime and sand may be observed mixed with it. These two substances are, however, evidently extraneous. From many experiments which I made I am convinced that after it has quitted its source, the water yields no deposit whatever; but it appears certain that the water, which, on rising from the spring, possesses a temperature of 112°, must be much warmer within the mountain, and that consequently its solvent power must be there much greater.

When a considerable quantity of it is evaporated, a small portion of silica and oxide of iron is found, a discovery that had been made by Signor Battisto Tessandori; and I have ascertained by experiments that these substances are obtained in the same state, and nearly in the same quantity in which I have stated them to be discovered in the brownish yellow deposit.

A small portion of oxide of iron is found in the Bath waters, where likewise it is accompanied with silica; nor is it improbable that this earth is in many cases the cause of the oxide of iron, from being dissolved in the water; and these facts combined, furnish us probably with an explanation of the manner in which ochre is generated. As to what may be the effect of the combination of oxide of iron and silica on animal bodies, it is the province of medical men to examine, and to determine upon, after long and adequate experiments.

On Tritoxide of Iron for sharpening Razors.
By a Correspondent.

Sir,—In your last number of the Focus of Philosophy, &c. you expressed a desire to learn what might be the result of trial made on the use of tritoxide of iron for sharpening razors, as recommended by M. Merimee; I therefore trouble you with what I have done myself in that matter. The surface of my face being, unfortunately for me, extremely tender and prone to inflammatory tubercles, I hailed the announcement of a means, whereby I might give a delicate and smooth edge to my razors: I assure you that I did not suffer the second day to pass over without making some of the tritoxide. But whether there be any nicety in the particular management of the process, or whether I have misunderstood your report from M. Merimee, I know not, but the thing has not succeeded with me. Let me tell you how I proceeded: first, I dried the muriate of soda, and then put equal parts of it, and of the sulphate of iron, into a crucible, which was kept at a full red heat for a long time, perhaps an hour, and constantly stirred. Now and then a little taken out and cooled, to ascertain whether it would assume the purple red colour said to be necessary; but it remained a simple brown. When cold, I washed it until the water was wholly tasteless. A powdery matter, consisting of brilliant particles, subsided, which I filtered and dried. The spangly appearance was then but partially to be seen, and the dried powder remained of a light brown colour. I put some of this on a very clean and even strap; but on applying the razor, I really think the sharpening effect was only just what would have been produced by any other hard powder. Being very anxious to accomplish my object, and not being satisfied that the process had been duly performed, as the colour of the powder ought, according to M. Merimee, to have been of a purple cast, I repeated the whole, but without stirring the mass at all, and urged it to a white heat. But although I every two or three minutes cooled a small portion, as a trial of the colour, I was not able to render it otherwise than brown; and I did not find any difference between the two powders, as yielded by the two processes, either in appearance or in effect.

I was not aware, until you mentioned, that a *smooth* edge is more of consequence than what is called a *sharp* edge, in cutting the beard. I could indeed readily comprehend that the smooth must be most acceptable in the case of my tender skin; and having failed in bringing the tritoxide of iron to any beneficial result, I resolved on trying one of the metallic razor-straps that you spoke of, made by Mr. Still of Leicester Street, Leicester Square. I have done so, and have more thanks to make to you for the recommendation, than I can shortly express; for, by the use of my metallic strap, I produce an edge, to which I scarcely know how to give a name; it is not merely sharpness, for the instrument is not felt. It seems to pass over the surface without cutting, and yet the beard is cleared away perfectly, so that the process of shaving, which had used to be, with me, always a matter of dread, and, when my face happened to be unusually tender, a torture too, is now so easy, and so pleasant, that I cannot express the personal gratification I receive. Perhaps, however, I ought to attribute something to the razor, for I bought one of Mr. Still at the same time I bought the metallic strap, being much pleased with the make of them, that is, a mere thin ribbon of steel, affixed in a strong iron back; the ribbon, or cutting part, being so thin that the edge can never be rounded by any mismanagement in honing or strapping. Having sent to him my own razors to be ground, I have as yet used the metallic strap with that one purchased of him. I shall conclude with my stating that, although I think the use of the soap on hones, as recommended by Mr. Reveley, far preferable to oil, or grease; yet I find that a very small portion of the latter does better than the former with Mr. Still's metallic strap.   I am, &c.

On the Breeding of Eels. By Sir ANTHONY CARLISLE.
Phil. Mag. No. 286.

Sir A. Carlisle having, some years since, suggested to several naturalists that the common eel procreated, exclusively, in the sea; he re-urges the opinion now, to induce such persons as have more leisure and opportunity than himself, to prosecute the inquiry. He grounds his opinion on the fact, which he states to be notorious, that "the common eel is never taken in fresh water, with either male or female organs distinctly formed." He says, they descend the rivers towards the sea; and are then caught in wears, &c.; but those grown eels never return up the rivers, and therefore perish in the ocean. At particular seasons, small eels ascend the rivers, in shoals; gradually attaining growth as they advance: thus they are always found larger at Oxford, than at the mouth of the Thames. Sir A. discovered in a conger eel a matured female roe; the ova being ripe for detachment from the parent membranes. On comparing this animal with the common eel, neither external nor internal difference was discoverable. On inquiry, he says, that, he "found the conger eel to be a regular breeding fish, with special sexual organs." He, therefore, infers that the "conger is the breeding eel; and that it never returns into fresh water, after its entrance into the ocean." Its habits being the reverse of those of the salmon, which retreats into fresh water for purposes of breeding. At Hastings, Sir Anthony put brook eels into sea water, and they enjoyed apparent vigour for several days. And can recollect, that in his youth, he has caught "river eels on the salt water side of a marsh sluice, at the mouth of the river Tees." He concludes with a suggestion, that, the river eels "require some years of sea growth, before they acquire the sexual parts; but no degree of fresh water growth developes those organs in a river eel."

We must consider the above as merely conjectural matter, to call forth more extensive and accurate observations; and thereby lay us a firmer foundation for belief. Some recollections of our own would go to render Sir Anthony Carlisle's hypothesis extremely doubtful as applicable to local peculiarities. We well remember catching eels of all sizes, in a very small brook in Staffordshire; which could scarcely have been supplied with young fry from the ocean; its situation being so remote. Indeed, according to Sir A.'s doctrine, very small eels could not be found so far from the sea, for they must have fed into greater magnitude during their course. That they were really eels, we may presume from their being constantly taken, and eaten, as such, by gentlemen of general intelligence, resident in that neighbourhood. They were found from a magnitude barely visible, up to that of a pound; or even more.

Literary Intelligence.

Mr. Doehart is composing a work on the interior of Africa, from the river Gambia to the town of Sego, visited by Mungo Park. Mr. D. accompanied Major Gray for some time; and, finally, proceeded alone on his tour of research. Mr. D., we believe, returned to England in the early part of February.

Major Gray, who has been a long time in the interior of Africa, and had the command of a large party, with the view of pursuing the route of Mungo Park down the Niger, and through the continent, has returned to England lately from Sierra Leone. We trust that the Major will publish to the world some valuable results of an undertaking from which he will know how much was expected.

Early in the month of May will be published, in one vol. royal 4to., illustrated by numerous engravings, the Fossils of the South Downs, or Illustrations of the Geology of Sussex, by Gideon Mantell, F. L. S.

THE FOCUS

OF

PHILOSOPHY, SCIENCE, AND ART.

No. V.]   MAY 1, 1822.   [Vol. I.

On Facilitating the Conveyance of Carriages along Iron, and Wood Rail-ways, Tram-ways, and other Roads. By BENJAMIN THOMPSON, Patentee.

(Continued from page 534 of this vol.)

WE now proceed to the detail of labour performed, and velocity in execution, by the steam-engines working carriages on a coal line in the north.

The situation where the experiment has been made, favoured the trial in no other respect than as affording a ready means for doing so, in yielding the required power at once from two steam-engines used in drawing loaded waggons up inclined planes. In other respects the site is unfavourable.

Upon the waggon-way from Ouston Colliery, in the county of Durham, seven miles from Newcastle, leading to the river Tyne, four miles below that place, and in length seven miles and a quarter, the stage was selected upon which this new method of conveyance has been put in force.

The distance of the two engines spoken of from each other is 2315 yards; the upper end whereof is a steep inclined plane 323 yards long, up which the carriages are drawn by the Ayton engine; and the remaining portion, which is 1992 yards, has been heretofore worked by ten powerful horses, the ascent of it being 65¼ feet, but not a regular acclivity. The engine at the lower end was for the purpose of drawing loaded waggons up an inclined plane extending 387 yards in the contrary direction, or towards the colliery.

The horse-way referred to has been in no respect changed for the trial. The line has considerable curves in it, and its ascent is such, and so variable, as not to admit of the waggons returning by their own gravity. The two engines, in addition to their former work, have been made to reciprocate with each other over the whole length of the horse-road, according to the mode described in the foregoing specification upon the second, third, and fourth stages.

Six loaded waggons, coupled together, carrying the same number of Newcastle chaldrons, or 15 tons 18 cwt. of coals, pass upward at a speed of $10\frac{1}{4}$ feet per second, or 7 miles an hour, with the greatest ease and certainty, affording a dispatch by no means derived previously from the use of animal power. The two extremities being visible to each other are furnished with flags, to give alternate signals of the readiness of the waggons to proceed. When the atmosphere is hazy and the flags cannot be seen, signals are made by drawing forward the rope three or four yards, with the engine, at that end from which the waggons are intended to go, and which is instantly perceived at the other end. And in the dark (for the work is daily prosecuted during five or six hours' absence of light at this period of the year) signals are given by a fire kept at each end for lighting the workmen, which is shut from, or opened to, the view of the opposite extremity by means of a door. A person accompanies the waggons constantly, seated in a chair fixed securely upon the fore end of one of the soles of the leading waggon of the set, which is easily removed from one to another. The use of such attendant is to disengage the hauling-rope from the waggons, by means of a spring catch, in the event of any sudden emergency, such as the breaking of a wheel or rail, or the hazard of running down any object, the stage in question lying over a common. Friction-wheels, of cast iron, weighing 14lb. each, having an axle of malleable iron, turned in a lathe, and weighing 1lb., running upon a frame of oak, are placed eight yards asunder on the straight parts of the way, and five yards from each other along the curves. For the latter purpose they are put into frames of iron and wood, which allow of an inclined position to any angle. The requisite inclination of the wheel, or that which is best suited to the curvature of the road, is soon found out by the road wrights. The greatest deviation from a vertical line found necessary in the present case was 45 degrees. The angle properly adapting the leaning friction-wheel is that which allows of neither an upward or downward stress of the rope, but which presents the wheel in such a manner as that the strain of the rope shall be in a line at right angles with the axis.

The friction-wheels are eleven inches diameter, with a groove 2¼ inches deep, opening from a narrow bottom to 4¼ inches at the top. The inclining wheels have a cast iron horn projecting five inches from the frame at its under side, to receive and guide the rope into the groove. The wheels are all made to run on oak bearings, and are greased once every day: they act well, and run in the lightest possible manner, occasioning a friction incredibly small when their number (350) and the length and weight of ropes are considered; for, in order to preserve and keep safe the ropes, they are both housed every night, the last set of loaded waggons being drawn up without the tail or passive rope, and in the morning *that* rope being first conveyed upwards with a single empty waggon by a horse, which performs the task without difficulty at the common working pace of 2¼ miles per hour.

The application just detailed having been for some time in a full and constant course of work, the patentee has been enabled to calculate the cost, as compared with the former mode of conveyance; and he estimates the saving in favour of his invention to be upwards of 500*l.* per annum.

He is proceeding with preparations for the extension of it, upon the same road, in continuation towards the Tyne, from the upper or Ayton engine, with which another engine of 14 horses power (not necessarily so large, but applied, because the owners of the colliery happened to have it lying useless, for a six-horse engine would have been sufficiently powerful) to be erected at the distance of 2664 yards, will have to reciprocate. An opportunity will be afforded, at the same time, of running the loaded waggons forward, by their gravity, a further distance of 3596 yards, according to the mode described over the fifth stage in the specification, the declination not being sufficient for the adoption of self-acting planes. The saving along this portion of the road is calculated to be not less than 430*l.* per annum. When completed it will perfect a chain of operations by fixed engines, of more than five miles in length, without the aid of a single horse.

Preparations are further making for carrying the same method into use, in the county of Northumberland, on the waggon-way from Fawdon Colliery, by the erection of a six-horse engine, to reciprocate with another engine which has for some time drawn loaded waggons up an inclined plane three-quarters of a mile in length. The distance between, and over, which these engines are mutually to act, is 2398 yards, and the annual saving will be 480*l.* and upwards. Thus an aggregate saving of between 14 and 1500*l.* will be made, in the place of, and where the cost had heretofore amounted to, 2200*l.*

In these three instances 27 waggon horses of the largest description, together with their drivers, will be dispensed with; and, judging from the practical result first detailed, (the two alterations in progress having more favourable lines of road than it), the business will be accomplished in much less time than before. It is proper here to observe, that half as many more waggons as are at present sent from both the collieries might be conveyed within the period of an ordinary working day, without any further charge, save the ropes, which, taking in the same ratio as the previous estimates (though they must be less), would be 263*l.* per annum; while the expense of horses and drivers would rise proportionately with the increased quantity.

By augmenting the leadings, therefore, one half, the annual savings, as compared with the horse system, would be 2300*l.*

Enough has been advanced to show that the conveyance along waggon-ways may be greatly facilitated, and the charges reduced, upon the reciprocating principle, by fixed engines. There is no other mode applicable in these cases but that of animal power, the roads being too variable, as well as too steep in their undulations, for locomotive engines.

The remark in the specification, that "there is no country, however uneven or variable in its surface, but that may, by this method, be traversed," will be rather strikingly manifested upon the Ouston waggon-way; as likewise the beneficial application of the system upon roads gently ascending, descending, or dead level. And yet the inventor cannot refrain from observing, that a new line of way, laid out with the express intention of having his invention applied on it, might be very much more conveniently adapted than any of the instances adduced.

Seven miles an hour is the speed he has here chosen, because it appeared to him, under all circumstances, to be the best calculated; but, generally speaking, he would prefer a quicker movement, and is induced to think that ten miles an hour is a more desirable rate upon a road where all the other dependent operations could be rendered simultaneous. Fast as this may possibly appear, he is convinced that loaded waggons may be made to travel even 12 miles an hour with perfect safety over a well laid rail-road; and as an expeditious conveyance is of the highest importance wherever much work is required to be done, it is probable that, possessing the means, the greatest practicable speed would commonly be preferred. There is no method of conveyance in use from which this rapidity of motion can be obtained but that of the alternating action of fixed engines. Locomotive steam-engines are incapable of it, for they ill sustain the working rate of horses, being, from their very nature, unsuited to the shocks and tremulous motion which, upon the most perfect roads, they must necessarily be subjected to.

Locomotive machines affording the only other mode of conveyance applicable, as a substitute for that by horses, the patentee is led to extend his remarks upon them.

The methods of Blenkinsop, Chapman, and Brunton are grounded on principles that supply the means of surmounting tolerably steep acclivities—all others depend on the resistance offered by the iron rails or plates to the surfaces of the wheels, for the application of power to the purpose of locomotion; and it becomes an object, consequently, in those cases, to *create* as much friction as possible at the contact of the wheels with the rails or plates. A quarter of an inch rise in every yard of way may, however, be considered as the greatest acclivity they can be rendered capable of overcoming with a load. The friction thus occasioned and otherwise, together with the movement of the machine itself, causes so extravagant a dissipation of power, as to leave, comparatively, but a small portion effective of that which the engine really applies; so that it is not safe to calculate on its yielding regularly more than about 35 per cent. of the force exerted. One supernumerary engine to every three, or at the most four, will be found necessary, together with the incessant and vigilant care of a superintending mechanic, to secure a tolerable degree of certainty. Numerous and costly trials have been made upon the locomotive principle, but for the most part given up; and it may be justly questioned whether, in any instance, a saving has been gained, compared with horse labour. In one case, where the experiment was made at a charge of several thousand pounds, with the best possibly executed engines, the plan was abandoned, and horses again resorted to, because not only of the trouble and inconvenience attending it, but the expense also.

There is another consideration, adverse to it, of no small importance, namely, the increased expenditure which is called for in the first instance.

The heavy cumbrous weight of the engines, requires a stout and massive road, very far exceeding what would be necessary for the common loads to be conveyed. In this part of the kingdom (Newcastle on Tyne), where the iron-ways are allowed to have attained the most advanced state of improvement, the greatest weight borne is a Newcastle chaldron of coals, which, by statute, is 53 cwt.

Such loads require a road of less than two thirds the weight of iron indispensable for the other purpose; but a long, extensive, and very active experience of more than twenty years has convinced the patentee that burthens of from a ton to a ton and a half, where circumstances allow of it, are, in every respect, the most convenient as well as the most economical for conveyance. A road for such use would take little more than one third the weight of iron required for the locomotive plan; would be made considerably cheaper in other respects also; would be less liable to injury, and more easily kept in good working condition.

The application of fixed reciprocating engines requires no more than a single way; sidings or passings being necessary only at the stages, by which alone about a fifth of all the materials would be saved; for six sidings, of 70 yards each, are necessary in every mile of horse-way. Another striking advantage possessed by this mode over horses and locomotive engines has just occurred. A good deal of snow fell in the night before last, and the ground was thickly covered at the hour of commencing work yesterday morning. No hindrance, however, arose from it, as the waggons proceeded at once in the usual manner, although it would have taken an hour or two to set horses off, and locomotive engines (depending on the friction of the wheels upon the rails) could not have travelled at all throughout the day. It ought to have been noticed before, that the wheels of those machines have scarcely any hold of the rails in wet weather.

The amount of work to be done must determine the number of waggons in the set, their travelling speed, and consequently (with the ascents to be overcome) the powers of the various engines. Not only, therefore, in the ultimate use, but also in the original cost, much is to be saved by the reciprocating plan of fixed engines in the place of horse labour, or locomotive powers.

Electro-Magnetic Experiments. By MM. VAN BECK, Prof. VAN REES, and Prof. MOLL.
Edinburgh Phil. Journal, No. 12, p. 220.

The experiments reported by the above named gentlemen, are the continuance of the series detailed in the Edinburgh Journal, and laid before our readers by us at page 301 of this volume. The present will be found not less interesting than the former, and the more valuable by the simplicity in form of some instruments to which they have given rise.

The experimentalists tried the effect of discharges, from

an electrical battery, on plates, discs, and solid cylinders, with some curious results.

A steel plate, in the form of a right angled parallelogram, having a plane of glass over it; on which last rested a brass wire in the direction of the length of the plate; was, by an electrical discharge through the wire, rendered magnetic. Each half of the plate, longitudinally, indicating opposite poles.

On carrying the wire over a square steel plate (the glass being interposed) in lines cutting the plate into four compartments, and passing the electrical discharge; the qualities of the imparted magnetism were similar in the diagonal quarters of the steel plate: the right hand quarter below, and the left hand quarter above, being south; the other two quarters, taken diagonally, were north. If the poles of contact of the wire with the electrical jar had been reversed, we presume that the compartments of the plate would have exhibited reversed signs. But the next results are the most worthy of our particular attention.

A steel cylinder, solid, with the exception of a bored axis, to receive a glass tube through it, containing a brass wire communicating with the leyden battery, was not magnetically affected by the electrical discharge. And when a cylinder divided into two equal longitudinal portions; but bound closely together, by brass rings; and the wire carried through a glass tube in its axis, as above, was subjected to an electrical discharge, it did not indicate any magnetic power so long as the respective halves remained in contact; but, when separated, each displayed opposite poles: the magnetic indications ceasing, and renewing, as the portions of the cylinder were united or separated. We do not recollect any fact having resulted from former experiments that could have led us to anticipate such a result as this; and therefore judge it to be the more worthy of particular remark.

A circular plate of steel, with a tube and wire passing through its centre, at right angles with its plane, and subjected to the electrical discharge, remained equally incapable as the cylinder of indicating magnetic power while entire;

but when divided through the centre, each half of the plate showed opposite poles.

It would appear from these results that the circular form is unfavourable for the indication and action of the magnetic current: perhaps it is essential to these signs, when the metallic mass be great, that there be points or terminating lines from, or to, which excitement can be established, by a facility to external agency. In the electrified and insulated sphere there is an increased power of electrical retention; but still it will impart or receive electrical matter according to its positive or negative condition, that matter not being rendered absolutely incapable of motion by the form of the body it may occupy, though much governed by such circumstance: for we know that a pointed, or rough, conductor speedily loses its electricity; while a globular, or smooth one, will long retain it. The great distinction between an electrized and a magnetized body consists in the former having a tendency to an exhausting, the latter to a renewing, current.

A steel needle, placed perpendicularly, in a ribbon of brass, that was partly covered with a glass plate, on which was a brass wire receiving the electrical discharge, became magnetic.

An instrument to display the agency of the galvanic circulation, in imparting magnetism to the conducting wire, is described as of this form: A very thin brass wire, suspending a square copper plate, passes upwards into a hollow tube, nearly eight inches long; formed of thin quills inserted end into end, and hanging horizontally from an untwisted thread of silk. The wire, on entering the tube, is carried along its axis to the nearest extremity; and then wound spirally round the outside of the tube, to the other end; where it re-enters its axis, and passes on to perforate the quill again; and, with its spare extremity, suspend a plate of zinc. We should state that this outward perforation of the quill tube, by the wire, is about as far from the one extreme end of the tube, as the inward perforation is from the other. The copper and zinc plates are kept separate, and in the same plane, by a slip of wood, uniting their faces. On taking the whole up by the silk thread, and lowering the metallic discs into diluted acid;

a magnet, brought near the apparatus, indicated a strong polarity in the latter.

"Again, a plane, of coiled brass wire, about 20 inches in diameter, was sustained by its two projecting extremities, terminating in cups of mercury; forming a moveable azimuth; and the poles of a galvanic battery being brought into contact with the mercury, the plane of the coil assumed a perpendicularity with the magnetic meridian.

"These instruments, on account of their simplicity, are presumed to supersede M. Ampere's, which are so well known to the philosophical world.

On Electro-Magnetism. By M. Prechtl, of Vienna.
Gilbert's Annalen, Vol. xvii. No. 3.

M. P. coiled a steel wire in a close sheath round a cylinder, and drew the pole of a magnet from one extremity of the spiral to the other, in a line parallel to its axis. The coil became a magnet, possessing the following properties:

Along the whole length, one side of the spiral has the north pole; the opposite has the south.

At every point in the length, these transversal magnetisms are equally strong.

The ends of the spiral do not indicate differently from points in the length, the coil being similar in condition to the voltaic conjunctive wire.

Like the conjunctive wire, if held over a magnetic needle in the declination plane, it repels the north pole of the needle right or left, according as its transversal magnetism may flow to the left or right; even as far as 90 degrees.

If a magnetic pole be carried spirally round the coil, the latter becomes magnetized longitudinally; and the poles will be found at the extremities of the spiral, like a common magnetized steel wire: therefore the transversal and longitudinal magnetisms are not compatible.

The phenomena are not limited to transversal magnetism with single polarity; as may be proved thus: Take four bar-magnets, about a quarter of an inch thick; provide a small disk of wood, with an aperture of an inch diameter in the centre, and four grooves cut in the face of the disk, leading from the circumference inwards; in which place the magnetic bars, with their narrow edges outwards, and their ends projecting into the aperture. A north pole, alternating with a south, so that the ends, terminating opposite each other, may bear similar polarity. Then adjust the whole so that they may touch the circumference of a steel wire coil, half an inch in diameter. Draw the spiral wire through the opening, and between the four magnets, so that the cylindric coil may not revolve on its axis; but that the direction of each individual magnetic pole may remain in the same plane with the axis; or the wire will acquire the longitudinal magnetism. Or, instead of the wire coil, we may use a massive cylinder of steel; which, when treated in a similar manner, will acquire the compound transversal magnetism, without its extremities indicating any greater intensity of power than the individual coils. These transversal magnets, with manifold polarities, have all the properties of the single transversal ones; but are still more analogous with the electrical conjunctive wire; for *under* the manifold polarized magnet, the deviation of the needle is the reverse of that *above* it.

We cannot omit observing here, that the effect of the magnetic bars, on the steel cylinder, is distinctly different from that of the discharge of an electrical battery, as related in our preceding paper; where it is shown that, although magnetic power was certainly imparted by the battery to a steel cylinder, yet it remained dormant until the cylinder was divided in the direction of its axis.

But a transversal magnet may be produced, with multiplied poles; or rather, a multiple of magnets; as thus: Furnish a ring of steel wire, five or six inches diameter, with as many poles as can be applied to its circumference. Lay the ring flat, and apply to its outer edge the two poles of the horseshoe magnet whose extremities are as close as they can be had. Remove it, and apply it to successive portions round the entire ring, at distances equal to the width of its own poles. Each contact of the magnet will produce another magnet in a portion of the ring.

This steel ring is presumed to represent a section of this manifold polarized transversal magnet; exhibiting, relatively to the greater extension, and smaller number of the existing magnetisms, the phenomena resulting from a section of the conjunctive wire. In each part, the north end is above, and on the right hand; the south below, and on the left.

On the Effects of Magnetism on Chronometers.
By R. Lecount, Esq.
Edinb. Philosophical Journal, No. 12, p. 268.

Mr. Lecount, after remarking on the coincidence of Mr. Barlow's opinion with his own, that the cause of aberration in the chronometer, so far as may be imputable to magnetic effect, is owing to a portion of fixed magnetism in the steel of the balance or its spring; goes on to observe that the makers should be cautious in guarding against this condition of the steel. And he extends this injunction to all the parts of the chronometer made of that metal. If there be "fixed magnetism in the balance, and variable magnetism in the spindles of the wheels, the rate may be altered by any considerable variation in the dip; as the direction and strength of the variable magnetism will thereby become changed; and if these conditions relatively become reversed, the fixed magnetism will be in the spindles; and the variable in the balance." To correct this, Mr. L. recommends that, in tempering the steel, the cooling metal should lie at right angles with the dipping needle: when cooled in the direction of the dipping needle, small steel bodies acquire a fixed magnetism. Experience teaches Mr. L. that the chronometer should never be placed near the ship's compass. Mr. L. concludes with stating that he can suggest to artists an easy method of forming the teeth of small wheels into arcs of the epicycloid.

Observations on the Chronometrical Arrangements now carried on at the Royal Observatory, under the Authority of the Lords Commissioners of the Admiralty; tending to show their Inadequacy to the Purpose for which they were designed. By JAMES SOUTH, F. R. S.

Mr. South comments on the manner in which the trials of chronometers is instituted at the Royal Observatory, and shows the defects thereof. The accuracy of the chronometer being an object of such paramount importance to the mariner, we shall present nearly the whole of Mr. S.'s paper; omitting such parts of it only as may be dispensed with, without injury to the expression of its purport.

Mr. S. sets out with considering the letter published in the Gazette by the Lords of the Admiralty; and which letter had its effect in so far as the accumulation of time-keepers might be desired; for we are told that upwards of thirty were sent by their respective makers or proprietors. What with the tenor of the advertisement, and the quantity of articles collected in hand, we may truly hold the Royal Observatory as a mart for the sale of chronometers. But we will insert the letter alluded to.

"*Admiralty Office, June,* 25, 1821.

"The Lords Commissioners of the Admiralty, being desirous of increasing the number of chronometers for the use of his Majesty's Navy, and of encouraging the improved manufacture of that important article, do hereby give notice, that a depot for the reception of chronometers is opened at the Royal Observatory of Greenwich, where the makers will be permitted to deposit their chronometers, in order to their being tried, and ultimately purchased for the use of the navy, or of being disposed of by the proprietors to private purchasers.

"And, for further encouragement, their Lordships will purchase, at the end of each year, the chronometer which shall have kept the best time, at the price of 300*l.*, and the second best at the price of 200*l.*, provided that there have been above ten chronometers in the competition, and that the said best chronometers shall keep their rates within certain limits to be hereafter stated. The other chronometers their Lordships may purchase, as they may think proper, at such sums as may be agreed upon with the makers; and their Lordships have reason to expect, that their annual rate of purchase, for some years to come, will be not less than ten chronometers in each year.

"Every facility will be afforded to the makers, who may place their chronometers in the depot, for disposing of any of them to private purchasers; and every information will be afforded to purchasers as to the rates of going of the chronometers, of which a strict account will be kept, under the direction of the Astronomer Royal and Board of Longitude.

"The further conditions and regulations connected with this arrangement, may be learned of the Astronomer Royal, at Greenwich, or of the Hydrographer of this office.

"J. W. CROKER."

"London Gazette, June 26, 1821."

Mr. S. now proceeds to consider the means adopted at the Observatory, as well as the neglect of certain tests that are essential to the forming of an accurate judgment. He says—

"The essentials of a good chronometer are these; that its rate should be uniform; undisturbed to any extent by alterations either of position or of temperature. A chronometer which answers these conditions may be considered fit for nautical, or (when a clock cannot be procured) for general astronomical purposes.

"If, then, such be the attributes of a good chronometer, it may be right to inquire what are the means that should be employed to determine, with the greatest certainty, whether a chronometer does or does not possess them. Having settled this matter, we shall see how far the trials to which the chronometers now in the depot are submitted, accord with these; and we shall then be enabled to draw such inferences as the comparison may warrant.

"Now, the rate of a chronometer is usually deduced from daily comparisons made with a good clock adjusted commonly to mean time; I would, however, prefer immediate comparisons with the transit clock, that being always considered the best in an observatory, and unless there are substantial reasons to the contrary, I would unquestionably have the chronometer adjusted to sidereal time, by which all trouble of reduction will be spared, and the errors arising from the unsatisfactory nature of solar transits entirely precluded.

"Should, however, necessity oblige us to have our chronometer show mean time, there is one circumstance which we may avail ourselves of in comparing it with the sidereal clock. The acceleration of sidereal on mean time is such, that the former gains on the latter one second in about six minutes; now the box chronometer usually beats half seconds, and consequently synchronises with the clock's pendulum twice in this time; these instants are, with a little attention on the part of the comparer, so easily ascertained, that, to make an error in the comparison equivalent to one twentieth, or even one fiftieth part of a second, would be almost unpardonable. When pocket chronometers are compared, the same principle may be acted upon. These generally beat five times in two seconds, but, owing to the seconds' circle being ill divided, and the seconds' hand not accurately centred, equal accuracy cannot be expected.

"The instrument, whether large or small, is always included in a box, whose base and top are connected together by four sides, which we will denominate A, B, C, D. As sent home by the maker, it will be unclamped and horizontal; in this state, therefore, it should for a few days be compared with the clock, and if its rate seem uniform, let it now, clamped in its gimbols, be placed vertical, by making the box rest upon the side A; on the day following move it one quadrant, by placing the box upon the side B; on the next day, vary its position another quadrant, by resting its box upon the side C; and on the subsequent day let it be passed through the remaining quadrant, by making its box rest upon the side D: it may then be restored to its horizontal position, and if, on repeating these experiments, examination should detect no material difference in the daily rates, a great point will be gained. During these observations the temperature should be kept as equable as possible; the thermometer, therefore, should be frequently appealed to, otherwise the inferences deduced will be liable to some suspicion.

"Having gone thus far, it will be prudent to unclamp it, and try whether a slight motion given to it will be productive of any alteration in its rate; and for this purpose it may advantageously be carried quickly up and down stairs frequently during the day; may be placed in a carriage driven quickly through the paved streets; or, should this be inconvenient, it may be slung over a servant's shoulders, who shall ride with it for a few miles on a hard-trotting horse. If proof against these trials, it may be clamped, and the same experiments repeated. Should no material alteration of its rate be elicited by these various contrivances, it may be said to have answered the first condition.

"Let it now be placed for twenty-four hours in a temperature such as may at any time be obtained, say 50° of Fahr., its rate well determined, and on the next day let the temperature of the room be raised to 80°, and the day following to 110°; now, if on examination of the daily rates it should seem a matter of indifference whether the temperature is 50, 80, or 110, it will only remain to put it to the most severe test of any, namely, that of exposing it to temperatures below 32 on one day, and from 110 to 120 the next day: in the ordinary winter seasons, the former is not difficult; but, when natural cold cannot be had, artificial may; for frigorific mixtures are not expensive: and as to the latter, it is always within our reach. To what extent cold may be safely employed I do not know; it is a subject upon which it was my intention to have made some experiments during the last winter, had it not proved too mild for the purpose. There seem, however, to be doubts as to what degree of cold the oil will usually bear without losing its fluidity, as also what diminution of temperature the spring will endure, without having its elasticity impaired. Perhaps also, under instantaneous exposures to intense cold, a slight deposition of water upon the spring might occur, which, if it lead to the oxidation of the metal, would unquestionably injure its power. From experience, however, I well know that a temperature of 20° on one day may be succeeded by one of 110° on the next day, with perfect safety to chronometrical economy; and, I also know, that extremes such as these, are trials that few, very few chronometers will bear, without having their rates materially deranged. A chronometer, therefore, satisfying these conditions, as also the former, may be indeed pronounced good, and is fit for nautical, or, when a clock cannot be procured, for general astronomical purposes.

"But it may be asked, is it not to be expected that a chronometer which shall in one position keep a better rate than twenty others, will retain its superiority under every other circumstance? To this I unhesitatingly reply, no. A chronometer may go well whilst horizontal, and ill whilst vertical; and *vice versâ,* or it may go well whilst in a state of quiescence, and ill when put in motion; it may go well when placed in an atmosphere which is temperate, and ill when exposed to extremes of heat and cold.

"An instance occurred to me three years ago in a box chronometer, made purposely for me by one of our first artists, which, while it remained horizontal, kept its rate remarkably well; but when placed vertical its rate was so much altered, that further trials of it till it had been returned to the maker were altogether useless. Again, the same chronometer was incapable of sustaining considerable alterations of temperature, although slight differences produced no sensible effect: again, on its return to me, the motion of a carriage occasioned some deviation from its rate, an evil which its maker afterwards completely remedied. But in these instances just alluded to, the defects were removed; in another instance, however, the attempts have not been so successful; in the early part of last year a gold pocket chronometer was made for me by the same person, and although, whilst horizontal and quiescent, it would even under severe alterations of temperature dispute the prize with most, still it would not bear alteration of position without altering its rate; it has on this account been twice or thrice returned to the maker for correction; but, notwithstanding all his pains and labour, he has not succeeded, for he informed me two or three days ago that it was still imperfect; and he is apprehensive that, to enable it to satisfy the only condition wanting, (for it is in every other respect an invaluable instrument,) will probably for ever baffle his endeavours.

"Again, during the last spring two pocket chronometers were placed under my care, by Major-General Sir Thomas Brisbane, K. C. B. The one of them was of gold, the other of silver; the former was an old favourite, the latter was deemed of no value, and considered scarcely to merit the name of a chronometer; they were included in their respective boxes, and their rates ascertained daily by comparisons with my transit clock; the gold one kept on the same second for a fortnight or three weeks, but the silver one did not; at this time being occasionally employed in inquiries into the differences of longitude of my observatory and that of Greenwich, the gold one amongst some others was deemed suitable for the purpose, its error as also those of its co-travellers were well ascertained before they were dispatched hence, and immediately on their return home comparisons were again made; on contrasting the errors which they now had with those which respectively belonged to them previous to their being sent away, (the proportional rates for the interval having been applied to them,) this gold chronometer which had kept a more uniform rate than any whilst quiescent, was so much affected by the journey, that a deviation from its rate amounting to more than a second was the result, whilst the others may be considered as having suffered no sensible inconvenience, for a tenth of a second was the maximum of alteration observed in either. Finding this occurrence where it was least likely to have been anticipated, I suspected that perhaps the error might have been my own, originating in inaccurate comparison; to put this matter to the test, all the same chronometers were transmitted, as also was the silver one on the day following, and the same precautions being taken prior to their dispatch, and subsequent to their return, the same results relative to the gold one were obtained; whilst the silver one, when the proportional rate for the intervening time had been applied, gave precisely the observed error. This was no accidental circumstance, the experiments, somewhat modified, were several times repeated, and uniformly with similar results. Observing the valuable property possessed by the silver one, I returned it to its maker, requesting him to lessen its rate, which was cumbersome; this being effected, I frequently carried it about in my pocket, together with the gold one, and whilst I could place no reliance upon the latter, the former scarcely ever led me into an error of the time exceeding one or two-tenths of a second, notwithstanding it sometimes met with rather rough usage; indeed, this almost despised chronometer was one of the best that I ever saw. That it was difference of position which occasioned the error found in the gold one, was inferred from a knowledge that it would bear very well considerable alterations of temperature. A chronometer, intended for the pocket, should be rigorously indeed examined, as to the effect produced upon it by alterations of position, seeing that the mere reclining of its wearer on a couch, may lead to considerable alterations of rate: indeed, from many opportunities of judging, I am inclined to believe, that it is more difficult to procure a good pocket, than a good box, chronometer.

" I have here only alluded to some of the instances which have occurred under my own observation, where chronometers, good in one respect, were bad in another. Others might have been adduced, but those already mentioned, will, I hope, suffice. They are assertions, it is true, the particulars of which are not brought forward; but the like are so frequently occurring, that he, indeed, can have had no experience who has not found them practically correct. To make a chronometer keep a good rate, when exposed to no change of position except what it must necessarily undergo in the act of winding, or to such change of temperature as it may usually meet with in a drawing-room, is neither hard nor difficult; but to enable it to sustain it in alterations of position, as well as of temperature, such as I have hinted at, is no easy task. These latter qualities depend upon the accuracy of its adjustment, and perhaps I might add, upon the uniformity of the materials of which the spring and balance are constructed, desiderata not to be arrived at without considerable sacrifices of time and labour. It is these, in fact, which so much enhance its value. But lest it should be supposed that I am giving to these adjustments more importance than they really merit, I shall only say, that two of our first-rate makers have sold as common silver watches, for the trifling sum of twenty-five pounds, what were in every respect equally well constructed with their best chronometers, and which wanted only the labours of adjusting to render them such; nor was the plan abandoned, till it was found that these watches occasionally got into the hands of persons for whom they were not made, who, ignorant of the terms upon which they had originally been sold, were sometimes enabled to bring their maker's name into disrepute.

"But it may perhaps be urged, than the plan of experimenting which I have here proposed, although very well in theory, is too difficult for practice. To this I can only reply, that a box chronometer is now before me, which has, *propriâ personâ*, undergone, and *satisfactorily* undergone, the *very* trials here alluded to: and, what is more important for the Lords Commissioners of the Admiralty to be informed of, *is*, that for a chronometer such as this, I gave to its good and honest maker (Mr. Molyneux) the sum of fifty guineas.

"If, however, their Lordships should deem it right, *still* to have their chronometrical affairs conducted at the Royal Observatory, (and as to the propriety of this, among scientific men, there seems some doubt,) I will indulge a hope, and a sincere one it is, that if 500*l. must* be annually given for two chronometers, that two may be procured, at least as *good*, as any private individual may get for ONE.

"Whether, also, it was necessary to decoy chronometers to Greenwich, by promising 500*l*. for what is worth but ONE, will perhaps admit of doubt. I cannot, however, but think, that a sufficient emulation would have been excited amongst the real makers, (and in this instance none others are worthy of consideration,) had the Lords of the Admiralty engaged annually to have published in the *London Gazette* the *name* and *residence* of that artist whose work had been declared the best, whilst the 400*l*., thus annually saved, might be appropriated to some scientific purpose, (for I would protect it from Humean fangs,) and perhaps to none better than restoring to its *pristine* excellence the *Nautical Almanac*, or *Astronomical Ephemeris*.

"But, to return from this digression; by reference to the preceding pages it will be seen what are the requisites of a good chronometer, and what are the means which, *if* adopted, seem most likely to enable us to select the good, and reject the bad. Having also shown that a chronometer may be good in one respect, yet bad in another, it remains that we should see how far the mode of trial sanctioned by the Admiralty, and carried on under its authority, accords with that which we have considered indispensable.

"The Admiralty places its chronometer horizontal, and daily comparisons with a good clock are enforced: our plan also requires this. The Admiralty exposes its chronometers to alterations of temperature, such as are to be met with in a common sitting-room; our plan does the same. We try our chronometer vertically, and in different directions of its axis; the Admiralty does no such thing. We try the effect of motion upon our chronometer; the Admiralty does no such thing. We expose ours to extremes of cold; the Admiralty does no such thing. We try ours in extremes of heat; the Admiralty does no such thing. We compare the various results produced by these alterations of circumstances upon our chronometer, because we wish to take not *any thing* for granted; the Admiralty having ascertained one fact, and that, perhaps, of the least importance, takes *every thing else* for granted. We *take* all this trouble that we may get a good chronometer; the Admiralty *saves* all this trouble, and will probably get a BAD ONE.

"On comparison, therefore, of the two modes, knowing, as I do, and showing, as I trust I have done, that the various trials I have advised are necessary, the only inference I can draw is, that the chronometrical arrangements at present conducted under the sanction, and by the authority, of the Lords Commissioners of the Admiralty, are INADEQUATE TO THE PURPOSES FOR WHICH THEY WERE DESIGNED."

On the Magnetism of Red Hot Iron, &c. By Mr. BARLOW.

Mr. Barlow having instituted a series of experiments to determine the relative magnetic power in different kinds of iron and steel on the needle, found the following result:—

	Pro. Power.		Pro. Power.
Malleable Iron	100	Shear Steel, soft	66
Cast Iron	84	Ditto, hard	53
Cast Steel, soft	74	Blistered Steel, hard	53
Blistered Steel, soft	67	Cast Steel, hard	49

Such being the relative powers of these bodies in deflecting the magnetic needle from its natural line.

Observing that the hardest iron and steel had the least magnetic influence, he tried the effect of relative degrees of heat, and found that malleable iron which when cold, stands, as above, at the head of the scale; when heated, ranks the lowest. And that cast iron which when cold is the least powerful, is when heated, the most so, being nearly as three to one. This fact is, however, applicable, comparatively, only to the relative conditions of the iron, as malleable or cast: for in the trials cold we see that the latter, although least powerful as compared with the malleable iron, was still superior in power to every quality of steel.

Between the white heat of the iron (when magnetism disappeared) and the blood-red heat (when magnetism was most intense) there was an intermediate action, during the changes from bright red and red, being contrary in attraction to that of the blood-red and cold. This negative attraction being least in those positions where the natural cold attraction is greatest; greater where the latter is least; and at a maximum when in that position where the cold attraction is zero; that is, in the plane of no attraction, if the needle be duly near to the bar.

The bars experimented with, were 25 inches long and an inch and half square, *inclined in the direction of the dipping needle*. The distance from 5 to 9 inches; and the nearer, the more powerful. The quantity of negative attraction amounted to as much as 50°.

From a hasty experiment made by ourselves, we are inclined to think that the partial heating of polarized iron may be worthy of Mr. Barlow's attention. We presented the lower extremity of a poker, possessing manifest polarity, to the compass, at about 5 inches distance, and at right angles with the needle. The deflection amounted to 15°. On heating the end to a white heat, and presenting it, the deflection was about 18°. On cooling, it sank to 15° again. But on heating it fully red, and plunging it for a minute into cold water, then wiping it dry, we found the deflection produced equal to 20°; re-heating it to a white heat, the deflection was nearly 25°; but it now remains at 20°, whether hot or cold.

Practical Rules for the Determination of the Radii of a double Achromatic Glass. By J. F. W. Herschel, Esq. F. R. S., &c.   Edin. Phil. Jour. No. 12, p. 361.

At the judicious request of Dr. Brewster, Mr. Herschel is pleased to present this abstract of his paper in the Philosophical Transactions, on the above subject, in a plain form, divested of all algebraical expression. For the public, we thank him; and should be glad to observe such simplicity of expression, on all practical subjects, a little more general. Without meaning any thing disrespectful to the higher mathematics, we would almost dare to assert that the truths explainable through such instrumentality only, may be sought for with a kind of supercilious philosophy; but are seldom essential to the purposes of life: and, therefore, more dignified than useful. The philosopher, as we think, never shines with so much intrinsic lustre, as when he levels the operations of nature to comprehension by plain capacities. In such case, the pleasure of study is enhanced by a consciousness of beneficent utility. We beg not to be misunderstood, as totally ignorant of the value of the profounder mathematics; or as desiring vulgarly to restrain such researches; we only mean that their records should be limited, rather to such works as the Transactions of learned Societies, than confound and disgust the plain reader of periodical popular journals. In some of these latter, simple expression is scarcely to be met with; algebraical formulæ being almost entirely substituted for the vernacular tongue: this looks mighty learned, but is really mighty ridiculous. We must not say that 2 and 2 make 4; that would be plain and vulgar; we must say $2 + 2 = 4$. But we will dismiss the further consideration of this unwelcome subject, and come to Mr. Herschel's valuable communication. He begins with remarking that, it is of the first importance for the artisan to be well informed as to the qualities of the different kinds of glass he may have to form into the requisite lenses; the refractive and dispersive powers being always to be ascertained before calculations can be properly instituted for the respective radii of focal surface: this should be done by grinding small portions into prisms or lenses, and subjecting them to trial as to " the deviation of the most luminous rays," or the best foci. Mr. H. states the inequality of chromatic dispersive power, in different kinds of glass, to be a defect that, with the double object glass, cannot be remedied. All that can be done, being, to work them to the same compound focus for the two brightest and most contrasted colours; these, experience leads him to conclude, are the bright red, bordering on orange; and the vivid blue, passing into green. " Supposing (says he) these rays perfectly united, all the rest will be nearly so; and the two extremities of the spectrum will both deviate one way from the exact focus, while the intermediate portion will deviate the other; thus producing the phenomenon always observed in a well adjusted achromatic telescope when thrown out of focus, viz. a purple or lilac fringe surrounding the image of a white object, on one side of the focus, and a green on the other. This is the criterion of a good adjustment of the foci; and to go beyond this point, with the ordinary materials, seems hopeless." Mr. H. advises the workman, when by trial he have found the ratio of the focal lengths of the component lenses in the proportion of their dispersions, to leave rather a preponderance on the side of the crown or convex lens, gradually reducing the curvature of one of its surfaces, until the purple and green fringes bound a white object on a black ground; when thrown out of the focus. Then, by accurate experiment, determine the focal length of each of the component lenses; and divide the one by the other, when the ratio of dispersive powers will result. Or, knowing the exact radii of the tools, the refracted powers of the media may be resolved.

Of the various mathematical elucidations, given for the solution of this problem, founded on the above data, Mr. H. prefers that of M. Clairant, in which the two internal surfaces of the compound glass were worked to equal radii, the one convex, and the other concave; and cemented together to save the light, otherwise lost by the reflection of two surfaces; but his indices of refraction (1·600 and 1·55) are stated, by Mr. H., to be too high for practical purposes.

By Mr. Herschel's method, the spherical aberration is wholly corrected; both for parallel, and moderately divergent, rays; producing, as he asserts, " a telescope equally perfect for terrestrial and astronomical purposes;" but still more important practical conditions result:—as

1st. That the assigned curvatures are more moderate than any other hitherto proposed on theoretical grounds.

2d. That the curvatures of the exterior surfaces of the compound lens, vary within narrower limits, by the variation in refractive or dispersive powers, than are likely to occur in practice. Mr. H. says that, he has shown in his paper " that a double object glass will be nearly free from aberration, provided the radius of the exterior surface of the crown lens be 6·72, and of flint 14·2; the focal length of the combination being 10·00, and the radii of the interior surfaces being computed from these data, by the formula given in all elementary works on optics, so as to make the focal lengths of the two glasses in the direct ratio of their dispersive powers."

Mr. H. directs the component lens to consist of the anterior or outer one a double convex of crown glass; the posterior or inner one of flint, and concavo-convex; the concavity of the latter receiving the convexity of the former.

3d. The interior surfaces so nearly coincide, that, equal radii may be used in working them, without any sensible error resulting; for when the dispersive ratio be as low as even 0·75, the difference in curvature would be less than $\frac{1}{40}$ part of each.

The dimensions given in the table presume the refractive power of the crown lens to be 1·524; that of the flint 1·585; and the compound focal length to be 10; whence, by aid of the table, may be calculated the proportions of construction on any assignable scale.

Mr. Herschel then proceeds to show how the artisan should estimate the relative proportions by the tabular data, when his scale of construction or powers may vary from them; and works an example in illustration: which we do not abstract, because we think that any intelligent workman will discern at once, from the table itself, how he must calculate his proportions.

We take the liberty of offering to Mr. Herschel, on the part of practical opticians, our best thanks for the result of his labours. The telescope is so useful, and so instructive, an implement of philosophical research; that he who contributes to the perfection of its form, not only merits, but *must obtain*, the grateful applause of mankind.

TABLE. Dimensions of an Aplanatic Double Object-glass.

Refractive Index of Crown Lens = 1·524
Refractive Index of Flint Lens = 1·585
Compound Focal Length, 10·000

Dispersive Ratio	0·50	0·55	0·60	0·65	0·70	0·75
1st Surface, Convex						
Radius for the above Refractive Indices	6·7485	6·7184	6·7069	6·7316	6·8279	7·0816
Variation of Radius for a change of +0·010 in Ref. Index of Crown Gl.	+0·0500	+0·0740	+0·0676	+0·0563	+0·0395	−0·0174
Variation of Radius for a change of +0·010 in Ref. Index of Flint Gl.	−0·0036	−0·0011	+0·0037	+0·0125	+0·0312	+0·0568
2nd Surface, Convex — Radius	4·2827	3·6332	3·0488	2·5208	2·0422	1·6073
3d Surface, Concave — Radius	4·1575	3·6006	3·0640	2·5566	2·0831	1·6450
4th Surface, Convex						
Radius for the above Refractive Indices	14·3697	14·5353	14·2937	13·5709	12·3154	10·5186
Variation of Radius for a change of +0·010 in Ref. Index of Crown Gl.	+0·9921	+1·0080	+1·1049	+1·1614	+1·1613	+1·0847
Variation of Radius for a change of +0·010 in Ref. Index of Flint Gl.	−0·3962	−0·5033	−0·5659	−0·6323	−0·7570	−0·7201
Focal Length of the Crown Lens	4·0	4·5	5·0	3·5	3·0	2·5
Focal Length of the Flint Lens	6·6667	8·1818	10·0000	5·3846	4·2858	3·3333

On the Extraordinary Darkness that was observed in some parts of the United States and Canada, in the month of November 1819. By FREDERICK HALL, Professor of Mathematics and Natural Philosophy in Middlebury College, Vermont. (Memoirs of the American Academy of Arts and Sciences, Vol. IV. part 3, p. 893.)

This phenomenon first attracted my attention on the morning of the 9th of November 1819. I rose at a quarter before seven, and found it much darker than it ordinarily is in the evening at the time of full moon. It snowed fast for about an hour; this was succeeded by a moderate rain, which continued most of the day. Being occupied, I took no farther notice of the uncommon darkness till about 9 o'clock. At this time, the obscurity, instead of diminishing, had considerably increased. The thermometer stood at 34°. A strong, steady, but not violent wind, blew from the south.

The darkness was so great, that a person, when sitting by a window, could not see to read a book, in small type, without serious inconvenience. Several of the students in the college studied the whole day by candle-light. A number of the mechanics in this village were unable to carry on their work without the assistance of lamps.

The sky exhibited a pale yellowish-white aspect, which, in some degree, resembled the evening twilight a few moments before it disappears. Indeed we had little else but twilight through the day; and such, too, as takes place when the sun is five or six degrees below the horizon. The colour of objects was very remarkable. Every thing I beheld wore a dull, smoky, melancholy appearance. The paper, on which I was writing, had the same yellowish-white hue as the heavens. The fowls showed that peculiar restlessness that was remarked in them during the total eclipse of the sun in 1806. Some of them retired to roost. The cocks crowed several hours incessantly, as they do at the dawning of day.

At 3 P. M. the sky brightened up a little, but in the evening the darkness became more extraordinary. A person could not discern his hand, held directly before his eyes. It was next to impossible for a person to find his way even in streets where he had been long accustomed to walk.

The sun was concealed from our view, nearly the whole time, from Monday evening to Friday morning. It did occasionally appear, but was always of a deep blood-red colour; and the apparent magnitude was at least one-third larger than usual. This was very striking on Friday, about nine in the morning. A dense, yellow vapour was then passing slowly over its enlarged disc. The spectacle was viewed by many with astonishment.

The darkness was not confined to this immediate vicinity. It was as great seventy miles west (in the State of New York) as at this place. And here I beg leave to insert an extract of a letter, on this subject, from Noadiah Moore, Esq. of Champlain, N. Y. a well informed and highly respectable gentleman.

"The darkness was first noticed on the night of the 6th November, when the day closing with a hazy atmosphere, the night became so exceedingly dark as to render the sense of sight wholly useless. The horse and his rider were in equal uncertainty. The moon, though near the full, produced no sensible change as it rose. Even the faint *profile* of the landscape, so important a guide to the benighted traveller, was lost in intense obscurity. The atmosphere continued to be clouded by dense vapours until the 9th; when the darkness greatly increased. A light snow covered the ground. It blew a strong gale from the south. The clouds, from which fine drops of rain were continually descending, resembled the pitchy blackness of the smoke of a furnace; they moved in a wild and hurried manner through the heavens, and, at times, seemed to be closing down upon the earth. Several claps of distant thunder were heard, and in a town adjoining, a heavy shower ensued.

"The water caught in this shower was observed to be much discoloured. A quantity caught in a clean vessel, exposed in a situation where it fell directly from the heavens, was preserved for many days in a corked phial, and did not wholly deposit its colouring matter. In appearance it was not unlike water impregnated with soot. As to the degree of darkness which prevailed, it may be observed, that writing, reading, or needle-work, could not be properly performed without candles. Indeed, candles were used during most of the day in many of the houses and workshops. Towards the evening it brightened up a little, but night brought darkness tangible."

The darkness was observed throughout the northern portion of this State, and in several parts of Canada. At Montpelier, about forty miles north east of this place, it is said to have been greater than it was here. A gentleman, from that town, informed me that the darkness there was so great, that the Speaker of the House of Representatives could not distinguish the countenances of the members, so as to determine who was addressing him. The same gentleman added, that where he stopped to dine, he was obliged to make use of a candle to distinguish the different kinds of food which were placed before him.

In the small quantity of water which fell from the atmosphere, I did not observe any extraordinary colour, or smell, or taste. It is stated in *Le Courier du Bas-Canada*, " that the water was of a black colour, as if it had been impregnated with a large proportion of soot; and several persons who had tasted it, discovered the taste of soot. This colour the water retained a considerable time." I have read remarks of a similar kind in the newspapers from various parts of New England. Had the fall of water here been more copious, I should probably have noticed the peculiarity above described.

The appearance of the heavens during the late period of darkness, was very much like that which is frequently occasioned by extensive fires in the woods. An effect, similar in kind, but far inferior in degree, was produced a few years since, by the fires which raged several weeks, and consumed most of the underwood on the Green Mountains opposite this place. The darkness observed at that time was very considerable, and the sky was of a pale yellowish-red aspect.

The cause assigned by Dr. Williams, for the uncommon darkness of 1780, is perhaps the most satisfactory which could be given. But in the present case, no similar cause can be supposed, at least in New England. No great fires were destroying our woodlands. It was too late in the season. The combustible matter of the forests was not sufficiently dry.

The darkness of 1780 occurred in May, after a long period of dry weather; that of 1819 in November, without being preceded by any unusual drought, especially in this part of the country. The former lasted only thirteen or fourteen hours; the latter nearly a week.

The cause of this phenomenon, whatever it may be, is undoubtedly to be sought at a considerable distance to the south of New England. Many persons in this vicinity, as well as myself, observed, that when the wind blew most powerfully from a southerly quarter, it brought with it a vast quantity of smoke, or of something much resembling it; and that the sky was then the darkest; that when the wind shifted, and blew a short time in any other direction, the atmosphere was in a degree cleared of this smoky matter. During the time the darkness lasted, there was for the most part a pretty strong wind from the south. On Friday morning it changed to the west, and continued to blow for some time from that quarter. The unusual obscurity gradually disappeared, and objects, both in the heavens and upon the earth, soon assumed their ordinary aspect.

Since writing the above, I have seen an article in the "Missionary," of the 12th of November—a very respectable paper—printed at Mount Zion, Hancock Co. Georgia, relating to this phenomenon. It is stated, that "the atmosphere had been very smoky for about a fortnight preceding: so much so, that it had literally intercepted the rays of the sun at noon during a part of this time, and seriously affected the eyes." "It is doubtless," added the writer, "occasioned by great fires in the Indian territories. The wind has blown almost invariably from that direction for some time."

That the late darkness had its origin in some of our most southern states, or in the territories belonging to them, can, I think, hardly be questioned. It is by no means improbable that it was occasioned by fires, running on those immense prairies that furnish annually such vast quantities of combustible materials. We are told that these prairies "are covered with a coarse kind of grass, which, before the country is settled in their vicinity, grows to the height of six or seven feet." (See Atwater's Letters to Professor Silliman on the

Prairies of the West, published in *The American Journal of Science*, vol. i. p. 116.) This vegetation, another writer observes, "becomes sufficiently dry to burn during the long dry season, called the *Indian Summer*; which commences usually in October, and continues a month and a half or two months, during which the vegetation is killed by the frost, and dried by the sun; the wet prairies are also dried, and before the season has expired, the grass is perfectly combustible." (See R. W. Well's communication on Prairies, published in the same work, vol. i. p. 334.) In order the more easily to take their game, and to facilitate travelling from one hunting ground to another, the Indians, we are informed, occasionally set fire to the prairies "towards the close of the Indian summer."

We present the above to our readers as a phenomenon of singular occurrence, extent, and duration. If the conjecture be correct, that the obscurity arose from the conflagration of herbage, the extent of burnt surface must have been immense.

On the Existence of Mercury in the Ocean. By M. PROUST.

1. Hilaire Rouëlle remarked, a long while ago, that whenever he purified the crude salt of the custom-house in silver basins, they became covered here and there with those spots which are particular to mercury.

2. The same salt, decomposed by sulphuric acid, always gave, in the top of the retorts, small quantities of a sublimate decidedly mercurial.

3. The fact generally known of whitening yellow metals, by putting them for some time into crude or rough salt, added to the preceding results, determined Rouëlle to announce that there was no doubt of the existence of mercury in marine salt.

4. Among the preparations which came to me from Paris to Spain, to furnish the laboratory of the artillery there, were a dozen bottles of fuming muriatic acid, which had been prepared in the laboratory of the druggist, Charlard: all these bottles contained mercury. I at first perceived it, from an amalgam of tin and mercury being left on dissolving

some tin in the acid; and afterwards I directly ascertained its presence by purifying the acid in the usual manner, and examining the residuum left; it contained mercury mixed with oxide of iron. It was sufficient indeed to pour a few drops of the proto-muriate of tin into the acid to precipitate the mercury in powder. Hence, then, mercury incontestably exists in the custom-house salt of France.

5. In Spain, the government put to sale the rock-salt of the mines of Cordova and Minglanilla. The first time that I purified the salt sold at Madrid, in a silver basin, I remarked the same spots as those noticed by Rouëlle.

6. Having used all the muriatic acid of Paris, I procured some from the manufactory of acids at Cadahalso. That which was sent to me, had been procured by means of calcined clay. It contained iron, and, to my surprise, mercury also. From that time I remarked, in my course of lectures, the singular accordance between the salt of France and Spain in this respect.

The presence of mercury in rock salt is not astonishing, but when it is found also in the salt produced by evaporation from sea water, there is greater difficulty, because it must be supposed to be in solution. There needs not, I think, more facts or better proved ones, than those mentioned, to establish with certainty the existence of mercury in the sea water of this period, and that it has existed also in those which, by evaporation or condensation, have given rise to the deposits of rock salt. All the chemists of the last century, but one, speak of the mercury of marine salt, probably from observations analogous to those I have mentioned, and Rouëlle remarked it before me.

There is nothing as yet demonstrated in the origin of rock salt; nevertheless, if it should ultimately be proved that the principal known mines contain mercury, it would be a new demonstration that the waters of the ocean had concurred in producing them; a consequence which has been already drawn from the discovery of potash in the waters of the ocean, and in rock salt.

An experiment I have desired to make for a long time, but for which the opportunity has not yet offered, is to attach a plate of gold, of two or three inches surface, to some part of a ship, where it would be continually plunged in the water. Half an ounce of gold laminated, would be amply sufficient; all that is required is, to ascertain whether, at the end of a long voyage, it had become amalgamated; but the person who would successfully make the experiment must not forget that if the plate is lost, it is probably because it would readily detach itself, nothing scarcely being so fragile as gold penetrated by mercury. As to the expense, I shall readily bear it with pleasure. Application may be made to M. Lucas, agent of the Institute, who will immediately give the value to any person willing to take charge of the experiment.—*Memoires du Muséum*, vii. 479.

If it be eventually established that the waters of the ocean hold mercury in solution, we shall perhaps be able to account for some facts not hitherto well understood. The public spirit of M. Proust is as fully established by his liberal sacrifice to science, as his devotion to its pursuits has long rendered him celebrated for, especially in the department of chemistry.

Examination of the Blood and its Action in the different Phenomena of Life.
By J. L. Prevost, M. D., and J. A. Dumas.
Bibliotheque Universelle.

We here present some results of experiments that merit our readers' particular attention. There was a time, and that not very far back, when physiologists contended with violence respecting the form and magnitude of the particles of blood: perhaps this indecent zeal was too furious and too disgraceful to maintain itself long; and so perished, doctrine and all, through its very excess. We are not in any great danger, now, of running mechanical principle too hard, to serve physiological purposes: and therefore whether the globules be spherical or elliptical; of easy or difficult transit; is not matter of fear or hope. The main facts are those of the blood bearing an individuality of character in the respective classes of animals; a knowledge of which may eventually aid future physiological research.

"If we submit," say these gentlemen, "to the action of the voltaic pile, the white of an egg, it is decomposed, the coagulated albumen is carried to the positive pole, the caustic soda to the negative. This experiment, which we owe to Mr. Brande, demonstrates that the white of egg ought to be regarded as an albumenate of soda, with excess of base. We have submitted to a very careful microscopic examination, the coagulum which is produced in these circumstances, and it is not without satisfaction that we have seen very distinct globules similar in every thing to those of the blood, &c.; the same appearance, the same diameter, the same disposition to form ranges or aggregates. This remarkable result appears proper to throw some light on the animal secretions, and in particular on the formation of the chyle." They measured the dimensions of the globules of blood in different animals, by the method of Captain Kater. The following is their table of results:—

Name of the Animal.	Real diameter in parts of an English Inch.	Name of the Animal.	Real diameter in parts of an English Inch.
Callitriche d'Afr.	$\frac{1}{3000}$	Grey Mouse	$\frac{1}{4275}$
Man	$\frac{1}{3750}$	White Mouse	do.
Dog	do.	Sheep	$\frac{1}{5000}$
Rabbit	do.	Horse	do.
Pig	do.	Mule	do.
Hedgehog	do.	Ox	do.
Guinea pig	do.	Chamois	$\frac{1}{5450}$
Muscardin	do.	Stag	do.
Ass	$\frac{1}{4175}$	She goat	$\frac{1}{7200}$
Cat	$\frac{1}{4275}$		

Sir Everard Home, Captain Kater, and Dr. Wollaston, make the mean dimension of the human globule $\frac{1}{5000}$ of an inch.

Dr. Young, in his introduction to "Medical Literature," published in 1813, states:—

Diameter of the globule of the blood of the calf $\frac{1}{6000}$ of an inch.
—Human blood diluted with water $\frac{1}{6000}$
—Human blood, after being several days in water $\frac{1}{5000}$
—Blood of the mouse $\frac{1}{4620}$
—Blood of the thornback $\frac{1}{1000}$

Messrs. Prevost and Dumas find the globule circular

(spherical?) in all the mammiferæ; varying in size, with that of the animal; elliptical in birds, varying only in the greater axis; elliptical in all cold blooded animals. The colourless globule, in the centre of each, always is $\frac{1}{7500}$ of an inch; whatever may be the animal to which it belongs. Animals bled to syncope, died, if water, or serum of blood, at 100° Fahr. were injected into the veins. When so bled the transfusion of blood from a similar animal restored the apparent corpse to life and health. If the transfusion be from a different kind of animal, but with similar globules, the relief will be imperfect, and death ensue within five or six days. The pulse is accelerated; the animal heat declines; but the breathing is regular. Mucous and bloody stools instantly follow the transfusion, and continue during life. By injecting circular globules into the veins of a bird, life is soon terminated in spasmodic exhaustion. Transfusion into a rabbit, from a cow, or a sheep, whether the blood were fresh, or kept cool for 12 or 24 hours, restored the animal after the bleeding. Ducks die convulsed by transfusion from the sheep. Birds have died by transfusion, apparently before the first syringeful of injection could have passed into the vein. From these facts, the experimenters consider transfusion into the human system as very absurd and dangerous, until we have more knowledge on the subject.

As a general caution against rash enterprize, we think with those gentlemen that transfusion into human subjects should not be had recourse to hastily; but we do not understand what the *absurdity* of a trial can consist in; for if they have given us plain truth, and nothing more, there is much to be hoped from such a means of restoration, when all other common remedies have failed us. And possibly we may hereafter find that the other members of the mammalia tribe, as the cow, &c. can supply a restorative in more cases than that of suspended animation.

On the Influence of Green Fruits on the Air, before their Maturity. By M. TH. DE SAUSSURE.

M. de Saussure's opinions on this subject are opposed to those of M. Berard's dissertation, which received the approbation of the Institute; an approval which, it appears, was by no means sanctioned by the Sçavans of Paris. M. de S. says—

"When I was occupied in my *researches on vegetation*, (pages 57 and 129,) with the action of green fruits on the atmospheric air, I admitted that they produced the same effects as the leaves, or that they poured out, like them, oxygenous gas, by the decomposition of the carbonic acid; with this difference, that, in an equal volume, they decomposed much less. My experiments on this subject indicate, that grapes in the state of verjuice, and the green fruit of the *solanum pseudo-capsicum*, exposed to the sun, and adhering to the plant and soil, which make them grow, add oxygen to the air contained in the vessel in which they are enclosed; whilst the same fruits, in circumstances otherwise equal, destroy the oxygen of the vessel, when it contains hydrate of lime. This substance, by absorbing the carbonic acid which they form, and that which they receive from the soil, prevents the oxygen from making its appearance, which would otherwise have been disengaged.

"In the experiments which I published, the disengagement of oxygen gas had not the same success when the fruits were detached from the plant that bore them. Like the leaves, they absorbed oxygen gas from the air in obscurity, replacing it in a volume nearly equal to the fruit, by an equal quantity of carbonic acid gas; but in the sun they decomposed only in part the acid gas produced during the night, whilst on the plant they decomposed it altogether. This partial and purely accidental difference depended evidently on the decay or loss of the vegetative force which a fruit must suffer when it is detached from its plant, and which receives no nourishment; and this difference ought not to affect the experiments which led to the conclusion that green fruits comport themselves in the air, as the leaves do. These experiments offered, moreover, merely a confirmation of the principle which supposes that the faculty of emitting oxygen gas in the sun is essential to the green herbaceous parts in a state of vegetation."

M. Berard maintained that green fruits do not effect or

undergo changes, similar to leaves, in the sun-shine; neither decomposing carbonic acid gas, nor disengaging oxygen gas. "They," says M. B., "at all periods of their growth, form carbonic acid with oxygen; absorbing more of the latter in the sun than in the shade."

M. de Saussure states, that to determine such a question, it is necessary for us to discard those fruits whose colour is feeble, as least adapted to exhibit the disengagement of oxygen gas. He recapitulates thus—

"1. Green fruits have the same influence on the air, in sun-shine and obscurity, as the leaves; the action differs only in being less intense than that of the latter.

"2. They cause the disappearance, during the night, of the oxygen gas of their atmosphere, and they replace it by carbonic acid gas, which they partially absorb; this absorption is usually less in the open air than under a receiver.

"3. In equal volume, they consume more oxygen in the dark, when they are distant from, than when they are near to, their maturity.

"4. During their exposure to the sun, they disengage, in whole or in part, the oxygen of the carbonic acid which they have imbibed during the night, and leave no trace of this acid in their atmosphere. Several fruits detached from the plant, add also oxygen gas to air which contained no carbonic acid. When their vegetation is very feeble or languishing, they corrupt the air in every circumstance, but less in the sun than in the shade.

"5. Green fruits detached from the plant, and exposed to the successive action of the night and of the sun, change the air little or nothing in purity and volume; the slight variations, which we observe in this respect, depend either on their greater or less faculty of elaborating carbonic acid, or on their composition, which is modified according to their degree of maturity.

"6. Green fruits decompose, in whole or in part, not only the carbonic acid which they have produced during the night, but also that which we add artificially to their atmosphere. When we make the latter experiment, with fruits which are aqueous, and which, such as apples and grapes, elaborate but slowly the carbonic acid gas, we perceive that they absorb in the sun, a portion of gas much greater than a like volume of water could do in a similar mixture. Thereafter they disengage the oxygen of the absorbed acid, and appear thus to elaborate it in their interior.

" 7. Their faculty of decomposing carbonic acid, becomes feebler as they ripen.

" 8. They appropriate, during their vegetation, the oxygen and hydrogen of the water, making it lose the liquid state.

" 9. These results are sometimes to be observed only in volumes of air, which exceed 30 or 40 times the volume of the fruit, and by weakening much the heating action of the sun. If we neglect these precautions, several fruits corrupt the air, even in the sun, by forming carbonic acid with the ambient oxygen. But still in the latter case, the mere comparison of their effect in the shade, with that which they produce under the successive influence of the night and of the sun, demonstrates that they decompose the carbonic acid.

" 10. The differences between the results of M. Berard and mine, proceed principally from his enclosing the fruits in a space which was only six or eight times greater than their own volume, and which was too narrow for them not to suffer by the neighbourhood or contact of the sides of the receiver heated by the sun. Some succulent plants *(plantas grasses)* resist this trial, and my results with the *cactus* may have induced this chemist to treat fruits by the same process; but several of them require more tender management, not only than the fleshy plants, but even than the most delicate leaves. I think also that he ought to have nourished the fruits with a small quantity of water; the appearance of freshness which he found in them after the experiment, might have some weight, if he had been operating on leaves, which lose their look and consistence by the least drying; but it has little value for thick and fleshy fruits, which may be deteriorated and lose their weight, without giving any such indication by inspection alone."

Account of the Hot Springs of Furnas, in the Island of St. Michael. By J. W. WEBSTER, M. D.

Dr. Webster's History of the Island of St. Michael.

The hot springs of the Valle das Furnas render this the most interesting spot in St. Michael. The valley is nearly twelve miles in circumference, and is bounded on every side by mountains of various height. Its form, like that of the other inclosed valleys, which have already been described, is nearly circular, but its surface has considerable irregularity, rising here and there into small hills. A part of it is under tolerable cultivation, and it is inhabited by a few peasants. It is watered by many streams that wind through the plantations till they unite to form a small river, called Ribeira Quente, or Warm River. After a circuitous course, the Ribeira Quente flows through a deep ravine, and empties itself into the sea on the southern side of the island at the base of Pico da Vigia.

The mountains surrounding this valley are composed chiefly of pumice; but compact lava and rocks of the trachyte family are seen on the face of many of the precipices. The columnar structure and vertical arrangement of these rocks are quite distinct in some places; in others, beds of the porphyry and pumice appear to alternate. They are sometimes separated by layers of fine sand or ashes. A few pieces of slaggy lava and scoriæ, are occasionally found at the foot of the mountains, but there are no large collections or beds of them.

At the bottom of one of the precipices, I found a number of pieces of a rock analogous to amygdaloid, and at the same time porphyritic. Each piece is composed of angular portions, apparently fragments, which are united by a yellowish white siliceous substance, approaching in some respects to calcedony. It is hard and opaque, and has somewhat of a waxy lustre. The cavities on which the amygdaloidal character of this rock depends, contain a small quantity of mealy and radiated zeolite.

The hot springs are situated towards one extremity of the valley, beyond a few cottages composing the village of Furnas. They are not seen at any distance, being surrounded by small hills, some of which, there is great reason to believe, owe their origin in part, if not altogether, to the springs themselves. They are generally covered with short shrubs, but some of them are wholly devoid of any traces of vegetation. They are composed of clay of different degrees of compactness, which is variously, and often beautifully coloured by iron, under different degrees of oxidation. The clay is intermixed with fine pumice and masses of siliceous sinter. As we pass along the narrow road from the village to this spot, the gradual change from a fertile to a barren soil is observed, and within a few yards of the hot springs, nearly all traces of vegetation are lost. At the extremity of the road the ground is almost snow white, and then acquires a reddish tinge; this increases in intensity and brightness, and finally passes through an infinite variety of shades to a deep brown. Here and there, patches and veins of a bright yellow and purple colour, add to the singular aspect of this remarkable spot. The clay is in some places so much indurated as to retain an imperfect slaty character, but most of it is soft, and has an earthy aspect. It does not feel perfectly smooth when rubbed, but is full of hard grains, which are exceedingly minute; and when a mass of it is diffused in water, a quantity of fine siliceous particles is separated. Is has many of the characters of tripoli. It is used by the peasants as an external application for cutaneous diseases, and is undoubtedly beneficial in some particular cases, from the quantity of sulphur it contains. Large pieces of siliceous sinter, of a grey colour, are imbedded in it, and it is covered in some parts by the same substance, which has accumulated upon it in layers, from an eighth of an inch to an inch in thickness. Near the extremity of the road, the beds of clay have been cut through to the depth of six or eight feet, and their structure is well displayed.

The vicinity of the springs is indicated by the increased temperature of the earth, a sulphureous odour, and the escape of vapour or steam from every crack and fissure in the ground. The temperature of the clay continues to increase as we advance, and a greater quantity of vapour is at last seen slowly ascending from the springs themselves.

The volumes of smoke and steam rolling upwards from the surface to a great height, till they are gradually diffused through the atmosphere, or mingle with the heavier clouds that crown the summit of the mountains, produce a striking effect. The confused rumbling and hissing noise that is heard for some time before we arrive in sight of the springs, increases at last to an incessant and terrific roar, and seems to issue from the very spot on which we stand. The earth returns a hollow sound, and great caution is required to avoid stepping into the pools and streams of boiling water, with which its surface is covered.

The quantities of hot water discharged through the innumerable orifices in the ground is prodigiously great, and the different streams unite, forming a small river, that, still hot, joins the Ribeira Quente. The largest springs are termed Caldeiras, or boilers, and a shallow basin of earthy matter has been formed round each of them, by depositions from the water. Much of the water is constantly retained within these reservoirs, and its surface is more or less agitated by the escape of sulphuretted hydrogen gas, and the ejection of the water from below. The temperature of some of these springs on the 2d day of December, between three and four o'clock P. M., the thermometer standing at 63° Fahrenheit, the barometer at 29·4, was as follows:

207°	200°	96°	137°	208°
190	134	170	73	114
184	94	122	171	147

The basin of the largest spring, particularly designated as "The Caldeira," is circular, and between twenty and thirty feet in diameter. The water in this boils with much greater violence than in any other caldeira, and distinct loud explosions occur at short intervals, which are succeeded by a very perceptible elevation of the centre of the body of water within the basin. This is attended with a loud hissing noise, and the escape of great quantities of sulphuretted hydrogen gas, steam, and sulphureous acid vapour. On account of the high temperature and vast quantities of steam, it is dangerous to approach near the spring, except on the windward side. The cattle, however, are often seen standing on the opposite side, to free themselves, as it is supposed, from vermin. The peasants are in the habit of placing baskets filled with lupines, beans, and other vegetables, on the edge of the basin, where they are speedily cooked.

From the great Caldeira, the water is conveyed to two or three small buildings, which are used as bathing houses. The temperature of the water being so high, reservoirs have been sunk, by removing the earth to the depth of a foot or two, into which the hot water is conducted, and allowed to cool; it is then received into bathing houses, and its temperature raised at pleasure by the admission of more water immediately from the caldeira. The water is turbid, from the presence of a large quantity of aluminous earth, but which gives to it a peculiarly soft feel.

A few yards from the principal caldeira, is an elevation about fifty feet in height, and probably as many in extent, composed of alternate layers, of a coarser variety of sinter, and clay, including grass, ferns, and reeds, in different states of petrifaction. Not many years since, the side of this hill fell in, and discovered a deep and frightful cavern: smoke and steam at present issue from it in vast quantity, accompanied by a tremendous noise. The hill, indeed, appears to be a dome, covering an extensive abyss, from which, by another outlet nearer the summit, hot mud and stones have been occasionally ejected. Looking down through the opening, a body of water is seen boiling with great violence. An appalling roar is incessantly reverberated from side to side within the dome, and is increased, at short intervals, by sudden and violent explosions. The surface of this hill, the sides of the cavern, and the innumerable crevices in the ground, are coated with sulphur; in obtaining specimens of which, I found the heat and acid fumes almost suffocating. Every stone has been more or less changed, while not a shrub or plant flourishes for many yards around. The thermometer introduced into the fissures immediately rose to 120°, and in some places to 123° Fahrenheit.

Sulphur is so abundant and pure, that it might be collected in quantities sufficient to export; wherever a loose stone lies over one of the fissures, or where many stones are loosely heaped together, their under surfaces are soon covered with it; and by placing tiles, as is done at Solfatra, on which the sulphur could collect, an abundant supply of it would be obtained.

Wherever the water has flowed, depositions of siliceous sinter have accumulated, and circular basins, composed entirely of this substance, have been here and there formed round a spring. The siliceous matter rises, in many places, eight or ten inches above the level of the water, and is often exceedingly beautiful. Grass, leaves, and similar substances which have been exposed to the influence of the water, are more or less incrusted with silex, and exhibit all the progressive steps of petrifaction; some being soft, and differing but little from their natural state; while others are partly converted into stone, or are entirely consolidated. In many instances, alumina is the mineralizing material, which is likewise deposited from the hot waters. I found branches of the ferns which now flourish on the island, completely petrified, preserving the same appearance as when vegetating, excepting the colour, which is now ash grey. Fragments of wood occur, more or less changed, and one entire bed, from three to five feet in depth, is composed of the reeds so common on the island, completely mineralized, the centre of each joint being filled with delicate crystals of sulphur, in elongated, double four-sided pyramidical crystals, with a highly resinous lustre.

Round the springs, where the water has dashed irregularly over the edge of the basins, the depositions of siliceous matter are rough, and often present an appearance similar to those of Iceland, which have been so well compared, by Sir George Mackenzie, to the heads of cauliflowers. The variety of siliceous sinter, which is most abundant in St. Michael, is in layers from a quarter to a half inch in thickness, which are accumulated on each other, to the height often of a foot and upwards, constituting distinct and wide strata, many yards in extent. These strata are always parallel, and for the most part horizontal, but in some places they are slightly undulating. Between the layers of this substance is a loose white powder, which, on examination, is found to be nearly pure silex, with a small proportion of alumina. When moist, it is nearly gelatinous. The colour of the slaty variety is pearl-grey; externally it is dull, but on the fresh fracture has a glistening lustre, and is translucent on the edges. The fracture is nearly smooth, inclining a little to conchoidal. It scratches glass with ease, and has a specific gravity of 2·107. It is infusible before the common blowpipe.

Another variety of sinter has a snow-white colour, and is externally wrinkled, abounding in slight depressions and protuberances, which are almost circular. This is found in delicate crusts, and often covers irregularly shaped masses of the other varieties. It has a very beautiful semi-opalescent lustre. The crusts are brittle, and seldom exceed the tenth of an inch in thickness. Their specific gravity is 1·886. Upon masses of a kind of conglomerate of altered lava and pumice, I noticed a very beautiful variety of fiorite, in small circular cup-shaped portions, the edges of which are of a pure flesh-red, becoming gradually fainter, till the centres are perfectly snow-white.

Another variety has the following characters: its colour is snow-white, reddish and yellowish-white, passing, in some specimens, to yellowish-grey. It occurs in long, slender, capillary filaments, from one to four inches in length. The filaments cross each other in every direction. On the cross fracture, viewed with a microscope, a lustre between vitreous and pearly is observed. It is translucent, brittle, and light. When reduced to powder, and rubbed over the surface of a plate of glass, it scratches it. Its specific gravity is 1·866. It is insoluble in nitric, muriatic, or sulphuric acids, and is infusible before Brooke's blowpipe. A portion of this mineral was examined by my friend Dr. Dana, who found it " fusible into a perfectly transparent glass, when mixed with an alkali, and that six grains of it, in fine powder intensely ignited in a platina crucible for fifteen minutes, lost 0·98125 grains, equal to 16·35 per cent." It appears from Dr. Dana's analysis, to consist of silex 83·65; water 16·35. It thus differs from the siliceous depositions of Iceland and Ischia, in the large proportion of water it contains, and in the absence of alumina and lime. It may be considered an hydrate of silex with more propriety than the hyalite of Frankfort, which M. Bucholz regards as such, and which contains but 6·33 of water. It appears to be a new variety of siliceous sinter, and deserves to be designated by an appropriate name. From the island in which it occurs, I propose to call it Michaelite.

Wherever cavities exist in the large masses of sinter, and in the hills formed by that substance, and the fragments of lava and pumice, the silex has assumed a stalactitic form; and the stalactites are from one to two inches in length, and their surfaces are often covered with small brilliant crystals of quartz. It is impossible to convey any adequate idea of the beauty and variety of forms under which silex appears in St. Michael, and mineralogists can here be supplied with specimens far surpassing those from any other localities as yet described.

Another variety of stalactite that occurs here is composed principally of alumina. These stalactites are rough and earthy, and their length is from one to six inches.

The more compact masses of sinter broken down by the weather, and other causes, have been cemented together, with portions of obsidian, pumice, and scoriæ, into very beautiful breccia, which is in some places sufficiently hard to admit a good polish. The cement is siliceous sinter. The different substances of which this mass is composed, exhibit a great variety of colour, and the fractured surface is curiously mottled with green, red, grey, white, yellow, and black, in every variety of shade. Some of the portions have external characters analogous to those of wax-opal, and many are striped and spotted, while others are porphyritic. This breccia is evidently of recent formation, and appears indeed to be actually forming at this time in those parts of the beds where it is soft, and the cement gelatinous. The alteration which the rock has undergone, in many places, where exposed to the steam and acid vapours, is remarkable. The different substances composing it have lost their colours, and have now a pretty uniform degree of whiteness, the brecciated structure remaining. The fragments are soft, and in many places have acquired a distinctly argillaceous character. Some of the elevations composed of this breccia are upwards of thirty feet in height. Wherever cavities occur in it, they are lined with small stalactites; and botryoidal concretions of pearl-sinter (fiorite of Thomson) and alum appear under the form of a delicate efflorescence, or in minute crystals.

Besides the hot springs already noticed, there are some others of less importance in different parts of the Valley of the Furnas, and bathing houses have been erected in their vicinity. There are also many cold springs, the waters of which are abundant in carbonic acid and sulphuretted hydrogen gases, and they are strongly chalybeate. They occur in various parts of the plain, and some of them are so near the hot springs, that the thumb may be placed in one of the former, the temperature of which is 70° or 80°, and the first finger of the same hand in one of the latter, at the temperature of 190° or 200°. The ground over which the water from the cold spring passes, is covered with a thin coating of oxide of iron, and many of the loose stones have a beautiful metallic stain, which is sometimes iridescent.

Description of the Slide of Alpnach. By the late Professor PLAYFAIR. From his Works, just published.

" On the south side of Pilatus, a considerable mountain near Lucerne, are great forests of spruce fir, consisting of the finest timber, but in a situation which the height, the steepness, and the ruggedness of the ground, seemed to render inaccessible. They had rarely been visited but by the chamois hunters, and it was from them, indeed, that the first information concerning the size of the trees and the extent of the forest appears to have been received. These woods are in the canton of Unterwalden, one of those in which the ancient spirit of the Swiss republics is the best preserved; where the manners are extremely simple, the occupations of the people mostly those of agriculture; where there are no manufactures, little accumulation of capital, and no commercial enterprise. In the possession of such masters, the lofty firs of Pilatus were likely to remain long the ornaments of their native mountain.

"A few years ago, however, Mr. Rupp, a native of Wirtemberg, and a skilful engineer, in which profession he had been educated, indignant at the political changes effected in his own country, was induced to take refuge among a free people, and came to settle in the canton of Schwytz, on the opposite side of the lake of Lucerne. The accounts which he heard there of the forest just mentioned determined him to visit it, and he was so much struck by its appearance, that, long and rugged as the descent was, he conceived the bold project of bringing down the trees by no other force than their own weight into the lake of Lucerne, from which the conveyance to the German Ocean was easy and expeditious. A more accurate survey of the ground convinced him of the practicability of the project.

"He had by this time resided long enough in Switzerland to have both his talents and integrity in such estimation, that he was able to prevail on a number of the proprietors to form a company, with a joint stock, to be laid out in the purchase of the forest, and in the construction of the road along which it was intended that the trees should slide down into the lake of Lucerne, an arm or gulph of which fortunately approaches quite near to the bottom of the mountain. The sum required for this purpose was very considerable for that country, amounting to nine or ten thousand pounds; three thousand to be laid out on the purchase of the forest from the community of Alpnach, the proprietors of it, and the rest being necessary for the construction of the singular railway by which the trees were to be brought down. In a country where there is little enterprise, few capitalists, and where he was himself a stranger, this was not the least difficult part of Mr. Rupp's undertaking.

"The distance which the trees had to be conveyed is about three of the leagues of that country, or, more exactly, 46,000 feet. The medium height of the forest is about 2500 feet; which measure I took from General Pfyffer's model of the Alps, and not from any actual measurement of my own. The horizontal distance just mentioned, when reduced to English measure, making allowance for the Swiss foot, is 44,252 feet, eight English miles and about three furlongs. The declivity is therefore one foot in 17.68; the medium angle of elevation 3° 14″ 20′.

"This declivity, though so moderate on the whole, is, in many places, very rapid; at the beginning of the inclination it is about one-fourth of a right angle, or about 22° 30′; in many places it is 20°, but no where greater than the angle first mentioned, 22° 30′. The inclination continues of this quantity for about 500 feet, after which the way is less steep, and often considerably circuitous, according to the directions which the ruggedness of the ground forces it to take.

"Along this line the trees descend, in a sort of trough, built in a cradle form, and extending from the forest to the edge of the lake. Three trees, squared, and laid side by side, form the bottom of the trough; the tree in the middle having its surface hollowed, so that a rill of water received from distance to distance, over the side of the trough, may be conveyed along the bottom, and preserve it moist. Adjoining to the central part, (of the trough,) other trees, also squared, are laid parallel to the former, in such a manner as to form a trough, rounded in the interior, and of such dimensions as to allow the largest trees to lie, or to move along quite readily. When the direction of the trough turns, or has any bending, of which there are many, its sides are made higher and stronger, especially on the convex side, or that from which it bends, so as to provide against the trees bolting or flying out, which they sometimes do, in spite of every precaution. In general, the trough is from five to six feet wide at top, and from three to four in depth, varying, however, in different places, according to circumstances.

"This singular road has been constructed at considerable expense; though, as it goes, almost for its whole length, through a forest, the materials of construction were at hand, and of small value. It contains, we are told, thirty thousand trees; it is, in general, supported on cross timbers, that are themselves supported by uprights fixed in the ground; and these cross timbers are sometimes close to the surface; they are occasionally under it, and sometimes elevated to a great height above it. It crosses in its way three great ravines, one at the height of 64 feet, another at the height of 103, and the third, where it goes along the face of a rock, at that of 157; in two places it is conveyed under ground. It was finished in 1812.

" The trees which descend by this conveyance are spruce firs, very straight, and of great size. All their branches are lopped off; they are stripped of the bark, and the surface, of course, made tolerably smooth. The trees, or logs, of which the trough is built, are dressed with the axe, but without much care.

" All being thus prepared, the tree is launched with the root end foremost, into the steep part of the trough, and in a few seconds acquires such a velocity as enables it to reach the lake in the short space of six minutes; a result altogether astonishing, when it is considered that the distance is more than eight miles, that the average declivity is but one foot in seventeen, and that the route which the trees have to follow is often circuitous, and in some places almost horizontal.

" Where large bodies are moved with such velocity as has now been described, and so tremendous a force of course produced, every thing had need to be done with the utmost regularity; every obstacle carefully removed that can obstruct the motion, or that might suffer by so fearful a collision. Every thing, accordingly, with regard to launching off the trees, is directed by telegraphic signals. All along the slide, men are stationed, at different distances, from half a mile to three quarters, or more, but so that every station may be seen from the next, both above and below. At each of these stations, also, is a telegraph, consisting of a large board like a door, that turns at its middle on a horizontal axle. When the board is placed upright, it is seen from the two adjacent stations; when it is turned horizontally, or rather parallel to the surface of the ground, it is invisible from both. When the tree is launched from the top, a signal is made by turning the board upright; the same is followed by the rest, and thus the information is conveyed, almost instantaneously, all along the slide, that a tree is now on its way. By and bye, to any one that is stationed on the side, even to those at a great distance, the same is announced by the roaring of the tree itself, which becomes always louder and louder; the tree comes in sight when it is perhaps half a mile distant, and in an instant after shoots past, with the noise of thunder and the rapidity of lightning. As soon as it has reached the bottom, the lowest telegraph is turned down, the signal passes along all the stations, and the workmen at the top are informed that the tree has arrived in safety. Another is set off as expeditiously as possible; the moment is announced, as before, and the same process is repeated, till all the trees that have been got in readiness for that day have been sent down into the lake.

"When a tree sticks by accident, or when it flies out, a signal is made from the nearest station, by half depressing the board, and the workmen from above and below come to assist in getting out the tree that has stuck, or correcting any thing that is wrong in the slide, from the springing of a beam in the slide; and thus the interruption to the work is rendered as short as possible.

"We saw five trees come down; the place where we stood was near the lower end, and the declivity was inconsiderable, (the bottom of the slide nearly resting on the surface,) yet the trees passed with astonishing rapidity. The greatest of them was a spruce fir, a hundred feet long, four in diameter at the lower end, and one foot at the upper. The greatest trees are those that descend with the greatest rapidity; and the velocity as well as the roaring of this one was evidently greater than of the rest. A tree must be very large, to descend at all in this manner; a tree, Mr. Rupp informed us, that was only half the dimensions of the preceding, and therefore only an eighth part of its weight, would not be able to make its way from the top to the bottom. One of the trees that we saw broke by some accident into two; the lighter part stopped almost immediately, and the remaining part came to rest soon after. This is a valuable fact; it appears from it that the friction is not in proportion to the weight, but becomes relatively less as the weight increases, contrary to the opinion that is generally received.

"In viewing the descent of the trees, my nephew and I stood quite close to the edge of the trough, not being more interested about any thing than to experience the impression which the near view of so singular an object must make on a spectator. The noise, the rapidity of the motion, the magnitude of the moving body, and the force with which it seemed to shake the trough as it passed, were altogether very formidable, and conveyed an idea of danger much greater than the reality. Our guide refused to partake of our amusement; he retreated behind a tree at some distance, where he had the consolation to be assured by Mr. Rupp, that he was no safer than we were, as a tree, when it happened to bolt from the trough, would often cut the standing trees clear over. During the whole time the slide has existed, there have been three or four fatal accidents, and one instance was the consequence of excessive temerity.

"I have mentioned that a provision was made for keeping the bottom of the trough wet; this is a very useful precaution; the friction is greatly diminished, and the swiftness is greatly increased by that means. In rainy weather the trees move much faster than in dry. We were assured that when the trough was every where in its most perfect condition, the weather wet, and the trees very large, the descent was sometimes made in as short a time as three minutes.

"The trees thus brought down into the lake of Lucerne are formed into rafts, and floated down the very rapid stream of the Reuss, by which the lake discharges its waters first into the Aar, and then into the Rhine. By this conveyance, which is all of it in streams of great rapidity, the trees sometimes reach Basle, in a few days after they have left Lucerne; and there the immediate concern of the Alpnach company terminated. They still continue to be navigated down the Rhine in rafts to Holland, and are afloat in the German Ocean in less than a month from having descended from the side of Pilatus, a very inland mountain, not less than a thousand miles distant. The late Emperor of France had made a contract for all the timber thus brought down.

"From the phenomena just described, I have deduced several conclusions, of which at present I can only give a very general account, without entering into any of the mathematical reasonings on which they rest.

"1. The rapidity of the descent is so extraordinary, it is so much greater than any thing that could have been anticipated, exceeding that of a horse at full speed, nearly in the ratio of 3 to 2, that the account seems to tread on the very verge of possibility, and to touch the line that divides between what may, and what cannot exist. The same question, therefore, I have no doubt, has occurred to many that occurred to myself, when I first heard of this extraordinary phenomenon.

"Is it possible that even if there were no friction, and if a body was accelerated along the line of swiftest descent, from a point 2500 feet above another, and horizontally distant from it by 44,009, that it could arrive at that lower point in three or even in six minutes? This was the first question that occurred to me, and at a distance from books as I was then, and in no condition to undertake any nice or difficult calculation, I could only satisfy myself by a rude approximation, that there was nothing in the reported circumstance that was without the limits of possibility. Had the result of the calculation been contrary, I should not only have disbelieved the report, but I should have doubted the testimony of my own senses.

"From a more accurate calculation I find that if no friction nor resistance took place, and if the moving body was allowed to take its flight in the line of the swiftest descent, that it would do so in less than sixty-six seconds. This is the minimum then of time, and we may rest assured, while the laws of nature continue the same that they are now, that no body, in the circumstances just described, can perform its journey in less time than the above.

"But though the descent of the trees at Alpnach contains nothing inconsistent with the acceleration of bodies by gravity, it is not to be reconciled with the notions concerning friction, that are usually received even in the scientific world.

"It is common to consider friction as a force bearing a certain proportion to the weight of the body moved, and as retarding the body by a force proportional to its weight, amounting to a fourth or fifth part, or when least to a tenth or twelfth part of gravity. A body, therefore, that was descending along an inclined plane, would be accelerated by its own gravity, minus the force of friction, a constant force that increased in proportion to the body.

"Now, in the present case, it will soon appear that the retardation is vastly less than would arise from any of these suppositions.

"Supposing it to be true, that friction in a given instance (the surface, the inclination, and the weight, being all given) acts as a uniformly retarding force, I have found that a body sliding along an inclined surface, under the acceleration of gravity, and the retardation of friction, will be accelerated, so that it will have at every point the velocity that would be acquired by falling by its own gravity from a line inclined to the horizon, that is drawn from the point where the body began to move, and that makes with the horizon an angle, the tangent of which is the fraction, that denotes the ratio of friction to gravity. The velocity of the moving body is therefore as the square root, of the portion of a vertical passing through the body, and reaching up to the line just mentioned, or the line of no acceleration.

"As the trees at Alpnach enter the lake with a considerable velocity, it is evident that the line of no acceleration, drawn from the top of the slide, does not reach the ground at the point where the slide ends, but is then still considerably above the surface; the tangent, therefore, of the angle which that line makes with the horizon, is much less than $\frac{1}{17}$. There is reason to think that it does not in reality amount to $\frac{1}{3}$ of this, and is therefore less than $\frac{1}{50}$. It follows, then, that the friction that trees suffer in the slide is less than one-fiftieth of their weight.

"Now, from what can we suppose the small proportion that friction in this instance, bears to the weight, to arise? It is not that the surfaces have a great smoothness or a fine polish. The logs that form the trough are coarsely dressed with the adze, and I observed that there was not even the precaution taken of making the grain of the wood lie downward, or toward the declivity. It was so in the tree, but not in the trees which composed the slide. It is not that any lubricating substance, oil, grease, soap, or black-lead, is interposed between their surfaces. Water is the only substance of this kind that is applied. We have fir rubbing on fir, which is supposed a case remarkably unfavourable to the diminution of friction. It can only arise, therefore, from a principle that some mechanical writers have suspected to exist, but which was never before, I think, proved by the direct evidence of facts, namely, that the force of friction does not increase in the proportion of the weight of the rubbing body, so that heavy bodies are, in reality, less retarded in their motion on an inclined surface than lighter bodies. Thus, the whole of the phenomena I have been describing, tend to prove, especially the fact I mentioned, that heavy trees made their way more easily than light ones, and that a tree must be of a certain magnitude to make its way to the bottom. Friction, therefore, does not bear even in the same materials a given ratio to the weight, but a ratio that evidently decreases as the weight increases; so that, in a fir of ordinary size it is $\frac{1}{10}$, or $\frac{1}{20}$, in one of 100 feet in length it is between $\frac{1}{50}$ and $\frac{1}{60}$. According to what law this change takes place, it would be most useful to investigate; it is an inquiry for those engineers who have strong machinery and great power ready at command.

"I must observe also, that I strongly suspect that friction diminishes with the velocity of the moving or sliding body. That it passes all at once when a body begins to move, to be only half of what it was when the body was at rest, is quite certain, and is proved by many experiments. It seems to me not unlikely that the same progress continues as the motion becomes greater. Perhaps in as much as friction is concerned, the pressure is lessened by the velocity, and the poet was not so far mistaken as he is generally supposed to be, when he said of his heroine

>   Illa vel intactæ segetis per summa volaret
>   Gramina, nec teneras cursu læsisset aristas.

However that be, we have a strong example here of the danger of concluding in many of the researches of mechanics, from experiments made on a small scale to the practice that is to be proceeded on in a great one. It requires some attention to enable us to discriminate between the cases where we can safely proceed from the small to the great, and those in which we cannot. A man, from finding that bodies of a pound or half a pound are in equilibrio when their distances from the fulcrum are inversely as their weights, might, without danger of error, transfer the conclusion to weights of hundreds of tons, or to whole planets, were it possible to make the experiment on so large a scale. But when he finds that the friction of a body of a pound or a hundred weight, is one-fourth of the weight, he cannot, with equal safety, presume that the same will hold when bodies of immense weight and size come to rub against one another. There are many other cases of the same kind. In general, when our experiments lead to the knowledge of a fact and not of a principle, there is caution required in extending the conclusions beyond the limits by which the experiments have been confined. This is the case with the experiments on friction, where we know only facts, and have no principle to guide us; that is, we have not been able to connect the facts with any of the known and measurable properties of body. In the case of the lever, we have connected the fact with the inertia of matter, and the equality of action and reaction. We have, therefore, a right to repose confidence on the one, when extended, though not on the other.

"That friction belongs to the cases in which great caution is necessary in extending the conclusions of experiments, is indeed most strongly evinced by the operations that have now been described, the result of which is such as could not have been anticipated from those experiments. The danger here, however, is quite of an opposite kind from that which commonly takes place in such instances. The experiments on the small scale, usually represent the thing as more easy than it is upon the great, and engage us in attempts that prove abortive, and are followed by disappointments and even ruin. In the present case, the experiments on the small scale represent the thing as more difficult than when tried on a great one it is found to be, and would lead us, by an error, the direct opposite of the last, to conclude things to be impracticable that may be carried into effect with ease. Had the ingenious inventor of the slide at Alpnach been better acquainted with the received theories of friction, or the experiments on which they are founded, even those that are the best, and on the greatest scale, such as those of another most skilful engineer, M. Coulomb, or had he placed more faith in them, he would never have attempted the great work in which he has so eminently succeeded."

The editor of the Edinburgh Philosophical Journal laments that the Professor commits some theoretical errors relative to friction; heavy bodies being less retarded by friction on inclined planes than light bodies; and friction diminishing with velocity: both of which positions have resulted from actual experiment. The same gentleman observes, that on the evening when the paper was read, he suggested to the Professor, Coulomb's discovery that when the touching surfaces were small compared with the pressure, the friction diminished as the velocity increased. It is further supposed that Professor Playfair intended to review his paper, for he declined to have it printed in the Transactions of the Royal Society of Edinburgh.

On Refraction. By JOSEPH READE, M. D.

Philosophical Magazine, No. 287, p. 200.

Our readers will recollect that Dr. Reade has been presented to them before, and by referring back to pages 131, 150, and 193 of this volume, our review may be seen of his successive papers in the Philosophical Magazine. The Doctor has resumed the subject in the last number of that journal, and we now lay before our friends the further arguments he advances to overthrow the doctrine of refraction.

Dr. R. commences with the following experiment. He placed a half crown at the bottom of a cylindrical tumbler, and poured water over it. On looking through the side of the glass, with the eye in the plane of level of the water, or a little above it, he saw the coin. He then intercepted the direct view of the coin from the eye, by a fillet of cloth round the outside of the bottom of the glass; yet he still could see the coin as before, n the plane of the water's surface. And then asks, "Is there not a reflected image formed perpendicularly over the piece of money, capable of being seen by an eye above, below, and on a line with the surface? Does this reflected image send rays, or rather an image, to the spectator's eye?" "To see", says he, "is to believe." Very true; we cannot perhaps mistake the *fact;* but we may, the *cause*.

We agree with Dr. R. that on looking from *below*, a reflection of the rays impresses an image on the eye; but we cannot assent to the assumption of there being any vision of the object at all, when the eye be placed exactly in the plane of the water's surface: at an elevation, however small, *above* that plane, the object may certainly be seen, but this cannot be by *reflection;* for where is the reflecting plane? When the eye be placed *above* the level of the water, we contend that the rays entering the eye are *emergent* not *reflectent*, as from the object through the water. When the eye be *below* the water level, the rays are reflected downwards from the plane of air, in contact with that level. These are the points we contended for in our former observations; and we cannot yet see reason to yield in any degree from our persuasion. These principles lead us to maintain that there is not an image formed at the surface, visible to the eye when above the water level; but that we see the object by the flowing rays becoming divergently refracted, on passing from the denser into the rarer medium. As to Dr. R.'s assertion that on looking down through the water on the half crown, we see the coin one-fourth nearer to the eye; we can merely remark that such a fact would militate directly against his doctrine of the existing image; because the distance of such image must ever be governed by the distance of the eye from it; and not by any fixed mathematical ratio. In short, according to Dr. R.'s theory, the distance of the image from the eye must be governed by the elevation or depression of the one or the other, relatively. We deny his position that "When the eye is placed immediately over the half crown, looking down into the water, we see the image, not the piece of money, one-fourth nearer to the eye: here there can be no refraction, no ratio of 3 to 4. In fact, this simple experiment rebels against all the laws of optics." Whether Snellius were, or were not, correct in his estimate of proportions, we cannot stop to contend; for we think the point not worthy of notice; but we say again, that in viewing the coin as above stated, we do not see any image; we see the half crown itself. Further, we contend that the rays do not flow parallel to the eye, from the coin, through the water and ambient air, although the eye be placed perpendicularly over the centre of the money. The rays flowing upwards from the centre, proceed to the eye without deviation from a right line; but those issuing more remotely from the central point will be divergently refracted from the line joining that point and the eye, in direct proportion with the distance of the issuing rays from that centre; consequently, the rays flowing from the circumference of the coin will be most refracted. The Doctor seems to forget that, from a visible object, rays are issuing in every direction from every point; subject of course (as we hold) to the refractions of their media: and this diffusion of rays in all directions, from individual points, enables us to see a whole, or a part, wherever the light may not be intercepted by an opaque body.— The Doctor, pursuing the research by experiments with the prism, urges the propriety of his principles with, as we humbly think, no better effect. Our general objection would apply to the doctrine attempted to be established, on a wider basis; namely, that we are not inclined to admit the existence of any *image*, formed by the rays, at any point; whether of reflection or refraction; we consider the *image* as formed *in the eye alone*; and that the crossings or bendings of rays, produced by the passage of light through media of different densities, do not form any representation of the object. We have hitherto used the word *image* in compliance with custom; but we beg leave to disclaim all acknowledgment of its proper application, except as to the refractive effect of the optical operation of the eye. This view, if correct, is fatal to the Doctor's theory; which is founded on the existence of an external image, urged as a constant attendant on vision; for the surface of the cornea is external as to the eye. " Cut a square piece of paper about the size of a half crown, and let it be dipped in a tumbler of clear water; on looking at it, it appears as if split into two papers, giving a simple but conclusive illustration of these reflected images."

We concur with the Doctor that this experiment is simple, and conclusive; but not as illustrating the positions he would uphold; for in our mind, not any thing could have been better devised to show the fallacy of his principles. Let any one place the paper horizontally on the surface of the water, the eye being *above* the level; then on pushing the paper gradually downwards, an image (we use the common expression) is seen on the surface, and the object below. If the eye be *below* the water level, and the paper swim on the surface, we see only the object. If the paper be depressed, we see the object magnified in the body of the water; and a reflection of it from the surface; both of which conditions we have particularly explained in our former pages.

The Doctor then adverts to a paper of his, published in an earlier number of the Philosophical Magazine; wherein he endeavoured to show that the mind receives its impression from an image formed on the cornea. This too, we beg leave to deny. The rays of light flowing from an object, and falling on the cornea, are not *arrested there, to form an image*: they are transmitted *through* the cornea, and refracted by the aqueous, crystalline, and vitreous humours, to form an image on the *retina*; if any image at all be formed, any where.

We consider this paper of Dr. Reade's as but a repetition of his previous assertions; not as containing any proof of their accuracy: for we really cannot perceive that his argument strengthens by extension. And if more potent demonstrations, than have yet appeared, cannot be advanced to subvert the Newtonian doctrine of refraction, we need not labour hard to justify the veneration we entertain for it. We do not say this as meaning disrespect to Dr. R. in the remotest degree; for, although we must array ourselves against his opinions, we can duly appreciate the time and trouble he bestows in detecting, and refuting, what to his conceptions may be erroneous.

Observations on the Temperature of Mines in Cornwall. By Mr. M. P. MOYLE.

Annals of Philosophy, No. 16, p. 308.

Mr. Moyle has been induced, he says, to publish these remarks on the subject of subterranean temperature, in consequence of the great difference of result obtained by Mr. Fox in the Dolcoath mine, from that obtained by his own experiments. Mr. F. found the temperature at 10 fathoms to be 50°·18 Fahrenheit, and at 240 fathoms, 82°·04. A jet of water issuing from a vein being constantly at that heat. And asks " what more evident proof can be given of the great heat of the interior state of the globe?" Mr. M. is of opinion that the temperature was merely local, and not to be found at some distance from the spring. He presumes that the increase of heat to be observed at low depths, in mines, is to be attributed to the number of men working in that atmosphere; the lower the level, the more numerous are the miners; amounting to 400 or more at different levels in the Dolcoath mine alluded to. The perspiration, respiration, and radiation from so many animal bodies must, Mr. M. judges, have a very sensible effect on the temperature of the galleries, as well as on their walls. Nor does he allow that Mr. F.'s having placed the bulb of his thermometer " six inches in the body of the rock " is any proof of the temperature observed being naturally that of the earth around.

We agree with Mr. Moyle that the temperature of the air in the crevices must be that, or nearly that, of the gallery; but we cannot think that the animal heat, generated and diffused in the galleries, could at all affect the temperature of the substance of the rock. He states that the mean should always be taken at a distance from the body of the workmen; and to show that these are points of importance, he tells us that " In the Wheal Unity (the same mine Mr. Fox visited) one of the galleries to the western part of the mine, at the depth of about 150 fathoms, which had not been worked for more than 12 months, at the extreme end, there being no current, I found the temperature was just 65°; while the working part, at the same depth, was 74°." Again " In

Wheal Trumpet tin mine, the extreme eastern part, at 75 fathoms in depth, has not been worked for 18 months. This gallery has no other communication with any other part of the mine for a distance of more than twenty fathoms in length. Here the temperature was, two months since 52°: the working part 30 fathoms distant, at the same time, and at the same depth, was 67°; the temperature of the open atmosphere being 60°. At the 86 fathom gallery in this mine, the water that issues from the vein was 51°; while the air of the same place was 68°·7." Mr. M. further says that, as an example of old mines long abandoned, "At the adit level of Old Frevenen tin mine, 14 fathoms from the surface, the temperature was less by 4° than the common atmosphere; most probably owing to the stillness of the air, and not being subject to such quick variations of temperature as on the surface. A shaft in this mine being full of water from the bottom to the adit level, the water proved 2°·5 lower than the atmosphere at the surface; which, in my opinion, clearly proves that had the bottom of this mine (about 110 fathoms) been much warmer than the surface of the earth, its heat would, in the course of eight years, which is the time since she ceased working, have been communicated to this water generally, especially as this shaft is always overflowing; and in which case it would be indicated by the thermometer." Besides, he adds that he could "prove that considerable variation in the temperature of a part of a mine is caused by the different currents of air; being in some places very still and confined, and in others, a few feet distant, so strong that a candle is instantly blown out." He therefore concludes that Mr. Fox has experimented in places where the workmen have been present, and consequently in an atmosphere heated by animal radiation.

Whether this may have been the case with Mr. Fox's experiments, is what we of course cannot determine; but we must say that we cannot infer error in all the observations of others: for we have results recorded, in proof of increasing temperature at increasing depths, which cannot be refuted by these objections: they not being applicable.

Experiments and Observations on the Communication between the Stomach and Urinary Organs; and on the propriety of administering Medicine by Injection into the Veins. By E. HALE, jun., M.D., &c.

North American Review, No. 34, p. 251.

We are told by the reviewer that these dissertations obtained the Boylston premiums for the years 1819 and 1821.

That there is a more direct communication between the stomach and the bladder, than that by the common digestive routine of the bowels, lacteals, &c., has long been suspected; and, we think, shown, by the common processes of nature. Indeed, we agree with the reviewer that the burthen of proof lies entirely on the opponents of this doctrine, who have to contend against common and notorious facts: and had no question ever existed on the subject, no further investigation would have been deemed necessary. We remember some angry controversy on the subject of urinary vomiting, exhibited in the Medical and Physical Journal, some years ago, by writers who consulted their passions, at least as much as they did their judgments or reputations, in endeavouring to bear down an opinion by harshness of manner, that they found too sturdy for their powers of reasoning. They could not well comprehend the process of nature whereby such a result should occur, and so they flatly denied the *fact*.

Experiments recorded by Sir Everard Home in 1818, established the fact of urinary secretion being independant of chylopoietic process; for after tying the pyloric orifice of the stomach, and injecting fluid through the œsophagus, part of the injected matter was found in the spleen, and part also in the urine. Subsequent experiments convinced that gentleman that the spleen was not the channel of urinary passage; but that the cardiac portion of the stomach has the power of dispatching fluids to the bladder, by some undetermined course, when the pyloric passage be closed.

The question then to be determined is, whether, having once got the fluids in this summary way into the circulation, they may not in the ordinary course of the functions be found in the bladder after the short period of time in which this is known to take place, without the necessity of supposing any more direct passage. The object of Dr. Hale is to show that they may, and in this we conceive he has perfectly succeeded.

With this view it was first necessary " to ascertain what length of time it would require for fluids to be carried from the stomach to the bladder, through the medium of the circulation. This can never be ascertained with any degree of precision; yet some approach to the knowledge desired may be made by estimating the rapidity and force of the blood in circulation." Supposing the whole quantity of blood in the body to be thirty pounds, and that thrown out at each contraction of the ventricle, which happens at least seventy times in a minute, to be two ounces; the complete circulation of any one definite portion of blood would be accomplished, according to Dr. Hale, in three minutes and twenty-five seconds; and calculating the quantity thrown out at each contraction at only one ounce and a half, the period would be only extended to five minutes and one second. Now, " the distance from the stomach to the kidneys, through the circulation, is that from the stomach to the heart, through the lungs, back to the left side of the heart, and from the mouth of the aorta to the mouth of the emulgent arteries. This, at the most, cannot be supposed to exceed one half of an entire revolution; and is probably less than one fourth. The time requisite, therefore, as far as the circulation is concerned, for fluids to pass from the stomach to the kidneys, is not more than from two to three and a half minutes, leaving the remainder of the time which actually intervenes between their being taken in drink, and ejected in urine, for their absorption in the stomach, and their secretion and excretion in the kidneys and bladder."

This calculation, which is certainly within bounds, shows sufficiently that there is nothing at all improbable in supposing the passage of fluids to be effected through the circulation and kidneys. Dr. Hale, has, however, by a few well designed experiments, added new certainty to these conclusions. It is unnecessary to enter into any detail of experiments; the results to which they lead we shall state in his own words.

"1. The speedy discharge of watery urine after taking a large quantity of liquid in drink, is not occasioned by sympathetic excitement of the urinary organs, but by the actual excretion of the fluid received.

"2. The same portions of fluid, which are received into the stomach, begin, under certain circumstances at least, to be collected in the bladder within twenty minutes from the time when they are taken.

"3. When a large quantity of fluid is taken, the excretion of urine is greatly increased; but the increase does not bear any very exact proportion to the quantity of drink. The increased discharge begins in about twenty minutes, is at its height in about an hour, and terminates, generally, in less than two hours.

"4. When a liquid, which is coloured with rhubarb, is taken, the colour of the rhubarb appears in the urine: and its appearance in that excretion is not at all confined to the time of the increased discharge, which is occasioned by the quantity of fluids received.

"5. When a liquid, which is of such a nature as to admit of ready detection in the animal fluids, is taken into the stomach, if the quantity is sufficiently large to affect the whole mass of blood, it will be found in the blood drawn from the veins, as soon as in the urine; although it will continue to appear in the urine after it has disappeared from the blood.

"6. When a quantity of colouring matter, sufficient to affect the whole mass of blood is taken, mixed with a large quantity of liquid, the colour appears in the urine, as soon, at least, as the excretion *begins* to be increased, and is at the deepest before the increase of urine is at its height; but if the quantity of colouring matter be only a little more than sufficient to tinge the amount of liquids taken, it does not appear in the urine until after a considerable quantity of watery urine has been passed, and does not give its deepest colour until some time after the excretion has diminished."

"7. The rapidity, with which fluids pass from the stomach to the bladder, is not increased by increasing their quantity."

"8. It results from the whole, that the only mode by which fluids received into the stomach can pass into the bladder, is by absorption into the blood, and subsequent secretion by the kidneys."

The second dissertation, upon the propriety of administering medicine by injection into the veins, derives a peculiar interest, from the circumstance of one of the experiments having been performed upon the person of the author. Injections of various substances into the veins and arteries of animals have been frequently practised for the purpose of determining various physiological facts, and sometimes with the view of ascertaining the probable effects of medicines introduced in this way into the system; yet little seems, so far, to have been done to settle the question as to the expediency of the practice. Some instances are related by Dr. Hale, in which medicines were injected into the veins, nearly two hundred years ago, to whose efficacy, effects truly marvellous were attributed. On these, however, and with good reason, he places but little reliance.

There is a great difference in the effects of foreign substances according to the part of the circulating system into which they are first introduced, and the organ to whose vessels they are first distributed. When the injection is made into the carotid artery, so that the first contact is upon the brain, almost every thing, even venous blood and serum, produces instant death. Water alone, or some substance very much diluted with it, can be introduced with impunity. In other parts of the arterial system, however, where the blood is first distributed to other organs of a less delicate structure and a less important function, the consequences are not necessarily fatal. Into the veins, a great variety of substances may be injected without danger to the life of the animal employed, although, generally speaking, some sensible effects are produced by their presence in the circulating system. "I have injected into the jugular veins of many dogs," says Bichat, "bile taken from the gall bladder of other dogs, which I opened at the same time. For the first few days they appeared to be weary, did not eat, were much altered, their eyes were heavy, and they were constantly lying down; but after some time, they gradually regained their former vigour. I afterwards employed human bile in these experiments; the result was the same, except that many times the animal had hiccough and vomiting some time after the injection. In one instance a dog died in three hours after the experiment; but it was because I made use of that extremely black fluid that is sometimes found in the gall-bladder instead of bile."

The same experiments were repeated, with the substitution of saliva and nasal mucus suspended in water for the bile, and with similar but less marked effects. Urine, of the strongest kind, was also injected in a number of instances. It was fatal in only one, and that upon the seventh day; but the animals were usually made much sicker by it, than by the other substances employed.

"There is no doubt," says the same writer, "that the different substances which can be introduced with the chyle into the blood, may be the cause of various diseases. Is it not the blood which carries to the brain the narcotic principles which produce sleep? Does it not carry turpentine and cantharides to the kidneys, mercury to the salivary glands, &c.? Inject opium, wine, &c. into the veins, and you will stupify the animal, the same as if you had given them by the stomach. Physiologists were, at one time, much engaged with the introduction of medicinal infusions into the veins of living animals. They circulated by these infusions, purgatives, emetics, and a thousand other foreign substances, the contact of which the blood bore, without occasioning any other accident to the animal, than that of vomiting or alvine evacuations, if they were emetics or purgatives, and a greater or less general derangement, if they were other foreign substances, which had no affinity with any particular organ. The caustics, as the nitric and sulphuric acids, and other very irritating substances, have alone caused death in these curious experiments."

Of the results of all the various experiments, which have been performed by different individuals, with regard to the injection of fluids into the veins, Dr. Hale observes, "that they are different in different cases, and sometimes give rise to opposite inferences; but the general effect of the whole is to lead to the belief, that the effects of medicinal substances are not materially different, in consequence of the modes of their introduction into the system."

The experiments of Fontana, for instance, offer different results from those obtained by Brodie, Magendie, and Orfila, in their investigation of the effects of the different poisons, when introduced into the circulation.

Fontana, as quoted by our author, found that the oil or water of cherry laurel, although a virulent and deadly poison when taken into the stomach, is almost inert when taken into the circulation by a wound or by injection into the veins. Brodie, Magendie, and Orfila, however, found that arsenic or tartar emetic, when injected into the veins, produced nearly the same effects, as when taken into the stomach, except that they were more violent in degree. The opposite results of these different physiologists are, we conceive, attributable to the different nature of the substances employed, Fontana having used a vegetable, and the other individuals mineral poisons in their experiments. The striking differences between the different classes of poisons are sufficiently well known.

The experiments of Dr. Hale were performed, with one exception, upon rabbits, and the substances injected were some of the common articles of the materia medica. Comparative trials were instituted, in which the same articles were administered by the mouth, in order to ascertain precisely their relative operation. In the first experiment two rabbits were taken, and two drachms of castor oil administered to each—to one by injection into the vein, to the other in the usual way. On the latter, no sensible effect was produced. In the former, copious operation took place from the bowels, which continued for some hours. A few days after this experiment, the same animals were made the subject of another, in which a drachm and a half of an infusion of rhubarb was injected into the veins of the one which swallowed the oil in the former experiment, and two drachms of the same infusion administered by the mouth to the other, who had previously undergone injection; in the latter, a slight operation took place within the next twenty-four hours—but in the other, no sensible effect was produced.

The sixth, seventh, eighth, and ninth experiments were occupied in ascertaining the effects of medicinal substances when taken into the stomach of rabbits. Six drachms of an infusion of colocynth, containing the strength of about twenty-two grains of that drug—four drachms of an infusion of ipecacuanha, of about the same strength—four drachms of an infusion of rhubarb—two scruples of ipecacuanha in powder, were sucessively given to different subjects, without any operation, which could decidedly be pronounced to be produced by the medicine; certainly none upon the stomach. Ten grains of tartar emetic were then administered without any sensible operation, but the next morning the animal was found dead.

In the eleventh experiment, twenty grains of calcined magnesia were intended to be injected in five drachms of water. Scarcely half a drachm of the mixture was thrown in before convulsions ensued, and death was produced in less than four minutes. Death followed with equal rapidity after the injection of two drachms of undiluted alcohol, though the same animal had a few moments before borne two drachms of a mixture of equal parts of alcohol and water, without any very serious effects. A drachm and a half of a solution of tartrite of potass and soda was borne without any bad consequences, and seemed to cause a slight operation upon the bowels; but two drachms of the sulphate of magnesia, dissolved in half an ounce of water, caused death before one third of the quantity could be injected. The injections were all made into the jugular vein.

But the most interesting and important experiment was that performed upon his own person; and it is, we believe, the only well authenticated one, in modern times at least, in which any medicinal substance has been injected into the veins of the human subject. The substance selected in this instance was castor oil, and the quantity, half an ounce, a small dose for an adult. This was thrown in at an opening made in one of the veins of the arm, commonly selected for bleeding, and at the temperature of about seventy degrees. The intrepidity, resolution, and perseverance with which this experiment was designed and performed were not a little remarkable; and it was accomplished under circumstances of difficulty and embarrassment, which would have made almost any operator, particularly in his own person, shrink from following up his undertaking. His sensations after the experiment are best detailed in his own words.

"I felt very well for a short time after the operation was finished. The first unusual sensation that I perceived, was a peculiar feeling, or taste of oiliness in the mouth, a little after twelve o'clock; (about ten minutes after the oil had been completely injected;) very soon after, while I was washing the blood from my arm and hands, and was talking in very good spirits, I felt a slight nausea with eructations, and some commotion in the bowels, then a singular and indescribable feeling seemed very suddenly to ascend to my head. At the same instant I felt a slight stiffness of the muscles of the face and jaw, which cut short my speaking in the middle of a word, accompanied by a bewildered feeling in my head, and a slight faintness. I sat down, and in a few moments recovered myself a little."

For two hours after the completion of the experiment, Dr. Hale continued to experience a strange sensation in his head, a degree of nausea, the oily taste in his mouth, and a tendency to alvine evacuation evinced by wandering pains, &c. in his bowels, but without any real operation. The former symptoms left him after this period, but these deceptive feelings in the bowels remained through the evening, though there was no operation at any time which could be attributed to the oil.

The next day some unpleasant symptoms ensued, of a different character.

"I had some pain in the head, and was all day much inclined to chilliness, though without true rigors. My arm was quite painful through the day. I had some fever and loss of appetite, and felt altogether too ill to make any use of my faculties, either of body or mind. This state continued several days; and when I began to recover from it, I found my strength so much diminished, that it required two or three weeks to restore it to its former vigour."

These symptoms, we conceive, however, and we presume

Dr. Hale to be of the same opinion, are to be in a very considerable degree attributed to the sympathy of the system with the injury to the arm occasioned by the operation, and not to the effect of the presence of the oil in the circulation. They were not different in their nature, nor greater in degree, than might be expected from the violence done to the parts about the vein. And although they would not be necessarily always the consequence of such an operation, yet so great is the probability of their occurrence, as to form an almost insurmountable objection to the adoption of the practice.

But in addition to these unpleasant consequences, there seems to be sufficient ground on other considerations to relinquish the expectation of finding in the injection of medicines into the veins, an advantageous mode of introducing them into the system.

" On a review of the whole subject," says Dr. Hale, " we find that the evacuations, occasioned by the operation of emetics and cathartics, might be procured quite as effectually, and even more so, by injecting them into the veins, as by introducing them into the stomach; but that it would be dangerous in the extreme to administer in this manner any of the emetics, or of the more powerful cathartics; and that the injection of even the milder cathartics is attended by much more pain and inconvenience, than can be counterbalanced by any advantages that it seems to promise. We must, therefore, regard this mode of administering medicines as too full of dangers to be entitled to confidence."

In this conclusion we perfectly agree, and presume that few, after the experience of Dr. Hale, will be inclined to put it again to the test of experiment, either on themselves or others. For all practical purposes, there can be little room for difference of opinion about the expediency of adopting the injection of medicinal substances as a means of curing diseases. Whatever may be the results of this operation upon other animals, they never can inspire sufficient confidence to justify us in making our fellow beings the subjects of such a series of severe and hazardous experiments, as would be necessary in order to establish the practice upon a sure basis; so that even were it determined as a matter of physiological interest, that similar results follow from the injection of medicinal substances, in man as in other animals, we conceive that few would be hardy enough to take upon themselves the risk and responsibility of the operation, in cases of disease.

Dr. Hale states very candidly, in his introduction, some of the objections to experiments upon living animals, and observes, with great truth, that " thousands of animals have died in the cause of physiological science, whose deaths have scarcely added any thing to our knowledge of the laws or properties of the human system." Now we are not at all disposed to deny, that there are questions in physiology which can only be decided by means of experiments on living animals; and such experiments, when performed in the course of a regular train of investigation, may be made to throw much light upon some of the dark points in the science of life. But their necessity and importance has been, we conceive, very much overrated. They have been, and are resorted to, as modes of proof upon the most trivial occasions, and too often unlimited confidence has been placed upon the deductions drawn from them, when they least deserved it.

Experiments have an imposing air when brought in support of any opinion, and they are too apt to command our implicit belief, without a sufficient examination of their claim to it. Yet surely men are as liable to be mistaken in the results of the experiments they perform, as they are to be wrong in the opinions they hold. Before we give full faith to deductions from experiments made upon living animals, we ought to assure ourselves that the operator is competent to the undertaking. The qualities necessary to it are rarely to be met with; one should have, not only the anatomical knowledge and manual dexterity of the most accomplished surgeon; but a thorough acquaintance with the whole science of physiology, and more especially of the particular subject before him. He should add also to these qualifications a clear, unprejudiced, and philosophical mind, capable of drawing accurate inferences from the phenomena that occur. Yet these circumstances are seldom taken into consideration, and an *experiment* would be received as conclusive from a quarter, whence an *opinion* merely would meet with little regard.

But it should be recollected, that there are probably more men qualified to form an *opinion* deserving of attention, than to perform an *experiment*; the latter presupposing even more rare qualities than the former. And, besides, when we decide between the comparative value of opinion and argument on the one hand, and experiment upon the other, we ought to consider that we are more competent judges of the former, than of the latter; we can estimate the weight and importance of men's arguments, and the grounds of their reasoning; but we cannot their powers of observing accurately, or of reporting truly. Hence the remark, we believe of Dr. Cullen, that there were more false facts than false theories in medicine, is found abundantly true.

We have only to look at the history of some physiological questions for evidence of the truth of these remarks; in which, after some important facts have been brought to light with regard to them by men of genius, they have been involved in fresh darkness by the accumulation around them of a mass of ill-contrived and ill-digested experiments. Let us not be mistaken; we do not intend to deny, that experiments upon living animals, performed by those competent to the task, with relation to subjects which are capable of being illustrated in this way, and without such injury and laceration of organs as throw into complete disorder all the functions of the system, may be of much service in enlightening some parts of the science of physiology. But when they are performed in the mere wantonness of philosophy, with scarce any other definite object, than that of gaining a name by eliciting some striking phenomena in the struggles of nature, which shall have the air of important discoveries, they are useless at best.

That we do not exaggerate in speaking on this subject, we think will be made evident by the following sketch of some *interesting* experiments on vomiting, performed within a few years at Paris.

M. Magendie, in order to prove that the stomach was inert in the act of vomiting, asserts, that when two fingers were introduced through an incision into the abdomen, the stomach was found not to act itself, but to be compressed between the diaphragm and abdominal muscles; that if the incision was enlarged so as to bring the stomach out of the wound, vomiting ceased, and the stomach remained quiet, although tartar emetic was injected into the veins; that if the abdominal muscles are cut away, vomiting is still produced by the compression of the stomach against the linea alba by the diaphragm, but that if this latter organ be incapacitated by dividing the phrenic nerves, vomiting is at an end. To crown all, M. Magendie removed the stomach, substituted a pig's bladder, which he connected with the œsophagus, and then having sewed up the abdomen, injected tartar emetic into the veins, and succeeded in producing vomiting.

So far all seems very well; but another inquirer, M. Maingault, having taken up the same subject, arrived by experiments performed, like Magendie, on living animals, at results directly opposite. He succeeded in producing vomiting, by strangulating an intestine, and by injecting tartar emetic, after dividing the abdominal muscles, cutting them off from the body, dividing the phrenic nerves, and even after completely removing the diaphragm itself. *Memoir sur le Vomissement*, 1813.

We know of no way of reconciling conclusions so diametrically opposite from a course of investigation so similar in each case; and fear there is no other mode of deciding the controversy, but by engaging afresh in the perpetration of these truly edifying experiments.

There are other sources of investigation, from which, if we are willing to resort to them, we can derive nearly all the information and the facts which we need. Nature presents, in the different kinds of animals, the organs and functions so variously constructed and so variously combined, that by tracing out their history accurately through all their varieties, we can come at the truth on most difficult subjects, as well as by having recourse to experiments upon living animals. Nature, in fact, does that which is equivalent to the experiments we perform, by presenting to us, in different classes of animals, the organs in those combinations and under those relations and circumstances, which it is the object of our operations to establish. Thus, it has been doubted by some whether the bile were formed in the liver, or in the gall-bladder, or in both. How are we to proceed, if we would settle the question by experiment on living animals? We must lay open the abdomen and dissect out the liver, or tie the duct which communicates it with the common biliary canal, or have recourse to some other expedient more ingenious still. How does Haller decide this question? By comparative anatomy. "It is found," says he, "that in many, even large animals, true bile is prepared by a liver alone, without any gall-bladder. That, on the other hand, no animal has a gall-bladder, without having also a liver—and none a gall-bladder so far separated from the liver, but that it is either connected with it directly or communicates with its excretory duct. We conclude then, that a liver is necessary for the secretion of bile, but that a gall-bladder is not necessary—and that it passes from the liver into the gall-bladder." Now who will doubt which method of investigation is most likely to give a satisfactory result? We are convinced that many subjects which still remain involved in obscurity, notwithstanding the innumerable experiments made upon living animals in order to illustrate them—and we may mention particularly the functions and relations of the nervous system—might be placed in a much clearer point of view, by throwing upon them the light which may be derived from the careful study of comparative anatomy and general physiology.

On the Effects produced on the Human Countenance by Paralysis of the different Systems of Facial Nerves. By JOHN SHAW, Esq. Journal of Science, No. 25, p. 120.

Mr. Shaw having resumed this subject, we are now able to present our readers with a continuation of it, from pages 234 and 261, of this volume.

Mr. S. proposes to further elucidate this most interesting object of inquiry, by the detail of cases, illustrating the facts of the portio dura and 5th pair, being nerves specifically appropriated to distinct effect.

He states that the two systems will seldom, or never, be found paralyzed at the same time. If future experience confirm this idea, it may lead to important conclusions.

Also, that if the actions influenced by the unaffected nerves, of the one set, be excited; the distortion, arising from the paralysis of the other set, will disappear for the time. The first case is that of " complete paralysis of those actions of the muscles of the face, which are regulated by one of the nerves of the superadded or additional system: viz. the portio dura, or respiratory nerve of the face."

Rebecca Larkin, 12 years of age, possesses good faculties of mind. She lost the use of her limbs when two years old, but regained her powers in a few months; and about seven years since, her mother first discovered a distortion of countenance. This is not perceptible when her face is quiet; but when excited, as in laughter, it is much distorted; in consequence of the muscles of the left side only being in action. When the laughter be violent it is all on the left side; the right remaining unmoved. And when making an effort to laugh, with the right side, the angle of the mouth is raised; but by an action evidently regulated by the fifth pair: and the countenance is said to assume an excessive drollery of expression, similar to that of a certain public mimic, to whom allusion was made in our former pages. On attempting to whistle, she could not close the right side of the mouth: but she could purse it up, by aid of the fifth pair influencing the orbicularis muscle; and when blowing, she could sound a whistle placed in her mouth; but in doing so, the right cheek did not contract: it remained distended like a leathern bag; the muscles being in such a condition as they would be if the right portio dura had been divided.

To determine the actions influenced by the fifth, it was observed that, during eating, the buccinator muscle was active; indeed she preferred eating on that side, and had always done so. This showed, says Mr. S., " that the same muscles of the mouth that were paralytic in those actions which are subservient to expression and respiration, were perfect in any voluntary action."

Ammonia was inhaled by the left nostril only; and the expression of sneezing confined to it. The left nostril being closed, the right could not snuff, nor sneeze, though the eyes watered with the strength of the vapour.

The right nostril was irritated by a feather; and the symptoms of approaching sneezing were excited on the left side; proving the power of the fifth pair.

The right orbicularis oculi was weaker than the left; and wasted. She cannot exert it as she can the left. When sneezing or laughing, it is unmoved. She cannot frown, nor corrugate the right eye-brow; but she has a power over the muscles of the head, apparently analogous with that over the right cheek, when attempting to laugh; nor can she close the eye-lid when startled: all which defects are imputed to the paralysis of the portio dura, because resembling those exhibited by the dog, whose corresponding nerve was cut.

She has lost the power of vision in her right eye; but the motions of the iris are perfect. Mr. Shaw conjectures that there is less sympathy between the retina and iris, in paralysis of different nerves of the head, than has been generally supposed.

Having ascertained that the actions excited by the portio dura were the only ones in the face paralyzed by nervous disease, he examined those of the limbs and body, (which are supplied with nerves from the original class) and found them all perfect.

The next case noticed is one of hemiplegia following apoplexy—J. Cooper. Resembles that of an old paralytic; the right side being affected. The arm and leg powerless; intellects impaired; and memory gone. When made to laugh, the right cheek sympathizes slightly with the left. When he blows, the right buccinator acts fully. When the nostrils are irritated by ammonia, the muscular actions preparatory to sneezing, are equal on both sides; therefore, the muscles on both sides are presumed to be perfect in action, as regulated by the respiratory or portio dura; and comparable with the condition of the muscles as related in the last case, when sneezing was excited.

Next Mr. S. inquires respecting the actions dependant on the fifth pair. The right cheek, and side of the mouth, are lower than the left. Could not, by the buccinator, remove bread put into the right side of the mouth; but this power was perfect in the left. Saliva flows from the right side. Could not hold a pencil, &c. on the right side of the mouth.

He was insensible to the prick of a needle on the right cheek, but not on the left: the same respectively, when hairs were plucked from his beard.

Being satisfied of the defective state of the fifth, in power over the muscles of the face and cheek, and influence on the sensibility of the skin; Mr. S. proceeded to examine the nose. Ammonia excited similar actions in both nostrils; showing symptoms of sneezing; therefore the nerve on the paralyzed side was in a state different from that in the last case. The power of the fifth being tried, not any effort could be produced by tickling the right nostril, but the left was excitable.

The eye and eye-lids being examined, the ball of the eye followed a moving pencil; proving the powers of the musculi oculi. The pupil was not noticed: but, in other cases of hemiplegia, it has been found most dilated on the paralytic side.

The orbicularis oculi, and corrugator supercilii, on the right side, could be completely excited: evincing, as Mr. S. thinks, that the actions of the eye-brow, which are defective under paralysis of the portio dura, are perfect in common palsy. We think it may be prudent to pause before we lay this down as an aphorism; for possibly the further researches of Mr. Shaw, and others, may require the expression to be in some degree modified.

The levator palpebræ, partly supplied by the fifth, is slightly paralyzed; but paralysis of the levator palpebræ, and iris, being common, and often unattended by palsy, differ, in nervous influence, from the muscles of the cheeks.

The tongue appeared perfect in its muscular functions, so that the motor linguæ, or ninth nerve, was in a healthy state. Mr. S. suggests that this nerve does not wholly control the motions of the tongue; for in cutting it in a dog, he could lap milk, but had lost the power of swallowing.

Mr. S. next examined the powers of taste and sense in the tongue, as regulated by the third branch of the fifth pair. On the paralyzed side, sensibility was wanting; and so was the power of taste. Examining the shoulders, and muscles of respiration of the chest and abdomen, it was found that, in long inspiration, or attempt to sneeze, the shoulders were alike raised; but, on making a voluntary effort to raise the right shoulder, the loss of power equalled that over the leg of the same side.

Not any difference was perceptible to the hand, when applied to the shoulders and ribs on both sides, during hard respiration.

Mr. Shaw concludes this case with suggesting that, in common hemiplegia, the respiratory nerves of the chest are as little affected as the portio dura of the face; and by the facility of respiration, proves a distinction from disorder in the par vagum and other respiratory nerves. And he infers from the two foregoing cases the truth of his proposition, " that *when either system of nerves be attacked by disease, the symptoms are different.* It only requires that a number of cases should be detailed to prove that *the two systems are seldom or never affected at the same time."* A conclusion that, however probable, must, at present, be received " cum grano salis."

The following case is considered, by Mr. Shaw, as a very uncommon one, and as particularly illustrating the distinction between the two foregoing.—Mr. Cæsar Hawkins had taken the history of the earlier stages of the case very carefully.

Phipps, a bricklayer, living in Brunswick Mews, Bryanstone Square, fell thirty feet down from a scaffold. The right clavicle was broken; the right loin and hip were bruised; a contusion was received on the head; a puffiness formed behind the right ear; with bleeding from the ear and nose.

When taken to the hospital, on the 1st of September, he was in a state of stupor, but recovered in the course of the day: and for several days, appeared to suffer from concussion only. On the fourth day the angle of the mouth was observed to be drawn aside; and also that there was an inequality in the state of the pupils. On the 6th, when asleep, the right eye was observed to be more than half open. On the 1st of October he was made an out patient. On the 17th, Mr. Shaw and Mr. Hawkins visited him: they found the face resembling that of a paralytic from apoplexy;—the mouth was drawn strongly to the left side, and the distortion extreme, at every effort of expression. The right side of the face passive, while the left is active; cannot close the lips; nor blow: evidently from inaction of the right side, owing to defective power in the respiratory nerve.

Next as to the powers of the fifth pair. Right cheek, and right side of the mouth, hung down bag-like, totally powerless. The buccinator equally so.

Sensibility in the left cheek perfect; in the right wanting: the same as to the sides of the jaws. Also, as to the muscles of the nostrils. Excitability of the fifth, on the interior, omitted to be tried.

Eye-lids and eye-brow, as in paralysis of portio dura; being both powerless.

As to the fifth of the eye, and eye-lids; there was an apparent anomaly; both sides being equally sensible, leading these gentlemen to suspect, from " this, and the state of the levator palpebræ, that the first division of the fifth was not so much affected as the second and third." The right masseter and temporalis muscles were perfect; explainable, perhaps, as Mr. S. conjectures, by a better knowledge of the divisions of the fifth. The muscles of the right eye had power; but did not act in unison with those of the left: for he saw double. The pupils were alike in power. The injury behind the ear has lost all superficial trace; but he remains very deaf. The tongue is perfect, in all its motions; whence Mr. S. infers the perfection of the motor linguæ, or ninth, and the glosso pharyngeal. With respect to the fifth of the tongue, it was noticed that, taste and sensibility were totally wanting on the right side.

The fauces and larynx were in good states: for he could swallow and utter.

The neck, shoulders, and leg of the right side were perfect in power, on the 16th of November; though the face was paralyzed as much as ever. Mr. Shaw proceeds to observe on the case thus:

" This case differs from the common examples of partial paralysis of the face; and also, from those of hemiplegia. From the first, not only in there being evident marks of paralysis while the muscles of the face are at rest; but in the power of the muscles being lost during the action of eating; and also in the sensibility of the skin of the same side being, in a great measure, destroyed. The first difference that we observed in it, from one of common hemiplegia is, that the paralysis is confined to the face. Secondly, that the paralysis is on the same side with that on which the head is injured. Thirdly, that the palsy is more evident, when the patient is made to sneeze or laugh; showing that in this instance the muscles are deficient, not only in the powers which they receive from the fifth, but also in the influence given by the seventh. The cause of the paralysis in this case is, I think, to be ascribed, not to any affection of the brain generally; but to an injury of the portio dura, and a great part of the fifth; either at their origin; or in their passage through the bones of the head."

Mr. Shaw's reasons for so concluding are, that the quality and degree of the powers injured, resemble, in part, those defects ensuing when the portio dura be cut. The bleeding from the ear and deafness he considers to have arisen from injury done to the petrous portion of the temporal bone, whereby the fifth, in its passage from the brain, has been impaired. And that the sense of taste and touch being lost, on the right side of the tongue, (not *always* the consequence of apoplexy,) is caused by injury sustained by the third division of the fifth; the phenomena according with those presenting when the fifth be divided.

Mr. S. requests attention to the circumstance of perfection in the functions of the organs of respiration and circulation (which are supplied with nerves from the superadded system) in a patient, who has entirely lost muscular power of one side. He urges on our notice, as an important fact that, paralysis of the *face alone*, may generally be attributed to some *local* cause; and, therefore, to be less considered as a subject of apprehension. Mr. S., after pointing out the utility of a correct knowledge of the nervous distributions on the face, as guiding the knife of a judicious operator, concludes thus:

"The importance of the discussion is sufficiently proved by the circumstance, that not less than eighteen cases of different kinds of paralysis, the causes of which were hitherto but very imperfectly understood, have come within my limited opportunities of observation, in the course of the last twelve months."

We will not trouble our readers with a repetition of the estimate we put upon this object of research. Fortunately, it is in able hands; and we feel the fullest confidence that some useful practical results will ensue from its further pursuit. At all events, it constitutes a demonstrated proof of the necessity of a diligent study in this part of anatomical inquiry; and that, to be useful, the medical attendant must be a learned neurologist.

An Account of the Cultivation of Mushrooms. By Mr. THOMAS ROGERS, Gardener to EDWARD JENKINS, Esq. F. H. S., Thorpe Hall near Peterborough.

Transactions of London Horticultural Society.

Having met with considerable success in the cultivation of *Mushrooms*, both as regards the quantity and the quality of the produce, I am naturally led to ascribe it to the method I have practised. I will first speak of the preparation of the spawn, which I manage in the following manner.

I collect pure cow-dung, not fresh, but such as I happen to find in the park, the fields, or the farm-yard; with this I mix the scrapings of roads, in the proportion of one half of the latter article to one of the former, adding to it about one third or a fourth of vegetable mould, obtained from leaves or decayed sticks. These ingredients being well worked up together, the compost is formed into bricks about nine inches long, three and a half broad, and two thick. The bricks are exposed to the air and sun, and suffered to attain such a degree of solidity, as to bear a considerable pressure, but not to dry hard. They are then removed to a shed, for the purpose of being laid up in *strata*. Three or four rows are first placed on the ground, with interstices of about one inch in width between the rows and the bricks: into these interstices or spaces, loose spawn, such as is found in the litter of old mushroom beds, is scattered; and over the whole surface of the layer, such spawny litter is likewise spread. Should there be no old mushroom beds at hand to furnish the scatterings, some spawn bricks must be broken to pieces in order to supply them. The first layer having been thus treated, another is put upon it, and likewise interspersed and covered with spawn and litter from old beds. A third and fourth stratum may be laid on, or more, and regulated in the same manner. The whole pile being completed according to the quantity that is required, it is covered over with hot stable dung, and litter; and in two, three, or more weeks, according to the state of the weather, the bricks are filled with spawn, and may be laid by for use. I will not hazard an opinion, whether the cow-dung itself contains the element of spawn, or only acts the part of a *matrix* or receptacle; but this I can state, that mushroom spawn is generated in other dung, besides horse-dung; for I once found it plentifully in pigeon's dung. As I have used this preparation of spawn for a length of time, the essence of cow-dung must entirely preponderate in my composition; though the origin of the spawn should at first have been derived from horse-dung. I may add, that, when managed in the manner I have described, it yields spawn as productive as any that can be obtained. I was formerly taught to believe that it was essential to mix a portion of horse-dung in the bricks; but my experience has since convinced me, that cow-dung alone answers the purpose. The spawn is generated in it plentifully, and of a good quality.

It is of importance that the bricks alluded to should not be left in a situation which would cause the spawn to work; an effect which would be produced by moisture, combined with warmth. Therefore, when the spawn is bred, the bricks must be laid in a dry place, to prevent the process of germination. The spawn must not be suffered to advance towards the rudiments of the mushroom, which consist in little threads or fibres; for in this state it ceases to be useful in spawning a bed. As soon as the rudiments are formed, they must be left undisturbed, or they perish. They will grow into a mushroom on the spot where they are developed; but when removed or torn up, they are destroyed. A piece of spawn which appears in filaments or fibres, is no longer applicable to a mushroom bed: it may produce a mushroom in itself, but can serve no other purpose. The spawn that is to be inserted in a bed, and to receive its developement there, must not be gone so far, but should only have the appearance of indistinct white mould.

The spawn being duly prepared, the beds are next to be considered. I have generally made them in a shed, against the wall, sloping from the wall, downwards; about two feet high at the back, and perhaps a little less than one foot in front. The materials for the bed are horse-dung mixed with litter, such as is commonly used for hot-beds: dry leaves may be added; or the greater part, if not the entire bed, may consist of leaves. I do not employ the dung fresh, but after it has lain on a dunghill, and has been frequently turned and well worked. There must be no rank heat in it, for the spawn would be killed by an excess of warmth. The temperature of the bed should be between 50° and 60°: from 52° to 55° may be quite sufficient. When the temperature is reduced to a proper state, the spawn is inserted. If the bed happen to be dry, I put a layer of moist manure, of the same quality, from the dunghill, upon the spawn; or if, on the other hand, the bed be too moist, I put a layer of drier manure over it: these layers I make about two inches thick. The mode of spawning is the usual one; namely, the bricks are broken into small pieces, which are inserted at three or four inches distance from one another. The beds are earthed over about one inch and a half thick, and ultimately covered with hay of different thickness, according to the state of the season. I have never made use of fire heat; but always succeeded in regulating the temperature of my beds by means of covering. I scarcely ever have occasion to water the beds, owing to the materials of which they are composed.

The produce from beds of this description has been ample, and the quality of the mushrooms excellent, rich, and well flavoured: they are of great size and thickness, when suffered to grow; one, for example, weighed eighteen ounces. They yield abundance of juice, when dressed, or prepared for catsup. There is no doubt that their quality depends upon the manner in which they are nourished: if they are meagerly fed, their flavour and substance will be poor in proportion. Thence, artificial mushrooms are, generally, richer and higher flavoured than those which grow naturally: and again, among the artificial produce, those will surpass which are reared on large and deep beds.

The Method of Propagating choice Dahlias, by grafting their Shoots on the Tubers of the Roots of the more common kinds. By Mr. THOMAS BLAKE, Gardener to JAMES VERE, Esq. F. H. S., Kensington Gore, in a letter to the Secretary of the L. H. S.

Sir,—In compliance with your desire, I send you an account of my manner of propagating *Double Dahlias* on the roots of single ones. Should it be thought deserving a place in the Transactions of the Horticultural Society, I shall be gratified by the distinction shown to my communication.

Necessity is the mother of invention; and so it operated with me in the subject now before you: for, not being able to procure plants of Double Dahlias, but having opportunities of obtaining cuttings from my brother gardeners, I was induced to try the experiment of grafting them, in preference to striking the cuttings, which is a tedious process. I first attempted it last year, but began too late to succeed well; for unless the new plant form eyes for the succeeding year, it is nothing more than annual; and the work must be done early to effect this object. In the present season I have succeeded beyond my most sanguine expectations, and therefore proceed to give you the details of my practice.

The cutting intended for the graft should be strong, and short-jointed, having on it two or more joints or buds; it must be also procured as soon in the season as possible:

when obtained, select a good tuber of a single sort, taking especial care that it has no eyes; with a sharp knife (for a dull edge would mangle the fleshy root, make it jagged, and so prevent a complete adhesion) cut off a slice from the upper part of the root, making, at the bottom of the part so cut, a ledge whereon to rest the graft; this is recommended, because you cannot tongue the graft as you do a wood shoot, and the ledge is useful in keeping the cutting fixed in its place while you tie it: next, cut the scion sloping, to fit; and cut it so that a joint may be at the bottom of it, to rest on the aforesaid ledge: a union may be effected without the ledge, provided the graft can be well fixed to the tuber; but the work will not then be so neat. It is of advantage, though not absolutely necessary, that a joint should be at the end of the scion, for the scion will occasionally put forth new roots from that lower joint: the stem is formed from the upper joint: I therefore procure the cuttings with the two lower joints as near together as possible. After the graft has been tied, a piece of fine clay, such as is used for common grafting, must be placed round it: then put the root in fine mould, in a pot of such a size as will bury the graft half way in the mould: place the pot in a little heat, in the front of a cucumber or melon frame, if you chance to have one in work at the time: I prefer the front, for the greater convenience of shading and watering, which are required. A striking-glass may be put over the graft, or not, as you please. In about three weeks the root should be shifted into a larger pot, if it be too soon to plant it in the border, which will probably be the case; for, supposing the work was begun in March, the plant cannot go out till the end of May; so that the shifting will be very essential, to promote its growth till the proper season of planting out shall arrive.

The specimens I have sent for exhibition will show how perfectly the new plant is formed on, and united to, the old root: you will also observe, that the eyes from whence the shoots of next year are to proceed, are only on that part which was next the graft; whilst the old tuber remains solely to furnish nutriment to the new plants, from the roots which issue from its lower end. I, remain, Sir, &c.

An Improved Mode of propagating Trees, &c. by Laying. By SAMUEL TAYLOR, Esq. of Moston, near Manchester.

Technical Repository, No. IV. p. 263.

The editor of the Repository states that this method of propagating trees was many years since communicated to him by Mr. Taylor. It resembles the usual process of laying carnations, pinks, &c., and is effected nearly similar to that recommended by Mr. Judd for Forcing the Vine, as described in our present volume, page 285. "Incisions or slits are made below the foot-stalk of each leaf, and extended a little above it; and by cutting off, carefully, the sharp spurs, or ends, of each tongue, so as to cause them to throw out a semicircle of fibres; instead of a few at the points only. The branch is then to be secured by hooks or pegs placed between each incision, to the surface of the earth, if that can be conveniently accomplished, by bending down the branch: or, if that cannot be done, placed in a broad pan or pot, supported upon a proper stand: and it must be covered with earth to the depth of about an inch only, the end of the branch remaining uncovered. The branch being thus supplied with nourishment from the parent tree, will soon shoot out, *both roots and stems, from each foot-stalk:* and when properly struck, may be cut across, between each layer, and taken up carefully, so as to disturb the fibres of the root as little as may be, and planted out: and thus *form a new tree from each individual foot-stalk.*"

These methods of propagation have the important advantage of excluding the casualties of seminal growth, as well as that of yielding a multiple of the original at a far more matured stage of production.

Account of a Method of forcing Asparagus, practised by Mr. Wm. Ross, Gardener to Edward Ellice, Esq., Wyke House, &c. By JOSEPH SABINE, Esq., F.R.S. and Sec.

Transactions of the London Horticultural Society.

The general appearance of the forced asparagus, used at table in the months of December, January, and February, is a sufficient indication of defective management in its production. When I first examined the method practised by Mr. Thomas Hogg, for forcing early potatoes (of which an account is given in this work), it occurred to me, that the same principle might be applied to raising early asparagus, viz. that of placing the roots of the plants over a substratum, not in a state of fermentation, and by introducing into the bed the warmth necessary to force them, from hot linings to the sides; for I considered that the weak and drawn state of forced asparagus is occasioned by the action of the dung immediately on its root.

My opinions, I think, are confirmed by the successful practice of Mr. William Ross, who, in the month of January, had some of the strongest asparagus I ever noticed at that season. He sent a sample, at my request, to the General Meeting of the Horticultural Society in February last, and has given me the following account of his practice. The pits in which his *succession pines* are kept in the summer, have at bottom a layer of leaves, about eighteen inches deep, covered with the same thickness of tan, which becomes quite cold when the pines are removed. In one of the pits he spread over the entire surface of the old tan a quantity of asparagus roots, which he covered with six inches more of tan, and applied linings of hot dung, successively renewed, round the sides, keeping up thereby a good heat. This was done in the middle of December, and in five weeks the crop was fit for use. As soon as the shoots made their appearance, and during the day-time, he took off the lights, introducing as much air as possible, which gave them a good natural colour, and the size was nearly as large as if they had been produced in the open ground, at the usual season.

I observed to Mr. Ross that I thought the plan would be improved if the roots were planted in mould, rather than in tan; in this point he agreed with me, observing, that he would nevertheless retain the underlayer of eighteen inches of tan, which, he was convinced, would be of great service, since it so readily admitted the passage of the heat; and that he should, in all cases, prefer the use of a bed so constructed, to the cold dung-beds of Mr. Hogg, on which he grows the early potatoes, which, from having lain together for some time, become too compact for the heat to penetrate into them easily.

From the above observations, I hope the gardener will be able to take such hints as will improve the practice in this part of his business. To insure perfect success, it is expedient to have good roots to place in the bed; the usual plan of taking them from the exhausted old beds of the garden is bad. If they are past their best, and unfit to remain in the garden, they cannot be in a good state for forcing. Young roots, four years old from the seed, are much preferable: they are costly, if they are to be purchased every year; but, where there is sufficient space, a regular sowing for this particular purpose should be made annually, and thus a succession of stock secured.

On an Insect which is occasionally very injurious to Fruit Trees. By WILLIAM SPENCE, Esq., F. L. S.

Transactions of the London Horticultural Society.

My attention was first attracted to this insect some years ago, by observing small masses of saw-dust-like excrement, the usual indication of the presence of larvæ, protruding from the edges of the cankered parts of a very diseased summer *apple*-tree, of the name of which I am ignorant. On cutting off a portion of the wood, I found many small white larvæ inhabiting cavities which they had excavated between the bark and the alburnum, and sometimes wholly in the latter, upon which they seemed to feed. These larvæ were of different sizes, and amongst them were several chrysales, which having detached, and placed under a glass, they produced in a few days the *tortrix wœberana*, a small moth very abundant in the garden, and thus proved to be the purest of the larvæ.

I at first supposed that these insects, like many others, deposited their eggs only upon parts of the trees previously diseased. Even on this supposition, their injurious effects would be very considerable, as it was clear that they every year greatly enlarged the extent of the canker, not merely by devouring the neighbouring alburnum, but by forming numerous cells in it, which when quitted by the chrysales, are filled with water by every shower, and thus become the source of more speedy and extensive decay. Many of the cankers in the tree above alluded to, have eaten half way through the small trunk and branches, which if not sheltered by a wall, must have been long ago broken off by the wind.

This tree is a remarkable example of the effect of partial decortication, as recommended by Dr. Darwin (Phytologia, p. 378), in inducing the production of flower instead of leaf-buds. Not only the bark, but half the trunk, as above observed, is eaten through in many places; yet though a new twig is scarcely ever put forth, it never fails to be laden with blossom and fruit. Here I may observe that a similar result, as to the increased produce of fruit, and the paler green of the leaves, with that above referred to by Dr. Darwin, I have myself seen on a branch of a *pear*-tree, from which nearly a complete cylinder of bark had been gnawed by cattle. It was filled with fruit, while not a pear was to be seen on the rest of the tree.

Narrower examination, however, has shown me, that their attacks are by no means confined to the diseased parts of fruit-trees; nor directed, as I first conjectured, against the *apple*-tree only. Being more anxious to ascertain the economy of an injurious insect, than desirous of preserving the tree which they chiefly attacked, I took no steps for extirpating them; and they have in consequence, seemed to increase every year since I first observed them, and last year carried on their operations so extensively, as to threaten more serious injury in return for my forbearance, than I had calculated upon. Not only were they more than usually abundant near the margins of all the old cankers, but I observed their masses of excrement adhering, in every direction, to the surface of the healthiest *pear* and *apple*-trees in the garden; and wherever these indications appeared, the application of the knife always detected the caterpillar beneath.

It is thus evident that where they abound, no other cause is wanting to generate canker and disease. Though their attacks upon the bark and alburnum should not at first be extensively injurious, the admission of water into their empty cells, and frequent repetitions of the mischief, must, in the end, cause rottenness; and it is perhaps not improbable that to these insects should be often primarily attributed the canker laid to the charge of the soil, or the mode of cultivation.

After these prefatory remarks I shall proceed to describe the insect in its different states, adding such observations as have occurred to me upon its economy, and the most probable means of extirpating it.

Eggs. I have never been able to detect any of these upon the parts of the tree where I conjecture they are laid; but several were deposited on the side of a glass jar, under which I had kept the two sexes from their first exclusion. They are lentiform, flat below, slightly convex above, smooth, pale red in the middle, with a white and apparently membranous margin. Altogether they very much resemble the seeds of the common garden *stock*, except that they are not above one-fourth of the size; and they presented an appearance so very dissimilar to that of the eggs of insects in general, that I for some time overlooked them.

Larva. The eggs above mentioned, not having produced any larvæ, I am unable to say any thing as to the precise period at which they are hatched; but from observations made on those found in the fruit-trees, I conjecture that they appear very shortly after the eggs are laid, and immediately proceed to insinuate themselves beneath the bark. When full grown, they are from four lines to half an inch long, and about a line broad; and wholly of a dull semi-transparent white colour, except the head, which is pale chesnut, which with the adjoining segment is also sometimes tinged. In some specimens, an obscure reddish line runs along the body, which is owing to the red colour of the fluid contained in it. The body, besides the head, consists of twelve segments, which, owing to the wrinkles in the three first, are not very easily counted. To each of the three first segments below, are affixed the usual pair of clawed feet, the claws of which are sometimes yellowish; and a pair of tubercular, or false feet, as they are often called, are attached to the 6th, 7th, 8th, 9th, and 12th (or last) segments: so that, in all, the insect has, as is usual in this tribe, sixteen feet; six clawed, and ten tubercular. Each of the segments above, is furnished with from four to six slightly elevated protuberances or mamillæ, more polished than the rest of the body, of a rather darker colour, and having one, and sometimes two, short stiff white hairs proceeding from each. As these mamillæ seem to furnish the best characters for discriminating these larvæ from others of the same tribe closely allied to them, it will be necessary to advert to their number and position more narrowly.

There are none on the first segment. On the second, third, and last, are four placed in a transverse line: and on each of the remaining segments, that is, from the fourth to the eleventh inclusive, are six, one on each side and four in the middle, forming a square, of which the two anterior are larger and nearer to each other than the two posterior. It is to be observed that this description applies only to the *back* of the larva, as both the belly and sides have other similar mamillæ, which it is unnecessary to particularise. The period in which these insects exists in the larva state, is, as far as my observations extend, about a year; during the whole of which, except in winter, when they probably lie torpid, they are employed in boring into the bark and alburnum. As the female moth seems to deposit her eggs through the whole summer, the larvæ may be always met with, and of very different sizes.

Chrysalis. The larvæ which are then full grown, and these are the greater number, assume the state of chrysalis about the latter end of *May,* soon after which time many of the empty husks from which the moths have escaped, may be seen projecting from the bark : and from this period, to the end of summer, others, lying still undisclosed within their silk-lined cavities, are found on cutting into the wood. The chrysalis has the usual sub-conical shape of those of the tribe of *tortrices.* It is about one-third of an inch long, and a line broad in the widest part; of a pale yellow colour when first disengaged from the larva, but nearly brown when mature; and smooth, except that each abdominal segment is set with two transverse lines of aculei, or little teeth, pointing towards the tail, of which those in the line nearest the head are larger and fewer in number than those in the line next the tail. These aculei, which are found in the chrysalis of most species of *tortrix*, evidently serve for enabling the insect, when in this state, to move itself to the entrance of the orifice in the bark, previously to escaping in its perfect form. The tail when viewed under a lens, is found to be furnished with seven or eight minute hooks.

Perfect insect. After remaining in the chrysalis state about ten days, the moth breaks forth. Of this the following is a description:

Tortrix Wœberana.

T. Upper wings chocolate-brown, variegated with orange and silver streaks.

Pyralis Wœberana. *Fabricius Mant. Ins.* II. p. 230. No. 52.—*Ent. Syst.* III. i i. p. 259. No. 71.

Tortrix Wœberana. *Wiener Verzeichniss, 4to. edit.* 126. 9.; *8vo. edit.* II. 43. *Fam.* B. *No.* 9.—*Haworth Lepidopt. Brit.* p. 457, No. 201.

Phalæna Tortrix Wœberana. *Gmelin Syst. Nat.* I. p. 2511. —*Turton's Translation,* III. p. 350—*Brahm Insekten Kalender* II. p. 252. No. 145—*De Villers Ent. Linn.* IV. p. 525.

Tortrix ornatana. *Hübner Schmet. Tort.* 32. 6.

Description.—Head brown, margined behind with orange. *Proboscis* short, pale yellow, spirally convoluted between the palpi, which are large, subtriangular, yellow, the apex and minute terminal joint, black. *Antennæ* one-third the length of the body, setaceous, not pectinate, brown, the first joint, which is thicker than the rest, yellow. *Thorax* brown, with two interrupted irregular transverse bars of orange. *Upperwings* brown, beautifully variegated with many irregular streaks of orange, and a few of silver. The silver streaks are situate chiefly next the margin: one just above the middle of the wing, anteriorly dividing into a fork, whose ends approach the margin; another below the middle, extending in a curved direction nearly to the apex, and sending off anteriorly two or three branches towards the margin. These silver lines are margined with orange, as are two other short transverse silver lines near the inner angle of the apex of the wing, which include a small silver spot, and two longitudinal orange bars. Besides numerous orange streaks and marks, which it is unnecessary to describe minutely, the wings are characterised at the outer margins by about six short oblique yellow spots. At the apex they are fringed with brown cilia, which in some lights have a metallic shade, and are interrupted by two longitudinal bars of yellow cilia. *Under-wings*, above wholly of a brownish black, except at the outer margin from the base to the middle, where they are white. At the apex they are fringed with cilia, white at the apex, and circumscribed just above the brown base with a very fine and almost imperceptible white line. Under-side of the *body* and *legs* of a silvery or pearly white; the tibiæ and tarri of the latter ringed with black. Length of the body about one-third of an inch; of the wings, when expanded, from half to three quarters of an inch.

Long as the above description may seem, it will not be deemed too minute by any one acquainted with the difficulty of discriminating many of the minuter species of this tribe of insects; nor could I have contracted it consistently with the object I have in view, that of enabling any gardener to recognise the moth in question.

How long these moths live after being excluded from the chrysalis, I am not able to say; but, from analogy, and the circumstance that some which I reared under a glass jar did not survive above a week, I conclude their term of existence does not much exceed that period. Hence as I find them in my garden from May to the middle of August, it is clear that they are not, like many other insects, confined to one term of exclusion, but are issuing from the chrysalis throughout the whole summer: in greater number, however, in June than afterwards. In the day-time they usually remain sitting at rest on the trunks and branches of the trees from which they have emerged: flying about, like other moths, only in the night. The sexes, judging from those I reared under glass, copulate soon after their exclusion from the chrysalis; and as the female, as remarked by Brahm, is not provided with any instrument for piercing the bark, it is probable that she deposits her eggs on the outside of it, the young larvæ subsequently making their way into the tree.

The only work in which I have found any allusion to the economy of this insect, is a German publication, Brahm's *Insekten Kalender*. In this it is briefly observed, that the larvæ winter in the trunks of *apricot* and *almond-trees*, upon the sap of which they are supposed to live, and to which it is conjectured they are very injurious.

With regard to the best mode of destroying these insects, when their attacks are injurious, I have nothing better to offer than a few imperfect hints. The first and most essential process evidently is, to cut away the edges of the cankers where they are chiefly found, making the wound smooth, and covering it with any composition likely to prevent the moth from depositing her eggs there again. One precaution is necessary, to put into boiling water, or bury at a considerable depth, the cut or pieces of decayed bark containing the larvæ; which, if left near the tree, would soon crawl from their holes and remount it; thus defeating the labour of the horticulturist, who, often, from neglecting a slight additional trouble, loses the benefit of more painful exertions.

Rösell tells us (Insekten Belustigung, I. iv. 171.) that the German gardeners, after collecting from their cabbages, with unwearied industry, whole baskets full of the destructive Noctua Brassicæ, bury them in a shallow hole in the earth; thus unwittingly counteracting their object in the most effectual way. For as this insect naturally undergoes its metamorphosis under ground, and many of the larvæ are full grown, they assume the chrysalis form in the hole into which they have been thrown, and in a few weeks emerge in the moth state, ready to lay thousands of eggs for a new brood.

Where the larvæ have been found to have insinuated themselves generally into the rough bark of old trees, it would probably be advisable to adopt Mr. Knight's judicious recommendation on another occasion, and scrape off the whole of the lifeless bark, and such portions of the alburnum, as are injured; a process which, there can be no doubt, would be advantageous to the tree in other respects pointed out by Mr. Knight. Where projecting saw-dust-like masses show that the larva has attacked even smooth-barked trees, the insertion of a blunt pricker into the hole would probably, in most cases, suffice to destroy it, and do less injury to the tree than suffering it to attain its growth. But the mode which I should recommend in this, as in the case of almost all insects injurious to the horticulturist, is to employ children in the summer months to destroy the moths themselves, giving a small premium for every ten or twenty they collect; and increasing it as the number become lessened. When taught where to look for them, they would discover numbers on the bark of the trees; and if provided with gause clasp-nets, would find it a most healthy and interesting occupation to catch them when made to fly, by shaking the trees and bushes in which they repose. The destruction of every female moth, before the deposition of its eggs, may be fairly calculated to prevent the existence of some hundreds of larvæ; and thus in any garden not in the neighbourhood of others where the same methods are neglected, the whole race might in a few years be extirpated.

On an Improved Glaze for Porcelain. By Mr. JOHN ROSE, of Coalport, Cheshire. In a letter to the Secretary of the Society of Arts.

" Sir,—Having for some time made use of a glaze for porcelain which gives me great satisfaction, and into the composition of which neither lead nor arsenic are admitted, I beg leave to submit the same to the consideration of the Society of Arts, &c.

" The common glaze for porcelain and the finer kinds of earthenware, contains a considerable proportion of glass of lead: this ingredient, however, on account of its being mixed with a certain proportion of siliceous earth and other vitrifiable materials, unites with them into a glass, which, although easily fusible, is not in the least corroded or acted on by any articles of food. It is not, therefore, from the apprehension of any injury to the health of those who use vessels of porcelain, that the use of lead in the glaze is objectionable: but because it is extremely liable to combine with and degrade the more delicate colours, especially those given by preparations of chrome and of gold. This is particularly the case in the more expensive and elaborate products, which, on account of the multiplicity of their colours, require to be repeatedly heated or *fired*. I trust, therefore, that the Society will consider the communication of a receipt for glazing, in which the above mentioned defects are avoided, as worthy of their favourable notice.

"The principal ingredient of my glaze is felspar, of a somewhat compact texture and a pale flesh-red colour, which forms veins in a slaty rock adjoining to the town of Welsh Pool, in Montgomeryshire. This material being freed from all adhering pieces of slate and of quartz, is ground to a fine powder; and being thus prepared, I mix, with 27 parts of felspar, 18 of borax, 4 of Lynn sand, 3 of nitre, 3 of soda, and 3 of Cornwall China clay. This mixture is to be melted to a frit; and is then to be ground to a fine powder, 3 parts of calcined borax being added previously to the grinding.

"The specimens accompanying this letter, are,
" 1. The felspar in its rough state.
" 2.   Do.   ground to a fine powder.
" 3. Some of the glaze ready prepared for dipping.
" 4. Specimens of porcelain glazed.
" 5.   Do.   both glazed, and afterwards painted, in order to show the solidity and brilliancy of the colours when used on this glaze.   I am, Sir, &c."

The Society placed some specimens in the hands of artists for trial: they were found to bear varied degrees of heat very well, without specks or spits: and even without injuring pinks and chrome greens: or chipping like the French glazes.

On the Use of Coal Tar, to prevent the Dry Rot in Timber.
By H. C. JENNINGS, Esq. In a letter addressed to the Editor of the Technical Repository.

Mr. Jennings was requested by Mr. Hume, the member of Parliament, to assist a gentleman named Good in experiments to ascertain whether the use of coal tar, adopted in the Navy at the suggestion of Sir Robert Seppings, were not injurious, by the emission of unwholesome vapours, dangerous by their inflammability, and destructive to the wood, and copper and iron fastenings. Mr. J. says, that the Navy Board conducted itself most liberally, by granting every information to aid his judgment; and that Mr. Hume was equally so in desiring that every fair caution should be taken to ascertain the truth. The whole of the above charges against the tar were, as Mr. J. states, fully disproved in the presence of a large assemblage of gentlemen; many of them members of Parliament.

We think Mr. J. goes a little too far in considering the bituminous vapour as almost a *desideratum* on board: for he attributes to it most important powers; such as being antiphthisical; and a stomachic: curing consumption, and exciting appetite. We think that the Faculty will assent to these inferences rather cautiously. We have seen tar vapour used in, perhaps, more instances of the kind than Mr. J. has, (we say this without meaning any thing disrespectful,) but in not one has it mitigated the severity of disease; and in some, it has been most decidedly injurious. It, in short, is one of those trifling placebos that rapidly succeed each other in ephemeral favour. We too, as well as Mr. J., have heard some strange reports relative to the impregnation of timber with tar, as a means of preventing the dry rot. We would simply inquire *who* was the real author of this suggestion, and *how* it came that until Sir R. Seppings *subsequently* brought it forward, it was not adopted, although long since proposed to the Government? Perhaps correct answers to these queries might show the world (what is already too well known by individuals) that there is no little danger in communicating with public men on matters of science.

We could illustrate this fact in the history of a certain character, well known in the metropolis, who being erroneously supposed a man of singular ingenuity, is received by public bodies, and the ignorant world, as a very peripatetic encyclopædia; containing not only all that ever was, but that ever can be, known; and who is perpetually besieging patentees and the patent office. Strip the daw of his borrowed plumes.—Take from him all that confidence has imparted to him; or that art has extorted by him; and then what will remain, worthy of other distinction than the disgrace of surreptitious fame?

Suppose a gallant officer to have invented a very improved means of effecting a purpose of the first practical consequence to the State; and on consulting a servant of the Crown is advised by him to think no farther about it, as not being adaptable. Suppose him not satisfied with the adverse opinion, and that he shortly afterwards present his plan to an eminent public Board, where he is informed that the party he had consulted had presented the very thing, claiming it as his own, and that it was in the course of adoption; with an intimation that he could not have come at the other gentleman's invention by fair means. And now, suppose the officer to draw from his pocket the *original* model, of which the one before him was a palpable duplicate, as proved by a letter produced by him from the pretender. Suppose him to urge his own real invention in vain, although the Board acknowledge the " incorrectness," as they softly term it, of his pretended friend. And when the officer declares he will publicly assert his priority of right, it is hinted that by so doing, *he will infallibly stop his own promotion!*

We obtrude these remarks, to put scientific gentlemen on their guard in communications with public men: for it should ever be recollected that a public body will not scruple to do that in its collective, which the members composing it would scorn to do in their individual, capacity.

On Purifying the Water of the River Seine, at Paris.

Technical Repository, No. IV. p. 316.

The editor quotes the letter of a correspondent, to show the simple but effectual means of purifying water, adopted by a patent institution at Paris, employing upwards of two hundred persons. "The water is pumped into vessels about twenty feet deep, and as many in width, where it reposes twelve hours. The clear water is then raised into another vessel, from whence it flows into long and shallow cisterns; in the sides of which a great number of sponge filtres are placed; and the sponges are renewed every hour. From the sponge filtres it finds its way into square shallow cisterns, each of which has, at the bottom, a bed of clean Fontainbleau sand; then a bed of pounded charcoal; then another bed of clean sand; and, lastly, at the top, a bed of coarse river sand; (these last mentioned filtres are renewed every six hours,) and this is the last operation previous to its distribution."

"They seem to take a pleasure in showing the whole of these respectable works to strangers. Four horses are constantly at the pumps, which obliges them to keep twelve for this purpose. I asked the superintendant why they had not a steam engine. The proprietor, he said, had inquired the cost of such a machine; but the dearness of fuel forbade its use."

This process is easily imitated, for domestic use, by laying charcoal, in gross powder, and coarse sand, in alternate layers of an inch thick, in a deep flower pot, or sieve, (a piece of linen being previously placed over the inside of the bottom, to prevent the charcoal and sand from running off,) the upper layer should be covered with a piece of flannel, to prevent the water, as it falls into the vessel, from forming pits on the filtering mass: and it should not be suffered to fall on the filter faster than it can drain through. This may be regulated by the fall being through a common cock. By this simple means, water may be rendered perfectly clear of insects, and bright as crystal.

On Argand Lamps, with concentric Wicks.

Annales de Chimie et de Physique.

Messrs. Arago and Fresnel, charged by the Director-general *des Ponts et Chaussées* with experiments on the improvement of the illumination of light-houses, have paid particular attention to the subject of lamps with concentric wicks, the advantages of which had long been noticed by the late Count Rumford, but which were still liable to great objections on account of the difficulty of regulating the flame.

Messrs. Arago and Fresnel have completely succeeded in obviating this objection, by applying to the sockets the happy idea by which M. Carcel has succeeded in bringing his single Argand lamps to such a high degree of perfection, which consists in keeping the wick always moistened with more oil than it can consume. In this way, the oil being constantly renewed, no part of it is detained in contact with the socket long enough to be heated to its boiling point, and the flame does not pass over the edge of the socket, if thus moistened with a current of fresh oil. In these lamps of Messrs. Arago and Fresnel, however, the oil is not supplied by a rack-work machinery, as in those of Carcel; but the reservoir, which is on a higher level than the socket, receives air by a tube sliding in a leather collar, which may be raised or depressed at will, and thus regulates the level of the flow of oil. The superabundant oil falls into a recipient placed below the socket, which is emptied into the upper reservoir when the lamp is put out.

This apparatus, which may be adopted with great propriety for light-houses, would, however, be very inconvenient for domestic use, on account of the great size required for the upper and lower reservoirs; and therefore in these cases it would be better to adopt the ingenious mechanism of M. Carcel.

It is not sufficient for regulating the combustion merely to have a superabundant supply of oil; for in some cases the flow of it must be so rapid as to empty the largest reservoirs in a very little time. It is necessary, therefore, to give a suitable height to the chimney; for it will easily be seen that the greater the height, the more rapidly the air flows in, and cools the edges of the socket. When the chimney is too low, the socket heats, and the flame becomes longer and redder: when, on the other hand, the chimney is too high, the flame is indeed white, but cannot acquire the requisite intensity; and is kept constantly wavering and unsteady, owing to the too great rapidity of the current of air. Experience alone can determine in each instance the most convenient height of the chimney; but as it ought to vary with the state of the air, and the temperature of the atmosphere, a tube of plate iron, composed of two pieces, one sliding within the other, and moved by rack-work, has been fitted to the chimney, which gives any required length of draught. The frame which supports the chimney can also be raised or depressed, as in the lamps of Carcel, so as to put the elbow of the chimney in the most favourable position for the combustion; for this circumstance, as is well known, has much influence on the whiteness of the flame.

Lastly, each of the concentric wicks may be separately raised or sunk by a rack, and the stem which supports the ring passes through the inner part of the socket, whilst the ring slides upon the latter, bayonet fashion, so that it may be taken off and replaced at pleasure. This arrangement has allowed the inventors to suppress the small tubes which are commonly fixed within the sockets to support the wick ring; for in the lamps with concentric wicks, where the heat is always very intense, it was found that the oil which constantly moistened these tubes gave out too great a quantity of gas, and, besides, diminished the passage of air through them, thus producing a jet of flame higher in this point than over the rest of the socket. After all, what perhaps is the most important circumstance to be attended to in these concentric burners, and one which can only be determined by actual experiment, is to regulate accurately the interval between the wicks, so as to produce the best possible effect. If they are set too far from each other, the flames do not heat each other mutually, and their colour becomes red; if, on the other hand, they are too near, the space left for the passage of air is too small for complete combustion of the oil; whence results a great lengthening of the jets of flame, which are also red at the top and give out smoke. This last defect might be removed by lengthening the chimney, but then the current of air would become so rapid, that a notable quantity of oil would be dispersed in vapour without undergoing combustion.

Messrs. Arago and Fresnel were spared the trouble of making many adjustments of this point, for at their first trials they were fortunate enough to hit upon the proper distance at which to place their concentric wicks. The first which they made bore only two wicks, and answered extremely well, according to the opinion of Captain Kater, of the Royal Society of London, who was present at the experiment in October, 1819. It produced as much light as five of Careel's lamps, and its consumption of oil hardly equalled that of four and a half. This result agrees in the main with what Count Rumford has remarked on the economy of these concentric lamps, though not entirely to the same degree as he has led us to expect. But the burners with three and with four concentric wicks, which Messrs. Arago and Fresnel have since constructed, and which give as much light as ten to twenty of Carcel's lamps, have not afforded so regular and decided a saving in the consumption of oil. Taking the mean of many experiments, it appeared on the whole, that the quantity of oil consumed was pretty exactly proportional to the light given out.

It is necessary that the superabundant oil which flows off from the wicks, and is caught in a recipient, should be at least equal to what is consumed; so that a receiver of double size is required for the supply of oil, unless Carcel's mechanism is adopted. However, the oil that has thus passed through the wicks unconsumed, does not appear to have undergone any alteration, and may always be mixed with the fresh oil for the following lighting. These burners with three or four concentric wicks will, therefore, present no advantage for domestic economy, but they may be adopted where it is wanted to collect a large body of light in a small focus. In this way they might illuminate a large hall or theatre, being attached to the ceiling underneath a large plate or disk, composed of small silvered mirrors, and arranged in a concave hemispherical form. Such a lamp would supersede the use of lustres, which are often in the way of the sight of the audience in the highest boxes.

M. Arago has had the idea of applying to the illumination of light-houses the lamps with two concentric wicks alone in those cases where large parabolic reflectors are employed, by which means the effect may be increased without multiplying the number of reflectors. When this lamp was placed in the focus of a fine parabolic mirror of M. Lenoir, of 31 inches diameter, it was found that the intensity of light in its axis was one and a half times greater than that which the same reflector produced with a single wick lamp, and that the total effect (that is to say, the sum of the divergent rays reflected horizontally) was increased in the proportion of 2·7 to 1. Thus it appears that in any apparatus of this kind composed of similar reflectors, the effect may be almost tripled by the substitution of the double-wicked lamps, at a greater proportional expense, however, than the increase in the intensity of light.

As to the lamps with three or four concentric wicks, they consume too much oil to be adapted to parabolic mirrors. Their application to light-houses can only become useful in placing them in the centre of the system of lenses proposed by M. Tresnel, which is about to be executed under the authority of the Director-general *des Ponts et Chaussées*. In this instance, the object is to unite in one common focus, and in a small volume, the whole of the light employed; and it is for this sole purpose that these triple and quadruple wicks have been constructed. They will answer the purpose required very effectually, by the whiteness and the intensity of the light, and they also will simplify the service of the light-house. They have the additional advantage, as experience has shown, to undergo much less diminution of light, through the carbonization of the wicks than the common lamps; for after twelve or thirteen hours' burning of the quadruple wick, the intensity of light was found to be lessened only by a fifth part. This, doubtless, depends on the intense heat produced, which promotes the ascension of the oil in the wicks.

On a Process for analyzing Gunpowder. Extracted from the Register of the Committee for the Direction of Powder and Saltpetre. Annales de Chimie et de Physique.

The method of analyzing gunpowder, usually employed, consists in lixiviating it with water to extract the nitre, and then digesting the residue with potash, to dissolve the sulphur; after which the charcoal is left untouched. Though this process appears quite easy and simple, the execution of it is attended with some difficulties: nevertheless, it should not be entirely rejected, and, indeed, it is the one which should be adopted where the object is to obtain directly the proportion of charcoal. In this case it would be right to analyze two portions of the powder; one should be lixiviated, to separate the nitre, and the entire residue dried and weighed; the other portion should be mixed with its weight of potash and some water, and heated; the sulphur will then dissolve rapidly along with the nitre, and the residue should be washed till all sulphureous flavour is lost; or, better, till acetite of lead is not blackened by the washings; and the charcoal that remains should be weighed and dried. In this way, by obvious calculation, the weight of each ingredient is found separately; and one process serves to verify the other.

By this method, however, the estimation of the proportion of charcoal is liable to some incorrectness, and for a like reason that of the sulphur; consequently, if the weight of the sulphur alone could be determined by analysis, it would be much more exact. This object is attained in the following method, the accuracy of which has been ascertained by repeated trials. It is as follows: first, dry a certain quantity of the powder, to learn the degree of moisture which it retains, which makes the valuation of the charcoal more exact, as the latter is found only by subtraction from the weight of two other ingredients. Then lixiviate the dry powder, to dissolve out the nitre, evaporate the solution to dryness, and fuse the nitre which it contains before weighing it.

To obtain the sulphur, fuse five grammes of the dried powder with an equal weight of pure subcarbonate of potash, at least one that contains no sulphate; pulverize the mixture in a mortar, then add five grammes of nitre, and twenty of common salt. When the whole is intimately mixed, put it into a platina crucible, standing amongst red-hot charcoal: the combustion of the sulphur goes on quietly, and soon the mass becomes white. The operation is then finished: withdraw the crucible from the fire, and, when cold, dissolve the saline mass in water, saturate it with pure nitric or muriatic acid, and precipitate the sulphuric acid which it contains by means of muriate of barytes. There are two ways of managing this precipitation; the first, and the most generally adopted, is to put the barytic salt into the solution till there is a slight, but decided, excess of it; and then to collect the product of sulphate of barytes. This process requires numerous washings, which must be performed at long intervals, on account of the slowness with which the barytic sulphate settles; particularly at the last, when, if it has not stood a good while, it will often pass with the clear liquid through the pores of the filtre. If the sulphate of barytes is washed on a filtre, a new inconvenience arises; the dried sulphate must either be scraped off the filtre, or weighed with the paper, both which methods are very liable to inaccuracies.

The other manner of precipitating the sulphate from the solution, is to make, before-hand, a solution of muriate of barytes of known strength; and to add as much of this, to the solution containing the sulphate, as is exactly enough to separate all the sulphuric acid. When the precipitation is nearly completed, the barytic liquid should be added only by drops, waiting between each addition till the liquor has become clear; or else, filtering a small portion in a small tube, and testing it with the barytic solution. The same filtre will serve for the whole operation. There is no danger here of the sulphate of barytes passing through the pores of the filtre; for this only takes place when the solution no longer contains any, or hardly any, saline matter, as happens when the sulphate has been washed many times with water.

The quantity of sulphuric acid, and consequently that of the sulphur whence it has been produced in the former part of the process, is given by that of the muriate of barytes employed; for the weight of the atom of sulphur being 20·116, and that of the crystallized muriate of barytes being 152·44, the sulphur contained in the sulphuric acid will be to the muriate of barytes used as 20·116 to 152·44.

This process, which may be generally adopted, is particularly applicable in those cases where the sulphate of barytes carries down with it other matters in its precipitation, making it difficult to estimate it by actual weighing. Its correctness may be depended on to a five-hundreth, or even a thousandth part; but as the barytic solution should be added drop by drop, which cannot be done correctly by mere pouring from a phial, on account of the trickling down of the liquid from the wetted edges, a small glass tube should be used, blown into a bulb in the middle, and drawn out into a capillary point at the lower end, and passed through the cork which closes the phial of barytic solution. Some of this liquid is to be sucked up into the bulb, and then let to fall, drop by drop, into the solution of the sulphate; the flow of the drops being regulated by placing the finger over the upper opening of the tube. The bottle of barytic solution, with the tube, should be weighed both before and after using it, that the quantity employed may be exactly ascertained; and still more, to ensure accuracy, the bottle should be thin, and should hold not more than about twice as much liquid as will be wanted, that the balance may not be overcharged. Even the last drop of solution that is used in making the precipitation should not be reckoned; but its weight should be subtracted from the whole quantity employed. The weight of a single drop is found, by separately weighing a number of drops, fifty for example, and taking a fiftieth part of this amount.

The nitre and sulphur of the gunpowder being thus accurately determined, the weight of the charcoal is found by subtracting the two former from the whole sum.

Carbonate of potash has been recommended in this analysis, because it mixes readily with the gunpowder by rubbing: but caustic potash may be also used; only in this case some water must be added, and the mixture must be dried with a very gradual heat, to avoid the spurting, which is apt to occur whenever any solution of potash is dried up hastily. Lastly, we may add, that a platina crucible is not indispensible, the fusion may be performed in a glass matrass, or even a glass tube; it always cracks indeed on cooling, but none of its contents are spilled.

This process has long been in actual use in the laboratory of the Gunpowder-office; but, we may remark, that in Schweigger's journal, for January 1821, M. Hermbstaedt recommends the detonation with nitre for the analysis of gunpowder. He first mixes equal parts of the gunpowder with pure nitre, then projects the mixture in small portions in a platina crucible, containing two parts of the same nitre in fusion: he then saturates the solution of the saline mass with nitric acid, and afterwards adds nitrate of barytes to obtain the sulphuric acid in combination with barytes in the precipitate. The author asserts, that this method is very exact; but, on repeating this process with attention, we shall find a sulphureous smell after each projection of the materials into the crucible, showing that a portion of the sulphur burns off on the surface, and is dissipated. Besides which, a part of the mixture is also driven out of the crucible, and dispersed in the form of white smoke. The addition of potash, or its carbonate, is indispensibly necessary, to prevent any portion of the sulphur from being volatilized; the common salt serves to render the deflagration less tumultuous.

On the Smut in Wheat. BAKER's Treatise.
Phil. Mag. No. 287, p. 228.

Take a double handful of good clean wheat, wash it well in clear water in a hand-basin or other utensil, rub the seed well between the hands *in the water,* and change the water several times until it comes from the seed quite clear: then sow half of the washed seed in a corner of the farm garden, or on some other convenient spot, but be careful not to use a rake for covering the seed, that had been recently used in the barn or elsewhere amongst smutted wheat, or even amongst the straw of that wheat. The first part of the wheat being disposed of, procure some smut balls, having no kernels of wheat amongst them; break the balls in a sample-bag, and put the other half of the washed wheat into the same bag; shake the wheat and the smut powder well together, and allow the wheat to remain in the bag one or two days, when it will have become dry, and the smut powder have effected the inoculation; then sow that seed upon a spot of ground contiguous, but not immediately adjoining to where the former handful of seed had been sown. The reason for not depositing one parcel of seed immediately adjoining to the other is, to guard against the probability of the two parcels of seed becoming intermixed, through the agency of birds, mice, &c. as an accident of that nature would render the experiment incomplete; whereas, if it is properly conducted, the result will assuredly be satisfactory: so much so, that the produce of the first sample will be without smut, and that of the second, will be smutted, more or less (probably half smut balls) according to the state of the smut powder at the time the inoculation was effected. Smut balls taken from old wheat are not so liable to communicate the disease, as those taken from new wheat: this phenomenon is owing to the eggs of the smut insect becoming addled, or rendered effete, when kept beyond the season assigned by nature for their procreation or re-production: hence old wheat seed is less liable to produce smut than new wheat; but this depends in some measure upon the manner in which the old wheat had been kept; if in stacks, the insect's eggs will not have been entirely destroyed, because of the air having been excluded from those situated in the middle of the stack; but in the event of the wheat being thrashed out a considerable time previously, the eggs will have become addled, from exposure to air. The same position holds good in regard to the eggs of other insects, reptiles, or birds: one law of Nature rules the whole; and it even extends to the germ of vegetables, for we see that old wheat seed kept in stacks vegetates better that when kept in granaries. This explanation will sufficiently account for the contrariety of opinion respecting the eligibility of using old wheat for seed, whether for producing a full crop of wheat, or as a prevention of smut.

On the Preservation of Grain. By M. CLEMENT DE-
SORMES. Journal de Physique.

Journal of Science, No. 25, p. 165.

M. Desormes ascertained that vegetable and animal substances might be preserved *ad libitum*, if protected from insect depredators; by keeping seeds, &c. in a perfectly dry state: moisture being essential to insect existence. He suggests the use of large iron cylinders or parallelopipeds to be entirely filled with the grain: and that not any air be admitted which has not been previously passed through lime. But the air in the interstices, varying with the fluctuations of atmospheric pressure and temperature, is allowed to escape by a valve at the top; and a renewed supply passing over lime, and then through another valve at the bottom of the granary. To facilitate occasional inspection of the grain, he proposes one or more vertical wells, closed at the top and bottom, with sliding valves, whereby the grain may be examined. This plan, it is justly observed by the editor of the Journal of Science, offers the important advantage of saving the expense of human labour in turning the grain; and he proceeds to show not only that the charge of a granary on a large scale, might be cheaper than one of brick work; but also, how it should be constructed. We will present this to our readers, in his own words, because we think it worthy of particular attention.

"The expense, we believe, will be much less to build an iron than a common granary; so much so, that we have no doubt farmers will eventually preserve their grain in a similar way. Supposing the house to be formed of large iron plates, with flanges for bolting them together, with packing of lead, as in water pipes, it will be most economically and conveniently made in the quadrangular form. Across the bottom of one end, an iron pipe, having a number of small holes, or thin slits, might be laid, from the middle part of which a similar pipe would rise to the top. This might be the receptacle of the lime, reduced to pieces about the size of a plum. A valve at top, opening freely inwards, would admit the external air, when the equilibrium required it.

At the other end of the chamber, but near to the middle height, might be placed another horizontal iron pipe, also perforated with little holes, from the middle of which would ascend a vertical tube, considerably above the top of the magazine. Here would be fitted a valve, opening outwards. If the grain had been stored in a somewhat damp state, then a current of desiccated air could be easily determined through it, so as to render it speedily dry, by establishing a small fire in the *eduction* pipe above the top of the chamber. Thus a constant current of air would pass down through the lime, and, in its hygrometrically dry state would sweep through the body of grain, necessarily robbing it of its pernicious moisture. We need not enter into further particulars concerning the number and forms of these pipes, &c., which will suggest themselves to every man of sound scientific principles. In such a magazine, we believe that well-cured grain might be preserved for any length of time without deterioration; and at no further expense than the interest of money on the first cost of the building. A penthouse roof should be stretched over the chamber, to screen the workmen from rain when they are introducing or discharging grain, inspecting its condition, or changing the lime, which may be easily done by having a false bottom to its cylinder, capable of being drawn up by an iron rod fixed in its centre. The openings in the top should be shut, after Glauber's plan, with grease-lute."

On the Preservation of Manure. By M. de Fellenberg.

Bibliotheque Universelle, 1822, Jan. 23.

We present this, as bearing an analogy with the preceding article, both in importance, and the character of interest it is proposed to serve. We cannot do better than give the method as described in M. de F.'s own words:

"Those who are most careful whom I have known in Switzerland, obtain an advantageous result by spreading the dung of the stables very regularly in thin layers on the heap, and pressing each down by frequent treading, so as to make a close and compact mass, which is surrounded by a kind of twist made with the tubes of litter, of which the ends are turned towards the interior of the heap, so as to retain the fluid parts which might otherwise escape. These persons, satisfied with their process, in as much as it prevents all mouldiness and decomposition of their manure, do not seek after the cause of their success, nor after any improvement which the instructed agriculturist may desire. By making the heap of manure very dense, and by excluding in that manner the influence of air, one may completely prevent fermentation and decomposition; but in pressing the heap, the tubes of straw, which ought to become filled and impregnated with the fluid parts of the manure, are flattened and broken. I gain the same advantage by making my heaps of dung so, that they shall be compact and without vacuities, but without pressing them. I moisten them abundantly with fluid manure, as soon as they are begun to be formed; and this moistening, or watering, is repeated each time that, from the elevation of vapours from the heap, it is judged that fermentation is commenced. By means of this process, the fermentation is continually checked. Whatever might have evaporated from the dung, is returned to the interior by the fluid thrown on the surface, which fluid is properly the essence of the dung; the tubes of straw, which served as litter, are impregnated, and this fluid forms certain chemical combinations, which enrich the mass both in its quality and quantity."

Observations on the Use of Prussic Acid in Phthisis Pulmonalis. Read before the Academy of Medicine of Philadelphia. By JOSEPH G. NANCREDI, M. D.

Philadelphia Journal of Med. and Phys. Sciences, vol. ii.

The diversity of opinions, which has lately arisen, in relation to the effects of the hydro-cyanic or prussic acid, in the treatment of phthisis pulmonalis, while its very powerful action on the human system is admitted on all sides, seems to point out this new article of the materia medica as an interesting subject of medical investigation. Whether we consider the inquiry as having reference solely to the new remedy, which has excited so much attention; or whether we view it as drawing anew our observations towards a disease, the inefficient treatment of which has ever been the disgrace of our science; every one of us will agree that no subject can be more deserving our study and reflection. If, on the one hand, the total failure of the many attempts to discover a cure for phthisis be calculated to destroy our ardour in what may, by some, be considered a hopeless pursuit; on the other, a short insight into the baneful ravages of this fatal disease is well calculated to arouse our attention, and urge us on to new efforts. Where is the physician, who can look at our bills of mortality, and see without feelings of the deepest mortification, the inefficiency of medicine exemplified in the ravages of consumption? To limit our examination to the year which has just elapsed, we shall perceive that one-sixth part of the mortality in the four largest cities of the United States is the result of this disease.

Case I.—The first case which appeared to me likely to test its efficacy, was that of Mrs. H., a patient of the Philadelphia Dispensary, aged about 45 years, and who was at that time labouring under symptoms of confirmed phthisis. She had tried in vain many remedies, before her admission to the care of the Institution. After resorting to the usual ineffectual modes of treatment, I had recourse to Dr. Majendie's plan, and prescribed the acid. It had been prepared with care, and was recommended to me as being precisely of the same strength as that used in Europe. Two drops were directed to be taken in pure water each day; and the dose to be gradually increased, until the patient, in the course of one week, had reached the dose of ten drops daily. Yet no visible effect was perceptible: not only was no amelioration observed, but neither the constriction about the chest, nor head-ache, which are mentioned as frequently attending its exhibition in such large doses, were complained of. At the end of the second week, the dose had been increased to about thirty drops daily, without producing any effect whatever. I now felt discouraged: but having procured a quantity of fresh prepared acid, I had an opportunity of testing its strength. Two drops were put on the tongue of a kitten two weeks old: it was immediately seized with convulsions, and in about four seconds expired. The patient now began its use in doses of two drops daily for three days; then increasing in the ratio of three drops daily, until she took thirty drops in the twenty-four hours. At this period I could find no visible alteration; and with reluctance abandoned, in this case, the use of the medicine.

The instance of Mrs. H., who was an extremely irritable and nervous woman, and whose disease was complicated with asthma, could not be deemed a sufficient trial, even admitting it to be a fair one; and consequently was in no way likely to affect the question of the efficacy of the medicine. I soon found, among the patients of the Dispensary, a case which afforded some rational hope of success.

Case II.—John C., aged about 53 years, of a strong and muscular appearance, working in a brick-yard, had been troubled, for about two months in August 1819, with continual pain in the chest, dyspnœa, and cough, accompanied with some expectoration of a doubtful nature. The pain in the chest induced me to direct the loss of about fourteen ounces of blood; and, immediately after, he began the use of the acid, in daily doses of four drops, increasing two drops every day, until he had taken twenty-four in a day. He now informed me that his cough was somewhat better; and that his sleep, which had been very much disturbed by unpleasant dreams, and otherwise agitated, was more tranquil. The dose was continued thus for a few days; and then increased four drops daily, until the patient took daily 36 drops. The benefit derived had increased; his cough was better, and his sleep continued composed. The medicine was now at an end, and this case terminated here. It is, however, proper to mention, that I have seen him a month ago, still affected with slight cough, but which is considerably diminished. He is now enabled to pursue his work. I conclude, therefore, that in this case the prussic acid has been of some use.

Case III.—In November last, Robert N., a patient of the Dispensary, aged about 36 years, of a slender form, and by trade a carpenter, applied for medical assistance. He complained of a pain in the chest, great difficulty in breathing, or, as he expressed it, a shortness of breath, a dry cough, no expectoration, and occasional chills and night sweats. His pulse was tense and frequent. These symptoms had been gradually increasing for about six months, during which time the patient had lost considerable flesh. After taking, for a few nights, the ipecacuanha and opium combined, he began the use of the acid. At first he took it in very small doses, owing to the impression I was then under that its effects would be very powerful. But the second prescription, Nov. 28th, contained thirty drops in four ounces of water, edulcorated with gum arabic and sugar. The patient was directed to take a table-spoonful of the mixture three times each day; and he soon felt some amelioration in his feelings.

December 2d, the mixture being out, a new one, containing two drachms of prussic acid in the same vehicle, and accompanied with the same injunctions as to its doses, was directed. It was followed by increased benefit.

December 7th, one drachm of the acid in three ounces of water, edulcorated with gum arabic and sugar, which the patient is to take in table-spoonfuls every third hour. Robert states that his cough is considerably diminished.

December 13th, the same prescription is renewed, with manifest advantage.

December 18th, one drachm and a half in six ounces of water is prescribed to be used, in the same doses and at the same intervals. The patient continues improving. At no period since its first exhibition has he mentioned either nausea or head-ache.

Robert continued under the operation of the acid until the 20th of January, and then used, as a substitute and general tonic, the cold infusion of bark. His cough has nearly left him; and his appetite, appearance, and general feelings are about the same as previous to the invasion of the disease. He is discharged from the care of the Institution, and is now pursuing his trade.

CASE IV.—Mary P., aged about 22 years, had been affected for about three weeks with the usual symptoms of incipient phthisis, and pronounced to be affected with that disease by a respectable physician, who had visited her previous to my attendance. When I first called on her, on the 11th of February, I found the patient confined to her bed with continual fever, and a small, quick, and tense pulse. She had already used in vain several pectoral mixtures, and took, according to my directions, a fresh one, containing balsam tolu; but without deriving from either any relief whatever. Accordingly, very soon after my attendance commenced, the prussic acid was administered, in doses of one drop to the ounce of water, which doses were very soon increased. She is now taking it in doses of sixteen drops to four ounces of water,—a table-spoonful every two hours. Without exhausting your patience, Gentlemen, with details, which, by their repetition, may be tedious and uninteresting, I will merely state, that my patient is rapidly improving; so much so, that this day, the 11th of March, she informs me that she has not coughed more than twice or three times in the course of the last twenty-four hours. She is now sitting up, and has already acquired some flesh, and a slow and rational pulse.

Besides the cases already related, there are three others under care; but they are of too recent date to form at present any satisfactory conclusion. A suspension or a mitigation of some of the symptoms of a disease for a few hours, or even days, should never be admitted as positive testimony. It becomes proper, however, to state, that the patients are all under the impression that they derive benefit from this medicine.

It may, perhaps, be expected, that, in concluding these remarks, something should be offered tending to explain the modus operandi of the article under consideration. But, besides the want of sufficient experience to support the reputation which this new medicine has been supposed to deserve, no facts explaining its action, of a satisfactory nature, have as yet been offered by those more immediately concerned in its success. It has been compared to opium in some points of view, and it does appear to possess some sedative properties. That it acts in some cases by occasioning vertigo, head-ache, and a slight stricture across the chest, must be admitted; but these are merely temporary effects, and of very rare occurrence. In my limited circle of observation, I have not witnessed the alarming symptoms related by Dr. Magendie; nor have I so far been enabled to produce those very agreeable sensations which Dr. Granville informs us were visible in some of his patients.

Diffident, however, of my own results, and therefore particularly anxious that some of my colleagues should add confirmation to the facts herein stated, I have thought the following remarks not altogether uninteresting to those who may feel disposed to use this medicine.

There are several modes of preparing the prussic acid, three of which are recommended in the French codex, under the names of Scheele, Gay Lussac, and Vauquelin. The two latter are much stronger than the former; but all three lose their properties by exposure to light and air, in a very short time. To obviate this very serious objection, Dr. Cooper has prepared a solution of this acid in alcohol, and in this form it certainly is much more easily preserved than the other preparations. It would appear, however, that it is still subject to a slow decomposition, from the circumstance of its peculiar flavour, resembling that of bitter almonds, decreasing after being kept for a couple or three weeks; and therefore it becomes desirable that it should be renewed as often as possible.

I have used this last preparation in most of the cases referred to in these remarks. In no case have its bad effects been produced, although used in large doses. For instance, I am in the habit of prescribing it in the proportion of one drop of the acid to an ounce of water, a table-spoonful of the mixture to be repeated once, twice, or oftener, as it may be judged requisite, in the course of the day. In the case of Robert N., a mixture containing one drachm and a half of the acid in six ounces of water, was directed to be taken by table spoonfuls every third hour, and the patient was evidently benefited by its use. Yet this is but one case, and should not be considered as conclusive evidence in favour of such large doses: for my very worthy and experienced friend, Dr. Monges, of this city, informs me, that he prescribed this same article in a case of calculous phthisis a short time since; and that doses of one-sixteenth part of a drop, occasioned such an increase of the cough, and consequent irritation, as to induce him to abandon its use. He observed at the same time, that, in this instance, the particular circumstance of small portions of calculi being expectorated, perhaps in a more rapid manner in consequence of the exhibition of this medicine, may have prevented its beneficial effects.

One inference appears fairly deduced from the above facts; and that is, that we should receive with due caution the opinion contained in Dr. Elliotson's paper, (p. 40,) when he affirms that he does not hesitate to prescribe the acid for patients whom he has not an opportunity of seeing more than once a week, or who perhaps reside in the country. With an agent endowed with such powerful properties, it certainly would seem to require more circumspection than can be exercised under such circumstances.

If any additional motive could be required, to warn the profession from too hasty an adoption of either of the opposite conclusions contained in the papers referred to, without further experience on so interesting a subject, it will be found in a reference to the history of other medicines, which have had their day, and which have also been proposed with the hope of averting this scourge of the human race. Many of these, apparently gifted with powerful properties, and supported by the enthusiastic encomiums of highly respectable names, have nevertheless not been found capable of standing the test of practical experience, and have accordingly already been deprived of their short lived reputation and ill deserved fame.

We present the above article, because we feel how interesting any thing that may afford a hope of relief is in this dreadful malady. Not that we have much confidence in the proposed means ourselves: for we have lived long enough to witness the rise, decline, and fall of too many medical nostrums, held forth as little less than infallible in consumption. The dry vomit; Griffith's mixture; medicated airs; and digitalis; have each lived their short day of specific character. We apprehend that prussic acid will follow them, after a short career.

On a successful Method of Curing the Hydrophobia, as practised in the Ukraine.

Phil. Mag. No. 287, p. 223.

Although we confess ourselves to be somewhat sceptical as to the mode of curing this horrid malady, to be related below, we hold ourselves bound by duty to give all possible publicity to whatever may be even suggested for relief, in cases that have hitherto defied the anxious researches of the Faculty. The editor of the above journal delivers himself as follows:—

When Mr. Marochetti, an operator in the Hospital at Moscow, was in the Ukraine in 1813, in one day fifteen persons applied to him for cure, having been bitten by a mad dog. Whilst he was preparing the remedies, a deputation of several old men made its appearance to request him to allow a peasant to treat them; a man who for some years past enjoyed a great reputation for his cures of hydrophobia, and of whose success Mr. Marochetti had heard much. He consented to their request under these conditions: 1st, that he, Mr. Marochetti, should be present at every thing done by the peasant; 2dly, in order that he might be more fully convinced that the dog was really mad, he (Mr. M.) should select one of the patients, who should be treated according to the medical course usually held in estimation. A girl of six years old was chosen for this purpose. The peasant gave to his fourteen patients a strong 'decoction' of the *Summit*, and *Fl. Genista luteæ tinctoriæ*, (about 1½lb. daily,) and examined twice a day under the tongues, where, as he stated, small knots, containing the poison of the madness, must form themselves. As soon as these small knots actually appeared, and which Mr. Marochetti himself saw, they were opened, and cauterised with a red-hot needle; after which the patient gargled with the decoction of the *Genista*. The result of this treatment was, that all the fourteen (of whom only two, the last bitten, did not show these knots) were dismissed cured at the end of six weeks, during which time they drank this decoction. But the little girl, who had been treated according to the usual methods, was seized with hydrophobic symptoms on the seventh day, and was dead in eight hours after they first took place. The persons dismissed as cured were seen three years afterwards by Mr. Marochetti, and they were all sound and well. Five years after this circumstance (in 1818) Mr. Marochetti had a new opportunity in Podolia of confirming this important discovery. The treatment of twenty-six persons, who had there been bitten by a mad dog, was confided to him; nine were men, eleven women, and six children. He gave them at once a decoction of the *Genista*, and a diligent examination of their tongues gave the following result: Five men, all the women, and three children, had the small knots already mentioned; those bitten worst, on the third day, others on the fifth, seventh, and ninth; and one woman, who had been bitten but very superficially in the leg only, on the twenty-first day. The other seven also, who showed no small knots, drank the *decoctum genistæ* six weeks, and all the patients were cured.

In consequence of these observations, Mr. Marochetti believes that the hydrophobic poison, after remaining a short time in the wound, fixes itself for a certain time under the tongue, at the openings of the ducts of the ' glandular submaxiller,' which are at each side of the tongue-string, and there forms those small knots, in which one may feel with a probe a fluctuating fluid, which is that hydrophobic poison. The usual time of their appearance seems to be between the third and ninth day after the bite; and if they are not opened within the first twenty-four hours after their formation, the poison is re-absorbed into the body, and the patient is lost beyond the power of cure. For this reason, Mr. Marochetti recommends that such patients should be immediately examined under the tongue, which should be continued for six weeks, during which time they should take daily 1½lb. of the *decoct. Genist.* (or four times a day the powder, one drachm *pro dosi*). If the knots do not appear in the day time, no madness is to be apprehended; but as soon as they show themselves, they should be opened with a lancet, and then cauterised, and the patient should gargle assiduously with the above-mentioned *decoction*.

We hasten to convey to our readers this important discovery, (which we borrow from the Petersburgh Miscellaneous Treatises in the Realm of Medical Science for 1821,) which certainly deserves the full attention of all medical practitioners; and which, if confirmed by experience, may have the most beneficial results.

Account of Natural Ice-Houses in Connecticut. By BENJAMIN SILLIMAN, Professor of Mineralogy in Yale College.

American Journal of Science.

That ice is perpetual in some climates is notorious. That it is so even in those of the Torrid Zone, upon mountains which rise to the height of three miles, is also well known. It is, however, a rare occurrence, even in cold climates, that ice is perennial on ground which possesses no more than the common elevation.

An instance of this kind has, however, recently come to our knowledge. It exists in the state of Connecticut, in the township of Meriden, mid-way between Hartford and Newhaven. This natural ice-house is situated in about 42° of north latitude, nearly twenty miles from the sea, and at the elevation of probably not more than two hundred feet above its level.

The country is a part of the secondary trap region of Connecticut, and is marked by numerous distinct ridges of greenstone, which present lofty mural precipices, and, from their number, contiguity, and parallelism, they often form narrow precipitous defiles, filled more or less with fragments of rocks, of various sizes, from that of a hand stone to that of a cottage. These fragments are the detritus or debris of these mountains, and every one in the least acquainted with such countries, knows how much they always abound with similar ruins.

In such a defile the natural ice-house in question is situated. On the south-western side there is a trap ridge of naked perpendicular rock, which, with the sloping ruins at the base, appears to be four hundred feet high; the parallel ridge which forms the other side of the defile is probably not above forty feet high, but it rises abruptly on the eastern side, and is covered on the other by wood, which occupies the narrow valley also. This valley is moreover choked, in an astonishing degree, with the ruins of the contiguous mountain-ridge, and exhibits many fragments of rock which would fill a large room. As the defile is very narrow, these fragments have in their fall been arrested here, by the low parallel ridge, and are piled on one another in vast confusion, forming a series of cavities which are situated among and under these rocks. Many of them have reposed there for ages, as appears from the fact that small trees (the largest that the scanty soil, accumulated by revolving centuries, can support,) are now growing on some of these fragments of rock. Leaves also, and other vegetable remains, have accumulated among the rocks and trees, and choked the mouths of many of the cavities among the ruins. This defile, thus narrow, and thus occupied by forest, and by rocky ruins, runs nearly north and south, and is completely impervious to the sun's rays, except when he is near the meridian. Then, indeed, for an hour, he looks into this secluded valley; but the trees, and the rocks, and the thick beds of leaves, scarcely permit his beams to make the slightest impression.

It is in the cavities, beneath the masses of rocks already described, that the ice is formed. The ground descends a little to the south, and a small brook appears to have formed a channel among the rocks. The ice is thick, and well consolidated, and its gradual melting in the warm season, causes a stream of ice-cold water to issue from this defile. This fact has been known to the people of the vicinity for several generations, and the youth have, since the middle of the last century, been accustomed to resort to this place in parties, for recreation, and to drink the waters of the cold-flowing brook.

It was on the 23d of last July (1821), in the afternoon of a very hot day, when the thermometer was probably as high as 85° Fahr. that, under the guidance of Dr. Hough, we entered this valley. After arriving among the trees, and in the immediate vicinity of the ice, there was an evident chilliness in the air; and, very near the ice, the air was (compared with the hot atmosphere which we had just left) rather uncomfortably cold. The ice was only partially visible, being covered by leaves, and screened from view by the rocks; but a boy descending with a hatchet, soon brought up large firm masses. One of these, weighing several pounds, we carried twenty miles, to Newhaven, where it was exhibited to various persons, and some of it remained unmelted during two succeeding nights; for it was in being on the morning of the third day.

The local circumstances which have been detailed, will probably account for this remarkable *locality* of ice, and scarcely need any illustration or comment.

This is not the only instance of the kind existing among the trap rocks of Connecticut. There is a similar place seven miles from Newhaven, near the Middletown Road, in the parish of Northford, and township of Branford. The ice here also (as we are assured) endures the year round. This place we have not visited, but we are assured that it is at the bottom, or on the declivity of a trap ridge. Several years ago, we had the ice of this place brought to us into Newhaven, in the hottest weather of midsummer. Like that of Meriden, it is very solid; but, like that also, it is soiled with leaves and dirt; and although it is unfit to be put into liquids which are to be swallowed, it is as good as any ice for mere cooling.

It is perhaps worthy of being mentioned, that an artificial ice-house, within the knowledge of the writer, is situated on the top of a ridge of trap in Connecticut. The excavation was made simply, by removing the loose pieces of trap rock, which are here piled in enormous quantities, but composed of fragments of very small size. These loose pieces of stone, with the air in the cavities, are better non-conductors of heat than the ground which usually surrounds ice-houses; for the ice keeps remarkably well in this elevated ice-house. Perhaps this will aid us also in explaining the phenomena of the natural ice-houses that have been mentioned.

It may not be useless, before dismissing this article, to mention, that the roof of an ice-house should be painted white, and that it should be thatched with straw, beneath the ordinary wood-roof. The surface of the roof thus becomes reflecting, and non-absorbing, and the substance non-conducting in relation to heat. We can speak from experience of the efficacy of this arrangement.

On the Rock-crystal of Primitive Marble. By M. Ripetti, of Florence. Bibliotheque Universelle.

Journal of Science, p. 231.

These crystals are found either in hollow geodes, completely closed, on the insides of which the crystals are set irregularly; or, isolated in the mass of Carrara marble. In the last case, frequently opaque. Calcareous sparry crystals in the vicinity are considered such certain indications of the rock-crystal, as to be denominated *spies*. M. Ripetti says that " there is frequently found in the hollow crystalline cavities at Carrara and elsewhere, a very limpid liquid, slightly sapid, and more or less abundant. I have lately had occasion to verify this fact, very common, as I have been told, in the valley of the Upper Pianello. There I have not only found in these cavities prismatic crystals, but I have seen a very transparent and slightly acid liquid come out of them as the workmen had said; and who further add, that they sometimes find it in such quantity as to quench their thirst with it, being led to the place by the appearance of the *lucica*. This is not all, and that which follows is still more extraordinary. In the spring of 1819, M. del Nero, proprietor of an excavation in the *Fossa de l'Angelo*, being engaged in sawing out the shaft of a large column, of the required length, for the temple of St. Francois at Naples, discovered a *lucica* in the interior of the marble, about which the workmen penetrated the rock, and found a cavity much larger than usual, lined with crystals, and containing above a pound and a half of the fluid in question. In this cavity there was seen also, with astonishment, a protuberance as large as the fist, transparent, and which appeared to have all the other characters of rock-crystal. M. del Nero, delighted to find himself possessor of one of the finest specimens of hyalin quartz which had ever been seen in the country, endeavoured to raise it at the base; but to his inexpressible surprise he found an elastic and pasty substance, which took any form he pleased under his hand, but which was not long becoming hard, and taking on the appearance of calcedony or porcelain. Provoked by the circumstance, the proprietor threw it from him amongst the fragments of the rocks, where this specimen, which would have interested the curious so highly, was lost. He affirmed to me, and his assertion was repeated by other witnesses worthy of confidence, that the same fact has occurred more than once, and I made him promise that if he again had the opportunity, he would impress some seal on the soft matter, and, when hard, send it to me at Florence, with the water which the cavity might contain."

On a new Property of the Ordinary Crystal with two Axes.

In the Bibliotheque Universelle, M. Fresnel records his recent discovery " that in crystals with two axes of double refraction, the ordinary ray undergoes variations of velocity and refraction, analogous to the extraordinary ray, but confined within less extended limits."

On an Improved Rail-way and Carriages.

By H. R. PALMER, Esq. Tech. Repository, No. 4, p. 287.

The editor of the Repository describes the rail-way as consisting of a single rail only, and the carriage as having two wheels, one following the other, instead of four, in the usual construction. The load is placed in two receptacles, one on each side of the rail; "and so much below the points of suspension, that, although the weights may be very unequally divided, yet a very considerable difference indeed would be requisite to disturb the equilibrium. Mr. Palmer proposes much advantage from the use of this novel invention, and particularly in carrying the rail-way on a level (or not, as may be required) across valleys;—the horse, whilst tracking the carriage along the rail by means of a rope or line affixed to it in the manner of a barge on a canal, passing down and up the descent and ascent along a common road or path. The saving, in point of original expense in forming such a road, is expected by Mr. Palmer to be very considerably less than in one made, on the ordinary construction with two rails; and the cost of keeping it in repair, he believes, will be very trifling indeed. It is certainly a bold innovation on the ordinary practice of making rail-ways; and we sincerely wish the inventor that success which his ingenuity so fairly entitles him to derive from his invention."

In order to load a large mass of bulky material, we should suppose the wheels must be of considerable diameter. If this construction can be carried into practical effect, it will doubtless save one half in friction; a point of no little consequence as to economy in horse power; as well as to wear.

On Steam Carriages. By Mr. W. SIMMONS.
London Journal of Arts, &c. No. 16, p. 196.

In a letter addressed to the editor of the above journal, Mr. S. makes some very judicious observations on the difficulties presenting to the locomotive steam carriage. First, as to the adaptation of means whereby the carriage shall, as it were, take hold of the road; the mere rotation of the wheels not being considered sufficiently *tactive*, (if we may presume to coin a word) to effect an ascending, or curved, course. Second, the noise made by the engine, and the darting forth of the condensed steam, would inevitably frighten every horse that heard or saw it. Third, the heavy toll that must be paid for the weight of the apparatus. But this objection Mr. S. thinks, an act of Parliament might remove. So should we too; did we not feel sure that the agricultural interest, in the two Houses, will not be brought to look very complacently on an instrument that, in so far as it can operate, must directly diminish demand for the produce of the soil.

Another objection is also suggested; and we think it will well deserve the consideration of steam-carriage speculators: viz. will the steam-carriage bear competition against horse power? We think not; if Providence should send us another productive year or two: for in such case, horses may be kept by every man, above a state of want. Mr. S. states that $\frac{7}{17}$ of an engine's power is lost in drawing its own weight. And he instances that at Orrell rail-road " there are two locomotive engines in constant action; but it is found absolutely necessary to have three; one being kept in repair to supply the place of either of the other two, when one of them becomes unfit for action."

On the Manufacture of White Lead. By Mr. J. Sadler.

Mr. Sadler has obtained a patent for his " new and improved method, or process, of manufacturing carbonate of lead, formerly denominated cerusse; but now commonly called white lead."

This process consists in adding carbonic acid to subacetate of lead; that is, the liquor plumbi subacetatis of the Pharmacopœia Londinensis, or extract of Goulard, as it is commonly called. But we will give Mr. S.'s own words.

" Place a solution of subacetate of lead (*liquor plumbi subacetatis*) in a cask, or vessel, either closed or open (though closed is preferable); then introduce into the same vessel, carbonic acid, either in a state of gas or solution. Use frequent agitation of the ingredients, to favour the combination of the carbonic acid with the oxide of lead. A precipitate is then formed, consisting of carbonate of lead; that is, of white lead or cerusse."

We object to this kind of specification, because it is too loose. And we must also beg leave to express a doubt as to the declared result. How are we to reconcile this formation of carbonate of lead with the tables of elective affinity? And further, how are we to account for the formation of subacetate of lead by *boiling carbonate of lead in acetous acid*, (which every chemical tyro has done, or can do,) if Mr. S.'s process be faithfully recorded?

Description of a new Safety Lamp. By J. Murray, Esq. Lecturer on Chemistry. Edin. Phil. Journ. No. 12, p. 292.

Mr. Murray, in his communication, describes his lamp as consisting of " two concentric cylinders of thick glass; the intermediate space being filled with water by a pipe at the top, having an air escape aperture on the opposite side. Over the flame of the wick (which is placed within the inner cylinder) is a bell or funnel, with a double recurved pipe issuing from its summit, and passing below the lamp; terminating immediately under a single central aperture (the excess is, of course, disengaged by the usual aperture at the top of the cylinder, and mingled with the explosive atmosphere rising from below) and passing to the flame of the lamp. This is, again, mixed more intimately at its immediate ingress, where it passes through the apertures represented on each side of the lamp." A circular band of lead at the base preserves the lamp in the perpendicular. Mr. M. says that the lamp is a self regulator. That it has been submitted to the " ordeal of explosive atmospheres with complete success." We sincerely wish it may fulfil the benevolent purpose for which it has been constructed.

A Method of making hard Black Lead Drawing Pencils for Artists. By Mr. CORNELIUS VARLEY.

Technical Repository, No. IV. p. 286.

These pencils are not made of black lead hardened, but by a mixture of that substance, ground into fine powder, with shell lac, and subjected to a melting heat. This compound must be repeatedly powdered and re-melted, until it be perfectly incorporated: then to be sawed into slips, and glued into cedar as usual. The hardness will be governed by the proportion of shell lac. Mr. Varley, it is said, invented this method about 1814: and Mr. Bankes, of Keswick, now makes his pencils, of very excellent qualities, in the same manner. But it seems that the inventions of these gentlemen have been totally independent of each other; not any communication having taken place between them on the subject.

On an Economical Mode of manufacturing Oil Gas. By DANIEL WILSON, Esq.

Technical Repository, No. IV. p. 286.

Mr. Wilson is much applauded by the editor of the Repository, for his proposed use of the oleaginous seeds, for the supply of combustible gas. The gas is recommended to be generated by close distillation of the seeds in retorts, in a manner similar to the process with coal; and by saving the expense of crushing the seeds and pressing the oil, is presumed to be a suggestion of great importance to countries where these seeds are abundantly cultivated, as France and Holland. It is said that, "the carbon afforded by the combustion of the seeds, is highly essential to the production of the gas; and it may also be subsequently employed as a valuable substitute for lamp black."

Mr. W. we are informed "(in conjunction with Mr. Aaron Manby, of the Horseley's Company Iron Works, near Tipton, in Staffordshire), has already contracted to light one of the principal districts of Paris, including the Tuilleries, the Palais Royale, and one of the chief streets for trade in that metropolis." And also, that "he is about to light the city of Lyons with oil gas thus produced."

We cannot refrain from stating our inability to conceive wherein the carbon of the seeds, during the generation of the gas, can contribute in a degree "highly essential" to the process. Indeed, we are inclined rather to think its presence must have a retarding effect; for we are to bear in mind, that the *gas* can arise only from *the decomposition of the extricated oil*. Since this notice came under our eye, we have distilled linseed in a close retort. The matter issuing was evidently *gas*, not *oleous vapour*; and therefore the oil must have been *decomposed*. And to this effect, we repeat, that we do not comprehend how the carbon could contribute. The gas was exceedingly fine and subtle, but it did not yield a body of illuminating flame; it resembled the fine blue jet of a flame before a blow-pipe. As to the carbonized seeds, they were hard, difficultly pulverized, and the powder was far removed from that soft velvety feel which we had expected. Perhaps, however, we might not have preserved such a nice degree of heat as may be necessary. We have only to state these resulting facts, and leave them to be corrected, or improved upon, by others.

On the application of Peat to the production of Gas for the purpose of Illumination.

London Journal of Arts, No. XVI. p. 216.

All nature will be tortured (as the old chemists termed it) for the production of combustible gas, now we have once discovered the gaseous means of illumination. Here we have another substance laid under contribution to our convenience. The dark peat moss of Scotland " will produce gas, equal, in quantity and quality, to that of coal; and possessing the additional and valuable advantage of being in a great measure free from those offensive and noxious effluvia emitted by gas obtained from the latter material." It is also said, that " the gentleman who made these experiments has, also, by a cheap and simple preparation of the peat, given it a consistency and durability not inferior to that of coal; rendering it thus not only a valuable fuel, but, at the same time, improving its capability for producing gas." A brewery at Edinburgh has been brilliantly lighted with peat gas.

Gas from Coal Tar and Saw-dust.

In the last Journal of Science, Literature, &c. we have the following—" Gas from Coal Tar. It has been found, by experiment, that the coal tar liquor, which is sometimes considered as waste, by those who make gas, if mixed with dry saw-dust, exhausted logwood, or fustic, to the consistence of paste, and allowed to remain till the water has drained off; two cwt. of the mass being put into the retort, will produce more gas, and be less offensive, than the same quantity of canal coal. This process will probably be found very convenient, in some circumstances, for the consumption of the tar produced by the distillation of coal in gas works."

We take it for granted that the editor of the Journal has not put this matter to the test of experiment; or he would have withheld his encomiums as to the quantity and inoffensiveness of the gas so generated. We do not hesitate to declare that, of all the materials we have subjected to distillation, with a view to the produce of combustible gas, (and we have tried many,) we have not met with the equal of common saw-dust for the acrimony of its vapours; nor do we think it yields so much gas as an equal weight of coal. It deposits a larger portion of tar than the latter. The mixture recommended is no better.

On Bleaching.

It is stated, in the London Journal of Arts, that a Mr. Crookshank, of Dublin, has greatly improved the process of bleaching, by decomposing the oxymuriate of lime, and disengaging the chlorine; and also that it has been tried largely and successfully.

How is it, we would ask, that this mode of process should be advantageous; when the impregnation of water with chlorine, as originally practised, is not considered expedient? We cannot understand any existing difference between the one mode and the other, as to the ultimate purpose of obtaining a solution of simple chlorine.

On a Green Colour by means of Tobacco.

Philosophical Mag. No. 286, p. 145.

It seems that M. Brugnatelli's experiments are leading to multiplied results in the hands of others. Tobacco is now said, by a gentleman named Willich, in a letter to the Editor of the Philosophical Magazine, to be capable of yielding a good green with sulphate of copper. Perhaps it will be found, that most vegetable matter may have this tendency. Mr. Willich states that M. Bizio's use of coffee led him to try several vegetable substances; and that he "succeeded in producing a green colour, brighter than by using coffee, and possessing chemical properties somewhat different." He formed "a strong decoction of tobacco, by boiling it for some time in pure water; then adding solution of sulphate of copper; and precipitating with carbonate of potassa. The precipitate, when dry, is of a light green colour. Mixed with linseed oil, it became darker and brighter, and very like a rich grass green. Dissolved in nitric acid, it formed a green solution. It also tinges sulphuric acid of a green colour. Not acted upon by water, alcohol, or ether." Dr. Tilloch observes, that the specimens sent to him by Mr. W. are of a most beautiful colour; and he thinks will probably prove highly useful in the arts.

We apprehend that the precipitate will be too sparing in quantity, to admit of its application to painting, in the large way; such as house-painting, &c.; where a durable green is so much wanted.

Extraordinary Productiveness of the Orange Trees of the Island of St. Michael.

Dr. Webster, in his History of this Island, relates that the oranges of St. Michael are celebrated for their fine flavour, and abundant sweet juice; when left to ripen on the trees, they are inferior to none in the world. The lemons have less juice than those of some other countries, and the demand for them is inconsiderable. The orange and lemon trees blossom in the months of February and March. At this time, the glossy green of the old leaves, the light, fresh tints of those just shooting forth, the brilliant yellow of the ripe fruit, and the delicate white and purple of the flower, are finely contrasted with each other, presenting one of the most beautiful sights imaginable. The trees generally attain the height of fifteen or twenty feet. The usual produce of a good tree, in common years, is from 6000 to 8000 oranges or lemons. Some instances of uncommon productiveness have occurred; a few years since, 26,000 oranges were obtained from one tree, and 29,000 have been gathered from another. These quantities have never been exceeded.

Power of Fascination in the Rattle Snake.
Philosophical Mag. No. 285.

It would appear, by the two following instances, that the terror in which animals hold this reptile, by paralyzing their muscular efforts, leads to the supply of its sustenance; for it has been said that even birds, which are placed out of its direct reach, cannot escape its rapacity.

" A friend in South Carolina, to whom I was on a visit, invited me to a morning walk round his plantation, and recommended our fowling pieces as companions. The day proved to be very sultry; and while my friend proceeded to give some directions to a gang of his negroes at a distance, he advised me to take the benefit of a shade formed by a wood adjoining the field in which we then were. I took the hint; and while leaning on the fence, (which was constructed on a bank between two dry ditches,) I was alarmed by the rattle of a snake very near me. I instantly sprung on the top rail of the fence, and the next moment discovered the monster in one of the ditches, within ten feet of the spot where I was seated. As I levelled my gun at his head, and was in the act of pulling the trigger, his tail ceased to vibrate. Conscious, from his position, that I was not the object of his regard, and that I was in no danger from him, and confident I could destroy him at any moment I pleased, I sat still to observe his further movements. As his eyes seemed to be riveted to a particular spot, I followed their direction, and discovered a wood rat. At the moment of my first seeing this little animal, he was rising from a crouching posture, and endeavouring to retire by a retrograde movement. This attempt was immediately followed by a second tremendous exercise of the rattle, and the rat again sunk to the ground. I witnessed several repetitions of this operation; and the result was, that at length the rat appeared perfectly exhausted, the snake advanced towards its prey, and was in the act of taking it into his mouth, when I discharged my two barrels at his head, and killed him on the spot. Whether any of my pellets struck the rat, I am unable to say; but, after the closest search, we could detect no mark of violence about his body, and he was dead when I took him up.

"Some years after the foregoing circumstance had taken place, as I was accompanying a lady to church in a gig, we were alarmed by the rattle of a snake by the road side. After I had tranquillized the horse, and prevailed on the lady to hold the reins, I returned to the spot from whence the noise seemed to issue, and soon discovered the subject of our alarm. The monster was lying in a coil, ready to strike, but manifested no concern at my approach. Having armed myself with a long fence rail, I was in the act of crushing his head, when I saw a rabbit in the very same posture and condition which the rat had exhibited. The fall of weapon disabled the snake, and I soon dispatched him. The rabbit I took into my hands, without any effort on its part to resist or escape, and deposited it in my companion's lap; but it died before we reached the church. I am confident that the animal had sustained no bodily injury either from the snake or myself."

www.ingramcontent.com/pod-product-compliance
Lightning Source LLC
Chambersburg PA
CBHW081141230426

43664CB00018B/2767